Complete Router Configurations!

The companion CD contains complete router configurations for each end-of-chapter case study. The configurations are in PDF for printing, and in plain text files that can easily be loaded into your own routers. Depending on specifics, you may need to edit the configuration to suit the specific interface types and addressing used in your test bed.

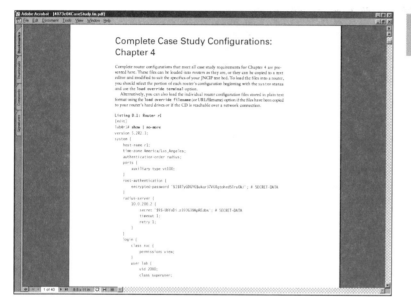

JUNOS Technical Documentation in PDF!

We have provided a variety of technical and software documentation to help you further your Juniper knowledge, including:

- JUNOS Internet Configuration Guides
- JUNOS Internet Software Command Reference
- JUNOS software release notes

SYBEX

JNCIP: Juniper Networks Certified Internet Professional Study Guide

Juniper Networks Certified Internet Professional, M-series, T-series Routers (JNCIP-M) exam (code CERT-JNCIP-M)

LAB SKILLS	CHAPTER
1. Initial Configuration and Platform Troubleshooting	
Use terminal server to access router console ports	1
Configure OoB management network and host name	1
Create user accounts and system authentication options	1
Configure syslog parameters	1
Configure network management and NTP	1
Determine JUNOS software version and perform upgrades	1
Configure chassis alarms and redundancy	1
2. Interface Configuration and Testing	
Configure Loopback interfaces	2
Configure POS interfaces	2
Physical properties	
Logical properties	
POS encapsulation options (Cisco HDLC, Frame Relay, and PPP)	
Configure ATM interfaces	2
Physical properties	
Logical properties	
Point-to-point	
Point-to-multipoint	
Traffic shaping	
Configure Ethernet interfaces	2
Physical properties	
Logical properties	
VLAN tagging and VRRP	
MAC address filtering	
Aggregated interfaces	2
Leaky bucket rate limiting	2
Unnumbered interfaces	2
3. OSPF Configuration and Testing	
Multi-area configuration	3
Network types	3
Broadcast, Point-to-Point, Multipoint, and NBMA	

SYBEX

LAB SKILLS	CHAPTER
Authentication	3
Stub and not-so-stubby areas	3
Address summarization and filtering between areas	3
Virtual links	3
Policy	3
Route redistribution	
Route tagging	
RIP configuration	
Metrics, timers, and various other "knobs"	3

4. IS-IS Configuration and Testing

Multi-Level IS-IS configuration	4
Default route origination	
Network types	4
Authentication	4
Hello and LSP authentication	
IS-IS policy	4
Summarization, filtering, and route leaking	
Route Redistribution	
Metrics, timers, and various other "knobs"	4

5. IBGP Configuration and Testing

IBGP peering	5
IBGP policy	
IBGP authentication	5
Route reflection	5
Confederations	5
IBGP timers and various other "knobs"	5

6. EBGP Configuration and Testing

EBGP peering	6
Multihop and multipath	
EBGP authentication	
Routing policy	6
Route damping	
Martian filters	
Local preference, MED, next hop self, etc.	
Miscellaneous EBGP knobs	6

> **NOTE** Exam objectives are subject to change at any time without prior notice and at Juniper Network's sole discretion. Please visit Juniper Networks Technical Certification Program website (http://www.juniper.net/certification) for the most current exam objectives listing.

SYBEX

JNCIP:
Juniper Networks Certified Internet Professional
Study Guide

JNCIP:
Juniper™ Networks Certified Internet Professional
Study Guide

Harry Reynolds

San Francisco • London

Associate Publisher: Neil Edde
Acquisitions & Development Editor: Maureen Adams
Production Editor: Mae Lum
Technical Editors: Peter Moyer, Josef Buchsteiner
Copyeditor: Linda Stephenson
Compositor: Jill Niles
Graphic Illustrator: Tony Jonick
CD Coordinator: Dan Mummert
CD Technician: Kevin Ly
Proofreaders: Nelson Kim, David Nash, Nancy Riddiough, Monique van den Berg
Indexer: Ted Laux
Book Designers: Bill Gibson, Judy Fung
Cover Designer: Archer Design
Cover Illustrator/Photographer: Bruce Heinemann, PhotoDisc

Library of Congress Card Number: 2002110012

ISBN: 0-7821-4073-4

SYBEX and the SYBEX logo are either registered trademarks or trademarks of SYBEX Inc. in the United States and/or other countries.

The CD interface was created using Macromedia Director, COPYRIGHT 1994, 1997-1999 Macromedia Inc. For more information on Macromedia and Macromedia Director, visit http://www.macromedia.com.

SYBEX is an independent entity from Juniper Networks Inc. and is not affiliated with Juniper Networks Inc. in any manner. This publication may be used in assisting students to prepare for a Juniper JNCIP-M exam. Neither Juniper Networks Inc. nor SYBEX warrants that use of this publication will ensure passing the relevant exam. Juniper is either a registered trademark or a trademark of Juniper Networks Inc. in the United States and/or other countries.

TRADEMARKS: SYBEX has attempted throughout this book to distinguish proprietary trademarks from descriptive terms by following the capitalization style used by the manufacturer.

The author and publisher have made their best efforts to prepare this book, and the content is based upon final release software whenever possible. Portions of the manuscript may be based upon pre-release versions supplied by software manufacturer(s). The author and the publisher make no representation or warranties of any kind with regard to the completeness or accuracy of the contents herein and accept no liability of any kind including but not limited to performance, merchantability, fitness for any particular purpose, or any losses or damages of any kind caused or alleged to be caused directly or indirectly from this book.

Manufactured in the United States of America

10 9 8 7 6 5 4 3 2 1

SYBEX

To Our Valued Readers:

As internetworking technologies continue to pervade nearly every aspect of public and private industry worldwide, the demand grows for individuals who can demonstrate they possess the skills needed to manage these technologies. Recognizing this need, Juniper Networks—the leading provider of Internet infrastructure solutions that enable ISPs and other telecommunications companies to meet the demands of Internet growth—recently restructured its certification program to provide a clear path for the acquisition of these skills. Sybex is proud to have partnered with Juniper Networks and worked closely with members of the Juniper Networks Technical Certification Program to develop this Official Study Guide for the Juniper Networks Certified Internet Professional certification.

Just as Juniper Networks is committed to establishing measurable standards for certifying those professionals who work in the cutting-edge field of internetworking, Sybex is committed to providing those professionals with the means of acquiring the skills and knowledge they need to meet those standards. It has long been Sybex's desire to help individuals acquire the technical knowledge and skills necessary to excel in the IT industry.

The authors and editors have worked hard to ensure that this Official Juniper Networks Study Guide is comprehensive, in-depth, and pedagogically sound. We're confident that this book will exceed the demanding standards of the certification marketplace and help you, the Juniper Networks certification candidate, succeed in your endeavors.

Good luck in pursuit of your Juniper Networks certification!

Neil Edde
Associate Publisher—Certification
Sybex, Inc.

This book is dedicated to my wife Anita, and to my daughters, Christina and Marissa. Anita, your willingness to "step up" and take in the slack afforded me the time I needed to complete this work; this book would not have been possible without you in my life. I thank and commend you all for tolerating the extension cords required to power my "pop lab" and for putting up with that pesky circuit breaker that needed resetting every time someone used the hairdryer. Thanks for accommodating me in this, my labor of love.

Acknowledgments

There are numerous people who deserve a round of thanks for assisting with this book. I would first like to thank Jason Rogan and Patrick Ames, who got this project started in the first place, and in the case of Jason, for providing editorial services to ensure that the certification program was not compromised. I would also like to thank Mae Lum, Linda Stephenson, and Maureen Adams at Sybex for keeping me on schedule and for getting the whole thing rolling. A very big thank-you goes out to the technical editors, Peter Moyer and Josef Buchsteiner. Both Peter and Josef worked very hard to keep me and the resulting book honest.

I would also like to thank Juniper Networks and my manager, Scott Edwards, for making this effort possible through arrangements that allowed me to access, borrow, or buy the equipment needed to build the test bed that formed the basis of this book.

—Harry Reynolds

Sybex would like to thank electronic publishing specialist Jill Niles and indexer Ted Laux for their valuable contributions to this book.

Contents at a Glance

Introduction   *xv*

Chapter 1   Initial Configuration and Platform Troubleshooting   1

Chapter 2   Interface Configuration and Testing   59

Chapter 3   OSPF Configuration and Testing   153

Chapter 4   IS-IS Configuration and Testing   255

Chapter 5   IBGP Configuration and Testing   373

Chapter 6   EBGP Configuration and Testing   479

Glossary   619

Index   *655*

Contents

Introduction   *xv*

Chapter   1   Initial Configuration and Platform Troubleshooting   1

Task 1: Access Routers Using a Terminal Server   2
    Console Connections   3
Task 2: Configure the OoB Management Network   8
Task 3: Create User Accounts   10
    Configuring the Root Account   11
Configuring the Lab Account   14
    Verify the Lab Account   15
Configure the Ops Account   17
    Verify the Ops Account   19
Task 4: Configure Syslog Parameters   20
    Verify Syslog Operation   21
Task 5: Configure Network Management and NTP   22
    Configure SNMP   22
    Configure NTP   24
Task 6: Perform General Maintenance and Software Upgrade   28
Task 7: Configure Chassis Alarms and Redundancy   33
Your Initial System Configuration   34
    Using Cut and Paste   38
Summary   41
Case Study: Initial System Configuration   42
    Configuration Requirements   42
    Configuration Examples   43
    The Completed Case Study Configuration   51
Spot the Issues: Review Questions   55
Spot the Issues: Answers   57

Chapter   2   Interface Configuration and Testing   59

Loopback Interfaces   60
Configuring Your lo0 Interface   61
Verify Your lo0 Interface Configuration   61
POS Interfaces   64
    Physical Properties for POS Interfaces   65
    Logical Properties of POS Interfaces   68
    Verifying POS Interface Operation   69
    Encapsulation Options for POS Interfaces   71
    Summary of POS Interface Configuration   89
ATM Interfaces   89
    Physical Properties for ATM Interfaces   90

Configuring ATM Interface Logical Properties   91
Verifying ATM Operation   93
Multipoint ATM Connections   97
ATM Traffic Shaping   98
ATM Interface Summary   100
Ethernet Interfaces   101
Ethernet Interface Physical Configuration   101
Ethernet Interface Logical Properties   102
MAC Address Filtering   111
Ethernet Interface Summary   114
Aggregated Interfaces   114
Aggregated Ethernet   114
Aggregated SONET   117
Leaky Bucket Rate Limiting   119
Configure Leaky Bucket Rate Limiting   119
Verify Leaky Bucket Rate Limiting   121
Unnumbered Interfaces   124
Configure Unnumbered Interfaces   125
Verify Unnumbered Interfaces   126
Summary   128
Case Study: Interface Configuration   129
Case Study Configurations   132
Spot The Issues: Review Questions   149
Spot The Issues: Answers   151

Chapter   3   OSPF Configuration and Testing   153

Multi-Area Configuration   154
r4 OSPF Configuration   155
r5 OSPF Configuration   157
r3 OSPF Configuration   159
Area 1 Configuration   161
OSPF Network Types   166
Multipoint Network Types   166
NBMA Network Types   168
Troubleshooting Network Type Problems   172
OSPF Authentication   173
Verify OSPF Authentication   176
Stub and Not-So-Stubby Areas   179
Stub Areas   179
Stub Area Deployment   180
Not-So-Stubby Areas (NSSA)   188
Address Summarization   194
Configure Summarization   194
Virtual Links   198

OSPF Routing Policy   201
    Configure OSPF Routing Policy   201
Metrics and Various Other Knobs   222
Summary   227
Case Study: OSPF   228
    OSPF Case Study Analysis   230
    OSPF Case Study Configurations   243
Spot the Issues: Review Questions   251
Spot the Issues: Answers   254

Chapter   4   IS-IS Configuration and Testing   255

Multi-Level IS-IS Configuration   256
    IS-IS Configuration   258
    Configure *r5* for IS-IS Operation   264
    Configure *r3* for IS-IS Operation   267
    Area 49.0002 Configuration   270
    Verify Overall IS-IS Operation   272
IS-IS Network Types   277
    The Designated Intermediate System   278
IS-IS Authentication   278
    Configure Authentication on *r5*   278
    Configure Authentication on *r3* and *r4*   280
    Configure Authentication in Area 49.0002   282
    Troubleshoot IS-IS Authentication   283
IS-IS Policy   286
    Route Leaking and Summarization   286
    Route Redistribution   297
Miscellaneous IS-IS Knobs   313
Summary   318
Case Study: IS-IS   319
    IS-IS Case Study Analysis   321
    IS-IS Case Study Configurations   345
Spot the Issues: Review Questions   366
Spot the Issues: Answers   370

Chapter   5   IBGP Configuration and Testing   373

Initial IBGP Peering   374
    IBGP Policy   377
IBGP Authentication   383
    Configure Authentication   383
IBGP Route Reflection   386
    Configure Route Reflection   387
    Verify Route Reflection   395

IBGP Confederations 402
Configure a Confederation 402
Verify Confederation Operation 413
Save Confederation Configuration 420
Miscellaneous IBGP Timers and Knobs 421
IBGP Preference and Load Balancing 422
Modify IBGP Timers 426
Configure Passive Mode 427
Use Local Preference and Communities 429
Summary 439
Case Study: IGBP 440
IBGP Case Study Analysis 442
IBGP Case Study Configurations 460
Spot the Issues: Review Questions 472
Spot the Issues: Answers 476

Chapter   6   EBGP Configuration and Testing   479
Initial EBGP Peering 481
C2 EBGP Peering 484
C1 EBGP Peering 487
P1 EBGP Peering 493
T2 EBGP Peering 498
T1 EBGP Peering 500
EBGP and Policy 504
EBGP Import Policy 504
EBGP (and IBGP) Export Policy 520
Confirm Forwarding Paths 540
Miscellaneous EBGP Timers and Knobs 541
AS Loops 542
Influence Incoming Traffic Flow 543
Set Local Preference Directly 547
Summary 549
Case Study: EBGP 550
EBGP Case Study Analysis 554
EBGP Case Study Configurations 589
Spot the Issues: Review Questions 612
Spot the Issues: Answers 617

Glossary   619
Index   655

Table of Case Studies

Initial System Configuration   42

Interface Configuration   129

OSPF   228

IS-IS   319

IGBP   440

EGBP   550

Introduction

Greetings and welcome to the world of Juniper Networks. This introductory section serves as a location to pass on to you some pertinent information concerning the Juniper Networks Technical Certification Program. In addition, you'll find information about how the book itself is laid out and what it contains. Finally, we'll review some technical information that you should already know before reading this book.

Juniper Networks Technical Certification Program

The Juniper Networks Technical Certification Program (JNTCP) consists of two platform-specific, multitiered tracks. Each exam track allows participants to demonstrate their competence with Juniper Networks technology through a combination of written proficiency and hands-on configuration exams. Successful candidates demonstrate a thorough understanding of Internet technology and Juniper Networks platform configuration and troubleshooting skills.

The two JNTCP tracks focus on the M-series Routers & T-series Routing Platforms and the ERX Edge Routers, respectively. While some Juniper Networks customers and partners work with both platform families, it is most common to find individuals working with only one or the other platform. The two different certification tracks allow candidates to pursue specialized certifications, which focus on the platform type most pertinent to their job functions and experience. Candidates wishing to attain a certification on both platform families are welcome to do so, but are required to pass the exams from each track for their desired certification level.

 This book covers the M-series & T-series track. For information on the ERX Edge Routers certification track, please visit the JNTCP website at http://www.juniper.net/certification.

M-series Routers & T-series Routing Platforms

The M-series Routers certification track consists of four tiers. They include the following:

Juniper Networks Certified Internet Associate (JNCIA)   The Juniper Networks Certified Internet Associate, M-series, T-series Routers (JNCIA-M) certification does not have any prerequisites. It is administered at Prometric testing centers worldwide.

Juniper Networks Certified Internet Specialist (JNCIS)   The Juniper Networks Certified Internet Specialist, M-series, T-series Routers (JNCIS-M) certification also does not have any prerequisites. Like the JNCIA-M, it is administered at Prometric testing centers worldwide.

Juniper Networks Certified Internet Professional (JNCIP)   The Juniper Networks Certified Internet Professional, M-series, T-series Routers (JNCIP-M) certification requires that candidates first obtain the JNCIS-M certification. The hands-on exam is administered at Juniper Networks offices in select locations throughout the world.

Juniper Networks Certified Internet Expert (JNCIE)   The Juniper Networks Certified Internet Expert, M-series, T-series Routers (JNCIE-M) certification requires that candidates first obtain the JNCIP-M certification. The hands-on exam is administered at Juniper Networks offices in select locations throughout the world.

FIGURE I.1   JNTCP M-series Routers & T-series Routing Platforms certification track

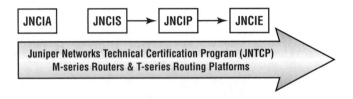

   The JNTCP M-series Routers & T-series Routing Platforms certification track covers the M-series and T-series routing platforms as well as the JUNOS software configuration skills required for both platforms. The lab exams are conducted using M-series routers only.

Juniper Networks Certified Internet Associate

The JNCIA-M certification is the first of the four-tiered M-series Routers & T-series Routing Platforms track. It is the entry-level certification designed for experienced networking professionals with beginner-to-intermediate knowledge of the Juniper Networks M-series and T-series routers and the JUNOS software. The JNCIA-M (exam code JN0-201) is a computer-based, multiple-choice exam delivered at Prometric testing centers globally for U.S.$125. It is a fast-paced exam that consists of 60 questions to be completed within 60 minutes. The current passing score is set at 70 percent.

JNCIA-M exam topics are based on the content of the Introduction to Juniper Networks Routers, M-series (IJNR-M) instructor-led training course. Just as IJNR-M is the first class most students attend when beginning their study of Juniper Networks hardware and software, the JNCIA-M exam should be the first certification exam most candidates attempt. The study topics for the JNCIA-M exam include:

- System operation, configuration, and troubleshooting
- Routing protocols—BGP, OSPF, IS-IS, and RIP
- Protocol-independent routing properties
- Routing policy
- MPLS
- Multicast

---

70 Percent Seems Really Low!

The required score to pass an exam can be one indicator of the exam's difficulty, but not in the way that many candidates might assume. A lower pass score on an exam does *not* usually indicate an easier exam. Ironically, it often indicates the opposite—it's harder.

The JNTCP exams are extensively beta tested and reviewed. The results are then statistically analyzed based on multiple psychometric criteria. Only after this analysis is complete does the exam receive its appropriate passing score. In the case of the JNCIA-M exam, for example, requiring the passing score to be higher than 70 percent would mean that the exam's target audience would have been excluded from passing. In effect, the exam would have been more difficult to pass. Over time, as more exam statistics are collected, or the exam questions themselves are updated, the passing score may be modified to reflect the exam's new difficulty level. The end result is to ensure that the exams are passable by the members of the target audience for which they are written.

Please be aware that the JNCIA-M certification is *not* a prerequisite for further certification in the M-series Routers & T-series Routing Platforms track. The purpose of the JNCIA-M is to validate a candidate's skill set at the Associate level and it is meant to be a stand-alone certification fully recognized and worthy of pride of accomplishment. Additionally, it can be used as a stepping stone before attempting the JNCIS-M exam.

Juniper Networks Certified Internet Specialist

The JNCIS-M was originally developed as the exam used to prequalify candidates for admittance to the practical hands-on certification exam. While it still continues to serve this purpose, this certification has quickly become a sought-after designation in its own right. Depending on the candidates' job functions, many have chosen JNCIS-M as the highest level of JNTCP certification needed to validate their skill set. Candidates also requiring validation of their hands-on configuration and troubleshooting ability on the M-series and T-series routers and the JUNOS software use the JNCIS-M as the required prerequisite to the JNCIP-M practical exam.

The JNCIS-M exam tests for a wider and deeper level of knowledge than does the JNCIA-M exam. Question content is drawn from the documentation set for the M-series routers, the T-series routers, and the JUNOS software. Additionally, on-the-job product experience and an understanding of Internet technologies and design principles are considered to be common knowledge at the Specialist level.

The JNCIS-M (exam code JN0-302) is a computer-based, multiple-choice exam delivered at Prometric testing centers globally for U.S.$125. It consists of 75 questions to be completed in 90 minutes. The current passing score is set at 70 percent.

The study topics for the JNCIS-M exam include:

- Advanced system operation, configuration, and troubleshooting
- Routing protocols—BGP, OSPF, and IS-IS
- Routing policy
- MPLS
- Multicast
- Router and network security
- Router and network management
- VPNs
- IPv6

 There are no prerequisite certifications for the JNCIS-M exam. While JNCIA-M certification is a recommended stepping stone to JNCIS-M certification, candidates are permitted to go straight to the Specialist (JNCIS-M) level.

Juniper Networks Certified Internet Professional

The JNCIP-M is the first of the two one-day practical exams in the M-series Routers & T-series Routing Platforms track of the JNTCP. The goal of this challenging exam is to validate a candidate's ability to successfully build an ISP network consisting of seven M-series routers and multiple EBGP neighbors. Over a period of eight hours, the successful candidate will perform system configuration on all seven routers, install an IGP, implement a well-designed IBGP, establish connections with all EBGP neighbors as specified, and configure the required routing policies correctly.

This certification establishes candidates' practical and theoretical knowledge of core Internet technologies and their ability to proficiently apply that knowledge in a hands-on environment. This exam is expected to meet the hands-on certification needs of the majority of Juniper Networks customers and partners. The more advanced JNCIE-M exam focuses on a set of specialized skills and addresses a much smaller group of candidates. You should carefully consider your certification goals and requirements, for you may find that the JNCIP-M exam is the highest-level certification you need.

The JNCIP-M (exam code CERT-JNCIP-M) is delivered at one of several Juniper Networks offices worldwide for U.S.$1,250. The current passing score is set at 80 percent.

The study topics for the JNCIP-M exam include:

- Advanced system operation, configuration, and troubleshooting
- Routing protocols—BGP, OSPF, IS-IS, and RIP
- Routing policy
- Routing protocol redistribution
- VLANs
- VRRP

The JNCIP-M certification is a prerequisite for attempting the JNCIE-M practical exam.

Juniper Networks Certified Internet Expert

At the pinnacle of the M-series Routers & T-series Routing Platforms track is the one-day JNCIE-M practical exam. The *E* stands for Expert and they mean it—the exam is the most challenging and respected of its type in the industry. Maintaining the standard of excellence established over two years ago, the JNCIE-M certification continues to give candidates the opportunity to distinguish themselves as the truly elite of the networking world. Only a few have dared attempt this exam, and fewer still have passed.

The new eight-hour format of the exam requires that candidates troubleshoot an existing and preconfigured ISP network consisting of 10 M-series routers. Candidates are then presented with additional configuration tasks appropriate for an expert-level engineer.

The JNCIE-M (exam code CERT-JNCIE-M) is delivered at one of several Juniper Networks offices worldwide for U.S.$1,250. The current passing score is set at 80 percent.

The study topics for the JNCIE-M exam *may* include:

- Expert-level system operation, configuration, and troubleshooting
- Routing protocols—BGP, OSPF, IS-IS, and RIP
- Routing protocol redistribution
- Advanced routing policy implementation
- Firewall filters
- Class of service
- MPLS
- VPNs
- IPv6
- IPSec
- Multicast

 Since the JNCIP-M certification is a prerequisite for attempting this practical exam, all candidates who pass the JNCIE-M will have successfully completed two days of intensive practical examination.

Registration Procedures

JNTCP written exams are delivered worldwide at Prometric testing centers. To register, visit Prometric's website at http://www.2test.com (or call 1-888-249-2567 in North America) to open an account and register for an exam.

The JNTCP Prometric exam numbers are:

- JNCIA-M—JN0-201

- JNCIS-M—JN0-302

JNTCP lab exams are delivered by Juniper Networks at select locations. Currently the testing locations are:

- Sunnyvale, CA

- Herndon, VA

- Amsterdam, Holland

Other global locations are periodically set up as testing centers based on demand. To register, send an e-mail message to Juniper Networks at `certification-testreg@juniper.net` and place one of the following exam codes in the subject field. Within the body of the message, indicate the testing center you prefer and which month you would like to attempt the exam. You will be contacted with the available dates at your requested testing center. The JNTCP lab exam numbers are:

- JNCIP-M—CERT-JNCIP-M

- JNCIE-M—CERT-JNCIE-M

Recertification Requirements

To maintain the high standards of the JNTCP certifications, and to ensure that the skills of those certified are kept current and relevant, Juniper Networks has implemented the following recertification requirements, which apply to both certification tracks of the JNTCP:

- All JNTCP certifications are valid for a period of two years.

- Certification holders who do not renew their certification within this two-year period will have their certification placed in *suspended mode*. Certifications in suspended mode are not eligible as prerequisites for further certification and cannot be applied to partner certification requirements.

- After being in suspended mode for one year, the certification is placed in *inactive mode*. At that stage, the individual is no longer certified at the JNTCP certification level that has become inactive and the individual will lose the associated certification number. For example, a JNCIP holder placed in inactive mode will be required to pass both the JNCIS and JNCIP exams in order to regain JNCIP status; such an individual will be given a new JNCIP certification number.

- Renewed certifications are valid for a period of two years from the date of passing the renewed certification exam.

- Passing an exam at a higher level renews all lower-level certifications for two years from the date of passing the higher-level exam. For example, passing the JNCIP exam will renew the JNCIS certification (and JNCIA certification if currently held) for two years from the date of passing the JNCIP exam.

- JNCIA holders must pass the current JNCIA exam in order to renew the certification for an additional two years from the most recent JNCIA pass date.

- JNCIS holders must pass the current JNCIS exam in order to renew the certification for an additional two years from the most recent JNCIS pass date.

- JNCIP and JNCIE holders must pass the current JNCIS exam in order to renew these certifications for an additional two years from the most recent JNCIS pass date.

 The most recent version of the JNTCP Online Agreement must be accepted for the recertification to become effective.

JNTCP Nondisclosure Agreement

Juniper Networks considers all written and practical JNTCP exam material to be confidential intellectual property. As such, an individual is not permitted to take home, copy, or re-create the entire exam or any portions thereof. It is expected that candidates who participate in the JNTCP will not reveal the detailed content of the exams.

For written exams delivered at Prometric testing centers, candidates must accept the online agreement before proceeding with the exam. When taking practical exams, candidates are provided with a hard-copy agreement to read and sign before attempting the exam. In either case, the agreement can be downloaded from the JNTCP website for your review prior to the testing date. Juniper Networks retains all signed hard-copy nondisclosure agreements on file.

 Candidates must accept the online JNTCP Online Agreement in order for their certifications to become effective and to have a certification number assigned. You can do this by going to the CertManager site at http://www.certmanager .net/juniper.

Resources for JNTCP Participants

Reading this book is a fantastic place to begin preparing for your next JNTCP exam. You should supplement the study of this volume's content with related information from various sources. The following resources are available for free and are recommended to anyone seeking to attain or maintain Juniper Networks certified status.

JNTCP Website

The JNTCP website (http://www.juniper.net/certification) is the place to go for the most up-to-date information about the program. As the program evolves, this website is periodically updated with the latest news and major announcements. Possible changes include new exams and certifications, modifications to the existing certification and recertification requirements, and information about new resources and exam objectives.

The site consists of separate sections for each of the certification tracks. The information you'll find there includes the exam number, passing scores, exam time limits, and exam topics. A special section dedicated to resources is also provided to supply you with detailed exam topic outlines, sample written exams, and study guides. The additional resources listed next are also linked from the JNTCP website.

CertManager

The CertManager system (`http://www.certmanager.net/juniper`) provides you with a place to track your certification progress. The site requires a username and password for access, and you typically use the information contained on your hard-copy score report from Prometric the first time you log in. Alternatively, a valid login can be obtained by sending an e-mail message to `certification@juniper.net` with the word **certmanager** in the subject field.

Once you log in, you can view a report of all your attempted exams. This report includes the exam dates, your scores, and a progress report indicating the additional steps required to attain a given certification or recertification. This website is where you accept the online JNTCP agreement, which is a required step to become certified at any level in the program. You can also use the website to request the JNTCP official certification logos to use on your business cards, resumes, and websites.

Perhaps most important, the CertManager website is where all your contact information is kept up-to-date. Juniper Networks uses this information to send you certification benefits, such as your certificate of completion, and to inform you of important developments regarding your certification status. A valid company name is used to verify a partner's compliance with certification requirements. To avoid missing out on important benefits and information, you should ensure your contact information is kept current.

Juniper Networks Training Courses

Juniper Networks training courses (`http://www.juniper.net/training`) are the best source of knowledge for seeking a certification and to increase your hands-on proficiency with Juniper Networks equipment and technologies. While attendance of official Juniper Networks training courses doesn't guarantee a passing score on the certification exam, it does increase the likelihood of your successfully passing it. This is especially true when you seek to attain JNCIP or JNCIE status, where hands-on experience is a vital aspect of your study plan.

Juniper Networks Technical Documentation

You should be intimately familiar with the Juniper Networks technical documentation set (`http://www.juniper.net/techpubs`). During the JNTCP lab exams (JNCIP and JNCIE), these documents are provided in PDF on your PC. Knowing the content, organizational structure, and search capabilities of these manuals is a key component for a successful exam attempt. At the time of this writing, hard-copy versions of the manuals are provided only for the hands-on lab exams. All written exams delivered at Prometric testing centers are closed-book exams.

Juniper Networks Solutions and Technology

To broaden and deepen your knowledge of Juniper Networks products and their applications, you can visit `http:///www.juniper.net/techcenter`. This website contains white papers, application notes, frequently asked questions (FAQ), and other informative documents, such as customer profiles and independent test results.

Group Study

The Groupstudy mailing list and website (`http://www.groupstudy.com/list/juniper.html`) is dedicated to the discussion of Juniper Networks products and technologies for the purpose of preparing for certification testing. You can post and receive answers to your own technical questions or simply read the questions and answers of other list members.

Tips for Taking Your Exam

Time, or the lack thereof, is normally one of the biggest factors influencing the outcome of JNCIP-M certification attempts. Having to single-handedly configure numerous protocols and parameters on seven routers while in a somewhat stressful environment often serves as a rude wake-up call early in the JNCIP-M candidate's first attempt.

Although the product documentation is provided during the exam, you will likely run short on time if you have to refer to it more than once or twice during your exam. The successful candidate will have significant practice time with the JUNOS software CLI, and will be experienced with virtually all aspects of protocol configuration, so that commands can be entered quickly and accurately without the need for user manuals.

Although troubleshooting is not a specific component of the exam, many candidates may spend a good portion of their time fault-isolating issues that result from their own configuration mistakes or that result from unanticipated interactions between the various protocols involved. Being able to quickly assess the state of the network, and to rapidly isolate and correct mistakes and omissions, are critical skills that a successful JNCIP candidate must possess.

The JNCIP-M exam is scored in a non-linear fashion—this means that a candidate can lose points for a single mistake that happens to affect multiple aspects of their network. The goal of this grading approach can be summed up as "We grade on results, as opposed to individual configuration statements, and your grade will be determined by the *overall* operational state of your network at the end of the exam." This is a significant point, and one that needs some elaboration, because many candidates are surprised to see how many points can be lost due to a single mistake on a critical facet of the exam.

Non-linear grading   The JNCIP-M exam is made up of several sections, and each section is worth a number of points. Missing too many of the criteria within one section can result in zero points being awarded for the entire section, even if the candidate configured some aspects of the task correctly! Getting zero points on a section almost always results in an insufficient number of total points for a passing grade. The goal of this grading approach is to ensure that the JNCIP candidate is able to at least get the majority of each task right. Put another way, "How can you be deemed a *Professional* if you cannot get a significant portion of your OSPF or IS-IS configuration correct?"

Results-based grading   Because of the numerous ways that JUNOS software can be configured to effect a common result and because a *Professional* should be able to configure a network that is largely operational, the JNCIP-M exam is graded based on overall results. So a serious error in a critical section of the exam can spell doom for the candidate, even if other sections of the candidate's configuration may be largely correct. For example, consider the case of a candidate who makes a serious mistake in their IGP configuration. With a dysfunctional IGP, there is a high probability that the candidate's IBGP, EBGP, and policy-related tasks will exhibit operational problems, which will result in point loss in this section, even though the IBGP, EBGP, and policy-related configuration might be configured properly. The moral of this story is make sure that you periodically spot-check the operation of your network, and that you quickly identify and correct operational issues before moving on to subsequent tasks.

Here are some general tips for exam success:

- Arrive early at the exam center, so you can relax and review your study materials.

- Read the task requirements *carefully*. Don't just jump to conclusions. Make sure that you're clear about what each task requires. When in doubt, consult the proctor for clarification. Don't be shy, because the proctor is there mainly to ensure you understand what tasks you are being asked to perform.

- Because the exam is graded based on your network's overall operation, moving on to later tasks when you are "stuck" on a previous task is not always a good idea. In general, you should not move on if your network has operational problems related to a previous task. If you get stuck, you might consider "violating" the rules by deploying a static route (or something similar) in an attempt to complete the entire exam *with* an operational network. You should then plan to revisit your problem areas using any remaining time *after* you have completed all remaining requirements. The point here is that you will likely experience significant point loss if your network has operational problems, so violating some restrictions in an effort to achieve an operational network can be a sound strategy for reducing overall point loss when you are stuck on a particular task.

- Pay attention to detail! With so much work to do and so many routers to configure, many candidates make "simple" mistakes that relate to basic instructions such as log file naming, login class names, etc.

- Use cut and paste judiciously. Cut and paste can be a real time-saver, but in many cases it can cost a candidate precious time when the configurations of the routers differ significantly or when mistakes are made because the candidate did not correctly adjust parameters before loading the configuration into the next router.

- Read each section (and perhaps the whole exam) fully before starting to type on the consoles. In many cases, the ordering of the requirements for a given section may result in the candidate having to revisit each router many times. By carefully reading all the requirements first, the candidate may be able to save time by grouping requirements so that each router needs to be configured only once.

- Know and prepare for the current test version. At the time of this writing, the production JNCIP-M exam and this book were synchronized to the same JUNOS software version. Before showing up for the exam, the candidate should determine the software version currently deployed in the JNCIP-M testing centers. If newer versions of JUNOS software are rolled out, the well-prepared candidate should study the release notes for the new software and compare any new features or functionality to the current JNCIP-M study guide and preparation road maps to ensure that exam updates will not catch them unprepared.

  It is important to note that the JNCIP-M certification requirements may not change just because a newer software version has been deployed in the lab, because there are many reasons to periodically upgrade the code used in the exam. Please also note that while the exam requirements may not change, the syntax used to establish a given level of functionality may evolve with new software releases.

JNCIP-M exam grading occurs at the end of the day. Results are provided by e-mail within ten business days.

JNCIP Study Guide

Now that you know a lot about the JNTCP, we need to provide some more information about this text. We begin with a look at some topics and information you should already be familiar with and then examine what topics are in the book. Finally, we discuss how to utilize this resource and the accompanying CD.

What You Should Know Before Starting

If you are familiar with networking books, you might be a little surprised that Chapter 1 starts with routing configuration. Rather than beginning with the Open Systems Interconnection (OSI) model common to books in our industry, we instead dive headfirst into the details of a typical JNCIP-level configuration task involving the establishment of an out-of-band management network and initial system configuration. This philosophy of *knowing the basics* is quite ingrained in the Juniper Networks Education courseware and certification exams, so we follow that assumption.

This means that you should be knowledgeable and conversant in the following topics in the context of Juniper Networks M-series Routers or T-series Routing Platforms. Please refer to other Juniper Networks Study Guides published by Sybex for assistance in gaining this knowledge.

- The basic components of the Juniper Networks routers, including hardware composition and the operation of JUNOS software

- M-series and T-series interfaces, both permanent and transient

- JUNOS software protocol-independent properties, which include static, aggregate, generated, and martian routes

- JUNOS software routing policies, including route filtering, route redistribution, and routing attribute modification

- JUNOS software support of the Routing Information Protocol (RIP)

- JUNOS software support of the Open Shortest Path First (OSPF) protocol

- JUNOS software support of the Intermediate System to Intermediate System (IS-IS) protocol

- JUNOS software support of the Border Gateway Protocol (BGP), in both its internal (IBGP) and external (EBGP) forms

Scope of the Book

While this book does provide the reader with a "feel" for the JNCIP-M exam, doing well on the exam will also involve getting some hands-on experience with M-series and T-series routers to practice the scenarios covered in each chapter. This book serves as a guide to readers who have access to a test bed that is specifically designed for JNCIP exam preparation. However, this book was also written so that adequate preparation can be achieved when the reader combines on-the-job experience with a careful study of the tips and examples contained in this book. The bottom line is that hands-on experience is critical in gaining the proficiency and troubleshooting skills required to successfully pass the JNCIP-M exam.

This book provides the reader with sample configuration scenarios that closely parallel those used in the actual JNCIP-M exam. At the time of writing, this book completely addressed all aspects of the production JNCIP-M exam. In fact, many of the configuration scenarios actually exceed the difficulty level of the current exam so that readers may be better prepared for their certification attempt.

 The operational output and configuration examples demonstrated throughout this book are based on JUNOS software version 5.2R2.3.

What Does This Book Cover?

This book covers design, configuration, and troubleshooting skills that are commensurate with the knowledge and skill set expected of a JNCIP-M candidate. The material closely parallels the actual JNCIP-M environment, in that each configuration example is characterized as a series of requirements and restrictions with which the resulting configuration and network behavior must comply. The reader is walked through each configuration scenario with equal emphasis placed on the correct configuration syntax and on the operational mode commands used to confirm proper operation, as defined by the restrictions placed on each configuration task. In many cases, the reader is made privy to tips and tricks that are intended to save time, avoid common pitfalls, and provide insight into how the JNCIP-M exam is graded. Knowing the techniques that are used by the exam proctors to assess the state of the candidate's network will often allow the candidate to correct his or her own mistakes before it is too late!

Each chapter begins with a list of the lab skills covered in that chapter, with the chapter body providing detailed examples of how the corresponding functionality can be quickly configured and verified. A full-blown case study typical of what the JNCIP-M candidate will encounter in the actual exam is featured near the end of each chapter. Each case study is designed to serve as a vehicle for review and as the basis for lab-based study time. Solutions to the case study configuration requirements and tips for verifying proper operation are provided at the end of each case study. Each chapter ends with review questions to highlight (and therefore prevent) mistakes that are commonly seen when JNCIP exams are graded.

The book consists of the following material:

- Chapter 1 provides detailed coverage of initial system configuration and related network management tasks. This type of configuration is typical of that normally performed on a brand-new system, and these tasks are characteristic of how the JNCIP-M candidate will usually begin their testing day.

- Chapter 2 focuses on the configuration and testing of popular interface types including Ethernet, ATM, and Packet Over Sonet (POS) interfaces running PPP or Frame Relay.

- Chapter 3 adds the OSPF Interior Gateway Protocol (IGP) to the mix. Various applications of OSPF, including authentication, route redistribution, stub and not-so-stubby areas (NSSA), and route aggregation are covered.

- Chapter 4 covers the Intermediate System to Intermediate System (IS-IS) routing protocol. Where possible, this chapter attempts to mirror the applications and features demonstrated for the OSPF routing protocol.

- Chapter 5 begins our journey into the BGP protocol by detailing the configuration and testing of the Interior Border Gateway Protocol (IBGP) in full mesh, confederation, and route reflection applications. BGP-related routing policy and route attribute manipulation are introduced in this chapter.

- Chapter 6 details the configuration and operational analysis of Exterior Border Gateway Protocol (EBGP) and provides a healthy dose of routing policy in the context of a service provider's network.

This book is written to mimic the actual JNCIP-M exam by having the reader add layers of complexity and increased functionality to a common network topology with each successive chapter. The decision to use a fixed topology allows the reader to focus on the "task at hand" instead of having to constantly adapt to new connectivity and address assignments. This layering approach helps to familiarize the reader with how the exam is structured, and also helps to reinforce the relationships between the various network protocols and applications that are covered.

How to Use This Book

This book can provide a solid foundation for the serious effort of preparing for the JNCIP-M exam. To best benefit from this book, we recommend the following study method:

- Read (and understand) the companion Juniper Networks Study Guides, such as the *JNCIA Study Guide* (Sybex, 2003), which are designed to prepare you for the lab-based nature of this book.

- When possible, you should gain access to a test bed of Juniper Networks M-series and/or T-series routers—preferably one that matches the topology used throughout this book. Accessing some routers is better than none, so get your hands on as many routers as you can. This book was designed to simulate the experience of actually working with Juniper Networks routers as closely as possible, recognizing that there is a substantial cost associated with the construction of a JNCIP-M test bed. Combining on-the-job experience with a careful analysis of the examples provided in this book will prepare you for the JNCIP-M exam.

- Follow along with the chapter body configuration examples and make sure you understand how network operation is validated against the scenario's requirements through the use of operational commands.

- Do not move on to the next chapter until you are confident that you can perform the case study configuration found at the end of each chapter in the time frames suggested—without the use of manuals and without any serious operational problems in the resulting network.

- Make sure you understand the answers to all the review questions at the end of each chapter. These questions are designed to prevent common mistakes!

- Use the JUNOS software documentation set for researching related information as needed. The documentation set for JUNOS software version 5.2 is included on the accompanying CD.

To learn all the material covered in this book, you'll have to apply yourself regularly and with discipline. Try to set aside the same amount of time every day to practice router configuration and network testing, and select a comfortable and quiet place to do so. If you work hard, you will be surprised at how quickly you demonstrate a professional level of proficiencies in the configuration and testing of networks based on JUNOS software and M-series/T-series platforms. Before you know it, you'll be finished with your JNCIP and on the way to becoming a JNCIE. Good luck and may the force be with you!

What's on the CD?

We worked very hard to provide some really great tools to help you with your certification process. The accompanying CD contains the following:

Complete Router Configurations

The companion CD contains complete router configurations for the case studies found at the end of each chapter. The configurations are available in PDF for printing, and as plain-text files for loading into your own routers. Depending on the situation, you may need to edit the configuration to suit the specific interface types and addressing used in your test bed.

JNCIP Study Guide in **PDF**

Sybex is also offering the Juniper Networks Certification books on their accompanying CDs so you can read the books on your PC or laptop. The *JNCIP Study Guide* is on this CD in Adobe Acrobat format. Acrobat Reader 5.1 with Search is also included on the CD.

This will be extremely helpful to readers who travel and don't want to carry a book, as well as to readers who find it more comfortable to read from their computer.

JUNOS software Documentation in **PDF**

Finally, the Juniper Networks documentation set for version 5.2 is included on the CD so that you can read these manuals on your PC or laptop. The documentation set is in Adobe Acrobat format. Acrobat Reader 5.1 with Search is also included on the CD.

About the Author and Technical Editors

Harry Reynolds, JNCIE #3, CCIE #4977, is the curriculum development manager and a Senior Education Services Engineer at Juniper Networks Inc. He has written numerous training courses and has presented data communications and internetworking training classes for the last 15 years for a variety of organizations. His e-mail address is `h.reynolds@dr-data.net`.

Jason Rogan is a Senior Engineer with Juniper Networks Inc. and Manager of the Juniper Networks Technical Certification Program (JNTCP). He is JNCIE #8 and a Juniper Networks Authorized Instructor.

Peter Moyer is a network consultant with the Professional Services group at Juniper Networks Inc. He holds a B.S. in Computer and Information Science from the University of Maryland and is JNCIE #2 and CCIE #3286. He can be partially blamed for the construction of the industry's toughest and most valuable IP networking exam, the JNCIE.

Josef Buchsteiner is a Senior Network Support Engineer with Juniper Networks Inc. in Amsterdam, The Netherlands. He is JNCIE #38.

Chapter

1

Initial Configuration and Platform Troubleshooting

JNCIP LAB SKILLS COVERED IN THIS CHAPTER:

- ✓ Use terminal server to access router console ports
- ✓ Configure OoB management network and host name
- ✓ Create user accounts and system authentication options
- ✓ Configure syslog parameters
- ✓ Configure network management and NTP
- ✓ Determine JUNOS software version and perform upgrades
- ✓ Configure chassis alarms and redundancy

In this chapter, you will be exposed to configuration tasks that are characteristic of those encountered when installing a brand-new M-series or T-series router. These initial configuration and maintenance tasks include setting up the Out of Band (OoB) management network, user accounts and permissions, the Network Time Protocol (NTP), syslog parameters, chassis alarms, redundancy, and maintaining JUNOS software.

You will learn numerous JNCIP-level configuration requirements along with the commands needed to correctly configure a Juniper Networks router for that task. Wherever possible, you will also be provided with techniques that can be used to verify the operation and functionality of the various elements that make up your system's configuration. The chapter concludes with a case study that is designed to closely approximate a typical JNCIP initial system configuration scenario. A router configuration that meets all case study requirements is provided at the end of the case study for comparison with your own configuration.

To kick things off, you will need to access the console ports of your assigned routers using reverse telnet connections though a terminal server. As you establish initial contact with each of your routers, you should make note of the types of routers provided in your test bed and be on guard for any symptoms of hardware malfunction or aberrant operation.

Faulty hardware is never intentionally given to a JNCIP candidate, but hardware failures do occur. In view of the time pressures associated with the JNCIP practical examination, you would be wise to bring suspicions of faulty hardware to the proctor's attention as soon as possible. The proctor will confirm whether there is actually a problem and may provide workaround instructions as needed. Before calling in the proctor, it is generally a good idea to try rebooting the router, because symptoms of bad hardware may be caused by software malfunctions that are sometimes cleared by a reboot.

Task 1: Access Routers Using a Terminal Server

As described in the introduction, your JNCIP test bed consists of seven freshly flashed M-series routers, a terminal server, and a 100Mbps Fast Ethernet LAN segment that will serve as your network's Out of Band (OoB) management network. Because your routers have a factory-fresh default configuration, you will not be able to telnet to the routers until you have correctly configured the OoB management network. Therefore, you should plan on accessing the console ports of the routers assigned to your station using an IOS-based (2517 or similar) terminal server to perform your initial configuration task. Since the actual examination does not involve non–Juniper Networks products, you will be instructed on how to use the particular terminal server used at your testing center.

Although you can use the router console ports for the duration of the examination, most candidates find that it saves time to open multiple telnet sessions (one per router) using the Out Of Band (OoB) management network that is configured during the examination. You should use the terminal server whenever you are performing router maintenance (such as upgrading JUNOS software), or when routing problems cause telnet access problems.

Console Connections

The OoB (Out of Band) management topology is illustrated in Figure 1.1. Based on this figure, you can see that the IP address of the terminal server is 10.0.1.101, and that its asynchronous interfaces are connected in ascending order to the console ports of each router that is associated with your test pod.

The testing center will provide you with both user EXEC and privileged EXEC mode passwords for the terminal server (or their equivalents should a non–IOS-based terminal server be in use). You'll sometimes need the privileged EXEC mode login to reset connections when you receive error messages about ports being busy or when you see messages about connections being refused. The following is an example of a typical login session to the terminal server:

```
telnet 10.0.1.101
Trying 10.0.1.101...
Connected to 10.0.1.101.
Escape character is '^]'.


User Access Verification

Password:
cert-ts>enable
Password:
cert-ts#
```

FIGURE 1.1   The Out of Band (OoB) management network

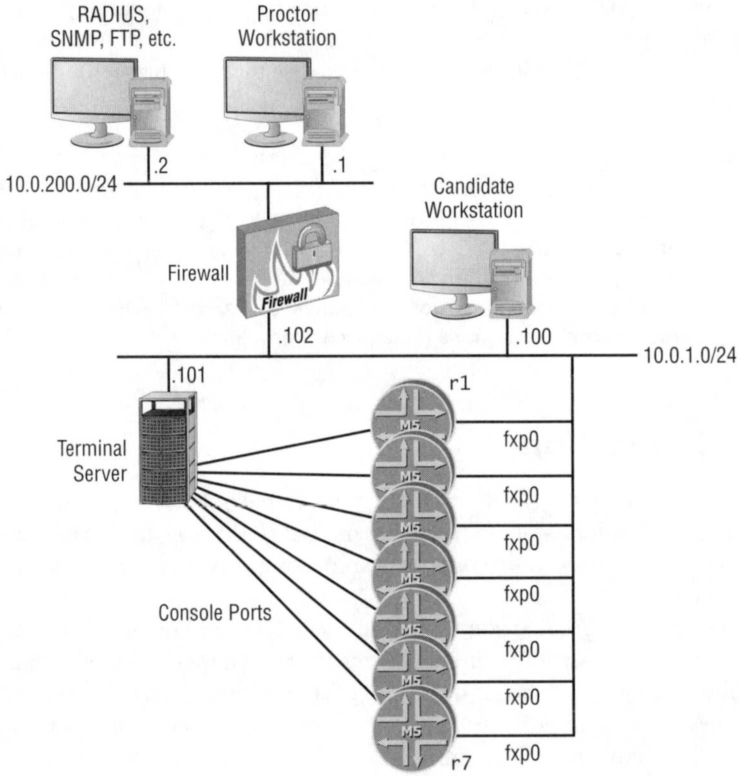

Depending upon the specifics of your test bed, you may want to configure symbolic name mappings on the terminal server to simplify the task of reverse telnetting. This will enable you to use symbolic names in lieu of specifying the reverse telnet port and IP address on the command line. In the preceding example, these name-to-address mappings have already been configured on the terminal server:

```
ip host r1 2001 10.0.1.101
ip host r2 2002 10.0.1.101
ip host r3 2003 10.0.1.101
ip host r4 2004 10.0.1.101
ip host r5 2005 10.0.1.101
ip host r6 2006 10.0.1.101
ip host r7 2007 10.0.1.101
```

In this configuration, you can see that port 2001 on the terminal server, which maps to its first asynchronous port, is associated with the symbolic name of r1. Now, to establish a reverse telnet connection to the console port of router 1, the user need only enter **r1** on the terminal server's command line. If host mappings have not been configured on your terminal server, you will need to specify the correct port identifier and IP address on the command line, as shown here:

```
cert-ts#telnet 10.0.1.101 2001
Trying 10.201.1.253, 2001 ... Open
<operator hits "enter">


Amnesiac (ttyd0)

login:
```

In the foregoing example, you can see that the reverse telnet session to r1 has succeeded, in that the router is now presenting its login prompt.

The Amnesiac prompt shown in the previous example is indicative of a router that is booting from a factory-fresh JUNOS software load, which, by definition, will not have a hostname configured. When preparing the lab for JNCIP testing, it is standard practice for the proctor to flash every router using removable media (PCMCIA) cards at the end of each certification attempt. This ensures that each new candidate will begin his or her test from a known starting point and will prevent possible difficulties caused by a previous candidate's tampering with the system's binaries or file structure.

Initial Console Login

Because the router is booting from a factory-fresh load, the only existing login account will be the user root. Initially, this account has no associated password. When logging in as root, the user is presented with the shell prompt, so the JUNOS software command-line interface (CLI) must be started manually as shown here:

```
login: root

--- JUNOS 5.2R1.4 built 2002-03-10 01:12:05 UTC

Terminal type? [vt100]
root@% cli
root>
```

Switching Among Reverse Telnet Sessions

Although the reverse telnet sessions can be opened in any order, it is highly recommended that you open the sessions to your routers in a sequential fashion. This will make it easy to switch among sessions using session numbers that map directly to corresponding router numbers. To regain the IOS command prompt, the user must enter an escape sequence consisting of a simultaneous Ctrl+Shift+6 followed by pressing the **x** key (the escape sequence is not echoed back to the user but is shown in angle brackets in the following to illustrate use of the escape sequence):

```
root> <control-shift-6 x>
pod2-ts#r2
Trying r2 (10.0.1.101, 2002)... Open


Amnesiac (ttyd0)

login:
```

After entering the escape sequence, the user is presented with an IOS prompt. If the user simply presses Enter at this point, the connection to r1 will be resumed. In this example, the user establishes a reverse telnet session to the next router (router 2) using the symbolic name r2. To switch between these two sessions, the user can now enter the escape sequence followed by the connection number, which will be either a 1 or a 2 at this stage:

```
login: <control-shift-6 x>
pod2-ts#1
[Resuming connection 1 to 10.0.1.101 ... ]


root>
```

Clearing Terminal Server Sessions

Although it's rarely necessary, sometimes you have to manually clear one or more reverse telnet sessions on the terminal server when connections cannot be correctly established to a given router's console port. This will require that you regain a privileged EXEC mode IOS command prompt to display and clear the problem line. Listing 1.1 is an example of this process. It demonstrates the clearing of Line 2 after a problem with access to r2 has been encountered:

Listing 1.1: Clearing Terminal Server Lines (IOS-Based Terminal Server)
```
pod2-ts#r2
Trying r2 (10.0.1.101, 2002)...
% Connection refused by remote host
```

```
pod2-ts#show line
```

Tty	Typ	Tx/Rx	A	Modem	Roty	AccO	AccI	Uses	Noise	Overruns
0	CTY		-	-	-	-	-	0	0	0/0
* 1	TTY	9600/9600	-	-	-	-	-	3	0	0/0
* 2	TTY	9600/9600	-	-	-	-	-	4	2031	0/0
3	TTY	9600/9600	-	-	-	-	-	3	1546	0/0
4	TTY	9600/9600	-	-	-	-	-	3	0	0/0
5	TTY	9600/9600	-	-	-	-	-	1	0	0/0
6	TTY	9600/9600	-	-	-	-	-	1	72050	3/0
7	TTY	9600/9600	-	-	-	-	-	1	19691	1/0
8	TTY	9600/9600	-	-	-	-	-	1	0	0/0
9	TTY	9600/9600	-	-	-	-	-	1	0	0/0
10	TTY	9600/9600	-	-	-	-	-	2	0	0/0
11	TTY	9600/9600	-	-	-	-	-	0	0	0/0
12	TTY	9600/9600	-	-	-	-	-	0	0	0/0
13	TTY	9600/9600	-	-	-	-	-	0	0	0/0
14	TTY	9600/9600	-	-	-	-	-	0	0	0/0
15	TTY	9600/9600	-	-	-	-	-	0	0	0/0
16	TTY	9600/9600	-	-	-	-	-	0	0	0/0
17	AUX	9600/9600	-	-	-	-	-	0	0	0/0
* 18	VTY		-	-	-	-	-	26	0	0/0
19	VTY		-	-	-	-	-	0	0	0/0
20	VTY		-	-	-	-	-	0	0	0/0
21	VTY		-	-	-	-	-	0	0	0/0
22	VTY		-	-	-	-	-	0	0	0/0

```
pod2-ts#clear line 2
[confirm]y [OK]
pod2-ts#r2
Trying r2 (10.0.1.101, 2002)... Open
<user hits enter>

Amnesiac (ttyd0)

login:
```

Reverse telnet sessions connect the user to a tty (asynchronous terminal line) on the terminal server. You will want to focus on tty sessions that have an asterisk (*) next to them, because this character indicates the line is in use. To clear a line, enter the **clear line** *n* command at the privileged EXEC mode prompt, and confirm the clear by entering **y** when prompted.

A Caution About Clearing Sessions

The "failure" described in Listing 1.1 was simulated by trying to open a second telnet session to port 2002 on the terminal server without first clearing the existing session. The operator should have simply entered the session number (2 in this case) to switch back to the previously established connection to resume the connection to router r2. Clearing sessions in the manner described can result in session numbers that are no longer directly related to router numbers, which can be very confusing—for example, the session associated with r2 might end up being number 8. When reverse telnet problems are detected, many candidates find it simpler to simply log out of an IOS-based terminal server, which causes the terminal server to clear all existing connections (after the user confirms). After reconnecting to the terminal server, the telnet sessions to all routers can be reestablished in the correct numeric sequence.

Task 2: Configure the OoB Management Network

Once you have opened reverse telnet sessions to each of the routers assigned to your test bed, you will want to configure and test the fxp0-based OoB management network and assign the correct hostname to each router. Once again referring to Figure 1.1, you can see that each router's fxp0 interface connects to a shared Ethernet segment with a logical IP subnet of 10.0.1.0/24. Also, the host value of each fxp0 address must match the router number, so router 1 will have the address 10.0.1.1 assigned to its fxp0 interface. The OoB management network must be reachable from the proctor's workstation, which is attached to subnet 10.0.200/24 behind a firewall router.

Because each router also requires a unique name, it makes sense to configure the router's hostname along with the OoB addressing and telnet service at this point. The following commands, entered on r1, will set the correct IP address and hostname for this exercise, and will enable the telnet service:

```
root> configure
Entering configuration mode

[edit]
root# set system host-name r1

[edit]
root# set interfaces fxp0 unit 0 family inet address 10.0.1.1/24

[edit]
root# set system services telnet
```

The resulting configuration is now as follows:

```
[edit]
root# show interfaces
fxp0 {
    unit 0 {
        family inet {
            address 10.0.1.1/24;
        }
    }
}

[edit]
root# show system
host-name r1;
services {
    telnet;
}
syslog {
    user * {
        any emergency;
    }
    file messages {
        any notice;
        authorization info;
    }
}
```

With the correct configuration now in r1, you decide to commit the changes to place them into effect:

```
[edit]
root# commit and-quit
commit complete
Exiting configuration mode

root@r1>
```

After the candidate configuration has been successfully committed, the router's command prompt takes on the newly assigned hostname. Although the configuration steps performed thus far will make telnet access available to the candidate, the router currently does not have a route back to the proctor's subnet, which will prevent proctor-initiated telnet connection to your routers. To rectify this situation, you must add a static route on each router for the 10.0.200/24 proctor subnet, using the firewall router (10.0.1.102) as the next hop. This route should have the `no-readvertise` tag to ensure the router does not inadvertently redistribute the static route in a later lab scenario. The following commands create the necessary static route and show the resulting configuration change:

```
[edit routing-options static route]
root@r1# set 10.0.200/24 next-hop 10.0.1.102 no-readvertise

[edit routing-options]
root@r1# show
static {
    route 10.0.200.0/24 {
        next-hop 10.0.1.102;
        no-readvertise;
    }
}
```

To confirm that the OoB management network and static routing are operational, try to ping the RADIUS/FTP server on the proctor subnet, like this:

```
root@r1> ping 10.0.200.2
PING 10.0.200.2 (10.0.200.2): 56 data bytes
64 bytes from 10.0.200.2: icmp_seq=0 ttl=255 time=1.228 ms
64 bytes from 10.0.200.2: icmp_seq=1 ttl=255 time=0.701 ms
^C
--- 10.0.200.2 ping statistics ---
2 packets transmitted, 2 packets received, 0% packet loss
round-trip min/avg/max/stddev = 0.701/0.964/1.228/0.264 ms
```

Based on the successful results shown in this output, things are now looking good for your OoB management network.

Task 3: Create User Accounts

When the OoB management network and its associated routing are confirmed to be operational, you will likely want to configure various user accounts. These accounts should make use of both local and remote authentication, and should also verify your ability to use `allow` and `deny` commands to provide local control of user authorization levels.

In the example shown in Table 1.1, the following accounts (and permissions) will be configured to demonstrate typical user account configuration and validation techniques.

TABLE 1.1   User Account Parameters

User	Password	Class/Permission	Notes
root	root	superuser	SSH with 1024-bit RSA public key authentication. Local password and RADIUS authentication criteria are the same as for user lab.
lab	lab	superuser	RADIUS/local password with automatic login in the event of RADIUS failure. RADIUS secret is *jni*.
ops	operator	Can view standard show interfaces output and conduct ping testing only.	RADIUS/local password, 5-minute inactivity time-out.

Configuring the Root Account

As noted in Table 1.1, the root user's account must be configured for SSH public key and RADIUS/local password authentication. The following commands configure the root account with the required SSH version 1 RSA public key (version 2 RSA keys are not supported at the time of this writing so a version 1 key must be loaded). It is important to note that the operator must manually add the opening and closing quotes (" ") so that white spaces in the key string do not cause syntax errors if the key is pasted from a terminal buffer. You could also choose to edit the ~/.ssh/authorized_keys file manually to add the public RSA key (by escaping to a shell and using vi), or you could transfer the key file to the router using the load-key-file option with an appropriate URL, such as ftp://user:password@hostname/file-name. However, the CLI paste approach demonstrated here is generally considered to be the most straightforward:

```
[edit system root-authentication]
root@r1# set ssh-rsa "key-data-pasted-from-terminal"
```

And now, to enable the SSH service on the router, which by default will support both SSH version 1 and 2:

```
[edit system]
root@r1# set system services ssh
```

Since the use of SSH public key authentication for the root account has no effect on local console-based logins, we also set the required root password:

```
[edit system]
root@r1# set root-authentication plain-text-password
New password:
Retype new password:
```

The following is the resulting configuration for the root account and the SSH service:

```
[edit system]
root@r1# show root-authentication
encrypted-password "$1$n/lx3$RNtF9uDlCsMsAL8gi/qA31"; # SECRET-DATA
ssh-rsa "1024 65537
1450752183928279843248252183502305532638140166345205866908088649146554470078439 2
8111405582237619829072232066626802021176342985734845637869610319998691546196249 4
3547969289443741778089801748344031384110736712267008043997289419567932079675341 0
7312228338991418693275832311709060479858146825449419051074168398032 83 root"; #
SECRET-DATA
```

```
lab@r2# show system services
ssh;
telnet;
```

Verify the Root Account

To confirm operation of the root account, you should test local authentication using the root password, and test SSH authentication using an appropriately configured session on your terminal emulator. The SSH session settings used in the SecureCRT application are shown in Figure 1.2; it should be noted that RSA (public key) has been selected as the authentication method (as opposed to password-based authentication).

FIGURE 1.2   SSH session settings for the root account

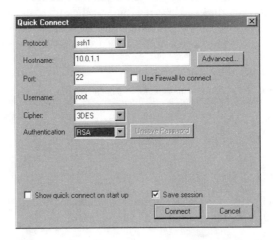

Generating SSH Key Pairs

The method used to generate your own SSH public/private key pair will vary based on SSH version and the particular client software being used.

For a Unix-like operating system   Generate a 1024-bit SSH version 1 RSA key pair using the ssh-keygen program with the –b flag set to *1024* and the -t flag set to *rsa1*. By default, the resulting public key will be written to $HOME/.ssh/identity.pub. The contents of this file would then be loaded into the router using the techniques described in the section "Configuring the Root Account" earlier in this chapter. Typical ssh-keygen output is shown here:

```
[harry@dr-data harry]$ ssh-keygen -b 1024 -t rsa1
Generating public/private rsa1 key pair.
Enter file in which to save the key (/home/harry/.ssh/identity):
Enter passphrase (empty for no passphrase):
Enter same passphrase again:
Your identification has been saved in /home/harry/.ssh/identity.
Your public key has been saved in /home/harry/.ssh/identity.pub.
The key fingerprint is:
d1:ac:20:9b:f6:82:04:06:09:69:11:57:66:8d:17:be harry@dr-data.net
```

After loading the resulting public key into the router, SSH connectivity can be tested:

```
[harry@dr-data harry]$ ssh -1 root -1 10.0.1.1
The authenticity of host '10.0.1.1 (10.0.1.1)' can't be established.
RSA1 key fingerprint is 10:e1:82:2f:6b:c3:9c:5e:84:d5:6c:0b:df:1c:3d:ea.
Are you sure you want to continue connecting (yes/no)? yes
Warning: Permanently added '10.0.1.1' (RSA1) to the list of known hosts.
Enter passphrase for RSA key '/home/harry/.ssh/identity':
Last login: Wed May 15 17:38:58 2002 from 10.0.1.201
--- JUNOS 5.2R2.3 built 2002-03-23 02:44:36 UTC


root@r1%
```

In this example, the -l switch was needed to indicate that the remote login name should be root instead of the user's local Unix login name, which would be harry in this case. The -1 was also needed to indicate that SSH version 1 should be used, because the SSH configuration on this author's Linux machine causes it to first try SSH version 2.

For the SecureCRT application   Generate a key pair by clicking the Advanced button in the SSH Quick Connect dialog box, followed by selecting the Create Identity File option in the resulting Advanced SSH Options dialog box, which will open the SecureCRT Key Generation Wizard. The wizard will guide you through the remaining key generation steps. When the Wizard completes, you will be prompted to enter the directory and key filenames for your newly generated secret and public keys. When using SecureCRT version 3.1.2, the default location and filename for the secret key is C:\Program Files\SecureCRT 3.0\identity. The public key will be stored in the same directory with a .pub file extension. As described in the previous "For a Unix-like Operating System" section, the contents of this public key file should be loaded into the router using the procedures outlined in the "Configuring the Root Account" section earlier in this chapter.

You will be asked to accept a "new host key" when testing SSH connectivity to the router for the first time, as shown in Figure 1.3.

FIGURE 1.3 Accepting a new host key

After accepting the host key, you will be prompted to enter the pass phrase associated with the session's private key. When the correct pass phrase is entered, you should be logged in as the root user and presented with a shell prompt.

Configuring the Lab Account

The following commands establish the lab account and associate the user with the superuser login class:

```
[edit system]
root@r1# set login user lab class superuser
[edit system]
root@r1# set login user lab authentication plain-text-password
New password:
Retype new password:
```

Because the lab, root, and ops accounts are to be authenticated through RADIUS, you must now configure the RADIUS server's properties. The RADIUS-related parameters needed for this task are configured with the following commands:

```
[edit system]
lab@r1# set radius-server 10.0.200.2 secret jni
```

If your test bench does not offer RADIUS support, you can reduce the delay associated with the failed RADIUS authentication requests by setting the retry and timeout parameters to 1.

To tell the system that RADIUS authentication is to be used first, you must specify `radius` as the first entry in the system's `authentication-order` list with the following command:

```
[edit system]
root@r1# set authentication-order radius
```

The resulting lab account and RADIUS configuration are shown next:

```
root@r1# show login user lab
class superuser;
authentication {
    encrypted-password "$1$nNISN$o7OGTEhEF5sOcgjS9pOLf0"; # SECRET-DATA
}
root@r1# show radius-server
10.0.200.2 secret "$9$NQVs4Pfz36A"; # SECRET-DATA
[edit system]
root@r1# show authentication-order
authentication-order radius;
```

Verify the Lab Account

To verify the lab account, we log out as **root** and reconnect as the `lab` user:

```
root@r1% exit
logout


r1 (ttyd0)


login: lab
Password:
Last login: Fri Mar  8 16:20:47 on ttyd0

--- JUNOS 5.2B3.1 built 2001-12-28 18:50:44 UTC

lab@r1>
```

Though the previous capture indicates that your user account is functional, notice the terminology "automatic login in the event of RADIUS failure" in Table 1.1, shown earlier. This should cause you to wonder what would happen if the RADIUS server should become unreachable. To simulate a RADIUS failure, the shared secret is changed to **foo** and the lab account is retested:

```
[edit system radius-server]
lab@r1# set 10.0.1.102 secret foo
```

```
[edit system radius-server]
lab@r1# commit and-quit
commit complete
Exiting configuration mode

lab@r1> quit


r1 (ttyd0)

login: lab
Password:
Local password:
Last login: Mon Apr  1 12:36:17 on ttyd0

--- JUNOS 5.2B3.1 built 2001-12-28 18:50:44 UTC

lab@r1>
```

Note the second prompt that asks for a local password. This indicates that automatic login is not functional. The problem lies in the omission of the `password` keyword in the system's `authentication-order` statement. Adding `password` after `radius` will cause the router to automatically verify the user's password against the local password database when access to the RADIUS server fails. To meet the configuration criteria, you must enter the following command to add `password` to the router's authentication order list:

```
[edit]
lab@r1# set system authentication-order password

[edit]
lab@r1# show system authentication-order
authentication-order [ radius password ];

[edit]
lab@r1# commit and-quit
commit complete
Exiting configuration mode
```

With the changes committed, we now retest the `lab` login:

```
lab@r1> quit


r1 (ttyd0)
```

```
login: lab
Password:
Last login: Mon Apr  1 12:41:09 on ttyd0

--- JUNOS 5.2B3.1 built 2001-12-28 18:50:44 UTC

lab@r1>
```

The user is now automatically logged in using the local password database when access to the RADIUS server is broken. After testing, you should reset the shared RADIUS secret to the correct value as specified in Table 1.1, shown earlier.

The local password database is not consulted when the RADIUS server returns an access reject message because of an unknown username or incorrect password being used. You will need to remove (or deactivate) the system's RADIUS configuration or change the authentication order to allow local logins if you feel that the RADIUS server has been misconfigured with regard to a given account's username or password.

Configure the Ops Account

You will now configure a user called ops that is only authorized to view the output of show interfaces and conduct ping testing.

The commands in Listing 1.2 configure the ops account and display the resulting configuration:

Listing 1.2: Commands for Configuring the Ops Account

```
[edit system login]
root@r1# set user ops class ops authentication plain-text-password
New password:
Retype new password:

[edit system login]
root@r1# set class ops permissions network

[edit system login class]
root@r1# set ops idle-timeout 5

[edit system login class]
root@r1# set ops allow-commands "show interfaces $"
```

```
[edit system login class]
root@r1# set ops deny-commands "traceroute|telnet|ssh"

[edit system login class]
root@r1# up

[edit system login]
root@r1# show user ops
uid 2002;
class ops;
authentication {
    encrypted-password "$1$SgJQQ$VYXXLPf9/TMOnb2ohWxOJ."; # SECRET-DATA
}

[edit system login]
root@r1# show class ops
idle-timeout 5;
permissions network;
allow-commands "show interfaces";
deny-commands "traceroute|telnet|ssh";
```

> Because these user account requirements involve custom settings of login class permissions, care should be taken to avoid the use of the predefined login classes (operator, read-only, superuser, and unauthorized). The parameters associated with these accounts cannot be modified. Depending on the JUNOS software version being used, you may be allowed to configure customized settings for the predefined login classes, but these changes will not actually have any effect on their default permissions.

This configuration example illustrates one possible solution to the ops account restrictions as specified in this example. In this case, we begin with a login class that contains only the network permission, which, by default, allows only access to the ping, telnet, traceroute, and SSH commands. Because the ops user should have access only to the ping utility, the deny-commands option was used with a regular expression to explicitly deny access to the telnet, traceroute, and SSH commands. In a similar fashion, the allow-commands option was included in the ops class to explicitly permit the use of the show interfaces command. Further, the nature of this allow-commands regular expression will not allow arguments such as detail or terse with the show interfaces command, so the ops user will be able to issue only the standard show interfaces command. In contrast, specifying show interfaces$ as the regular expression for allowed commands will provide access to the full range of options supported by the show interfaces command.

Verify the Ops Account

To confirm the ops login and account permissions, we log in as **ops** and verify that we have access to the standard show interfaces and ping commands. Listing 1.3 shows you this sequence. Based on the results shown in Listing 1.3, you can see that all the account restrictions for the **ops** user have been met.

Listing 1.3: Verify Ops Account Permissions
```
ops@r1> show ?
Possible completions:
  host                    Host name lookup service using domain name server
  interfaces              Show interface information

ops@r1> show interfaces
Physical interface: fe-0/0/0, Enabled, Physical link is Down
  Interface index: 10, SNMP ifIndex: 13
  Link-level type: Ethernet, MTU: 1514, Speed: 100mbps,
. . .

ops@r1> show interfaces fxp0 detail
error: permission denied for interfaces: detail

ops@r1> ping 10.0.1.102
PING 10.0.1.102 (10.0.1.102): 56 data bytes
64 bytes from 10.0.1.102: icmp_seq=0 ttl=255 time=0.560 ms
^C
--- 10.0.1.102 ping statistics ---
1 packets transmitted, 1 packets received, 0% packet loss
round-trip min/avg/max/stddev = 0.560/0.560/0.560/0.000 ms

ops@r1> tra
        ^
unknown command.
ops@r1> tel
        ^
unknown command.
ops@r1>
```

Task 4: Configure Syslog Parameters

Now that your user accounts are configured and you have confirmed that they work, you can move on to adjusting the default syslog parameters. The default syslog configuration on an M-series router will be similar to this example:

```
[edit]
lab@r1# show system syslog
user * {
    any emergency;
}
file messages {
    any notice;
    authorization info;
```

The default syslog settings will display emergency-level messages for all facility classes to any user that is logged in, and will log at the notice and info levels to the file messages for all facility classes and for the authorization class, respectively. The default archive settings will allow up to ten 128KB files that are not world-readable.

In this example, your goal is to modify the default syslog parameters to achieve the following criteria:

- Place authorization messages into a log file named auth
- Permit five copies of the auth file, each no larger than 5MB

The commands used to meet these requirements are as follows:

```
[edit system syslog]
lab@r1# delete file messages authorization

[edit system syslog]
lab@r1# set file auth authorization info

[edit system syslog]
lab@r1# set file auth archive files 5 size 5m
```

And here is the modified syslog stanza:

```
[edit system syslog]
lab@r1# show
user * {
    any emergency;
}
```

```
file messages {
    any notice;
}
file auth {
    authorization info;
    archive size 5m files 5;
}
```

Verify Syslog Operation

Verifying the modified syslog parameters is relatively simple. You can open a second telnet connection to the router and monitor the log files while you log in and out, or you can view the log files offline to confirm that authorization-related information is now being written to both the auth and messages log files. The second approach is illustrated next:

```
lab@r1> quit

r1 (ttyd0)

login: anything
Password:
Login incorrect
login: ^CClient aborted login

r1 (ttyd0)

login: lab
Password:
Last login: Mon Apr  1 14:33:26 on ttyd0

--- JUNOS 5.2B3.1 built 2001-12-28 18:50:44 UTC

lab@r1> show log auth
Apr  1 14:36:25 r1 login: 1 LOGIN FAILURE ON ttyd0
Apr  1 14:36:30 r1 login: login on ttyd0 as lab
```

When modifying the syslog configuration, care should be taken to ensure that the remaining default settings are left according to the lab scenario's instructions. For example, the following syslog configuration sets the default archive parameters of all files at the [edit system syslog] level and below to five files of 5MB each. Such a setting will also affect the size and number of the archived messages files stored on your router. Depending on the specifics of your configuration requirement, changing the default size and number of archived messages files could result in lost points on the JNCIP exam:

```
[edit system syslog]

lab@r1# show
archive size 5m files 5;
user * {
    any emergency;
}
file messages {
    any notice;
}
file auth {
    authorization info;
}
```

Task 5: Configure Network Management and NTP

Now that you have correctly set your syslog parameters, we next examine typical SNMP and NTP configuration requirements. SNMP can be used to pull statistics and operational status from your router, while the NTP protocol can be used to ensure that all of the routers in your test bench have an accurate and consistent time-of-day setting.

Configure SNMP

In the following example, we will configure SNMP with the parameters listed next. Refer to Figure 1.1, shown earlier, for addressing specifics:

- Only allow SNMP access from the SNMP server
- Only allow SNMP access over the fxp0 interface
- Use a community string of test
- Send all link up and down related traps to the SNMP server

  These requirements are met with the following SNMP configuration:

```
[edit snmp]
lab@r1# show
interface fxp0.0;
```

```
community test {
    clients {
        10.0.200.2/32;
    }
}
trap-group interface {
    categories link;
    targets {
        10.0.200.2;
    }
}
```

By default, SNMP requests will be accepted over any interface. Specifying one or more inter-face names under the `interface` keyword will cause SNMP requests on nonmatching interfaces to be ignored. Similarly, all clients are allowed to make requests by default; specifying one or more client IP addresses after the `clients` keyword causes requests from nonmatching clients to be ignored. This example includes a trap group named *interface* that has been configured to send link up and down traps to the SNMP server by including the `link` keyword under the `categories` hierarchy. By default, both SNMP versions 1 and 2 traps will be sent, but either version can be forced through appropriate trap group configuration.

SNMP uses community strings for authentication. Failure to include a community string will result in the denial of all SNMP requests, while specifying the wrong community string will result in otherwise legitimate requests being denied, so take care when configuring your SNMP community values, and pay special attention to the community string case as the strings are case sensitive. By default, SNMP clients are authorized to view only. Read and write access (SNMP get and put) can be granted by including the `read-write` keyword under the community definition as shown next:

```
[edit snmp]
lab@r1# set community test authorization read-write
```

Verify SNMP

The verification of correct SNMP configuration can be difficult without access to the SNMP management station. There are a few things you can do to test your SNMP configuration, how-ever. You can start by verifying that the router is now listening on UDP port 161, which is the port associated with SNMP requests:

```
lab@r1> show system connections
Active Internet connections (including servers)
Proto Recv-Q Send-Q Local Address        Foreign Address        (state)
tcp4    0      0   *.23                  *.*                    LISTEN
tcp4    0      0   *.22                  *.*                    LISTEN
tcp4    0      0   10.0.1.1.22           10.0.1.100.2346        ESTABLISHED
tcp4    0      0   *.666                 *.*                    LISTEN
```

```
udp46      0      0   *.161              *.*
udp4       0      0   *.161              *.*
udp4       0      0   *.500              *.*
udp46      0      0   *.1025             *.*
udp4       0      0   *.1024             *.*
udp4       0      0   *.*                *.*
udp4       0      0   *.123              *.*
```

Proper trap group operation can be verified by monitoring traffic on the system's OoB interface using the following steps. First, open a second telnet session to the router for the purpose of monitoring UDP traffic on the router's fxp0 interface. This is done using the following command:

```
root@r1> monitor traffic interface fxp0 matching udp
Listening on fxp0
```

Second, assign an arbitrary address to the router's lo0 interface in order to generate a link up trap. Once the configuration is committed, an SNMP trap should be generated on the router's fxp0 interface. If the trap group is configured correctly, you will see something that is similar to the following. Note that the destination address for the trap matches the address of the SNMP server shown earlier in Figure 1.1.

```
15:34:45.871146 Out 10.0.1.1.1024
  > 10.0.200.2.snmptrap:  C=interface Trap(36)
  E:2636.1.1.1.2.5 10.0.1.1 linkUp 1467547 [|snmp]
15:34:45.871250 Out 10.0.1.1.1024
  > 10.0.200.2.snmptrap:  C=interface V2Trap(35)
  system.sysUpTime.0=1467547 .iso.org.dod.internet=[|snmp]
```

You can monitor SNMP command response operation through SNMP protocol tracing, but the monitor traffic mechanism shown previously is the best way to verify that your router is sending SNMP traps as required.

After verifying the trap, be sure to remove any arbitrary addressing that you have assigned to the lo0 interface. Neglecting to do so could cause problems in a subsequent lab scenario.

Configure NTP

Once again, refer to Figure 1.1 for the addressing specifics needed to complete this task. In this example, you will need to configure your router as a unicast NTP client because the NTP server is not directly attached to your OoB management network and the lack of multicast/broadcast forwarding on the firewall router will prevent the use of multicast or broadcast client modes.

In this example, you will configure NTP on the local router to meet the following criteria:

- The router must synchronize to the NTP server.
- The router's clock cannot set automatically at boot.
- NTP version 4 must be used, with MD5 authentication using key ID 101 and a key value of jni.

The following configuration commands get us started on these criteria:

```
[edit system ntp]
lab@r1# set server 10.0.200.2 key 101
```

```
[edit system ntp]
lab@r1# set trusted-key 101
```

```
[edit system ntp]
lab@r1# set authentication-key 101 type md5 value jni
```

The first command tells the router to operate as an NTP client, and to include authentication key 101 in the messages it sends to the NTP server identified as 10.0.200.2. The second command specifies that messages containing a key ID of 101 are to be trusted, and the last command defines the key parameters by specifying the use of message digest 5 (MD5) and the key value of jni. Since NTP version 4 is the default for unicast NTP in JUNOS software 5.2, no NTP version–related configuration is necessary, but explicit version configuration is never a bad idea when you are unsure about the system's default version.

The resulting NTP configuration is shown next:

```
[edit system ntp]
lab@r1# show
authentication-key 101 type md5 value "$9$Q5J23/tleWLxd"; # SECRET-DATA
server 10.0.200.2 key 101;
trusted-key 101;
```

It should be noted that the boot-server statement has been omitted from the previous configuration, because its presence will cause the router to automatically synchronize its clock upon bootup using the ntpdate command, which would violate the NTP configuration requirements listed at the beginning of this example.

Verify NTP

To verify NTP operation, commit your changes and issue the show ntp associations command, as shown next:

```
lab@r1> show ntp associations
     remote           refid        st t when poll reach   delay   offset  jitter
==============================================================================
 10.0.200.2        LOCAL(0)        11 u   25   64    37   0.492  2542804 4000.00
```

Many operators find the output of this command to be confusing. The key to this display is the overall fate of the clock selection and synchronization process, which is indicated by various characters in the far left margin. In this example, the presence of a space in front of the `10.0.200.2` address indicates that the peer has been rejected due to failed sanity checks or a stratum level that is too high. Synchronization with a particular NTP server is indicated with an asterisk (*) in the left margin, and this is what we need to see for 10.0.200.2 before we can move on.

However, the non-zero delay and offset fields in the previous display indicate that NTP messages are being received from the server, and that the messages are being correctly authenticated, which is a good start. So what is preventing the local router from synchronizing with the NTP server? The answer lies in the NTP specification and the fact that it will not allow the NTP protocol to make gross adjustments in a system's clock. According to the NTP specification, synchronization requires that the two system clocks be off by at least 128 milliseconds, but no more than 128 seconds, before synchronization can begin. Use of the `boot-server` option will set the system's clock at boot time, regardless of how far off it may be from that of the specified server, but this option requires a reboot to take effect, and automatic clock setting at reboot is not permitted in this example.

So, it would seem that the solution to this dilemma is the manual setting of your router's clock to bring it to within 128 seconds of the server's clock. To obtain the NTP server's view of the time, you could manually decode NTP messages using tcpdump or `monitor traffic`, or you could take the easy route of telnetting into the NTP server to issue a `date` command. The following commands demonstrate the latter approach:

```
lab@r1> telnet 10.0.200.2
Trying 10.0.200.2...
Connected to 10.0.200.2.
Escape character is '^]'.

Red Hat Linux release 6.0 (Hedwig)
Kernel 2.2.17 on an i686
login: lab
Password:
Last login: Mon Apr  1 08:23:21 from yoda
[lab@ntp]$ date
Mon Apr  1 15:45:29 PST 2002
 [lab@ntp]$ exit
logout
Connection closed by foreign host.
```

Now that you know the server's view of the current time, you can manually set your router's clock as shown next:

```
lab@r1> set date 200204011545
Mon Apr  1 15:45:00 UTC 2002
```

Now, assuming that you have set the local router's clock accurately (and quickly), the two clocks should be within the limits needed for NTP synchronization. However, since the NTP protocol requires several successful packet exchanges before allowing synchronization, you will have to wait approximately five minutes to determine your relative success in this matter. Because NTP slowly steps a system's clock into synchronization, it may take a seemingly inordinate amount of time to get the proper NTP synchronization on all of your routers. You can tell when things are working correctly when you see a display containing an asterisk in the left margin, as shown next:

```
lab@r1> show ntp associations
     remote          refid        st t when poll reach   delay   offset  jitter
================================================================================
*10.0.200.2      LOCAL(0)       11 u   10   64   17    0.491  12.991  10.140
```

NTP operation is confusing to many exam candidates, and the delays associated with normal NTP operation have been known to cause some candidates to assume that they have made a mistake when things do not work as expected right away. When all else fails, remember that NTP works slowly, and that the system clocks have to be within 128 seconds of each other to get things synchronizing. Also, keep in mind that time zone settings will affect your local clock, and remember that non-zero values in the offset and delay fields of the `show ntp associations` command indicate successful communication and, when in use, authentication between your router and the NTP server. As a final tip, when all else has failed, you may want to try deactivating and reactivating the NTP configuration stanza to ensure that recent changes are in fact being put into effect after you commit them.

TIP   A possible shortcut to the problem of manual clock setting would be the use of the `boot-server` option coupled with a reboot to get your router's clocks initially synchronized to the NTP server's. Once you have obtained synchronization, you can simply remove the `boot-server` statement and move on with your life, with no one being the wiser as to how initial synchronization was achieved.

Set Your Local Time Zone

Even though your router is now synchronized with the NTP server, you will likely find that the local time is being displayed incorrectly because of the router's default use of the UTC time zone. The following commands show the router's view of the local time before and after the correct local time zone is configured:

```
lab@r1> show system uptime
Current time:      2002-04-02 01:35:42 UTC
System booted:     2002-04-01 18:33:27 UTC (07:02:15 ago)
Protocols started: 2002-04-01 18:33:17 UTC (07:02:25 ago)
Last configured:   2002-04-02 01:25:14 UTC (00:10:28 ago) by lab
 1:35AM  up  7:02, 2 users, load averages: 0.00, 0.00, 0.00
```

Though this author often works well past 6:00 P.M., it would be rare to see me working at 1:35 A.M.! The following commands correctly set the router's time zone based on the location of the test bed:

```
[edit]
lab@r1# set system time-zone America/Los_Angeles
lab@r1# commit and-quit
commit complete
Exiting configuration mode

lab@r1> show system uptime
Current time:       2002-04-02 01:36:00 UTC
System booted:      2002-04-01 18:33:27 UTC (07:02:33 ago)
Protocols started:  2002-04-01 18:33:17 UTC (07:02:43 ago)
Last configured:    2002-04-02 01:35:57 UTC (00:00:03 ago) by lab
5:36PM  up  7:03, 2 users, load averages: 0.08, 0.02, 0.01
```

The router's time of day now shows the correct value of 5:36 P.M.

Task 6: Perform General Maintenance and Software Upgrade

At this stage, your basic system configuration should be completed and its operational status confirmed. If you have not already looked for hardware anomalies or alarms, now might be a good time to issue some chassis/hardware related show commands to confirm that all is good to go with your gear. You should also take note of the JUNOS software version on each router, because an upgrade or a downgrade may be necessary to meet the requirements of your scenario. The following commands illustrate the most common ways of accessing the state of your hardware. The syntax and output can vary depending on M-series router type, but the general concept and results are similar for all Juniper Networks routers.

First, verify that there are no chassis alarms:

```
lab@r1> show chassis alarms

No alarms currently active
```

The lack of alarms indicates the router is free from serious hardware and environmental defects. Next, check out the general hardware environment of each router:

```
lab@r1> show chassis environment
Class Item                   Status      Measurement
```

```
Power  Power Supply A        OK
       Power Supply B        Absent
Temp   FPC Slot 0            OK        33 degrees C / 91 degrees F
       FEB                   OK        34 degrees C / 93 degrees F
       PS Intake             OK        29 degrees C / 84 degrees F
       PS Exhaust            OK        31 degrees C / 87 degrees F
Fans   Left Fan 1            OK        Spinning at normal speed
       Left Fan 2            OK        Spinning at normal speed
       Left Fan 3            OK        Spinning at normal speed
       Left Fan 4            OK        Spinning at normal speed
Misc   Craft Interface       OK
```

The missing power supply B is generally not an issue in a test bed, so all looks normal here. For even more information on the router's hardware, issue the following command:

```
lab@r1> show chassis hardware
Hardware inventory:
Item            Version  Part number  Serial number  Description
Chassis                               50779          M5
Midplane        REV 03   710-002650   HF2739
Power Supply A  Rev 04   740-002497   LK23083        AC
Display         REV 04   710-001995   AV8231
Host                                  bb00000792cd4801  teknor
FEB             REV 09   710-002503   HF2037         Internet Processor II
FPC 0
  PIC 0         REV 04   750-002992   HD4121         4x F/E, 100 BASE-TX
  PIC 1         REV 03   750-002971   HE5549         4x OC-3 SONET, MM
```

Based on this display, you can confirm you are working on an M5 router, with a single FPC (only one FPC is supported on an M5), equipped with a four-port Fast Ethernet PIC and a four-port OC-3 SONET PIC. It is worth noting that this router, as with all M5s, M10s, M160s, and M40e platforms, is IP II equipped. Because the IP II is needed for various enhanced functions, such as firewalls and VPNs, the absence of an IP II in any router making up your test bed is certainly worth noting. Similarly, you should take note of any service PICs available in your test bed. For instance, noting what routers have a tunnel PIC installed can be real handy if you later find yourself trying to decide on which pair of routers to use when a tunnel application is thrown your way.

Next, let's check the software versions on all the machines:

```
lab@r2> show version
Hostname: r2
Model: m5
JUNOS base [4.4R1.5]
```

```
JUNOS Kernel Software Suite [4.4R1.5]
JUNOS Routing Software Suite [4.4R1.5]
JUNOS Packet Forwarding Engine Support [4.4R1.5]
JUNOS Online Documentation Files [4.4R1.5]
. . .
```

While r2 is probably free from rust, it is running a rather old version of JUNOS software. Candidates taking the JNCIP exam are expected to know how to perform command line–based FTP transfers, and should be prepared to perform JUNOS software upgrades (or downgrades) using `jinstall`, `jbundle`, and individual `jbundle` components such as a `jroute` package, when called for. In this sample scenario, all routers must be running some form of 5.*x* release, so it looks like r2 is in line for some new bits pretty quickly.

Upgrading or downgrading an M-series router between 4.*x* and 5.*x* releases requires the use of a `jinstall` package due to the resulting change from a.out to ELF binaries; use of a `jinstall` package will affect both the system binaries and the JUNOS software components. Within a 4.*x* or 5.*x* release, the operator should use either a `jbundle` or individual j-package for upgrade or downgrade. Attempting to upgrade or downgrade between 4.*x* and 5.*x* releases using a `jbundle` package will result in wasted time, as the install script will abort without making any modifications to the system being upgraded or downgraded.

Since r2 is running a 4.*x* release, we know that we need to locate a 5.*x* related `jinstall` on the FTP server. The following capture illustrates typical FTP session commands and the actual file transfer. The capture begins by showing the initial FTP login:

```
lab@r2> ftp 10.0.200.2
Connected to 10.0.200.2.
220-cert-lab NcFTPd Server (free personal license) ready.
220-Warning!!!
220-This is a restricted computer system.
220-
220-ALL ACTIONS ARE LOGGED!
220
Name (10.0.200.2:lab): lab
331 User lab okay, need password.
Password:
230-You are user #1 of 3 simultaneous users allowed.
230-
230-Welcome to the FTP site.
230 Restricted user logged in.
Remote system type is UNIX.
Using binary mode to transfer files.
```

Now that we are logged into the FTP server, let's see what packages are available by obtaining a file listing:

```
ftp> ls
200 PORT command successful.
150 Opening ASCII mode data connection for /bin/ls.
-rw-r--r--   1 ftpuser   ftpusers   19538662 Apr  2 04:23 4.1R1.5-domestic.ls120.tgz
-rw-r--r--   1 ftpuser   ftpusers   19512433 Apr  2 04:23 4.1R1.5-domestic.pcm110.tgz
-rw-r--r--   1 ftpuser   ftpusers     433758 Apr  2 04:23 jbase-4.0B3-domestic.tgz
-rw-r--r--   1 ftpuser   ftpusers    7927224 Apr  2 04:23 jbundle-3.4R3.2.tgz
-rw-r--r--   1 ftpuser   ftpusers    6530202 Apr  2 04:23 jbundle-4.0R4.tgz
-rw-r--r--   1 ftpuser   ftpusers    7774361 Apr  2 04:23 jbundle-4.1R1.5.tgz
-rw-r--r--   1 ftpuser   ftpusers    8687924 Apr  2 04:23 jbundle-4.2R2.4-domestic.tgz
-rw-r--r--   1 ftpuser   ftpusers    9187867 Apr  2 04:23 jbundle-4.3R1.4-domestic.tgz
-rw-r--r--   1 ftpuser   ftpusers    9202130 Apr  2 04:23 jbundle-4.3R2-domestic.tgz
-rw-r--r--   1 ftpuser   ftpusers    9208526 Apr  2 04:23 jbundle-4.3R3-domestic.tgz
-rw-r--r--   1 ftpuser   ftpusers    9871826 Apr  2 04:23 jbundle-4.4B1.2-domestic.tgz
-rw-r--r--   1 ftpuser   ftpusers   10094406 Apr  2 04:23 jbundle-4.4R1.5-domestic.tgz
-rw-r--r--   1 ftpuser   ftpusers    6530202 Apr  2 04:23 jbundle-4_0R4.tgz
-rw-r--r--   1 ftpuser   ftpusers   24217723 Apr  2 04:23 jbundle-5.2R2.3-
domestic-signed.tgz
-rw-r--r--   1 ftpuser   ftpusers   19685721 Apr  2 04:23 jinstall-4.4R1.5-
domestic.tgz
-rw-r--r--   1 ftpuser   ftpusers   21543210 Apr  2 04:23 jinstall-5.2R2.3-
domestic.tgz
-rw-r--r--   1 ftpuser   ftpusers   21530984 Apr  2 04:23 jinstall-5.0B1.2-
domestic.tgz
226 Listing completed.
```

In this example, there are many packages from which to choose, but it has already been determined that a 5.x version of jinstall package is needed to satisfy the requirements of this example. In this case, the operator takes the "easy" way out by using the globbing character (*) in conjunction with the mget FTP transfer option, which results in a prompt for the transfer of each matching file:

```
ftp> mget jinstall*
mget jinstall-4.4R1.5-domestic.tgz? n
mget jinstall-5.2R2.3-domestic.tgz? y
200 PORT command successful.
150 Opening BINARY mode data connection for jinstall-5.2R2.3-domestic.tgz
(21543210 bytes)
```

```
226 Transfer completed.
21543210 bytes received in 22.07 seconds (953.15 Kbytes/s)
ftp>quit
```

Now that the correct 5.*x* jinstall package has been transferred to r2, the operator instructs the router to load the new software and to automatically reboot so that the new code is put into effect:

```
lab@r2> request system software add jinstall-5.2R2.3-domestic.tgz reboot
Installing package '/var/home/lab/jinstall-5.2R2.3-domestic.tgz' ...

WARNING:      This package will load JUNOS 5.2R2.3 software.
WARNING:      It will save JUNOS configuration files, log files, and SSH keys
WARNING:      (if configured), but erase all other files and information
WARNING:      stored on this machine.  This is the pre-installation stage
WARNING:      and all the software is loaded when you reboot the system.

Saving the config files ...
NOTICE: uncommitted changes have been saved in /var/db/config/juniper.conf.pre-
install
. . .
```

After the two reboots associated with jinstall package installation, r2 comes back up and the new code installation is confirmed:

```
lab@r2 show version
Hostname: r2
Model: m5
JUNOS Base OS boot [5.2R2.3]
JUNOS Base OS Software Suite [5.2R2.3]
JUNOS Kernel Software Suite [5.2R2.3]
JUNOS Routing Software Suite [5.2R2.3]
JUNOS Packet Forwarding Engine Support [5.2R2.3]
JUNOS Crypto Software Suite [5.2R2.3]
JUNOS Online Documentation [5.2R2.3]
```

Task 7: Configure Chassis Alarms and Redundancy

Some M-series routers support Routing Engine (RE) and system control board redundancy options. You should be familiar with the configuration and operation of the various redundancy features available on the M20, M160, M40e, and T640 platforms, and you should be familiar with the ways in which various problems can be mapped to system alarm states. An example system alarm and redundancy scenario might consist of the following requirements:

- Configure the router to generate a yellow alarm when the fxp0 interface goes down.

- Set RE0 to be the primary, and configure RE failover in the event of routing daemon failure. You may assume that the configuration files have already been mirrored on the two REs for this task.

- Ensure that failure of router flash will not affect the operation of your initial configuration.

Configure alarms   Alarms are configured at the [`edit chassis alarms`] configuration hierarchy. The following command is used to configure a yellow alarm upon detection of an fxp0 link down event:

```
[edit chassis alarm]
lab@r2# set management-ethernet link-down yellow
```

Configure redundancy   System redundancy is configured at the [`edit chassis redundancy`] configuration hierarchy. The following commands are used to explicitly configure RE0 as the primary RE, which is the default, and to evoke a switchover to RE1 in the event of routing daemon (`rpd`) failure. The following commands were issued on a M20 router, because the M5 platform does not support RE redundancy:

```
[edit]
lab@m20# set chassis redundancy routing-engine 0 master
```

```
[edit]
lab@m20# set system processes routing failover other-routing-engine
```

Perform a system snapshot   To ensure that a failure of the router's flash will not cause the loss of your initial system configuration, you must perform a system snapshot to mirror the contents of the router's flash onto the router's hard drive:

```
lab@r1> request system snapshot
umount: /altroot: not currently mounted
Copying / to /altroot.. (this may take a few minutes)
```

```
umount: /altconfig: not currently mounted
Copying /config to /altconfig.. (this may take a few minutes)

The following filesystems were archived: / /config
```

Resulting alarms and redundancy configuration   The configuration stanzas that resulted from the tasks in this example are shown next:

```
[edit]
lab@sanjose# show system processes
routing failover other-routing-engine;

[edit]
lab@sanjose# show chassis redundancy
routing-engine 0 master;

[edit]
lab@sanjose# show chassis alarm
management-ethernet {
    link-down yellow;
}
```

Your Initial System Configuration

After performing the configuration tasks outlined in this chapter, you have a configuration that resembles the complete router configuration example shown in Listing 1.4. If you have not already done so, you will now need to replicate the common portions of this configuration in all of the routers that make up your test bed so that this baseline functionality is available throughout your entire network before proceeding to the next chapter. The highlighted redundancy options shown in this example are supported only on the M20, M40e, M160, and T640 platforms.

Listing 1.4: *r1*'s Initial Configuration
```
[edit]
lab@r1# show | no-more
system {
    host-name r1;
    time-zone America/Los_Angeles;
    authentication-order [ radius password ];
```

```
    root-authentication {
        encrypted-password "$1$j5nxWQ9r$p6XQ9eKqpgsGe51DYySGI/"; # SECRET-DATA
        ssh-rsa "1024 65537
14507521839282798432482521835023055326381401663452058669080886491465544700784392
81114055822376198290722320666268020211763429857348456378696103199986915461962494
35479692894437417780898017483440313841107367122670080439972894195679320796753410
731222833899141869327583231170906047985814682544941905107416839803283 root"; #
SECRET-DATA
    }
    radius-server {
        10.0.1.102 secret "$9$.fQnEhrevL"; # SECRET-DATA
    }
    login {
        class ops {
            idle-timeout 5;
            permissions network;
            allow-commands "show interfaces";
            deny-commands "traceroute|telnet|ssh";
        }
        user lab {
            uid 2000;
            class superuser;
            authentication {
                encrypted-password "$1$nNISN$o7OGTEhEF5sOcgjS9pOLfO"; # SECRET-DATA
            }
        }
        user ops {
            uid 2002;
            class ops;
            authentication {
                encrypted-password "$1$SgJQQ$VYXXLPf9/TMOnb2ohWxOJ."; # SECRET-DATA
            }
        }
        user proctor {
            uid 2001;
            class superuser;
        }
    }
    services {
        ssh;
        telnet;
    }
```

```
        syslog {
        user * {
            any emergency;
        }
        file messages {
            any notice;
        }
        file auth {
            authorization info;
            archive size 5m files 5;
        }
    }
    processes {
        routing failover other-routing-engine;
    }
    ntp {
        authentication-key 101 type md5 value "$9$fQ39SyKM87"; # SECRET-DATA
        server 10.0.200.2 key 101;
        trusted-key 101;
    }
}
chassis {
    redundancy {
        routing-engine 0 master;
    }
    alarm {
        management-ethernet {          .
            link-down yellow;
        }
    }
}
interfaces {
    fxp0 {
        unit 0 {
            family inet {
                address 10.0.1.1/24;
            }
        }
    }
}
```

```
snmp {
    interface fxp0.0;
    community test {
        clients {
            10.0.200.2/32;
        }
    }
    trap-group interface {
        categories link;
        targets {
            10.0.200.2;
        }
    }
}
routing-options {
    static {
        route 10.0.200.0/24 {
            next-hop 10.0.1.102;
            no-readvertise;
        }
    }
}
```

The Case for Cut and Paste on the Exam

Time is a critical factor in the JNCIP examination, and any technique that can save time is well worth deploying during the lab. Deciding when a configuration is common enough to warrant pasting into the remaining routers is a decision that has to be made by each individual, and should be based on factors such as your familiarity with using load (merge|override) terminal, and the potential time savings that are expected. Cut and paste is a double-edged sword, and as with any such tool, you can cause serious problems by using it incorrectly in an effort to save time. For example, forgetting to change a lo0 address can result in duplicate router IDs (RIDs) in a subsequent OSPF scenario, and this type of problem can be very difficult to diagnose in the heat of battle. Generally speaking, it is advisable to paste configurations (or particular stanzas) into a text editor such as Word Pad, where you can easily edit the variables to suit the router that you plan to paste the configuration into.

Using Cut and Paste

The following commands illustrate how an edited version of the previous configuration can be pasted into r2. In this example, the only fields that required modification between the various routers are the hostname and fxp0 addressing:

```
root@host> configure
Entering configuration mode

[edit]
lab@host# load override terminal
[Type ^D to end input]
<select paste in emulation program>
system {
    host-name r2;
    time-zone America/Los_Angeles;
    authentication-order [ radius password ];

    . . .

        route 10.0.200.0/24 {
            next-hop 10.0.1.102;
            no-readvertise;
        }
    }
} <carriage return>
<control d>

load complete

[edit]
lab@host# commit and-quit
commit complete
Exiting configuration mode

lab@r2>
```

In the previous capture, operator input that is not echoed back is displayed in italics with "< >" delimiters. The first such occurrence is when the user selects Paste from their terminal emulation program after entering the load override terminal command. At the end of the capture, the operator enters a single carriage return to place a new line after the last curly brace, and then terminates the paste operation with the Ctrl+d key sequence (per the instructions provided at the beginning of the terminal paste operation). Because no errors are reported, the paste operation appears to have been successful. You now commit the new configuration, which results in the router's hostname becoming r2, as highlighted.

Pasting Individual Stanzas or Stanza Components

Using load override is pretty straightforward, but there are many instances when the wholesale replacement of the entire router configuration is not desired. It is also possible to paste in complete stanzas, or components from a particular stanza, though this can be a bit tricky. The following example shows the cut and paste of just the routing-options stanza. We start on r2 where we display the contents of its `routing-options` stanza:

```
[edit]
lab@r2# show routing-options
static {
    route 10.0.200.0/24 {
        next-hop 10.0.1.102;
        no-readvertise;
    }
}
```

The contents of the stanza, which is highlighted, are then selected and copied into your emulation program's capture buffer. To paste this snippet into r1, we use `load merge terminal`, and must be careful to include the configuration hierarchy `routing-options` before performing the paste operation so the router knows where to put the information that is pasted. In this example, we first delete the existing routing-options stanza on r1 to demonstrate that the paste was successful:

```
[edit]
root@r1# delete routing-options


[edit]
root@r1# show routing-options


[edit]
root@r1# load merge terminal
[Type ^D to end input]
routing-options static {
    route 10.0.200.0/24 {
        next-hop 10.0.1.102;
        no-readvertise;
    }
}-<carriage return>
```

```
<control-d>
load complete

[edit]
root@r1# show routing-options
static {
    route 10.0.200.0/24 {
        next-hop 10.0.1.102;
        no-readvertise;
    }
}
```

The procedure is similar when the goal is to paste a portion of a stanza, such as an individual static route. In this example, a static route to 1.1.1.1 has been added to r2, and this route will be pasted into r1:

```
[edit]
lab@r2# show routing-options
static {
    route 10.0.200.0/24 {
        next-hop 10.0.1.102;
        no-readvertise;
    }
    route 1.1.1.1/32 discard;
}
```

After copying the 1.1.1.1 static route into the capture buffer, it is pasted into r1 using the following commands. Note that the operator has correctly specified the destination of the pasted data by manually entering **routing-options static** before performing the paste:

```
[edit]
root@r1# load merge terminal
[Type ^D to end input]
routing-options static   route 1.1.1.1/32 discard;
/<carriage return>
<control-d>
load complete

[edit]
root@r1# show routing-options
```

```
static {
    route 10.0.200.0/24 {
        next-hop 10.0.1.102;
        no-readvertise;
    }
    route 1.1.1.1/32 discard;
}
```

Summary

This chapter provided configuration and operational mode examples for a variety of initial system configuration scenarios that are similar to the type of tasks that will confront a JNCIP candidate. At this stage, you should have a good idea of what types of configuration tasks will confront you as you begin your JNCIP examination, and you should now be comfortable with terminal server use and OoB management network establishment; creating user accounts and permissions; configuring SNMP, NTP, chassis alarms, system redundancy, and syslog; and general software maintenance procedures.

Case Study: Initial System Configuration

This section presents a list of initial system-configuration tasks that resemble the examples demonstrated throughout this chapter. For each configuration task, the relevant portions of a typical router configuration are shown and described. The complete configuration from one of the routers is provided at the end, to illustrate a known good solution for the configuration requirements provided in the case study.

Configuration Requirements

To complete this case study, you must configure all seven routers in your test bed to comply with the following criteria. It should take approximately 45 minutes to complete your configuration, and you should start with a factory-fresh JUNOS software install. A reasonable approximation of such an install will result if you load and commit the skeleton configuration found at the following location on routers running a 5.*x* JUNOS software version: /packages/mnt/jbase/sbin/ install/default-juniper.conf.

Whether you opt to flash your routers, or load the skeleton configuration file, your starting configuration should be similar to the following:

```
root@r1# show
system {
    syslog {
        user * {
            any emergency;
        }
        file messages {
            any notice;
            authorization info;
        }
    }
}
```

- Assign each router a hostname of the form *rn*, where *n* is a router number in the range of 1 through 7 inclusive.

- Configure the fxp0 network according to Figure 1.1, and ensure that you and the proctor station will have telnet access to all seven routers using the OoB management network.

- Modify the syslog parameters to log all interactive CLI commands to a file called rn-cli, where *n* is equal to the router number. Configure the CLI log to permit four archived copies that will be no larger than 128K, and ensure that CLI-related logging is also sent to

10.0.200.2, which is providing a remote syslog service. All other syslog parameters should be left at their default setting.

- Create user accounts and permissions based on Table 1.2.

TABLE 1.2   Case Study User Accounts

User/Password	Permissions	Notes
lab	superuser	Telnet, SSH version 2 only with password, and console
root	superuser	Console only
noc	View only	Telnet, SSH version 2 only with password, and console

- Ensure that all users are first authenticated through RADIUS, and that the local password database is not automatically consulted should the RADIUS server become unreachable. The RADIUS secret is juniper.

- Allow SNMP access from all IP addresses, but only allow SNMP request over the fxp0 interface. Use a community value of public for read-only access and private for read/write access. Send only version 1 authentication–related traps to the SNMP server.

- Configure all routers as broadcast NTP clients, and authenticate all messages using MD5, key ID 200, and key value juniper. Ensure that manual clock synchronization steps are not required. For this example, the NTP service is provided by 10.0.1.102.

- Ensure that all routers display the correct value for local time. You should assume that you are testing in Sunnyvale, California.

- Without using DNS, ensure that you can ping the proctor workstation using the name proctor.

- Configure the router to ignore management interface link status and enable the auxiliary console port for vt100 terminals.

Configuration Examples

Each of the case study requirements will now be echoed back along with the configuration commands that would typically be used to correctly meet the operational criteria. Due to the innate flexibility of JUNOS software, multiple solutions to the case study requirements will normally exist; for example, the operator could opt to deploy configuration groups for common configuration elements such as the RADIUS server and authentication order. The examples shown next attempt to show the most common and straightforward solutions to the configuration tasks. An example of configuration group usage to support RADIUS will be provided to demonstrate this flexibility and, indirectly, to demonstrate why a JNCIP candidate is graded on results and not on their particular configuration approach.

- Assign each router a hostname of the form **r*n***, where *n* is a router number in the range of 1 through 7 inclusive:

```
[edit]
root@host# set system host-name r2
[edit]
root@host# show system host-name
host-name r2;
```

- Configure the fxp0 network according to Figure 1.1, and ensure that you and the proctor station will have telnet access to all seven routers using the OoB management network:

```
[edit]
root@r2# set system services telnet


[edit interfaces]
root@r2# set fxp0 unit 0 family inet address 10.0.1.2/24


[edit routing-options]
root@r2# set static route 10.0.200.0/24 next-hop 10.0.1.102 no-readvertise
```

The resulting OoB-related configuration is now as follows:

```
[edit]
root@r2# show system services
telnet;


[edit]
root@r2# show interfaces fxp0
unit 0 {
    family inet {
        address 10.0.1.2/24;
    }
}
root@r2# show routing-options
static {
    route 10.0.200.0/24 {
```

```
        next-hop 10.0.1.102;
        no-readvertise;
    }
}
```

- Modify the syslog parameters to log all interactive CLI commands to a file called rn-cli,
  where *n* is the router number. Configure the CLI log to permit four archived copies that will
  be no larger than 128K, and ensure that CLI-related logging is also sent to 10.0.200.2,
  which is providing a remote syslog service. All other syslog parameters must be left at their
  default setting:

```
[edit system syslog]
root@r2# set file r2-cli interactive-commands any
```

```
[edit system syslog]
root@r2# set file r2-cli archive files 4
```

```
[edit system syslog]
lab@r1# set host 10.0.200.2 interactive-commands any
```

The modified syslog parameters are now displayed:

```
[edit system syslog]
lab@r1# show
user * {
    any emergency;
}
host 10.0.200.2 {
    interactive-commands any;
}
file messages {
    any notice;
    authorization info;
}
file r2-cli {
    interactive-commands any;
    archive files 4;
}
```

- Create user accounts and permissions based on Table 1.3.

TABLE 1.3 Case Study User Accounts

User/pass	permissions	Notes
lab	superuser	Telnet, SSH version 2 only with password, and console
root	superuser	Console only
noc	View only	Telnet, SSH version 2 only with password, and console

The commands used to correctly configure and display user account and permission settings are shown in Listing 1.5.

Listing 1.5: User Account Configuration
```
[edit system]
root@r2# set root-authentication plain-text-password
New password:
Retype new password:

[edit system login]
root@r2# set user lab class superuser

root@r2# set user lab authentication plain-text-password
New password:
Retype new password:

[edit system login]
root@r2# set class noc permissions view

[edit system login]
root@r2# set user noc class noc

[edit system login]
root@r2# set user noc authentication plain-text-password
New password:
Retype new password:

[edit]
root@r1# set system services ssh protocol-version v2

[edit]
lab@r2# set system services ssh root-login deny
```

```
[edit]
lab@r2# show system services
ssh {
    root-login deny;
    protocol-version v2;
}
telnet;

[edit]
root@r2# show system root-authentication
encrypted-password "$1$RTyGDGYG$ukqr37VGRgtohedSlruOk/"; # SECRET-DATA

[edit]
root@r2# show system login
class noc {
    permissions view;
}
user lab {
    class superuser;
    authentication {
        encrypted-password "$1$L6ZKKWYI$GxEI/7YzXes2JXDcHJvz7/"; # SECRET-DATA
    }
}
user noc {
    class noc;
    authentication {
        encrypted-password "$1$Z5Sb1eVg$R8.iZMCAMAOTdEeS2svvd0"; # SECRET-DATA
    }
}
```

By default, all users except root can log in via console, telnet, or SSH. The root user can log in by using either the console or SSH by default, so to meet the criteria for this case study you must disable root's ability to log in using SSH. The correct SSH version must also be set in this example, because the default JUNOS software behavior will support SSH versions 1 and 2.

- Ensure that all users are first authenticated through RADIUS, and that the local password database is not automatically consulted should the RADIUS server become unreachable. The RADIUS secret is juniper.

```
[edit system]
root@r2# set authentication-order radius
```

```
[edit system]
root@r2# set radius-server 10.0.200.2 secret juniper
```

The resulting system authentication configuration is now displayed:

```
[edit system]
root@r2# show radius-server
10.0.200.2 secret "$9$-UbYoDi.z39JG39ApREdbs"; # SECRET-DATA


[edit system]
root@r2# show authentication-order
authentication-order radius;
```

By omitting the password option from the system's authentication order statement, you ensure that the local password database is not automatically consulted when the RADIUS server becomes unreachable, which results in the operator being prompted for a local password in the event of RADIUS connectivity problems.

Configuration Groups

As previously mentioned, JUNOS software is extremely flexible, and this flexibility can translate to the ability to satisfy a configuration requirement using what can appear to be orthogonal approaches. Configuration groups provide excellent proof of this concept in that they allow common elements of a configuration to be specified at the [edit groups] configuration hierarchy. Once configured, these groups can then be applied to the appropriate level of the system's configuration to affect the inheritance of group-related configuration. You can override this group inheritance through explicit configuration where needed. For example, consider the following configuration group called authentication, which will result in the required RADIUS and authentication order behavior when applied as shown:

```
[edit]
lab@r1# show groups
authentication {
    system {
        authentication-order radius;
        radius-server {
            10.0.1.201 secret "$9$9ftBtOIylMNdsEcds24DjCtu"; # SECRET-DATA
        }
    }
}
```

```
[edit]
lab@r1# set system apply-groups authentication
```

To confirm the correct application of a configuration group, you should pipe configuration output through the `inheritance` filter as shown here:

```
[edit]
lab@r1# show system | match radius

[edit]
lab@r1# show system | display inheritance | match radius
## 'radius' was inherited from group 'authentication'
authentication-order radius;
radius-server {
```

You should practice with the effects of configuration group usage before deciding to deploy the technique on a live examination. Some candidates have been burned by failing to completely anticipate the effects of configuration group usage. For example, the inadvertent configuration (and operation) of an IGP on your fxp0 OoB management interface (which is never a good idea) can easily result when a configuration group is used to add protocol families to your interfaces in conjunction with a command such as `set protocol isis interface all`.

- Allow SNMP access from all IP addresses, but only allow SNMP request over the fxp0 interface. Use a community value of `public` for read-only access and `private` for read/write access. Send only version 1 authentication–related traps to the SNMP server:

```
[edit snmp]
root@r2# set interface fxp0

[edit snmp]
root@r2# set community public

[edit snmp]
root@r2# set trap-group foo categories authentication

[edit snmp]
root@r2# set trap-group foo targets 10.0.200.2

[edit snmp]
root@r2# set community private authorization read-write
```

The resulting configuration changes are now confirmed:

```
[edit snmp]
root@r2# show
interface fxp0.0;
community public;
community private {
    authorization read-write;
}
trap-group foo {
    version v1;
    categories authentication;
    targets {
        10.0.200.2;
    }
}
```

By including interface fxp0, you disallow access from all other interfaces. The lack of a client statement results in the default of access being allowed from all clients. The default for SNMP traps is to send both version 1 and version 2, so version 1 traps must be specified.

- Configure your routers as broadcast NTP clients, and authenticate all messages using MD5, key ID 200, key value juniper. Ensure that manual clock synchronization steps are not required. For this example, you may assume that the NTP service is provided by 10.0.1.102:

```
[edit system ntp]
root@r2# set authentication-key 200 type md5 value juniper

[edit system ntp]
root@r2# set trusted-key 200

[edit system ntp]
root@r2# set broadcast-client

[edit system ntp]
root@r2# set boot-server 10.0.1.102
```

Once again, the changes to the configuration are confirmed:

```
[edit system ntp]
root@r2# show
boot-server 10.0.1.102;
```

```
authentication-key 200 type md5 value "$9$KoAWX-YgJHqfVwqfTzCAvWL"; # SECRET-DATA
broadcast-client;
trusted-key 200;
```

Because manual synchronization is not permitted in this example, you must include the
`boot-server` statement to allow initial clock synchronization at boot. You must also configure
your router as a broadcast client to tell it to listen to NTP broadcasts. If all goes according to
plan, you should have NTP associations like the following example on all your routers after
they are rebooted; it should be noted that the server type (t) is now set to broadcast (b):

```
root@r1> show ntp associations
      remote           refid      st t when poll reach   delay   offset  jitter
==============================================================================
*10.0.1.102     LOCAL(1)          11 b   -   64  377   0.000   39.204   1.045
```

- Ensure that all routers display the correct value for local time. You should assume that you
  are testing in Sunnyvale, California:

```
[edit system]
root@r2# set time-zone America/Los_Angeles
```

There is no CLI option for America/Sunnyvale, but Los Angeles and the San Francisco Bay
Area are both on Pacific Time so this does the trick.

- Without using DNS, ensure that you can ping the proctor workstation using the name
  `proctor`.

You must configure a static host mapping to accomplish this task because DNS services are
not available in this example:

```
[edit system]
lab@r2# set static-host-mapping proctor inet 10.0.200.1
```

- Configure the router to ignore management interface link status and enable the auxiliary
  console port for vt100 terminals.

```
[edit chassis alarm]
lab@r2# set management-ethernet link-down ignore
```

```
[edit system ports]
lab@r2# set auxiliary type vt100
```

The Completed Case Study Configuration

The configuration of r2 is shown in Listing 1.6. This configuration satisfies all case study
requirements.

Listing 1.6: Case Study Configuration for *r2*

```
[edit]
lab@r2# show | no-more
version 5.2R2.3;
system {
    host-name r2;
    time-zone America/Los_Angeles;
    authentication-order radius;
   ports {
    auxiliary type vt100;
   }
    root-authentication {
        encrypted-password "$1$RTyGDGYG$ukqr37VGRgtohedSlruOk/"; # SECRET-DATA
    }
    radius-server {
        10.0.200.2 secret "$9$-UbYoDi.z39JG39ApREdbs"; # SECRET-DATA
    }
    login {
        class noc {
            permissions view;
        }
        user lab {
            uid 2000;
            class superuser;
            authentication {
                encrypted-password "$1$L6ZKKWYI$GxEI/7YzXes2JXDcHJvz7/"; #
SECRET-DATA
            }
        }
        user noc {
            uid 2001;
            class noc;
            authentication {
                encrypted-password "$1$Z5Sb1eVg$R8.iZMCAMAOTdEeS2svvd0"; #
SECRET-DATA
            }
        }
    }
    static-host-mapping {
        proctor inet 10.0.200.1;
    }
```

```
    services {
        ssh {
            root-login deny;
            protocol-version v2;
        }
        telnet;
    }
    syslog {
        user * {
            any emergency;
        }
        host 10.0.200.2 {
            interactive-commands any;
        }
        file messages {
            any notice;
            authorization info;
        }
        file r2-cli {
            interactive-commands any;
            archive files 4;
        }
    }
    ntp {
        boot-server 10.0.1.102;
        authentication-key 200 type md5 value "$9$KoAWX-YgJHqfVwqfTzCAvWL"; #
SECRET-DATA
        broadcast-client;
        trusted-key 200;
    }
}
chassis {
    alarm {
        management-ethernet {
            link-down ignore;
        }
    }
}
interfaces {
    fxp0 {
        unit 0 {
```

```
            family inet {
                address 10.0.1.2/24;
            }
        }
    }
}
snmp {
    interface fxp0.0;
    community public;
    community private {
        authorization read-write;
    }
    trap-group foo {
        version v1;
        categories authentication;
        targets {
            10.0.200.2;
        }
    }
}
routing-options {
    static {
        route 10.0.200.0/24 next-hop 10.0.1.102;
    }
}
```

You should now ensure that the remaining routers in your test bed have a similar initial system configuration. The use of cut and paste using `load override terminal` is recommended as a time-saving technique. You should attempt to validate as much of your initial configuration as possible using the techniques demonstrated in this chapter because "silly" mistakes such as fat-fingering the IP address associated with the proctor subnet are hard to spot when simply viewing the router's configuration.

Spot the Issues: Review Questions

1. Will the following login class provide **superuser** privileges while preventing the user's ability to enter the configuration mode?

    ```
    [edit system login]
    lab@t1# show class test
    permissions all;
    deny-commands "^config$";
    ```

2. Will this syslog configuration alter the default size of the messages file?

    ```
    [edit system syslog]
    lab@t1# show
    archive size 10m files 5;
    user * {
        any emergency;
    }
    file messages {
        any notice;
        authorization info;
        archive size 128m files 10;
    }
    file r1-cli {
        interactive-commands any;
        archive files 5;
    }
    ```

3. You must ensure that your router's cold start trap is sent to a non–directly attached SNMP server. What command is needed?

4. Your router is not synchronizing with the NTP server after a reboot. What could be wrong with this NTP configuration? (You may assume that the secret is correctly configured.)

    ```
    lab@t1# show system ntp
    boot-server 10.0.1.201;
    authentication-key 10 type md5 value "$9$2XoJDn6AIEy"; # SECRET-DATA
    server 10.0.1.201 key 10 version 3; # SECRET-DATA
    ```

5. How can you configure an M-series router to source all SNMP trap messages from its lo0 interface without affecting the source addresses of other traffic?

```
[edit]
lab@r4# show snmp
community public {
    clients {
        0.0.0.0/0 restrict;
        10.0.1.102/32;
    }
}
trap-options {
    source-address lo0;
}
```

Spot the Issues: Answers

1. No. The `deny-commands` regular expression incorrectly matches on the exact sequence `config`, which is not a valid command. A user in this class would still be able to use the `configure` command. The correct regular expression would be `^configure$`.

2. Yes. The global syslog archive parameters have been set to retain five 10MB files, and the operator's attempt at returning the messages file archive settings to the default setting of ten 128KB files has failed due to incorrect use of the Mega (`m`) suffix.

3. You will need to use the `backup-router` statement with the correct gateway address. The `backup-router` is used while the system is booting, and in the event that the routing daemon cannot be started.

4. The NTP configuration is missing the trusted-key definition. Without a list of trusted keys, the router will not use, or accept, `key-id` *10* in NTP messages.

5. You must use the `source-address` option at the [`edit snmp trap-options`] hierarchy when configuring SNMP. Use of `default-address-selection` at the [`edit system`] hierarchy affects all locally generated packets, not just SNMP.

Chapter

2

Interface Configuration and Testing

JNCIP LAB SKILLS COVERED IN THIS CHAPTER:

- ✓ **Configure Loopback interfaces**
- ✓ **Configure POS interfaces**
  - ▪ Physical properties
  - ▪ Logical properties
  - ▪ POS encapsulation options (Cisco HDLC, Frame Relay, and PPP)
- ✓ **Configure ATM interfaces**
  - ▪ Physical properties
  - ▪ Logical properties
  - ▪ Point-to-point
  - ▪ Point-to-multipoint
  - ▪ Traffic shaping
- ✓ **Configure Ethernet interfaces**
  - ▪ Physical properties
  - ▪ Logical properties
  - ▪ VLAN tagging and VRRP
  - ▪ MAC address filtering
- ✓ **Aggregated interfaces**
- ✓ **Leaky bucket rate limiting**
- ✓ **Unnumbered interfaces**

This chapter exposes the reader to a variety of JNCIP-level interface configuration scenarios while also describing common verification techniques that can be used to confirm proper interface operation.

M-series router interface configuration typically requires the setting of interface properties at both the physical and logical levels. Physical interface properties normally relate to media-specific criteria such as framing, CRC length, and device MTU, while logical properties relate to specific protocol families, logical units, and protocol-specific options such as IPv4 addresses or the protocol family's MTU.

Because specific interface technologies are normally isolated to a subset of the routers that make up your JNCIP test bed, this chapter provides interface configuration examples based on arbitrary router pairs as appropriate. The chapter ends with a large case study that involves the configuration and testing of all router interfaces that make up the sample JNCIP topology.

Loopback Interfaces

We begin our guided tour of interface configuration by assigning the correct IP address to the loopback (lo0) interfaces on your routers. The loopback interface is important because it is the default source of your router ID (RID), and is often used for IBGP peering. Because lo0 is a virtual interface, it represents the most stable IP address on your router.

It should be noted that while Juniper Networks routers permit the configuration of multiple IP addresses on a single logical unit, the router's loopback interface can only support a single logical unit, and this logical unit must use the default value of 0. Further, M-series routers can only support a single loopback interface instance, and this instance must be identified as 0. The lo0 interface will not support multipoint connectivity so you must be sure to assign a netmask that indicates a full 32 or 128 bits of host address, based on the use of IPv4 or IPv6, respectively.

Omitting the netmask when assigning a version 4 IP address will result in a default mask of /32 (a host address). This is ideal for loopback interfaces, but will result in commit errors on Ethernet interfaces, because these interfaces are inherently multipoint in nature and therefore will not support the attachment of a single-host device.

Table 2.1 provides the loopback addressing information for r3 and r4:

TABLE 2.1   Loopback Addressing for r3 and r4

Router	lo0 Address
r3	10.0.3.3/32
r4	10.0.3.4/32

Configuring Your lo0 Interface

The lo0 interface does not require any physical device configuration because it is a virtual device. The following commands correctly assign a /32-bit host address to logical unit 0 of the router's loopback interface based on the contents of Table 2.1:

```
[edit interfaces]
lab@r3# set lo0 unit 0 family inet address 10.0.3.3

[edit interfaces]
lab@r3# show lo0
unit 0 {
    family inet {
        address 10.0.3.3/32;
    }
}
```

Verify Your lo0 Interface Configuration

After you commit your lo0 configuration, you should be able to ping the router's loopback address. You can also use a show interfaces command to verify its status:

```
lab@r3> ping 10.0.3.3
PING 10.0.3.3 (10.0.3.3): 56 data bytes
64 bytes from 10.0.3.3: icmp_seq=0 ttl=255 time=8.148 ms
^C
--- 10.0.3.3 ping statistics ---
1 packets transmitted, 1 packets received, 0% packet loss
round-trip min/avg/max/stddev = 8.148/8.148/8.148/0.000 ms
```

```
lab@r3> show interfaces lo0
Physical interface: lo0, Enabled, Physical link is Up
  Interface index: 4, SNMP ifIndex: 7
  Type: Loopback, MTU: Unlimited
  Device flags   : Present Running Loopback
  Interface flags: SNMP-Traps
  Link flags     : None
  Input packets : 2
  Output packets: 2

  Logical interface lo0.0 (Index 3) (SNMP ifIndex 28)
    Flags: SNMP-Traps Encapsulation: Unspecified
    Protocol inet, MTU: Unlimited, Flags: None
      Addresses, Flags: Is-Default Is-Primary
        Local: 10.0.3.3
```

In this screen capture, you can see that the one and only address assigned to the lo0 interface is, by definition, both the preferred and primary addresses for the interface. The preferred address is used to source a packet when multiple addresses belonging to the same logical IP subnet (LIS) have been assigned, and the destination address of the packet identifies it as belonging to that particular subnet. In contrast, the primary address is used to source a packet when a particular interface is used for packet egress, but the destination address of the packet does not identify it as belonging to any of the subnets assigned to that particular interface. This situation is often the case when sending multicast or global broadcast packets (using address 255.255.255.255) because these types of addresses are not associated with any particular subnet or interface address assignments.

Because the primary address of the lo0 interface is used as the RID, you may need to manually configure a particular address to be the primary one in situations where you assign multiple addresses to a router's lo0 interface.

The following captures illustrate this point by assigning a second address to r3's lo0 interface:

```
[edit interfaces lo0]
lab@r3# set unit 0 family inet address 200.0.0.1

[edit interfaces lo0]
lab@r3# show
unit 0 {
    family inet {
        address 10.0.3.3/32;
        address 200.0.0.1/32;
    }
}
```

```
lab@r3> show interfaces lo0
Physical interface: lo0, Enabled, Physical link is Up
  Interface index: 4, SNMP ifIndex: 7
  Type: Loopback, MTU: Unlimited
  Device flags   : Present Running Loopback
  Interface flags: SNMP-Traps
  Link flags     : None
  Input packets : 2
  Output packets: 2

  Logical interface lo0.0 (Index 3) (SNMP ifIndex 28)
    Flags: SNMP-Traps Encapsulation: Unspecified
    Protocol inet, MTU: Unlimited, Flags: None
      Addresses, Flags: Is-Default Is-Primary
        Local: 10.0.3.3
      Addresses
        Local: 200.0.0.1
```

After committing, the results shown previously indicate that the lowest IP address on a particular logical unit is chosen as the primary address for that logical interface. If we assume that you wanted r3's RID to be 200.0.0.1, then you will need to manually configure the 200.0.0.1 address as the primary address on the lo0 interface. To set an address as primary, use the primary argument when assigning the address:

```
[edit interfaces lo0]
lab@r3# set unit 0 family inet address 200.0.0.1/32 primary

[edit interfaces lo0]
lab@r3# commit
commit complete

[edit interfaces lo0]
lab@r3# run show interfaces lo0
Physical interface: lo0, Enabled, Physical link is Up
  Interface index: 4, SNMP ifIndex: 7
  Type: Loopback, MTU: Unlimited
  Device flags   : Present Running Loopback
  Interface flags: SNMP-Traps
  Link flags     : None
  Input packets : 2
  Output packets: 2
```

```
Logical interface lo0.0 (Index 3) (SNMP ifIndex 28)
  Flags: SNMP-Traps Encapsulation: Unspecified
  Protocol inet, MTU: Unlimited, Flags: None
    Addresses
      Local: 10.0.3.3
    Addresses, Flags: Primary Is-Default Is-Primary
      Local: 200.0.0.1
```

WARNING   Because the router's lo0 address is used as a router ID in protocols such as OSPF and BGP, extra care should be taken when configuring your loopback interface. Problems relating to duplicate RIDs can be quite difficult to isolate and repair.

The 200.0.0.1 address should now be removed from your lo0 interface before proceeding, to ensure that it does not cause problems with subsequent lab activities.

Because JUNOS software permits multiple addresses on a single logical unit, care should be taken when correcting addressing mistakes; simply reassigning the correct address will normally result in the interface having two addresses—one being good, and the other bad. To save time, you might use the JUNOS software rename function to correct addressing mistakes. This saves you the trouble of having to explicitly delete the incorrect address, thereby helping you avoid the pitfall described previously. The following example shows how the **rename** command is used to reassign the existing fe-0/1/2 interface address from 10.0.1.1/24 to a new value of 10.0.1.200/30:

```
[edit interfaces fe-0/1/2]
lab@router# rename unit 0 family inet address 10.0.1.1/24 to address 10.0.1.200/30
[edit interfaces fe-0/1/2]
lab@router# show
unit 0 {
    family inet {
        address 10.0.1.200/30;
    }
}
```

POS Interfaces

With the correct loopback addressing in r3 and r4, we can now move on to common configuration requirements and testing techniques for Packet Over SONET (POS) interfaces. Figure 2.1 details the specifics of the POS interfaces connecting r3 and r4.

FIGURE 2.1 POS interface connecting r3 and r4

Physical Properties for POS Interfaces

The physical device properties of a POS interface determine its clocking, framing, CRC length, link-level encapsulation, and various other SONET parameters. A typical POS interface configuration could involve one or more of the following physical device criteria, which we will use in our example:

- 32-bit FCS (CRC)

- Payload scrambling enabled

- MTU of 4474 bytes

- SDH framing, path trace set to "JNCIP test bed"

- Internal timing

- Cisco HDLC encapsulation with 5-second keepalives

- Hold setting of 20 milliseconds

The following capture shows some of the default parameters for a POS interface on an M-series router. Based on this display, it is clear that additional device configuration will be needed to meet all of the criteria listed previously.

```
[edit interfaces so-0/2/0]
lab@r3# run show interfaces so-0/2/0
Physical interface: so-0/2/0, Enabled, Physical link is Up
  Interface index: 16, SNMP ifIndex: 19
  Link-level type: PPP, MTU: 4474, Clocking: Internal, SONET mode, Speed: OC3,
  Loopback: None, FCS: 16, Payload scrambler: Enabled
  Device flags   : Present Running
  Interface flags: Point-To-Point SNMP-Traps
  Link flags     : Keepalives
  Input rate     : 0 bps (0 pps)
  Output rate    : 0 bps (0 pps)
  SONET alarms   : None
  SONET defects  : None
```

This capture indicates that the default encapsulation of PPP (Point-to-Point Protocol) will need to be changed, as will the default 16-bit FCS (CRC) length and SONET framing mode.

Configuring POS Interface Physical Properties

The following commands configure the physical properties of r3's so-0/2/0 POS interface in accordance with the criteria listed previously:

```
[edit interfaces so-0/2/0]
lab@r3# set sonet-options fcs 32
```

```
[edit interfaces so-0/2/0]
lab@r3# set sonet-options path-trace "JNCIP test bed"
```

```
[edit interfaces so-0/2/0]
lab@r3# set hold-time up 20
```

```
[edit interfaces so-0/2/0]
lab@r3# set hold-time down 20
```

```
[edit interfaces so-0/2/0]
lab@r3# set encapsulation cisco-hdlc
```

```
[edit interfaces so-0/2/0]
lab@r3# set keepalives interval 5
```

This configuration, combined with the interface's default parameters, achieves all of the required configuration parameters with the exception of the need for SDH framing. Though rather unintuitive, the framing mode used for all the ports associated with a given SONET PIC is configured at the [edit chassis] hierarchy, as shown next:

```
[edit]
lab@r3# set chassis fpc 0 pic 2 framing sdh
```

The completed physical configuration of r3's so-0/2/0 POS interface is shown next:

```
[edit]
lab@r3# show interfaces so-0/2/0
keepalives interval 5;
hold-time up 20 down 20;
encapsulation cisco-hdlc;
sonet-options {
    fcs 32;
    path-trace "JNCIP test bed";
}
```

```
[edit]
```

```
lab@r3# show chassis fpc 0
pic 2 {
    framing sdh;
}
```

The results of a show interfaces extensive for r3's so-0/2/0 interface is displayed next. The following capture has been edited for brevity:

```
lab@r3> show interfaces so-0/2/0 extensive
Physical interface: so-0/2/0, Enabled, Physical link is Up
  Interface index: 16, SNMP ifIndex: 19, Generation: 19
  Link-level type: Cisco-HDLC, MTU: 4474, Clocking: Internal, SDH mode,
  Speed: OC3, Loopback: None, FCS: 32, Payload scrambler: Enabled
  Device flags   : Present Running
  Interface flags: Point-To-Point SNMP-Traps
  Link flags     : Keepalives
  Hold-times     : Up 20 ms, Down 20 ms
  Statistics last cleared: Never
  Traffic statistics:
   . . .
  Input errors:
   . . .
  Output errors:
   . . .
  SONET alarms   : None
  SONET defects  : None
  SONET PHY:              Seconds      Count  State
    PLL Lock                    0          0  OK
    PHY Light                   0          0  OK
  SONET section:
   . . .
  SONET line:
   . . .               0
  SONET path:
   . . .               0
  Received SDH overhead:
   . . .
  Transmitted SDH overhead:
   . . .
  Received path trace:
    00 00 00 00 00 00 00 00 00 00 00 00 00 00 00 00   . . . . . . . . . . . . . . . .
```

```
Transmitted path trace: JNCIP test bed
  4a 4e 43 49 45 20 74 65 73 74 20 62 65 64 00 00    JNCIP test bed..
HDLC configuration:
  Policing bucket: Disabled
  Shaping bucket : Disabled
  Giant threshold: 4486, Runt threshold: 5
. . .
```

According to current JUNOS software documentation, the interface hold time can range from 0 (the default) to 65,535 milliseconds, with the configured value being rounded up to the nearest whole second. Therefore, any hold-time setting between 1 and 1000 inclusive should produce the same 1-second interface transition hold-down.

The lack of the correct value for the received path trace value in the previous capture indicates that r4's so-0/1/0 POS interface has not been configured with compatible SONET framing. By default, path trace information should contain the router's host and transmitting interface name but instead r3 is showing null values for the received path trace. After configuring r4's so-0/1/0 interface with identical parameters to those of r3, the received path trace displays the expected value:

```
[edit]
lab@r3# run show interfaces so-0/2/0 extensive | match "path trace"
  Received path trace: JNCIP test bed
  Transmitted path trace: JNCIP test bed
```

Logical Properties of POS Interfaces

With the POS interface's physical properties correctly set, it is time to move on to configuring the interface's logical properties. Logical interface properties will normally involve the creation of logical units, the assignment of protocol families to these logical units, and the configuration of parameters associated with each particular protocol family as needed.

Configuring POS Interface Logical Properties

Typical configuration criteria for the logical properties of a POS interface might take the following form:

- Logical unit 0
- IPv4 family, MTU = 1600 bytes
- Address assignment based on Table 2.2

TABLE 2.2   POS Addressing for r3 and r4

Router	POS Interface Address
r3	172.16.0.3/32
r4	192.168.0.4/32

The only tricky part to this configuration assignment is the use of 32-bit host addresses on each end of the POS link, which creates two independent IP subnets that in turn require the use of the destination keyword to explicitly specify the address of the remote device. This is required in order to accommodate the proper routing of packets across the point-to-point link. The following commands correctly configure the logical properties of r3's POS interface:

```
[edit interfaces so-0/2/0 unit 0 family inet]
lab@r3# set mtu 1600

[edit interfaces so-0/2/0 unit 0 family inet]
lab@r3# set address 172.16.0.3 destination 192.168.0.4

[edit interfaces so-0/2/0 unit 0 family inet]
lab@r3# show
mtu 1600;
address 172.16.0.3/32 {
    destination 192.168.0.4;
}
```

Verifying POS Interface Operation

When r4's POS interface is correctly configured, you should be able to conduct ping testing to verify IP forwarding across the POS link. We begin our interface verification by confirming the POS interface is up at both the administrative and logical levels using the following command:

```
lab@r3> show interfaces so-* terse
Interface       Admin Link Proto Local           Remote
so-0/2/0        up    up
so-0/2/0.0      up    up    inet  172.16.0.3 --> 192.168.0.4
so-0/2/1        up    down
so-0/2/2        up    down
```

The resulting display indicates that r3's so-0/2/0 interface is administratively enabled, and that it is operational at the logical link layer, which in this example indicates that cisco-hdlc keepalives are being exchanged across the link. The presence of a configured logical unit on the POS interface also allows us to verify the correct setting of the keepalive timers:

```
lab@r3> show interfaces so-0/2/0
Physical interface: so-0/2/0, Enabled, Physical link is Up
  Interface index: 16, SNMP ifIndex: 19
  Link-level type: Cisco-HDLC, MTU: 4474, Clocking: Internal, SDH mode,
  Speed: OC3, Loopback: None, FCS: 32, Payload scrambler: Enabled
  Device flags   : Present Running
  Interface flags: Point-To-Point SNMP-Traps
  Link flags     : Keepalives
  Keepalive settings: Interval 5 seconds, Up-count 1, Down-count 3
  Keepalive: Input: 1 (00:00:00 ago), Output: 0 (never)
  Input rate     : 88 bps (0 pps)
  Output rate    : 0 bps (0 pps)
  SONET alarms   : None
  SONET defects  : None


  Logical interface so-0/2/0.0 (Index 4) (SNMP ifIndex 29)
    Flags: Point-To-Point SNMP-Traps Encapsulation: Cisco-HDLC
    Protocol inet, MTU: 1600, Flags: None
      Addresses, Flags: Is-Preferred Is-Primary
        Destination: 192.168.0.4, Local: 172.16.0.3
```

We now conduct a ping test to verify proper packet routing between r3 and r4:

```
lab@r3> ping 192.168.0.4 size 1540
PING 192.168.0.4 (192.168.0.4): 1540 data bytes
1548 bytes from 192.168.0.4: icmp_seq=0 ttl=255 time=2.548 ms
1548 bytes from 192.168.0.4: icmp_seq=1 ttl=255 time=2.435 ms
^C
--- 192.168.0.4 ping statistics ---
2 packets transmitted, 2 packets received, 0% packet loss
round-trip min/avg/max/stddev = 2.435/2.492/2.548/0.056 ms
```

Things look very good so far. Now for a flood ping stress test evoked with the rapid option:

```
lab@r3> ping rapid count 200 192.168.0.4 size 1540
PING 192.168.0.4 (192.168.0.4): 1540 data bytes
!!!!!!!!!!!!!!!!!!!!!!!!!!!!!!!!!!!!!!!!!!!!!!!!!!!!!!!!!!!!!!!!!!!!!!!!!!!!!!!!!!!!
!!!!!!!!!!!!!!!!!!!!!!!!!!!!!!!!!!!!!!!!!!!!!!!!!!!!!!!!!!!!!!!!!!!!!!!!!!!!!!!!!!!!
!!!!!!!!!!!!!!!!!!!!!!!!!!!!!!!!!!!!!!!!!!
--- 192.168.0.4 ping statistics ---
```

```
200 packets transmitted, 200 packets received, 0% packet loss
round-trip min/avg/max/stddev = 2.266/2.355/9.730/0.613 m
```

Based on these results, it would seem that congratulations on the successful configuration of a `cisco-hdlc` encapsulated POS interface are in order! In the next section, we will explore the remaining encapsulation options that are available for POS interfaces.

Encapsulation Options for POS Interfaces

A POS interface can be configured to operate with either the Cisco version of HDLC, Frame Relay, or PPP-based encapsulation. The use of `cisco-hdlc` (as illustrated in the previous section) is generally considered to be the most straightforward encapsulation approach because it supports very little in the way of configurable options. This section details common configuration requirements and testing techniques for Frame Relay and PPP encapsulations.

Configuring Frame Relay

The configuration of Frame Relay encapsulation requires the configuration of the `frame-relay` encapsulation type and the assignment of one or more DLCIs. In some cases, you may also have to modify the default data terminal equipment (DTE) line appearance and make modifications to the PVC management protocol parameters, depending on the network particulars that you need to accommodate. The PVC management protocol is often referred to as the Local Management Interface (LMI).

Running Frame Relay devices back-to-back requires that special attention be paid to the device type and keepalive settings because the default Frame Relay parameters will cause back-to-back connections to be declared **down** due to LMI keepalive malfunctions caused by the pairing of two Frame Relay DTEs. Also, the DLCI value must be the same at both ends of a back-to-back connection, because there will be no Frame Relay switch present to provide DLCI translation functions.

Typical Frame Relay configuration tasks are listed next. For simplicity, the same addressing and POS parameters used in the previous Cisco HDLC example will be retained in this example:

- Use DLCI 100
- Use the ITU Annex A version of PVC management protocol (LMI)
- Keepalive parameters:
  - DTE poll interval 5 seconds, full status every poll
  - Set a line **up/down** threshold of 2/3 events

Though not explicitly specified in the task listing, the requirement that keepalives be enabled forces you to configure one or both of the routers to operate as a Frame Relay DCE (data communications equipment) because pairing two DTEs will force you to disable PVC management protocol–based keepalives.

Two DCE devices would be paired to create a network-to-network interface (NNI) with bi-directional keepalives enabled by the inclusion of the `keepalives` keyword at the physical-device level.

This example begins by demonstrating the problems encountered with back-to-back Frame Relay DTE, and then moves on to show how these problems can be resolved by configuring one end of the link as a DCE. Because most of the keepalive parameters are dependent upon a device's status as either a DTE or DCE, the keepalive parameters will be configured after demonstrating the problems with DTE-DTE connections.

We begin r3's Frame Relay configuration by deleting the `keepalive` settings previously configured under `keepalives`. Frame Relay encapsulation has a unique set of LMI parameters that provide keepalive functionality:

```
[edit interfaces so-0/2/0]
lab@r3# delete keepalives
```

And now the initial Frame Relay configuration is performed:

```
[edit interfaces so-0/2/0]
lab@r3# set encapsulation frame-relay
```

```
[edit interfaces so-0/2/0]
lab@r3# set lmi lmi-type itu
```

```
[edit interfaces so-0/2/0]
lab@r3# set unit 0 dlci 100
```

The results of these commands are highlighted next; it is assumed that you have issued the same set of commands and DLCI assignment of 100 on r4's so-0/1/0 interface:

```
[edit interfaces so-0/2/0]
lab@r3# show
hold-time up 20 down 20;
encapsulation frame-relay;
lmi {
    lmi-type itu;
}
sonet-options {
    fcs 32;
    path-trace "JNCIP test bed";
}
unit 0 {
```

```
    dlci 100;
    family inet {
        mtu 1600;
        address 172.16.0.3/32 {
            destination 192.168.0.4;
        }
    }
}
```

In this example, we have assigned DLCI 100 to the interface's existing logical unit 0. You could have renamed or reassigned the logical unit to match the DLCI value, but a specific value for the logical unit is not a requirement in this example. The results of this basic Frame Relay configuration leave much to be desired, as the following captures demonstrate:

> Although many operators prefer to make interface unit numbers match the associated virtual connection identifiers, the unit 0 approach taken here has certain advantages, and is perfectly legal when an interface supports a single connection identifier and therefore requires only one logical unit. The use of non-zero unit numbers can cause problems if the operator forgets to explicitly include the correct unit number when placing the interface into a protocol such as OSPF or IS-IS. The use of unit 0 provides some relief in these cases, as the omission of a unit number will cause the default value of 0 to be assumed.

```
[edit interfaces so-0/2/0]
lab@r3# run show interfaces terse | match so-0/2/0
Interface         Admin Link Proto Local           Remote
so-0/2/0          up    down
so-0/2/0.0        up    down inet  172.16.0.3 --> 192.168.0.4
```

It would seem that our Frame Relay link is down. The following command provides additional information about the cause of the problem:

```
[edit interfaces so-0/2/0]
lab@r3# run show interfaces so-0/2/0
Physical interface: so-0/2/0, Enabled, Physical link is Up
  Interface index: 16, SNMP ifIndex: 19
  Link-level type: Frame-Relay, MTU: 4474, Clocking: Internal, SDH mode,
  Speed: OC3, Loopback: None, FCS: 32, Payload scrambler: Enabled
  Device flags   : Present Running
  Interface flags: Link-Layer-Down Point-To-Point SNMP-Traps
  Link flags     : Keepalives DTE
  ITU LMI settings: n391dte 6, n392dte 3, n393dte 4, t391dte 10 seconds
```

```
LMI: Input: 20 (00:00:00 ago), Output: 20 (00:00:02 ago)
Input rate      : 0 bps (0 pps)
Output rate     : 0 bps (0 pps)
SONET alarms    : None
SONET defects   : None

Logical interface so-0/2/0.0 (Index 4) (SNMP ifIndex 29)
  Flags: Device-Down Point-To-Point SNMP-Traps Encapsulation: FR-NLPID
Input packets : 57
Output packets: 46
  Protocol inet, MTU: 1600, Flags: None
    Addresses, Flags: Dest-route-down Is-Preferred Is-Primary
      Destination: 192.168.0.4, Local: 172.16.0.3
  DLCI 100
    Flags: Active
    Total down time: 0 sec, Last down: Never
Traffic statistics:
    Input  packets:              57
    Output packets:              46
```

Besides getting additional confirmation that the line is down, the show interfaces command provides a clue as to the nature of the problem. The LMI: portion of the display clearly indicates that LMI messages are being sent (Output) and received (Input), but despite this fact the line protocol remains down. A situation like this provides a strong indication that some type of incompatibility is causing the LMI messages to be ignored, because bit errors resulting from device malfunctions or device-level configuration mistakes would simply result in the discard of the corrupted messages causing the input/output counters to remain frozen. Before leaving this capture, take note of the default values for the LMI timers. To meet the requirements of this example, we will need to modify some of these timer values. The use of monitor traffic (tcpdump) will often provide you with important clues when you encounter interface problems. The following capture illustrates how traffic monitoring can be used in this example:

```
[edit interfaces so-0/2/0]
lab@r3# run monitor traffic interface so-0/2/0
Listening on so-0/2/0


16:36:33.972435  In Call Ref: 75, MSG Type: 95 LOCK-SHIFT-5
                IE: 01 Len: 1, LINK VERIFY
                IE: 03 Len: 2, TX Seq: 175, RX Seq:  49
```

```
16:36:35.883477 Out Call Ref: 75, MSG Type: 51 ITU LMI
                IE: 01 Len: 1, LINK VERIFY
                IE: 03 Len: 2, TX Seq: 145, RX Seq:  10

16:36:45.283870 Out Call Ref: 75, MSG Type: 51 ITU LMI
                IE: 01 Len: 1, LINK VERIFY
                IE: 03 Len: 2, TX Seq: 146, RX Seq:  10

16:36:45.672869  In Call Ref: 75, MSG Type: 95 LOCK-SHIFT-5
                IE: 01 Len: 1, LINK VERIFY
                IE: 03 Len: 2, TX Seq: 176, RX Seq:  49
^C
5 packets received by filter
0 packets dropped by kernel
```

These results indicate that both ends are generating status enquiries (message type 75), and that neither end is receiving a status message (message type 7D), which makes perfect sense when one recalls that the Frame Relay DCE device generates status messages in response to the receipt of a DTE-generated status enquiry. Also of interest in this capture is the fact that we have uncovered a configuration error on r4. The LMI messages sent from r4 are using the ANSI Annex D version of LMI, as indicated by the locking code-shift to national code set #5, which is not used in the ITU Q.933 Annex A version of the protocol. Because this example requires the use of ITU Annex A, we should consider ourselves lucky for catching this while there is still time for corrective action.

Now that we know the back-to-back pairing of Frame Relay DTEs has caused our problem, we can easily resolve the issue by configuring one of the routers as a DCE. In this case, we configure r4 as a DCE with the following commands (the incorrect LMI type is also corrected at this time):

```
[edit interfaces so-0/1/0]
lab@r4# set dce

[edit interfaces so-0/1/0]
lab@r4# set lmi lmi-type itu
```

After committing these changes, we once again monitor the LMI exchanges between r3 and r4:

```
[edit interfaces so-0/2/0]
lab@r3# run monitor traffic interface so-0/2/0
Listening on so-0/2/0
```

```
16:44:42.704152 Out Call Ref: 75, MSG Type: 51 ITU LMI
                IE: 01 Len: 1, LINK VERIFY
                IE: 03 Len: 2, TX Seq: 195, RX Seq:  13

16:44:42.704771  In Call Ref: 7d, MSG Type: 51 ITU LMI
                IE: 01 Len: 1, LINK VERIFY
                IE: 03 Len: 2, TX Seq:  14, RX Seq: 195

16:44:51.204457 Out Call Ref: 75, MSG Type: 51 ITU LMI
                IE: 01 Len: 1, LINK VERIFY
                IE: 03 Len: 2, TX Seq: 196, RX Seq:  14

16:44:51.205068  In Call Ref: 7d, MSG Type: 51 ITU LMI
                IE: 01 Len: 1, LINK VERIFY
                IE: 03 Len: 2, TX Seq:  15, RX Seq: 196

16:45:02.604939 Out Call Ref: 75, MSG Type: 51 ITU LMI
                IE: 01 Len: 1, LINK VERIFY
                IE: 03 Len: 2, TX Seq: 197, RX Seq:  15

16:45:02.605571  In Call Ref: 7d, MSG Type: 51 ITU LMI
                IE: 01 Len: 1, LINK VERIFY
                IE: 03 Len: 2, TX Seq:  16, RX Seq: 197

16:45:12.105339 Out Call Ref: 75, MSG Type: 51 ITU LMI
                IE: 01 Len: 1, FULL STATUS
                IE: 03 Len: 2, TX Seq: 198, RX Seq:  16

16:45:12.105965  In Call Ref: 7d, MSG Type: 51 ITU LMI
                IE: 01 Len: 1, FULL STATUS
                IE: 03 Len: 2, TX Seq:  17, RX Seq: 198
                IE: 57 Len: 3, DLCI 100: status   Active

^C
8 packets received by filter
0 packets dropped by kernel
```

The above results indicate the correct operation of the Frame Relay LMI protocol, as both link verify (keepalive) and DLCI status messages are being exchanged between r3 and r4. It is interesting to note that these results indicate that the LMI protocol is operating with the default settings of a 10-second poll interval with a full status exchange occurring every six polls (or once a minute). These parameters must now be adjusted to comply with the configuration requirements of this example. We begin by configuring the DTE device (r3) with the correct LMI parameters using the following commands:

```
[edit interfaces so-0/2/0]
lab@r3# set lmi t391dte 5

[edit interfaces so-0/2/0]
lab@r3# set lmi n391dte 1

[edit interfaces so-0/2/0]
lab@r3# set lmi n392dte 2

[edit interfaces so-0/2/0]
lab@r3# set lmi n393dte 3
```

The resulting configuration tells r3 to generate polls every five seconds (t391), to request full status with every poll (n391), and that it should consider the link **down** if two errors occur in any three monitored events (n392/n393). The resulting Frame Relay configuration for r3, our DTE, is shown next, with newly configured parameters highlighted:

```
lab@r3# show
hold-time up 20 down 20;
encapsulation frame-relay;
lmi {
    n391dte 1;
    n392dte 2;
    n393dte 3;
    t391dte 5;
    lmi-type itu;
}
sonet-options {
    fcs 32;
    path-trace "JNCIP test bed";
}
unit 0 {
    dlci 100;
    family inet {
        mtu 1600;
        address 172.16.0.3/32 {
```

```
            destination 192.168.0.4;
        }
    }
}
```

You must now enter the following commands on r4, which is functioning as the Frame Relay DCE:

```
[edit interfaces so-0/1/0]
lab@r4# set lmi n392dce 2

[edit interfaces so-0/1/0]
lab@r4# set lmi n393dce 3
```

The DCE maintains a poll expectation timer, T392, which must be set higher than the DTE's T391 poll timer for reliable operation. If these two values are set to the same value, the result will likely be a line that oscillates between the up and down states at periodic intervals. Since the default value for T392 is 15 seconds, it will require modification only when the DTE's T391 timer is set to a value greater than the default setting of 10.

The resulting DCE configuration from r4, with Frame Relay–related portions highlighted, is shown next:

```
[edit interfaces so-0/1/0]
lab@r4# show
dce;
hold-time up 20 down 20;
encapsulation frame-relay;
lmi {
    n392dce 2;
    n393dce 3;
    lmi-type itu;
}
sonet-options {
    fcs 32;
    path-trace "JNCIP test bed";
}
unit 0 {
    dlci 100;
    family inet {
        mtu 1600;
```

```
        address 192.168.0.4/32 {
            destination 172.16.0.3;
        }
    }
}
```

Verify Frame Relay

Once the configuration of both routers is complete, you can verify proper operation with ping testing. To confirm the settings of the LMI protocol, you can show the interface's parameters, or monitor the protocol's operation with `monitor traffic` as shown in the following examples:

```
lab@r3> show interfaces so-0/2/0
Physical interface: so-0/2/0, Enabled, Physical link is Up
  Interface index: 16, SNMP ifIndex: 19
  Link-level type: Frame-Relay, MTU: 4474, Clocking: Internal, SDH mode,
  Speed: OC3, Loopback: None, FCS: 32, Payload scrambler: Enabled
  Device flags   : Present Running
  Interface flags: Point-To-Point SNMP-Traps
  Link flags     : Keepalives DTE
  ITU LMI settings: n391dte 1, n392dte 2, n393dte 3, t391dte 5 seconds
  LMI: Input: 322 (00:00:03 ago), Output: 324 (00:00:03 ago)
  Input rate     : 0 bps (0 pps)
  Output rate    : 0 bps (0 pps)
  SONET alarms   : None
  SONET defects  : None

  Logical interface so-0/2/0.0 (Index 4) (SNMP ifIndex 29)
    Flags: Point-To-Point SNMP-Traps Encapsulation: FR-NLPID
  Input packets : 59
  Output packets: 48
    Protocol inet, MTU: 1600, Flags: None
      Addresses, Flags: Is-Preferred Is-Primary
        Destination: 192.168.0.4, Local: 172.16.0.3
    DLCI 100
      Flags: Active
      Total down time: 0 sec, Last down: Never
  Traffic statistics:
      Input  packets:              59
      Output packets:              48
```

The results of a show interfaces are as expected. The link is up and the counters indicate the transmission and reception of LMI-related messages. We now monitor traffic to confirm the specifics of LMI protocol operation:

```
lab@r3> monitor traffic interface so-0/2/0
Listening on so-0/2/0
17:16:17.584353 Out Call Ref: 75, MSG Type: 51 ITU LMI
               IE: 01 Len: 1, FULL STATUS
               IE: 03 Len: 2, TX Seq: 154, RX Seq: 227

17:16:17.584972  In Call Ref: 7d, MSG Type: 51 ITU LMI
               IE: 01 Len: 1, FULL STATUS
               IE: 03 Len: 2, TX Seq: 228, RX Seq: 154
               IE: 57 Len: 3, DLCI 100: status   Active

17:16:21.384512 Out Call Ref: 75, MSG Type: 51 ITU LMI
               IE: 01 Len: 1, FULL STATUS
               IE: 03 Len: 2, TX Seq: 155, RX Seq: 228

17:16:21.385131  In Call Ref: 7d, MSG Type: 51 ITU LMI
               IE: 01 Len: 1, FULL STATUS
               IE: 03 Len: 2, TX Seq: 229, RX Seq: 155
               IE: 57 Len: 3, DLCI 100: status   Active
```

Very nice! The time stamps and message contents indicate that we now have full status exchanges with every poll, and that polls are occurring every five seconds. This behavior demonstrates that, based on the requirements given for this configuration example, we have correctly configured a POS interface with Frame Relay encapsulation.

Point-to-Multipoint Frame Relay Connections

The previous Frame Relay examples have demonstrated point-to-point connection types. You should also be able to configure point-to-multipoint connections to create a non-broadcast multi-access (NMBA) topology as needed. Inverse ARP (IN-ARP) is often deployed on multipoint connections to eliminate the need for the manual mapping of local DLCI values to remote IP addresses. As of this writing, JUNOS software does not offer full IN-ARP support for Frame Relay or ATM interfaces. While an M-series router can be configured to respond to IN-ARP requests (as might be sent from another vendor's router), the Juniper Networks router cannot generate IN-ARP requests. As a result, you will need to manually configure all DLCI to remote IP address mappings when configuring multipoint connections with JUNOS software. IN-ARP response support can be configured on non–Juniper Networks equipment to eliminate the need for static mappings as desired.

The following example is based on the topology shown in Figure 2.2. Here, r1 is connected through a Frame Relay network to r2 and r3 using its so-0/0/0 interface. All routers in this example have been configured with a common IP subnet of 10.0.1/24, which represents the WAN cloud.

FIGURE 2.2   Multipoint Frame Relay connections

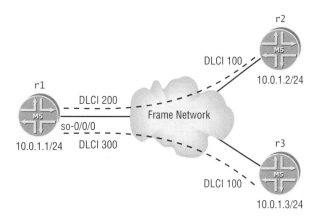

The following commands correctly configure r1 for this multipoint, NMBA application. Use of the multipoint keyword to support this application is worth noting:

```
[edit interfaces so-0/0/0]
lab@r1# set encapsulation frame-relay

lab@r1# set unit 0 multipoint

[edit interfaces so-0/0/0]
lab@r1# set unit 0 family inet address 10.0.1.1/24

[edit interfaces so-0/0/0 unit 0 family inet address 10.0.1.1/24]
lab@r1# set multipoint-destination 10.0.1.2 dlci 200

[edit interfaces so-0/0/0 unit 0 family inet address 10.0.1.1/24]
lab@r1# set multipoint-destination 10.0.1.3 dlci 300

[edit interfaces so-0/0/0 unit 0 family inet address 10.0.1.1/24]
lab@r1# up 3

[edit interfaces so-0/0/0]
lab@r1# show
encapsulation frame-relay;
```

```
unit 0 {
    multipoint;
    family inet {
        address 10.0.1.1/24 {
            multipoint-destination 10.0.1.2 dlci 200;
            multipoint-destination 10.0.1.3 dlci 300;
        }
    }
}
```

The key aspects of this multipoint configuration are the inclusion of the multipoint keyword and the static DLCI to IP mappings configured as arguments to the multipoint-destination keyword. If the remote routers (r3 and r2) have been configured for dynamic address mappings (IN-ARP support), then you must also include support for IN-ARP replies on r1 as shown in the following:

```
[edit interfaces so-0/0/0]
lab@r1# set unit 0 inverse-arp

[edit interfaces so-0/0/0]
lab@r1# show
encapsulation frame-relay;
unit 0 {
    multipoint;
    inverse-arp;
    family inet {
        address 10.0.1.1/24 {
            multipoint-destination 10.0.1.2 dlci 200;
            multipoint-destination 10.0.1.3 dlci 300;
        }
    }
}
```

Configuring PPP

JUNOS software supports PPP encapsulation on POS interfaces, but does not support many of the enhanced capabilities of PPP because of the lack of support for switched connections and the limited protocol support needed by a core IP router. The support of a limited subset of the PPP's capabilities makes the configuration of PPP relatively easy on an M-series router. Figure 2.3 shows the sample topology that will be used to demonstrate PPP configuration and interface verification.

FIGURE 2.3   PPP topology

Because r3 and r4 share a common /30 subnet in this example, the destination keyword is not needed for proper routing across the point-to-point link. The following commands delete the existing interface configuration and correctly configure r3's so-0/2/0 interface for basic PPP operation:

```
[edit interfaces so-0/2/0]
lab@r3# delete
Delete everything under this level? [yes,no] (no) yes

[edit interfaces so-0/2/0]
lab@r3# set unit 0 family inet address 192.168.0.5/30

lab@r3# show
unit 0 {
    family inet {
        address 192.168.0.5/30;
    }
}
```

Because PPP is by nature a point-to-point protocol, only one logical unit can be configured for a PPP-encapsulated interface and this logical unit must be unit 0. Also, because PPP encapsulation is the default encapsulation for POS interfaces, there is no need to explicitly configure the interface's encapsulation when basic PPP functionality is required.

Verifying PPP

The PPP transitions through various states before the interface becomes operational at the network layer (dead, link up, authentication, LCP open, and ultimately network control protocol [NCP] open for each configured protocol family). Configuration problems and incompatibilities can result in the PPP becoming stuck in a particular state. Knowing how PPP progresses through these various states and being able to determine that it is hung at a particular phase can greatly simplify PPP troubleshooting.

PPP makes use of a Link Control Protocol (LCP) to provide keepalive and link-level negotiation functions such as PPP address and control field compression. Generally speaking, problems with LCP establishment indicate hardware or transmission link problems, but can also be caused by incompatible LCP settings between the devices that terminate the link. At the time of this writing, JUNOS software does not support the configuration of LCP-related options such as address or control field compression, so the correction of any incompatibilities that arise will require the modification of the non–Juniper Networks device's settings.

Information on the state of the PPP can be obtained by viewing the interface, as shown next:

```
[edit interfaces so-0/2/0]
lab@r3# run show interfaces so-0/2/0
Physical interface: so-0/2/0, Enabled, Physical link is Up
  Interface index: 16, SNMP ifIndex: 19
  Link-level type: PPP, MTU: 4474, Clocking: Internal, SDH mode, Speed: OC3,
Loopback: None,
  FCS: 16, Payload scrambler: Enabled
  Device flags   : Present Running
  Interface flags: Point-To-Point SNMP-Traps
  Link flags     : Keepalives
  Keepalive settings: Interval 10 seconds, Up-count 1, Down-count 3
  Keepalive: Input: 97 (00:00:08 ago), Output: 97 (00:00:02 ago)
  LCP state: Opened
  NCP state: inet: Opened, inet6: Not-configured, iso: Not-configured, mpls:
Not-configured
  Input rate     : 40 bps (0 pps)
  Output rate    : 48 bps (0 pps)
  SONET alarms   : None
  SONET defects  : None

  Logical interface so-0/2/0.0 (Index 4) (SNMP ifIndex 29)
    Flags: Point-To-Point SNMP-Traps Encapsulation: PPP
    Protocol inet, MTU: 4470, Flags: None
      Addresses, Flags: Is-Preferred Is-Primary
        Destination: 192.168.0.4/30, Local: 192.168.0.5
```

From this display, you can see that the LCP has been correctly opened, and that it is exchanging keepalives across the link. Furthermore, we can see that the IPv4 Control Protocol (IPCP) connection has successfully entered the opened state, while the NCP connections for MPLS and ISO have not been opened because these protocol families have not been configured on the logical interface. The operation of PPP can also be verified through the use of traffic monitoring as shown in the following example:

```
[edit interfaces so-0/2/0]
lab@r3# run monitor traffic interface so-0/2/0
Listening on so-0/2/0
11:10:12.830818 Out LCP echo request          (type 0x09  id 0x88  len 0x0008)
11:10:12.831422  In LCP echo reply            (type 0x0a  id 0x88  len 0x0008)
```

```
11:10:18.776802  In LCP echo request        (type 0x09  id 0x7a  len 0x0008)
11:10:18.776817 Out LCP echo reply          (type 0x0a  id 0x7a  len 0x0008)
11:10:20.731145 Out LCP echo request        (type 0x09  id 0x89  len 0x0008)
11:10:20.731749  In LCP echo reply          (type 0x0a  id 0x89  len 0x0008)
^C
6 packets received by filter
0 packets dropped by kernel
```

The resulting output shows that bidirectional keepalives are being sent, which confirms that LCP is open and that the data link is capable of passing traffic. In the following capture, one end of the link is deactivated while the results are monitored at r3:

```
[edit interfaces so-0/2/0]
lab@r3# run monitor traffic interface so-0/2/0
Listening on so-0/2/0
11:13:04.582841  In LCP echo request         (type 0x09  id 0x8b  len 0x0008)
11:13:04.582849 Out LCP echo reply           (type 0x0a  id 0x8b  len 0x0008)
11:13:12.648573  In IPCP terminate request   (type 0x05  id 0x8c  len 0x0004)
11:13:12.648649 Out IPCP terminate acknowledge (type 0x06  id 0x8c  len 0x0004)
11:13:12.692233  In LCP terminate request    (type 0x05  id 0x8d  len 0x0004)
11:13:12.692246 Out LCP terminate acknowledge (type 0x06  id 0x8d  len 0x0004)
11:13:14.688520 Out LCP configure request    (type 0x01  id 0x9a  len 0x000a)
  LCP OPTION: Magic number                   (type 0x05 len 0x06 val 0x3cbdb0ac)
. . .
```

Here you can see that r4 initiates the teardown of the IP control protocol, and then follows up by tearing down the LCP session. After acknowledging r4's request for IPCP and LCP termination, r3 then tries to reestablish the link by generating LCP configure requests. The magic number option is used to provide loopback detection, and cannot be disabled in JUNOS software. LCP echoes will not be sent if keepalives are disabled with the no-keepalives option, but the LCP will still be opened to facilitate the operation of the various NCPs needed to support the configured protocol families.

Using CHAP Authentication

Though PPP authentication using the Password Authentication Protocol (PAP) or Challenge Handshake Authentication Protocol (CHAP) is normally associated with switched connections, recent versions of JUNOS software include support for the CHAP authentication option. To configure CHAP on a PPP interface, issue the following commands with the appropriate variables as needed for the specifics of your configuration:

```
[edit interfaces so-0/2/0]
lab@r3# set interfaces so-0/2/0 encapsulation ppp
```

```
[edit interfaces so-0/2/0 ppp-options]
lab@r3# set chap local-name r3 access-profile test
[edit interfaces so-0/2/0]
lab@r3# top
lab@r3# set access profile test client r4 chap-secret jni
```

The modified configuration is shown next with the CHAP and authentication-related options highlighted. PPP encapsulation must be explicitly configured before the operator can commit a configuration that makes use of ppp-options, even though PPP encapsulation is the default:

```
[edit]
lab@r3# show interfaces so-0/2/0
encapsulation ppp;
ppp-options {
    chap {
        access-profile test;
        local-name r3;
    }
}
unit 0 {
    family inet {
        address 192.168.0.5/30;
    }
}

lab@r3# show access
profile test {
    client r4 chap-secret "$9$a7GjqCA0BIc"; # SECRET-DATA
}
```

Because r4 has not yet been configured for CHAP authentication, we now have a link layer incompatibility that results in PPP getting stuck at the LCP open stage:

```
[edit]
lab@r3# run show interfaces so-0/2/0
Physical interface: so-0/2/0, Enabled, Physical link is Up
  Interface index: 16, SNMP ifIndex: 19
  Link-level type: PPP, MTU: 4474, Clocking: Internal, SDH mode, Speed: OC3,
Loopback: None,
  FCS: 16, Payload scrambler: Enabled
```

```
Device flags    : Present Running
Interface flags: Point-To-Point SNMP-Traps
Keepalive settings: Interval 10 seconds, Up-count 1, Down-count 3
Keepalive: Input: 0 (never), Output: 0 (never)
LCP state: Conf-ack-sent
NCP state: inet: Down, inet6: Not-configured, iso: Not-configured, mpls: Not-
configured
Input rate      : 104 bps (0 pps)
Output rate     : 136 bps (0 pps)
SONET alarms    : None
SONET defects   : None

Logical interface so-0/2/0.0 (Index 4) (SNMP ifIndex 29)
  Flags: Hardware-Down Point-To-Point SNMP-Traps Encapsulation: PPP
  Protocol inet, MTU: 4470, Flags: Protocol-Down
    Addresses, Flags: Dest-route-down Is-Preferred Is-Primary
      Destination: 192.168.0.4/30, Local: 192.168.0.5
```

Traffic monitoring on r3 provides useful clues in this case:

```
lab@r3# run monitor traffic interface so-0/2/0
Listening on so-0/2/0


11:52:25.730741  In LCP configure request      (type 0x01  id 0x10  len 0x000a)
  LCP OPTION: Magic number              (type 0x05 len 0x06 val 0x3cb67f61)
11:52:25.730767 Out LCP configure acknowledge   (type 0x02  id 0x10  len 0x000a)
  LCP OPTION: Magic number              (type 0x05 len 0x06 val 0x3cb67f61)
. . .


11:52:28.738220 Out LCP configure request      (type 0x01  id 0x81  len 0x000f)
  LCP OPTION: Magic number              (type 0x05 len 0x06 val 0x3cbda343)
  LCP OPTION: Authentication protocol   (type 0x03 len 0x05 val 0xc2 0x23 0x05 )
11:52:28.738844  In LCP configure negative ack  (type 0x03  id 0x81  len 0x0009)
  LCP OPTION: Authentication protocol   (type 0x03 len 0x05 val 0xc2 0x23 0x05 )
^C
6 packets received by filter
0 packets dropped by kernel
```

Here you can clearly see that r4's configure requests (In LCP) do not contain the authentication option. However, the LCP configure requests sent from r3 (Out LCP) indicate a desire to use

authentication. Because r4 has not been configured for CHAP, it refuses the LCP configure request received from r3, which results in a failure of the LCP open. After configuring r4 with CHAP authentication and a compatible secret, the PPP once again operates correctly as shown in the following:

```
1:58:56.975423  In LCP configure request       (type 0x01  id 0x02  len 0x000f)
   LCP OPTION: Magic number                   (type 0x05 len 0x06 val 0x3cba6a6b)
   LCP OPTION: Authentication protocol      (type 0x03 len 0x05 val 0xc2 0x23 0x05 )
11:58:56.975502 Out LCP configure request       (type 0x01  id 0x46  len 0x000f)
   LCP OPTION: Magic number                   (type 0x05 len 0x06 val 0x3cc218cf)
   LCP OPTION: Authentication protocol      (type 0x03 len 0x05 val 0xc2 0x23 0x05 )
11:58:56.975514 Out LCP configure acknowledge  (type 0x02  id 0x02  len 0x000f)
   LCP OPTION: Magic number                   (type 0x05 len 0x06 val 0x3cba6a6b)
   LCP OPTION: Authentication protocol      (type 0x03 len 0x05 val 0xc2 0x23 0x05 )
11:58:56.976093  In LCP configure acknowledge  (type 0x02  id 0x46  len 0x000f)
   LCP OPTION: Magic number                   (type 0x05 len 0x06 val 0x3cc218cf)
   LCP OPTION: Authentication protocol      (type 0x03 len 0x05 val 0xc2 0x23 0x05 )
11:58:56.976322  In   23 03 CHAP: Challenge,
Value=209b2a49005365580e3dac339d484b42, Name=r4
                 0103 0017 1020 9b2a 4900 5365 580e
11:58:56.977101 Out   23 03 CHAP: Challenge,
Value=6219ad3f7fa423050caefc3a1783da02, Name=r3
                 0147 0017 1062 19ad 3f7f a423 050c
11:58:56.977335 Out   23 03 CHAP: Response,
Value=73d43645397ad22e0c4115765663b581, Name=r3
                 0203 0017 1073 d436 4539 7ad2 2e0c
11:58:56.977864  In   23 03 CHAP: Response,
Value=d966a3b7137c35ad5f8b37267737aea8, Name=r4
                 0247 0017 10d9 66a3 b713 7c35 ad5f
11:58:56.977985 Out    4 03 CHAP: Success
                 0347 0004
11:58:56.978073 Out IPCP configure request       (type 0x01  id 0x48  len 0x0004)
11:58:56.978099  In    4 03 CHAP: Success
                 0303 0004
11:58:56.978114  In IPCP configure request       (type 0x01  id 0x04  len 0x0004)
11:58:56.978145 Out IPCP configure acknowledge   (type 0x02  id 0x04  len 0x0004)
11:58:56.978699  In IPCP configure acknowledge   (type 0x02  id 0x48  len 0x0004)
11:59:00.654824 Out LCP echo request             (type 0x09  id 0x49  len 0x0008)
11:59:00.655441  In LCP echo reply               (type 0x0a  id 0x49  len 0x0008)
```

Summary of POS Interface Configuration

Packet over SONET (POS) interfaces can be configured to run point-to-point protocols such as Cisco HDLC or PPP, and can operate with Frame Relay encapsulation for multipoint capabilities. Care must be taken when configuring a back-to-back Frame Relay connection due to the nature of the LMI keepalive mechanism and the need for a DTE-DCE line discipline on the data link. By default, M-series routers will function as Frame Relay DTEs, so either keepalives have to be disabled or one of the devices will need to be configured as a DCE.

Verification of a POS interface can be performed through ping testing, showing the interface, or by monitoring the traffic on that interface.

ATM Interfaces

The configuration of ATM interfaces is similar to that of Frame Relay because they both support multipoint operation through the use of virtual circuit (VC)–based multiplexing. ATM technology can be very complex, especially if the device supports switched VCs, multiple ATM Adaptation Layer (AAL) types, voice/date integration, and traffic shaping. The good news is that M-series routers currently support only Permanent Virtual Circuit (PVC) modes of ATM operation, so there is no need to deal with ATM forum/Q2931 call establishment signaling. Currently, there is support only for AAL5 Segmentation and Reassembly (SAR) functionality, which is relatively straightforward when compared to other AAL options defined by ATM technology.

 Juniper Networks routers can support any AAL type when the interface is configured for cell relay mode. A discussion of this capability is beyond the scope of this book.

ATM interfaces on M-series routers support point-to-point and multipoint connection types; traffic shaping; Operations, Administration, and Management (OAM) keepalive; and the ATM Forum's Integrated Local Management Interface (ILMI) for IP address and network interface registration. The following ATM configuration and verification examples are based on the topology shown in Figure 2.4. Based on the back-to-back nature of this initial ATM topology, the operator must be sure that the same VPI/VCI values are provisioned on both routers as in the case of back-to-back Frame Relay connection. Unlike the Frame Relay protocol, with ATM the use of the ILMI and link keepalives based on OAM cell exchanges are not affected by the absence of an ATM switch that normally functions as the User-to-Network Interface (UNI) DCE.

FIGURE 2.4   ATM interface topology

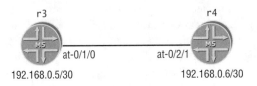

Physical Properties for ATM Interfaces
======================================

When implemented on a fiber optic–based SONET interface, the physical properties for an ATM interface are virtually identical to those detailed in the "Physical Properties for POS Interfaces" section earlier in this chapter. However, configuration at the physical-device level can include the following ATM-specific options:

- Support for the ILMI protocol
- Declaration of the maximum number of virtual circuits per virtual path (VP)

M-series routers also offer support for T3/E3-based ATM interfaces which, being copper-based, offer a different set of physical configuration options, some of which are listed next:

- Cell encapsulation mode (PLCP/Direct)
- CSU compatibility mode
- T3 C-bit parity
- Frame checksum (16- or 32-bit)
- Payload scrambling
- Loopback, line build, out, and BERT testing properties

The default setting for cell encapsulation is to use the Physical Layer Convergence Protocol (PLCP). Direct cell mapping is also supported, and is in fact required when the G.832 E3 line coding option has been selected. For proper operation, both ends of the T3/E3 ATM link must use the same cell-mapping approach.

This ATM interface configuration example will use the default physical device settings with the following ATM-specific options:

- No ILMI (default)
- Allow for VCI assignment of 3.300

The following commands correctly configure the physical properties of our SONET-based ATM interface:

```
[edit interfaces at-0/1/0]
lab@r3# set atm-options vpi 3 maximum-vcs 301
```

```
[edit interfaces at-0/1/0]
lab@r3# show
atm-options {
    vpi 3 maximum-vcs 301;
}
```

Because the ILMI protocol is disabled by default, the declaration of VP 3 and the maximum numbers of VCs that can in turn be supported within this VP complete the ATM-related physical device configuration. It may seem odd that the maximum VCI value specified in this example was 301 instead of the more intuitive setting of 300. This setting is needed because VCIs are zero indexed, which technically makes VCI 300 the 301st VCI instance. The ATM SAR ASIC allocates buffers based on the maximum number of VCIs supported in a specific virtual path, so you will be unable to commit a configuration that specifies a VCI number that lies outside the value specified by the maximum-vcs.

After committing the configuration, the results of a show interfaces indicate that all is well with the ATM physical layer settings on r3:

```
[edit interfaces at-0/1/0]
lab@r3# run show interfaces at-0/1/0
Physical interface: at-0/1/0, Enabled, Physical link is Up
  Interface index: 14, SNMP ifIndex: 12
  Link-level type: ATM-PVC, MTU: 4482, Clocking: Internal, SONET mode, Speed: OC3,
  Loopback: None, Payload scrambler: Enabled
  Device flags  : Present Running
  Link flags    : None
  Input rate    : 0 bps (0 pps)
  Output rate   : 0 bps (0 pps)
  SONET alarms  : None
  SONET defects : None
```

Configuring ATM Interface Logical Properties

As with a Frame Relay interface, the logical properties for ATM interfaces will include the specification of a protocol family and its associated addressing, along with the binding of one or more virtual circuit identifiers to logical units on the interface.

The criteria for the ATM logical properties configuration in this example are as follows:

- Logical unit 200, VPI 3, and VCI 200
- IPv4 family, with the addressing shown earlier in Figure 2.4
- NLPID encapsulation
- Unspecified Bit Rate (UBR) with no traffic shaping

> Because the JNCIP candidate is only required to configure a VCI 200, requiring support of a VCI 300 could be considered a "trick" in that it would be easy for the candidate to incorrectly set the maximum-vci option to a value of 300 with little chance of ever catching the 0-based indexing mistake. But genuine "experts" should be familiar with this nonintuitive maximum VCI issue, having come across the problem numerous times during their years of configuring ATM interfaces in the field. If nothing else, this ATM configuration example should stress the need for careful analysis of all tasks and operational requirements presented in your scenario, as well as the need to seek clarification from your exam proctor when you think a task may have hidden issues.

The following commands correctly configure r3 for this scenario. Because UBR is the default, no configuration is needed, or is in fact possible, for the UBR requirement posed in this configuration example:

```
[edit]
lab@r3# edit interfaces at-0/1/0 unit 200

[edit interfaces at-0/1/0 unit 200]
lab@r3# set family inet address 192.168.0.5/30

[edit interfaces at-0/1/0 unit 200]
lab@r3# set vci 3.200

[edit interfaces at-0/1/0 unit 200]
lab@r3# set encapsulation atm-nlpid
```

The interface configuration resulting from these commands is shown next:

```
[edit interfaces at-0/1/0]
lab@r3# show
atm-options {
    vpi 3 maximum-vcs 301;
}
unit 200 {
    encapsulation atm-nlpid;
    vci 3.200;
    family inet {
        address 192.168.0.5/30;
    }
}
```

Omitting the VPI value when configuring the VCI will result in the default VPI value of 0. Because this example calls for VPI 3, care must be taken to explicitly configure the correct VPI value.

The default encapsulation for ATM VCs is LLC/SNAP, so NLPID-based encapsulation must be configured at the logical unit/VCI level for compliance with this example's requirements. The default ATM connection type of point-to-point is a perfect match for this configuration example, so no connection type modification is necessary.

Similar commands are entered on r4 to create the ATM interface configuration shown here:

```
[edit interfaces at-0/2/1]
lab@r4# show
atm-options {
    vpi 3 maximum-vcs 301;
}
unit 200 {
    encapsulation atm-nlpid;
    vci 3.200;
    family inet {
        address 192.168.0.6/30;
    }
}
```

Verifying ATM Operation

With the point-to-point ATM configuration now committed in both r3 and r4, the operator can verify proper operation by displaying the interface's status or by conducting ping testing. We begin our verification with an example of the former:

```
[edit interfaces at-0/1/0]
lab@r3# run show interfaces terse at-0/1/0
Interface       Admin Link Proto Local              Remote
at-0/1/0        up    up
at-0/1/0.200    up    up    inet  192.168.0.5/30
```

The terse display indicates that the interface is up both administratively and at the logical-link layers, and confirms the use of logical unit 200 as required. The following command displays additional details on the operational status of the ATM interface and confirms the correct NLPID encapsulation:

```
[edit interfaces at-0/1/0]
lab@r3# run show interfaces at-0/1/0
```

```
Physical interface: at-0/1/0, Enabled, Physical link is Up
  Interface index: 14, SNMP ifIndex: 12
  Link-level type: ATM-PVC, MTU: 4482, Clocking: Internal, SONET mode, Speed: OC3,
  Loopback: None, Payload scrambler: Enabled
  Device flags    : Present Running
  Link flags      : None
  Input rate      : 0 bps (0 pps)
  Output rate     : 0 bps (0 pps)
  SONET alarms    : None
  SONET defects   : None

  Logical interface at-0/1/0.200 (Index 5) (SNMP ifIndex 30)
    Flags: Point-To-Point SNMP-Traps Encapsulation: ATM-NLPID
  Input packets : 0
  Output packets: 0
    Protocol inet, MTU: 4470, Flags: None
      Addresses, Flags: Is-Preferred Is-Primary
        Destination: 192.168.0.4/30, Local: 192.168.0.5
    VCI 3.200
      Flags: Active
      Total down time: 0 sec, Last down: Never
  Traffic statistics:
      Input  packets:                0
      Output packets:                0
```

To verify the operation of the ATM VC, the operator now issues a conventional ping from r3 to r4:

```
[edit interfaces at-0/1/0]
lab@r3# run ping count 2 192.168.0.6
PING 192.168.0.6 (192.168.0.6): 56 data bytes
64 bytes from 192.168.0.6: icmp_seq=0 ttl=255 time=1.371 ms
64 bytes from 192.168.0.6: icmp_seq=1 ttl=255 time=1.204 ms

--- 192.168.0.6 ping statistics ---
2 packets transmitted, 2 packets received, 0% packet loss
round-trip min/avg/max/stddev = 1.204/1.288/1.371/0.083 ms
```

The operator can also verify the ATM circuit using the atm option to the ping command as follows:

```
[edit interfaces at-0/1/0]
lab@r3# run ping atm vci 3.200 segment interface at-0/1/0
```

```
53 byte oam cell received on (vpi=3 vci=200): seq=1
53 byte oam cell received on (vpi=3 vci=200): seq=2
53 byte oam cell received on (vpi=3 vci=200): seq=3
```

Based on these results, it would seem that all is good with your initial ATM interface configuration!

 When conventional IP-level pings fail on an ATM interface, you should consider using the atm option, which generates OAM loopback cells (F5 level) at either the VCI segment or end-to-end connection levels. These non-IP pings can help isolate ATM and physical layer problems from those that relate to your IP layer configuration. Because this example illustrates a back-to-back connection, you will get the same result regardless of whether you evoke the command with the segment or end-to-end switches. When a switch is present, the segment-level ping will validate the ATM access link while the end-to-end level option will test the end-to-end operation of the virtual channel connection (VCC). You can also configure the background generation of OAM cells to verify link integrity using the oam-period option under the desired VCI.

Monitoring ILMI Operation

While the ILMI protocol can be used to provide link integrity testing between the ATM device and its attached switch, M-series routers only make use of the ILMI protocol for SNMP-related get and puts that are used to exchange ATM interface and IP address information for the devices that attach to a particular ATM access link. As with any command/response protocol, one can gain valuable insight and troubleshooting clues from monitoring the status and operation of the ILMI protocol.

ILMI is enabled on an ATM interface with the following command:

```
[edit interfaces at-0/1/0]
lab@r3# set atm-options ilmi
```

In order to commit this configuration, you must ensure that you have enabled support for the well-known 0.16 VPI/VCI value associated with the ILMI protocol at the physical-device level with the following command:

```
lab@r3# set atm-options vpi 0 maximum-vcs 17
```

The modified ATM configuration in r3 is shown next with the ILMI-related changes highlighted:

```
[edit interfaces at-0/1/0]
lab@r3# show
atm-options {
    vpi 3 maximum-vcs 201;
```

```
    vpi 0 maximum-vcs 17;
    ilmi;
}
unit 200 {
    encapsulation atm-nlpid;
    vci 3.200;
    family inet {
        address 192.168.0.5/30;
    }
}
```

After committing the ILMI change, the router creates a new logical unit that is associated with the 0.16 VPI/VCI value used by ILMI. Information about ILMI protocol operation can now be obtained by showing the interface:

```
lab@r3# run show interfaces at-0/1/0
Physical interface: at-0/1/0, Enabled, Physical link is Up
  Interface index: 14, SNMP ifIndex: 12
  Link-level type: ATM-PVC, MTU: 4482, Clocking: Internal, SONET mode, Speed:
OC3,
  Loopback: None, Payload scrambler: Enabled
  Device flags   : Present Running
  Link flags     : None
  Input rate     : 0 bps (0 pps)
  Output rate    : 248 bps (0 pps)
  SONET alarms   : None
  SONET defects  : None

  Logical interface at-0/1/0.200 (Index 4) (SNMP ifIndex 30)
    Flags: Point-To-Point SNMP-Traps Encapsulation: ATM-NLPID
  Input packets : 0
  Output packets: 0
    Protocol inet, MTU: 4470, Flags: None
      Addresses, Flags: Is-Preferred Is-Primary
        Destination: 192.168.0.4/30, Local: 192.168.0.5
    VCI 3.200
      Flags: Active
      Total down time: 0 sec, Last down: Never
  Traffic statistics:
      Input  packets:              0
      Output packets:              0
```

```
Logical interface at-0/1/0.32767 (Index 5) (SNMP ifIndex 31)
    Flags: Point-To-Point SNMP-Traps Encapsulation: ATM-VCMUX
 Input packets : 0
 Output packets: 91
    VCI 0.16
      Flags: Active, ILMI
      Total down time: 0 sec, Last down: Never
 Traffic statistics:
      Input  packets:                    0
      Output packets:                   91
```

The fact that ILMI packets are present only in one direction is a sure sign that the router is having problems communicating to the local ATM switch, or as is the case in this example, the presence of a device that has not been configured to support ILMI. After including ILMI support in r4's configuration, we can display information gleaned from ILMI exchanges:

```
lab@r3# run show ilmi all
Physical interface: at-0/1/0, VCI: 0.16
  Peer IP address: 192.168.0.6, Peer interface name: at-0/2/1
```

The results confirm that r3 is connected to r4's at- 0/2/1 interface, and that r4's IP address has in fact been set to 192.168.0.6.

Multipoint ATM Connections

The presence of an ATM switch allows for multipoint ATM connections. A typical multipoint topology is shown in Figure 2.5.

FIGURE 2.5   Multipoint ATM connections

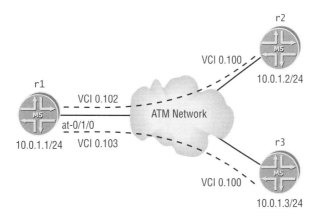

In this case, r1 is connected to both r2 and r3 using a single logical unit that has been associated with two remote destination IP addresses and the local connection identifier (VPI/VCI) used to reach each of them. The required ATM configuration for r1 is similar to that of a multipoint Frame Relay connection. The key difference between a multipoint and a point-to-point ATM connection is the inclusion of the `multipoint` and `multipoint-destination` keywords as shown in the following:

```
[edit interfaces at-0/1/0]
lab@r3# show
atm-options {
    vpi 0 maximum-vcs 201;
}
unit 200 {
    multipoint;
    family inet {
        address 10.0.1.1/24 {
            multipoint-destination 10.0.1.2 vci 102;
            multipoint-destination 10.0.1.3 vci 103;
        }
    }
}
```

As with Frame Relay, Juniper Networks M-series routers can respond to ATM Inverse ARP requests but cannot initiate them. Therefore, static VCI–to–IP address mapping is mandatory when configuring a Juniper Networks router for multipoint ATM operation. To allow the router to respond to an ATM inverse ARP request, include the `inverse-arp` keyword as part of the `multipoint-destination` configuration.

ATM Traffic Shaping

Juniper Networks M-series routers support ATM traffic shaping using either Constant or Variable Bit Rate (CBR/VBR) traffic parameters. Unspecified Bit Rate (UBR) is the default traffic shaping method. You can also configure a maximum queue length on each VC, a technique that is often used to put a finite bound on queue latency (at the cost of dropping traffic that is in excess of VC's shaping profile). To demonstrate the configuration and verification of ATM traffic shaping, you will now apply the following VBR shaping profile to the ATM connection between r3 and r4:

- Peak bit rate = 1Mbps (~2600 cells/second)
- Sustained bit rate = 500Kbps (~1300 cells/second)
- Maximum burst = 25 cells
- Maximum queue depth of 20 packets

You can also specify ATM traffic shaping rates in cells/second by using the suffix c after the desired cell rate, as in set shaping vbr peak 100c for a CBR shaping profile that generates 100 cells per second. Each such cell will carry about 48 bytes of user payload, which equates to a link level throughput of approximately 38.4Kbps. JUNOS software will convert cell-per-second rates into bit-per-second rates when the configuration is displayed.

The commands used to configuring this ATM shaping profile on r3 are shown in the following:

```
[edit interfaces at-0/1/0 unit 200]
lab@r3# set shaping queue-length 20

[edit interfaces at-0/1/0 unit 200]
lab@r3# set shaping vbr peak 1m sustained 500k burst 25
```

The resulting shaping configuration is shown next with highlights:

```
[edit interfaces at-0/1/0]
lab@r3# show
atm-options {
    vpi 3 maximum-vcs 201;
    vpi 0 maximum-vcs 17;
    ilmi;
}
unit 200 {
    encapsulation atm-nlpid;
    vci 3.200;
    shaping {
        vbr peak 1m sustained 500k burst 25;
        queue-length 20;
    }
    family inet {
        address 192.168.0.5/30;
    }
}
```

To verify that shaping is having an effect, we conduct large packet flood pings, both with shaping enabled and after shaping has been deactivated:

```
[edit interfaces at-0/1/0]
lab@r3# run ping size 64000 rapid count 5 192.168.0.6
```

```
PING 192.168.0.6 (192.168.0.6): 64000 data bytes
..!..
--- 192.168.0.6 ping statistics ---
5 packets transmitted, 1 packets received, 80% packet loss
round-trip min/avg/max/stddev = 1048.413/1048.413/1048.413/0.000 ms
```

A packet loss of 80 percent is pretty harsh, even for a flood ping. Now the `ping` test is repeated with shaping deactivated:

```
[edit interfaces at-0/1/0]
lab@r3# deactivate unit 200 shaping

[edit interfaces at-0/1/0]
lab@r3# commit
commit complete

[edit interfaces at-0/1/0]
lab@r3# run ping size 64000 rapid count 5 192.168.0.6
PING 192.168.0.6 (192.168.0.6): 64000 data bytes
!!!!!
--- 192.168.0.6 ping statistics ---
5 packets transmitted, 5 packets received, 0% packet loss
round-trip min/avg/max/stddev = 31.168/31.474/31.929/0.263
```

These results indicate that ATM shaping is working as expected.

ATM Interface Summary

ATM interface configuration and testing is similar to Frame Relay in that both interface types support multipoint capabilities using virtual circuit identifiers. ATM interfaces require explicit configuration of VP and maximum VC counts at the physical level, and these values must be adjusted to accommodate the 0-based indexing of VCI values. When a VP value is not specified, JUNOS software will assume a value of 0, so pay special attention when configuring ATM VCIs that do not make use of VP 0.

ATM ping testing can quickly isolate ATM problems from those caused by configuration mistakes made at the IP layer. The use of ILMI can provide information about the device that terminates the ATM access link, and its command/response nature can be used to confirm the integrity of an ATM access link. OAM cells should be enabled when keepalive functions are desired on an ATM interface. Lastly, ATM connections default to a UBR traffic shaping profile but can be configured to support traffic shaping using either CBR or VBR parameters.

Ethernet Interfaces

Juniper Networks routers support a variety of different Fast and Gigabit Ethernet PICs. The 12- and 48-port Fast Ethernet PICs supported in the M160 are capable of performing ingress rate limiting and dual-rate (10/100 Mbps) operation at either 10Mbps or 100Mbps, but all remaining Juniper Networks Fast Ethernet PICs require 100Mbps operation and can only be rate-limited through the configuration of IP II–related policers.

M-series Ethernet interfaces support VLAN tagging, 802.3ad link aggregation, and the Virtual Router Redundancy Protocol (VRRP), which is a standards-based protocol that is similar in function to Cisco's Hot Standby Router Protocol (HSRP). The configuration options supported by Fast and Gigabit Ethernet PICs are very similar, as are the verification mechanisms available to the operator.

This section focuses on Fast Ethernet links because they are the most common interface type found in a certification preparation lab.

Ethernet Interface Physical Configuration

The physical properties for Ethernet interfaces are set at the device and `fastether-options` or `gigether-options` portion of the configuration hierarchy, depending on the type of interface being configured. The physical options for Ethernet interfaces include the following:

- Half/full duplex mode (Fast-E only)
- Flow control
- Speed (12- and 48-port Fast-E PICs only)
- Loopback
- 802.3ad link aggregation
- Source address (MAC) filtering
- Encapsulation (to support Circuit Cross Connect [CCC] applications)
- VLAN tagging support
- Manual MAC address assignment
- Device MTU (Jumbo frames)

Figure 2.6 illustrates the topology used in this Ethernet configuration scenario. In this example, VLAN tagging and VRRP are required on the 10.0.5/24 subnet to which r1 and r2 attach, so your initial Fast Ethernet configuration will require that you enable VLAN tagging at the physical-device level with all other device properties remaining at their defaults.

The following command, issued on both r1 and r2, completes the necessary physical configuration of the Ethernet device to enable support of VLAN-tagged frames:

```
[edit interfaces fe-0/0/0]
lab@r1# set vlan-tagging
```

FIGURE 2.6   Ethernet configuration topology

r1
fe-0/0/0   .1
                  fe-0/0/1   10.0.4.0/24
.1
                                                        .3   r3
10.0.5/24 (VLAN 520)
10.0.6/24 (VLAN 530)
                                              fe-0/0/0
                                              fe-0/0/1
                                                        .3
r2
.2   fe-0/0/1
fe-0/0/0   .2   10.0.3.0/24

Ethernet Interface Logical Properties

The logical properties for Ethernet interfaces are configured at the logical-unit level, and will relate to the protocol family being configured. For example, the IP protocol is associated with ARP and static ARP entries can be added to a logical unit that supports the IP protocol family. You can also specify the encapsulation (Ethernet II, SNAP, LLC-SNAP) at the logical-unit level for traffic that is originated by the RE, but the default encapsulation associated with each protocol family rarely needs modification, and in some cases cannot be modified despite configuration attempts to the contrary. For example, IP and ARP always use Ethernet Version II (DIX) encapsulation, despite what may be configured under the logical unit.

M-series and T-series routers do not perform a translation of Ethernet framing for transit traffic, so that a frame that arrives using DIX encapsulation will always be forwarded using the same encapsulation, regardless of the encapsulation specified on that logical unit. The various encapsulation options listed for Ethernet interfaces only affect traffic generated locally by the RE.

The configuration requirements for this scenario are:

- IPv4 addressing as shown in Figure 2.6
- VLAN and VRRP requirements
    - VLAN IDs are 520 and 530.
    - Virtual IP (VIP) addresses = 10.0.5.253 and 10.0.6.253.
    - r1 is master of VLAN 520 when operational.

- r2 is master of VLAN 530 when operational.
- Ensure that the VIP is pingable on each VLAN.

r1's VLAN and VRRP Configuration

The following commands correctly configure r1 for this scenario:

```
[edit interfaces fe-0/0/0]
lab@r1# set unit 520 family inet address 10.0.5.1/24
```

```
[edit interfaces fe-0/0/0]
lab@r1# set unit 520 vlan-id 520
```

```
[edit interfaces fe-0/0/0 unit 520 family inet address 10.0.5.1/24]
lab@r1# set vrrp-group 1 virtual-address 10.0.5.253
```

```
[edit interfaces fe-0/0/0 unit 520 family inet address 10.0.5.1/24]
lab@r1# set vrrp-group 1 accept-data
```

These commands configured r1 to associate VLAN tag 520 with logical unit 520 on its fe-0/0/0 interface, assigned its IP address, and created VRRP group 1 that will use a VIP address of 10.0.5.253. The accept-data option tells the router to "violate" the VRRP specification by allowing it to respond to ICMP echo requests sent to the VIP address. According to the VRRP specification, the VIP master can only respond to ARP requests unless the current VIP is assigned to one of the master router's interfaces, in which case the VRRP master may respond to all traffic addressed to the VIP. This particular scenario does not require that there be any correlation between the logical unit number and the VLAN ID, but in this example the values have been matched.

The VLAN assignments used in the previous example will conflict with the VLAN ID range of 512–4094 reserved for VLAN-CCC applications. Because this configuration example does not involve the use of VLAN-CCC encapsulation, these VLAN ID assignments are perfectly valid.

Technicians are often confused by the default VRRP behavior of not allowing the VIP address to be pinged, most likely because they have become accustomed to being able to ping the VIP address used by Cisco's proprietary HSRP protocol. Without the accept-data option, you will not be able to test the VIP address by issuing pings. This behavior has been known to cause JNCIP candidates to engage in troubleshooting procedures to isolate a problem that does not even exist.

The VLAN 520 configuration in r1 is shown next:

```
lab@r1# show
vlan-tagging;
unit 520 {
    vlan-id 520;
    family inet {
        address 10.0.5.1/24 {
            vrrp-group 1 {
                virtual-address 10.0.5.253;
                accept-data;
            }
        }
    }
}
```

Because no priority value has been specified for VRRP group 1, the default value of 100 will be in effect. You will now add the configuration for VLAN 530 to r1, being careful to adjust priorities so that the correct VRRP mastership is achieved when r2 is later brought online:

```
[edit interfaces fe-0/0/0]
lab@r1# set unit 530 family inet address 10.0.6.1/24

[edit interfaces fe-0/0/0]
lab@r1# set unit 530 vlan-id 530

[edit interfaces fe-0/0/0]
lab@r1# edit unit 530 family inet address 10.0.6.1/24

[edit interfaces fe-0/0/0 unit 530 family inet address 10.0.6.1/24]
lab@r1# set vrrp-group 2 virtual-address 10.0.6.253

[edit interfaces fe-0/0/0 unit 530 family inet address 10.0.6.1/24]
lab@r1# set vrrp-group 2 accept-data

[edit interfaces fe-0/0/0 unit 530 family inet address 10.0.6.1/24]
lab@r1# set vrrp-group 2 priority 80
```

Because the priority setting for r1's VRRP group 2 (80) is lower than the default value of 100, the default priority setting in r2 will ensure that it becomes the master of VRRP group 2 when operational. The complete VLAN tagging and VRRP configuration for r1 is shown next:

```
[edit interfaces fe-0/0/0]
lab@r1# show
```

```
vlan-tagging;
unit 520 {
    vlan-id 520;
    family inet {
        address 10.0.5.1/24 {
            vrrp-group 1 {
                virtual-address 10.0.5.253;
                accept-data;
            }
        }
    }
}
unit 530 {
    vlan-id 530;
    family inet {
        address 10.0.6.1/24 {
            vrrp-group 2 {
                virtual-address 10.0.6.253;
                priority 80;
                accept-data;
            }
        }
    }
}
```

Because r2 has not yet been configured in this example, we expect to see that r1 is currently master of both VRRP groups. The following command verifies that this is the case:

```
lab@r1> show vrrp summary
Interface   Unit  Group  Type  Address    Int state  VR state
fe-0/0/0    520   1      lcl   10.0.5.1   up         master
                         vip   10.0.5.253
fe-0/0/0    530   2      lcl   10.0.6.1   up         master
                         vip   10.0.6.253
```

r2's VLAN and VRRP Configuration

The following commands correctly configure r2 for this scenario:

```
[edit interfaces fe-0/0/0]
lab@r2# set unit 520 family inet address 10.0.5.2/24
```

```
[edit interfaces fe-0/0/0]
lab@r2# set unit 520 vlan-id 520

[edit interfaces fe-0/0/0 unit 520 family inet address 10.0.5.2/24]
lab@r2# set vrrp-group 1 virtual-address 10.0.5.253

[edit interfaces fe-0/0/0 unit 520 family inet address 10.0.5.2/24]
lab@r2# set vrrp-group 1 accept-data

[edit interfaces fe-0/0/0 unit 520 family inet address 10.0.5.2/24]
lab@r2# set vrrp-group 1 priority 80
```

These commands configured r2 to associate VLAN tag 520 with its logical unit 520, assigned the interface's IP address, and configured VRRP group 1 to use the correct Virtual IP address of 10.0.5.253. Worthy of note is the fact that r2 has the priority of VRRP group 1 set to 80, which is lower than the default value of 100 in place on r1. This will ensure that r1 is master of VRRP group 1 when it is operational.

We next add the configuration for VLAN 530 to r2 using the same set of commands used to configure VRRP group 1. The priority of VRRP group 2 is left at the default value of 100 in this case, to ensure that r2 is the master of VRRP group 2 when operational. The completed r2 VRRP/VLAN configuration is shown next:

```
[edit]
lab@r2# show interfaces fe-0/0/0
vlan-tagging;
unit 520 {
    vlan-id 520;
    family inet {
        address 10.0.5.2/24 {
            vrrp-group 1 {
                virtual-address 10.0.5.253;
                priority 80;
                accept-data;
            }
        }
    }
}
unit 530 {
    vlan-id 530;
    family inet {
        address 10.0.6.2/24 {
            vrrp-group 2 {
```

```
                   virtual-address 10.0.6.253;
                   accept-data;
               }
           }
       }
   }
}
```

Verify Basic VRRP Operation

With both r1 and r2 configured as described earlier, we should see that r1 is master of VRRP group 1 while r2 is master of VRRP group 2. Furthermore, either router should take over mastership if the current master fails. The following steps confirm that this is the case:

```
lab@r1> show vrrp summary
Interface   Unit  Group  Type  Address   Int state  VR state
fe-0/0/0    520   1      lcl   10.0.5.1    up        master
                         vip   10.0.5.253
fe-0/0/0    530   2      lcl   10.0.6.1    up        backup
                         vip   10.0.6.253
```

Very good, just as we had expected: r1 is heading the charge for VRRP group 1 and is functioning as a backup for VRRP group 2. To verify that r1 will take over for VRRP group 2, we disable r2's fe-0/0/0 interface and redisplay VRRP status on r1:

```
[edit]
lab@r2# set interfaces fe-0/0/0 disable
[edit]
lab@r2# commit
```

```
lab@r1> show vrrp summary
Interface   Unit  Group  Type  Address   Int state  VR state
fe-0/0/0    520   1      lcl   10.0.5.1    up        master
                         vip   10.0.5.253
fe-0/0/0    530   2      lcl   10.0.6.1    up        master
                         vip   10.0.6.253
```

As expected, r1 has become master for both VRRP groups, which confirms that basic VRRP functionality is working as desired. Be sure to re-enable the fe-0/0/0 interface on r2 before proceeding. A thorough operator will perform a similar check for mastership switchover on r2 as well.

VRRP Authentication and Interface Tracking

With basic VRRP functionality working as planned, we will enhance the configuration by adding MD5 authentication and upstream interface tracking. Interface tracking is used to lower the priority of the current VRRP master should its upstream interface become inoperable. Based on Figure 2.6, we can see that both r1 and r2 should track the status of their respective fe-0/0/1 interfaces as these interfaces connect each of them to the upstream router r3.

The following commands add MD5 authentication to both VRRP groups; they must be entered on both r1 and r2 for proper operation. The authentication key value will be set to jni in this example:

```
[edit interfaces fe-0/0/0 unit 530 family inet address 10.0.5.1/24]
lab@r1# set vrrp-group 1 authentication-type md5

[edit interfaces fe-0/0/0 unit 530 family inet address 10.0.5.1/24]
lab@r1# set vrrp-group 1 authentication-key jni

[edit interfaces fe-0/0/0 unit 530 family inet address 10.0.6.1/24]
lab@r1# set vrrp-group 2 authentication-type md5

[edit interfaces fe-0/0/0 unit 530 family inet address 10.0.6.1/24]
lab@r1# set vrrp-group 2 authentication-key jni
```

The next set of commands instructs the router to deduct 30 from its current priority level (100 by default) should its fe-0/0/1 interface become inoperable. For r2, this command will need to be entered under VRRP group 2:

```
[edit interfaces fe-0/0/0 unit 520 family inet address 10.0.5.1/24 vrrp-group 1]
lab@r1# set track interface fe-0/0/1 priority-cost 30
```

The Fast Ethernet configuration for r1 is shown in Listing 2.1, including the configuration of its fe-0/0/1 interface that is now being tracked by VRRP group 1:

Listing 2.1: VRRP Configuration for *r1*
```
[edit]
lab@r1# show interfaces
fxp0 {
    unit 0 {
        family inet {
            address 10.0.1.1/24;
        }
    }
}
fe-0/0/0 {
    vlan-tagging;
    unit 520 {
        vlan-id 520;
        family inet {
```

```
                address 10.0.5.1/24 {
                    vrrp-group 1 {
                        virtual-address 10.0.5.253;
                        accept-data;
                        authentication-type md5;
                        authentication-key "$9$3BYX/A0vMX7-w"; # SECRET-DATA
                        track {
                            interface fe-0/0/1.0 priority-cost 30;
                        }
                    }
                }
            }
        }
        unit 530 {
            vlan-id 530;
            family inet {
                address 10.0.6.1/24 {
                    vrrp-group 2 {
                        virtual-address 10.0.6.253;
                        priority 80;
                        accept-data;
                        authentication-type md5;
                        authentication-key "$9$rhkKWxJZjHqf"; # SECRET-DATA
                    }
                }
            }
        }
    }
    fe-0/0/1 {
        unit 0 {
            family inet {
                address 10.0.4.1/24;
            }
        }
    }
}
```

Verify VRRP Interface Tracking

Once the configurations of r1 and r2 have been modified with the authentication and interface tracking–related configuration, you can verify that tracking is working by deactivating the tracked interface and confirming that the expected change in VRRP group mastership occurs. For this example, we will monitor the VRRP state on r2, both before and after r1's fe-0/0/1 interface is deactivated:

```
lab@r2> show vrrp summary
Interface   Unit  Group  Type   Address      Int state  VR state
fe-0/0/0    520   1      lcl    10.0.5.2     up         backup
                         vip    10.0.5.253
fe-0/0/0    530   2      lcl    10.0.6.2     up         master
                         vip    10.0.6.253
```

Now we disconnect, disable, or deactivate the tracked interface on r1 (fe-0/0/1), and verify that r2 becomes master for both VRRP groups:

```
lab@r2> show vrrp summary
Interface   Unit  Group  Type   Address      Int state  VR state
fe-0/0/0    520   1      lcl    10.0.5.2     up         master
                         vip    10.0.5.253
fe-0/0/0    530   2      lcl    10.0.6.2     up         master
                         vip    10.0.6.253
```

It would appear that both the MD5 authentication and interface tracking aspects of your VRRP configuration are working as designed. When interface-tracking issues are suspected, you can obtain detailed information on the status of tracking using this command:

```
lab@r1> show vrrp track
Track if    State Cost  Interface    Group  Cfg Run VR State
fe-0/0/1.0  down  30    fe-0/0/0.520 1      100 70  backup
```

This display confirms that r1 is tracking the state of its fe-0/0/1.0 interface and that it will deduct 30 from the VRRP priority of interface fe-0/0/0.520 when the tracked interface's state is other than up. You can also see the VRRP group's configured priority (the default 100 in this case) as well as its current running priority, which is now 70, due to the tracked interface being down. This display confirms that all is working with your final VRRP configuration.

When all else fails and your VRRP configuration is not working, you should enable VRRP tracing and monitor the trace file for real-time debug output. A typical VRRP-tracing configuration and some of the output generated by unplugging r1's tracked interface are shown in the following, with key information highlighted:

In this example, the tracked interface was entered as **fe-0/0/1**, which resulted in the default logical unit (0) being tracked on this interface. You should always explicitly enter a unit number when unit values other than the default are in use. VRRP-tracking problems will result when the default unit number is inadvertently tracked on an interface that is not using unit number 0.

```
[edit]
lab@r1# show protocols vrrp
traceoptions {
    file vrrp;
    flag state;
    flag general;
}
```

This tracing configuration causes VRRP state and general activities to be logged to a file called vrrp. We now monitor the file as r1's tracked interface is disconnected:

```
lab@r1> monitor start vrrp
```

```
*** vrrp ***
Apr 10 23:50:38 vrrpd_rts_async_ifd_msg, Received Async message for: fe-0/0/1
Apr 10 23:50:38 vrrpd_update_track_if_entry
Apr 10 23:50:38 vrrpd_update_track_if_entry : fe-0/0/1.0 : fe-0/0/
0.002.008.010.000.005.001.001
Apr 10 23:50:38 vrrpd_rts_update_track_if for fe-0/0/1.0
Apr 10 23:50:38 vrrpd_rts_get_track_if_state for fe-0/0/1.0
Apr 10 23:50:38 Interface fe-0/0/1 ifindex: 3 flags 0x8001
Apr 10 23:50:38 Interface fe-0/0/1 ifl ifindex: 4 flags 0x8000
Apr 10 23:50:38 vrrpd_rts_get_track_if_state : fe-0/0/1.0 : down
Apr 10 23:50:38 vrrpd_update_track_priority : 100
Apr 10 23:50:38 vrrpd_update_track_priority: 70
Apr 10 23:50:39 vrrp_fsm_update IFD: fe-0/0/0.002.008.010.000.005.001.001 event:
backup
Apr 10 23:50:39 vrrp_fsm_backup: fe-0/0/0.002.008.010.000.005.001.001 state
from: master
Apr 10 23:50:39 Signalled dcd (PID 1672) to reconfig
```

The trace output shown here displays the change in r1's priority due to the state change interface fe-0/0/1, and also shows the loss of VRRP group mastership that results from the reduction in priority.

MAC Address Filtering

By default, Fast and Gigabit Ethernet interfaces will accept frames from all source MAC addresses. You can limit frame acceptance based on the source MAC address by using the source-filtering option and a corresponding list of MAC addresses that can be accepted. To demonstrate this feature, we will continue to use the topology illustrated in Figure 2.6 and configure r3's fe-0/0/0 interface to meet the following criterion:

▪ Only accept frames sent from r1's fe-0/0/1 interface.

The following configuration on r3 correctly configures the source address filtering requirements of this configuration example. To obtain the MAC address being used by r1's fe-0/0/1
interface, you can either examine the ARP cache on r3 or show the fe-0/0/1 interface on r1. This
example demonstrates the ARP cache examination approach:

```
lab@r3# run ping 10.0.4.1 count 1
PING 10.0.4.1 (10.0.4.1): 56 data bytes
64 bytes from 10.0.4.1: icmp_seq=0 ttl=255 time=0.635 ms

--- 10.0.4.1 ping statistics ---
1 packets transmitted, 1 packets received, 0% packet loss
round-trip min/avg/max/stddev = 0.635/0.635/0.635/0.000 ms
```

The ARP cache is now examined to obtain the MAC address for address 10.0.4.1:

```
[edit]
lab@r3# run show arp
MAC Address        Address          Interface
00:b0:d0:10:73:2f  10.0.1.100       fxp0.0
00:a0:c9:b2:f8:cb  10.0.3.2         fe-0/0/1.0
00:a0:c9:6f:7b:3e  10.0.4.1         fe-0/0/0.0
Total entries: 3
```

We now know that r1's fe-0/0/1 interface will be using MAC address 00:a0:c9:6f:7b:3e.
Armed with this information, we can proceed with the source address filter configuration on r3:

```
[edit interfaces fe-0/0/0 fastether-options]
lab@r3# set source-filtering

[edit interfaces fe-0/0/0 fastether-options]
lab@r3# set source-address-filter 00:a0:c9:6f:7b:3e

[edit interfaces fe-0/0/0 fastether-options]
lab@r3# up
```

The resulting configuration is:

```
[edit interfaces fe-0/0/0]
lab@r3# show
fastether-options {
    source-filtering;
    source-address-filter {
        00:a0:c9:6f:7b:3e;
    }
```

```
}
unit 0 {
      family inet {
        address 10.0.4.3/24;
    }
}
```

The resulting configuration on r3 will cause it to reject any frames received on its fe-0/0/0 interface that do not contain a source MAC address of 00:a0:c9:6f:7b:3e.

Verify MAC Address Filtering

To confirm that the MAC address filter is working, we first ping r3 using r1's burned-in MAC address, and then retry the ping after manually setting a new MAC address on r1's fe-0/0/1 interface:

```
[edit interfaces fe-0/0/1]
lab@r1# run ping 10.0.4.3 count 1
PING 10.0.4.3 (10.0.4.3): 56 data bytes
64 bytes from 10.0.4.3: icmp_seq=0 ttl=255 time=0.568 ms

--- 10.0.4.3 ping statistics ---
1 packets transmitted, 1 packets received, 0% packet loss
round-trip min/avg/max/stddev = 0.568/0.568/0.568/0.000 ms
```

The pings using the burned-in MAC address work as expected. We now assign a new MAC address to r1's fe-0/0/1 interface:

```
[edit interfaces fe-0/0/1]
lab@r1# set mac 00:a0:c9:6f:7b:3d

[edit interfaces fe-0/0/1]
lab@r1# commit
commit complete

[edit interfaces fe-0/0/1]
lab@r1# run ping 10.0.4.3 count 1
PING 10.0.4.3 (10.0.4.3): 56 data bytes
^C
--- 10.0.4.3 ping statistics ---
1 packets transmitted, 0 packets received, 100% packet loss
```

Great—packets sent to r4 with the new MAC address fail as expected. This behavior confirms that the source address filter is working as intended.

Ethernet Interface Summary

This section provided typical JNCIP-level Ethernet configuration examples and common verification techniques. Using several examples, we detailed a typical VRRP configuration scenario that used both authentication and interface tracking and provided examples of source address filtering.

Aggregated Interfaces

JUNOS software supports the aggregation of Ethernet and SONET interfaces through the creation of a virtual device that is associated with one or more physical interfaces. All physical interfaces that make up such an aggregated device must operate at a common speed, and in the case of Ethernet, must also operate in full-duplex mode with VLAN tagging. You cannot aggregate Ethernet interfaces that have not been configured for VLAN tagging. Aggregated interfaces are an example of inverse multiplexing in that a single high-speed link is achieved through the bundling of multiple lower-speed links.

Aggregated Ethernet

This example will demonstrate the configuration and testing of an aggregated Ethernet interface. The requirements for this example are these:

- Create an aggregated Ethernet link between r3 and r5 using VLAN tag 100.
- Ensure the aggregated device is only marked up when there are at least two functional interfaces associated with the bundled interface.

Figure 2.7 shows the aggregated Ethernet topology used in this example.

FIGURE 2.7   Aggregated Ethernet

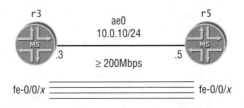

We begin by defining the first aggregated Ethernet device (ae0) on r3:

```
[edit interfaces ae0]
lab@r3# set vlan-tagging
```

```
[edit interfaces ae0]
lab@r3# set unit 100 vlan-id 100
```

```
[edit interfaces ae0]
lab@r3# set unit 100 family inet address 10.0.10.3/24
```

```
[edit interfaces ae0]
lab@r3# set aggregated-ether-options minimum-links 2
```

These commands create the ae0 aggregated Ethernet device and assign it the correct IP address and VLAN ID. By default, an aggregated interface will be marked up if there is at least one physical interface associated with the bundle. Because this example requires a minimum of 200Mbps of bandwidth between r3 and r5, the minimum link value must be set to at least 2.

To enable support for aggregated devices, you must configure the number of aggregated devices that can be supported in the router chassis. By default, this value is 0, which disables the support of aggregated devices. Because this scenario requires only one aggregated Ethernet device, the aggregated device count must be set to at least 1, but could be set higher with no ill effects. You configure aggregated Ethernet support in the router chassis with the following command:

```
[edit chassis]
lab@r3# set aggregated-devices ethernet device-count 1
```

Next, we configure each Fast Ethernet port that is to be a member of the ae0 interface. As shown previously in Figure 2.7, r3 and r5 are connected via four Fast Ethernet ports that belong to a PIC installed in slot 0 of FPC 0. The following commands enable link aggregation and associate all four of the FE ports with the ae0 aggregated device:

```
[edit interfaces]
lab@r3# set fe-0/0/0 fastether-options 802.3ad ae0
```

```
[edit interfaces]
lab@r3# set fe-0/0/1 fastether-options 802.3ad ae0
```

```
[edit interfaces]
lab@r3# set fe-0/0/2 fastether-options 802.3ad ae0
```

```
[edit interfaces]
lab@r3# set fe-0/0/3 fastether-options 802.3ad ae0
```

The resulting configuration for aggregated Ethernet support on r3 is shown next:

```
lab@r3# show interfaces ae0
vlan-tagging;
aggregated-ether-options {
    minimum-links 2;
}
unit 100 {
```

```
        vlan-id 100;
        family inet {
            address 10.0.10.3/24;
        }
    }
}

[edit]
lab@r3# show interfaces fe-0/0/0
fastether-options {
    802.3ad ae0;
}

[edit]
lab@r3# show chassis aggregated-devices
ethernet {
    device-count 1;
}
```

Though not shown, the configuration of the three remaining Fast Ethernet ports is identical to that shown for fe-0/0/0. After committing this configuration in r3, we confirm the status of the ae0 device:

```
lab@r3> show interfaces ae0
Physical interface: ae0, Enabled, Physical link is Up
  Interface index: 20, SNMP ifIndex: 33
  Link-level type: Ethernet, MTU: 1518, Speed: 400mbps, Loopback: Disabled,
  Source filtering: Disabled, Flow control: Disabled, Minimum links needed: 2
  Device flags   : Present Running
  Interface flags: SNMP-Traps
  Current address: 00:90:69:6d:9b:f0, Hardware address: 00:90:69:6d:9b:f0
  Input rate     : 0 bps (0 pps)
  Output rate    : 0 bps (0 pps)

  Logical interface ae0.100 (Index 6) (SNMP ifIndex 34)
    Flags: SNMP-Traps VLAN 100 Encapsulation: Aggregate
    Statistics      Packets         pps         Bytes       bps
    Bundle:
        Input :             0           0             0       0
        Output:             0           0             0       0
    Protocol inet, MTU: 1500, Flags: None
      Addresses, Flags: Is-Preferred Is-Primary
        Destination: 10.0.10/24, Local: 10.0.10.3, Broadcast: 10.0.10.255
```

Based on the highlighted portion of this display, we see that all criteria for the aggregated Ethernet configuration example have been met. After a similar configuration has been added to r5, we can verify that the aggregated interface will actually carry data by conducting ping testing using the addresses associated with the ae0 device.

Aggregated SONET

The configuration and verification of an aggregated SONET link are almost identical to those processes in the previous Ethernet aggregation example. The requirements for this configuration example are:

- Create an aggregated SONET link between r3 and r5.
- Ensure the aggregated device provides at least 280Mbps of bandwidth.

Figure 2.8 shows the aggregated SONET topology used in this example.

FIGURE 2.8   Aggregated SONET

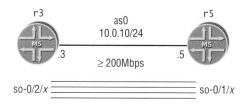

Because the configuration of an aggregated SONET link is so similar to the example already given for aggregated Ethernet, we will cut to the chase by going straight to a working configuration for r3 based on the requirements of the SONET aggregation scenario:

```
[edit]
lab@r3# show chassis aggregated-devices
sonet {
    device-count 1;
}

[edit]
lab@r3# show interfaces as0
aggregated-sonet-options {
    minimum-links 2;
    link-speed oc3;
}
unit 0 {
    family inet {
        address 10.0.10.3/24;
```

```
    }
}


[edit]
lab@r3# show interfaces so-0/2/0
sonet-options {
    aggregate as0;
}
```

Because the speed of a POS interface is not indicated by the interface name, an aggregated SONET device requires explicit configuration of bundle member interface speed. To verify that the requirements of the configuration example have been met, we display the aggregated SONET interface's status using both the terse and standard displays:

```
lab@r3> show interfaces terse
Interface        Admin Link Proto Local            Remote
. . .
so-0/2/0         up    up
so-0/2/0.0       up    up    soagg --> as0.0
so-0/2/1         up    up
so-0/2/1.0       up    up    soagg --> as0.0
so-0/2/2         up    down
so-0/2/2.0       up    down  soagg --> as0.0
so-0/2/3         up    down
so-0/2/3.0       up    down  soagg --> as0.0
as0              up    up
as0.0            up    up    inet  10.0.10.3/24
. . .
```

The terse output indicates that the aggregated SONET link is up, and also shows that two of the four member interfaces are down at the link level. Since only two members are required for the aggregated bundle to be considered active, the down state of SONET ports so-0/2/2 and so-0/2/3 does not cause the as0 device to be marked as down. The standard interface output also confirms the correct operation and configuration for this SONET aggregation configuration task:

```
lab@r3> show interfaces as0
Physical interface: as0, Enabled, Physical link is Up
  Interface index: 21, SNMP ifIndex: 43
  Link-level type: PPP, MTU: 4474, Speed: 311040kbps, Minimum links needed: 2
  Device flags   : Present Running
  Interface flags: SNMP-Traps
  Link flags     : Keepalives
  Keepalive settings: Interval 10 seconds, Up-count 1, Down-count 3
```

```
Input rate      : 0 bps (0 pps)
Output rate     : 0 bps (0 pps)

Logical interface as0.0 (Index 6) (SNMP ifIndex 48)
  Flags: Point-To-Point SNMP-Traps Encapsulation: Aggregate
  Statistics         Packets        pps      Bytes    bps
  Bundle:
     Input :              0           0        0      0
     Output:              0           0        0      0
  Protocol inet, MTU: 4470, Flags: None
    Addresses, Flags: Is-Preferred Is-Primary
      Destination: 10.0.10/24, Local: 10.0.10.3
```

Leaky Bucket Rate Limiting

Most M-series router interfaces support transmit and receive rate limiting using a leaky-bucket algorithm that acts to shape the traffic leaving or arriving on a particular interface. Currently, all interface types support this type of rate limiting, with the exception of ATM, Fast Ethernet, and Gigabit Ethernet interfaces. Internet Processor II (IP II) policers employ a token bucket-policing scheme and can be deployed on any interface type.

Configure Leaky Bucket Rate Limiting

This configuration example will demonstrate leaky-bucket configuration and verification techniques using the topology shown in Figure 2.9.

FIGURE 2.9   Leaky bucket rate limiting

The criteria for this configuration are as follows:

- Limit r3's so-0/2/0 interface to operate at no more than five percent of the OC-3c interface's bandwidth. Do not rate limit r5's so-0/1/0 interface.
- Use default encapsulation.
- Ensure that excess data is not delivered and do not allow bursting.

The following commands correctly configure the transmit bucket on r3's so-0/2/0 interface:

```
[edit interfaces so-0/2/0]
lab@r3# set transmit-bucket rate 5
```

```
[edit interfaces so-0/2/0]
lab@r3# set transmit-bucket threshold 0
```

```
[edit interfaces so-0/2/0]
lab@r3# set transmit-bucket overflow discard
```

This configuration sets the bucket's drain rate to five percent of the ~148Mbps OC-3 payload rate (approximately 7.43Mbps), and sets a burst threshold of 0 to disable bursting above the bucket's specified rate. To ensure that excess data is never delivered, the discard action has been configured for data that overflows the bucket. Because M-series router PICs cannot support SONET payload scrambling in conjunction with leaky bucket traffic shaping, the operator must explicitly disable the default SONET payload scrambling behavior in order to commit the rate-limiting configuration:

```
[edit interfaces so-0/2/0]
lab@r3# set sonet-options no-payload-scrambler
```

Although the configuration scenario states that r5's so-0/1/0 interface is not to be rate-limited, you must disable SONET payload scrambling on this interface to make it compatible with r3's setting. Failure to do this will result in a communications failure, with the primary symptom being a device down flag at the logical-interface level.

After configuring the interface's receive bucket with identical parameters, r3's so-0/2/0 interface configuration is shown with token bucket-related entries highlighted:

```
[edit interfaces so-0/2/0]
lab@r3# show
receive-bucket {
    overflow discard;
    rate 5;
    threshold 0;
}
transmit-bucket {
    overflow discard;
    rate 5;
    threshold 0;
```

```
}
sonet-options {
    no-payload-scrambler;
}
unit 0 {
    family inet {
        address 10.0.10.3/24;
    }
}
```

Verify Leaky Bucket Rate Limiting

You can view leaky bucket–related statistics and configuration settings by using the `extensive` switch with the `show interfaces` command. The following example highlights the leaky bucket–related fields. The extensive output shown next has been edited for brevity:

```
lab@r3> clear interfaces statistics all

lab@r3> show interfaces so-0/2/0 extensive
Physical interface: so-0/2/0, Enabled, Physical link is Up
  . . .
  FCS: 16, Payload scrambler: Disabled
  Device flags    : Present Running
  Interface flags: Point-To-Point SNMP-Traps
  Link flags      : Keepalives
  Hold-times      : Up 0 ms, Down 0 ms
  . . .
  Input errors:
    Errors: 0, Drops: 0, Framing errors: 0, Runts: 0, Giants: 0, Bucket drops: 0,
    Policed discards: 0, L3 incompletes: 0, L2 channel errors: 0, L2 mismatch
timeouts: 0,
    HS link CRC errors: 0, HS link FIFO overflows: 0
  Output errors:
    Carrier transitions: 0, Errors: 0, Drops: 0, Aged packets: 0,
    HS link FIFO underflows: 0
  . . .
  HDLC configuration:
    Policing bucket: Enabled, Bit rate: 5 , Threshold: 0
    Shaping bucket : Enabled, Bit rate: 5 , Threshold: 0
    Giant threshold: 4484, Runt threshold: 3
  . . .
```

The highlighted fields in this display indicate that leaky bucket rate limiting has been correctly configured for this example. To further test the effects of your rate-limiting configuration, you can use r5 to generate flood pings targeted at r3 by issuing a **ping rapid count 20000 size 4000 10.0.10.4** command while the traffic level on r3's so-0/2/0 interface is monitored.

The use of the Routing Engine to generate flood pings is not recommended in a production network because the internal fxp1 link between the RE and PFE is intended for other purposes. The fact that control traffic will take priority over ICMP messages will cause variations in your test results in a production network, especially when routing protocols are converging. Note that the extremely large packet size used in this example was chosen to maximize the amount of traffic produced by the RE. The 4474-byte MTU settings on the SONET interfaces will cause packets of this size to be fragmented by the PFE in both directions.

Figure 2.10 shows the observed traffic load on r3 when the leaky-bucket policer is deactivated, while Figure 2.11 shows the effects of enabling the leaky buckets.

FIGURE 2.10   Deactivated leaky buckets

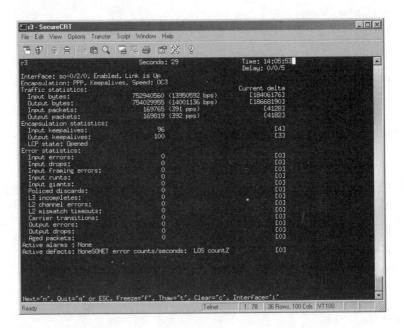

FIGURE 2.11   Leaky buckets activated

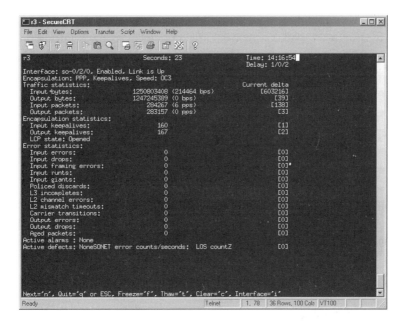

Figure 2.10 shows that, in the absence of leaky-bucket policing, the flood pings coming from r5 produce approximately 14Mbps of input traffic on r3's so-0/2/0 interface. Note that the input and output traffic are balanced, which indicates that r3 is able to respond to the ICMP echo packets received from r5.

Figure 2.11 shows the r3's so-0/2/0 interface's input rate has dropped to approximately 214Kbps once the policers are activated on r3. This is because virtually none of the fragmented ICMP packets are allowed to pass through r3's receive bucket unscathed. This point is evidenced by the low output rate of 48bps, which indicates that the r3's RE is not able to reassemble the IP packet fragments such that no echo response traffic can be sent back to r5.

You may wonder why the input rate at r3 is not closer to the expected value of 7.4Mbps. This behavior is the result of the `monitor interface` command being designed to tabulate only the amount of valid layer 3, or IP, traffic observed. In this case, the 4474-byte MTU of the SONET interfaces means that the discard of a single byte of data will result in the loss of (and failure to count) the remaining 4473 bytes associated with that packet.

Changing the data size to 4000 bytes on r5 allows the echo request packets to pass through r3's receive bucket, causing r3's so-0/2/0 interface to register a receive rate of approximately 5.7Mbps with no observed bucket-induced drops. This value begins to approach the maximum data rate associated with the configured rate limit, which confirms proper rate-limiting to the extent possible, considering the coarse nature of tests conducted with RE-generated traffic streams.

To further confirm that the packet loss is related to the leaky buckets, r3's interface statistics are cleared and the bucket's drop count is displayed both before and after r5 generates exactly 20 flood pings using a 40,000-byte packet size. The results indicate that each attempt to send an ICMP echo packet with a 40,000-byte data field results in six bucket drops on r3:

```
lab@r3> clear interfaces statistics all

lab@r3> show interfaces so-0/2/0 extensive | match Bucket
    Errors: 0, Drops: 0, Framing errors: 0, Runts: 0, Giants: 0, Bucket drops: 0,
    Policing bucket: Enabled, Bit rate: 5 , Threshold: 0
    Shaping bucket : Enabled, Bit rate: 5 , Threshold: 0
```

After r5 generates 20 40,000-byte packets, r3's bucket drops are once again displayed:

```
lab@r3> show interfaces so-0/2/0 extensive | match Bucket
    Errors: 0, Drops: 0, Framing errors: 0, Runts: 0, Giants: 0, Bucket drops: 120,
    Policing bucket: Enabled, Bit rate: 5 , Threshold: 0
    Shaping bucket : Enabled, Bit rate: 5 , Threshold: 0
```

Unnumbered Interfaces

JUNOS software supports the deployment of point-to-point interfaces that are not assigned IP network numbers. For these links to become functional, they must be associated with the router ID for advertisement to adjacent routers using your IGP. The router will use the system's default address as the source address for packets that originate on an unnumbered link, and the routing process will try to use the default address as the source of the router ID for protocols like BGP and OSPF. It is recommended that you assign a non-Martian address to the router's lo0 interface for use as the default address even though the default address can be obtained from any interface with a valid address. In the event that a usable address is not found on the lo0 interface, the router will use the primary address associated with the system's primary interface as the default address. By default, the system's primary interface will be fxp0 unless the primary keyword is specified under another router interface.

For more information on Martian and non-Martian addresses, refer to Chapter 6, "EBGP Configuration and Testing." Additional information on filtering packets due to invalid source or destination address (Martians) can also be found in section 5.3.7 of RFC 1812, "Requirements for IP Version 4 Routers," F. Baker (June 1995).

Figure 2.12 illustrates a typical unnumbered interface application. In this example, packets sent over the unnumbered interface from r3 to r5 will use r3's lo0 address as the packet's source address.

FIGURE 2.12   Unnumbered interfaces

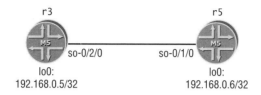

IGP needed for routing across unnumbered link

Configure Unnumbered Interfaces

To configure an unnumbered interface, simply omit the address from the inet protocol family as shown in the following example. Also, make sure that at least one interface, preferably the router's lo0, has an address that does not appear in the router's Martian address table so that the address may be used to source packets sent over the unnumbered link.

```
[edit interfaces]
lab@r3# show so-0/2/0
unit 0 {
    family inet;
}

[edit interfaces]
lab@r3# show lo0
unit 0 {
    family inet {
        address 192.168.0.5/32;
    }
}
```

JUNOS software Default Martian Table

Juniper Networks M-series and T-series routers come from the factory with a default Martian table that causes common Martian addresses to be hidden. The following command is used to display the default Martian entries for the inet.0 routing table:

```
lab@router> show route martians table inet.0


inet.0:
            0.0.0.0/0 exact -- allowed
            0.0.0.0/8 orlonger -- disallowed
            127.0.0.0/8 orlonger -- disallowed
            128.0.0.0/16 orlonger -- disallowed
            191.255.0.0/16 orlonger -- disallowed
            192.0.0.0/24 orlonger -- disallowed
            223.255.255.0/24 orlonger -- disallowed
            240.0.0.0/4 orlonger -- disallowed
```

Verify Unnumbered Interfaces

Unnumbered interfaces are tested and verified in the same way as their numbered counterparts, with the exception that an IGP (or static) route is needed to conduct ping testing due to the source address being "remote" from the perspective of the peer that is directly attached to the unnumbered link. Also, because the link itself is unnumbered, you will have to ping an address associated with the remote router to generate traffic across the unnumbered link.

Because traceroute will no longer indicate that packets have visited the unnumbered link, you may ask whether a particular unnumbered link is being used for data transport, especially if multiple unnumbered links have been provisioned between a pair of routers. To verify which unnumbered link is being used for a particular destination address, you can inspect the router's forwarding table, or you can force traffic over the unnumbered link of choice using the bypass-routing option on the ping command line to allow the specification of the egress interface for the ICMP packet.

Real World Scenario

Minimize Mistakes by Renaming

JNCIP candidates often make "silly" mistakes when dealing with the time pressures and stress of a lab-based examination. The fact that JUNOS software will allow you to configure nonexistent interfaces, with no warnings or alarms, means that it is possible to spend a lot of time on an interface configuration, only to later find that the configuration has had no effect because it was applied to the wrong interface. Rather than deleting the bogus configuration and re-creating it under the correct interface, you should consider using the JUNOS software CLI rename feature, which will often save you valuable lab time. Using rename is also an excellent way to correct IP addressing mistakes, because it allows you to correct an address without first having to delete the incorrect address assignment.

The use of rename is demonstrated here, where we determine that the operator has incorrectly configured r4's Frame Relay interface as so-0/2/0.

```
[edit interfaces]
lab@r4# show so-0/2/0
dce;
hold-time up 20 down 20;
encapsulation frame-relay;
lmi {
    n392dce 2;
    n393dce 3;
    lmi-type itu;
}
sonet-options {
    fcs 32;
    path-trace "JNCIP test bed";
}
unit 0 {
    dlci 100;
    family inet {
        mtu 1600;
        address 192.168.0.4/32 {
            destination 172.16.0.3;
        }
    }
}
```

Recognizing the mistake, the operator now saves the day with a quick rename command:

```
[edit interfaces]
lab@r4# rename so-0/2/0 to so-0/1/0
```

The results of the renaming operation are now confirmed:

```
lab@r4# show so-0/1/0
dce;
hold-time up 20 down 20;
encapsulation frame-relay;
lmi {
    n392dce 2;
    n393dce 3;
    lmi-type itu;
}
sonet-options {
    fcs 32;
    path-trace "JNCIP test bed";
}
unit 0 {
    dlci 100;
    family inet {
        mtu 1600;
        address 192.168.0.4/32 {
            destination 172.16.0.3;
        }
    }
}
```

Summary

JNCIP candidates will be expected to configure a variety of interface types during their lab exam. Successful candidates will be fluent with virtually all of the options that exist for any given interface type, and will possess the skills needed to quickly verify the proper operation of their interfaces.

   This chapter provided configuration scenarios and verification techniques for SONET, ATM, and Ethernet interface types and also covered common point-to-point and multipoint configuration requirements, including the specific issues that surround the various keepalive protocols and how they are impacted by back-to-back connections. This chapter also provided examples of VLAN tagging, VRRP, and interface aggregation.

Case Study: Interface Configuration

The following case study is designed to simulate a typical JNCIP interface configuration scenario. You will need to refer to the information contained in the lab topology shown in Figure 2.13 and the criteria specified in Table 2.3 for the information needed to complete this case study. It is assumed that you will be applying your interface configuration to the initial system configuration that was performed in Chapter 1, "Initial Configuration and Platform Troubleshooting."

FIGURE 2.13 Interface case study topology

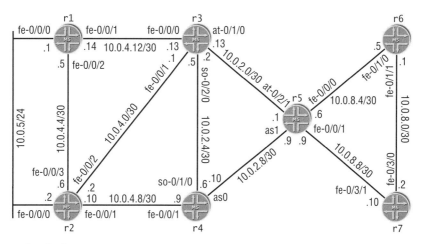

Loopbacks

r1 = 10.0.6.1
r2 = 10.0.6.2
r3 = 10.0.3.3
r4 = 10.0.3.4
r5 = 10.0.3.5
r6 = 10.0.9.6
r7 = 10.0.9.7

TABLE 2.3   Interface Configuration Criteria

Router	Interface	L2	Logical Unit	Comment
r1	fe-0/0/0	150	—	VRRP group 1, VIP 10.0.5.200, master when link to r3 is up, authenticate with plain-text password jnx
	fe-0/0/1	200	200	VLAN tagging
	fe-0/0/2	—	—	Only accept frames sent from r2's fe-0/0/3 MAC address
	lo0	—	—	—
r2	fe-0/0/0	—	—	VRRP backup for r1
	fe-0/0/1	—	—	Half-duplex
	fe-0/0/2	—	—	—
	fe-0/0/3	—	—	Only accept frames sent from r1's fe-0/0/2 MAC address
	lo0	—	—	—
r3	fe-0/0/0	—		
	fe-0/0/1	—	—	—
	so-0/2/0	100	—	Frame Relay, ITU LMI, 15-second polls, 30-millisecond hold-time, threshold/events ratio of 2:3 for line up or down
	at-0/1/0	VP 5 VC 35	—	10-second keepalives, link up/down criteria = 2, ILMI-enabled, 50Mbps shaping with no bursts
	lo0	—	—	—
r4	fe-0/0/1	—	—	Disable flow control
	so-0/1/0	—	—	—
	as0	—	—	SDH framing, path trace set to r4-jnx. Members so-0/1/1 and so-0/1/2

TABLE 2.3   Interface Configuration Criteria *(continued)*

Router	Interface	L2	Logical Unit	Comment
	lo0	—	—	—
r5	fe-0/0/0	—	—	—
	fe-0/0/1	—	—	—
	at-0/2/1	—	—	10-second keepalives, two out of three for link up/down, ILMI-enabled, shaping to 50Mbps with no bursts
	as1	—	—	Path trace set to r5-jnx, members so-0/1/0 and so-0/1/1
	lo0	—	—	—
r6	fe-0/1/0	—	—	—
	fe-0/1/1			Device MTU = 4000
	lo0	—	—	—
r7	fe-0/3/0	—	—	—
	fe-0/3/1	—	—	—
	lo0	—	—	—

Entries with "—" are either non-applicable or left to the operator's discretion. The setting of these parameters may be contingent on the values specified for adjacent router interfaces, so read all details carefully!

It would seem that you have your work cut out for you, considering that you have seven routers to configure and that each of them can have up to five interfaces with varying requirements. It is expected that a JNCIP candidate will be able to complete this case study in approximately one hour with no mistakes. Sample interface configurations from all seven routers will be provided at the end of the case study for comparison to your own configurations. Some tasks may have multiple solutions, so differences between the provided examples and your own configuration do not automatically indicate that a mistake has been made. In the end, you will be graded on the overall functionality of your configuration and its compliance with any stipulations provided in your configuration task.

Case Study Configurations

The interface-related portions of each router configuration are displayed in Listings 2.2 through 2.8. While these configurations are known to meet the requirements of the case study, other solutions are also possible. Where appropriate, the correct operation of key interface configuration criteria is demonstrated with the appropriate operational mode commands.

Listing 2.2: *r1* **Interface Configuration**

```
[edit]
lab@r1# show interfaces
fe-0/0/0 {
    vlan-tagging;
    unit 0 {
        vlan-id 150;
        family inet {
            address 10.0.5.1/24 {
                vrrp-group 1 {
                    virtual-address 10.0.5.200;
                    authentication-type simple;
                    authentication-key "$9$dVw2a5T3nCu"; # SECRET-DATA
                    track {
                        interface fe-0/0/1.200 priority-cost 30;
                    }
                }
            }
        }
    }
}
fe-0/0/1 {
    vlan-tagging;
    unit 200 {
        vlan-id 200;
        family inet {
            address 10.0.4.14/30;
        }
    }
}
fe-0/0/2 {
    fastether-options {
        source-filtering;
```

```
        source-address-filter {
            00:a0:c9:6f:70:0d;
        }
    }
    unit 0 {
        family inet {
            address 10.0.4.5/30;
        }
    }
}

fxp0 {
    unit 0 {
        family inet {
            address 10.0.1.1/24;
        }
    }
}
lo0 {
    unit 0 {
        family inet {
            address 10.0.6.1/32;
        }
    }
}
```

The following command verifies that the correct interface is being tracked as part of r1's VRRP configuration. Forgetting to specify a logical unit, and therefore getting the default value of 0, is a common mistake.

```
lab@r1> show vrrp track
Track if      State Cost  Interface Group  Cfg  Run VR State
fe-0/0/1.200  up    30    fe-0/0/0.0  1    100  100 master
```

Listing 2.3: *r2* Interface Configuration
```
[edit]
lab@r2# show interfaces
fe-0/0/0 {
    vlan-tagging;
```

```
    unit 0 {
        vlan-id 150;
        family inet {
            address 10.0.5.2/24 {
                vrrp-group 1 {
                    virtual-address 10.0.5.200;
                    priority 80;
                    authentication-type simple;
                    authentication-key "$9$ZdDHmtpB1hr"; # SECRET-DATA
                }
            }
        }
    }
}
fe-0/0/1 {
    speed 100m;
    link-mode half-duplex;
    fastether-options {
        no-flow-control;
    }
    unit 0 {
        family inet {
            address 10.0.4.10/30;
        }
    }
}
fe-0/0/2 {
    unit 0 {
        family inet {
            address 10.0.4.2/30;
        }
    }
}
fe-0/0/3 {
    fastether-options {
        source-filtering;
        source-address-filter {
            00:a0:c9:6f:7b:84;
        }
    }
```

```
        unit 0 {
            family inet {
                address 10.0.4.6/30;
            }
        }
    }
    fxp0 {
        unit 0 {
            family inet {
                address 10.0.1.2/24;
            }
        }
    }
    lo0 {
        unit 0 {
            family inet {
                address 10.0.6.2/32;
            }
        }
    }
}
```

The following commands verify VRRP and the overall interface state at r2. The confirmation that r2 is acting as VRRP backup indicates that VRRP has been correctly configured and that authentication is working between r1 and r2 (if r1 and r2 were not communicating, they would both claim mastership of VRRP group 1).

```
lab@r2> show vrrp summary
Interface   Unit  Group  Type  Address     Int state VR state
Fe-0/0/0    0     1      lcl   10.0.5.2    up        backup
                         vip   10.0.5.200


lab@r2> show interfaces terse
Interface        Admin Link Proto Local            Remote
fxp0             up    up
fxp0.0           up    up    inet  10.0.1.2/24
fe-0/0/0         up    up
fe-0/0/0.0       up    up    inet  10.0.5.2/24
fe-0/0/1         up    up
fe-0/0/1.0       up    up    inet  10.0.4.10/30
fe-0/0/2         up    up
fe-0/0/2.0       up    up    inet  10.0.4.2/30
fe-0/0/3         up    up
```

```
fe-0/0/3.0        up    up    inet   10.0.4.6/30
gre               up    up
ipip              up    up
lo0               up    up
lo0.0             up    up    inet   10.0.6.2          --> 0/0
lsi               up    up
pimd              up    up
pime              up    up
tap               up    up
```

Listing 2.4 details the interface configuration of r3, which must function as the Frame Relay DTE in order to meet the requirement that it generate a poll every 15 seconds. r3's DTE appearance requires that r4 be set to function as the DCE to accommodate the LMI keepalive protocol aspects of this case study. r3 also requires SDH framing on its so-0/2/0 interface to be compatible with r4, which in turn must run SDH framing on all of the ports associated with SONET PIC 0/1 to meet the requirements specified for its connection to r5.

Listing 2.4: *r3* Interface Configuration

```
[edit]
lab@r3# show chassis
fpc 0 {
    pic 2 {
        framing sdh;
    }
}
alarm {
    management-ethernet {
        link-down ignore;
    }
}

lab@r3# show interfaces
fe-0/0/0 {
    vlan-tagging;
    unit 0 {
        vlan-id 200;
        family inet {
            address 10.0.4.13/30;
        }
    }
}
```

```
fe-0/0/1 {
    unit 0 {
        family inet {
            address 10.0.4.1/30;
        }
    }
}

at-0/1/0 {
    atm-options {
        vpi 0 maximum-vcs 17;
        vpi 5 maximum-vcs 36;
        ilmi;
    }
    unit 35 {
        vci 5.35;
        shaping {
            cbr 50m;
        }
        oam-period 10;
        oam-liveness {
            up-count 2;
            down-count 2;
        }
        family inet {
            address 10.0.2.2/30;
        }
    }
}
so-0/2/0 {
    hold-time up 30 down 30;
    encapsulation frame-relay;
    lmi {
        n392dte 2;
        n393dte 3;
        t391dte 15;
        lmi-type itu;
    }
    unit 100 {
        dlci 100;
```

```
                family inet {
                    address 10.0.2.5/30;
                }
            }
        }
        fxp0 {
            unit 0 {
                family inet {
                    address 10.0.1.3/24;
                }
            }
        }
        lo0 {
            unit 0 {
                family inet {
                    address 10.0.3.3/32;
                }
            }
        }
```

The following command verifies r3's Frame Relay interface configuration:

```
[edit]
lab@r3# run show interfaces so-0/2/0
Physical interface: so-0/2/0, Enabled, Physical link is Up
  Interface index: 16, SNMP ifIndex: 19
  Link-level type: Frame-Relay, MTU: 4474, Clocking: Internal, SDH mode, Speed:
OC3, Loopback: None,
  FCS: 16, Payload scrambler: Enabled
  Device flags   : Present Running
  Interface flags: Point-To-Point SNMP-Traps
  Link flags     : Keepalives DTE
  ITU LMI settings: n391dte 6, n392dte 2, n393dte 3, t391dte 15 seconds
  LMI: Input: 248 (00:00:11 ago), Output: 249 (00:00:11 ago)
  Input rate     : 0 bps (0 pps)
  Output rate    : 0 bps (0 pps)
  SONET alarms   : None
  SONET defects  : None

  Logical interface so-0/2/0.100 (Index 9) (SNMP ifIndex 42)
    Flags: Point-To-Point SNMP-Traps Encapsulation: FR-NLPID
  Input packets : 296717
```

```
Output packets: 297430
  Protocol inet, MTU: 4470, Flags: None
    Addresses, Flags: Is-Preferred Is-Primary
      Destination: 10.0.2.4/30, Local: 10.0.2.5
  DLCI 100
    Flags: Active
    Total down time: 0 sec, Last down: Never
Traffic statistics:
    Input  packets:              296717
```

One key aspect of r4's configuration is the need for a t392 timer setting that is greater than the 15-second default. This increase is needed to make r4 compatible with the increased setting of r3's t391 poll timer. The path trace requirements for r4's aggregated SONET link to r5 must be specified at the physical SONET device portion of the configuration hierarchy because the as0 device does not support the specification of sonet-options. As shown next in Listing 2.5, r4's configuration also includes support for SDH framing and the aggregated SONET device setting necessary to support its aso interface.

Listing 2.5: *r4* Interface Configuration
```
[edit]
lab@r4# show chassis
aggregated-devices {
    sonet {
        device-count 1;
    }
}
fpc 0 {
    pic 1 {
        framing sdh;
    }
}

[edit]
lab@r4# show interfaces
fe-0/0/1 {
    speed 100m;
    link-mode half-duplex;
    fastether-options {
        no-flow-control;
    }
    unit 0 {
        family inet {
```

```
                address 10.0.4.9/30;
            }
        }
    }
    so-0/1/0 {
        dce;
        hold-time up 30 down 30;
        encapsulation frame-relay;
        lmi {
            n392dce 2;
            n393dce 3;
            t392dce 25;
            lmi-type itu;
        }
        unit 100 {
            dlci 100;
            family inet {
                address 10.0.2.6/30;
            }
        }
    }
    so-0/1/1 {
        sonet-options {
            path-trace r4-jnx;
            aggregate as0;
        }
    }
    so-0/1/2 {
        sonet-options {
            path-trace r4-jnx;
            aggregate as0;
        }
    }
    as0 {
        aggregated-sonet-options {
            minimum-links 2;
            link-speed oc3;
        }
        unit 0 {
            family inet {
```

```
                address 10.0.2.10/30;
            }
        }
    }
    fxp0 {
        unit 0 {
            family inet {
                address 10.0.1.4/24;
            }
        }
    }
    lo0 {
        unit 0 {
            family inet {
                address 10.0.3.4/32;
            }
        }
    }
}
```

A Common Mistake

Leaving r4's t392 at its default setting of 15 seconds is a common mistake, and one that is not readily apparent to the majority of technicians. Having the same setting for the t391 and t392 timers will result in a line that suffers from periodic service outages, which are likely to go unnoticed during your other lab activities. The following syslog entries illustrate typical line bounce frequency for the case where r4 mistakenly uses the default 15-second t392 setting for this case study:

```
Apr 20 17:01:36 r4 mib2d[578]: SNMP_TRAP_LINK_DOWN: ifIndex 25, ifAdminStatus
up(1), ifOperStatus down(2), ifName so-0/1/0
Apr 20 17:03:33 r4 last message repeated 2 times
Apr 20 17:12:27 r4 last message repeated 3 times
Apr 20 17:22:02 r4 last message repeated 3 times
```

The configuration of r5 (Listing 2.6) is similar to that of r4 and r3. The tricky part here is the need to set the aggregated device number to a value greater than 1 because of the requirement that it support an as1 device. SDH framing is also needed on r5's SONET PIC to be compatible with the SDH framing in use on r4's aggregated so-0/1/1 and so-0/1/2 interfaces. r4 is using SDH framing on these interfaces as a side effect of having to run SDH framing on its so-0/1/0 interface that connects it to r3.

Listing 2.6: *r5* **Interface Configuration**

```
[edit]
lab@r5# show chassis
aggregated-devices {
    sonet {
        device-count 2;
    }
}
fpc 0 {
    pic 1 {
        framing sdh;
    }
}

[edit]
lab@r5# show interfaces
fe-0/0/0 {
    unit 0 {
        family inet {
            address 10.0.8.6/30;
        }
    }
}
fe-0/0/1 {
    unit 0 {
        family inet {
            address 10.0.8.9/30;
        }
    }
}
so-0/1/0 {
    sonet-options {
        path-trace r5-jnx;
        aggregate as1;
    }
}
so-0/1/1 {
    sonet-options {
        path-trace r5-jnx;
        aggregate as1;
```

```
        }
    }
    at-0/2/1 {
        atm-options {
            vpi 0 maximum-vcs 17;
            vpi 5 maximum-vcs 36;
            ilmi;
        }
        unit 35 {
            vci 5.35;
            shaping {
                cbr 50m;
            }
            oam-period 10;
            oam-liveness {
                up-count 2;
                down-count 2;
            }
            family inet {
                address 10.0.2.1/30;
            }
        }
    }
    as1 {
        aggregated-sonet-options {
            minimum-links 2;
            link-speed oc3;
        }
        unit 0 {
            family inet {
                address 10.0.2.9/30;
            }
        }
    }
    fxp0 {
        unit 0 {
            family inet {
                address 10.0.1.5/24;
            }
        }
```

```
}
lo0 {
    unit 0 {
        family inet {
            address 10.0.3.5/32;
        }
    }
}
```

The following commands help to verify the operation of r5's ATM and aggregated interfaces. The support of ILMI requires the declaration of VP 0 because ILMI uses VPI/VCI 0/16.

```
lab@r5> show interfaces as1
Physical interface: as1, Enabled, Physical link is Up
  Interface index: 21, SNMP ifIndex: 31
  Link-level type: PPP, MTU: 4474, Speed: 311040kbps, Minimum links needed: 2
  Device flags   : Present Running
  Interface flags: SNMP-Traps
  Link flags     : Keepalives
  Keepalive settings: Interval 10 seconds, Up-count 1, Down-count 3
  Input rate     : 48 bps (0 pps)
  Output rate    : 48 bps (0 pps)

  Logical interface as1.0 (Index 12) (SNMP ifIndex 33)
    Flags: Point-To-Point SNMP-Traps Encapsulation: Aggregate
    Statistics        Packets        pps        Bytes        bps
    Bundle:
        Input :          424          0         6195          0
        Output:           12          0         1056          0
    Protocol inet, MTU: 4470, Flags: None
      Addresses, Flags: Is-Preferred Is-Primary
        Destination: 10.0.2.8/30, Local: 10.0.2.9
```

The previous display indicates that the aggregated SONET interface is operational. Now to check on path trace requirements, as shown next:

```
lab@r5> show interfaces so-0/1/1 extensive | match trace
  Received path trace: r4-jnx
  Transmitted path trace: r5-jnx
```

The path trace settings also appear to be correct. An interesting side effect of configuring r5 with the ability to support two aggregated SONET devices is the automatic creation of an as0 interface. Because this interface is not being used, it is expected to be down, as shown in the following:

```
lab@r5# run show interfaces terse | match as
so-0/1/0.0      up     up     soagg --> as1.0
so-0/1/1.0      up     up     soagg --> as1.0
as0             up     down
as1             up     up
as1.0           up     up     inet   10.0.2.9/30
```

Next we verify the correct operation of r5's ATM interface:

```
lab@r5> show interfaces at-0/2/1
Physical interface: at-0/2/1, Enabled, Physical link is Up
  Interface index: 19, SNMP ifIndex: 27
  Link-level type: ATM-PVC, MTU: 4482, Clocking: Internal, SONET mode, Speed:
OC3, Loopback: None,
  Payload scrambler: Enabled
  Device flags   : Present Running
  Link flags     : None
  Input rate     : 0 bps (0 pps)
  Output rate    : 0 bps (0 pps)
  SONET alarms   : None
  SONET defects  : None

  Logical interface at-0/2/1.35 (Index 8) (SNMP ifIndex 21)
    Flags: Point-To-Point SNMP-Traps Encapsulation: ATM-SNAP
  Input packets : 1143
  Output packets: 1143
    Protocol inet, MTU: 4470, Flags: None
      Addresses, Flags: Is-Preferred Is-Primary
        Destination: 10.0.2.0/30, Local: 10.0.2.1
    VCI 5.35
      Flags: Active, OAM, Shaping
      CBR, Peak: 50mbps
      OAM, Period 10 sec, Up count: 2, Down count: 2
      Total down time: 0 sec, Last down: Never
```

```
   OAM F5 cell statistics:
    Total received: 1142, Total sent: 1142
    Loopback received: 1142, Loopback sent: 1142
    RDI received: 0, RDI sent: 0
    AIS received: 0
 Traffic statistics:
     Input  packets:                1143
     Output packets:                1143


 Logical interface at-0/2/1.32767 (Index 9) (SNMP ifIndex 20)
   Flags: Point-To-Point SNMP-Traps Encapsulation: ATM-VCMUX
 Input packets : 2
 Output packets: 2
    VCI 0.16
     Flags: Active, ILMI
     Total down time: 0 sec, Last down: Never
 Traffic statistics:
     Input  packets:                2
     Output packets:                2
```

The ATM interface status display indicates that all requirements have been met, and that the interface is operating normally.

There is little to note in the interface configurations for r6 and r7 (Listings 2.7 and 2.8), except the need for Jumbo frame support on the r6-r7 Fast Ethernet link. Though it is only specified for r6, r7 must also have a compatible device MTU set for proper operation with r6.

Listing 2.7: *r6* Interface Configuration

```
[edit]
lab@r6# show interfaces
fe-0/1/0 {
    unit 0 {
        family inet {
            address 10.0.8.5/30;
        }
    }
}
fe-0/1/1 {
    mtu 4000;
    unit 0 {
        family inet {
            address 10.0.8.1/30;
```

```
            }
        }
    }
    fxp0 {
        unit 0 {
            family inet {
                address 10.0.1.6/24;
            }
        }
    }
    lo0 {
        unit 0 {
            family inet {
                address 10.0.9.6/32;
            }
        }
    }
}
```

Proper MTU setting is confirmed by displaying the interface's operational status at r6:

```
lab@r6# run show interfaces fe-0/1/1
Physical interface: fe-0/1/1, Enabled, Physical link is Up
  Interface index: 11, SNMP ifIndex: 13
  Link-level type: Ethernet, MTU: 4000, Speed: 100mbps, Loopback: Disabled,
  Source filtering: Disabled, Flow control: Enabled
  Device flags   : Present Running
  Interface flags: SNMP-Traps
  Current address: 00:90:69:6d:98:00, Hardware address: 00:90:69:6d:98:00
  Input rate     : 0 bps (0 pps)
  Output rate    : 0 bps (0 pps)
  Active alarms  : None
  Active defects : None

  Logical interface fe-0/1/1.0 (Index 14) (SNMP ifIndex 29)
    Flags: SNMP-Traps Encapsulation: ENET2
  Input packets : 0
  Output packets: 1
    Protocol inet, MTU: 3982, Flags: None
      Addresses, Flags: Is-Preferred Is-Primary
Destination: 10.0.8.0/30, Local: 10.0.8.1, Broadcast: 10.0.8.3
```

Listing 2.8: *r7* **Interface Configuration**

```
[edit]
lab@r7# show interfaces

fe-0/3/0 {
    mtu 4000;
    unit 0 {
        family inet {
            address 10.0.8.2/30;
        }
    }
}
fe-0/3/1 {
    unit 0 {
        family inet {
            address 10.0.8.10/30;
        }
    }
}
fxp0 {
    unit 0 {
        family inet {
            address 10.0.1.7/24;
        }
    }
}
lo0 {
    unit 0 {
        family inet {
            address 10.0.9.7/32;
        }
    }
}
```

Spot The Issues: Review Questions

1. Why is a commit error returned for the following interface configuration?

    ```
    [edit interfaces so-0/2/0]
    lab@r3# show
    no-keepalives;
    encapsulation frame-relay;
    transmit-bucket {
        overflow discard;
        rate 10;
        threshold 100;
    }
    unit 0 {
        multipoint;
        family inet {
            address 10.1.0.3/24 {
                multipoint-destination 10.1.0.4 dlci 400;
            }
        }
    }
    ```

2. What is needed in the following configuration to ensure that the aggregated interface can always provide at least 270Mbps of bandwidth (assuming you are bundling OC-3c links)?

    ```
    [edit interfaces as0]
    lab@r4# show
    aggregated-sonet-options {
        link-speed oc3;
    }
    unit 0 {
        family inet {
            address 10.0.2.10/30;
        }
    }
    ```

3. What commands are needed to enable ILMI on an ATM interface?

4. You have two routers on a point-to-point link with /32 address assignments that cause the routers to be on different logical IP subnets. What configuration option is needed for proper routing across this link?

5. How is remote IP address–to–local VC identifier mapping performed on a Juniper Networks router?

6. What change is required to make the following VRRP configuration valid?

```
[edit]
lab@r1# show interfaces fe-0/3/0
vlan-tagging;
unit 0 {
    vlan-id 150;
    family inet {
        address 10.0.5.1/24 {
            vrrp-group 1 {
                virtual-address 10.0.5.200;
                authentication-type simple;
                authentication-key "$9$dVw2a5T3nCu"; # SECRET-DATA
                track {
                    interface so-0/0/0.0 priority-cost 30;
                }
            }
        }
    }
}


lab@r3# show interfaces so-0/0/0
hold-time up 30 down 30;
encapsulation frame-relay;
lmi {
    n392dte 2;
    n393dte 3;
    t391dte 15;
    lmi-type itu;
}
unit 100 {
    dlci 100;
    family inet {
        address 10.0.2.5/30;
    }
}
```

Spot The Issues: Answers

1. Payload scrambling cannot work in conjunction with leaky bucket rate limiting. Because payload scrambling is enabled by default, this configuration requires the setting of `no-payload-scrambler` under `sonet-options`.

2. You need to include a minimum links setting of at least 2. By default, an aggregated interface requires only one bundle member to be declared operational.

3. You must enable ILMI under `atm-options`, and you must configure support for the associated VP/VCI by defining VP 0 as supporting at least 17 VCIs.

4. The `destination` keyword is required to explicitly define the neighbor address that is reachable over the p-t-p link.

5. The lack of complete support for inverse ARP requires that the operator perform static mappings using the `multipoint-destination` keyword. The router can be configured to respond to inverse ARP request to eliminate the need for similar static mappings on the remote device, assuming it has full inverse ARP support.

6. The problem lies in the tracked interface's logical unit value of 0, which is nonexistent on the interface that is being tracked. For proper operation, you must track interface so-0/0/0.100.

Chapter

3

OSPF Configuration and Testing

JNCIP LAB SKILLS COVERED IN THIS CHAPTER:

- ✓ Multi-area configuration
- ✓ Network types
  - Broadcast, Point-to-Point, Multipoint, and NBMA
- ✓ Authentication
- ✓ Stub and not-so-stubby areas
- ✓ Address summarization and filtering between areas
- ✓ Virtual links
- ✓ Policy
  - Route redistribution
  - Route tagging
  - RIP configuration
- ✓ Metrics, timers, and various other "knobs"

This chapter details various JNCIP-level OSPF configuration scenarios, and provides examples of the verification methods that can be used to confirm the proper operation of the OSPF protocol. I'm assuming that your configurations are currently based on the case study criteria presented at the end of Chapters 1 and 2. You will now be adding the OSPF protocol to your test bed. If you are unsure as to the state of your routers, you should compare your configuration against those provided at the end of Chapters 1 and 2, and verify that all of your router interfaces are operational before proceeding.

Proper Interior Gate Protocol (IGP) operation is a critical factor in the JNCIP exam. Many of the product features and capabilities you will be expected to configure throughout the exam rely on your IGP for routing within your Autonomous System (AS). Internal Border Gateway Protocol (IBGP) peering is a common example of how a protocol or service can depend on the correct operation of your IGP. Because the IGP provides the information needed to route between loopback addresses, IBGP peering between loopback interfaces can only succeed when your IGP is operational.

Because IGP problems can produce operational problems in wide-ranging and numerous aspects of your configuration, the rapid and effective isolation of IGP problems is a critical lab skill that a successful JNCIP candidate must master. For example, you can differentiate between IGP and IBGP problems by conducting ping tests between the loopback addresses of the routers in question. By taking care to source the pings from each router's loopback address, you can confirm that the IGP is, or is not, providing the routing services needed to establish your loopback-based IBGP peering sessions. Assuming that these tests fail, the realization that you are dealing with an IGP connectivity problem will ensure that you will not waste valuable time chasing down nonexistent IBGP problems.

Multi-Area Configuration

The OSPF protocol supports the partitioning of a routing domain into multiple areas. The use of multiple areas will generally improve protocol scalability, as most link-state advertisement (LSA) types are not flooded across area boundaries. This means that a given router must only maintain a complete link-state database (LSDB) for the areas to which it actually connects. Distance vector–based routing is used between areas based on metrics that are carried in summary LSAs, which are generated by Area Border Routers (ABRs).

We begin our OSPF configuration example with the network topology shown in Figure 3.1.

FIGURE 3.1 Multi-area OSPF

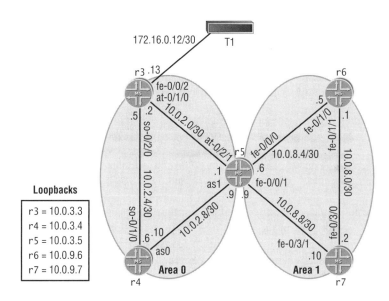

Referring to Figure 3.1, you can see that r5 will need to function as an ABR between the backbone (area 0) and transit area 1. To complete this configuration example, your OSPF configuration must meet the following criteria:

- Router ID (RID) based on lo0 address.
- lo0 address must be reachable via OSPF.
- Loopback addresses from backbone routers appear as summaries in area 1.
- The link between r3 and T1 must appear in area 0 as an intra-area route. Ensure that no adjacencies can be established on this interface.

r4 OSPF Configuration

We begin by configuring r4 as an internal backbone router with the following commands:

```
[edit protocols ospf]
lab@r4# set area 0 interface lo0 passive
```

```
[edit protocols ospf]
lab@r4# set area 0 interface as0
```

```
[edit protocols ospf]
lab@r4# set area 0 interface so-0/1/0.100
```

These commands enable the main OSPF protocol instance, and place r4's lo0, its aggregated SONET interface as0, and its so-0/1/0.100 interfaces into area 0. By default JUNOS software will obtain the OSPF router ID from the first interface that is detected with a non-Martian address. Because lo0 is always the first interface examined when rpd starts, explicit configuration of the RID under `routing-options` is rarely necessary. Simply assigning the desired IP address to the lo0 interface results in a stable and deterministic router ID.

JUNOS software automatically advertises a stub route to the interface from which the RID is obtained; therefore it is not actually necessary to explicitly configure lo0 as an OSPF interface to meet the lo0 connectivity requirements of this configuration example.

 Manually configuring the RID under `routing-options` will affect connectivity to the lo0 address, as the router will no longer include a stub route for its lo0 interface. You will have to enable OSPF on the lo0 interface, as done in the previous example, if lo0 connectivity is required and you have assigned the RID manually.

Omitting the lo0 interface from your OSPF configuration results in the lo0 address being advertised as a stub network in the router LSAs (type 1 LSAs) that are generated and flooded into all areas to which a given router attaches. Because your backbone routers must advertise their loopback addresses as a network summary route (LSA type 3) into the non-backbone areas, explicit association of the lo0 interface with the backbone area is required to meet the criteria of this example.

Because adjacencies cannot be formed on the router's lo0 interface, it has been configured to run as a passive interface in area 0. This prevents the unnecessary generation of hello packets and the general waste of compute cycles that would otherwise occur if lo0 were set as an active OSPF interface.

The resulting configuration for r4 is shown next:

```
[edit protocols ospf]
lab@r4# show
area 0.0.0.0 {
    interface lo0.0 {
        passive;
    }
    interface as0.0;
    interface so-0/1/0.100;
}
```

It is worth noting that the correct logical interface has been specified for r4's so-0/1/0 interface. Omitting the logical unit number when specifying the interface name results in OSPF running on unit 0, which is the default logical unit number.

Verify OSPF on *r4*

After committing the initial OSPF configuration, we can display r4's OSPF interfaces to confirm proper backbone configuration. In the absence of other OSPF routers, we expect to find that r4 has no neighbors, and therefore, no adjacencies:

```
[edit protocols ospf]
lab@r4# run show ospf interface
Interface         State    Area       DR ID      BDR ID     Nbrs
as0.0             PtToPt   0.0.0.0    0.0.0.0    0.0.0.0       0
lo0.0             DRother  0.0.0.0    0.0.0.0    0.0.0.0       0
so-0/1/0.100      PtToPt   0.0.0.0    0.0.0.0    0.0.0.0       0
```

As predicted, r4 has no neighbors, but the display does indicate that the correct interfaces have been placed into area 0. To confirm that r4's lo0 address is reachable as an area 0 internal route, we display the contents of r4's router LSA:

```
[edit protocols ospf]
lab@r4# run show ospf database detail

    OSPF link state database, area 0.0.0.0
Type      ID              Adv Rtr          Seq       Age  Opt  Cksum  Len
Router  *10.0.3.4         10.0.3.4         0x80000001  163  0x2  0x1bc4  60
  bits 0x0, link count 3
  id 10.0.2.8, data 255.255.255.252, type Stub (3)
  TOS count 0, TOS 0 metric 1
  id 10.0.3.4, data 255.255.255.255, type Stub (3)
  TOS count 0, TOS 0 metric 0
  id 10.0.2.4, data 255.255.255.252, type Stub (3)
  TOS count 0, TOS 0 metric 1
```

As required, r4 is reporting its lo0 address as a stub link in its area 0 router LSA. We can also confirm that r4 has correctly obtained its RID from its lo0 address. You may need to restart routing to establish the correct RID, especially if the OSPF process was started before a non-Martian address was assigned to lo0.

r5 OSPF Configuration

The following commands define the correct interface and area associations needed by r5, which will function as an ABR:

```
[edit protocols ospf]
lab@r5# set area 0 interface lo0 passive
```

```
[edit protocols ospf]
lab@r5# set area 0 interface at-0/2/1.35
```

```
[edit protocols ospf]
lab@r5# set area 0 interface as1
```

With all the area 0 interfaces specified, we now move on to area 1:

```
[edit protocols ospf]
lab@r5# set area 1 interface fe-0/0/0
```

```
[edit protocols ospf]
lab@r5# set area 1 interface fe-0/0/1
```

The resulting multi-area configuration for r5 is shown next:

```
[edit protocols ospf]
lab@r5# show
area 0.0.0.0 {
    interface lo0.0 {
        passive;
    }
    interface at-0/2/1.35;
    interface as1.0;
}
area 0.0.0.1 {
    interface fe-0/0/0.0;
    interface fe-0/0/1.0;
}
```

Verify OSPF on *r5*

After committing r5's OSPF configuration, we expect to see an adjacency to r4, and the correct interface-to-area associations as indicated next:

```
[edit protocols ospf]
lab@r5# run show ospf interface
```

Interface	State	Area	DR ID	BDR ID	Nbrs
as1.0	PtToPt	0.0.0.0	0.0.0.0	0.0.0.0	1
at-0/2/1.35	PtToPt	0.0.0.0	0.0.0.0	0.0.0.0	0
lo0.0	DRother	0.0.0.0	0.0.0.0	0.0.0.0	0
fe-0/0/0.0	DR	0.0.0.1	10.0.3.5	0.0.0.0	0
fe-0/0/1.0	DR	0.0.0.1	10.0.3.5	0.0.0.0	0

```
[edit protocols ospf]
lab@r5# run show ospf neighbor
  Address         Interface          State    ID           Pri  Dead
  10.0.2.10       as1.0              Full     10.0.3.4      128   37
```

These results confirm the presence of an OSPF adjacency between r4 and r5, and also confirm that the correct interface-to-area associations have been configured. Because r5 is an ABR, we can now examine a non-backbone area's link-state database to confirm that loopback addresses from backbone routers are being correctly injected into other areas as network summary LSAs:

```
[edit protocols ospf]
lab@r5# run show ospf database netsummary area 1

    OSPF link state database, area 0.0.0.1
  Type       ID              Adv Rtr          Seq       Age  Opt  Cksum  Len
  Summary *10.0.2.0         10.0.3.5         0x80000001  489  0x2  0x3d04  28
  Summary *10.0.2.4         10.0.3.5         0x80000001  489  0x2  0x1f1d  28
  Summary *10.0.2.8         10.0.3.5         0x80000001  489  0x2  0xec4c  28
  Summary *10.0.3.4         10.0.3.5         0x80000001  489  0x2  0x1C1d  28
  Summary *10.0.3.5         10.0.3.5         0x80000001  489  0x2  0x831   28
```

This display indicates that r5 has generated several network summary LSAs for area 1, and that two of these summary LSAs are correctly reporting the loopback addresses of r4 and r5.

r3 OSPF Configuration

The following commands are entered on r3 to complete the configuration of the backbone area:

```
[edit protocols ospf]
lab@r3# set area 0 interface fe-0/0/2 passive
```

```
[edit protocols ospf]
lab@r3# set area 0 interface lo0 passive
```

```
[edit protocols ospf]
lab@r3# set area 0 interface at-0/1/0.35
```

```
[edit protocols ospf]
lab@r3# set area 0 interface so-0/2/0.100
```

The configuration of r3 is now as follows:

```
[edit protocols ospf]
lab@r3# show
```

```
area 0.0.0.0 {
    interface fe-0/0/2.0 {
        passive;
    }
    interface lo0.0 {
        passive;
    }
    interface at-0/1/0.35;
    interface so-0/2/0.100;
}
```

By setting r3's fe-0/0/2 interface as passive, you ensure that no adjacencies can be formed over the interface and that the route to 172.16.0.12/30 will be injected into area 0 as an internal route. The passive setting on r3's fe-0/0/2 interface is needed to meet the requirements of this configuration example.

Verify OSPF on *r3*

With the backbone area configured, you expect to see that r3 has detected neighbors on both its at-0/1/0.35 and so-0/2/0.100 interfaces, and that the link to T1 is correctly reported in its router LSA:

```
lab@r3> show ospf interface
Interface            State      Area         DR ID         BDR ID        Nbrs
at-0/1/0.35          PtToPt     0.0.0.0      0.0.0.0       0.0.0.0          1
fe-0/0/2.0           DRother    0.0.0.0      0.0.0.0       0.0.0.0          0
lo0.0                DRother    0.0.0.0      0.0.0.0       0.0.0.0          0
so-0/2/0.100         PtToPt     0.0.0.0      0.0.0.0       0.0.0.0          1

lab@r3> show ospf neighbor
  Address        Interface         State     ID           Pri  Dead
10.0.2.1         at-0/1/0.35       Full      10.0.3.5     128   32
10.0.2.6         so-0/2/0.100      Full      10.0.3.4     128   35
```

These results confirm the correct interface and area settings are present in r3's OSPF configuration, and also verify that r3 has the expected adjacencies to r4 and r5. Next we will examine the contents of r3's router LSA to confirm the presence of the 172.16.0.12/30 prefix:

```
lab@r3> show ospf database router advertising-router 10.0.3.3 detail

    OSPF link state database, area 0.0.0.0
  Type      ID           Adv Rtr        Seq         Age  Opt  Cksum   Len
  Router  *10.0.3.3      10.0.3.3       0x80000003  103  0x2  0xbbf1  96
    bits 0x0, link count 6
```

```
id 10.0.3.5, data 10.0.2.2, type PointToPoint (1)
TOS count 0, TOS 0 metric 1
id 10.0.2.0, data 255.255.255.252, type Stub (3)
TOS count 0, TOS 0 metric 1
id 172.16.0.12, data 255.255.255.252, type Stub (3)
TOS count 0, TOS 0 metric 1
id 10.0.3.3, data 255.255.255.255, type Stub (3)
TOS count 0, TOS 0 metric 0
id 10.0.3.4, data 10.0.2.5, type PointToPoint (1)
TOS count 0, TOS 0 metric 1
id 10.0.2.4, data 255.255.255.252, type Stub (3)
TOS count 0, TOS 0 metric 1
```

As expected, we see that the external link to T1 is being reported as an OSPF stub route, as shown with highlights.

Area 1 Configuration

The following commands correctly configure r6 for operation as an internal area 1 router:

```
[edit protocols ospf]
lab@r6# set area 1 interface fe-0/1/0
```

```
[edit protocols ospf]
lab@r6# set area 1 interface fe-0/1/1
```

The specification of r6's lo0 interface is not necessary to meet the requirements of this example. The default JUNOS software behavior will result in r6 using the configured lo0 address as its RID, which in turn results in the automatic advertisement of this address as a stub route in r6's router LSA. The configuration of r7 is nearly identical to that of r6, with the only differences relating to interface-naming particulars. The configuration of r6 is shown next:

```
[edit protocols ospf]
lab@r6# show
area 0.0.0.1 {
    interface fe-0/1/0.0;
    interface fe-0/1/1.0;
}
```

Verify Overall OSPF Operation

The various spot checks performed thus far have all indicated the expected OSPF behavior and operation. This author has found that the following commands, which should be issued on an ABR, prove invaluable when the goal is to quickly assess the operational state of a multi-area

OSPF configuration. The first command verifies that we have the expected number of router LSAs, which is 6 in this case, 3 in area 0, and 3 in area 1:

```
lab@r5> show ospf database router area 0

    OSPF link state database, area 0.0.0.0
 Type      ID              Adv Rtr         Seq        Age  Opt  Cksum  Len
 Router    10.0.3.3        10.0.3.3        0x80000003 1604 0x2  0xbbf1 96
 Router    10.0.3.4        10.0.3.4        0x80000003 1611 0x2  0x373e 84
 Router   *10.0.3.5        10.0.3.5        0x80000005 305  0x2  0x3446 84
```

As expected, three router LSAs have been flooded in area 0, one of which has been generated by r5 itself. The following confirms that area 1 also has the expected number of router LSAs:

```
lab@r5> show ospf database router area 1

    OSPF link state database, area 0.0.0.1
 Type      ID              Adv Rtr         Seq        Age  Opt  Cksum  Len
 Router   *10.0.3.5        10.0.3.5        0x80000008 374  0x2  0x9020 48
 Router    10.0.9.6        10.0.9.6        0x80000005 337  0x2  0x5f2e 60
 Router    10.0.9.7        10.0.9.7        0x80000004 338  0x2  0xa6db 60
```

The resulting display indicates that three routers currently belong to area 1, which is the expected result based on the topology being configured. It is interesting to note that r5 has generated two router LSAs, one that is flooded into area 0 and another that is flooded into area 1.

When dealing with a large number of routers, it will sometimes prove helpful to pipe the results of these types of commands to the CLI's `match` and `count` functionalities:

```
lab@r5> show ospf database router | match router | count
Count: 6 lines
```

Considering that the ABR has generated two router LSAs, the five routers that make up this multi-area OSPF network is expected to produce a total of six router LSAs, so the results of this command indicate that all routers are present and that each router has at least one functional adjacency. Because the whole purpose of OSPF is to build a routing table, it might be wise to verify that the correct routing tables are being built as a result of all this LSA flooding. While the operator can always display the routing table and/or conduct ping testing to the various addresses that make up the test bed, this author has found it beneficial to perform spot checks such as the following, which quickly confirms that the loopback addresses of all remote routers are present as OSPF routes:

```
lab@r5> show route protocol ospf | match /32
10.0.3.3/32        *[OSPF/10] 00:35:19, metric 1
10.0.3.4/32        *[OSPF/10] 00:53:09, metric 1
```

```
10.0.9.6/32        *[OSPF/10] 00:15:07, metric 1
10.0.9.7/32        *[OSPF/10] 00:14:50, metric 1
224.0.0.5/32       *[OSPF/10] 00:53:14, metric 1
```

This display, taken from r5, confirms that the loopback addresses from the four remote routers are present as OSPF routes. r5's loopback address is not displayed here, because from r5's perspective, this address is not learned via OSPF. The 224.0.0.5/32 route is the ALL-OSPF router multicast address, and is always present as an OSPF route. Broken adjacencies are sure to cause grief during a lab-based examination, so you should verify the state of all adjacencies before considering your OSPF configuration complete. There are no shortcuts here. You will need to manually display and inspect the adjacency status on several of the routers that make up your JNCIP practice rack to verify the state of all adjacencies.

Because it takes at least two routers to form an adjacency, there is no need to check every router in the test bed for adjacency status. By choosing wisely, one can minimize the number of routers that must be checked in order to confirm that all adjacencies are functional. For example, displaying the adjacency status on the DR (or BDR) will allow the quick confirmation of all adjacencies associated with a broadcast network.

We next display OSPF adjacency information from r3, r4, and r7, to verify the adjacency status of all five routers in the test bed:

```
lab@r3> show ospf neighbor
  Address          Interface         State     ID         Pri  Dead
  10.0.2.1         at-0/1/0.35       Full      10.0.3.5   128  32
  10.0.2.6         so-0/2/0.100      Full      10.0.3.4   128  35

lab@r5> show ospf neighbor
  Address          Interface         State     ID         Pri  Dead
  10.0.2.10        as1.0             Full      10.0.3.4   128  32
  10.0.2.2         at-0/2/1.35       Full      10.0.3.3   128  31
  10.0.8.5         fe-0/0/0.0        Full      10.0.9.6   128  35

lab@r7> show ospf neighbor
  Address          Interface         State     ID         Pri  Dead
  10.0.8.1         fe-0/3/0.0        ExStart   10.0.9.6   128  35
  10.0.8.9         fe-0/3/1.0        Full      10.0.3.5   128  32
```

While r3 and r5 show the proper adjacency counts and state, it would seem from these displays that there is a problem with the adjacency between r6 and r7.

Troubleshooting Adjacency Problems

Those experienced with OSPF adjacency formation and troubleshooting will recall that, after achieving two-way communications, OSPF neighbors wishing to form an adjacency will enter the state of "Exchange Start" for the purpose of exchanging the contents of their LSDBs. After exchanging the database contents, and receiving acknowledgments from the remote router, the adjacency transitions to the *full* state. In this example, r6 and r7 are stuck at the exchange-start phase of adjacency formation. Because the exchange-start state confirms that both routers have successfully exchanged IP packets, there is little point in performing ping testing to fault isolate this type of problem.

One of the best ways to troubleshoot OSPF adjacency problems is to deploy tracing with special attention placed on hello packet exchanges, database descriptions, and any error messages that may be occurring. The following `traceoptions` configuration on r7 focuses on these message types:

```
lab@r7# show protocols ospf traceoptions
file ospf;
flag hello detail;
flag error detail;
flag database-description detail;
```

The result of monitoring the *ospf* trace file is shown next. To minimize clutter, r7 has its fe-0/3/1 interface disabled during the trace operation. The trace begins after the neighbor state is cleared:

```
lab@r7> clear ospf neighbor
```

```
Apr 24 12:18:58 RPD_OSPF_NBRDOWN: OSPF neighbor 10.0.8.1 (fe-0/3/0.0) state
changed from Exchange to Down due to Kill all neighbors
Apr 24 12:18:58 OSPF DR is 10.0.9.7, BDR is 0.0.0.0
Apr 24 12:18:59 OSPF sent Hello 10.0.8.2 -> 224.0.0.5 (fe-0/3/0.0)
Apr 24 12:18:59    Version 2, length 44, ID 10.0.9.7, area 0.0.0.1
Apr 24 12:18:59    checksum 0xdC1c, authtype 0
Apr 24 12:18:59    mask 255.255.255.252, hello_ivl 10, opts 0x2, prio 128
Apr 24 12:18:59    dead_ivl 40, DR 10.0.8.2, BDR 0.0.0.0
Apr 24 12:19:00 OSPF rcvd Hello 10.0.8.1 -> 224.0.0.5 (fe-0/3/0.0)
Apr 24 12:19:00    Version 2, length 48, ID 10.0.9.6, area 0.0.0.1
Apr 24 12:19:00    checksum 0xcf14, authtype 0
Apr 24 12:19:00    mask 255.255.255.252, hello_ivl 10, opts 0x2, prio 128
Apr 24 12:19:00    dead_ivl 40, DR 10.0.8.1, BDR 0.0.0.0
Apr 24 12:19:00 RPD_OSPF_NBRUP: OSPF neighbor 10.0.8.1 (fe-0/3/0.0) state
changed from Init to ExStart due to Two way communication established
```

So far, all has been normal with the OSPF packet exchange and adjacency formation. The establishment of the two-way state confirms that the two routers agree on the area number, its type (transit in this case), logical IP subnet information, timer settings (hello and dead interval), etc. The trace output continues next, where we can see the exchange of database description messages:

```
Apr 24 12:19:00 OSPF DR is 10.0.9.7, BDR is 10.0.9.6
Apr 24 12:19:00 OSPF sent DbD 10.0.8.2 -> 10.0.8.1 (fe-0/3/0.0)
Apr 24 12:19:00    Version 2, length 32, ID 10.0.9.7, area 0.0.0.1
Apr 24 12:19:00    checksum 0x7790, authtype 0
Apr 24 12:19:00    options 0x42, i 1, m 1, ms 1, seq 0xa0f1da0, mtu 3986
```

After correctly establishing their roles as master or slave for the database synchronization exchange, we next see 10.0.8.2 sending a database description packet to 10.0.8.1:

```
Apr 24 12:19:01 OSPF sent Hello 10.0.8.2 -> 224.0.0.5 (fe-0/3/0.0)
Apr 24 12:19:01    Version 2, length 48, ID 10.0.9.7, area 0.0.0.1
Apr 24 12:19:01    checksum 0xbd12, authtype 0
Apr 24 12:19:01    mask 255.255.255.252, hello_ivl 10, opts 0x2, prio 128
Apr 24 12:19:01    dead_ivl 40, DR 10.0.8.1, BDR 10.0.8.2
Apr 24 12:19:01 OSPF rcvd DbD 10.0.8.1 -> 10.0.8.2 (fe-0/3/0.0)
Apr 24 12:19:01    Version 2, length 32, ID 10.0.9.6, area 0.0.0.1
Apr 24 12:19:01    checksum 0x66a2, authtype 0
Apr 24 12:19:01    options 0x42, i 1, m 1, ms 1, seq 0xa0f3843, mtu 1500
Apr 24 12:19:01 OSPF now slave for nbr 10.0.8.1
. . .
```

After some hello exchanges, we next see r7 (10.0.8.2) receiving a database description packet from r6 (10.0.8.1). A short while later, the following trace output is observed:

```
. . .
Apr 24 12:19:06 OSPF rcvd DbD 10.0.8.1 -> 10.0.8.2 (fe-0/3/0.0)
Apr 24 12:19:06    Version 2, length 32, ID 10.0.9.6, area 0.0.0.1
Apr 24 12:19:06    checksum 0x66a2, authtype 0
Apr 24 12:19:06    options 0x42, i 1, m 1, ms 1, seq 0xa0f3843, mtu 1500
Apr 24 12:19:06    Duplicate
Apr 24 12:19:06 OSPF resend last DBD to 10.0.8.1
```

Though perhaps not obvious, the lack of database description acknowledgment, and the indication that duplicate database description packets are being sent, indicate that the two routers are discarding each other's database descriptions.

Because the majority of configuration problems (or bit errors) would prevent the establishment of two-way communications, this problem must relate to the nature of the database description packets themselves. Closer inspection of the trace output reveals that the database description packets sent by r7 have an IP layer MTU of 3986, while the packets sent by r6 indicate that the default MTU setting of 1500 bytes is in place. After correctly setting r6's fe-0/1/1 interface MTU to the correct value of 4000 as specified in the interface case study, the r6 to r7 adjacency can be correctly established:

```
lab@r7> show ospf neighbor
   Address        Interface        State    ID         Pri  Dead
  10.0.8.1        fe-0/3/0.0       Full     10.0.9.6    128  35
  10.0.8.9        fe-0/3/1.0       Full     10.0.3.5    128  32
```

Now that all adjacencies have been confirmed, the initial OSPF multi-area configuration example can be considered a success!

OSPF Network Types

OSPF operates differently over broadcast, point-to-point, point-to-multipoint, and NBMA networks. For example, Designated Routers (DRs) are only elected on the broadcast and NBMA network types, and the default hello interval for Juniper Networks routers is 10 seconds for all network types except NBMA, which use a 30-second hello interval. It should be obvious to the reader of this book that incorrect or mismatched network type settings can result in adjacency formation problems.

By default, LAN interfaces operate as a broadcast (LAN) network type, while all other interface types default to point-to-point operation unless the multipoint keyword is used to configure a multipoint ATM or Frame Relay connection.

Multipoint Network Types

Figure 3.2 illustrates a typical multipoint connection that connects r3 to r4 and r5 over a Frame Relay network in a star topology. The lack of a virtual circuit connection between r4 and r5 differentiates this multipoint topology from a fully meshed NBMA topology.

To correctly configure OSPF for this application, the operator must include the neighbor statement under each multipoint OSPF interface declaration. JUNOS software currently does not support automatic neighbor discovery. The use of the multipoint keyword in the so-0/2/0 interface configuration automatically enables point-to-multipoint OSPF operation so the OSPF network type does not require explicit setting in this example. The following code snippets correctly configure r3 for this multipoint OSPF application:

```
[edit]
lab@r3# show interfaces so-0/2/0
no-keepalives;
encapsulation frame-relay;
unit 0 {
    multipoint;
    family inet {
```

```
        address 10.1.0.3/24 {
            multipoint-destination 10.1.0.4 dlci 400;
            multipoint-destination 10.1.0.5 dlci 500;
        }
    }
}

[edit]
lab@r3# show protocols ospf
area 0.0.0.0 {
    interface so-0/2/0.0 {
        neighbor 10.1.0.4;
        neighbor 10.1.0.5;
    }
}
```

FIGURE 3.2   Multipoint OSPF network

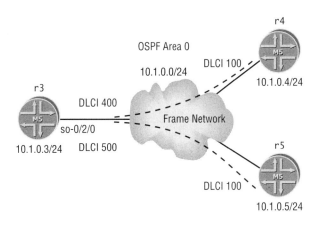

Use of the multipoint keyword requires the configuration of one or more neighbor state-ments to map remote IP addresses to local DLCI connection identifiers. Proper OSPF operation is determined using standard OSPF testing methodology, starting with the determination of r3's OSPF interface state:

```
[edit]
lab@r3# run show ospf interface detail
Interface            State    Area          DR ID        BDR ID       Nbrs
so-0/2/0.0           PtToPt   0.0.0.0       0.0.0.0       0.0.0.0      2
Type P2MP, address 10.1.0.3, mask 255.255.255.0, MTU 4470, cost 1
```

DR addr 0.0.0.0, BDR addr 0.0.0.0, adj count 2
Hello 10, Dead 40, ReXmit 5, Not Stub

The highlighted fields in this capture confirm that r3's so-0/2/0.0 interface is considered by OSPF to be a point-to-multipoint interface. The empty DR and BDR fields are to be expected since the DR function is not present on multipoint network types. The neighbor count of 2 correctly reflects the neighbors that were manually configured on r3. We will now confirm r3's adjacency state, as shown next:

```
[edit]
lab@r3# run show ospf neighbor
  Address        Interface         State    ID         Pri  Dead
  10.1.0.5       so-0/2/0.0        Full     10.0.3.5   128  38
  10.1.0.4       so-0/2/0.0        Full     10.0.3.4   128  39
```

Based on the show ospf interface and show ospf neighbor displays, we can confirm that OSPF is correctly operating over this multipoint topology.

NBMA Network Types

Figure 3.3 illustrates a typical NBMA topology in which a full mesh of virtual circuit connections is provided between r3, r4, and r5. Even though this network will work fine using the default point-to-multipoint mode, it may be necessary to configure an NBMA network for interoperability with another vendor, to achieve maximum protocol efficiency for networks that meet the full mesh requirements of an NBMA, or to meet the specific configuration requirements for your examination scenario. When configured for NBMA operation, the OSPF protocol will endeavor to elect both a DR and BDR, in effect treating the WAN cloud as a LAN that happens to lack link-level broadcast.

FIGURE 3.3 NBMA OSPF topology

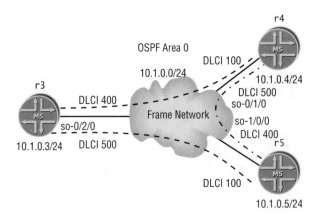

NBMA configuration is very similar to that of the multipoint case. The key differences relate to the inclusion of the `eligible` keyword after each neighbor that is considered capable of functioning as the DR, and the need to specify the network type as `nbma`. The `poll-interval` parameter is associated with NMBA networks, and functions to reduce the rate of hello packet transmission to neighbors that are assumed to be down. In essence, the hello interval is used to maintain adjacencies that are operational while the poll interval is used to solicit the formation of an adjacency with a neighbor that is currently marked as down. The default poll interval of 90 seconds has been left in place for this example. The OSPF configuration of all three of the nodes that form the OSPF NBMA topology are shown in Listings 3.1 through 3.3.

Listing 3.1: *r3* **OSPF Configuration**

```
[edit]
lab@r3# show protocols ospf
area 0.0.0.0 {
    interface so-0/2/0.0 {
        interface-type nbma;
        neighbor 10.1.0.4 eligible;
        neighbor 10.1.0.5;
    }
}
```

Listing 3.2: *r4* **OSPF Configuration**

```
[edit]
lab@r4# show protocols ospf
area 0.0.0.0 {
    interface so-0/1/0.0 {
        interface-type nbma;
        neighbor 10.1.0.3 eligible;
        neighbor 10.1.0.5;
    }
}
```

Listing 3.3: *r5* **OSPF Configuration**

```
[edit]
lab@r5# show protocols ospf
area 0.0.0.0 {
    interface so-1/0/0.0 {
        interface-type nbma;
        priority 0;
        neighbor 10.1.0.3;
        neighbor 10.1.0.4;
    }
}
```

In this example, r3 and r4 have defined each other as being DR-eligible while r5 has been left in the default state of ineligible. To ensure operational consistency, r5 should have its local DR priority set to 0, as highlighted in the previous capture, so that it does not try to elect itself the DR for the NBMA network. r5's neighbor statements do not require the `eligible` keyword because its presence affects only the hello generation behavior of a router that considers itself to be DR-eligible.

It must be stressed that the `eligible` tag does not really affect a router's ability to become the DR, so much as to control the exchange of hello packets among a subset of routers that could be elected as the DR. Once elected as the DR, that router must send hello packets to all neighbors, whether they are listed as DR-eligible or not.

The net result of this configuration, and the rules that govern OSPF operation over an NBMA network, will therefore be:

1. r5 can never be the DR because it has a priority of 0.

2. Upon network activation, r3 and r4 will exchange hello packets for the purposes of electing a DR.

3. Once a DR is elected, the DR router will send hellos to all listed neighbors, which includes r5. r5 must in turn generate hello packets in response to the receipt of a hello packet from any node that considers itself to be the DR or BDR.

This behavior guarantees hellos will be exchanged between any two eligible routers—as is necessary for the proper functioning of the OSPF DR election algorithm—and that the total volume of hello packets can be dramatically reduced on a large NBMA topology by limiting the number of DR-eligible routers to a small subset of the total router population.

Who Uses This NBMA Stuff Anyway?

From a purely practical perspective, the fact that most ATM and Frame Relay topologies are configured to provide less than a full mesh of connectivity, coupled with the increased link speed of modern broadband access technologies, makes the whole motivation for NBMA support somewhat moot. Many industry gurus believe that VC-based WAN backbones should always be configured as a collection of point-to-point links or as a point-to-multipoint network. You should be prepared to configure all OSPF network types, popular or not, as part of your lab scenario.

Based on the rules that govern OSPF operation over NBMA networks and the current state of configuration in our example, we expect to find that r3 will have adjacencies to both r4 and r5, and that r3 will be functioning as either the DR or BDR based on the results of the DR election algorithm. Proper operation is verified with the following commands, starting with the determination that we have the proper NBMA interface configuration:

```
[edit]
lab@r3# run show ospf interface extensive
```

```
Interface              State   Area         DR ID          BDR ID        Nbrs
so-0/2/0.0             DR      0.0.0.0      10.0.3.3       10.0.3.4        2
Type NBMA, address 10.1.0.3, mask 255.255.255.0, MTU 4470, cost 1
DR addr 10.1.0.3, BDR addr 10.1.0.4, adj count 2, priority 128
Hello 30, Poll 90, Dead 120, ReXmit 5, Not Stub
```

The highlights in the previous capture confirm that r3's OSPF interface correctly shows the NBMA network type, and also confirms the election of a DR and BDR for the NBMA topology. Other fields in this display show the default settings for the priority, hello, and poll timer parameters; these values should be contrasted to the default settings for broadcast, point-to-point, and multipoint network types. Proper adjacency formation and additional DR election functionality is verified with the following command:

```
[edit]
lab@r3# run show ospf neighbor detail
  Address        Interface        State       ID            Pri  Dead
  10.1.0.5       so-0/2/0.0       Full        10.0.3.5       0   118
    area 0.0.0.0, opt 0x0, DR 10.0.1.3, BDR 10.0.1.4
  10.1.0.4       so-0/2/0.0       Full        10.0.3.4      128  118
    area 0.0.0.0, opt 0x42, DR 10.1.0.3, BDR 10.1.0.4
    Up 00:02:13, adjacent 00:00:49
```

Because r5 is not listed as a DR-eligible neighbor, its DR priority setting should be set to 0, and this is confirmed in the highlighted portions of the previous capture. The DR priority is configured under the NBMA interface, and is used to influence the outcome of the DR election process. The following command will ensure that r4 will win a DR election contest should it be pitted against r3:

```
[edit protocols ospf area 0.0.0.0]
lab@r4# set interface so-0/1/0.0 priority 200
```

The DR function in OSPF is not preemptive. Therefore, even with its higher priority setting, r4 will not be able to "overthrow" r3 as the DR if r3 is already functioning in that capacity, which means that the first router to boot will tend to be the DR as long as it does not have a priority setting of 0. The DR priority setting would come into play if network connectivity were to be restored between r3 and r4 after being disrupted long enough for both routers to have elected themselves as the DR for the 10.1.0.0/24 subnet. Because there can be only one DR, the router with the lower priority will defer to the higher priority router in this case.

After committing this change and restarting the routing daemon on both r4 and r5, we wait for the DR election algorithm to complete, and then confirm that the results are as expected:

```
[edit protocols ospf area 0.0.0.0]
lab@r3# run show ospf neighbor detail
```

```
     Address        Interface           State    ID          Pri  Dead
     10.1.0.4       so-0/2/0.0          Full     10.0.3.4    200  110
       area 0.0.0.0, opt 0x42, DR 10.1.0.4, BDR 10.1.0.3
       Up 00:01:02, adjacent 00:01:02
     . . .
```

The results shown confirm that r4 has won the DR election contest, and also display r5's modified DR priority setting.

Troubleshooting Network Type Problems

As previously mentioned, incorrect network type settings will normally result in OSPF adjacency failures. The following trace configuration and the resulting output, which was taken from r3, illustrate symptoms that are typically associated with incompatible network type settings. These captures are based on the topology shown in Figure 3.4.

FIGURE 3.4   Incorrect OSPF network types

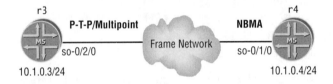

The trace configuration is committed on r3, and you monitor the results:

```
[edit protocols ospf]
lab@r3# show
traceoptions {
    file ospf;
    flag hello detail;
    flag error detail;
}
area 0.0.0.0 {
    interface so-0/2/0.0;
}
```

The trace configuration is committed on r3, and you monitor the results:

```
[edit protocols ospf]
lab@r3# run monitor start ospf

[edit protocols ospf]
lab@r3#
*** ospf ***

. . .
```

```
Apr 24 15:05:09 OSPF sent Hello -> 224.0.0.5 (so-0/2/0.0)
Apr 24 15:05:09   Version 2, length 44, ID 10.0.3.3, area 0.0.0.0
Apr 24 15:05:09   checksum 0xef1c, authtype 0
Apr 24 15:05:09   mask 255.255.255.0, hello_ivl 10, opts 0x2, prio 128
Apr 24 15:05:09   dead_ivl 40, DR 0.0.0.0, BDR 0.0.0.0
Apr 24 15:05:19 OSPF sent Hello -> 224.0.0.5 (so-0/2/0.0)
Apr 24 15:05:19   Version 2, length 44, ID 10.0.3.3, area 0.0.0.0
Apr 24 15:05:19   checksum 0xef1c, authtype 0
Apr 24 15:05:19   mask 255.255.255.0, hello_ivl 10, opts 0x2, prio 128
Apr 24 15:05:19   dead_ivl 40, DR 0.0.0.0, BDR 0.0.0.0
Apr 24 15:05:22 OSPF rcvd Hello 10.1.0.4 -> 10.1.0.3 (so-0/2/0.0)
Apr 24 15:05:22   Version 2, length 44, ID 10.0.3.4, area 0.0.0.0
Apr 24 15:05:22   checksum 0xe4b2, authtype 0
Apr 24 15:05:22   mask 255.255.255.0, hello_ivl 30, opts 0x2, prio 128
Apr 24 15:05:22   dead_ivl 120, DR 10.1.0.4, BDR 0.0.0.0
Apr 24 15:05:22 OSPF packet ignored: hello interval mismatch 30 from 10.1.0.4
```

The trace output shows that r3 is generating hellos with a 10-second interval as expected for the default point-to-point OSPF network type, while r4, which is set for NBMA operation, is sending hellos with a 30-second interval. The last line of the trace output clearly indicates that r3 scoffs at r4's hello parameters as it complains of the timer mismatch. The most obvious symptom of this network type incompatibility is the lack of neighbor detection and adjacency formation, as highlighted next:

```
[edit protocols ospf]
lab@r3# run show ospf neighbor


[edit protocols ospf]
lab@r3# run show ospf interface
Interface          State   Area        DR ID        BDR ID       Nbrs
so-0/2/0.0         PtToPt  0.0.0.0     0.0.0.0      0.0.0.0      0
```

OSPF Authentication

The OSPF protocol can support the authentication of packet exchanges to ensure that adjacencies and LSA flooding are confined to a set of trusted nodes. Authentication options include the default setting of *none,* the use of a simple password, or a Message Digest 5 (MD5) encoded checksum. Authentication support is configured at the OSPF area–level hierarchy. The individual authentication passwords (or keys) are then specified on a per-interface basis within that area's configuration stanza.

MD5 authentication requires that communicating stations share both the key value and a corresponding key-id. Specifying the same secret with two different key-ids will result in authentication failures.

Your next assignment is to add OSPF authentication according to the criteria listed next. You should refer back to Figure 3.1 as needed for topology details:

- Backbone area uses MD5 key = *jni*, key-id = 10.
- Area 1 uses a plain-text password of *jnx*.

The following commands correctly configure the authentication type for area 0 and area 1:

```
[edit protocols ospf]
lab@r5# set area 0 authentication-type md5
```

```
[edit protocols ospf]
lab@r5# set area 1 authentication-type simple
```

The next set of commands configure the MD5 specifics for all backbone area interfaces:

```
[edit protocols ospf area 0.0.0.0]
lab@r5# set interface at-0/2/1.35 authentication-key jni key-id 10
```

```
[edit protocols ospf area 0.0.0.0]
lab@r5# set interface as1.0 authentication-key jni key-id 10
```

Authentication parameters are not needed on the router's lo0 interface because adjacencies and LSP flooding will not occur over this interface. The next set of commands configure the simple password authentication that is required for area 1:

```
[edit protocols ospf area 0.0.0.1]
lab@r5# set authentication-type simple
```

```
[edit protocols ospf area 0.0.0.1]
lab@r5# set interface fe-0/0/0 authentication-key jnx
```

```
[edit protocols ospf area 0.0.0.1]
lab@r5# set interface fe-0/0/1.0 authentication-key jnx
```

The modified OSPF configuration for r5 is shown next. The newly added authentication-related entries are highlighted:

```
lab@r5# show protocols
ospf {
    area 0.0.0.0 {
        authentication-type md5; # SECRET-DATA
        interface lo0.0 {
            passive;
        }
        interface at-0/2/1.35 {
            authentication-key "$9$QgSo3/tleWLxd" key-id 10; # SECRET-DATA
        }
        interface as1.0 {
            authentication-key "$9$WjsXNbiHmfT3" key-id 10; # SECRET-DATA
        }
    }
    area 0.0.0.1 {
        authentication-type simple; # SECRET-DATA
        interface fe-0/0/0.0 {
            authentication-key "$9$Kw2WX-UDkqfz"; # SECRET-DATA
        }
        interface fe-0/0/1.0 {
            authentication-key "$9$32M9/A0vMXxds"; # SECRET-DATA
        }
    }
}
```

After committing the authentication changes on r5, we expect to see the loss of all adjacencies until compatible authentication settings are put into place on the remaining routers. The lack of detected neighbors in the following display confirms these expectations:

```
[edit protocols ospf area 0.0.0.1]
lab@r5# run show ospf interface
Interface          State    Area       DR ID       BDR ID      Nbrs
as1.0              PtToPt   0.0.0.0    0.0.0.0     0.0.0.0      0
at-0/2/1.35        PtToPt   0.0.0.0    0.0.0.0     0.0.0.0      0
lo0.0              DR       0.0.0.0    10.0.3.5    0.0.0.0      0
fe-0/0/0.0         DR       0.0.0.1    10.0.3.5    0.0.0.0      0
fe-0/0/1.0         DR       0.0.0.1    10.0.3.5    0.0.0.0      0
```

Verify OSPF Authentication

OSPF authentication problems normally result in the same types of neighbor detection and adjacency failures that could also be attributed to numerous problems at the OSPF, IP, link, or physical layers. The operator can quickly isolate physical, link, and IP layer problems through ping testing to a directly connected OSPF router. You should suspect authentication-related problems when ping testing succeeds in the face of OSPF neighbor discovery failures.

Sometimes, the use of monitor traffic will make authentication problems obvious. The following example shows a capture taken from r5's fe-0/0/0 interface:

```
[edit]
lab@r5# run monitor traffic interface fe-0/0/0 extensive
Listening on fe-0/0/0

08:34:44.426378 Out 0:90:69:69:70:0 1:0:5e:0:0:5 ip 78: 10.0.8.6 > 224.0.0.5:
OSPFv2-hello 44: rtrid 10.0.3.5 area 0.0.0.1 auth "jnx^@^@^@^@^@" E mask
255.255.255.252 int 10 pri 128 dead 40 dr 10.0.8.6 nbrs [tos 0xc0]  [ttl 1] (id
48338)

08:34:48.854579  In 10.0.8.5 > 224.0.0.5:  OSPFv2-hello 44: rtrid 10.0.9.6 area
0.0.0.1 E mask 255.255.255.252 int 10 pri 128 dead 40 dr 10.0.8.5 nbrs [tos
0xc0]  [ttl 1] (id 32032)
```

This output clearly shows that simple password authentication is present in the hello packets sent out r5's fe-0/0/0 interface. The plain text password value of *jnx*, which has been padded to the required 8 bytes, is clearly displayed in this output. In contrast, the hello packets received by r5 lack any authentication fields.

The following capture, taken from r5's ATM interface, illustrates the difference between the simple password and MD5-based authentication techniques:

```
lab@r5# run monitor traffic interface at-0/2/1 extensive
Listening on at-0/2/1

08:47:43.044735  In 10.0.2.2 > 224.0.0.5:  OSPFv2-hello 44: rtrid 10.0.3.3
backbone E mask 255.255.255.252 int 10 pri 128 dead 40 nbrs [tos 0xc0]  [ttl 1]
(id 22522)

08:47:47.948227 Out aa aa 03 00-00-00 0800: 10.0.2.1 > 224.0.0.5:  OSPFv2-hello
44: rtrid 10.0.3.5 backbone auth MD5 E mask 255.255.255.252 int 10 pri 128 dead
40 nbrs [tos 0xc0]  [ttl 1] (id 48763)
```

Once again, it is clear that received packets have no authentication information while the packets being sent by r5 carry an MD5-based hash. In contrast to the simple password example, it is impossible to ascertain the MD5 secret that is being used to produce the MD5 hash. You will therefore need to reset the MD5 hash in all routers if you suspect that mismatched MD5 secrets have been configured.

Protocol Tracing

While monitoring traffic has the benefit of being "quick and dirty," the more or less raw output pales in comparison to the well-cooked information provided by JUNOS software protocol tracing. The following tracing configuration has been added to r5, which is still the only router configured for authentication at this stage of the configuration example:

```
[edit]
lab@r5# show protocols ospf
traceoptions {
    file ospf;
    flag error detail;
    flag hello detail;
}
```

This tracing configuration produced the following output, which makes the nature of the problem obvious to even a casual observer:

```
[edit]
lab@r5# run monitor start ospf


*** ospf ***
Apr 25 08:51:11 OSPF packet ignored: authentication type mismatch (0) from
10.0.8.10
Apr 25 08:51:11 OSPF rcvd Hello 10.0.8.10 -> 224.0.0.5 (fe-0/0/1.0)
Apr 25 08:51:11    Version 2, length 44, ID 10.0.9.7, area 0.0.0.1
Apr 25 08:51:11    checksum 0xd611, authtype 0
Apr 25 08:51:11    mask 255.255.255.252, hello_ivl 10, opts 0x2, prio 128
Apr 25 08:51:11    dead_ivl 40, DR 10.0.8.10, BDR 0.0.0.0
Apr 25 08:51:11 OSPF packet ignored: authentication type mismatch (0) from
10.0.2.10
Apr 25 08:51:11 OSPF rcvd Hello 10.0.2.10 -> 224.0.0.5 (as1.0)
. . .
```

After adding the appropriate authentication settings to the remaining routers in area 0 and area 1, we once again have a functional IGP as indicated by the following operational mode commands:

```
[edit]
lab@r5# run show ospf interface
```

Interface	State	Area	DR ID	BDR ID	Nbrs
as1.0	PtToPt	0.0.0.0	0.0.0.0	0.0.0.0	1
at-0/2/1.35	PtToPt	0.0.0.0	0.0.0.0	0.0.0.0	1
lo0.0	DR	0.0.0.0	10.0.3.5	0.0.0.0	0
fe-0/0/0.0	BDR	0.0.0.1	10.0.9.6	10.0.3.5	1
fe-0/0/1.0	BDR	0.0.0.1	10.0.9.7	10.0.3.5	1

As shown previously, neighbors have once again been detected on r5's interfaces. We will now confirm adjacency status for r5's neighbors:

```
[edit]
lab@r5# run show ospf neighbor
```

Address	Interface	State	ID	Pri	Dead
10.0.2.10	as1.0	Full	10.0.3.4	128	34
10.0.2.2	at-0/2/1.35	Full	10.0.3.3	128	35
10.0.8.5	fe-0/0/0.0	Full	10.0.9.6	128	32
10.0.8.10	fe-0/0/1.0	Full	10.0.9.7	128	32

Excellent! These results indicate that all of r5's adjacencies have been correctly established. The next command quickly assesses the overall state of the OSPF routing domain by confirming that all routers have flooded a router LSA within their respective areas:

```
[edit]
lab@r5# run show ospf database router
```

OSPF link state database, area 0.0.0.0

Type	ID	Adv Rtr	Seq	Age	Opt	Cksum	Len
Router	10.0.3.3	10.0.3.3	0x8000000d	169	0x2	0xa7fb	96
Router	10.0.3.4	10.0.3.4	0x80000017	166	0x2	0xf52	84
Router	*10.0.3.5	10.0.3.5	0x80000013	173	0x2	0x1854	84

OSPF link state database, area 0.0.0.1

Type	ID	Adv Rtr	Seq	Age	Opt	Cksum	Len
Router	*10.0.3.5	10.0.3.5	0x80000043	31	0x2	0x264f	48
Router	10.0.9.6	10.0.9.6	0x8000006c	59	0x2	0x70b7	60
Router	10.0.9.7	10.0.9.7	0x8000003f	35	0x2	0x3c0b	60

The OSPF database on r5 indicates that router LSAs (type 1 LSAs) have been generated by each of the five routers in this topology. While these results do not prove that all routers have the expected number of adjacencies, the results do indicate that every router in the network has at least one functional adjacency as evidenced by the successful flooding of router LSAs.

Stub and Not-So-Stubby Areas

The performance and scalability of link-state routing protocols like OSPF are to a large degree determined by the volume and frequency of LSA flooding, because these factors impact the size of a router's LSDB and number of times it must perform SPF calculations as a result of network changes. In many cases, the majority of information flooded throughout an OSPF routing domain, and thereby contained in the OSPF LSDB, will relate to AS external routes, which are routes that have been redistributed into OSPF from another protocol such as RIP, direct, or BGP. Stub and not-so-stubby areas (NSSA) were developed to eliminate the need to carry AS external routing information in non-transit areas.

Stub Areas

A stub area does not allow the flooding of AS external routing information into that area from the backbone, or out of that area into the backbone. The result is that LSA types 5 and 7 will not be present in a stub area. ASBR-summary LSAs (type 4s) are not generated to a stub area, as the lack of type 5 external LSAs makes the need to know the route to the originating ASBR a non-issue.

Routers within a stub area rely on default routes, originated by the area's ABRs, to reach AS external destinations. Internal routers in a stub area simply choose the metrically closest ABR for the forwarding of packets destined for delivery to external addresses.

 Juniper Networks routers do not automatically generate a default route when operating as an ABR attached to a stub or not-so-stubby area. With JUNOS software, you must configure a default metric before a default route will be advertised!

Network summary LSAs (type 3s) are generated by ABRs to summarize their SPF cost to destinations within their attached areas. Other routers compute their SPF cost to each ABR, and then add (as in distance vector routing!) the metric received in summary LSAs to compute the shortest path to inter-area destinations. Summary LSAs are advertised into a stub area by default, but can be restricted with the `no-summaries` option. The contents of the summary LSAs allow internal routers in a stub area to compute shortest paths to destinations in other areas (inter-area) so that packets are forwarded to the ABR that lies along the shortest path to that destination.

Totally Stubby Areas

A stub area that has been configured to block summary LSAs is often referred to as a *Totally Stubby Area* because internal routers will now have to rely on the default route received from the metrically closest ABR to reach both inter-area and AS external destinations. The behavior of a TSA is very similar to that of an IS-IS level 1 area, in that both require default routing to reach destinations outside of that router's area. As mentioned earlier, you can create a TSA in JUNOS software by including the `no-summaries` option as part of the stub area's definition. If desired, you can prevent routing to destinations outside of a stub area by omitting the `default-metric` statement, thus preventing the generation of the default route into that stub area.

By their very nature, Totally Stubby Areas are black holes looking for a place to happen. You should always be on guard when configuring a TSA because achieving connectivity to inter-area destinations from within a TSA can be tricky, and the loss of inter-area connectivity could be overlooked in the heat of battle—resulting in major problems in your network's operation down the road.

Stub Area Deployment

In the next section you will configure a stub area comprising routers r1, r2, r3, and r4, as shown in Figure 3.5.

FIGURE 3.5   OSPF stub areas

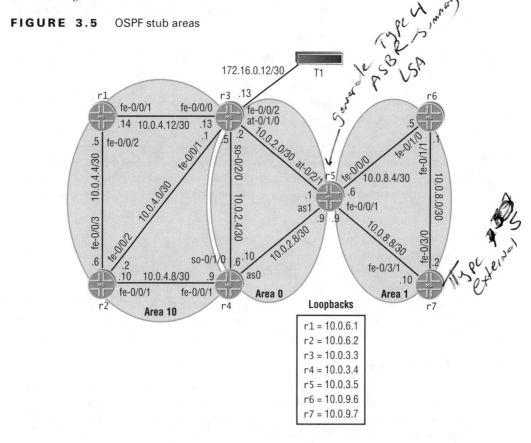

To better demonstrate the stub area concept, and to make things a bit more interesting, r7 will first be made into an ASBR so that AS external flooding behavior can be observed.

The criteria for this configuration task are as follows:

- Advertise the prefix 200.0.0/24 as an AS external from r7.
- r1 and r2 are internal area 10 routers.
- No type 5 LSAs are allowed in area 10.
- Loopback addresses of all routers must be reachable from area 10.
- No static routes permitted in area 10.

External LSA Generation

The first set of commands creates a static route on r7 and the policy needed to redistribute the route into another routing protocol:

```
[edit routing-options]
lab@r7# set static route 200.0.0/24 reject
```

```
[edit routing-options]
lab@r7# top
```

The static route redistribution policy is now created:

```
[edit]
lab@r7# edit policy-options policy-statement stat
```

```
[edit policy-options policy-statement stat]
lab@r7# set term 1 from protocol static
```

```
[edit policy-options policy-statement stat]
lab@r7# set term 1 from route-filter 200.0.0/24 exact
```

```
[edit policy-options policy-statement stat]
lab@r7# set term 1 then accept
```

```
[edit policy-options policy-statement stat]
lab@r7# set term 2 then reject
```

You next apply the *stat* policy to the OSPF protocol as an export policy:

```
[edit protocols]
lab@r7# set protocols ospf export stat
```

The static route to 200.0.0/24 points to *reject* in this example, so that traceroutes to this address will complete with a "destination unreachable" message. The 200.0.0/24 route is used here strictly for purposes of external LSA generation, so using a discard next hop would result in time-outs when performing ping or traceroute testing to addresses that are encompassed by this prefix. The `stat` policy, as applied to the OSPF routing protocol, tells r7 to redistribute into OSPF all active routes that match the `200.0.0.0/24 exact` route filter statement. The use of a discriminating route filter is used here to prevent the inadvertent redistribution of other static routes, such as the one associated with your fxp0 OoB network (in the event that you neglected to add the `no-advertise` tag when it was defined).

External LSA Verification

After committing the change on r7, we confirm all is well by verifying the presence of the resulting type 5 and type 4 LSAs in r5's LSDB:

```
[edit]
lab@r5# run show ospf database extern
    OSPF external link state database
 Type      ID             Adv Rtr        Seq       Age  Opt  Cksum   Len
 Extern    200.0.0.0      10.0.9.7       0x80000002  25  0x2  0xea04  36


[edit]
lab@r5# run show ospf database asbrsummary

    OSPF link state database, area 0.0.0.0
 Type      ID             Adv Rtr        Seq       Age  Opt  Cksum   Len
 ASBRSum  *10.0.9.7        10.0.3.5      0x80000001  38  0x2  0xad81  28

    OSPF link state database, area 0.0.0.1
```

Perfect. We see the external LSA advertising the route to 200.0.0.0/24 is being generated by r7, which is now an ASBR, and we also see the ASBR-summary LSA (LSA type 4) as generated by r5, the ABR, which is used to advertise reachability information for ASBRs in area 1.

Because previously generated LSAs can remain in the LSDB for up to one hour (3600 seconds), it is often helpful to purge the OSPF LSDB to prevent confusion due to the presence of LSAs that should no longer be in the database. The purge switch to the `clear ospf database` command causes the router to reflood all the LSAs in its LSDB with an indication that their lifetime has reached 3600 seconds. This causes all routers in the OSPF domain to regenerate the LSAs that they consider valid, which in turn results in a clean and tidy LSDB that will greatly enhance your viewing pleasure.

Stub Area Configuration

The following commands correctly configure area 10 as a stub area, beginning with the configuration changes required on r3.

```
[edit protocols ospf]
lab@r3# set area 10 stub default-metric 10

[edit protocols ospf]
lab@r3# set area 10 interface fe-0/0/0.200

[edit protocols ospf]
lab@r3# set area 10 interface fe-0/0/1
```

These commands correctly configure area 10 as a stub area on r3, and instruct r3 (the ABR) to generate a default route with a metric of 10 into the stub area. The presence of this default route will enable packet forwarding from the stub area to external destinations. The OSPF configuration for r3 is shown next with stub area–related entries highlighted:

```
[edit protocols ospf]
lab@r3# show
area 0.0.0.0 {
    authentication-type md5; # SECRET-DATA
    interface fe-0/0/2.0 {
        passive;
        authentication-key "$9$I3jhyKsYoJGi" key-id 10; # SECRET-DATA
    }
    interface lo0.0 {
        passive;
    }
    interface at-0/1/0.35 {
        authentication-key "$9$a1GjqCAOBIc" key-id 10; # SECRET-DATA
    }
    interface so-0/2/0.100 {
        authentication-key "$9$hOuyeWg4ZUjq" key-id 10; # SECRET-DATA
    }
}
area 0.0.0.10 {
    stub default-metric 10;
    interface fe-0/0/0.200;
    interface fe-0/0/1.0;
}
```

r4's stub area configuration is virtually identical to that performed on r3, because the only differences are those that relate to interface particulars. Though not shown, it is assumed that you have completed and committed the stub area configuration on r4 based on the example shown previously for r3.

The following commands are entered on r1 to correctly configure stub area 10:

```
[edit protocols ospf]
lab@r1# set area 10 stub

[edit protocols ospf]
lab@r1# set area 10 interface fe-0/0/1.200

[edit protocols ospf]
lab@r1# set area 10 interface fe-0/0/2
```

There is no need for the default-metric option on r1, as this knob applies only to an ABR. The resulting configuration for r1 is shown next. It should be noted that we have correctly specified the logical interface for the r1-to-r3 Fast Ethernet link, which is using VLAN tagging and logical unit 200:

```
[edit protocols ospf]
lab@r1# show
area 0.0.0.10 {
    stub;
    interface fe-0/0/1.200;
    interface fe-0/0/2.0;
}
```

The configuration of stub area 10 on r2 is shown next, and is very similar to that of r1:

```
[edit protocols ospf]
lab@r2# show
area 0.0.0.10 {
    stub;
    interface fe-0/0/1.0;
    interface fe-0/0/2.0;
    interface fe-0/0/3.0;
}
```

Stub Area Verification

Common OSPF operational mode commands will now be used to verify that the requirements of the stub area configuration example have been met. We start by confirming the adjacency status of r1:

```
[edit protocols ospf]
lab@r1# run show ospf neighbor
```

Address	Interface	State	ID	Pri	Dead
10.0.4.13	fe-0/0/1.200	<u>Full</u>	10.0.3.3	128	35
10.0.4.6	fe-0/0/2.0	<u>Full</u>	10.0.6.2	128	39

The adjacency between r1 and r3 confirm that they agree on the area number and the area type (stub areas set the "E" bit in the OSPF header's options field), which is a good sign. Now to confirm that external LSAs are not being flooded into area 10, we issue the following command:

```
[edit protocols ospf]
lab@r1# run show ospf database extern

[edit protocols ospf]
lab@r1#
```

As per the requirements of the OSPF stub area configuration example, r7's type 5 LSA is not present in the LSDB of routers in area 10. The following actions will confirm the presence of the default route, and the resulting ability to reach external destinations:

```
lab@r1> show route protocol ospf | match 0.0.0.0
0.0.0.0/0          *[OSPF/10] 00:08:27, metric 11
```

The default route is present, and shows the expected metric of 11, which represents the costs of the r1-r3 link (1) added to the advertised cost of the default route (10). The next command confirms that r1 does not have a route to any prefix that starts with 200/8, which is expected because of the lack of type 5 flooding into a stub area.

```
lab@r1> show route protocol ospf 200/8
```

As expected, no matching routes are returned by r1. We now confirm that external destinations are reachable from within the stub area:

```
lab@r1> traceroute 200.0.0.1
traceroute to 200.0.0.1 (200.0.0.1), 30 hops max, 40 byte packets
 1  10.0.4.13 (10.0.4.13)  0.351 ms  0.243 ms  0.221 ms
 2  10.0.2.1 (10.0.2.1)  0.675 ms  0.664 ms  0.875 ms
 3  10.0.8.10 (10.0.8.10)  0.857 ms  0.700 ms  0.876 ms
 4  10.0.8.10 (10.0.8.10)  0.858 ms !H  0.700 ms !H  0.862 ms !H
```

The traceroute succeeds, ironically by virtue of it terminating with an indication that the destination is unreachable (the "!H")! This is the expected result, and the reason why the static routes used in this example have their next hops set to reject instead of discard. Refer to the "External LSA Generation" section earlier in this chapter for more information on the use of reject vs. discard next hops. These results prove that routers in stub area 10 can use the default route to reach external destinations. Because summary LSAs are permitted in area 10, r1 and r2 should have complete inter-area routing for your OSPF network. This is confirmed with the following commands:

```
lab@r1> show ospf database netsummary
```

```
    OSPF link state database, area 0.0.0.10
 Type      ID               Adv Rtr           Seq        Age  Opt  Cksum  Len
Summary   0.0.0.0          10.0.3.3          0x80000006  372  0x0  0x62dd  28
Summary   0.0.0.0          10.0.3.4          0x80000005  481  0x0  0x5ee1  28
Summary   10.0.2.0         10.0.3.3          0x80000008   58  0x0  0x59e4  28
Summary   10.0.2.0         10.0.3.4          0x80000005  346  0x0  0x63db  28

. . . .


Summary   10.0.9.7         10.0.3.4          0x80000003  913  0x0  0xe54a  28
Summary   172.16.0.12      10.0.3.3          0x80000005  818  0x0  0xd1ae  28
Summary   172.16.0.12      10.0.3.4          0x80000003  913  0x0  0xd9a6  28
```

This (edited) output confirms that numerous network summary LSAs (type 3s) are present in r1's LSDB. To quickly verify that inter- and intra-area routes are present, we confirm that OSPF routes exist for all loopback addresses:

```
lab@r1> show route protocol ospf | match /32
10.0.3.3/32        *[OSPF/10] 00:17:02, metric 1
10.0.3.4/32        *[OSPF/10] 00:17:02, metric 2
10.0.3.5/32        *[OSPF/10] 00:17:02, metric 2
10.0.6.2/32        *[OSPF/10] 00:17:02, metric 1
10.0.9.6/32        *[OSPF/10] 00:17:02, metric 3
10.0.9.7/32        *[OSPF/10] 00:17:02, metric 3
224.0.0.5/32       *[OSPF/10] 00:53:23, metric 1
```

With seven routers in the test bed, we expect to see OSPF routes to six remote router loopback addresses. Because r1's loopback address was not learned through OSPF, its absence in the previous display is also as expected. These results confirm that all aspects of the stub area configuration example have been met.

Totally Stubby Areas

Now that area 10's stub behavior has been confirmed, your new goal is to convert area 10 into a totally stubby area that meets the following criteria:

- r1 and r2 are internal area 10 routers.
- No type 5 or type 3 LSAs in area 10.
- Loopback addresses of all routers reachable from area 10.
- No static routes in area 10.

Based on the specified criteria and our existing configurations, it should be apparent that to meet the new criteria, all we must do is eliminate the type 3 LSAs that differentiate a stub area from a totally stubby area. The following command, issued on area 1's ABRs only, does the trick:

```
[edit protocols ospf area 0.0.0.10]
lab@r4# set stub no-summaries
```

Knowing all the OSPF LSA numbers and types, which routers generate them, and how they are used, is crucial for lab-based examinations. For example, you may be given a requirement with wording to the effect of "block LSA type 3's." Not knowing that a type 3 LSA is a network summary will make an otherwise simple configuration requirement seem much more difficult. The no-summaries option will likely not jump out at you when you are looking for something that references a type 3 LSA.

After committing this change on r3 and r4, the conversion of area 10 from a stub area to a totally stubby area should be complete.

Verify Totally Stubby Area Operation

To confirm that all requirements for this example have been met, we simply need to verify that summary LSAs are no longer contained in area 10's LSDB, and that we still have inter-area connectivity through the default route generated by the ABRs:

```
lab@r1> show ospf database netsummary

    OSPF link state database, area 0.0.0.10
 Type       ID              Adv Rtr          Seq      Age  Opt  Cksum  Len
 Summary  0.0.0.0         10.0.3.3         0x80000007  265  0x0  0x60de  28
 Summary  0.0.0.0         10.0.3.4         0x80000006  279  0x0  0x5ce2  28
```

As hoped for, the only summaries that are present in area 10 are those being used to describe the default routes that are being introduced by area 10's ABRs (r3 and r4). The next command verifies that inter-area routes are no longer present in the totally stubby area:

```
lab@r1> show route protocol ospf | match /32
10.0.6.2/32        *[OSPF/10] 00:38:16, metric 1
224.0.0.5/32       *[OSPF/10] 01:14:37, metric 1
```

We see that the lack of summaries has caused the disappearance of all inter-area routes. We now trace a route to both external and inter-area destinations to confirm that the connectivity requirements have been met:

```
lab@r1> traceroute 200.0.0.1
traceroute to 200.0.0.1 (200.0.0.1), 30 hops max, 40 byte packets
 1  10.0.4.13 (10.0.4.13)  0.359 ms  0.246 ms  0.219 ms
 2  10.0.2.1 (10.0.2.1)  0.649 ms  0.654 ms  0.875 ms
 3  10.0.8.10 (10.0.8.10)  0.856 ms  0.709 ms  0.872 ms
 4  10.0.8.10 (10.0.8.10)  0.861 ms !H  0.701 ms !H  0.872 ms !H
```

The trace to the external prefix works, so connectivity to inter-area destinations is now confirmed by tracing the route to the loopback address of r6:

```
lab@r1> traceroute 10.0.9.6
traceroute to 10.0.9.6 (10.0.9.6), 30 hops max, 40 byte packets
 1  10.0.4.13 (10.0.4.13)  0.335 ms  0.248 ms  0.222 ms
 2  10.0.2.1 (10.0.2.1)  0.942 ms  0.673 ms  0.872 ms
 3  10.0.9.6 (10.0.9.6)  0.857 ms  0.696 ms  0.874 ms
```

These results confirm the proper operation of area 10 as a totally stubby area.

Not-So-Stubby Areas (NSSA)

A stub area does not receive external routing information from the backbone, which is great for the reduction of LSDB size, but this restriction on type 5 LSAs cuts both ways, because a stub area cannot introduce external routing into the backbone either. A not-so-stubby area (NSSA) addresses this issue by defining a new LSA type (type 7) that allows an NSSA to support the presence of ASBRs and their corresponding external routing information. By default, type 7 external LSAs are converted by the NSSA's ABRs into conventional type 5 LSAs for flooding throughout the routing domain. The translation of type 7 LSAs to type 5 LSAs can be controlled at the ABR using area range statements with the `restrict` keyword.

As with stub areas, an NSSA is identified through a special setting in the OSPF options field (the *N* bit) with the intent being the assurance that all routers in a NSSA agree on the area's type; adjacencies will not form if two routers disagree as to the area's type. JUNOS software allows the filtering of network summary LSAs (LSA type 3s) into a NSSA, despite the wording of RFC 1587 that indicates network summary LSAs *must* be imported into a NSSA to ensure that OSPF internal routes will always be chosen over AS external routes. While no official name exists for such a beast, this author feels it is valid to refer to a NSSA that is configured to filter network summaries as a Totally Not-So-Stubby Area (TNSSA).

Not-So-Stubby Area Configuration

To demonstrate NSSA configuration and operation, area 10 will be converted into an NSSA that must comply with the following criteria:

- No type 5 or type 3 LSAs in area 10.

- Define and redistribute static route 3/8 into OSPF from r1 using a metric of 10. You must ensure that all routers adjust this metric to reflect their OSPF cost to reach r1.

- Inter-area and external prefixes must be reachable from area 10.

- No other static routes are permitted in area 10.

The following commands get things started on r1 by defining the static route and the policy needed to correctly redistribute it into OSPF with type 1 external metric:

```
[edit routing-options]
lab@r1# set static route 3/8 reject
```

```
[edit]
lab@r1# edit policy-options policy-statement r1-stat

[edit policy-options policy-statement r1-stat]
lab@r1# set term 1 from protocol static

[edit policy-options policy-statement r1-stat]
lab@r1# set term 1 from route-filter 3/8 exact

[edit policy-options policy-statement r1-stat]
lab@r1# set term 1 then metric 10

[edit policy-options policy-statement r1-stat]
lab@r1# set term 1 then external type 1
```

By setting the external metric to a type 1, you ensure that each router will increase the metric based on its cost to the advertising ASBR. By default, routes redistributed into OSPF use a type 2 metric, which does not increase based on the OSPF cost to the originating ASBR. A working policy is shown next:

```
[edit]
lab@r1# show policy-options
policy-statement r1-stat {
    term 1 {
        from {
            protocol static;
            route-filter 3.0.0.0/8 exact;
        }
        then {
            metric 10;
            external {
                type 1;
            }
            accept;
        }
    }
}
```

The policy is then applied to r1's main OSPF instance as export:

```
[edit]
lab@r1# set protocols ospf export r1-stat
```

The following commands convert area 10 from a stub area to a NSSA. The commands shown next for r1 also need to be entered and committed on r2:

```
[edit protocols ospf area 0.0.0.10]
lab@r1# set nssa
```

Wow, that seemed too easy! The modified OSPF configuration for r1 is as follows with the NSSA-related changes highlighted:

```
[edit protocols ospf area 0.0.0.10]
lab@r1# show
nssa;
interface fe-0/0/2.0;
interface fe-0/0/1.200;
```

After committing the changes on r1, the loss of all adjacencies is expected due to the area type mismatch. This condition will persist until all routers in area 10 have been reconfigured to view the area as a NSSA.

```
[edit protocols ospf area 0.0.0.10]
lab@r1# commit
commit complete
```

```
[edit protocols ospf area 0.0.0.10]
lab@r1# run show ospf neighbor
```

The following commands, entered on both r3 and r4, correctly configure the NSSA's ABRs:

```
[edit protocols ospf area 0.0.0.10]
lab@r4# set nssa no-summaries default-lsa type-7 metric-type 2
```

```
[edit protocols ospf area 0.0.0.10]
lab@r4# set nssa default-lsa default-metric 10
```

The modified NSSA ABR configuration is shown next with highlights:

```
edit protocols ospf area 0.0.0.10]
lab@r4# show
nssa {
    default-lsa {
        default-metric 10;
        metric-type 2;
        type-7;
    }
```

```
    no-summaries;
}
interface fe-0/0/1.0;
```

Once again, a `default-metric` setting is required to trigger the generation of the default route needed for routing to external (and in this example, inter-area) destinations. Normally, the default route injected into a NSSA will be a type 3 (network-summary), so configuration of a type 7–based default route and the inclusion of the `no-summaries` statement are needed to comply with the "no type 3 LSA" restriction of this configuration example. The external metric type for the default route is not specified in the configuration criteria, and so is left to the exam candidate's discretion. In this example, a type 2 metric (the default) has been explicitly configured.

NSSA Verification

The same set of commands used to verify stub area operation will now be applied to the NSSA. We start by confirming there are no type 5 or type 3 LSAs in area 10:

```
lab@r1> show ospf database netsummary

    OSPF link state database, area 0.0.0.10


lab@r1> show ospf database extern


lab@r1>
```

Assuming that the external and summary LSAs are still present in the ABRs, these results confirm that we are dealing with some type of totally stubby area, as both type 5 and type 3 LSAs are being filtered at the ABRs. We now confirm the area's type and the correct operation of r1's OSPF export policy:

```
lab@r1> show ospf database nssa

    OSPF link state database, area 0.0.0.10
Type      ID              Adv Rtr           Seq        Age   Opt  Cksum  Len
NSSA    0.0.0.0         10.0.3.3        0x80000003  1276  0x0  0xc3f2  36
NSSA    0.0.0.0         10.0.3.4        0x80000003  1429  0x0  0xbdf7  36
NSSA    *3.0.0.0        10.0.6.1        0x80000001    42  0x8  0xe9b1  36
```

Most excellent! The presence of type 7 LSAs confirms the area's type as a NSSA, and the highlighted portion of this output also confirms that r1 is exporting its 3/8 static route. It can also be observed that both of the area's ABRs are correctly sourcing a default route into the NSSA. By adding the `detail` switch, we can also confirm the correct metric setting and external metric type for the 3/8 route being advertised by r1, as highlighted in the following:

```
lab@r1> show ospf database nssa detail
```

```
     OSPF link state database, area 0.0.0.10
  Type        ID                  Adv Rtr           Seq       Age  Opt  Cksum  Len
NSSA      0.0.0.0             10.0.3.3          0x80000003  1504 0x0  0xc3f2  36
  mask 0.0.0.0
  Type 2, TOS 0x0, metric 10, fwd addr 0.0.0.0, tag 0.0.0.0
NSSA      0.0.0.0             10.0.3.4          0x80000003  1657 0x0  0xbdf7  36
  mask 0.0.0.0
  Type 2, TOS 0x0, metric 10, fwd addr 0.0.0.0, tag 0.0.0.0
NSSA      *3.0.0.0            10.0.6.1          0x80000001   270 0x8  0xe9b1  36
  mask 255.0.0.0
  Type 1, TOS 0x0, metric 10, fwd addr 10.0.6.1, tag 0.0.0.0
```

We now compare the metric seen in area 10 with that being calculated by routers in other areas to verify the type 1 external metric has been adjusted to reflect each router's OSPF cost to reach r1:

```
lab@r6> show route 3/8

inet.0: 28 destinations, 28 routes (28 active, 0 holddown, 0 hidden)
+ = Active Route, - = Last Active, * = Both


3.0.0.0/8           *[OSPF/150] 00:06:33, metric 14, tag 0
                     > to 10.0.8.6 via fe-0/1/0.0
```

The route entry for the 3/8 prefix in r6 reveals that the initial metric value of 10 has been increased by 4, which confirms that a type 1 metric has been attached to the routes as per the configuration requirements. However, you may have noticed that r6's cost to reach route 3/8 seems a bit higher than expected, considering that the three links that separate r6 from r1 should each have an OSPF cost of 1. Because this discrepancy may indicate a configuration problem or hardware malfunction, further investigation is warranted. To determine if an interface is down, we display the route to r1's lo0 interface as seen from r6:

```
lab@r6> show route 10.0.6.1

inet.0: 28 destinations, 28 routes (28 active, 0 holddown, 0 hidden)
+ = Active Route, - = Last Active, * = Both


10.0.6.1/32         *[OSPF/10] 00:27:34, metric 3
                     > to 10.0.8.6 via fe-0/1/0.0
```

Based on these results, we can conclude that all links are functional between r6 and r1, as the route metric of 3 correctly reflects the summation of the OSPF cost, which by default is 1 for any link that is equal to or faster than 100Mbps for each of the three links that make up the optimal path between r6 and r1. The following sidebar explains why there is a metric discrepancy between the OSPF route to r1's loopback address and the OSPF metric associated with the external prefix being advertised by r1. For our purposes, we can conclude that all is working as per design and move on with the task of NSSA verification.

 Real World Scenario

Metric Mania

Because r6 crosses three links to reach r1, a path metric of *3* is the expected (and confirmed) value. Knowing that 10 + 3 is 13 can cause confusion when it is noted that the external route to 3/8 shows a path metric of 14. This confusion might cause some exam candidates to try chasing down what is perceived to be a problem, when in fact the network is behaving normally.

The answer to this riddle lies in the way that the ABRs in a NSSA translate type 7 LSAs into type 5 LSAs for flooding throughout the OSPF domain. Because multiple ABRs can exist in a NSSA, having each ABR translate the type 7 LSAs could produce extra flooding traffic that would result in more or less redundant LSDB entries. The NSSA specification addresses this problem by indicating that the type 7–to–type 5 translation should be performed by the ABR with the highest RID on behalf of the entire NSSA. While this approach improves protocol scalability, it comes at the potential cost of less-than-ideal routing in some topologies (such as in this case, where packets from r6 that are destined for r1 are being forced to endure an extra hop through r4) and can result in the whole NSSA being black-holed if the ABR that is performing type 7 translation should lose its connectivity to the backbone while maintaining connectivity to the NSSA. Some vendors can enable LSA translations on all NSSA ABRs (in violation of the RFC), but at this time JUNOS software does not support this behavior. The traceroute output shown here confirms that the metric at r6 is higher than expected due to the behavior described previously:

```
[edit]
lab@r6# run traceroute 3.0.0.1
traceroute to 3.0.0.1 (3.0.0.1), 30 hops max, 40 byte packets
 1  10.0.8.6 (10.0.8.6)  0.330 ms  0.245 ms  0.215 ms
 2  10.0.2.10 (10.0.2.10)  0.269 ms  0.246 ms  0.232 ms
 3  10.0.4.10 (10.0.4.10)  0.180 ms  0.167 ms  0.155 ms
 4  10.0.4.5 (10.0.4.5)  0.496 ms  0.694 ms  0.378 ms
 5  10.0.4.5 (10.0.4.5)  0.363 ms !H  0.690 ms !H  0.376 ms !H
```

To test that the default route is providing connectivity to routes outside of area 10, we perform a few traceroutes to key targets such as r6's loopback and the external route 200.0.0.0/24 coming from r7:

```
[edit]
lab@r1# run traceroute 10.0.9.6
traceroute to 10.0.9.6 (10.0.9.6), 30 hops max, 40 byte packets
 1  10.0.4.13 (10.0.4.13)  0.351 ms  0.249 ms  0.222 ms
 2  10.0.2.1 (10.0.2.1)  0.724 ms  1.166 ms  0.872 ms
 3  10.0.9.6 (10.0.9.6)  0.859 ms  1.191 ms  0.876 ms

lab@r2# run traceroute 200.0.0.1
traceroute to 200.0.0.1 (200.0.0.1), 30 hops max, 40 byte packets
 1  10.0.4.1 (10.0.4.1)  0.393 ms  0.315 ms  0.234 ms
 2  10.0.2.1 (10.0.2.1)  1.281 ms  0.494 ms  0.359 ms
 3  10.0.8.10 (10.0.8.10)  0.356 ms  0.655 ms  0.374 ms
 4  10.0.8.10 (10.0.8.10)  0.360 ms !H  0.665 ms !H  0.368 ms !H
```

The success of these traceroutes confirms that all NSSA requirements have been achieved.

Address Summarization

OSPF is capable of supporting classless addressing functions such as subnetting and supernetting because it includes a network mask in conjunction with the prefixes carried in the various LSAs that are used to advertise reachability. The ability to support discontiguous subnets and address summarization is one of the main benefits that OSPF provides when compared to classful protocols like RIP version 1.

Address summarization and filtering can be performed at ABRs by specifying one or more area-range statements at either the[edit protocols ospf area area-number] or [edit protocols ospf area area-number nssa] hierarchical levels, depending on what types of routes are being summarized. An area range statement contained within the nssa stanza is used only to coalesce or filter type 7 LSAs before they are translated into type 5 externals for submission to the backbone area. In contrast, an area range statement specified in the area area-number stanza is used only to summarize and filter intra-area prefixes.

Configure Summarization

Route summarization and NSSA external route filtering will be demonstrated in the following configuration tasks:

- Summarize all the intra-area prefixes into the backbone area.
- Block the 3/8 static route from leaving area 10.

This configuration example begins with the configuration of route summarization on r5. We first examine the current state of r3's routing table, as it relates to the prefixes assigned to area 1. This "before-and-after" approach will best demonstrate the effects of address summarization.

The proposed summarization prefix and mask pair of 10.0.8/23 is first used to filter the routing table contents of r5. This allows the candidate to accurately gauge the summarization effect that will result when the same prefix/mask is configured as part of an area range statement:

```
lab@r3# run show route protocol ospf 10.0.8/23

inet.0: 29 destinations, 31 routes (29 active, 0 holddown, 0 hidden)
+ = Active Route, - = Last Active, * = Both

10.0.8.0/30        *[OSPF/10] 00:04:38, metric 3
                    > via at-0/1/0.35
10.0.8.4/30        *[OSPF/10] 00:04:38, metric 2
                    > via at-0/1/0.35
10.0.8.8/30        *[OSPF/10] 00:04:38, metric 2
                    > via at-0/1/0.35
10.0.9.6/32        *[OSPF/10] 00:04:38, metric 2
                    > via at-0/1/0.35
10.0.9.7/32        *[OSPF/10] 00:04:38, metric 2
                    > via at-0/1/0.35
```

These results demonstrate that all of area 1's internal prefixes can be correctly summarized with a 10.0.8.0/23 prefix and mask. Knowing that the summarization mask is valid, the following command is now used to configure the summarization of the prefixes in area 1:

```
[edit protocols ospf area 0.0.0.1]
lab@r5# set area-range 10.0.8/23
```

> When performing summarization for an OSPF area, do not forget to also summarize the loopback addresses, unless otherwise required by your lab scenario.

The modified configuration for area 1's ABR (r5) is shown next with the summarization changes highlighted:

```
[edit protocols ospf area 0.0.0.1]
lab@r5# show
area-range 10.0.8.0/23;
authentication-type simple; # SECRET-DATA
interface fe-0/0/0.0 {
    authentication-key "$9$Kw2WX-UDkqfz"; # SECRET-DATA
```

```
}
interface fe-0/0/1.0 {
    authentication-key "$9$32M9/AOvMXxds"; # SECRET-DATA
}
```

After committing the change, we again look at r3's routing table for area 1 prefixes:

```
lab@r3> show route 10.0.8.0/23

inet.0: 25 destinations, 27 routes (25 active, 0 holddown, 0 hidden)
+ = Active Route, - = Last Active, * = Both

10.0.8.0/23        *[OSPF/10] 00:00:08, metric 3
                   > via at-0/1/0.35
```

Good—the fewer routes the better! From the perspective of a backbone router, a single prefix/mask pair now represents all of area 1's destinations. Prior to summarization, five prefix/mask pairings were needed to correctly route packets into area 1. We now add the required summarization and filtering to area 10's ABRs with the following commands:

```
[edit protocols ospf area 0.0.0.10]
lab@r3# set area-range 10.0.4.0/22

[edit protocols ospf area 0.0.0.10]
lab@r3# set nssa area-range 3/8 restrict
```

A key point to this task is the need to specify an area range both at the area and NSSA levels of the configuration. The NSSA-related area range statements control type 7 translations, and so allow the summarization and filtering of external routes in a NSSA. There is no mechanism in JUNOS software to summarize or filter type 5 LSAs using area-range statements. Options for the control of type 5 LSAs include the configuration of external route aggregates at the source ASBR, or the deployment of stub areas, which automatically filter external routes.

The resulting NSSA configuration for the route summarization and NSSA external route-filtering tasks are shown next with highlighted changes:

```
[edit protocols ospf area 0.0.0.10]
lab@r3# show
nssa {
    default-lsa {
        default-metric 10;
        metric-type 2;
        type-7;
    }
    no-summaries;
```

```
     area-range 3.0.0.0/8 restrict;
}
area-range 10.0.4.0/22;
interface fe-0/0/1.0;
interface fe-0/0/0.0;
```

Once again we judge the effects of summarization by examining a backbone router that does not attach to area 10, which in this example happens to be r5:

```
lab@r5> traceroute 10.0.6.2
traceroute to 10.0.6.2 (10.0.6.2), 30 hops max, 40 byte packets
 1  10.0.2.2 (10.0.2.2)  1.621 ms  1.526 ms  1.089 ms
 2  10.0.6.2 (10.0.6.2)  1.039 ms  1.000 ms  0.624 ms
```

With reachability to area 10 confirmed, we now check for proper summarization:

```
lab@r5> show route 10.0.6.2

inet.0: 23 destinations, 25 routes (23 active, 0 holddown, 0 hidden)
+ = Active Route, - = Last Active, * = Both

10.0.4.0/22        *[OSPF/10] 00:00:27, metric 3
                    > via at-0/2/1.35


lab@r5> show route 10.0.4.5

inet.0: 23 destinations, 25 routes (23 active, 0 holddown, 0 hidden)
+ = Active Route, - = Last Active, * = Both

10.0.4.0/22        *[OSPF/10] 00:02:03, metric 3
                    > via at-0/2/1.35
```

The same aggregate route is returned for the area's physical and loopback addresses, which indicates that summarization is working. It may be acceptable to send two aggregates for an area—one encompassing the physical addresses and another to advertise the loopback address space—especially if the two address blocks are discontiguous.

Lastly, we confirm that the external route is being properly filtered at the NSSA boundaries with the following command issued on r5:

```
lab@r5> show route 3/8

lab@r5>
```

The lack of a route to 3/8 on r5 indicates that the external route is being properly filtered by r3 and r4.

Virtual Links

OSPF allows the creation of a virtual link that can be used to repair a partitioned backbone, or to connect a discontiguous area to the backbone. Though virtual links are generally considered evidence of poor network design, the prepared JNCIP exam candidate will be able to configure and test them as required.

The following configuration task is designed to illustrate the configuration and operational aspects of a virtual link:

- Ensure that r7 can ping destinations in area 10 when r5 loses backbone connectivity (as shown in Figure 3.6).

FIGURE 3.6   OSPF virtual links

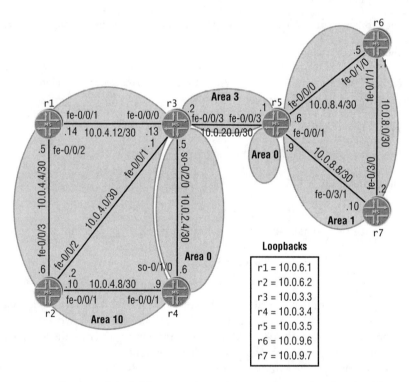

Figure 3.6 provides a modified OSPF topology showing that r5 has lost backbone connectivity due to the deactivation of its at-0/1/0 and as1 interfaces. This topology also shows the addition of a new area, area 3, which has already been configured between r5 and r3. r5's area 3 definition is shown in the following:

```
[edit]
lab@r5# show protocols ospf area 3
interface fe-0/0/3.0;
```

Because summary LSAs should be exchanged only over the backbone area, the loss of backbone connectivity will result in connectivity problems between areas 10 and 1, as shown in the following screen dumps. A key point is that even though r5 is receiving a summary LSA for the 10.0.4/22 area 10 aggregate from r3, the router refuses to install the route. This is because r6 expects to receive such summaries via area 0, not area 3:

```
lab@r5> show ospf database netsummary extensive advertising-router 10.0.3.3 area 3

    OSPF link state database, area 0.0.0.3
 Type       ID                 Adv Rtr          Seq      Age  Opt  Cksum  Len
 Summary  10.0.2.4            10.0.3.3         0x80000005  137  0x2  0x1922  28
   mask 255.255.255.252
   TOS 0x0, metric 1
   Aging timer 00:57:43
   Installed 00:02:16 ago, expires in 00:57:43, sent 00:02:17 ago
 Summary  10.0.3.3            10.0.3.3         0x80000005  137  0x2  0x2019  28
   mask 255.255.255.255
   TOS 0x0, metric 0
```

Despite the presence of area 0 and area 10 summary LSAs, r5 has not installed any of the routes because the summaries were not received over the backbone area:

```
lab@r5> show route 10.0.4/22

lab@r5>

lab@r5> show route 10.0.3.3

lab@r5>
```

To restore connectivity over the partitioned backbone, you will need to establish a virtual link that transits area 3 and interconnects r5 to the backbone-attached r3. Virtual links are always configured under area 0 and can be configured only on an ABR. By definition, any router with a virtual link becomes a backbone router, and one end of the virtual link must terminate at a router that is actually backbone attached.

The following commands configure a virtual link on r5 and display the resulting virtual link configuration:

```
[edit protocols ospf area 0]
lab@r5# set virtual-link neighbor-id 10.0.3.3 transit-area 3

[edit protocols ospf area 0.0.0.0]
lab@r5# show | match virtual
virtual-link neighbor-id 10.0.3.3 transit-area 0.0.0.3;
```

With the definition of the virtual link, you have effectively re-attached r5 to area 0 by instructing it to establish a virtual adjacency to r3 by transiting area 3. It should be noted that the virtual link endpoints are defined based on the remote router's RID, not its physical address, and that the virtual link can only cross one transit area. Once committed, we confirm that r5 is now trying to establish an adjacency with r3:

```
lab@r5> show ospf interface
Interface      State      Area          DR ID          BDR ID      Nbrs
lo0.0          DR         0.0.0.0       10.0.3.5       0.0.0.0        0
vl-10.0.3.3    PtToPt     0.0.0.0       0.0.0.0        0.0.0.0        0
fe-0/0/0.0     BDR        0.0.0.1       10.0.9.6       10.0.3.5       1
fe-0/0/1.0     BDR        0.0.0.1       10.0.9.7       10.0.3.5       1
fe-0/0/3.0     DR         0.0.0.3       10.0.3.5       10.0.3.3       1
```

The presence of a virtual link "interface" confirms that r5 is trying to communicate with the backbone-attached router identified as 10.0.3.3. The lack of a neighbor on the virtual link is due to the fact that r3's virtual link back to r5 has not yet been configured.

The following command is now entered (and committed) on r3 to complete the definition of the virtual link:

```
[edit protocols ospf area 0.0.0.0]
lab@r3# set virtual-link neighbor-id 10.0.3.5 transit-area 3
```

We now recheck the status of the virtual link from the perspective of r6:

```
lab@r5> show ospf neighbor
  Address        Interface        State     ID           Pri  Dead
10.0.20.2        vl-10.0.3.3      Full      10.0.3.3       0   31
10.0.8.5         fe-0/0/0.0       Full      10.0.9.6     128   32
10.0.8.10        fe-0/0/1.0       Full      10.0.9.7     128   35
10.0.20.2        fe-0/0/3.0       Full      10.0.3.3     128   39
```

The full adjacency status is a very good sign. The next command confirms the presence of the aggregate route for area 10 on r5:

```
lab@r5> show route 10.0.4/22

inet.0: 21 destinations, 21 routes (21 active, 0 holddown, 0 hidden)
+ = Active Route, - = Last Active, * = Both

10.0.4.0/22        *[OSPF/10] 00:00:43, metric 3
                    > to 10.0.20.2 via fe-0/0/3.0
```

The aggregate route's presence indicates that the configuration of the virtual link was successful. The final check is to confirm that r7 can now reach area 10 destinations:

```
[edit]
lab@r7# run traceroute 10.0.6.2
traceroute to 10.0.6.2 (10.0.6.2), 30 hops max, 40 byte packets
 1  10.0.8.9 (10.0.8.9)  0.366 ms  0.294 ms  0.239 ms
 2  10.0.20.2 (10.0.20.2)  0.322 ms  0.284 ms  0.256 ms
 3  10.0.6.2 (10.0.6.2)  0.211 ms  0.244 ms  0.189 ms
```

After confirming the operation of the virtual link backbone, you should restore backbone connectivity on r5 by reactivating its at-0/2/1.35 and as1 interfaces. After r5 reestablishes its area 0 adjacencies, the virtual link and area 3 definitions should be removed from r3 and r5. The results of this traceroute confirm that r5's area 0 interfaces have been correctly reactivated:

```
[edit]
lab@r7# run traceroute 10.0.6.2
traceroute to 10.0.6.2 (10.0.6.2), 30 hops max, 40 byte packets
 1  10.0.8.9 (10.0.8.9)  0.347 ms  0.247 ms  0.217 ms
 2  10.0.2.2 (10.0.2.2)  0.870 ms  0.657 ms  0.876 ms
 3  10.0.6.2 (10.0.6.2)  0.500 ms  0.675 ms  0.368 ms
```

OSPF Routing Policy

Export policy can be applied to OSPF to accommodate route redistribution, route tagging, and metric manipulation at ASBRs. JUNOS software does not support the application of import policy for link-state routing protocols such as OSPF. This makes sense when remembering that OSPF exchanges LSAs, not routes, and trying to filter or block incoming LSAs could lead to inconsistent LSDBs, which in turn could result in a protocol malfunction. LSA filtering can only be performed at area borders by deploying stub areas or through the use of area range statements as previously demonstrated in this chapter.

The use of routing policy to accomplish route redistribution has already been demonstrated several times in this chapter, as has the use of policy to set the metric value and type for a redistributed static route. The following configuration example will demonstrate the interaction between route redistribution and global route preference and will also provide examples of RIP configuration and testing in JUNOS software.

Configure OSPF Routing Policy

The topology for this configuration example is shown in Figure 3.7, and the configuration criteria are listed after the figure.

FIGURE 3.7   OSPF policy and redistribution

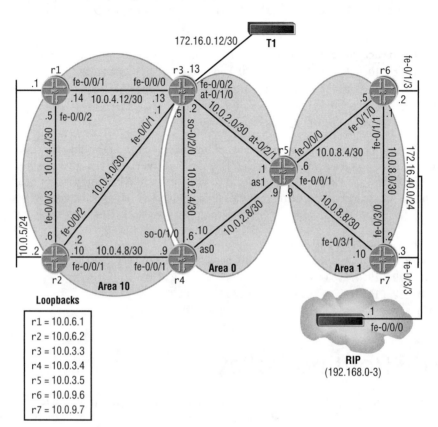

- Redistribute the 10.0.5/25 subnet from both r1 and r2 with a metric of 50 and a route tag value of 420. The metric value must remain 50 on all routers.
- Advertise the 10.0.5/24 prefix to the RIP router from both r6 and r7.
- Advertise RIP routes 192.168.0/24 through 192.168.3/24 into area 1 from both r6 and r7.
- Ensure that the RIP router, r6, and r7 can reach destinations on the 10.0.5/24 subnet.
- No single point of failure should isolate the RIP router from reaching the 10.0.5/24 subnet.

RIP Router Configuration

The pertinent portions of the RIP router configuration are shown and described next:

```
[edit]
lab@rip# show protocols rip
```

```
group test {
    export rip;
    neighbor fe-0/0/0.0;
}
```

The RIP stanza creates a RIP group called *test* containing the RIP router's fe-0/0/0 interface. The members of the *test* group will export routes based on a policy called *rip*, the contents of which is shown next:

```
lab@rip# show policy-options
policy-statement rip {
    term 1 {
        from protocol [ static rip ];
        then accept;
    }
}
```

The *rip* policy will redistribute routes learned through the static or RIP protocols into the RIP protocol. Odd as it may seem, the default JUNOS software export policy for RIP is to reject everything, even RIP routes! This makes RIP unique in the JUNOS software environment because all other protocols have a default export policy that will accept routes learned from that particular protocol. The end result is that export policy is almost always needed when using RIP, even when it is deployed in a simple point-to-point topology with the intent of simply exchanging RIP routes. This policy will cause the RIP router to advertise all active static and RIP routes to r6 and r7, with the exception of routes that are suppressed due to split horizon.

The RIP router's routing-options stanza contains the various 192.168.x static route definitions that are set to silent discard in this example (this is equivalent to "null 0" in Cisco's IOS):

```
[edit]
lab@rip# show routing-options
static {
    route 192.168.0.0/24 discard;
    route 192.168.1.0/24 discard;
    route 192.168.2.0/24 discard;
    route 192.168.3.0/24 discard;
    }
```

The RIP router's interface configuration correctly sets the addressing for the RIP subnet, and assigns host addresses from each of the 192.168.x static routes to the lo0 address so that pings to host-id *1* on each 192.168.x subnet will complete normally:

```
[edit]
lab@rip# show interfaces
. . .
```

```
fe-0/0/0 {
    unit 0 {
        family inet {
            address 172.16.40.1/24;
        }
    }
}
lo0 {
    unit 0 {
        family inet {
            address 192.168.0.1/32;
            address 192.168.1.1/32;
            address 192.168.2.1/32;
            address 192.168.3.1/32;
        }
    }
}
```

r1 and *r2* OSPF Redistribution Policy

We begin our configuration by creating and applying a policy that will redistribute the 10.0.5/24 direct route from r1 and r2 into OSPF. The following policy works for the requirements of this configuration example; other policy approaches could also be used with similar results. Because the default external metric type is type 2, there is no need to explicitly state the metric type to meet the requirements of this configuration scenario:

```
[edit policy-options policy-statement direct]
lab@r2# show
term 1 {
    from {
        protocol direct;
        route-filter 10.0.5.0/24 exact;
    }
    then {
        metric 50;
        tag 420;
        accept;
    }
}
```

To confirm the redistribution, tagging, and proper connectivity to the 10.0.5/24 subnet, we verify the route's presence and confirm reachability from r7:

```
lab@r7> show route 10.0.5/24

inet.0: 30 destinations, 34 routes (30 active, 0 holddown, 0 hidden)
+ = Active Route, - = Last Active, * = Both


10.0.5.0/24        *[OSPF/150] 00:00:13, metric 50, tag 420
                    > to 10.0.8.9 via fe-0/3/1.0
```

These results confirm that the metric, metric type, and tag values are correct (a type 1 metric would have been incremented above the initial setting of 50, so this must be a type 2 metric). We now confirm that r7 can reach the 10.0.5/24 subnet:

```
[edit]
lab@r7# run traceroute 10.0.5.1
traceroute to 10.0.5.1 (10.0.5.1), 30 hops max, 40 byte packets
 1  10.0.8.9 (10.0.8.9)  0.335 ms  0.248 ms  0.216 ms
 2  10.0.2.10 (10.0.2.10)  0.280 ms  0.244 ms  0.234 ms
 3  10.0.4.10 (10.0.4.10)  0.618 ms  0.694 ms  0.379 ms
 4  10.0.5.1 (10.0.5.1)  0.362 ms  0.700 ms  0.377 ms
```

These results prove that the redistribution of 10.0.5/254 from area 10 is working properly, and that the metric and tag values have been correctly set.

Configure RIP and Redistribution Policy on *r6*

You will now configure r6 to redistribute routes from OSPF to RIP, and in the reverse direction, from RIP back into OSPF. We begin with the following command that configures r6 to run RIP on its fe-0/1/3 interface:

```
[edit protocols rip]
lab@r6# set group rip neighbor fe-0/1/3
```

The resulting RIP configuration is now as follows:

```
[edit protocols rip]
lab@r6# show
group rip {
    neighbor fe-0/1/3.0;
}
```

After committing the changes, we verify that RIP routes are being received from the RIP router:

```
[edit protocols rip]
lab@r6# commit
commit complete

[edit protocols rip]
lab@r6# run show route protocol rip

inet.0: 28 destinations, 28 routes (28 active, 0 holddown, 0 hidden)
+ = Active Route, - = Last Active, * = Both

192.168.0.0/24     *[RIP/100] 00:00:04, metric 2
                    > to 172.16.40.1 via fe-0/1/3.0
192.168.1.0/24     *[RIP/100] 00:00:04, metric 2
                    > to 172.16.40.1 via fe-0/1/3.0
192.168.2.0/24     *[RIP/100] 00:00:04, metric 2
                    > to 172.16.40.1 via fe-0/1/3.0
192.168.3.0/24     *[RIP/100] 00:00:04, metric 2
                    > to 172.16.40.1 via fe-0/1/3.0
224.0.0.9/32       *[RIP/100] 00:00:04, metric 1
```

As previously discussed, the default input policy for RIP is to accept RIP routes and the default RIP export policy is to reject everything, even routes learned through RIP. To effect the redistribution of these RIP routes into OSPF, you must now write and apply a routing policy that will accept RIP routes for export into OSPF:

```
[edit policy-options policy-statement rip-ospf]
lab@r6# set term 1 from protocol rip

[edit policy-options policy-statement rip-ospf]
lab@r6# set term 1 then accept

[edit policy-options policy-statement rip-ospf]
lab@r6# set term 2 then reject
```

The resulting RIP to OSPF redistribution policy is shown next:

```
[edit policy-options policy-statement rip-ospf]
lab@r6# show
term 1 {
    from protocol rip;
    then accept;
```

```
}
term 2 {
    then reject;
}
```

The *rip-ospf* policy is now applied to OSPF as an export policy:

```
[edit]
lab@r6# set protocols ospf export rip-ospf
```

With the export policy in place on r6, we confirm the presence of the 192.168.*x*/24 routes on r5 to verify that RIP-to-OSPF redistribution is working:

```
lab@r5> show route 192.168/16

inet.0: 28 destinations, 30 routes (28 active, 0 holddown, 0 hidden)
+ = Active Route, - = Last Active, * = Both

192.168.0.0/24      *[OSPF/150] 00:01:00, metric 2, tag 0
                    > to 10.0.8.5 via fe-0/0/0.0
192.168.1.0/24      *[OSPF/150] 00:01:00, metric 2, tag 0
                    > to 10.0.8.5 via fe-0/0/0.0
192.168.2.0/24      *[OSPF/150] 00:01:00, metric 2, tag 0
                    > to 10.0.8.5 via fe-0/0/0.0
192.168.3.0/24      *[OSPF/150] 00:01:00, metric 2, tag 0
                    > to 10.0.8.5 via fe-0/0/0.0
```

So far, so good. All the RIP routes are present on r5 as OSPF external routes, and these routes should now be present in the backbone area. The global preference for these external routes will be 150 by default. With RIP to OSPF redistribution working properly, you should now create and apply the policy needed to redistribute the 10.0.5/24 route from OSPF into RIP. The policy shown next will accommodate the requirements of this configuration example, but other policy approaches can also work:

```
[edit policy-options policy-statement ospf-rip]
lab@r6# show
term 1 {
    from {
        protocol ospf;
        route-filter 10.0.5.0/24 exact;
    }
    then accept;
}
term 2 {
```

```
        then reject;
}
```

We now apply the *ospf-rip* policy as export to the *rip* group using the following command:

```
[edit]
lab@r6# set protocols rip group rip export ospf-rip
```

After committing this change, we confirm that the 10.0.5/24 route is now present on the RIP router:

```
lab@rip> show route 10/8

inet.0: 16 destinations, 16 routes (16 active, 0 holddown, 0 hidden)
+ = Active Route, - = Last Active, * = Both

10.0.5.0/24         *[RIP/100] 00:01:38, metric 2
                    > to 172.16.40.2 via fe-0/0/0.0
```

Great, the route is present and active on the RIP router. We now confirm that the RIP router can ping destinations on the 10.0.5/24 subnet:

```
lab@rip> traceroute 10.0.5.1
traceroute to 10.0.5.1 (10.0.5.1), 30 hops max, 40 byte packets
 1  172.16.40.2 (172.16.40.2)  0.202 ms  0.232 ms  0.095 ms
 2  * * *
^C
```

Bummer—despite the presence of the 10.0.5/24 route, the ping and traceroute tests are failing. Because the traceroute results indicate that the RIP router is correctly forwarding the packet to r6, we once again verify that r6 has connectivity to 10.0.5/24:

```
[edit]
lab@r6# run traceroute 10.0.5.1
traceroute to 10.0.5.1 (10.0.5.1), 30 hops max, 40 byte packets
 1  10.0.8.6 (10.0.8.6)  0.330 ms  0.257 ms  0.220 ms
 2  10.0.2.10 (10.0.2.10)  0.285 ms  0.245 ms  0.233 ms
 3  10.0.4.10 (10.0.4.10)  0.176 ms  0.167 ms  0.157 ms
 4  10.0.5.1 (10.0.5.1)  0.508 ms  0.677 ms  0.368 ms
```

This is very strange. The RIP router forwards the packet to r6, and r6 can get to 10.0.5/24, but the RIP router cannot get to 10.0.5/24. Any ideas? A valuable clue can be gained by performing the traceroute from r6 with a packet that is sourced from its fe-0/1/3 interface:

```
[edit]
lab@r6# run traceroute 10.0.5.1 source 172.16.40.2
```

```
traceroute to 10.0.5.1 (10.0.5.1) from 172.16.40.2, 30 hops max, 40 byte packets
 1  *^C
```

The results obtained when the RIP router sources its traceroute from its lo0 interface are also quite revealing:

```
[edit]
lab@rip# run traceroute 10.0.5.1 source 192.168.0.1
traceroute to 10.0.5.1 (10.0.5.1) from 192.168.0.1, 30 hops max, 40 byte packets
 1  172.16.40.2 (172.16.40.2)  0.202 ms  0.224 ms  0.093 ms
 2  10.0.8.6 (10.0.8.6)  0.316 ms  0.292 ms  0.278 ms
 3  10.0.2.10 (10.0.2.10)  0.346 ms  0.307 ms  0.295 ms
 4  10.0.4.10 (10.0.4.10)  0.232 ms  0.230 ms  0.219 ms
 5  10.0.5.1 (10.0.5.1)  0.590 ms  0.358 ms  0.475 ms
```

The information gleaned by sourcing the traceroute from the non-default interfaces reveal the true nature of the problem—which, it would seem, has nothing to do with our OSPF and RIP redistribution policies. The real issue here is the lack of OSPF routes for the 172.16.40.*x* addressing being used on the r6-to-RIP router link. Listing r6's fe-0/1/3 interface as passive under the OSPF process, or redistributing the 172.16.40.0/24 address from either the RIP router, or r6, will resolve this issue. Being inherently lazy, this author has opted to make a single change on the RIP router that will solve this problem for now for r6, and later for r7:

```
[edit routing-options]
lab@rip# set static route 172.16.40/28 discard
[edit routing-options]
lab@rip# commit
commit complete
```

The 172.16.40/28 static route will be redistributed into RIP, and from there into OSPF, by both r6 and r7. This ensures that routers within the OSPF domain will know how to route packets back to the 172.16.40/28 subnet. The effects are confirmed after the change has been committed:

```
[edit routing-options]
lab@rip# run traceroute 10.0.5.1
traceroute to 10.0.5.1 (10.0.5.1), 30 hops max, 40 byte packets
 1  172.16.40.2 (172.16.40.2)  0.199 ms  0.228 ms  0.096 ms
 2  10.0.8.6 (10.0.8.6)  0.333 ms  0.292 ms  0.275 ms
 3  10.0.2.10 (10.0.2.10)  0.331 ms  0.306 ms  0.295 ms
 4  10.0.4.10 (10.0.4.10)  0.237 ms  0.229 ms  0.217 ms
 5  10.0.5.1 (10.0.5.1)  0.470 ms  0.357 ms  0.479 ms
```

Based on these results, it would appear that most of the configuration requirements have been met for this configuration example, at least as far as the configuration and operation of r6 is concerned. You must now complete the configuration by ensuring that both r6 and r5 perform OSPF and RIP route redistribution to ensure that neither r6 nor r7 represents a single point of failure in the network.

Real World Scenario

Why a /28 Netmask for a /24 Subnet?

The reader may find it odd that a static route for the 172.16.40/24 subnet was created with a 28-bit mask in this example. This approach was used to ensure that the static route would be active, and therefore eligible for export, when compared against the directly connected 172.16.40/24 subnet, because direct routes have a higher global preference than static routes. Because the /28 mask is more specific than the /24 direct route, the static route will now be considered active, and the /28 mask encompasses host addresses in the range of 1–15, which meets all connectivity requirements of this configuration example. This approach was taken because it eliminated the need for export policy route-filter statements that would otherwise have been needed to prevent the redistribution of other direct routes (such as the 192.168.x.1/32 lo0 addresses) on the RIP router.

Configure RIP and Policy on *r7*

To complete the OSPF policy task, the operator in this example has decided to mirror the RIP and routing policy configuration of r6 into r7, because this can be performed easily using load merge terminal and because this configuration appears to be working great for r6.

Because the use of load merge can be an important timesaver, the operational steps needed to rapidly modify r7 with the RIP and redistribution policy–related configuration from r6 are outlined next.

First, the operator displays the protocol and policy-options stanzas from r6's configuration, as shown in Listing 3.4:

Listing 3.4: *r6*'s Protocol and Policy Stanzas

```
[edit]
lab@r6# show protocols
ospf {
    export rip-ospf;
    area 0.0.0.1 {
        authentication-type simple; # SECRET-DATA
        interface fe-0/1/0.0 {
            authentication-key "$9$GEjkPpu1Icl"; # SECRET-DATA
        }
        interface fe-0/1/1.0 {
            authentication-key "$9$/hZQAu18LN-wg"; # SECRET-DATA
        }
```

```
        }
    }
rip {
    group rip {
        export ospf-rip;
        neighbor fe-0/1/3.0;
    }
}
```

```
policy-statement rip-ospf {
    term 1 {
        from protocol rip;
        then accept;
    }
    term 2 {
        then reject;
    }
}
policy-statement ospf-rip {
    term 1 {
        from {
            protocol ospf;
            route-filter 10.0.5.0/24 exact;
        }
        then accept;
    }
    term 2 {
        then reject;
    }
}
```

After verifying that the information is generic enough to apply to r7's environment, the highlighted portions shown in Listing 3.4 are removed, the RIP interface name is changed, and curly braces are added as shown in Listing 3.5:

Listing 3.5: Modified Protocol and Policy Stanzas
```
protocols {
rip {
    group rip {
        export ospf-rip;
```

```
        neighbor fe-0/3/3.0;
    }
}
            }
policy-options {
policy-statement rip-ospf {
    term 1 {
        from protocol rip;
        then accept;
    }
    term 2 {
        then reject;
    }
}
policy-statement ospf-rip {
    term 1 {
        from {
            protocol ospf;
            route-filter 10.0.5.0/24 exact;
        }
        then accept;
    }
    term 2 {
        then reject;
    }
}
        }
```

The resulting code is then loaded into r7 using the `load merge terminal` option. After the
load completes, the operator manually applies the `rip-ospf` policy as an OSPF export policy
and commits the configuration. Many operators find that having to remember where the curly
braces go, and what statements still have to be configured after the merge is performed, makes
the whole "pasting from a terminal thing" too much bother for all but the most compelling of
cases. In the final analysis, the time saved from cut-and-paste operations may be negligible, or
may be significant, depending on your typing skill and overall familiarity with the JUNOS software command-line interface (CLI).

 WARNING   Opting for `load override terminal` would have left you feeling relieved that
your old config was only a `rollback 1` away, or at least you will be relieved
once you realize that you have just blown away r7's configuration by overwriting it with a few measly code snippets intended only to augment its configuration with RIP support and route redistribution policies.

Verify OSPF Policy and Redistribution

After adding the RIP configuration and redistribution policies to r7, we now verify that all is well with our network by confirming the RIP router has two next hops for 10.0.5/25 (both r6 and r7 should be advertising the route to the RIP router), and that the RIP router can reach destinations on the 10.0.5/24 subnet:

```
lab@rip> show route 10/8

inet.0: 15 destinations, 15 routes (15 active, 0 holddown, 0 hidden)
+ = Active Route, - = Last Active, * = Both

10.0.5.0/24          *[RIP/100] 00:49:33, metric 2
                     > to 172.16.40.2 via fe-0/0/0.0
```

Darn, there should be two viable and equal-cost next hops for the RIP router. Based on these results, it looks like r7 is not correctly redistributing the 10.0.5/25 prefix. We will investigate the missing next hop in a bit, but we might as well verify forwarding to the 10.0.5/24 subnet while we are on the RIP router:

```
lab@rip> traceroute 10.0.5.1
traceroute to 10.0.5.1 (10.0.5.1), 30 hops max, 40 byte packets
 1  172.16.40.2 (172.16.40.2)  0.196 ms  0.230 ms  0.096 ms
 2  172.16.40.3 (172.16.40.3)  0.148 ms  0.141 ms  0.128 ms
 3  172.16.40.2 (172.16.40.2)  0.159 ms  0.167 ms  0.158 ms


 . . .
29  172.16.40.2 (172.16.40.2)  0.989 ms  0.999 ms  0.987 ms
30  172.16.40.3 (172.16.40.3)  1.021 ms  1.029 ms  1.020 ms
lab@rip>
```

Not good, unless of course you like packet loops! As is so often the case when performing mutual route redistribution, we have managed to create a packet loop somewhere in the network. Seems like we should poke around on r7 due to the indication that it is not advertising the 10.0.5/24 route to the RIP router:

```
lab@r7> show route 10.0.5/24

inet.0: 30 destinations, 36 routes (30 active, 0 holddown, 0 hidden)
+ = Active Route, - = Last Active, * = Both

10.0.5.0/24          *[RIP/100] 00:37:48, metric 2
                     > to 172.16.40.2 via fe-0/3/3.0
```

Interesting. r7 is using a 10.0.5/24 route learned through RIP from r6, which explains why r7 was not listed as a next hop on the RIP router—split horizon is preventing r7 from advertising the 10.0.5/24 prefix back out the interface it was learned on. A quick look at r6 confirms the presence of a loop:

```
lab@r6> show route 10.0.5/24

inet.0: 28 destinations, 34 routes (28 active, 0 holddown, 0 hidden)
+ = Active Route, - = Last Active, * = Both

10.0.5.0/24        *[OSPF/150] 00:37:59, metric 2, tag 0
                    > to 10.0.8.2 via fe-0/1/1.0
```

From these displays, we see that r7 is forwarding packets addressed to 10.0.5/24 through r6 based on a RIP route, while r6 forwards these packets back to r7 based on an OSPF route. As with most tragedies, this mess is caused by a number of individual factors that happen to combine and interact in such a way that the end result can be almost impossible to predict, and in many cases, difficult to diagnose when observed. To better understand what has gone wrong, we need to analyze the network's operation both before and after redistribution was enabled on r7. Figure 3.8 illustrates the situation that existed before r7 was configured to run RIP.

FIGURE 3.8   Single redistribution point

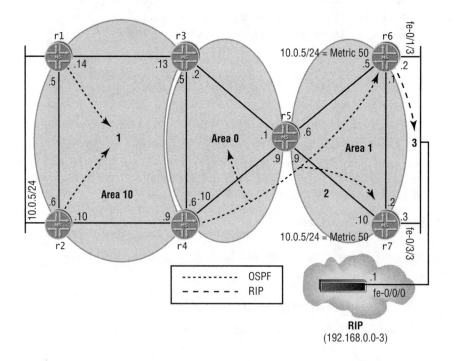

At step 1 we have r1 and r2 flooding type 7 LSAs (NSSA) that advertise the 10.0.5/24 prefix with a type 2 metric setting of 50. r4, the ABR with the highest RID, then translates the type 7 LSAs into a single type 5 that is flooded throughout all non-stub areas, as shown at step 2. Both r6 and r7 receive a copy and install an OSPF route to 10.0.5/24 that correctly points toward r5 with an external metric of 50. This OSPF route is then exported to the RIP segment by r6 where it is received by the RIP router at step 3 of Figure 3.8.

Figure 3.9 shows the effects of bringing r7's RIP and redistribution configuration online, and explains how this packet loop is being created.

FIGURE 3.9   Two redistribution points

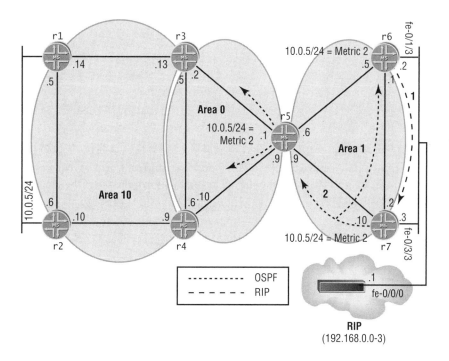

At step 1 on Figure 3.9 we see that, in this case, r6 generates a RIP update before r7, causing r7 to receive a RIP advertisement from r6 that indicates reachability to 10.0.5/24. Because r7's rip-ospf policy accepts all RIP routes, and because the global preference value of RIP is preferred over the default preference value assigned to OSPF external routes, r7 installs the RIP route as active and, true to its export policy, proceeds to redistribute it back into OSPF. This is shown at step 2. By default, r7 attaches a metric value to the route that is equal to the metric that would have been advertised by RIP, which in this example is 2. When r5 and r6 receive r7's external LSA, they both install r7 as the next hop to 10.0.5/24, due to the lower metric value advertised by r7's LSA.

Now that the reason for the packet loop has been diagnosed, the following section will discuss and demonstrate the most common ways of resolving this type of problem.

RIP Import Policy

It is generally considered that the best approach to this problem is to create and apply a RIP import policy that prevents r6 and r7 from accepting each other's routes. There are many ways to write such an import policy, but techniques that use the from next-hop or route filter matching conditions are most common. Typical RIP import policy solutions are shown next:

```
[edit]
lab@r6# show policy-options policy-statement rip-in
term 1 {
    from {
        protocol rip;
        next-hop 172.16.40.1;
    }
    then accept;
}
term 2 {
    then reject;
}
```

The policy shown previously is written with a positive approach, and so requires a *reject all* term to override the default RIP import policy. The policy shown next uses the same principles, but involves less typing:

```
[edit]
lab@r7# show policy-options policy-statement rip-in
from {
    protocol rip;
    next-hop 172.16.40.2;
}
then reject;
```

And lastly, a typical route filtering approach is shown in the following:

```
[edit policy-options]
lab@r7# show policy-statement rip-in
term 1 {
    from {
        route-filter 192.168.0.0/22 orlonger;
    }
    then accept;
}
```

```
term 2 {
    then reject;
}
```

Either of these policies will resolve the packet loop problem when applied to r6 and r7 as a RIP import policy. RIP import policy cannot be applied at the global or group levels, so you apply your import policy at the `neighbor` level of the RIP configuration hierarchy with the following command:

```
[edit protocols rip]
lab@r7# set group rip neighbor fe-0/3/3.0 import rip-in

[edit]
lab@r7# show protocols rip
group rip {
    export ospf-rip;
    neighbor fe-0/3/0.0 {
        import rip-in;
    }
}
```

The RIP import policy method is generally considered the "best" approach to this dilemma, because it results in both r6 and r7 considering the RIP routes as active, and therefore both routers will be exporting the RIP routes into OSPF as external LSAs. This is an important point because two viable next hops may be required by the specifics of your examination. Also, both r6 and r7 will forward over an optimal path to the RIP router, which may not occur with the alternative solution that is described next. The "optimal" behavior that was described previously is demonstrated in the following capture taken from r5. This screen dump shows that external LSAs are being received from both r6 and r7:

```
lab@r5> show ospf database extern
    OSPF external link state database
 Type      ID             Adv Rtr        Seq        Age  Opt  Cksum   Len
 . . .
 Extern    192.168.0.0    10.0.9.6       0x80000001 261  0x2  0x87c6  36
 Extern    192.168.0.0    10.0.9.7       0x80000001 251  0x2  0x81cb  36
 Extern    192.168.1.0    10.0.9.6       0x80000001 261  0x2  0x7cd0  36
 Extern    192.168.1.0    10.0.9.7       0x80000001 251  0x2  0x76d5  36
 . . .
```

With two sets of LSAs confirmed, the presence of two OSPF next hops for the RIP routes is now confirmed on r5:

```
lab@r5> show route 192.168/16

inet.0: 22 destinations, 22 routes (22 active, 0 holddown, 0 hidden)
+ = Active Route, - = Last Active, * = Both

192.168.0.0/24     *[OSPF/150] 00:00:01, metric 2, tag 0
                   > to 10.0.8.5 via fe-0/0/0.0
                     to 10.0.8.10 via fe-0/0/1.0
192.168.1.0/24     *[OSPF/150] 00:00:06, metric 2, tag 0
                     to 10.0.8.5 via fe-0/0/0.0
                   > to 10.0.8.10 via fe-0/0/1.0
192.168.2.0/24     *[OSPF/150] 00:00:06, metric 2, tag 0
                     to 10.0.8.5 via fe-0/0/0.0
                   > to 10.0.8.10 via fe-0/0/1.0
192.168.3.0/24     *[OSPF/150] 00:00:06, metric 2, tag 0
                   > to 10.0.8.5 via fe-0/0/0.0
                     to 10.0.8.10 via fe-0/0/1.0
```

Global Preference and OSPF Export Policy

The loop condition can also be resolved by adjusting the global preference associated with either RIP or OSPF externals to cause r6 and r7 to prefer OSPF external routing information to that learned through RIP, while also filtering the 10.0.5/24 route from OSPF redistribution. The following command sets the RIP preference to 160, which will cause OSPF externals (150) to be preferred. This command is needed on both r6 and r7:

```
[edit protocols rip]
lab@r7# set group rip preference 160
```

The change in route preference combined with the application of the modified OSPF export policy shown next to both r6 and r7 eliminates the packet loop, and results in both r6 and r7 being listed as next hops for the 10.0.5/24 prefix on the RIP router:

```
[edit policy-options]
lab@r7# show policy-statement rip-ospf
term 1 {
    from {
        protocol rip;
        route-filter 10.0.5.0/24 orlonger reject;
        route-filter 0.0.0.0/0 orlonger;
    }
```

```
        then accept;
}
term 2 {
        then reject;
}
```

Failing to change the protocol preference will result in only one next hop for 10.0.5/24 on the RIP router, because one of the ASBR routers (r6 or r7) will otherwise learn about and install the 10.0.5/25 route from RIP advertisements received over the RIP subnet, which prevents that router from sending the 10.0.5/24 prefix to the RIP router because of split horizon. The following capture displays the correct number of next hops for the 10.0.5/24 prefix, as seen from the RIP router:

```
lab@rip> show route 10/8

inet.0: 15 destinations, 15 routes (15 active, 0 holddown, 0 hidden)
+ = Active Route, - = Last Active, * = Both


10.0.5.0/24          *[RIP/100] 00:05:33, metric 2
                        to 172.16.40.2 via fe-0/0/0.0
                     > to 172.16.40.3 via fe-0/0/0.0
```

While the route preference/OSPF export approach works to break the loop and results in the RIP router correctly seeing two next hops for the10.0.5/24 prefix, this solution is a bit messy because one of the two ASBRs will wind up installing the other ASBR's externals as the active routes. This situation will lead to less-than-optimal forwarding from that ASBR, because packets addressed to the RIP prefixes will now be forwarded through the other ASBR instead of being sent directly to the RIP router. Another side effect of this approach is that only one ASBR will be redistributing the RIP routes into OSPF at any given time because the RIP routes will be inactive on one of the ASBRs, and only active routes can be exported through policy. Should the ASBR with active RIP routes fail, the remaining ASBR will once again install and redistribute the RIP routes (due to the loss of the OSPF externals from the failed ASBR) so fail-over is still possible with this approach.

This situation is demonstrated in the next set of captures, starting with the confirmation that in this case r6 has redistributed the RIP routes as OSPF externals:

```
[edit]
lab@r7# run show ospf database extern
    OSPF external link state database
  Type      ID               Adv Rtr         Seq         Age  Opt  Cksum  Len
  . . .
  Extern    192.168.0.0      10.0.9.6        0x80000002  806  0x2  0x85c7 36
  Extern    192.168.1.0      10.0.9.6        0x80000002  806  0x2  0x7ad1 36
  . . .
```

The lack of external LSAs from r7 is explained by the results of the following command:

```
[edit]
lab@r7# run show route 192.168.0.0

inet.0: 29 destinations, 36 routes (29 active, 0 holddown, 0 hidden)
+ = Active Route, - = Last Active, * = Both

192.168.0.0/24      *[OSPF/150] 00:05:49, metric 2, tag 0
                    > to 10.0.8.1 via fe-0/3/0.0
                    [RIP/160] 12:44:56, metric 2
                    > to 172.16.40.1 via fe-0/3/3.0
```

This capture shows that r7 (in this case) has received the OSPF externals from r6 and, due to the modified route preference, has installed them as the active routes. Because the RIP routes are not active in r7, we expect to find that r7 does not redistribute the RIP routes as OSPF externals, and that r7 will forward through r6 to get to the RIP router, which is a suboptimal path for this topology:

```
lab@r7# run traceroute 192.168.0.1 source 172.16.40.3
traceroute to 192.168.0.1 (192.168.0.1) from 172.16.40.3, 30 hops max, 40 byte
packets
 1  172.16.40.2 (172.16.40.2)  0.211 ms  0.126 ms  0.098 ms
 2  192.168.0.1 (192.168.0.1)  0.166 ms  0.140 ms  0.125 ms
```

Because the RIP router knows only the 10.0.5/24 prefix, the traceroute from r7 requires the source option; otherwise r7 sources the packet from the 10.0.8.0/30 subnet, which is unknown to the RIP router. The extra hop through r6 can be observed in the previous capture.

Various other techniques could also be used to solve this mutual route redistribution problem. For example, global route preferences can remain at their default settings if the exam candidate applies the appropriate OSPF export *and* RIP import policies in unison. Another common variation to the route preference solution involves writing the OSPF export policy so that the redistributed routes have a metric that is greater than that being reported in the external LSA originating from area 10 (via the translation performed by the NSSA ABR r4). The higher metric setting in the LSAs generated by r6 and r7 will cause the routers in area 1 to forward through r5 for 10.0.5/24 destinations, which again breaks the loop. The following OSPF export policy combined with the route preference modification described previously illustrates this technique. Here, the metric setting of 400 causes the routers in area 1 to ignore the 10.0.5/24 prefix being advertised by r6 and r7 in preference of the lower metric reported in the LSA being flooded by r4:

```
[edit policy-options policy-statement rip-ospf]
lab@r6# show
term 1 {
    from protocol rip;
```

```
    then {
        metric 400;
        accept;
    }
}
term 2 {
    then reject;
}
```

It should be clear from these examples that JUNOS software routing policy is extremely flexible, and that this flexibility normally translates into more than one viable solution for most of the problems you will encounter in the lab. Unfortunately, this flexibility also means that there are numerous ways in which you can manage to break your network through mistakes in your routing policy or in the way that the policy is applied.

In the end, it is only the results of your policy that will matter in the JNCIP examination. It is therefore suggested that you keep your policy as simple as possible, and that you always verify correct policy behavior, because common mistakes are often difficult to catch when one simply views the policy statements.

The final verification of the OSPF policy task is to confirm that r1 and r2 have the correct connectivity to the RIP router. As the RIP router is being told only about the 10.0.5/24 subnet, ping and traceroute tests will require that you make use of the local or source switches, respectively, if you perform the tests from either r1 or r2, as shown next:

```
lab@r1> traceroute 192.168.0.1
traceroute to 192.168.0.1 (192.168.0.1), 30 hops max, 40 byte packets
 1  10.0.4.13 (10.0.4.13)  0.341 ms  0.252 ms  0.217 ms
 2  10.0.2.1 (10.0.2.1)  0.787 ms  0.663 ms  0.876 ms
 3  10.0.8.10 (10.0.8.10)  0.853 ms  0.691 ms  0.878 ms
 4  *^C
```

Here the trace times out as the packet is sourced from r1's fe-0/0/1 interface by default. Using the source switch and the correct interface address resolves this problem:

```
lab@r1> traceroute 192.168.0.1 source 10.0.5.1
traceroute to 192.168.0.1 (192.168.0.1) from 10.0.5.1, 30 hops max, 40 byte packets
 1  10.0.4.13 (10.0.4.13)  0.403 ms  0.291 ms  0.262 ms
 2  10.0.2.1 (10.0.2.1)  0.537 ms  0.614 ms  0.375 ms
 3  10.0.8.10 (10.0.8.10)  0.294 ms  0.676 ms  0.375 ms
 4  192.168.0.1 (192.168.0.1)  0.443 ms  0.649 ms  0.374 ms
```

A Time for Static Routes?

Though arbitrary use of static routes is normally forbidden in lab examinations, when you are hung up on a problem and afraid of running low on time, the decision to deploy a static route is well worth considering. Unauthorized static routes may result in far less point loss than would otherwise occur if you were to leave a packet loop in place or end up running out of time because you could not work through a particularly difficult problem. Though each individual will have to weigh all factors and come to a personal decision, throwing in a static route so that you can get moving on the remaining configuration tasks can be a sound examination strategy. Ideally, you will be able to revisit the problem and resolve the issue during any spare time left over at the end of all your configuration tasks.

Metrics and Various Other Knobs

You should be familiar with all the OSPF options and knobs before attempting a lab examination. The following section will demonstrate how some of the remaining OSPF configuration parameters may be deployed in a lab scenario. Traffic Engineering (TE)–related OSPF options are beyond the scope of the JNCIP examination and are therefore not covered in this book.

To finish this section, you must complete the following tasks:

- Ensure that r5 can load-balance to area 10 internal destinations by adjusting metrics.

- Configure r6 so that other routers will not forward transit traffic through it. Your OSPF adjacencies must stay up, and you cannot change interface metrics directly.

- Configure the aggregated SONET link between r3 and r4 to reflect a 4-second propagation delay.

The first configuration task requires that we determine how r5 is currently forwarding traffic into area 10, our NSSA:

```
lab@r5> show route 10.0.4/22

inet.0: 28 destinations, 30 routes (28 active, 0 holddown, 0 hidden)
+ = Active Route, - = Last Active, * = Both

10.0.4.0/22          *[OSPF/10] 00:09:58, metric 3
                      > via at-0/2/1.35
```

At present, r5 is displaying only one path to area 10's internal destinations, as represented by the 10.0.4/22 summary LSA. We can gain a clue as to why r4 is not being used by examining the LSDB:

```
lab@r5> show ospf database netsummary area 0 detail

    OSPF link state database, area 0.0.0.0
```

Type	ID	Adv Rtr	Seq	Age	Opt	Cksum	Len
Summary	10.0.4.0	10.0.3.3	0x80000083	734	0x2	0x3b82	28

  mask 255.255.252.0
  TOS 0x0, metric 2

| Summary | 10.0.4.0 | 10.0.3.4 | 0x8000005e | 874 | 0x2 | 0x8957 | 28 |

  mask 255.255.252.0
  TOS 0x0, metric 3
. . .

From this display we can see that the summary metric received from r4 is higher than that being received from r3, which explains why load balancing is not occurring. Fixing this problem requires that the candidate understand that summary metrics are set based upon the highest metric associated with the summary's contributing routes, and that the lack of a direct link between r4 and r1 is causing r4's summary to reflect a higher cost than that sent by r3. You can correct this problem by adding 1 to the metric value of r3's fe-0/0/0 and fe-0/0/1 interfaces as shown next:

```
[edit protocols ospf]
lab@r3# set area 10 interface fe-0/0/0 metric 2

[edit protocols ospf]
lab@r3# set area 10 interface fe-0/0/1 metric 2
```

After committing the changes on r3, we confirm that load balancing is now possible from r5:

```
lab@r5> show route 10.0.4/22

inet.0: 28 destinations, 30 routes (28 active, 0 holddown, 0 hidden)
+ = Active Route, - = Last Active, * = Both

10.0.4.0/22        *[OSPF/10] 00:02:03, metric 4
                    > via as1.0
                      via at-0/2/1.35
```

r5 now shows two equal-cost paths to area 10's internal routes. The next configuration requirement is to configure r6 so that other routers avoid sending transit traffic toward it. Because you cannot disrupt your adjacencies and you are not permitted to configure interface metrics directly, you pretty much have to use the overload knob as shown next. Before modifying r6 to indicate that its database is overloaded, we first confirm that it is a viable next hop for transit traffic:

```
lab@r5> show route 10.0.8/30

inet.0: 28 destinations, 30 routes (28 active, 0 holddown, 0 hidden)
```

```
+ = Active Route, - = Last Active, * = Both

10.0.8.0/30        *[OSPF/10] 00:00:36, metric 2
                   > to 10.0.8.5 via fe-0/0/0.0
                     to 10.0.8.10 via fe-0/0/1.0
```

Now, you configure r6 to appear overloaded:

```
[edit]
lab@r6# set protocols ospf overload

[edit]
lab@r6# commit
commit complete
```

You now confirm the effects as seen from r5:

```
lab@r5> show route 10.0.8/30

inet.0: 28 destinations, 30 routes (28 active, 0 holddown, 0 hidden)
+ = Active Route, - = Last Active, * = Both

10.0.8.0/30        *[OSPF/10] 00:02:36, metric 2
                   > to 10.0.8.10 via fe-0/0/1.0
```

Good, r5 now sees only r7 as a viable next hop when forwarding to the 10.0.8.0/30 subnet. Examining r6's router LSA displays the result of setting the overload option, which causes transit interface metrics to be set to the maximum value:

```
lab@r5> show ospf database router detail advertising-router 10.0.9.6

    OSPF link state database, area 0.0.0.0
Type      ID                 Adv Rtr           Seq       Age  Opt  Cksum  Len

    OSPF link state database, area 0.0.0.1
Type      ID                 Adv Rtr           Seq       Age  Opt  Cksum  Len
Router    10.0.9.6           10.0.9.6          0x80000192  28  0x2  0xf60a  60
  bits 0x2, link count 3
  id 10.0.8.5, data 10.0.8.5, type Transit (2)
  TOS count 0, TOS 0 metric 65535
  id 10.0.8.1, data 10.0.8.1, type Transit (2)
  TOS count 0, TOS 0 metric 65535
```

```
id 10.0.9.6, data 255.255.255.255, type Stub (3)
TOS count 0, TOS 0 metric 0
```

The last configuration requirement in this section is to correctly set OSPF to factor in a 4-second propagation delay between r4 and r5. This is accomplished by setting the OSPF `transit-delay` value at both ends of the aggregated SONET interface that interconnects r4 and r5. The following setting causes the lifetime of all LSAs flooded over r4's aggregated link to be reduced by the alleged 4-second propagation delay of the interface. This `transit-delay` setting must also be configured on r5:

```
[edit protocols ospf area 0.0.0.0 interface as0.0]
lab@r4# set transit-delay 4
```

```
[edit protocols ospf area 0.0.0.0 interface as0.0]
lab@r4# show
transit-delay 4;
authentication-key "$9$3.1g/A0vMX7-w" key-id 10; # SECRET-DATA
```

Troubleshoot an Adjacency Problem

You have noticed an adjacency formation problem between r3 and r4 in the topology shown in the following graphic:

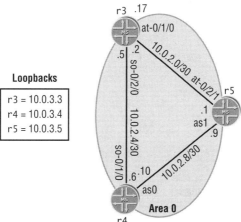

Displaying the adjacency status returns the following:

```
[edit interfaces lo0]
lab@r3# run show ospf neighbor
```

Address	Interface	State	ID	Pri	Dead
10.0.2.1	at-0/1/0.35	Full	10.0.3.5	128	36
10.0.2.6	so-0/2/0.100	Down	0.0.0.0	0	106

You can ping r4's 10.0.2.6 address from r3, and the OSPF area 0 stanzas of both routers are as shown:

```
[edit]
lab@r3# show protocols ospf area 0
authentication-type md5; # SECRET-DATA
interface at-0/1/0.35 {
    authentication-key "$9$I-EhyKsYoaUH" key-id 1; # SECRET-DATA
}
interface so-0/2/0.100 {
    interface-type nbma;
    authentication-key "$9$6M9/CpBW87Nb2" key-id 1; # SECRET-DATA
    neighbor 10.0.2.6 eligible;
}
interface lo0.0;
[edit]

lab@r4# show protocols ospf area 0
authentication-type md5; # SECRET-DATA
interface so-0/1/0.100 {
    interface-type nbma;
    authentication-key "$9$42JUH/9pu1h" key-id 1; # SECRET-DATA
    neighbor 10.0.4.5 eligible;
}
interface as0.0 {
    authentication-key "$9$AXiLuBEx7Vb2a" key-id 1; # SECRET-DATA
}
interface lo0.0;
```

Displaying the LSDB on r3 provides an invaluable clue as to the source of the problem. Can you spot the issue?

```
[edit]
lab@r3# run show ospf database router area 0

    OSPF link state database, area 0.0.0.0
```

Type	ID	Adv Rtr	Seq	Age	Opt	Cksum	Len
Router	10.0.3.3	10.0.3.3	0x80000009	396	0x2	0x7814	72
Router	*10.0.3.4	10.0.3.4	0x80000091	2	0x2	0x8491	72
Router	10.0.3.5	10.0.3.5	0x8000000a	384	0x2	0x1f41	84

Tracing hello and error messages indicates that r3 is sending hellos out its so-0/2/0.100 interface, but no hellos are shown as being received and no errors are evident in the trace output. The nature of the problem is evident in this hello message sent from r3 to r4. Have you determined the problem yet?

```
Jun 11 12:08:16 OSPF sent Hello 10.0.2.5 -> 10.0.2.6 (so-0/2/0.100)
Jun 11 12:08:16   Version 2, length 44, ID 10.0.3.4, area 0.0.0.0
Jun 11 12:08:16   checksum 0x0, authtype 2
Jun 11 12:08:16   mask 255.255.255.252, hello_ivl 30, opts 0x2, prio 128
Jun 11 12:08:16   dead_ivl 120, DR 0.0.0.0, BDR 0.0.0.0
```

If you have determined that r3 is incorrectly using a router ID that rightfully belongs to r4, then a self high-five is in order! This problem is the result of incorrectly assigning r4's loopback address to r3, which has resulted in duplicate RIDs and a broken adjacency between r3 and r4.

Summary

This chapter provided numerous examples of OSPF configuration tasks that are similar to those you may encounter while taking your JNCIP lab examination. You should now feel comfortable with the commands needed to configure and validate a multi-area OSPF network using a mixture of transit, stub, and NSSA area types. You should also be able to use area-range statements to filter and summarize network summaries and external routes in a NSSA. OSPF authentication options were also demonstrated, as was the use of protocol tracing to diagnose operational problems caused by incorrect or incompatible configurations.

The use of JUNOS software policy to effect route redistribution, tagging, and metric manipulation was also demonstrated along with the operational commands that can be used to determine the operational status of your OSPF IGP. The following case study is designed to review critical OSPF configuration tasks in a configuration scenario designed to simulate the JNCIP testing environment.

Case Study: OSPF

The following case study is designed to simulate a typical JNCIP OSPF configuration scenario. You should refer to the criteria listing and Figure 3.10, the case study topology, for the information needed to complete the OSPF case study. It is assumed that you will be building your OSPF configuration on top of the interface configuration that was left from the case study at the end of Chapter 2. You should remove any protocol, policy, and static route configurations related to the previous examples given in this chapter from all seven routers before starting.

It is expected that a prepared JNCIP exam candidate will be able to complete this case study in approximately one hour, and that the resulting OSPF network will have no serious operational problems. Sample OSPF configurations for all seven routers are provided at the end of the case study to compare with your own configurations. Multiple solutions to the same requirement are often possible, so differences between these sample configurations and those created by you will not necessarily indicate that mistakes have been made. Because you are graded on the overall functionality of your IGP, and its conformance to the specified configuration criteria, various operational mode commands will be shown to allow you to compare the behavior of your network to a known good example.

FIGURE 3.10 OSPF case study topology

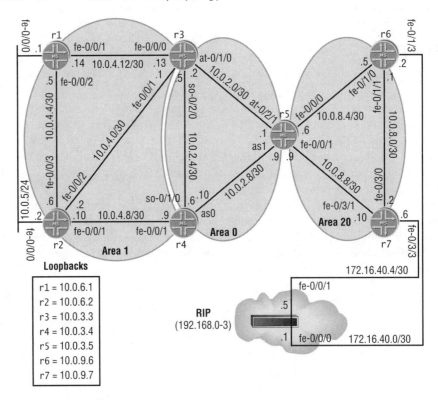

To complete this case study, you must ensure that your OSPF configuration meets the following criteria:

- RID based on lo0 address and reachable via OSPF for all routers.

- Loopback addresses from the backbone must appear as summary LSAs in area 20.

- The 10.0.5/25 subnet between r1 and r2 must appear in area 0 as an external route. Ensure that no adjacencies can be established over this subnet.

- Set the metric of the 10.0.5/24 route to reflect an initial value of 10 and ensure that all routers adjust this value to reflect their internal OSPF cost. Tag this route with the value *420*.

- Ensure that r1 never generates a network LSA.

- No type 3 or type 5 LSAs in area 1.

- You must elect a DR on the 10.0.2.4/30 subnet.

- Summarize all routes (internal and external) into the backbone area, including the 192.168.*x*/24 routes from the RIP router. You must not modify the RIP router's configuration.

- Area 0 must use md5 authentication with secret of *jnx*. Configure r6 and r7 to advertise 10.0.5/24 to the RIP router, and ensure that the rip metric sent by r7 is higher than that sent from r6.

- Advertise the 172.16.40.*x* RIP router subnets as OSPF internal routes, while ensuring that no adjacency can be established over these interfaces.

- Except for r5, ensure that no single ABR or link failure will break communications between area 1 routers and the RIP router.

- Optimize routing based on bandwidth, and ensure that all Fast Ethernet interfaces are automatically assigned a metric of 10. You may manually set metrics as needed to allow load balancing from r5 to area 1 internal destinations.

- No static routes.

- The 10.0.5/24 subnet must be reachable from the RIP router and the path must be optimal.

In this case study, the RIP router is preconfigured and its configuration cannot be modified. Key aspects of the RIP router's configuration are shown in Listing 3.6.

Listing 3.6: RIP Router's Configuration

```
[edit]
lab@rip# show policy-options
policy-statement rip {
    term 1 {
        from protocol [ static rip ];
        then accept;
    }
}
```

```
[edit]
lab@rip# show routing-options static
route 192.168.0.0/24 receive;
route 192.168.1.0/24 receive;
route 192.168.2.0/24 receive;
route 192.168.3.0/24 receive;
route 192.168.4.0/24 receive;

[edit]
lab@rip# show interfaces lo0
unit 0 {
    family inet {
        address 192.168.0.1/32;
        address 192.168.1.1/32;
        address 192.168.2.1/32;
        address 192.168.3.1/32;
        address 192.168.4.1/32;
    }
}
```

OSPF Case Study Analysis

Each configuration requirement for the case study will now be matched to the necessary configuration steps, and will be confirmed operational within all specified case study guidelines. We begin with the first two configuration criteria:

- RID based on lo0 address and reachable via OSPF for all routers.

- Loopback addresses from the backbone must appear as summary LSAs in area 20.

As long as you do not manually specify a RID, your router's RID will be based on its lo0 address. By including the lo0 interface under the area 0 configuration of backbone routers, you ensure that the lo0 address will be injected as a network summary into other areas. These requirements are met with the highlighted configuration entry shown next:

```
[edit]
lab@r3# show protocols ospf area 0
authentication-type md5; # SECRET-DATA
interface at-0/1/0.35 {
    authentication-key "$9$I-EhyKsYoaUH" key-id 1; # SECRET-DATA
}
interface so-0/2/0.100 {
    interface-type nbma;
```

```
    authentication-key "$9$6M9/CpBW87Nb2" key-id 1; # SECRET-DATA
    neighbor 10.0.2.6 eligible;
}
interface lo0.0;
```

The results are now confirmed in area 20:

```
lab@r7> show ospf database netsummary advertising-router 10.0.3.5

    OSPF link state database, area 0.0.0.20
 Type      ID              Adv Rtr          Seq      Age  Opt  Cksum  Len
 Summary  10.0.2.0        10.0.3.5         0x80000008 1036 0x2  0x61d3  28
 Summary  10.0.2.4        10.0.3.5         0x8000000c  900 0x2  0x6db9  28
 Summary  10.0.2.8        10.0.3.5         0x80000007  765 0x2  0x131b  28
 Summary  10.0.3.3        10.0.3.5         0x80000007  736 0x2  0x4ce2  28
 Summary  10.0.3.4        10.0.3.5         0x80000007  601 0x2  0x42eb  28
 Summary  10.0.3.5        10.0.3.5         0x80000007  465 0x2  0xfb37  28
 Summary  10.0.7.255      10.0.3.5         0x80000007  436 0x2  0x5cb6  28
```

We next deal with the following configuration criteria:

- The 10.0.5/25 subnet between r1 and r2 must appear in area 0 as an external route. Ensure that no adjacencies can be established over this subnet.

- Set the metric of the 10.0.5/24 route to reflect an initial value of *10* plus OSPF internal cost. Tag this route with the value *420*.

- Ensure that r1 never generates a network LSA.

You must use OSPF export policy on both r1 and r2 to make the 10.0.5/24 subnet appear as an external route in the backbone area. There is no need to run OSPF on the 10.0.5/24 subnet, but if you do, you must include the `passive` keyword on r1 and r2's fe-0/0/0 interface to prevent adjacency formation. The OSPF export policy must set the correct metric type (a type 1 metric will be increased to reflect internal OSPF cost), initial metric value, and tag setting. The priority setting of 0 on r1's OSPF interfaces ensures it can never be a DR or BDR, and that it can therefore never generate a network LSA in accordance with your configuration requirements. The highlights in the screen captures shown next call out the configuration additions needed to address the requirements listed previously:

```
[edit]
lab@r1# show protocols ospf
export external;
reference-bandwidth 1g;
area 0.0.0.1 {
    nssa;
```

```
    interface fe-0/0/2.0 {
        priority 0;
    }
    interface fe-0/0/1.200 {
        priority 0;
    }
}
```

```
lab@r1# show policy-options
policy-statement external {
    term 1 {
        from {
            route-filter 10.0.5.0/24 exact;
        }
        then {
            metric 10;
            tag 420;
            external {
                type 1;
            }
            accept;
        }
    }
    term 2 {
        then reject;
    }
}
```

The DR status of r1 is now confirmed:

```
lab@r1> show ospf interface
Interface         State      Area       DR ID       BDR ID      Nbrs
fe-0/0/1.200      DRother    0.0.0.1    10.0.3.3    0.0.0.0        1
fe-0/0/2.0        DRother    0.0.0.1    10.0.6.2    0.0.0.0        1
```

The status of DRother indicates that r1 is neither the DR nor the BDR, despite being one of only two nodes on a broadcast network. This proves that r1 is not eligible to become the DR or BDR. The following test confirms proper operation of the r1 and r2 OSPF export policy:

```
lab@r5> show ospf database extern detail
    OSPF external link state database
```

```
Type       ID                  Adv Rtr        Seq      Age Opt Cksum  Len
Extern   10.0.5.0            10.0.3.4       0x80000002 170 0x2 0xed80  36
   mask 255.255.255.0
   Type 1, TOS 0x0, metric 30, fwd addr 0.0.0.0, tag 0.0.1.164
```

The 10.0.5/24 prefix appears in the backbone as an external LSA. The metric type, value, and tag setting all appear correct (note that the metric value has increased to reflect r5's cost to the advertising ASBR). In this display, the tag is shown in dotted decimal notation. To view its decimal setting, you can view the resulting route:

```
lab@r5> show route 10.0.5/24

inet.0: 26 destinations, 29 routes (26 active, 0 holddown, 0 hidden)
+ = Active Route, - = Last Active, * = Both

10.0.5.0/24          *[OSPF/150] 00:27:12, metric 36, tag 420
                     > via as1.0
```

The following configuration requirements must now be addressed:

- No type 3 or type 5 LSAs in area 1.
- You must elect a DR on the 10.0.2.4/30 subnet.
- Area 0 must use md5 authentication with a secret of *jnx*.

You must configure area 1 as a NSSA with the no-summaries option to meet the area's LSA restrictions. The default-metric option instructs the ABRs to generate the default route needed for area 1 routers to reach inter-area and external destinations. The type-7 keyword is needed to ensure that the default route is generated as a NSSA type 7 LSA, which is in accordance with the requirement that there be no type 3 LSAs in area 1:

```
[edit]
lab@r3# show protocols ospf area 1
nssa {
    default-lsa {
        default-metric 1;
        type-7;
    }
    no-summaries;
}
. . .
```

The following commands confirm that no type 3 or type 5 LSAs are present in area 1:

```
[edit]
lab@r3# run show ospf database netsummary area 1

   OSPF link state database, area 0.0.0.1

[edit]
lab@r3# run show ospf database extern area 1

[edit]
lab@r3#
```

The DR requirement for the 10.0.2.4/30 subnet means that you must configure the Frame Relay link between r3 and r4 as an NBMA network so that the DR election algorithm is performed. While it is odd to see a point-to-point WAN link running in NBMA mode, this is a legal NBMA topology and can be fully justified with plans for future backbone expansion. This approach also proves useful for practicing WAN interface configurations in a test bed that forces back-to-back connections due to lack of switching gear.

This example shows a correct area 0 authentication configuration from r3. The key-id value of *1* was not specified in the case study, and so was left to the operator's discretion. This key-id value must be used in all backbone routers for proper area 0 authentication. You can also see that the so-0/2/0.100 interface has been correctly configured for OSPF NBMA operation:

```
[edit]
lab@r3# show protocols ospf area 0
authentication-type md5; # SECRET-DATA
interface at-0/1/0.35 {
    authentication-key "$9$I-EhyKsYoaUH" key-id 1; # SECRET-DATA
}
interface so-0/2/0.100 {
    interface-type nbma;
    authentication-key "$9$6M9/CpBW87Nb2" key-id 1; # SECRET-DATA
    neighbor 10.0.2.6 eligible;
}
interface lo0.0;
```

The following confirms that authentication and DR router election is functional. The presence of neighbors on area 0 interfaces indicates that compatible authentication has been configured, and it is clear from the following output that a DR and BDR have been elected on the so-0/2/0.100

interface in keeping with its NBMA network type. Though not shown, all area 0 adjacencies are confirmed to be in the full state:

```
[edit]
lab@r3# run show ospf interface
Interface          State   Area      DR ID         BDR ID        Nbrs
at-0/1/0.35        PtToPt  0.0.0.0   0.0.0.0       0.0.0.0          1
lo0.0              DR      0.0.0.0   10.0.3.3      0.0.0.0          0
so-0/2/0.100       DR      0.0.0.0   10.0.3.3      10.0.3.4         1
fe-0/0/0.0         DR      0.0.0.1   10.0.3.3      0.0.0.0          1
fe-0/0/1.0         BDR     0.0.0.1   10.0.6.2      10.0.3.3         1
```

We next examine the following configuration criterion:

- Summarize all routes (internal and external) into the backbone area. You must not modify the RIP router's configuration.

Internal route summarization is performed by the ABRs, and is configured under areas 1 and 20. Your summarization must include the area's physical, loopback, and RIP router subnets as applicable. Area 1 summarization is configured as shown next:

```
[edit]
lab@r3# show protocols ospf area 1
nssa {
    default-lsa {
        default-metric 1;
        type-7;
    }
    no-summaries;
}
area-range 10.0.4.0/22;
interface fe-0/0/0.0 {
    metric 20;
}
interface fe-0/0/1.0 {
    metric 20;
}
```

Because there is only one NSSA external route in area 1, there is no need for NSSA summarization through an area range specified within the NSSA stanza. Summarization for area 20, as configured on r5, is shown next:

```
[edit]
lab@r5# show protocols ospf area 20
```

```
area-range 172.16.40.0/28;
area-range 10.0.8.0/21;
interface fe-0/0/0.0;
interface fe-0/0/1.0;
```

Because type 5 LSAs can be summarized only at the originating ASBR, the summarization of the 192.168.*x*/24 RIP routes must be performed on r6 and r7 using OSPF export policy and a locally configured aggregate route, as shown next. The presence of any 192.168.*x*/24 RIP routes will cause the aggregate route to be active:

```
[edit]
lab@r7# show policy-options policy-statement ospf-out
term 1 {
    from {
        protocol aggregate;
        route-filter 192.168.0.0/22 exact;
    }
    then accept;
}
term 2 {
    then reject;
}

[edit]
lab@r7# show routing-options aggregate
route 192.168.0.0/22;
```

Address summarization is confirmed in area 0 with the commands shown in Listing 3.7:

Listing 3.7: Verify Address Summarization in the Backbone
```
[edit]
lab@r3# run show route 192.168/16

inet.0: 27 destinations, 28 routes (27 active, 0 holddown, 0 hidden)
+ = Active Route, - = Last Active, * = Both

192.168.0.0/22     *[OSPF/150] 01:14:08, metric 0, tag 0
                    > via at-0/1/0.35

[edit]
lab@r3# run show route 10.0.8.0
```

```
inet.0: 27 destinations, 28 routes (27 active, 0 holddown, 0 hidden)
+ = Active Route, - = Last Active, * = Both

10.0.8.0/21        *[OSPF/10] 00:13:58, metric 26
                    > via at-0/1/0.35

[edit]
lab@r3# run show route 10.0.9.0

inet.0: 27 destinations, 28 routes (27 active, 0 holddown, 0 hidden)
+ = Active Route, - = Last Active, * = Both

10.0.8.0/21        *[OSPF/10] 00:14:03, metric 26
                    > via at-0/1/0.35

lab@r5> show route 10.0.4.0

inet.0: 26 destinations, 29 routes (26 active, 0 holddown, 0 hidden)
+ = Active Route, - = Last Active, * = Both

10.0.4.0/22        *[OSPF/10] 01:16:25, metric 36
                    > via at-0/2/1.35

lab@r5> show route 10.0.6.0

inet.0: 26 destinations, 29 routes (26 active, 0 holddown, 0 hidden)
+ = Active Route, - = Last Active, * = Both

10.0.4.0/22        *[OSPF/10] 01:16:33, metric 36
                    > via at-0/2/1.35
```

The results shown in Listing 3.7 confirm that the internal and external addresses associated with the non-backbone areas are being correctly summarized before injection into the backbone area.

We now address the following configuration criteria:

- Configure r6 and r7 to advertise 10.0.5/24 to the RIP router. Ensure that the rip metric sent by r7 is higher than that sent from r6.

- Advertise the 172.16.40.x RIP router subnets as OSPF internal routes, while ensuring that no adjacency can be established over these interfaces.

For the first of the two requirements, r7 is configured to set the metric of advertised routes to *2*, which is higher than the metric of *1* associated with the routes sent by r6. The *rip-out* export policy causes the OSPF route 10.0.5/24 to be exported into RIP:

```
[edit]
lab@r7# show protocols rip
group rip {
    metric-out 2;
    export rip-out;
    neighbor fe-0/3/3.0 {
        import rip-in;
    }
}
```

```
[edit]
lab@r7# show policy-options policy-statement rip-out
term 1 {
    from {
        protocol ospf;
        route-filter 10.0.5.0/24 exact;
    }
    then accept;
}
term 2 {
    then reject;
}
```

To address the second requirement, both r6 and r7 have been configured to list their RIP router interfaces as passive under OSPF. This prevents adjacency formation while causing the associated routes to be advertised as OSPF internals:

```
[edit]
lab@r7# show protocols ospf
export ospf-out;
reference-bandwidth 1g;
area 0.0.0.20 {
    interface fe-0/3/0.0;
    interface fe-0/3/1.0;
    interface fe-0/3/3.0 {
        passive;
    }
}
```

To prevent loops and the possibility of inefficient routing, a RIP import policy has been defined (and applied to RIP) to ensure that r6 and r7 will accept only the 192.168.*x*/24 routes from the RIP router:

```
[edit]
lab@r7# show policy-options policy-statement rip-in
term 1 {
    from {
        protocol rip;
        route-filter 192.168.0.0/22 orlonger;
    }
    then accept;
}
term 2 {
    then reject;
}
```

```
[edit]
lab@r7# show protocols rip
group rip {
    metric-out 2;
    export rip-out;
    neighbor fe-0/3/3.0 {
        import rip-in;
    }
}
```

We next analyze the following requirement:

- Except for r5, ensure that no single ABR or link failure will break communications between area 1 routers and the RIP router.

To achieve this requirement, you must ensure that both r3 and r4 are generating a default route into area 1, and that both r6 and r7 are advertising the aggregate for the RIP routes. Load balancing from the RIP router will not function because of the different metrics being advertised by r6 and r7, but the failure of r6 will not isolate the RIP router once network reconvergence is complete. The following commands confirm that the redundancy requirements have been met:

```
lab@r1> show ospf database nssa
```

```
    OSPF link state database, area 0.0.0.1
Type     ID              Adv Rtr          Seq        Age  Opt  Cksum   Len
NSSA     0.0.0.0         10.0.3.3         0x80000007  692 0x0  0xdd5e  36
NSSA     0.0.0.0         10.0.3.4         0x80000007 1246 0x0  0xd763  36
```

The presence of two default routes in area 1 confirms that the loss of either r3 or r4 will not isolate area 1 routers. We now confirm that both r6 and r7 are advertising the RIP aggregate:

```
lab@r5# run show ospf database extern
    OSPF external link state database
 Type      ID              Adv Rtr          Seq        Age  Opt  Cksum  Len
 Extern   10.0.5.0         10.0.3.4         0x8000000b  380  0x2  0xdb89  36
 Extern   192.168.0.0      10.0.9.6         0x80000003 1313  0x2  0x60f0  36
 Extern   192.168.0.0      10.0.9.7         0x80000009  451  0x2  0x4efb  36
```

We now verify that the RIP router correctly points to r6 when forwarding to 10.0.5/24, until r6 has its RIP interface deactivated:

```
[edit]
lab@rip# run show route protocol rip

inet.0: 16 destinations, 16 routes (16 active, 0 holddown, 0 hidden)
+ = Active Route, - = Last Active, * = Both

10.0.5.0/24        *[RIP/100] 02:02:48, metric 2, tag 420
                    > to 172.16.40.2 via fe-0/0/0.0


[edit]
lab@r6# deactivate interfaces fe-0/1/3


[edit]
lab@r6# commit
commit complete
```

After taking r6 out of the equation, you confirm that r7 takes over:

```
[edit]
lab@rip# run show route protocol rip

inet.0: 16 destinations, 16 routes (16 active, 0 holddown, 0 hidden)
+ = Active Route, - = Last Active, * = Both

10.0.5.0/24        *[RIP/100] 00:00:09, metric 3, tag 420
                    > to 172.16.40.6 via fe-0/0/1.0
```

Great—the RIP router fails over to r7 as expected, so we can reactivate r6's fe-0/1/3 inter-face. We now address the following (and last) configuration requirement:

- Optimize routing based on bandwidth, and ensure that all Fast Ethernet interfaces are auto-matically assigned a metric of *10*, excepting manual settings needed to allow load balancing from r5 to internal destinations in area 1.

To meet this requirement, you must set the OSPF reference bandwidth to 1 Gig on all routers, which will result in an automatic metric setting of *10* for 100Mbps interfaces. The default OSPF reference bandwidth of 100Mbps had caused all interface used in this sample JNCIP test bed to have a metric of *1*, which results in path optimization based on hop count. To achieve the required load balancing at r5, you must manually set metrics in area 1 (so that both r3 and r4 advertise the same metric in their network summary) and you must set the metric of the aggre-gated SONET link so that it has the same OSPF cost as the slower ATM link. The load-balancing requirement can be met with an asymmetric metric assignment on the aggregated SONET inter-face, which is the approach taken in the following, in that the default metric has been left in place for r4's as0 interface:

```
[edit]
lab@r3# show protocols ospf
reference-bandwidth 1g;
area 0.0.0.1 {
    nssa {
        default-lsa {
            default-metric 1;
            type-7;
        }
        no-summaries;
    }
    area-range 10.0.4.0/22;
    interface fe-0/0/0.0 {
        metric 20;
    }
    interface fe-0/0/1.0 {
        metric 20;
    }
}
area 0.0.0.0 {
    . . .
```

```
[edit]
lab@r5# show protocols ospf area 0
authentication-type md5; # SECRET-DATA
interface lo0.0;
interface at-0/2/1.35 {
    authentication-key "$9$LaA7dskqf5F/" key-id 1; # SECRET-DATA
}
interface as1.0 {
    metric 6;
    authentication-key "$9$LBa7dskqf5F/" key-id 1; # SECRET-DATA
}
```

You now confirm the correct load-balancing behavior at r5:

```
[edit]
lab@r5# run show route 10.0.4/22

inet.0: 26 destinations, 28 routes (26 active, 0 holddown, 0 hidden)
+ = Active Route, - = Last Active, * = Both

10.0.4.0/22        *[OSPF/10] 00:53:46, metric 36
                      via as1.0
                    > via at-0/2/1.35
10.0.5.0/24        *[OSPF/150] 00:53:46, metric 36, tag 420
                    > via as1.0
```

The presence of a single next hop for the 10.0.5/24 prefix is not a problem because this is not an area 1 internal route.

The last check is to verify RIP router connectivity and optimal forwarding paths through your network, in accordance with this stipulation:

- The 10.0.5/24 subnet must be reachable from the RIP router using optimal paths.

Forwarding to 10.0.5/24 from area 20 is confirmed with the following test performed at the RIP router:

```
lab@rip> traceroute 10.0.5.1
traceroute to 10.0.5.1 (10.0.5.1), 30 hops max, 40 byte packets
 1  172.16.40.2 (172.16.40.2)  0.194 ms  0.248 ms  0.095 ms
 2  10.0.8.6 (10.0.8.6)  0.326 ms  0.295 ms  0.277 ms
 3  10.0.2.10 (10.0.2.10)  0.331 ms  0.314 ms  0.294 ms
 4  10.0.4.10 (10.0.4.10)  0.234 ms  0.256 ms  0.218 ms
 5  10.0.5.1 (10.0.5.1)  0.314 ms  0.296 ms  0.283 ms
```

The results of the RIP router traceroute indicate that it is forwarding through r6, so we now know that r6 will use the path shown in the traceroute to reach the 10.0.5/24 subnet. Some candidates may be thrown by the extra hop caused by r5 forwarding through r4 instead of r3. This inefficiency is the result of r4 having a higher RID than r3, and therefore being the only ABR that is performing the type 7 to type 5 LSA translations for the NSSA. This is confirmed by changing the traceroute target to the address owned by r2, which confirms optimal forwarding:

```
lab@rip> traceroute 10.0.5.2
traceroute to 10.0.5.2 (10.0.5.2), 30 hops max, 40 byte packets
 1  172.16.40.2 (172.16.40.2)  0.196 ms  0.229 ms  0.094 ms
 2  10.0.8.6 (10.0.8.6)  0.332 ms  0.294 ms  0.276 ms
 3  10.0.2.10 (10.0.2.10)  0.330 ms  0.307 ms  0.294 ms
 4  10.0.5.2 (10.0.5.2)  0.238 ms  0.228 ms  0.220 ms
```

We now verify that r7 can also reach the 10.0.5/24 subnet using an optimal path, because the failure of r6 would cause r7 to become part of the forwarding path:

```
lab@r7> traceroute 10.0.5.2
traceroute to 10.0.5.2 (10.0.5.2), 30 hops max, 40 byte packets
 1  10.0.8.9 (10.0.8.9)  0.351 ms  0.257 ms  0.216 ms
 2  10.0.2.10 (10.0.2.10)  0.274 ms  0.247 ms  0.243 ms
 3  10.0.5.2 (10.0.5.2)  0.179 ms  0.169 ms  0.155 ms
```

OSPF Case Study Configurations

The configuration changes needed to complete the OSPF IGP case study for all routers in the test bed are provided in Listings 3.8 through 3.14.

Listing 3.8: *r1* OSPF-Related Configuration

```
[edit]
lab@r1# show policy-options
policy-statement external {
    term 1 {
        from {
            route-filter 10.0.5.0/24 exact;
        }
        then {
            metric 10;
            tag 420;
            external {
                type 1;
            }
```

```
            accept;
        }
    }
    term 2 {
        then reject;
    }
}

[edit]
lab@r1# show protocols ospf
export external;
reference-bandwidth 1g;
area 0.0.0.1 {
    nssa;
    interface fe-0/0/2.0 {
        priority 0;
    }
    interface fe-0/0/1.200 {
        priority 0;
    }
}
```

Listing 3.9: *r2* **OSPF-Related Configuration**
```
[edit]
lab@r2# show protocols ospf
reference-bandwidth 1g;
area 0.0.0.1 {
    nssa;
    interface fe-0/0/1.0;
    interface fe-0/0/2.0;
    interface fe-0/0/3.0;
}

[edit]
lab@r2# show policy-options
policy-statement external {
    term 1 {
        from {
            route-filter 10.0.5.0/24 exact;
        }
        then {
```

```
            metric 10;
            tag 420;
            external {
                type 1;
            }
            accept;
        }
    }
    term 2 {
        then reject;
    }
}
```

Listing 3.10: *r3* **OSPF-Related Configuration**
```
[edit]
lab@r3# show protocols ospf
reference-bandwidth 1g;
area 0.0.0.1 {
    nssa {
        default-lsa {
            default-metric 1;
            type-7;
        }
        no-summaries;
    }
    area-range 10.0.4.0/22;
    interface fe-0/0/0.0 {
        metric 20;
    }
    interface fe-0/0/1.0 {
        metric 20;
    }
}
area 0.0.0.0 {
    authentication-type md5; # SECRET-DATA
    interface at-0/1/0.35 {
        authentication-key "$9$I-EhyKsYoaUH" key-id 1; # SECRET-DATA
    }
    interface so-0/2/0.100 {
        interface-type nbma;
```

```
        authentication-key "$9$6M9/CpBW87Nb2" key-id 1; # SECRET-DATA
        neighbor 10.0.2.6 eligible;
    }
    interface lo0.0;
}
```

Listing 3.11: *r4* OSPF-Related Configuration

```
[edit]
lab@r4# show protocols ospf
reference-bandwidth 1g;
area 0.0.0.1 {
    nssa {
        default-lsa {
            default-metric 1;
            type-7;
        }
        no-summaries;
    }
    area-range 10.0.4.0/22;
    interface fe-0/0/1.0;
}
area 0.0.0.0 {
    authentication-type md5; # SECRET-DATA
    interface so-0/1/0.100 {
        interface-type nbma;
        authentication-key "$9$42JUH/9pu1h" key-id 1; # SECRET-DATA
        neighbor 10.0.4.5 eligible;
    }
    interface as0.0 {
        authentication-key "$9$AXiLuBEx7Vb2a" key-id 1; # SECRET-DATA
    }
    interface lo0.0;
}
```

Listing 3.12: *r5* OSPF-Related Configuration

```
[edit]
lab@r5# show protocols ospf
reference-bandwidth 1g;
area 0.0.0.0 {
    authentication-type md5; # SECRET-DATA
    interface lo0.0;
```

```
    interface at-0/2/1.35 {
        authentication-key "$9$LaA7dskqf5F/" key-id 1; # SECRET-DATA
    }
    interface as1.0 {
        metric 6;
        authentication-key "$9$LBa7dskqf5F/" key-id 1; # SECRET-DATA
    }
}
area 0.0.0.20 {
    area-range 172.16.40.0/28;
    area-range 10.0.8.0/21;
    interface fe-0/0/0.0;
    interface fe-0/0/1.0;
}
```

Listing 3.13: *r6* **OSPF- and RIP-Related Configuration**
```
[edit]
lab@r6# show routing-options aggregate
route 192.168.0.0/22;

[edit]
lab@r6# show policy-options
policy-statement rip-in {
    term 1 {
        from {
            protocol rip;
            route-filter 192.168.0.0/22 orlonger;
        }
        then accept;
    }
    term 2 {
        then reject;
    }
}
policy-statement ospf-out {
    term 1 {
        from {
            protocol aggregate;
            route-filter 192.168.0.0/22 exact;
        }
```

```
            then accept;
        }
        term 2 {
            then reject;
        }
    }
    policy-statement rip-out {
        term 1 {
            from {
                protocol ospf;
                route-filter 10.0.5.0/24 exact;
            }
            then accept;
        }
        term 2 {
            then reject;
        }
    }

[edit]
lab@r6# show protocols
ospf {
    export ospf-out;
    reference-bandwidth 1g;
    area 0.0.0.20 {
        interface fe-0/1/0.0;
        interface fe-0/1/1.0;
        interface fe-0/1/3.0 {
            passive;
        }
    }
}
rip {
    group rip {
        export rip-out;
        neighbor fe-0/1/3.0 {
            import rip-in;
        }
    }
}
```

Listing 3.14: *r7* OSPF- and RIP-Related Configuration
```
[edit]
lab@r7# show routing-options aggregate
route 192.168.0.0/22;

[edit]
lab@r7# show policy-options
policy-statement rip-in {
    term 1 {
        from {
            protocol rip;
            route-filter 192.168.0.0/22 orlonger;
        }
        then accept;
    }
    term 2 {
        then reject;
    }
}
policy-statement ospf-out {
    term 1 {
        from {
            protocol aggregate;
            route-filter 192.168.0.0/22 exact;
        }
        then accept;
    }
    term 2 {
        then reject;
    }
}
policy-statement rip-out {
    term 1 {
        from {
            protocol ospf;
            route-filter 10.0.5.0/24 exact;
        }
        then accept;
    }
    term 2 {
```

```
        then reject;
    }
}

[edit]
lab@r7# show protocols
ospf {
    export ospf-out;
    reference-bandwidth 1g;
    area 0.0.0.20 {
        interface fe-0/3/0.0;
        interface fe-0/2/1.0;
        interface fe-0/3/3.0 {
            passive;
        }
    }
}
rip {
    group rip {
        metric-out 2;
        export rip-out;
        neighbor fe-0/3/3.0 {
            import rip-in;
        }
    }
}
```

Spot the Issues: Review Questions

1. You have to configure simple OSPF authentication, but you are not provided with the secret being used by the remote router. How can you determine the correct secret?

2. r3 is an ASBR in a NSSA, and you need to summarize the external routes 192.168.0/24 through 192.168.3/24. What is wrong with the following configuration?

```
[edit protocols ospf]
lab@r3# show
reference-bandwidth 1g;
area 0.0.0.1 {
    nssa {
        default-lsa {
            default-metric 1;
            type-7;
        }
        no-summaries;
    }
    area-range 10.0.4.0/22;
    area-range 192.168.0.0/22;
    interface fe-0/0/0.0 {
        metric 20;
    }
    interface fe-0/0/1.0 {
        metric 20;
    }
}
```

3. Based on the following configuration, will the router's loopback address be advertised into OSPF, and if so, what type of LSA will be used to report the lo0 address?

```
[edit]
lab@r3# show routing-options
static {
    route 10.0.200.0/24 {
        next-hop 10.0.1.102;
        no-readvertise;
    }
}
router-id 10.0.3.3;

[edit]
lab@r3# show protocols ospf
```

```
reference-bandwidth 1g;
area 0.0.0.1 {
    nssa {
        default-lsa {
            default-metric 1;
            type-7;
        }
        no-summaries;
    }
    area-range 10.0.4.0/22;
    interface fe-0/0/0.0 {
        metric 20;
    }
    interface fe-0/0/1.0 {
        metric 20;
    }
}
area 0.0.0.0 {
    authentication-type md5; # SECRET-DATA
    interface at-0/1/0.35 {
        authentication-key "$9$I-EhyKsYoaUH" key-id 1; # SECRET-DATA
    }
    interface so-0/2/0.100 {
        interface-type nbma;
        authentication-key "$9$6M9/CpBW87Nb2" key-id 1; # SECRET-DATA
        neighbor 10.0.2.6 eligible;
    }
}
```

4. You have just configured area 20 as a stub, but you note that external LSAs are still in the LSDB as shown next. Is this a problem?

```
[edit]
lab@r7# set protocols ospf area 20 stub

[edit]
lab@r7# commit
commit complete

[edit]
lab@r7# run show ospf database

    OSPF link state database, area 0.0.0.20
```

Type	ID	Adv Rtr	Seq	Age	Opt	Cksum	Len
Router	*10.0.9.7	10.0.9.7	0x80000002	88	0x0	0x2584	72

OSPF external link state database

Type	ID	Adv Rtr	Seq	Age	Opt	Cksum	Len
Extern	10.0.5.0	10.0.3.4	0x80000039	620	0x2	0x7fb7	36
Extern	192.168.0.0	10.0.9.6	0x8000001c	1579	0x2	0x2e0a	36
Extern	*192.168.0.0	10.0.9.7	0x80000064	701	0x2	0x9757	36

5. Your goal is to advertise only 192.168.*x*/24 routes to a RIP neighbor. What is wrong with the following RIP export policy?

```
[edit]
lab@r6# show policy-options policy-statement broke
term 1 {
    from {
        protocol rip;
        route-filter 192.168.0.0/16 orlonger;
    }
}
then accept;
```

6. What is needed to make a Juniper Networks router generate a default route into a stub or NSSA?

Spot the Issues: Answers

1. You will need to monitor the traffic being sent by the remote router with the tcpdump or `monitor traffic` CLI command to actually view the secret. Showing the configuration will display only the hash of the secret, and tracing indicates only that there is a problem with authentication.

2. The area-range statement for the 192.168.*x* summary is incorrectly specified. To summarize external LSAs in a NSSA, you must include the `area-range` statement within the NSSA stanza. The example shown will summarize only 192.168.*x*/24 routes if they are area 1 internals.

3. The router's loopback address will not be advertised into OSPF because the RID was explicitly specified under `routing-options`. Omitting an explicit RID declaration will cause the router to advertise its loopback address as a stub route in the router LSAs it generates. If the loopback interface is placed into a particular area, then a network summary LSA is used to report the loopback interface route in all other areas to which that router attaches.

4. No, this is normal. The external LSAs will be flushed when they have reached max-age. If their presence serves to distract you, you can expedite their demise by purging the OSPF LSDB.

5. The problem with this policy is that the `first term is not` associated with a terminating action. So all routes, whether they match term 1 or not, are evaluated by the second term, which accepts all routes from all protocols. The fact that the last term in a policy can be unnamed, as is this case in this example, can make spotting this type of policy problem very difficult. To meet the requirements of accepting only 192.168.*x*/24 RIP routes for export, your RIP export policy will need to have an accept action associated with term 1. An explicit reject action for all other routes is not required since this is the default policy for RIP export. Both of the following policy examples will work as desired:

    ```
    [edit policy-options]
    lab@r6# show policy-statement not-broke1
    term 1 {
        from {
            protocol rip;
            route-filter 192.168.0.0/16 orlonger;
        }
        then accept;
    }


    [edit policy-options]
    lab@r6# show policy-statement not-broke2
    from {
        protocol rip;
        route-filter 192.168.0.0/16 orlonger accept;
    }
    ```

6. You must configure a default metric under the stub or NSSA area. This is often missed because default route origination is automatic for stub areas when using Cisco's IOS.

Chapter 4

IS-IS Configuration and Testing

JNCIP LAB SKILLS COVERED IN THIS CHAPTER:

- ✓ **Multi-Level IS-IS configuration**
    - ▪ Default route origination
- ✓ **Network types**
- ✓ **Authentication**
    - ▪ Hello and LSP authentication
- ✓ **IS-IS policy**
    - ▪ Summarization, filtering, and route leaking
    - ▪ Route Redistribution
- ✓ **Metrics, timers, and various other "knobs"**

This chapter details various JNCIP-level IS-IS configuration scenarios, and provides examples of the verification methods that can be used to confirm proper IS-IS protocol operation. It is assumed that your configurations are currently based on the case study criteria presented at the end of the initial system and interface configuration chapters. You will now be adding the IS-IS protocol to this test bed. If you are unsure as to the state of your routers, you should compare your configuration against those provided at the end of Chapters 1 and 2, and verify that all of your router interfaces are operational before proceeding.

As described in the previous chapter, the proper operation of your IGP will play a critical role in the overall success of your JNCIP lab attempt. Serious problems with your IGP's operation will almost guarantee that you will experience malfunctions with higher-level protocols and services like BGP or RSVP signaling, and the cascading effects of the cumulative point loss that will occur in such situations will virtually assure that you will experience little joy at the end of your testing day. A successful JNCIP exam candidate must possess the practical skills and protocol knowledge necessary to proficiently configure and troubleshoot the IS-IS protocol in a variety of network scenarios as demonstrated in this chapter.

Because the overall purpose of OSPF and IS-IS are essentially identical, this chapter will demonstrate IS-IS configuration and testing using topologies and configuration requirements that parallel the examples used in the previous chapter wherever possible. The fact that IS-IS supports only the point-to-point and broadcast network types means that you will be mercifully spared the need to configure multipoint and NBMA network types.

This chapter concludes with a case study that is designed to approximate a typical JNCIP IS-IS configuration scenario. The results of key operational mode commands are provided in the case study analysis section so that you can also compare the behavior of your network to a known good example. Router configurations that meet all case study requirements are provided at the end of the case study for comparison with your own configurations.

Multi-Level IS-IS Configuration

Like OSPF, the IS-IS protocol supports the partitioning of a routing domain into multiple levels. The use of multiple levels will generally improve protocol scalability, as level 2 (backbone) Link State Protocol Data Units (LSPs) are normally not flooded into a level 1 area.

Briefly stated, an IS-IS level 2 area is analogous to the OSPF backbone area (0), while a level 1 area operates much as an OSPF Totally Stubby Area, in that a default route is normally used to reach both inter-level and AS external routes. Unlike OSPF, IS-IS area boundaries occur between routers, such that a given Intermediate System (IS) is always wholly contained within a particular area. Level 1 adjacencies can only be formed between routers that share a common area number, while a level 2 adjacency can be formed between routers that may or may not share an area number. Juniper Networks M-series routers support the IS-IS protocol strictly for use in building IP routing tables. There is no support for the routing of OSI Connectionless Network Service (CLNS) network layer packets.

We begin our IS-IS configuration example with the network topology shown in Figure 4.1.

FIGURE 4.1   Multi-level IS-IS

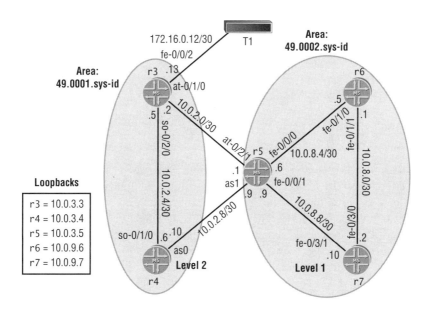

Referring to Figure 4.1, you can see that r5 will need to function as a level 1/level 2 router to interconnect the level 2 backbone (area 49.0001) and the level 1 area (49.0002) containing r6 and r7. To complete this configuration example, your IS-IS configuration must meet the following criteria:

- The System ID (SysID) must be based on the router's IPv4 lo0 address.

- Loss of any individual interface must not totally disrupt the router's IS-IS operation.

- The IPv4 lo0 addresses of all routers must be reachable via IS-IS.

- The link between r3 and T1 must appear in area 49.0001 as an intra-area route. Ensure that no IS-IS adjacencies can be established on this interface.

- The loopback addresses of level 2 routers may not appear in a level 1 area.

- Only one adjacency per router pairing is permitted.

IS-IS Configuration

We begin by configuring r4 as a level 2 IS-IS router based on the topology shown earlier in Figure 4.1. To enable IS-IS routing on a Juniper Networks router, you must add the iso protocol family to each IS-IS interface, assign your router's IS-IS address, and enable the IS-IS routing instance. What follows are step-by-step instructions on how to configure IS-IS and confirm its operation.

Configure Interface Support of IS-IS PDUs

The following commands are required to add the iso protocol family to all of r4's interfaces that are expected to run IS-IS. Failing to include the iso family will cause IS-IS to be disabled on that interface, because such an interface will not be able to send or receive link-level IS-IS PDUs:

```
[edit interfaces]
lab@r4# set so-0/1/0 unit 100 family iso
```

```
[edit interfaces]
lab@r4# set as0 unit 0 family iso
```

The IS-IS protocol will not operate until you have assigned a NET to one of your router's interfaces. The term *NET* is a fancy word for the IS-IS address that will uniquely identify a given router within an IS-IS routing domain. You must assign the NET to the router's lo0 interface to meet this example's requirement that "loss of any individual interface must not totally disrupt the router's IS-IS operation." You must also ensure that the NET is in some way traceable to the IPv4 address assigned to the router's lo0 address. The following command correctly configures r4's NET for this example:

```
[edit interfaces lo0 unit 0 family iso]
lab@r4# set address 49.0001.0100.0000.3004.00
```

Though perhaps not intuitive, the IS-IS address (NET) that has been assigned to r4 is interpreted as follows:

- The Authority and Format Identifier (AFI) value of *49* indicates a private use/locally assigned ISO NET.

- The area number is *0001*.

- The 6-byte System ID (SysID) is set to encode the router's IPv4 lo0 address in Binary Coded Decimal (BCD) format using three BCD digits for each decimal-delimited portion of corresponding IPv4 address. The resulting SysID is interpreted as 10.0.3.4, which meets the configuration requirements of this example. Although numerous mapping approaches could be used to satisfy the requirements of this example, e.g., 0010.0000.0034, it is highly recommended that you adopt a consistent transcoding algorithm to ensure ease of SysID interpretation, and to help prevent the assignment of a duplicate SysID.

- The Selector field is set to *00*, which makes this an ISO NET and not a Network Service Access Point Address (NSAPA). You should always specify an all-zeros selector byte for proper IS-IS operation.

The IS-IS related interface configuration of r4 is displayed in Listing 4.1. The highlights call out the recently added IS-IS configuration:

Listing 4.1: *r4* IS-IS Interface Configuration

```
[edit]
lab@r4# show interfaces as0
aggregated-sonet-options {
    minimum-links 2;
    link-speed oc3;
}
unit 0 {
    family inet {
        address 10.0.2.10/30;
    }
    family iso;
}
[edit]
lab@r4# show interfaces so-0/1/0
dce;
hold-time up 30 down 30;
encapsulation frame-relay;
lmi {
    n392dce 2;
    n393dce 3;
    t392dce 25;
    lmi-type itu;
}
unit 100 {
    dlci 100;
    family inet {
        address 10.0.2.6/30;
    }
    family iso;
}
[edit]
lab@r4# show interfaces lo0
unit 0 {
    family inet {
```

```
            address 10.0.3.4/32;
    }
    family iso {
        address 49.0001.0100.0000.3004.00;
    }
}
[edit]
lab@r4# show interfaces fxp0
unit 0 {
    family inet {
        address 10.0.1.4/24;
    }
}
```

WARNING
To help guard against inadvertent use of IS-IS on the OoB management network, you should avoid adding the iso family to the router's fxp0 interface. If you are using configuration groups to expedite the addition of protocol families, you must use caution to ensure either that the configuration group does not "catch" the fxp0 interface or that you explicitly disable IS-IS on the fxp0 interface when making use of the interface all option shown in this chapter. IGP adjacency formation over the OoB network can be disastrous because your routers will be inclined to forward traffic over the fxp0 subnet (because of the lower metric associated with this path), in conjunction with the fact that transit traffic is not supported over the fxp0 interface. Can you say "black hole"?

Configure *r4*'s IS-IS Routing Instance

The following commands are used to enable the main IS-IS instance and to correctly associate r4's IS-IS capable interfaces with IS-IS level 2 operation. Unlike OSPF, you must explicitly list the router's lo0 interface under the [edit protocols isis] stanza, as this interface is the source of the router's NET, and therefore must be configured as an IS-IS interface. The lo0 interface will operate in the passive mode by default, which is ideal because adjacency formation can never occur on a virtual interface anyway.

```
[edit protocols isis]
lab@r4# set interface lo0 level 1 disable

[edit protocols isis]
lab@r4# set interface as0 level 1 disable

[edit protocols isis]
lab@r4# set interface so-0/1/0.100 level 1 disable
```

By disabling level 1 IS-IS operation on r4's area 49.0001 interfaces, you ensure that at most one adjacency (level 2) can be formed between each router pair in area 49.0001. The JUNOS software default is to enable interface operation at both levels 1 and 2, which would result in two adjacencies forming, and subsequent point loss on your exam because the criteria for this example limits you to one adjacency per router pairing. The resulting configuration of r4's main IS-IS routing instance is shown here:

```
[edit protocols isis]
lab@r4# show
interface so-0/1/0.0 {
    level 1 disable;
}
interface as0.0 {
    level 1 disable;
}
interface lo0.0 {
    level 1 disable;
}
```

Verify IS-IS on *r4*

After committing the initial IS-IS configuration, we can display the state of r4's IS-IS interfaces to confirm their proper configuration and level assignment. The results indicate that r4's as0, so-0/1/0.100, and lo0 interfaces are enabled for IS-IS operation at level 2 only. As expected, no Designated Intermediate System (DIS) has been elected because of the lack of broadcast interface types on r4:

```
lab@r4> show isis interface
IS-IS interface database:
Interface          L CirID Level 1 DR      Level 2 DR      L1/L2 Metric
as0.0              2  0x1 Disabled         Point to Point       10/10
lo0.0              0  0x1 Disabled         Passive               0/0
so-0/1/0.100       2  0x1 Disabled         Point to Point       10/10

lab@r4>
```

In the absence of other IS-IS routers, we expect to find that r4 has no neighbors and, therefore, no adjacencies:

```
lab@r4> show isis adjacency

lab@r4>
```

As predicted, r4 currently has no IS-IS adjacencies. We can obtain additional information about the default IS-IS timers and source of the router's NET by using the `detail` switch, as shown next:

```
lab@r4> show isis interface detail
IS-IS interface database:
as0.0
  Index: 10, State: 0x6, Circuit id: 0x1, Circuit type: 2
  LSP interval: 100 ms, CSNP interval: disabled
  Level Adjacencies Priority Metric Hello (s) Hold (s) Designated Router
    2            0      64    10         9       27
lo0.0
  Index: 3, State: 0x7, Circuit id: 0x1, Circuit type: 0
  LSP interval: 100 ms, CSNP interval: disabled, Sysid: r4
  Level Adjacencies Priority Metric Hello (s) Hold (s) Designated Router
    2            0      64     0 Passive
so-0/1/0.100
  Index: 11, State: 0x6, Circuit id: 0x1, Circuit type: 2
  LSP interval: 100 ms, CSNP interval: disabled
  Level Adjacencies Priority Metric Hello (s) Hold (s) Designated Router
    2            0      64    10         9       27
```

This display confirms that the lo0 interface is the source of the router's NET, that no adjacencies have been formed, and that the default (non–Designated Intermediate System [DIS]) hello and hold timers are being used on all interfaces except lo0, which does not use them because of its passive mode of operation.

IS-IS Timers

Unlike OSPF, IS-IS will permit adjacency formation between systems that have been configured to use different hello timers. The `hold` interval is used to inform the remote system how long the adjacency can be considered valid in the absence of received hello LSPs. By default, the hold value is three times the configured hello interval, but both parameters can be set independently. The default ratio means that an adjacency can be maintained even if two out of three hello packets are lost. JUNOS software will automatically reduce an interface's hold and hello intervals by ⅔rds (3-second hellos and 9-second hold time) should the router be elected the DIS for the network that attaches to that interface. This enables the rapid detection of DIS failures. The IS-IS hold times at each level are unrelated to each other, so you may configure an interface's level 1 and level 2 timers differently with no ill effects.

The last step in confirming IS-IS operation on r4 is to examine the LSDB:

```
lab@r4# run show isis database
IS-IS level 1 link-state database:
LSP ID                      Sequence Checksum Lifetime Attributes
r4.00-00                      0x8   0xa284     1195 L1 L2
  1 LSPs


IS-IS level 2 link-state database:
LSP ID                      Sequence Checksum Lifetime Attributes
r4.00-00                      0xc   0xbab3     1195 L1 L2
  1 LSPs
```

Many exam candidates are surprised to find their router contains a level 1 database entry when they know that all of the router interfaces have been set to run level 2 only. The lone level 1 LSP is the result of disabling level 1 operation on the router's interfaces but not in the IS-IS routing instance itself. This LSP can never leave your router, and no level 1 LSPs can be received from other routers in the routing domain until IS-IS level 1 operation is enabled on at least one interface. A detailed examination of the LSDB confirms that the level 1 LSP is not advertising any prefixes (as yet, no interfaces are enabled for level 1 operation), and also confirms that the level 2 LSP is advertising the route to all three of r4's IS-IS subnetworks:

```
[edit]
lab@r4# run show isis database detail
IS-IS level 1 link-state database:

r4.00-00  Sequence: 0x8, Checksum: 0xa284, Lifetime: 818 secs

IS-IS level 2 link-state database:

r4.00-00  Sequence: 0xd, Checksum: 0xb8b4, Lifetime: 1176 secs
    IP prefix:             10.0.2.4/30 Metric:      10 Internal
    IP prefix:             10.0.2.8/30 Metric:      10 Internal
    IP prefix:             10.0.3.4/32 Metric:       0 Internal
```

If the presence of this LSP serves as a distraction, you can disable IS-IS level 1 in the routing instance by issuing a **set protocols isis level 1 disable** command. This command is not used here because r4 is expected to require level 1 capabilities at a later point in this chapter's examples.

Configure *r5* for IS-IS Operation

Though not shown here, r5's IS-IS configuration begins with the addition of the iso family to its as1, at-0/2/1.35, fe-0/0/0, fe-0/0/1, and lo0 interfaces using the commands that were shown for r4 in the section "Configure Interface Support of IS-IS PDUs" earlier in this chapter. The following commands define the correct interface and area associations needed by r5, which functions as a L1/L2 router in this example:

```
[edit protocols isis]
lab@r5# set interface lo0 level 1 disable

[edit protocols isis]
lab@r5# set interface at-0/2/1.35 level 1 disable

[edit protocols isis]
lab@r5# set interface as1 level 1 disable

[edit protocols isis]
lab@r5# set interface fe-0/0/0 level 2 disable

[edit protocols isis]
lab@r5# set interface fe-0/0/1 level 2 disable
```

The resulting multi-level configuration for r5 is shown next:

```
[edit protocols isis]
lab@r5# show
interface fe-0/0/0.0 {
    level 2 disable;
}
interface fe-0/0/1.0 {
    level 2 disable;
}
interface at-0/2/1.35 {
    level 1 disable;
}
interface as1.0 {
    level 1 disable;
}
interface lo0.0 {
    level 1 disable;
}
```

An alternative, but equally functional, configuration for r5 makes good use of the `interface all` keyword to save some typing:

```
[edit protocols isis]
lab@r5# show
interface fe-0/0/0.0 {
    level 2 disable;
}
interface fe-0/0/1.0 {
    level 2 disable;
}
interface all {
    level 1 disable;
}
```

Many operators feel that this alternative configuration "contradicts itself" in that intuition tells them that the `interface all level 1 disable` statement should affect all interfaces, and thereby cause problems with r5's Fast Ethernet interfaces, which are supposed to operate at level 1. This author likes to view the apparent quandary from a "longest match" perspective, in that the router will always override less specific configurations, such as `interface all`, with more specific information such as `interface fe-0/0/0 level 2 disable`. In this case, the fe-0/0/0 statement is more specific than the `all` keyword, so the router does the right thing by enabling level 1 only on the Fast Ethernet interfaces and level 2 only on all other interfaces. You should pay extra attention to the `show isis interfaces` command results when using this approach. You may find the router is running IS-IS on an unintended interface, such as fxp0, due to the non-specific nature of the `all` keyword.

Verify IS-IS on *r5*

After committing r5's IS-IS configuration, we expect to see an adjacency to r4, and the correct interface-to-area associations as demonstrated next:

```
[edit]
lab@r5# run show isis interface
IS-IS interface database:
Interface         L CirID Level 1 DR    Level 2 DR      L1/L2 Metric
as1.0             2 0x1 Disabled        Point to Point      10/10
at-0/2/1.35       2 0x1 Disabled        Point to Point      10/10
fe-0/0/0.0        1 0x2 r5.02           Disabled            10/10
fe-0/0/1.0        1 0x3 r5.03           Disabled            10/10
lo0.0             0 0x1 Disabled        Passive              0/0
```

These results confirm that r5's interfaces have been correctly configured with the `iso` family, and that the interfaces have been placed into the correct levels as stipulated by Figure 4.1, shown earlier. You can also see that r5 has elected itself as the DIS on its two broadcast-capable IS-IS interfaces. We now confirm the r4-to-r5 IS-IS adjacency:

```
[edit]
lab@r5# run show isis adjacency detail
r4
  Interface: as1.0, Level: 2, State: Up, Expires in 23 secs
  Priority: 0, Up/Down transitions: 1, Last transition: 00:11:13 ago
  Circuit type: 2, Speaks: IP, IPv6
  IP addresses: 10.0.2.10
```

These results confirm that r5 has a single level 2 adjacency to r4, whose IP address is 10.0.2.10. Because r5 is a L1/L2 attached router, we can now examine the level 1 link-state database associated with area 49.0002 to confirm that loopback addresses from backbone routers are not being advertised into the level 1 area. The contents of r5's LSDB are shown in Listing 4.2.

Listing 4.2: The Contents of *r5*'s IS-IS LSDB

```
[edit]
lab@r5# run show isis database detail
IS-IS level 1 link-state database:


r5.00-00  Sequence: 0x5, Checksum: 0x62c, Lifetime: 1123 secs
  IP prefix:                  10.0.8.8/30 Metric:       10 Internal
  IP prefix:                  10.0.8.4/30 Metric:       10 Internal


IS-IS level 2 link-state database:


r4.00-00  Sequence: 0x71, Checksum: 0xa9d4, Lifetime: 566 secs
  IS neighbor:               r5.00  Metric:       10
  IP prefix:                  10.0.2.4/30 Metric:       10 Internal
  IP prefix:                  10.0.2.8/30 Metric:       10 Internal
  IP prefix:                  10.0.3.4/32 Metric:        0 Internal


r5.00-00  Sequence: 0x6, Checksum: 0x10f1, Lifetime: 1123 secs
  IS neighbor:               r4.00  Metric:       10
  IP prefix:                  10.0.2.8/30 Metric:       10 Internal
  IP prefix:                  10.0.2.0/30 Metric:       10 Internal
  IP prefix:                  10.0.8.8/30 Metric:       10 Internal
  IP prefix:                  10.0.8.4/30 Metric:       10 Internal
  IP prefix:                  10.0.3.5/32 Metric:        0 Internal  0x2
0x831    28
```

This display indicates that r5's loopback interface has been correctly configured to run level 2 only. Had level 1 operation been enabled on lo0, r5 would have then included its loopback address in its level 1 LSP, thus violating the configuration requirements given for this example. You can also see that r5 has two level 2 LSPs, one of which was received from its adjacent neighbor, r4. It should be noted that like an OSPF Totally Stubby Area, no backbone (level 2) or external prefixes are leaked into a level 1 area by default. Level 1 prefixes are leaked up into the IS-IS backbone, however, as can be seen by the 10.0.8.*x*/30 prefixes in r5's level 2 LSP. Based on these results, we find that both r4 and r5 have been correctly configured for this example.

Configure *r3* for IS-IS Operation

The following commands are entered on r3 to complete the configuration of the level 2 backbone area. Once again, you may assume that r3's interfaces have been configured with the iso family and the correct NET, as demonstrated previously for r4:

```
[edit protocols isis]
lab@r3# set interface at-0/1/0.35 level 1 disable

[edit protocols isis]
lab@r3# set interface lo0 level 1 disable

[edit protocols isis]
lab@r3# set interface so-0/2/0.100 level 1 disable

[edit protocols isis]
lab@r3# set interface fe-0/0/2 passive

[edit protocols isis]
lab@r3# set interface fe-0/0/2 level 1 disable
```

The resulting IS-IS configuration for r3 is shown next:

```
[edit protocols isis]
lab@r3# show
interface fe-0/0/2.0 {
    passive;
    level 1 disable;
}
interface at-0/1/0.35 {
    level 1 disable;
}
```

```
interface so-0/2/0.100 {
    level 1 disable;
}
interface lo0.0 {
    level 1 disable;
}
```

By setting r3's fe-0/0/2 interface to passive, you ensure that no adjacencies can be formed over the interface and that the route to 172.16.0.12/30 will be injected into area 49.0001 as an internal route. Failing to set this interface as passive would result in loss of points on the JNCIP exam because there is no other way to correctly advertise the 172.16.0.12/30 route as an IS-IS internal prefix while also preventing adjacency formation. It is a good idea to disable level 1 operation on r3's fe-0/0/2 interface, even though it's passive, because this interface is associated with a level 2–only router and such configuration will keep r3's database tidy.

Verify IS-IS on *r3*

With the IS-IS backbone configured, you will expect to see that r3 has formed a single level 2 adjacency to each of its neighbors, and that the link to T1 is correctly reported in its level 2 LSP. You start by confirming the correct interface and IS-IS level configuration:

```
lab@r3> show isis interface
IS-IS interface database:
Interface          L CirID Level 1 DR     Level 2 DR        L1/L2 Metric
at-0/1/0.35        2   0x1 Disabled       Point to Point        10/10
lo0.0              0   0x1 Disabled       Passive                0/0
so-0/2/0.100       2   0x1 Disabled       Point to Point        10/10
```

The results leave something to be desired in that r3's fe-0/0/2 interface is not listed as an IS-IS interface. This could be the result of the interface being down, the lack of IS-IS instance configuration, or the lack of the iso family on the correct logical unit. A quick look at the interface's status confirms that the lack of family iso on the device's logical unit 0 is the cause of the problem:

```
[edit]
lab@r3# run show interfaces terse fe-0/0/2
Interface        Admin Link Proto Local                 Remote
fe-0/0/2         up    up
fe-0/0/2.0       up    up   inet  172.16.0.13/30
```

The following command adds the iso family to the correct logical unit on interface fe-0/0/2:

```
[edit interfaces]
lab@r4# set fe-0/0/2 unit 0 family iso
```

The results are now confirmed:

```
[edit]
lab@r3# run show isis interface
IS-IS interface database:
Interface          L CirID Level 1 DR      Level 2 DR         L1/L2 Metric
at-0/1/0.35        2   0x1 Disabled        Point to Point        10/10
fe-0/0/2.0         0   0x2 Disabled        Passive               10/10
lo0.0              0   0x1 Disabled        Passive                0/0
so-0/2/0.100       2   0x1 Disabled        Point to Point        10/10
```

You now confirm the correct IS-IS adjacency status for area 49.0001:

```
lab@r3> show isis adjacency
Interface          System        L State       Hold (secs) SNPA
at-0/1/0.35        r5            2 Up              22
so-0/2/0.100       r4            2 Up              25
```

Good, r3 has the required level 2 adjacencies to both r4 and r5 as required. Next, confirm the presence of the 172.16.0.12/30 route as an IS-IS level 2 route. We start by confirming the route's presence in r3's level 2 LSP:

```
[edit]
lab@r3# run show isis database r3 detail
IS-IS level 1 link-state database:


r3.00-00  Sequence: 0x12, Checksum: 0x53cd, Lifetime: 789 secs

IS-IS level 2 link-state database:


r3.00-00  Sequence: 0x15, Checksum: 0xb78a, Lifetime: 1052 secs
    IS neighbor:                   r4.00  Metric:        10
    IS neighbor:                   r5.00  Metric:        10
    IP prefix:           172.16.0.12/30 Metric:        10 Internal
    IP prefix:           10.0.2.4/30 Metric:          10 Internal
    IP prefix:           10.0.2.0/30 Metric:          10 Internal
    IP prefix:           10.0.3.3/32 Metric:           0 Internal
```

As required, the 172.16.0.12/30 prefix is being reported as an internal level 2 route. The last confirmation is to verify that other backbone routers have correctly installed this route. The following command is issued on r5:

```
[edit]
lab@r5# run show route protocol isis 172/8
```

```
inet.0: 16 destinations, 16 routes (16 active, 0 holddown, 0 hidden)
+ = Active Route, - = Last Active, * = Both

172.16.0.12/30    *[IS-IS/18] 14:19:29, metric 20, tag 2
                   > to 10.0.2.2 via at-0/2/1.35
```

As expected, r5 has installed the route as an IS-IS level 2 internal route as indicated by the tag 2 value (which denotes level 2) and the preference setting of 18.

Area 49.0002 Configuration

The following commands correctly configure r6 for operation as an IS-IS level 1 router in area 49.0002. You begin by configuring its interfaces with the iso family and the router's NET:

```
[edit interfaces]
lab@r6# set fe-0/1/0 unit 0 family iso
```

```
[edit interfaces]
lab@r6# set fe-0/1/1 unit 0 family iso
```

```
[edit interfaces lo0 unit 0]
lab@r6# set family iso address 49.0002.0100.0000.9006.00
```

The IS-IS routing instance for r6 is now configured. Because r6 is strictly a level 1 router, we disable all level 2 processing and save some typing by using **interface all**, as shown:

```
[edit protocols isis]
lab@r6# set level 2 disable
```

```
[edit protocols isis]
lab@r6# set interface all
```

The IS-IS configuration of r6 is shown below:

```
[edit protocols isis]
lab@r6# show
level 2 disable;
interface all;
```

The configuration of r7 is not shown here because it is virtually identical to that of r6 except for interface-naming specifics.

Area 49.0002 Verification

After committing the level 1 IS-IS configuration on both r6 and r7, we expect to find that a level 1 adjacency has formed between them:

```
lab@r6> show isis adjacency
Interface          System       L State      Hold (secs) SNPA
fe-0/1/1.0         r7           1 Up                   8  0:a0:c9:6f:7b:1a
```

With the level 1 adjacency confirmed up, we next verify proper DIS election on the broadcast interface between r6 and r7:

```
lab@r6> show isis interface
IS-IS interface database:
Interface          L CirID Level 1 DR      Level 2 DR       L1/L2 Metric
fe-0/1/0.0         1   0x2 r6.02           Disabled            10/10
fe-0/1/1.0         1   0x3 r7.02           Disabled            10/10
lo0.0              0   0x1 Passive         Disabled             0/0
```

The display indicates that r7 has won the DIS election on the 10.0.8.0/30 subnet. We confirm this by verifying that r7 has generated a pseudonode LSP for the broadcast network with r6 listed as the only neighbor:

```
lab@r6> show isis database r7 detail
IS-IS level 1 link-state database:

r7.00-00  Sequence: 0x3, Checksum: 0x7247, Lifetime: 539 secs
    IS neighbor:                    r7.02  Metric:       10
    IP prefix:              10.0.9.7/32 Metric:       0 Internal
    IP prefix:              10.0.8.8/30 Metric:      10 Internal
    IP prefix:              10.0.8.0/30 Metric:      10 Internal

r7.02-00  Sequence: 0x1, Checksum: 0xfdbc, Lifetime: 539 secs
    IS neighbor:                    r6.00  Metric:       0
    IS neighbor:                    r7.00  Metric:       0

IS-IS level 2 link-state database:
```

This display confirms that r7 is acting as the pseudonode for the 10.0.8.0/30 subnet, as indicated by its generation of an LSP with a non-zero selector field. Because all level 2 IS-IS processing has been disabled in r6 and r7, we find that the level 2 database is empty as expected.

Verify Overall IS-IS Operation

The spot checks performed thus far have returned the expected results for each of the two IS-IS areas in the configuration example outlined earlier in Figure 4.1, but the astute reader will have noticed that the command outputs displayed in the previous section indicate that r5 has not yet formed the required level 1 adjacencies to the routers in area 49.0002. The lack of an adjacency to the L1/L2-attached r5 results in the absence of the default route needed by level 1 routers to reach other areas:

```
lab@r7> show route protocol isis

inet.0: 11 destinations, 11 routes (11 active, 0 holddown, 0 hidden)
+ = Active Route, - = Last Active, * = Both

10.0.8.4/30         *[IS-IS/15] 00:26:23, metric 20, tag 1
                     > to 10.0.8.1 via fe-0/3/0.0
10.0.9.6/32         *[IS-IS/15] 00:26:23, metric 10, tag 1
                     > to 10.0.8.1 via fe-0/3/0.0


iso.0: 1 destinations, 1 routes (1 active, 0 holddown, 0 hidden)
```

Troubleshooting Adjacency Problems

The lack of an IS-IS adjacency between r5 and area 49.0002 routers could be the result of physical layer problems. This possibility is quickly eliminated through a quick round of ping testing, however:

```
lab@r6> ping 10.0.8.6
PING 10.0.8.6 (10.0.8.6): 56 data bytes
64 bytes from 10.0.8.6: icmp_seq=0 ttl=255 time=0.529 ms
64 bytes from 10.0.8.6: icmp_seq=1 ttl=255 time=0.451 ms
^C
--- 10.0.8.6 ping statistics ---
2 packets transmitted, 2 packets received, 0% packet loss
round-trip min/avg/max/stddev = 0.451/0.490/0.529/0.039 ms
```

These results indicate that physical layer connectivity between r6 and r5 is not the cause of the adjacency problem. Next, reconfirm that r5 has the necessary level 1 configuration:

```
lab@r5> show isis interface
IS-IS interface database:
```

Interface	L	CirID	Level 1 DR	Level 2 DR	L1/L2 Metric
as1.0	2	0x1	Disabled	Point to Point	10/10
at-0/2/1.35	2	0x1	Disabled	Point to Point	10/10
fe-0/0/0.0	1	0x2	r5.02	Disabled	10/10
fe-0/0/1.0	1	0x3	r5.03	Disabled	10/10
lo0.0	0	0x1	Disabled	Passive	0/0

The fact that both r5 and r6 have elected themselves as the DIS for the 10.0.8.4/30 subnet provides an indication that we are experiencing some type of "ships in the night" issue that results in each router ignoring the other's level 1 IS-IS packets.

As with the OSPF protocol, IS-IS tracing, with special attention placed on hello packet exchanges (and any error messages that may be occurring), is one of the best ways to troubleshoot adjacency formation problems. The following traceoptions configuration has been added to r6.

```
[edit protocols isis]
lab@r6# show traceoptions
file isis;
flag hello detail;
flag error detail;
```

The result of monitoring the isis trace file is shown in Listing 4.3:

Listing 4.3: IS-IS Tracing
```
[edit protocols isis]
lab@r6# run monitor start isis

[edit protocols isis]
lab@r6#
*** isis ***
May 17 17:24:43 Sending L1 LAN IIH on fe-0/1/0.0
May 17 17:24:43     max area 0, circuit type l1
May 17 17:24:43     No candidates for DR
May 17 17:24:43     hold time 27, priority 64, circuit id r6.02
May 17 17:24:43     speaks IP
May 17 17:24:43     speaks IPv6
May 17 17:24:43     IP address 10.0.8.5
May 17 17:24:43     area address 49.0002 (3)
May 17 17:24:44 Received L1 LAN IIH, source id 0100.0000.3005 on fe-0/1/0.0
May 17 17:24:44     intf index 2 addr 0.90.69.69.70.0, snpa 0:90:69:69:70:0
May 17 17:24:44     max area 0, circuit type l1, packet length 43
May 17 17:24:44     hold time 27, priority 64, circuit id 0100.0000.3005.02
May 17 17:24:44     speaks IP
May 17 17:24:44     speaks IPV6
```

```
May 17 17:24:44     IP address 10.0.8.6
May 17 17:24:44     area address 49.0001 (3)
May 17 17:24:44 ERROR: IIH from 0100.0000.3005 with no matching areas, interface
fe-0/1/0.0
May 17 17:24:44     local area  49.0002
May 17 17:24:44     remote area 49.0001 (3)
. . .
```

The trace output identifies the problem rather explicitly in this case. A level 1 router can only form an adjacency with routers in the same area, and r5 is identifying itself as belonging to area 49.0001. To resolve the problem, we reassign r5's NET using the following commands:

```
[edit interfaces lo0 unit 0 family iso]
lab@r5# delete address
```

```
[edit interfaces lo0 unit 0 family iso]
lab@r5# set address 49.0002.0100.0000.3005.00
```

The results are now confirmed:

```
[edit interfaces lo0 unit 0 family iso]
lab@r5# run show isis adjacency
Interface           System          L State      Hold (secs) SNPA
as1.0               r4              2 Up              25
at-0/2/1.35         r3              2 Up              22
fe-0/0/0.0          0100.0000.9006 1 New             23   0:a0:c9:69:c5:27
fe-0/0/1.0          r7              1 Up             24   0:60:94:51:c4:27
```

Excellent! The level 1 adjacencies are now forming correctly. It should be noted that even though r5's NET identifies itself as belonging to the level 1 area 49.0002, its lo0 interface has not been configured as a level 1 interface. This is important, because doing so would cause the route to r5's loopback to be injected into the level 1 area in violation of the configuration requirements specified in this example.

Verify Multi-Level Operation

The proper operation of the level 1 area is confirmed with the following command, the results of which indicate the presence of the required default route to the L1/L2-attached router and the absence of level 2 router loopback addresses:

```
[edit protocols isis]
lab@r6# run show route protocol isis

inet.0: 12 destinations, 12 routes (12 active, 0 holddown, 0 hidden)
+ = Active Route, - = Last Active, * = Both
```

```
0.0.0.0/0              *[IS-IS/15] 00:03:58, metric 10, tag 1
                       > to 10.0.8.6 via fe-0/1/0.0
10.0.8.8/30            *[IS-IS/15] 00:03:58, metric 20, tag 1
                       > to 10.0.8.6 via fe-0/1/0.0
                         to 10.0.8.2 via fe-0/1/1.0
10.0.9.7/32            *[IS-IS/15] 00:55:25, metric 10, tag 1
                       > to 10.0.8.2 via fe-0/1/1.0
```

```
iso.0: 1 destinations, 1 routes (1 active, 0 holddown, 0 hidden)
```

This author has found that issuing the following command on a L1/L2-attached router provides a quick check on the overall operation of an IS-IS network by confirming the presence of each IS-IS router and the setting of its SysID. The idea is similar to the verification of router LSAs on an OSPF ABR:

```
lab@r5> show isis hostname
IS-IS hostname database:
System Id       Hostname                          Type
0100.0000.3003 r3                                 Dynamic
0100.0000.3004 r4                                 Dynamic
0100.0000.3005 r5                                 Static
0100.0000.9006 r6                                 Dynamic
0100.0000.9007 r7                                 Dynamic
```

As required, all five routers are present and the unique assignment of SysID values is confirmed. The last check is to verify connectivity to the loopback address of level 2 routers from within the level 1 area:

```
lab@r7> traceroute 10.0.3.3
traceroute to 10.0.3.3 (10.0.3.3), 30 hops max, 40 byte packets
 1  10.0.8.9 (10.0.8.9)  0.357 ms  0.258 ms  0.215 ms
 2  10.0.3.3 (10.0.3.3)  0.915 ms  1.124 ms  0.877 ms

lab@r7> traceroute 10.0.3.4
traceroute to 10.0.3.4 (10.0.3.4), 30 hops max, 40 byte packets
 1  10.0.8.9 (10.0.8.9)  0.330 ms  0.244 ms  0.218 ms
 2  10.0.3.4 (10.0.3.4)  0.445 ms  0.368 ms  0.355 ms
```

The traceroutes to both r3 and r4 succeed as we had hoped, confirming the correct operation of your multi-level IS-IS configuration.

IS-IS Adjacencies and IP Addressing

The IS-IS protocol carries IP routing information in an opaque manner using Type Length Values (TLVs) that act as extensions to the IS-IS routing protocol. This point is significant because the opacity of these IP-related TLVs will allow an IS-IS adjacency to form across a subnet with IP addressing problems. In general, most individuals are more familiar with the operation of OSPF than IS-IS, and such readers may find this behavior unexpected, as the OSPF protocol will not form an adjacency when IP parameters are mismatched. The key point is that IS-IS adjacency formation does not validate the interface IP–related configuration, and this can lead to some tricky troubleshooting problems as demonstrated here. In this example, r6 has had its IP address changed from the correct setting of 10.0.8.5/30 to the incorrect value of 10.0.10.5/30. This change does not affect IS-IS adjacency formation, and connectivity to r5's 10.0.8.6 address is still possible, albeit with a less-than-optimal route:

```
[edit]
lab@r6# show interfaces fe-0/1/0
unit 0 {
    family inet {
        address 10.0.10.5/30;
    }
    family iso;
}
[edit]
lab@r6# run show isis adjacency
Interface          System       L State      Hold (secs) SNPA
fe-0/1/0.0         r5           1 Up                  22  0:90:69:69:70:0
fe-0/1/1.0         r7           1 Up                   7  0:a0:c9:6f:7b:1a
[edit]
lab@r6# run traceroute 10.0.8.6
traceroute to 10.0.8.6 (10.0.8.6), 30 hops max, 40 byte packets
 1  10.0.8.2 (10.0.8.2)  0.197 ms  0.123 ms  0.096 ms
 2  10.0.8.6 (10.0.8.6)  0.488 ms  0.435 ms  0.410 ms
```

Though not required by the IS-IS specification or the IP-related RFCs, newer versions of JUNOS software have been modified to prevent the establishment of an IS-IS adjacency when IP parameters are mismatched. This modified behavior is nice, but should not be counted on because of the version-specific nature of this feature.

IS-IS Network Types

The IS-IS protocol offers support only for the broadcast and point-to-point network types. You will not be able to configure the IS-IS protocol on a WAN interface configured with the `multipoint` keyword, unless multicast support is also included:

```
[edit interfaces so-0/1/0]
lab@r4# show
dce;
hold-time up 30 down 30;
encapsulation frame-relay;
lmi {
    n392dce 2;
    n393dce 3;
    t392dce 25;
    lmi-type itu;
}
unit 100 {
    multipoint;
    family inet {
        address 10.0.2.6/30 {
            multipoint-destination 10.0.2.5 dlci 100;
        }
    }
    family iso;
}
```

The lack of a multicast DLCI assignment makes this an illegal configuration:

```
[edit interfaces so-0/1/0]
lab@r4# commit check
[edit interfaces so-0/1/0 unit 100 family iso]
  'family iso;'
    Family ISO not allowed on non-multicast-capable multipoint interfaces
DCD_PARSE_ERROR: config file parse failed
error: configuration check-out failed
```

At the time of this writing, carrier support for multicast Frame Relay and ATM circuits is virtually nonexistent. The grounding of the JNCIP examination in "real world" service provider–like environments means that you are unlikely to see multicast Frame Relay or ATM-related configuration requirements in the lab. With the `multicast-dlci` keyword present, the candidate configuration will commit but IS-IS will still treat the WAN link as a point-to-point interface.

The Designated Intermediate System

IS-IS makes use of the Designated Router (DR) concept for the same reasons as the OSPF protocol. Since IS-IS does not support NBMA network types, it elects only a DIS on the broadcast network type associated with LAN interfaces. Unlike OSPF, the DIS function in IS-IS is preemptive, which means that a router with a preferred priority setting will overthrow the existing DIS to claim its rightful position on the network. Should the DIS priority be the same, the tie is broken based on the MAC address (also called a Subnetwork Point of Attachment [SNPA]), with the router possessing the highest MAC address being declared the winner. Additional differences between IS-IS and OSPF include the fact that IS-IS does not support the concept of a BDR, and that LAN-attached stations will form a full mesh of IS-IS adjacencies, while in OSPF, such stations will form adjacencies only to the DR and BDR but not among DROther routers.

IS-IS Authentication

The IS-IS implementation offered in JUNOS software supports both simple password and HMAC-MD5–based authentication mechanisms. One key difference between OSPF and IS-IS authentication support relates to the ability to configure authentication for IS-IS hellos, LSP exchanges, or both.

Your next assignment is to add IS-IS authentication according to the criteria listed next. You should refer back to Figure 4.1 for topology details.

- Backbone area authenticates both hello and LSP exchanges using MD5 with a key value of *jni*.
- Area 49.0002 uses a plain text password of *jnx* for hello authentication only.
- No routing disruption can occur in the backbone when adding authentication.

Configure Authentication on *r5*

The following commands correctly configure the authentication parameters for area 49.0001. Note that the inclusion of the `no-authentication-check` option is required to ensure that adjacencies are not disrupted by the addition of authentication to the IS-IS level 2 backbone:

```
[edit protocols isis]
lab@r5# set no-authentication-check
```

```
[edit protocols isis]
lab@r5# set level 2 authentication-type md5 authentication-key jni
```

The next set of commands adds the required hello authentication to each of r5's level 2 interfaces. Authentication is not configured on interface lo0 because LSP flooding and adjacency formation do not occur on this virtual interface:

```
[edit protocols isis]
lab@r5# set interface as1.0 hello-authentication-type md5
```

```
[edit protocols isis]
lab@r5# set interface as1.0 hello-authentication-key jni

[edit protocols isis]
lab@r5# set interface at-0/2/1.35 hello-authentication-type md5

[edit protocols isis]
lab@r5# set interface at-0/2/1.35 hello-authentication-key jni
```

Next, simple password authentication, as required for area 49.0002 hello exchanges, is configured on r5:

```
[edit protocols isis]
lab@r5# set interface fe-0/0/0 hello-authentication-type simple

[edit protocols isis]
lab@r5# set interface fe-0/0/0 hello-authentication-key jnx

[edit protocols isis]
lab@r5# set interface fe-0/0/1 hello-authentication-type simple

[edit protocols isis]
lab@r5# set interface fe-0/0/1 hello-authentication-key jnx
```

The modified configuration for r5 is shown next with the newly added authentication configuration highlighted:

```
[edit protocols isis]
lab@r5# show
no-authentication-check;
level 2 {
    authentication-key "$9$iqPQB1hSrv"; # SECRET-DATA
    authentication-type md5; # SECRET-DATA
}
interface fe-0/0/0.0 {
    hello-authentication-key "$9$VhsgJTQn6A0"; # SECRET-DATA
    hello-authentication-type simple; # SECRET-DATA
    level 2 disable;
}
interface fe-0/0/1.0 {
    hello-authentication-key "$9$iqPQB1hclM"; # SECRET-DATA
    hello-authentication-type simple; # SECRET-DATA
```

```
        level 2 disable;
}
interface at-0/2/1.35 {
    hello-authentication-key "$9$p-XmOIcN-wYgJ"; # SECRET-DATA
    hello-authentication-type md5; # SECRET-DATA
    level 1 disable;
}
interface as1.0 {
    hello-authentication-key "$9$gXaGi6/tuOR"; # SECRET-DATA
    hello-authentication-type md5; # SECRET-DATA
    level 1 disable;
}
interface lo0.0 {
    level 1 disable;
}
```

After committing the authentication changes on r5, we confirm that all level 2 adjacencies remain in place, despite the absence of compatible authentication settings on the remaining routers that make up the test bed:

```
[edit]
lab@r5# commit and-quit
commit complete
Exiting configuration mode

lab@r5> show isis adjacency
Interface            System          L State         Hold (secs) SNPA
as1.0                r4              2 Up                  19
at-0/2/1.35          r3              2 Up                  21
fe-0/0/0.0           r6              1 Up                   8  0:a0:c9:69:c5:27
fe-0/0/1.0           r7              1 Up                  23  0:60:94:51:c4:27
```

Configure Authentication on *r3* and *r4*

The authentication configuration for r3 and r4 is similar to that of r5. The only difference is the lack of area 49.0002 and level 1–related authentication, which is not required because these routers are only level 2–attached. The completed configuration for the remaining level 2 routers is shown here, starting with r3:

```
[edit protocols isis]
lab@r3# show
no-authentication-check;
```

```
level 2 {
    authentication-key "$9$nhTp9tOMWxNds"; # SECRET-DATA
    authentication-type md5; # SECRET-DATA
}
interface fe-0/0/2.0 {
    passive;
    level 1 disable;
}
interface at-0/1/0.35 {
    hello-authentication-key "$9$wx2oGzF/CtO"; # SECRET-DATA
    hello-authentication-type md5; # SECRET-DATA
    level 1 disable;
}
interface so-0/2/0.100 {
    hello-authentication-key "$9$yuZeMXaJDikP"; # SECRET-DATA
    hello-authentication-type md5; # SECRET-DATA
    level 1 disable;
}
interface lo0.0 {
    level 1 disable;
}
```

r4's configuration is very similar to that of r3:

```
[edit protocols isis]
lab@r4# show
no-authentication-check;
level 2 {
    authentication-key "$9$XX4NVYq.5QF/"; # SECRET-DATA
    authentication-type md5; # SECRET-DATA
}
interface so-0/1/0.100 {
    hello-authentication-key "$9$OQpxIhrVb24aU"; # SECRET-DATA
    hello-authentication-type md5; # SECRET-DATA
    level 1 disable;
}
interface as0.0 {
    hello-authentication-key "$9$SCLlvLoaUjHm"; # SECRET-DATA
    hello-authentication-type md5; # SECRET-DATA
    level 1 disable;
}
```

```
interface lo0.0 {
    level 1 disable;
}
```

Configure Authentication in Area 49.0002

The following commands correctly configure r7 for simple password-based authentication of hello messages. The use of `no-authentication-check` is not required in this area, so we expect to see the loss of adjacency to r6 when the changes are committed. The adjacency to r5, however, should remain operational because it's already being configured with compatible authentication parameters:

```
[edit protocols isis]
lab@r7# set interface all hello-authentication-type simple

[edit protocols isis]
lab@r7# set interface all hello-authentication-key jnx

[edit protocols isis]
lab@r7# commit
commit complete

[edit protocols isis]
lab@r7# run show isis adjacency
Interface           System        L State       Hold (secs) SNPA
fe-0/3/0.0          r6            1 Rejected           16  0:a0:c9:69:c1:e4
fe-0/3/1.0          r5            1 Up                  7  0:90:69:69:70:1
```

Just as predicted, the lack of compatible hello authentication in r6 results in the rejection of its hello packets. This situation will clear up when r6 is compatibly configured, as shown next:

```
[edit protocols isis]
lab@r6# show
level 2 disable;
interface all {
    hello-authentication-key "$9$RTtcrvY2aJDk"; # SECRET-DATA
    hello-authentication-type simple; # SECRET-DATA
}
```

The authentication changes are committed on r6, and the results are confirmed:

```
[edit protocols isis]
lab@r6# commit
commit complete
```

```
[edit protocols isis]
lab@r6# run show isis adjacency
Interface          System      L State      Hold (secs) SNPA
fe-0/1/0.0         r5          1 Up                  21  0:90:69:69:70:0
fe-0/1/1.0         r7          1 Initializing        22  0:a0:c9:6f:7b:1a

[edit protocols isis]
lab@r6# run show isis adjacency
Interface          System      L State      Hold (secs) SNPA
fe-0/1/0.0         r5          1 Up                  22  0:90:69:69:70:0
fe-0/1/1.0         r7          1 Up                  26  0:a0:c9:6f:7b:1a
```

Troubleshoot IS-IS Authentication

IS-IS authentication problems often result in the same types of neighbor detection and adjacency failures that can also be attributed to numerous problems at the IS-IS, link, or physical layers. The operator can quickly isolate physical and link layer problems through ping testing to a directly connected router. Authentication-related problems should be suspected when ping testing succeeds in the face of IS-IS adjacency failures. Adding the `no-authentication-check` option can quickly confirm if authentication is causing an adjacency problem because this causes the receiving router to ignore the authentication parameters (or lack thereof) in the IS-IS PDUs it receives.

Often, the use of `monitor traffic` will make authentication problems obvious. The following example shows a capture taken from r7's `fe-0/3/0` interface before r6 has been correctly configured for hello authentication:

```
[edit protocols isis]
lab@r7# run monitor traffic interface fe-0/3/0
Listening on fe-0/3/0
19:55:18.586402 Out iso isis 0:a0:c9:6f:7b:1a > 1:80:c2:0:0:14 len=49
                    L1 lan iih, circuit l1 only, holding time 27
                    source 1:0:0:0:90:7, length 49
                    lan id 1:0:0:0:90:7(2)
                    Supports protocols are CC 8E
                    IP address: 10.0.8.2
                    area addresses
                    49.0002 (3)
                    authentication data
                    016a 6e78
```

```
19:55:20.195900  In iso isis 0:a0:c9:69:c1:e4 > 1:80:c2:0:0:14 len=1492
                            L1 lan iih, circuit 11 only, holding time 27
                            source 1:0:0:0:90:6, length 1492
                            lan id 1:0:0:0:90:6(3)
                            neighbor addresses
                            0:a0:c9:6f:7b:1a
                            Supports protocols are CC 8E
                            IP address: 10.0.8.1
                            area addresses
                            49.0002 (3)
                            padding for 255 bytes
                            packet exceeded snapshot
```

This decode clearly shows that simple password authentication is present in the hello packets sent out r7's fe-0/3/0 interface. The plain text password value of *jnx* is displayed in hexadecimal form with 6a 6e 78 being ASCII code for the configured *jnx* key. In contrast, the hello packets received by r7 clearly lack the authentication field.

The following capture, taken from r5's aggregated SONET interface, illustrates the difference between the simple password and MD5-based hello packet authentication approaches:

```
[edit protocols isis]
lab@r5# run monitor traffic interface as1
Listening on as1
. . .
05:03:53.746131  In iso isis len=72
                            PTP iih, circuit 12 only, holding time 27
                            source 1:0:0:0:30:4, length 72
                            PTP adjacency status UP
                            Supports protocols are CC 8E
                            IP address: 10.0.2.10
                            area addresses
                            49.0001 (3)
                            authentication data
                            3661 755c 5532 ce85 645f a7d0 8b92 8934 69
```

Once again, it is clear that the received hello packet is carrying some type of authentication information. However, it is not obvious whether the packets are using simple password or MD5-based secrets. If you suspect that mismatched MD5 secrets have been configured, you will need to reset the MD5 key in all routers. Reverse engineering the MD5 hash is not possible, even with an ASCII code chart.

Protocol Tracing

While monitoring traffic has the benefit of being fast and dirty, the output will often leave much to the operator's interpretation, which is in stark contrast to the overt error messages that are sometimes seen with protocol tracing. The following tracing configuration has been added to r7:

```
[edit protocols isis]
lab@r7# show traceoptions
file isis;
flag error detail;
flag hello detail;
```

This tracing configuration produced the following output, which makes it hard to miss the authentication-related nature of the problem:

```
[edit]
lab@r7# run monitor start isis

lab@r7#
*** isis ***
May 17 20:08:57 Received L1 LAN IIH, source id r6 on fe-0/3/0.0
May 17 20:08:57     intf index 2 addr 0.a0.c9.69.c1.e4, snpa 0:a0:c9:69:c1:e4
May 17 20:08:57     max area 0, circuit type l1, packet length 1492
May 17 20:08:57     hold time 27, priority 64, circuit id r6.03
May 17 20:08:57     neighbor 0:a0:c9:6f:7b:1a (ourselves)
May 17 20:08:57     speaks IP
May 17 20:08:57     speaks IPV6
May 17 20:08:57     IP address 10.0.8.1
May 17 20:08:57     area address 49.0002 (3)
May 17 20:08:57 ERROR: IIH from r6 without authentication
May 17 20:08:57 ERROR: previous error from L1, source r6 on fe-0/3/0.0
```

Real World Scenario

How Can You Confirm Area 49.0001 Authentication Settings?

The presence of the `no-authentication-check` option in the backbone routers can cause incompatible or incorrect authentication parameters to go undetected. Before moving on, you should temporarily delete this option on a backbone router and verify that all level 2 adjacencies are maintained. After confirming that all is well, this option should be reinstated, as its presence is needed to show compliance with the specified configuration requirements.

```
[edit protocols isis]
lab@r5# delete no-authentication-check


[edit protocols isis]
lab@r5# commit
commit complete


[edit protocols isis]
lab@r5# run show isis adjacency
Interface          System        L State        Hold (secs) SNPA
as1.0              r4            2 Up                 23
at-0/2/1.35        r3            2 Up                 23
fe-0/0/0.0         r6            1 Up                  8  0:a0:c9:69:c5:27
fe-0/0/1.0         r7            1 Up                 20  0:60:94:51:c4:27
[edit protocols isis]
lab@r5# set no-authentication-check
[edit protocols isis]
lab@r5# commit
commit complete
```

IS-IS Policy

JUNOS software policy is used with IS-IS to configure route leaking, route summarization, and route redistribution. The configuration examples in this section demonstrate the use and verification of IS-IS routing policy.

Route Leaking and Summarization

Route leaking allows the injection of routing information from the IS-IS backbone into a level 1 area. The added routing information in the level 1 area reduces the area's reliance on the default route generated by level 2–attached routers, and can eliminate the potential for inefficient routing that can result from using the metrically closest attached router for all inter-area destinations.

To complete this configuration example, you will need to configure area 49.0003 and then apply routing policy to effect route leaking and route summarization for the area according to the following criteria:

- Leak level 2 loopback addresses into area 49.0003 and ensure optimal routing to these prefixes.

- Summarize area 49.0003 addresses into the backbone.

- Maintain connectivity between all router loopback addresses.

Area 49.0003 Initial Configuration

Before route leaking and summarization can be demonstrated, you must first correctly configure area 49.0003 as a level 1 area according to Figure 4.2.

FIGURE 4.2   Route leaking and summarization

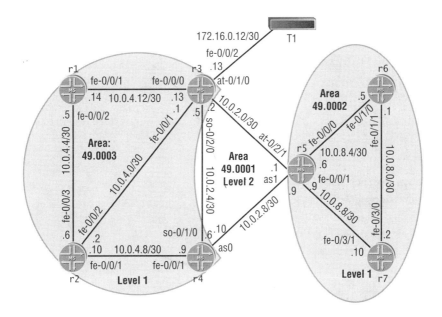

To complete the initial configuration of area 49.003, you will need to reassign the NET on both r3 and r4 (the current NET will prevent level 1 adjacency formation in area 49.0003), and configure the correct interfaces for level 1 operation. A working configuration from r4 is shown here with highlighted changes:

```
[edit]
lab@r4# show interfaces fe-0/0/1
speed 100m;
link-mode half-duplex;
```

```
fastether-options {
    no-flow-control;
}
unit 0 {
    family inet {
        address 10.0.4.9/30;
    }
    family iso;
}


[edit]
lab@r4# show interfaces lo0
unit 0 {
    family inet {
        address 10.0.3.4/32;
    }
    family iso {
        address 49.0003.0100.0000.3004.00;
    }
}
```

The modified IS-IS stanza on r4 includes the declaration of interface fe-0/0/1 as a level 1–only interface:

```
[edit]
lab@r4# show protocols isis
no-authentication-check;
level 2 {
    authentication-key "$9$XX4NVYq.5QF/"; # SECRET-DATA
    authentication-type md5; # SECRET-DATA
}
interface fe-0/0/1.0 {
    level 2 disable;
}
interface so-0/1/0.100 {
    hello-authentication-key "$9$0QpxIhrVb24aU"; # SECRET-DATA
    hello-authentication-type md5; # SECRET-DATA
    level 1 disable;
}
interface as0.0 {
    hello-authentication-key "$9$SCLlvLoaUjHm"; # SECRET-DATA
```

```
    hello-authentication-type md5; # SECRET-DATA
    level 1 disable;
}
interface lo0.0 {
    level 1 disable;
}
```

A functional configuration for a level 1 router in area 49.0003 is shown next for r1 with IS-IS additions highlighted:

```
[edit]
lab@r1# show interfaces fe-0/0/1
vlan-tagging;
unit 200 {
    vlan-id 200;
    family inet {
        address 10.0.4.14/30;
    }
    family iso;
}

[edit]
lab@r1# show interfaces fe-0/0/2
fastether-options {
    source-filtering;
    source-address-filter {
        00:a0:c9:6f:70:0d;
    }
}
unit 0 {
    family inet {
        address 10.0.4.5/30;
    }
    family iso;
}

[edit]
lab@r1# show interfaces lo0
unit 0 {
    family inet {
        address 10.0.6.1/32;
    }
```

```
    family iso {
        address 49.0003.0100.0000.6001.00;
    }
}
```

r1's IS-IS stanza correctly configures it as a level 1–only router:

```
[edit]
lab@r1# show protocols isis
level 2 disable;
interface all;
```

Area 49.0003 Verification

After completing the initial configuration for area 49.0003, you can quickly assess your work by verifying that the appropriate adjacencies and SysIDs are present in area 49.0003:

```
lab@r3> show isis adjacency
Interface            System          L State        Hold (secs) SNPA
at-0/1/0.35          r5              2 Up                21
fe-0/0/0.0           r1              1 Up                 7  0:a0:c9:6f:7b:3e
fe-0/0/1.0           r2              1 Up                26  0:a0:c9:6f:7a:ff
so-0/2/0.100         r4              2 Up                26
```

```
lab@r3> show isis hostname
IS-IS hostname database:
System Id       Hostname                                Type
0100.0000.3003  r3                                      Static
0100.0000.3004  r4                                      Dynamic
0100.0000.3005  r5                                      Dynamic
0100.0000.6001  r1                                      Dynamic
0100.0000.6002  r2                                      Dynamic
```

Configure Route Leaking

For this example, your IS-IS route-leaking configuration is performed on the L1/L2-attached routers that serve area 49.0003. You must use a policy that makes use of route filters to achieve the goal of leaking only the backbone area's loopback addresses. Before route leaking is configured, you first analyze the state of the routing table for level 1 routers in area 49.0003:

```
lab@r2> show route protocol isis

inet.0: 15 destinations, 15 routes (15 active, 0 holddown, 0 hidden)
+ = Active Route, - = Last Active, * = Both
```

```
0.0.0.0/0              *[IS-IS/15] 01:54:13, metric 10, tag 1
                          to 10.0.4.9 via fe-0/0/1.0
                        > to 10.0.4.1 via fe-0/0/2.0
10.0.4.12/30           *[IS-IS/15] 01:54:21, metric 20, tag 1
                          to 10.0.4.1 via fe-0/0/2.0
                        > to 10.0.4.5 via fe-0/0/3.0
10.0.6.1/32            *[IS-IS/15] 01:54:28, metric 10, tag 1
                        > to 10.0.4.5 via fe-0/0/3.0
```

From this display, we can see that backbone area loopback addresses are not yet present in area 49.0003. The following commands create the policy needed to correctly leak lo0 prefixes into area 49.0003:

```
[edit policy-options policy-statement leak]
lab@r4# set term 1 from protocol isis
```

```
[edit policy-options policy-statement leak]
lab@r4# set term 1 from level 2
```

```
[edit policy-options policy-statement leak]
lab@r4# set term 1 from route-filter 10.0.3/24 longer
```

```
[edit policy-options policy-statement leak]
lab@r4# set term 1 to level 1
```

```
[edit policy-options policy-statement leak]
lab@r4# set term 1 then accept
```

The completed policy is now displayed:

```
[edit policy-options policy-statement leak]
lab@r4# show
term 1 {
    from {
        protocol isis;
        level 2;
        route-filter 10.0.3.0/24 longer;
    }
    to level 1;
    then accept;
}
```

The route-leaking policy is now applied as an export policy to the IS-IS instance and the changes are committed:

```
[edit]
lab@r4# set protocols isis export leak

[edit]
lab@r4# commit
commit complete
```

Verify Route Leaking

The effects of your route-leaking policy are tested with the following commands:

```
lab@r2> show route protocol isis

inet.0: 17 destinations, 17 routes (17 active, 0 holddown, 0 hidden)
+ = Active Route, - = Last Active, * = Both

0.0.0.0/0          *[IS-IS/15] 01:57:53, metric 10, tag 1
                     to 10.0.4.9 via fe-0/0/1.0
                   > to 10.0.4.1 via fe-0/0/2.0
10.0.3.3/32        *[IS-IS/18] 00:00:54, metric 20, tag 1
                   > to 10.0.4.9 via fe-0/0/1.0
10.0.3.5/32        *[IS-IS/18] 00:00:54, metric 20, tag 1
                   > to 10.0.4.9 via fe-0/0/1.0
10.0.4.12/30       *[IS-IS/15] 01:58:01, metric 20, tag 1
                     to 10.0.4.1 via fe-0/0/2.0
                   > to 10.0.4.5 via fe-0/0/3.0
10.0.6.1/32        *[IS-IS/15] 01:58:08, metric 10, tag 1
                   > to 10.0.4.5 via fe-0/0/3.0
```

While these results are promising, r4's loopback address is absent in area 49.0003. This situation is caused by the policy being written to match on IS-IS level 2 routes coupled with the fact that r4 has learned about its own lo0 address from the direct protocol. This problem is easily rectified with the highlighted policy modification on r4:

```
[edit policy-options policy-statement leak]
lab@r4# show
term 1 {
    from {
        protocol isis;
        level 2;
        route-filter 10.0.3.0/24 longer;
```

```
        }
        to level 1;
        then accept;
}
term 2 {
    from {
            protocol direct;
            route-filter 10.0.3.0/24 longer;
    }
    to level 1;
    then accept;
}
```

Although the testing conducted with the 5.2 version of JUNOS software used in this test bed indicates that the `to level 1` criteria is not needed for the route leaking behavior specified in this example, such syntax is needed when the goal is to leak a prefix into either level 1 *or* level 2, but not into both levels 1 and 2. The `to level 1` syntax has been included here because it helps to reinforce the readers' awareness of route-leaking directionality. Also of note is the fact that this policy does not make use of a "reject all" term, which means the default IS-IS policy of leaking level 1 prefixes into level 2 has not been altered. The net result is the expectation that r4 will continue to leak level 1 routes into level 2 while also leaking specific level 2 prefixes into area 49.0003.

To complete the route-leaking configuration, a similar policy must be applied to r3. This will ensure that the suboptimal routing from area 49.0003 to backbone router loopback addresses, which is demonstrated next, does not occur:

```
lab@r1> traceroute 10.0.3.3
traceroute to 10.0.3.3 (10.0.3.3), 30 hops max, 40 byte packets
 1  10.0.4.6 (10.0.4.6)  0.219 ms  0.167 ms  0.115 ms
 2  10.0.4.9 (10.0.4.9)  0.353 ms  0.307 ms  0.286 ms
 3  10.0.3.3 (10.0.3.3)  0.504 ms  0.433 ms  0.421 ms
```

The extra hops in this capture are the result of having only one of the attached routers perform the route leaking. After applying the same route-leaking policy to r3, we see that optimal routing to level 2 lo0 addresses has been achieved:

```
lab@r1> traceroute 10.0.3.3
traceroute to 10.0.3.3 (10.0.3.3), 30 hops max, 40 byte packets
 1  10.0.3.3 (10.0.3.3)  0.513 ms  0.376 ms  0.346 ms
```

Configure Route Summarization

Because the IS-IS protocol does not offer support of area-range statements, route summarization requires the definition of an aggregate route and the policy needed to advertise this aggregate while suppressing the more specific prefixes. Before configuring summarization, analyze the route table of a backbone router with regard to area 49.0003 routes in order to better judge the effect of your route summarization configuration:

```
lab@r5> show route protocol isis 10.0.4/22

inet.0: 24 destinations, 24 routes (24 active, 0 holddown, 0 hidden)
+ = Active Route, - = Last Active, * = Both

10.0.4.0/30        *[IS-IS/18] 02:46:47, metric 20, tag 2
                    > to 10.0.2.2 via at-0/2/1.35
10.0.4.4/30        *[IS-IS/18] 00:02:27, metric 30, tag 2
                    > to 10.0.2.2 via at-0/2/1.35
                      to 10.0.2.10 via as1.0
10.0.4.8/30        *[IS-IS/18] 02:48:01, metric 20, tag 2
                    > to 10.0.2.10 via as1.0
10.0.4.12/30       *[IS-IS/18] 02:46:47, metric 20, tag 2
                    > to 10.0.2.2 via at-0/2/1.35
10.0.6.1/32        *[IS-IS/18] 00:02:34, metric 20, tag 2
                    > to 10.0.2.2 via at-0/2/1.35
10.0.6.2/32        *[IS-IS/18] 00:02:27, metric 20, tag 2
                    > to 10.0.2.2 via at-0/2/1.35
                      to 10.0.2.10 via as1.0
```

These results confirm that summarization into the backbone does not occur by default. You can configure r3 to advertise a summary, and to suppress the more specific level 1 routes, with the following policy and aggregate route definition:

```
[edit]
lab@r3# show policy-options policy-statement summ
term 1 {
    from protocol aggregate;
    to level 2;
    then accept;
}
term 2 {
    from {
        protocol isis;
        level 1;
    }
    to level 2;
    then reject;
}
```

Term 2 in this policy negates the default IS-IS policy of leaking level 1 routes into level 2, which is intended to prevent the advertisement of the specific prefixes in area 49.0003. The aggregate route for area 49.0003 prefixes is displayed next:

```
[edit]
lab@r3# show routing-options aggregate
route 10.0.4.0/22;
```

The *summ* policy is then applied to r3's IS-IS instance as an export policy:

```
[edit]
lab@r3# show protocols isis export
export [ leak summ ];
```

Verify Route Summarization

You can easily verify the results of your route summarization by once again displaying the contents of a backbone router's routing table, as it relates to area 49.0003 routes:

```
lab@r5> show route protocol isis 10.0.4/22

inet.0: 25 destinations, 25 routes (25 active, 0 holddown, 0 hidden)
+ = Active Route, - = Last Active, * = Both

10.0.4.0/22      *[IS-IS/165] 00:00:22, metric 20, tag 2
                  > to 10.0.2.2 via at-0/2/1.35
10.0.4.0/30      *[IS-IS/18] 03:04:49, metric 20, tag 2
                  > to 10.0.2.2 via at-0/2/1.35
10.0.4.4/30      *[IS-IS/18] 00:00:22, metric 30, tag 2
                  > to 10.0.2.10 via as1.0
10.0.4.8/30      *[IS-IS/18] 00:02:44, metric 20, tag 2
                  > to 10.0.2.10 via as1.0
10.0.4.12/30     *[IS-IS/18] 03:04:49, metric 20, tag 2
                  > to 10.0.2.2 via at-0/2/1.35
10.0.6.1/32      *[IS-IS/18] 00:00:22, metric 30, tag 2
                  > to 10.0.2.10 via as1.0
10.0.6.2/32      *[IS-IS/18] 00:00:22, metric 20, tag 2
                  > to 10.0.2.10 via as1.0
```

You can also assess the operation of the summarization policy by examining the contents of r3's LSPs:

```
lab@r5> show isis database r3 detail
IS-IS level 1 link-state database:
```

```
IS-IS level 2 link-state database:

r3.00-00  Sequence: 0x93, Checksum: 0x442, Lifetime: 413 secs
    IS neighbor:                      r4.00  Metric:      10
    IS neighbor:                      r5.00  Metric:      10
    IP prefix:              10.0.4.0/22 Metric:      10 External
    IP prefix:              10.0.2.4/30 Metric:      10 Internal
    IP prefix:              10.0.2.0/30 Metric:      10 Internal
    IP prefix:              10.0.4.0/30 Metric:      10 Internal
    IP prefix:             10.0.4.12/30 Metric:      10 Internal
    IP prefix:              10.0.3.3/32 Metric:       0 Internal
    IP prefix:           172.16.0.12/30 Metric:      10 Internal
```

These results confirm that r3 is correctly advertising the aggregate in its level 2 LSP, but also indicate that the 10.0.4.0/30 and 10.0.12.0/30 contributing routes are being incorrectly leaked (as indicated by the entries using at-0/2/1.35 as a next hop in r5's routing table and by their presence in r3's level 2 LSP). As you might expect, the problem here relates to the summarization policy, and the fact that it is not rejecting routes for directly connected interfaces that have IS-IS configured. Displaying one of these routes on r3 confirms this is indeed the case:

```
[edit]
lab@r3# run show route 10.0.4.12/30

inet.0: 26 destinations, 26 routes (26 active, 0 holddown, 0 hidden)
+ = Active Route, - = Last Active, * = Both

10.0.4.12/30       *[Direct/0] 2d 03:50:53
                    > via fe-0/0/0.0
10.0.4.13/32       *[Local/0] 2d 04:16:09
                      Local via fe-0/0/0.0
```

To correct this problem, the summarization policy on r3 is modified as highlighted next. This is just one example of many possible policy modifications that could have resolved the route summarization problem:

```
[edit policy-options policy-statement summ]
lab@r3# show
term 1 {
    from protocol aggregate;
    to level 2;
    then accept;
}
term 2 {
```

```
    from {
        route-filter 10.0.4.0/22 longer;
    }
    to level 2;
    then reject;
}
```

In this example, omitting the `to level 2` condition in term 2 would cause problems in area 49.0003 because routes matching the route-filter would then not be injected into any IS-IS level, and these routes should be present in the level 1 area. After applying the same summarization policy to r4, the results are once again verified on the backbone router r5:

```
lab@r5> show route 10.0.4/22

inet.0: 19 destinations, 19 routes (19 active, 0 holddown, 0 hidden)
+ = Active Route, - = Last Active, * = Both

10.0.4.0/22       *[IS-IS/165] 00:00:00, metric 20, tag 2
                    to 10.0.2.2 via at-0/2/1.35
                  > to 10.0.2.10 via as1.0
```

Very good, the summary route for area 49.0003 now has two viable next hops, and the more specific prefixes are no longer being injected into the level 2 area in accordance with the configuration requirements.

Route Redistribution

Export policy can also be applied to IS-IS to facilitate route redistribution and the manipulation of metrics at L1/L2-attached routers. JUNOS software does not support the application of import policy for link-state routing protocols like IS-IS because such policies could lead to inconsistent LSDB entries, which in turn could result in routing inconstancies. The filtering of LSPs is only possible in a multi-level topology, which will suppress the injection of level 2 LSPs into level 1 areas by default.

The use of routing policy to evoke route redistribution has already been demonstrated several times in this book, as has the use of policy to set the metric values for a redistributed static route. The following configuration scenario will demonstrate these capabilities as part of an IS-IS and OSPF mutual route redistribution scenario.

You will now add to the complexity of your network by configuring mutual route redistribution between IS-IS and OSPF as shown in Figure 4.3. The configuration criteria for this example follow the figure.

FIGURE 4.3 IS-IS route redistribution

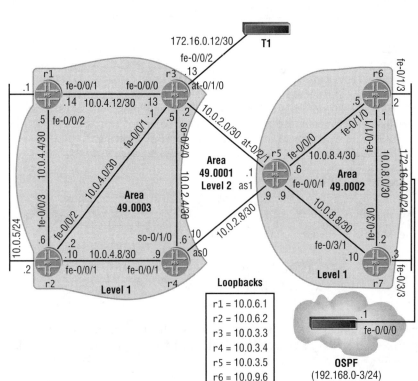

- Redistribute the 10.0.5/25 subnet from both r1 and r2 so that level 2 routers display a route metric of at least 500.

- r5 must be able to load balance to the 10.0.5/24 prefix.

- Redistribute the IS-IS default route from both r6 and r7 to the OSPF router.

- Redistribute OSPF routes 192.168.0/24 through 192.168.3/24 into area 49.0002 from both r6 and r7.

- Ensure that the OSPF router, r6, and r7 can reach destinations on the 10.0.5/24 subnet.

- Except for r5, no single point of failure can isolate the OSPF router from reaching the 10.0.5/24 subnet.

- Continue to advertise the area 49.0003 summary while suppressing more specific prefixes, except for the 10.0.5/24 route in accordance with the first requirement.

The OSPF Router's Configuration

The pertinent portions of the OSPF router's configuration are shown and described in the following. You may not modify the OSPF router's configuration in this configuration example:

```
[edit]
lab@ospf# show protocols
ospf {
    export ospf;
    area 0.0.0.1 {
        interface fe-0/0/0.0;
    }
}
```

The OSPF stanza defines OSPF area 1 operation with an export policy called *ospf*. The contents of this policy are as follows:

```
[edit]
lab@ospf# show policy-options
policy-statement ospf {
    term 1 {
        from protocol static;
        then accept;
    }
}
```

The *ospf* policy will redistribute routes learned through the static protocol into OSPF as AS externals. The OSPF router's `routing-options` stanza contains the various 192.168.x static route definitions, with their next hops set to discard in this example:

```
[edit]
lab@ospf# show routing-options
static {
    route 192.168.0.0/24 discard;
    route 192.168.1.0/24 discard;
    route 192.168.2.0/24 discard;
    route 192.168.3.0/24 discard;
    }
```

The OSPF router's interface configuration correctly sets the addressing for the OSPF subnet, and assigns host addresses from each of the 192.168.x static routes to the lo0 interface so that pings and traceroutes to host-id 1 on each 192.168.x subnet can complete successfully:

```
[edit]
lab@ospf# show interfaces
```

```
. . .
fe-0/0/0 {
    unit 0 {
        family inet {
            address 172.16.40.1/24;
        }
    }
}
lo0 {
    unit 0 {
        family inet {
            address 192.168.0.1/32;
            address 192.168.1.1/32;
            address 192.168.2.1/32;
            address 192.168.3.1/32;
        }
    }
}
```

IS-IS Redistribution on *r1* and *r2*

Your configuration begins by creating and applying a policy that will redistribute the 10.0.5/24 direct route from r1 and r2 into IS-IS with a metric of at least 500. The following policy will work for the requirements of this example, but other techniques are certainly possible:

```
[edit policy-options policy-statement direct]
lab@r1# show
term 1 {
    from {
        route-filter 10.0.5.0/24 exact;
    }
    then {
        metric 500;
        accept;
    }
}
```

The policy is applied to r1's IS-IS instance as an export policy, and the effects are confirmed on r5:

```
[edit]
lab@r5# run show route 10.0.5/24
```

```
[edit]
lab@r5#
```

The route's absence on r5 is not a good sign. Perhaps we should look closer to the route's source by examining r3's view of the situation?

```
[edit]
lab@r3# run show route 10.0.5/24

inet.0: 27 destinations, 27 routes (27 active, 0 holddown, 0 hidden)
+ = Active Route, - = Last Active, * = Both

10.0.5.0/24        *[IS-IS/160] 00:02:51, metric 73, tag 1
                    > to 10.0.4.14 via fe-0/0/0.0
```

Troubleshoot IS-IS Redistribution

The 10.0.5/24 route is present on r3, so r1's export policy must be doing something. The metric value of 73 is odd (both literally and in the context of this example), considering that the policy used to redistribute the route was configured to set the metric to 500. When faced with multiple symptoms such as these, this author would suggest that you prioritize the symptoms so that you can concentrate on resolving the most significant problems first. In this case, it is suggested that you resolve the route's absence on r5 before worrying about the incorrect metric, because in many cases connectivity problems will result in more point losses on your exam, which makes the missing route your highest priority. Besides, it is often the case that multiple symptoms will result from a common problem, so tackling the most significant issue first may result in less work overall.

The route's presence in r3 combined with its absence in r3's L2 LSP points to routing policy as the probable cause. There are really two issues at work here; one is general in nature while the other is somewhat specific to this example. The general problem relates to the fact that the default IS-IS export policy will not send level 1 external routes into the IS-IS backbone. The specific issue lies in the route-filter statement used in the existing *sum* policy that was designed to suppress the specific routes associated with area 49.0003, as the 10.0.5/24 route happens to fall within the aggregate 10.0.4/22, and is therefore being explicitly rejected. The problem area in the *sum* policy is highlighted next:

```
. . .
term 2 {
    from {
        route-filter 10.0.4.0/22 longer;
    }
    to level 2;
    then reject;
}
```

The highlighted policy modification punches a hole in term 2 to explicitly allow the 10.0.5/
24 prefix:

```
[edit policy-options policy-statement summ]
lab@r3# show
term 1 {
    from protocol aggregate;
    to level 2;
    then accept;
}
term 2 {
    from {
        route-filter 10.0.4.0/22 longer;
        route-filter 10.0.5.0/24 exact accept;
    }
    to level 2;
    then reject;
}
```

The use of an accept terminating action in conjunction with the 10.0.5/24 route-filter statement causes packets that match the route-filter exactly to be accepted while all other area 49.0003
prefixes are rejected by the terminating action associated with term 2. After committing the
modification to the *summ* policy on r3, the results are once again confirmed on r5:

```
[edit]
lab@r5# run show route 10.0.5/24

inet.0: 20 destinations, 20 routes (20 active, 0 holddown, 0 hidden)
+ = Active Route, - = Last Active, * = Both

10.0.5.0/24        *[IS-IS/165] 00:00:05, metric 73, tag 2
                    > to 10.0.2.2 via at-0/2/1.35
```

Good! The route is now present on r5, but the metric is still stuck at 73. This is a tricky problem
to solve, as its solution depends on an in-depth understanding of the IS-IS protocol and JUNOS
software behavior. The issue here relates to narrow vs. wide metrics, and the fact that the former
supports a maximum link cost of 63 and a total path cost of 1023. The use of narrow metrics
explains why the route's metric is stuck at 73. Neither r1 nor r3 can advertise a link metric
higher than 63, and the cost for r5 to reach r3 is 10, which results in the displayed metric value
of 73. By default, JUNOS software sends both wide and narrow metrics along with each route,
and when given the choice, Juniper Networks routers will opt to use the narrow metric. To

resolve this situation, you must modify the routers in areas 49.0003 and 49.0001 to use wide metrics only, with the following command:

```
[edit]
lab@r1# set protocols isis level 1 wide-metrics-only
```

After the change has been committed, the contents of r1's level 1 LSP is verified:

```
[edit]
lab@r1# run show isis database r1 detail
IS-IS level 1 link-state database:

r1.00-00  Sequence: 0x70, Checksum: 0x75bc, Lifetime: 1195 secs
    IS neighbor:                  r1.03  Metric:      10
    IS neighbor:                  r1.02  Metric:      10
    IP prefix:            10.0.4.4/30 Metric:      10 Internal
    IP prefix:           10.0.4.12/30 Metric:      10 Internal
    IP prefix:            10.0.6.1/32 Metric:       0 Internal
    IP prefix:            10.0.5.0/24 Metric:     500 Internal
. . .
```

The following command is now applied to r3 to enable its use of wide metrics only, in the level 2 area:

```
[edit]
lab@r3# set protocols isis level 2 wide-metrics-only
```

After the change is committed, the route is once again analyzed on r5:

```
[edit]
lab@r5# run show route 10.0.5/24

inet.0: 20 destinations, 20 routes (20 active, 0 holddown, 0 hidden)
+ = Active Route, - = Last Active, * = Both

10.0.5.0/24        *[IS-IS/18] 00:00:00, metric 520, tag 2
                   > to 10.0.2.2 via at-0/2/1.35
```

Good! Backbone routers now see a metric greater than 500, in accordance with the specified requirements. To complete this example, you must now apply the same IS-IS export policy to r2, and you must also set wide metrics only, on r2 and r4, as shown for r1 and r3. The added configuration is needed to comply with the redundancy requirements of this example. After making the changes, we expect to see two viable next hops for the 10.0.5/24 prefix on r5. Failing to disable narrow metrics on r4 will result in a single next hop on r5 (and point loss on your exam for not allowing load-balancing), because r5 will prefer the narrow metric sent from r4 to the wide metric that is advertised by r3. This situation is demonstrated in the following capture:

```
[edit]
lab@r5# run show route 10.0.5/24


inet.0: 20 destinations, 20 routes (20 active, 0 holddown, 0 hidden)
+ = Active Route, - = Last Active, * = Both


10.0.5.0/24         *[IS-IS/18] 00:00:02, metric 73, tag 2
                    > to 10.0.2.10 via as1.0
```

You now correctly disable level 2 narrow metrics on r4:

```
[edit]
lab@r4# set protocols isis level 2 wide-metrics-only


[edit]
lab@r4# commit
commit complete
```

After a few moments, we finally observe the required load-balancing behavior on r5:

```
[edit]
lab@r5# run show route 10.0.5/24


inet.0: 20 destinations, 20 routes (20 active, 0 holddown, 0 hidden)
+ = Active Route, - = Last Active, * = Both


10.0.5.0/24         *[IS-IS/18] 00:00:20, metric 520, tag 2
                    > to 10.0.2.2 via at-0/2/1.35
                      to 10.0.2.10 via as1.0
```

To complete this configuration example, connectivity to the 10.0.5/24 prefix is tested from the perspective of a level 1 router in area 49.0002:

```
lab@r7> traceroute 10.0.5.1
traceroute to 10.0.5.1 (10.0.5.1), 30 hops max, 40 byte packets
 1  10.0.8.9 (10.0.8.9)  0.338 ms  0.242 ms  0.216 ms
 2  10.0.2.2 (10.0.2.2)  0.777 ms  0.656 ms  0.878 ms
 3  10.0.4.2 (10.0.4.2)  0.565 ms  0.655 ms  0.379 ms
 4  10.0.5.1 (10.0.5.1)  0.690 ms  0.688 ms  0.878 ms
```

```
lab@r7> traceroute 10.0.5.2
traceroute to 10.0.5.2 (10.0.5.2), 30 hops max, 40 byte packets
 1  10.0.8.9 (10.0.8.9)  0.342 ms  0.241 ms  0.216 ms
 2  10.0.2.2 (10.0.2.2)  0.863 ms  1.162 ms  0.378 ms
 3  10.0.5.2 (10.0.5.2)  0.276 ms  0.643 ms  0.
```

The (highlighted) extra hop through r2 to reach the 10.0.5.1 address could be the normal result of IS-IS load balancing from r3 to r1 and r2, if we assume that r2 has been chosen as the current next hop for the 10.0.5/24 subnet. The following capture confirms this suspicion and proves that all is well with the route redistribution and redundancy requirements of your configuration:

```
lab@r3> show route 10.0.5.1

inet.0: 28 destinations, 28 routes (28 active, 0 holddown, 0 hidden)
+ = Active Route, - = Last Active, * = Both


10.0.5.0/24        *[IS-IS/15] 00:12:16, metric 510, tag 1
                      to 10.0.4.14 via fe-0/0/0.0
                    > to 10.0.4.2 via fe-0/0/1.0
```

Congratulations! You have met the requirements specified for the 10.0.5/24 prefix, with regard to its redistribution, metric setting, and backbone load-balancing capabilities.

While not required for this example, it is suggested that you now disable narrow metrics (at level 2) on r5, and at level 1 on r3 and r4. Mixing narrow and wide metrics within a single area can cause confusion down the road.

IS-IS and OSPF Redistribution on *r6*

You will now configure r6 to redistribute the default route from IS-IS into OSPF, and in the reverse direction, to redistribute the 192.168.*x*/24 OSPF routes into IS-IS. We begin with the following command that configures r6 to run OSPF on its fe-0/1/3 interface in area 1:

```
[edit protocols]
lab@r6# set ospf area 1 interface fe-0/1/3
```

After committing the changes, we verify that routes are now being received from the OSPF router:

```
[edit protocols]
lab@r6# run show route protocol ospf

inet.0: 20 destinations, 20 routes (20 active, 0 holddown, 0 hidden)
+ = Active Route, - = Last Active, * = Both
```

```
192.168.0.0/24      *[OSPF/150] 00:00:16, metric 0, tag 0
                     > to 172.16.40.1 via fe-0/1/3.0
192.168.1.0/24      *[OSPF/150] 00:00:16, metric 0, tag 0
                     > to 172.16.40.1 via fe-0/1/3.0
192.168.2.0/24      *[OSPF/150] 00:00:16, metric 0, tag 0
                     > to 172.16.40.1 via fe-0/1/3.0
192.168.3.0/24      *[OSPF/150] 00:00:16, metric 0, tag 0
                     > to 172.16.40.1 via fe-0/1/3.0
224.0.0.5/32        *[OSPF/10] 00:01:23, metric 1

iso.0: 1 destinations, 1 routes (1 active, 0 holddown, 0 hidden)
```

Great, r6 has formed an adjacency to the OSPF router. The next step is to write an export policy to redistribute the OSPF routes into IS-IS:

```
[edit]
lab@r6# edit policy-options policy-statement ospf-isis

[edit policy-options policy-statement ospf-isis]
lab@r6# set term 1 from protocol ospf

[edit policy-options policy-statement ospf-isis]
lab@r6# set term 1 from route-filter 192.168.0/22 longer

[edit policy-options policy-statement ospf-isis]
lab@r6# set term 1 then accept
```

The resulting OSPF to IS-IS redistribution policy is shown next:

```
[edit policy-options policy-statement ospf-isis]
lab@r6# show
term 1 {
    from {
        protocol ospf;
        route-filter 192.168.0.0/22 longer;
    }
    then accept;
}
```

The *ospf-isis* policy is now applied to the IS-IS instance as an export policy:

```
[edit]
lab@r6# set protocols isis export ospf-isis
```

With the export policy in place on r6 and the changes committed, we confirm the presence of the 192.168.*x*/24 routes on r5 to determine its effect:

```
[edit]
lab@r5# run show route 192.168.0/22

inet.0: 26 destinations, 26 routes (26 active, 0 holddown, 0 hidden)
+ = Active Route, - = Last Active, * = Both

192.168.0.0/24     *[IS-IS/160] 00:00:01, metric 10, tag 1
                    > to 10.0.8.5 via fe-0/0/0.0
192.168.1.0/24     *[IS-IS/160] 00:00:01, metric 10, tag 1
                    > to 10.0.8.5 via fe-0/0/0.0
192.168.2.0/24     *[IS-IS/160] 00:00:01, metric 10, tag 1
                    > to 10.0.8.5 via fe-0/0/0.0
192.168.3.0/24     *[IS-IS/160] 00:00:01, metric 10, tag 1
                    > to 10.0.8.5 via fe-0/0/0.0
```

So far, so good—all the OSPF routes are present on r5 as IS-IS level 1 external routes. To get the routes into the IS-IS backbone, you must now write an export policy on r5 instructing it to redistribute level 1 externals into level 2. The *l1-ext* policy shown here works well for our purposes:

```
[edit policy-options policy-statement l1-ext]
lab@r5# show
term 1 {
    from {
        protocol isis;
        level 1;
        route-filter 192.168.0.0/22 longer;
    }
    to level 2;
    then accept;
}
```

After applying the *l1-ext* as export to r5's IS-IS instance, the presence of the 192.168.*x* routes are confirmed on r3:

```
lab@r3> show route 192/8

inet.0: 33 destinations, 33 routes (33 active, 0 holddown, 0 hidden)
+ = Active Route, - = Last Active, * = Both
```

```
192.168.0.0/24      *[IS-IS/18] 00:00:01, metric 20, tag 2
                     > to 10.0.2.1 via at-0/1/0.35
192.168.0.1/32      *[IS-IS/18] 00:00:01, metric 21, tag 2
                     > to 10.0.2.1 via at-0/1/0.35
192.168.1.0/24      *[IS-IS/18] 00:00:01, metric 20, tag 2
                     > to 10.0.2.1 via at-0/1/0.35
192.168.2.0/24      *[IS-IS/18] 00:00:01, metric 20, tag 2
                     > to 10.0.2.1 via at-0/1/0.35
192.168.3.0/24      *[IS-IS/18] 00:00:01, metric 20, tag 2
                     > to 10.0.2.1 via at-0/1/0.35
```

In this example, r3 displays a preference of 18 for the 192.168.0/22 routes because the use of level 2 wide metrics on r5 prevents r3 from seeing the routes as level 2 externals, which have a default preference of 165. Refer back to the previous section, "Troubleshoot IS-IS Redistribution," for details on why wide metrics have been enabled in the level 2 backbone. With OSPF-to–IS-IS redistribution working properly at r6 and r5, you now create and apply the policy needed to redistribute the IS-IS default route from r6 into OSPF. The policy shown next will accommodate the requirements of this example, but other policy approaches are also workable.

```
[edit policy-options policy-statement default]
lab@r6# show
term 1 {
    from {
        route-filter 0.0.0.0/0 exact;
    }
    then accept;
}
```

Now apply the *default* policy as an export to OSPF using the following command:

```
[edit]
lab@r6# set protocols ospf export default
```

After committing the change, confirm that the default route is present on the OSPF router:

```
lab@ospf> show route protocol ospf
inet.0: 17 destinations, 17 routes (17 active, 0 holddown, 0 hidden)
+ = Active Route, - = Last Active, * = Both

0.0.0.0/0           *[OSPF/150] 00:02:47, metric 10, tag 1
                     > to 172.16.40.2 via fe-0/0/0.0
10.0.9.6/32         *[OSPF/10] 00:22:38, metric 1
                     > to 172.16.40.2 via fe-0/0/0.0
224.0.0.5/32        *[OSPF/10] 00:23:23, metric 1
```

The default route is present as required, but unfortunately so is the route to r6's loopback address. In accordance with the requirements of this example, you are to advertise *only* the default route to the OSPF router. Solving this problem can also be tricky. The issue relates to the JUNOS software behavior of automatically advertising a stub route to the interface from which the OSPF RID was obtained, as described in Chapter 3, "OSPF Configuration and Testing." To eliminate this route, you must manually assign r6's RID as shown:

```
[edit]
lab@r6# set routing-options router-id 10.0.9.6

[edit]
lab@r6# commit
commit complete
```

Once again, confirm the results from the perspective of the OSPF router:

```
lab@ospf> show route protocol ospf

inet.0: 16 destinations, 16 routes (16 active, 0 holddown, 0 hidden)
+ = Active Route, - = Last Active, * = Both

0.0.0.0/0            *[OSPF/150] 00:08:11, metric 10, tag 1
                      > to 172.16.40.2 via fe-0/0/0.0
224.0.0.5/32         *[OSPF/10] 00:28:47, metric 1
```

As required, r6 is now advertising only the default route to the OSPF router. With this 5.2 code base, a routing daemon restart was not required for the change in RID source to take effect. With some JUNOS software versions, you may have to restart routing (or for dramatic effect, reboot the router) in order to have the routing daemon begin using the new source of its RID. With the default route confirmed in the OSPF router, you decide to test connectivity to the 10.0.5/24 prefix before bringing r7 into the route redistribution fray:

```
lab@ospf> traceroute 10.0.5.1
traceroute to 10.0.5.1 (10.0.5.1), 30 hops max, 40 byte packets
 1  172.16.40.2 (172.16.40.2)  0.190 ms  0.123 ms  0.096 ms
 2  * * *
^C
```

This problem should seem familiar, as the very same issue arose in the OSPF-to-RIP redistribution example provided in Chapter 3. The issue is the lack of a route in the IS-IS routing domain for the 172.16.40/24 OSPF subnet used by the OSPF router when sourcing its packets. This is confirmed by using the source switch to the traceroute command as shown next:

```
lab@ospf> traceroute 10.0.5.1 source 192.168.0.1
traceroute to 10.0.5.1 (10.0.5.1) from 192.168.0.1, 30 hops max, 40 byte packets
```

```
1  172.16.40.2 (172.16.40.2)  0.190 ms  0.122 ms  0.094 ms
2  10.0.8.6 (10.0.8.6)  0.321 ms  0.289 ms  0.277 ms
3  10.0.2.2 (10.0.2.2)  0.756 ms  0.705 ms  0.874 ms
4  10.0.4.2 (10.0.4.2)  0.621 ms  0.673 ms  0.374 ms
5  10.0.5.1 (10.0.5.1)  0.628 ms  0.704 ms  0.875 ms
```

Because no restrictions have been placed on how you should handle this problem (other than your not being able to modify the OSPF router's configuration), you could opt for one of several solutions that include running IS-IS passive on the OSPF subnet, or the redistribution of the direct interface route from r6. Because the latter approach will also require a policy modification on r5 to tell it that it should also redistribute the 172.16.40/24 level 1 external into the backbone, this author has opted to go with the simpler passive IGP approach, as shown next:

```
[edit protocols]
lab@r6# set isis interface fe-0/1/3 level 2 disable

[edit protocols]
lab@r6# set isis interface fe-0/1/3 passive

[edit interfaces]
lab@r6# set fe-0/1/3 unit 0 family iso
```

After committing changes on r6, we again test reachability to 10.0.5/24 from the OSPF router:

```
lab@ospf> traceroute 10.0.5.1
traceroute to 10.0.5.1 (10.0.5.1), 30 hops max, 40 byte packets
1  172.16.40.2 (172.16.40.2)  0.195 ms  0.123 ms  0.094 ms
2  10.0.8.6 (10.0.8.6)  0.341 ms  0.304 ms  0.278 ms
3  10.0.2.2 (10.0.2.2)  0.777 ms  1.204 ms  0.876 ms
4  10.0.4.2 (10.0.4.2)  0.400 ms  0.682 ms  0.375 ms
5  10.0.5.1 (10.0.5.1)  0.845 ms  1.204 ms  0.872 ms
```

IS-IS and OSPF Redistribution on *r7*

With IS-IS to OSPF route redistribution working on r6, you must now configure r7 so that it too redistributes routes between IS-IS and OSPF. As always, the bidirectional redistribution of routes from multiple locations is a task fraught with the peril of a routing loop. Before attacking this problem, it might behoove you to consider that the default preference for the IS-IS default route is 15, while the OSPF external route that results from its redistribution into OSPF will have a preference of 150. This means that r6 and r7 will automatically "ignore" the redistributed default route should it later be received over the OSPF subnet. Further, if this default should be inadvertently re-advertised back into the IS-IS level 1 area, the level 1 external preference will be 160, which will result in the continued use of the default route being injected by r5, which is a level 1 internal with a preference of 15. The same preference settings should also cause r6 and r7 to make the "right" choice when presented with the 192.168.*x* routes as both OSPF routes and IS-IS level 1 external routes, which is to say that the routers will prefer the OSPF source as desired.

Based on the default route preference settings, it would seem that a loop will not occur if the somewhat sloppy export policy in use by r6 is simply copied over to r7, even though such a procedure did result in a routing loop when OSPF was used to redistribute routes to and from the RIP protocol in Chapter 3. To put the theory to the test, r6's export policies are copied and committed on r7. You should also configure r7's OSPF area 1, and passive IS-IS interface as shown for r6 in the previous section. Lastly, do not forget to add the manually assigned RID to r7 to prevent it from advertising a stub route to its loopback address.

Verify OSPF and IS-IS Redistribution

When the configuration of r7 is complete, the results are confirmed with the following commands, starting with the verification that the OSPF router sees two equal-cost next hops for the default route:

```
lab@ospf> show route protocol ospf

inet.0: 16 destinations, 16 routes (16 active, 0 holddown, 0 hidden)
+ = Active Route, - = Last Active, * = Both

0.0.0.0/0          *[OSPF/150] 00:01:32, metric 10, tag 1
                    > to 172.16.40.2 via fe-0/0/0.0
                      to 172.16.40.3 via fe-0/0/0.0
224.0.0.5/32       *[OSPF/10] 01:49:48, metric 1
```

We now confirm that r6 and r7 prefer the OSPF 192.168.*x*/24 externals, as received from the OSPF router, to the redistributed IS-IS level 1 externals:

```
[edit]
lab@r7# run show route 192/8

inet.0: 20 destinations, 21 routes (20 active, 0 holddown, 0 hidden)
+ = Active Route, - = Last Active, * = Both

192.168.0.0/24     *[OSPF/150] 00:01:26, metric 0, tag 0
                    > to 172.16.40.1 via fe-0/3/3.0
192.168.0.1/32     *[OSPF/10] 00:01:26, metric 1
                    > to 172.16.40.1 via fe-0/3/3.0
192.168.1.0/24     *[OSPF/150] 00:01:26, metric 0, tag 0
                    > to 172.16.40.1 via fe-0/3/3.0
192.168.2.0/24     *[OSPF/150] 00:01:26, metric 0, tag 0
                    > to 172.16.40.1 via fe-0/3/3.0
```

```
192.168.3.0/24      *[OSPF/150] 00:01:26, metric 0, tag 0
                    > to 172.16.40.1 via fe-0/3/3.0
```

You should also verify that the IS-IS level 1 default route is preferred to the OSPF external default on r6 and r7:

```
[edit]
lab@r6# run show route 3.3.3.3

inet.0: 20 destinations, 21 routes (20 active, 0 holddown, 0 hidden)
+ = Active Route, - = Last Active, * = Both

0.0.0.0/0           *[IS-IS/15] 02:14:46, metric 10, tag 1
                    > to 10.0.8.6 via fe-0/1/0.0
                    [OSPF/150] 00:15:57, metric 10, tag 1
                    > to 172.16.40.3 via fe-0/1/3.0
```

These results indicate that, as predicted, the default route preference settings for IS-IS and OSPF internal/external routes result in the routers just "doing the right thing" in that no loops have been created by the mutual route redistribution actions of r6 and r7. The last step is to confirm that r5 sees two equal-cost next hops for the redistributed 192.168.*x*/24 OSPF routes, which verifies that both r6 and r7 are correctly exporting the OSPF routes into IS-IS:

```
[edit]
lab@r5# run show route 192.168.0/24

inet.0: 27 destinations, 27 routes (27 active, 0 holddown, 0 hidden)
+ = Active Route, - = Last Active, * = Both

192.168.0.0/24      *[IS-IS/160] 00:06:11, metric 10, tag 1
                    > to 10.0.8.5 via fe-0/0/0.0
                    to 10.0.8.10 via fe-0/0/1.0
192.168.0.1/32      *[IS-IS/160] 00:07:21, metric 11, tag 1
                    > to 10.0.8.5 via fe-0/0/0.0
                    to 10.0.8.10 via fe-0/0/1.0
```

All indications point to a properly functioning, loop-free network, which will provide both optimal routing and the required redundancy. A few quick traceroutes provide the final confirmation that you have met the requirements of the route redistribution example:

```
lab@ospf> traceroute 10.0.5.1
traceroute to 10.0.5.1 (10.0.5.1), 30 hops max, 40 byte packets
 1  172.16.40.2 (172.16.40.2)  0.189 ms  0.123 ms  0.094 ms
 2  10.0.8.6 (10.0.8.6)  0.329 ms  0.288 ms  0.279 ms
```

```
3   10.0.2.2 (10.0.2.2)   1.029 ms   1.204 ms   0.876 ms
4   10.0.4.2 (10.0.4.2)   0.323 ms   0.677 ms   0.372 ms
5   10.0.5.1 (10.0.5.1)   0.924 ms   1.186 ms   0.874 ms
```

The OSPF router has the required connectivity through r6, so we quickly test that r7 can also correctly forward should it be chosen by the OSPF router as the forwarding next hop the next time a load-balancing hash is performed:

```
lab@r7> traceroute 10.0.5.1
traceroute to 10.0.5.1 (10.0.5.1), 30 hops max, 40 byte packets
1   10.0.8.9 (10.0.8.9)   0.326 ms   0.242 ms   0.216 ms
2   10.0.2.2 (10.0.2.2)   0.839 ms   0.657 ms   0.880 ms
3   10.0.4.2 (10.0.4.2)   0.499 ms   0.653 ms   0.379 ms
4   10.0.5.1 (10.0.5.1)   0.759 ms   0.697 ms   0.866 ms
```

The traceroutes produce the expected results, which brings this configuration example to a close. You will not need to source traffic from the 10.0.5/24 subnet when testing connectivity to the OSPF router from either r1 or r2 because this example provides a default route to the OSPF router, which affords it connectivity to the whole IS-IS routing domain.

Congratulations!

Miscellaneous IS-IS Knobs

You should be familiar with all IS-IS options and available knobs before attempting your lab examination, because the evolving nature of the test will make it hard to predict when you will need to enable what might be considered a corner-case knob. The following section will demonstrate how some of the remaining IS-IS configuration parameters may be deployed in a lab scenario based on Figure 4.3. Traffic Engineering (TE)–related OSPF options are beyond the scope of the JNCIP examination and are therefore not covered in this book.

To complete this section, you must perform the following tasks:

- Ensure that r2 cannot reach destinations outside of area 49.0003 while keeping all its IS-IS adjacencies up and without modifying its routing-options stanza.

- Configure r6 with a level 1 priority of 0.

- Ensure that r5 never generates a non-0 selector byte LSP for the 10.0.8.8/30 network.

- Configure the r3-r5 ATM link so that flooded LSPs are spaced at least 300 milliseconds apart.

The first configuration task requires that we determine how r2 is currently forwarding traffic into other areas:

```
lab@r2> show route 10.0.2.0

inet.0: 18 destinations, 18 routes (18 active, 0 holddown, 0 hidden)
```

```
+ = Active Route, - = Last Active, * = Both

0.0.0.0/0          *[IS-IS/15] 03:21:43, metric 10, tag 1
                    > to 10.0.4.9 via fe-0/0/1.0
                      to 10.0.4.1 via fe-0/0/2.0
```

As expected, r2 is using the default route produced by detecting the presence of a L1/L2-attached router to route to destinations outside of its level 1 area. There may be times, such as during a Denial of Service (DoS) attack, that you will not want a level 1 router to be able to forward traffic based on a default route. To prevent r2 from being able to reach inter-area destinations in accordance with the provided criteria, you must stop r2 from installing this default route without affecting the status of its IS-IS adjacencies. The following command is used to tell the router to ignore the presence of the attached bit in level 1 LSPs, which blocks the installation of the IS-IS default route:

```
[edit]
lab@r2# set protocols isis ignore-attached-bit
```

The results are confirmed by verifying that r2 no longer displays a default route for inter-area destinations:

```
lab@r2> show route 10.0.2.0

lab@r2>
```

The second and third configuration tasks relate to one another and are made difficult by the somewhat cryptic wording of the requirements. A reader who possesses a detailed understanding of the IS-IS protocol will realize that only an IS-IS DIS can generate non-0 selector byte LSPs as part of its pseudonode functionality. So to meet this requirement, you must ensure that r5 can never be elected as the IS-IS DIS for the 10.0.8.8/30 subnet, despite the need to set r6's DIS priority to 0!

This seemingly insurmountable task can only be accomplished by setting r5's priority to 0 and then manually assigning a MAC address to r5's fe-0/0/0 interface that is numerically lower than the MAC address in use by r6's fe-0/1/0 interface (or vice versa). Simply modifying r5's fe-0/0/0 interface priority will not suffice for this task, because the resulting priority tie with r6 will simply be resolved based on their burned-in MAC addresses. Though you may get lucky and find that r5 happens to lose the MAC address–based DIS election in your test bed, you would likely still lose points on the actual JNCIP exam for not taking the necessary precautions that would have allowed you to forsake the services of that fleeting mistress known as luck.

The following commands set the level 1 priority of r5's fe-0/0/0 interface to 0, and assigns a new MAC address that is numerically lower than r6's fe-0/1/0 MAC address, which in this test bed happens to be 00:90:69:32:11:3a:

```
[edit protocols isis]
lab@r5# set interface fe-0/0/0 level 1 priority 0
```

```
[edit interfaces fe-0/0/0]
lab@r5# set mac 00.00.00.00.00.11
```

The level 1 priority of r6 is now set to 0 with the following command. You can opt for a global change, as demonstrated here, or the explicit setting of the level 1 priority associated with its fe-0/1/0 interface:

```
[edit]
lab@r6# set protocols isis interface all level 1 priority 0
```

To confirm the expected behavior, we verify that r5 has not been elected the DIS on its fe-0/0/0 interface. Alternatively, we can examine the level 1 area's database to confirm that r5 has not generated a pseudonode LSP for the 10.0.8.4/30 subnet. Both approaches are shown here:

```
[edit]
lab@r5# run show isis interface fe-0/0/0
IS-IS interface database:
Interface            L CirID Level 1 DR      Level 2 DR      L1/L2 Metric
fe-0/0/0.0           1   0x2 r6.02           Disabled              5/5
```

As required, r6 has won the DIS election, despite its priority setting of zero.

```
[edit]
lab@r5# run show isis database r5 detail
IS-IS level 1 link-state database:

r5.00-00  Sequence: 0x1b, Checksum: 0x63a3, Lifetime: 3597 secs
   IS neighbor:                     r5.03  Metric:      5
   IS neighbor:                     r6.02  Metric:      5
   IP prefix:             10.0.2.0/23 Metric:     10 External
   IP prefix:             10.0.8.8/30 Metric:      5 Internal
   IP prefix:             10.0.8.4/30 Metric:      5 Internal


r5.03-00  Sequence: 0x9, Checksum: 0x1db, Lifetime: 3597 secs
   IS neighbor:                     r7.00  Metric:      0
   IS neighbor:                     r5.00  Metric:      0


IS-IS level 2 link-state database:

. . .
```

As expected, the only level 1, non-zero selector byte LSP generated by r5 refers to the 10.0.8.8/30 subnet by virtue of the neighbor report that includes r5 and r7. These results confirm that the requirements of this configuration task have been met.

 You may want to flush the IS-IS LSDB with the `clear isis` database command before you conduct your LSP analysis to ensure that stale LSPs, which can serve to add confusion, are no longer present.

The last requirement in this section is to configure the ATM interface between r3 and r5 so that flooded LSPs are spaced by at least 300 milliseconds. Controlling the rate of LSP flooding can be desirable on slow links, or when the device at the other end has processing limitations, because LSPs that are spaced too closely may be lost in such situations. The following command, entered on both r3 and r5, does the trick:

```
[edit protocols isis]
lab@r5# set interface at-0/2/1.35 lsp-interval 301
```

To confirm, we examine the interface's IS-IS parameters, being sure to compare the ATM interface's settings to the default LSP interval in use by its other point-to-point interface:

```
lab@r5> show isis interface detail
IS-IS interface database:
as1.0
  Index: 13, State: 0x6, Circuit id: 0x1, Circuit type: 2
  LSP interval: 100 ms, CSNP interval: disabled
  Level Adjacencies Priority Metric Hello (s) Hold (s) Designated Router
    2            1       64     10        9       27
at-0/2/1.35
  Index: 9, State: 0x6, Circuit id: 0x1, Circuit type: 2
  LSP interval: 301 ms, CSNP interval: disabled
  Level Adjacencies Priority Metric Hello (s) Hold (s) Designated Router
    2            1       64     10        9       27
. . .
```

Real World Scenario

A Monkey in Your Wrench?

A JNCIP candidate may be expected to demonstrate the ability to reverse engineer the configuration of an attached device by virtue of not being given the required details of its configuration. By way of example, consider the case where you must establish an adjacency to the OSPF router when its configuration is not made available to you. In such a situation, you will need to deploy various diagnostic utilities, such as protocol tracing or traffic monitoring, to determine the OSPF parameters that must be added to r6 and r7 for compatibility with the OSPF router (as shown earlier in Figure 4.3). The following example shows a candidate starting with a "bare bones" OSPF configuration that is intended only to enable OSPF protocol tracing:

```
[edit protocols ospf]
lab@r6# show
traceoptions {
    file test;
    flag hello detail;
    flag error detail;
}
area 0.0.0.0 {
    interface fe-0/1/3.0;
}
```

The results obtained from the trace file make it clear that the OSPF router is in area 1 and that authentication is not being used. The various time-stamps and tracing output also make the detection of the 8-second hello interval setting possible:

```
May 18 20:58:29 OSPF packet ignored: area mismatch (0.0.0.1) from 172.16.40.1
May 18 20:58:29 OSPF rcvd Hello 172.16.40.1 -> 224.0.0.5 (fe-0/1/3.0)
May 18 20:58:29    Version 2, length 44, ID 192.168.0.1, area 0.0.0.1
May 18 20:58:29    checksum 0x676d, authtype 0
May 18 20:58:29    mask 255.255.255.0, hello_ivl 8, opts 0x2, prio 128
May 18 20:58:29    dead_ivl 32, DR 172.16.40.1, BDR 0.0.0.0
May 18 20:58:32 OSPF sent Hello 172.16.40.2 -> 224.0.0.5 (fe-0/1/3.0)
May 18 20:58:32    Version 2, length 44, ID 10.0.9.6, area 0.0.0.0
May 18 20:58:32    checksum 0x1507, authtype 0
May 18 20:58:32    mask 255.255.255.0, hello_ivl 10, opts 0x2, prio 128
```

```
May 18 20:58:32   dead_ivl 40, DR 172.16.40.2, BDR 0.0.0.0
May 18 20:58:36 OSPF packet ignored: area mismatch (0.0.0.1) from 172.16.40.1
May 18 20:58:36 OSPF rcvd Hello 172.16.40.1 -> 224.0.0.5 (fe-0/1/3.0)
May 18 20:58:36   Version 2, length 44, ID 192.168.0.1, area 0.0.0.1
May 18 20:58:36   checksum 0x676d, authtype 0
May 18 20:58:36   mask 255.255.255.0, hello_ivl 8, opts 0x2, prio 128
May 18 20:58:36   dead_ivl 32, DR 172.16.40.1, BDR 0.0.0.0
```

Summary

This chapter provided numerous examples of IS-IS configuration tasks that are indicative of those you may encounter while taking your JNCIP lab examination. You should now feel comfortable with the commands needed to add the `iso` family to your router interfaces, and with the aspects of IS-IS routing instance configuration needed to support either level 1, level 2, or a level 1/level 2 configuration. IS-IS authentication options were also demonstrated, as was the use of protocol tracing to diagnose operational problems caused by incorrect or incompatible configurations.

The use of JUNOS software policy to effect IS-IS route leaking, summarization, and route redistribution were demonstrated, along with the operational commands that can be used to determine the status of your IS-IS IGP. The following case study reviews critical IS-IS configuration tasks in a configuration scenario designed to simulate the JNCIP testing environment.

Case Study: IS-IS

The following case study simulates a typical JNCIP-level IS-IS configuration scenario. You should refer to the criteria listing and the information in Figure 4.4, the case study topology, in order to complete the IS-IS case study. It is assumed that you will be adding the IS-IS related configuration on top of the interface configuration that was left from the case study at the end of Chapter 2, "Interface Configuration and Testing." You should therefore first remove any protocol, policy, family iso interface statements, and any static route–related configuration resulting from the examples given in this chapter from all your routers before beginning the case study. Ideally you will start the case study by reloading your Chapter 2 baseline configuration using load override.

It is expected that a JNCIP candidate will be able to complete this case study in approximately one hour, with the result being an IS-IS IGP that exhibits no serious operational problems. Sample IS-IS configurations from all seven routers are provided at the end of the case study for comparison with your own configurations. Multiple solutions are sometimes possible, so differences between the provided examples and your own configurations do not always indicate that mistakes have been made. Because you are graded on the overall functionality of your IGP and its conformance to the specified configuration criteria, various operational mode commands are included so that you may compare the behavior of your network to a known good example.

To complete this case study, your IS-IS configuration must meet the following criteria:

- lo0 addresses are reachable through IS-IS for all routers with an IS-IS SysID based on the lo0 address. Backbone router lo0 addresses must not be injected into area 49.0002 or 49.0001.

- Backbone area routes must be summarized into area 49.0001.

- The subnet between r3 and T1 must appear in area 49.0003 as an internal route. Ensure that no adjacencies can be established on this subnet.

- Redistribute the 10.0.5/24 route into the backbone such that area 49.0002–attached routers see a metric of at least 100.

- r5 and r6 must use a level 1 priority of 0.

- Ensure that r7 never functions as a pseudonode when its adjacencies are up.

- Summarize all routes (internal and external) into the backbone area.

- You may not modify or view the OSPF router's configuration.

- All areas must use hello authentication based on md5 with a secret of *jnx*. The backbone area must also authenticate LSPs using a simple password of *jnx*.

- Configure r6 and r7 to advertise the IS-IS default route to the OSPF router. Ensure that the OSPF router can load balance over the default route.

- Configure r6 and r7 to redistribute OSPF routes learned from the OSPF router into IS-IS.

- Except for r5, ensure that no single router or link failure will isolate r1, r2, or the OSPF router.

- Optimize routing based on bandwidth, and ensure that all Fast Ethernet interfaces are automatically assigned a metric of *5*.
- No static routes and no loops.
- Set the level 1 preference in area 49.0001 to *155*.
- You must not have suboptimal routing between r6, r7, and the OSPF router.
- Configure the network to keep LSPs that are up to 3600 seconds old.
- Only one adjacency is permitted between any two routers.

FIGURE 4.4   IS-IS case study topology

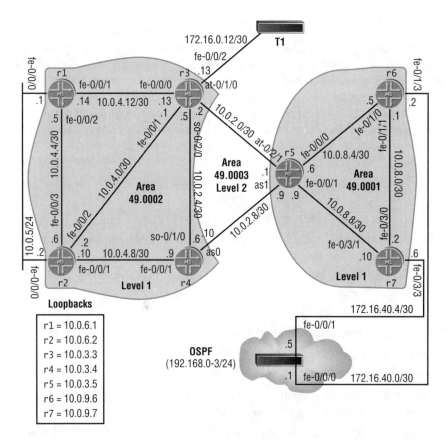

In this case study, the OSPF router is preconfigured and its configuration cannot be modified or viewed. You may assume, however, that it is configured to run OSPF, and that it has the policy statements needed to redistribute the 192.168.0-3/24 static routes into OSPF should an adjacency be formed.

IS-IS Case Study Analysis

Each configuration requirement for the case study will now be matched to one or more valid router configurations and the commands that can be used to confirm that the router is operating within all specified case study guidelines. We begin with these four criteria, as they serve to establish baseline IS-IS operation in each area:

- lo0 addresses are reachable through IS-IS for all routers with an IS-IS SysID based on the lo0 address. Backbone router lo0 addresses must not be injected into area 49.0002 or 49.0001.
- Optimize routing based on bandwidth, and ensure that all Fast Ethernet interfaces are automatically assigned a metric of 5.
- Configure the network to keep LSPs that are up to 3600 seconds old.
- Only one adjacency is permitted between any two routers.

To get basic IS-IS connectivity going, you must add the iso family to the correct logical units on all IS-IS interfaces, assign the router's NET to its lo0 address, and correctly configure the interface to level associations so that no interfaces are running at both levels 1 and 2. The following captures show typical IS-IS configurations from key routers throughout the network, starting with r4:

```
[edit]
lab@r4# run show interfaces terse
Interface        Admin Link Proto Local              Remote
fe-0/0/0         up    down
fe-0/0/1         up    up
fe-0/0/1.0       up    up   inet  10.0.4.9/30
                            iso
. . .
so-0/1/0         up    up
so-0/1/0.100     up    up   inet  10.0.2.6/30
                            iso
so-0/1/1         up    up
so-0/1/1.0       up    up   soagg --> as0.0
so-0/1/2         up    up
so-0/1/2.0       up    up   soagg --> as0.0
so-0/1/3         up    down
as0              up    up
as0.0            up    up   inet  10.0.2.10/30
                            iso
fxp0             up    up
fxp0.0           up    up   inet  10.0.1.4/24
fxp1             up    up
fxp1.0           up    up   tnp   4
```

```
. . .
lo0              up    up
lo0.0            up    up    inet  10.0.3.4              --> 0/0
                             iso   49.0002.0100.0000.3004.00
. . .
```

The IS-IS routing instance for r4 is shown next:

```
[edit]
lab@r4# show protocols isis
reference-bandwidth 500m;
lsp-lifetime 3600;
interface fe-0/0/1.0 {
    level 2 disable;
}
interface all {
    level 1 disable;
}
```

r4's configuration has the required iso family interface assignments, NET, and the correct interface-to-level associations, which in this case was achieved by disabling level 1 on all interfaces with the exception of interface fe-0/0/1. Care must be taken to ensure that you do not configure backbone router lo0 interfaces to operate at level 1 in order to meet the requirement that backbone lo0 addresses are not to be injected into area 49.0002 or 49.0001. The automatic metric requirement is achieved by assigning reference bandwidth of 500Mbps, and the default LSP lifetime is set to 3600 seconds as required. Correct interface-to-level mapping and the automatically calculated metric values are confirmed by displaying IS-IS interface status:

```
[edit]
lab@r4# run show isis interface
IS-IS interface database:
```

Interface	L	CirID	Level 1 DR	Level 2 DR	L1/L2 Metric
as0.0	2	0x1	Disabled	Point to Point	1/1
fe-0/0/1.0	1	0x2	r2.02	Disabled	5/5
lo0.0	0	0x1	Disabled	Passive	0/0
so-0/1/0.100	2	0x1	Disabled	Point to Point	3/3

The configuration of routers in level 1 areas will be similar to the example shown next, which is taken from r7:

```
[edit]
lab@r7# run show interfaces terse
Interface        Admin Link Proto Local                Remote
. . .
```

```
fe-0/3/0          up    up
fe-0/3/0.0        up    up    inet  10.0.8.2/30
                                iso
fe-0/3/1          up    up
fe-0/3/1.0        up    up    inet  10.0.8.10/30
                                iso
. . .
lo0               up    up
lo0.0             up    up    inet  10.0.9.7              --> 0/0
                                iso   49.0001.0100.0000.9007.00
. . .
```

The routing instance for a level 1 router r7 is configured as shown next:

```
[edit]
lab@r7# show protocols isis
reference-bandwidth 500m;
lsp-lifetime 3600;
interface all {
    level 2 disable;
}
```

The correct interface-to-level mappings are now confirmed on r7:

```
[edit]
lab@r7# run show isis interface
IS-IS interface database:
Interface         L CirID Level 1 DR     Level 2 DR     L1/L2 Metric
fe-0/3/0.0        1  0x2 r7.02           Disabled              5/5
fe-0/3/1.0        1  0x3 r5.03           Disabled              5/5
lo0.0             0  0x1 Passive         Disabled              0/0
```

At this stage, you should have the required number and type (either level 1 or level 2) of adjacencies between all seven routers. To quickly confirm, we verify that we have the expected number of SysIDs on a few strategic routers:

```
[edit]
lab@r3# run show isis hostname
IS-IS hostname database:
System Id       Hostname                            Type
0100.0000.3003 r3                                   Static
0100.0000.3004 r4                                   Dynamic
0100.0000.3005 r5                                   Dynamic
```

```
0100.0000.6001 r1                                          Dynamic
0100.0000.6002 r2                                          Dynamic
```

r3 has hostname entries that correctly reflect area 49.0003 and 49.0002 routers, as expected. We confirm area 49.0001 by performing the same command on r6:

```
[edit]
lab@r6# run show isis hostname
IS-IS hostname database:
System Id       Hostname                                   Type
0100.0000.3005 r5                                          Dynamic
0100.0000.9006 r6                                          Static
0100.0000.9007 r7                                          Dynamic
```

A test to confirm that backbone routers see IS-IS routes to all loopback addresses is now performed:

```
[edit protocols isis]
lab@r3# run show route protocol isis | match /32
10.0.3.4/32       *[IS-IS/18] 00:39:09, metric 3, tag 2
10.0.3.5/32       *[IS-IS/18] 00:39:09, metric 3, tag 2
10.0.6.1/32       *[IS-IS/15] 00:39:09, metric 5, tag 1
10.0.6.2/32       *[IS-IS/15] 00:39:09, metric 5, tag 1
10.0.9.6/32       *[IS-IS/18] 00:37:32, metric 8, tag 2
10.0.9.7/32       *[IS-IS/18] 00:36:27, metric 8, tag 2
```

As expected, there are six IS-IS routes on r3 that represent the loopback addresses of all remote routers. These results indicate that baseline IS-IS functionality is working as needed for the remaining configuration tasks. You will now add authentication as per this requirement:

- All areas must use hello authentication based on md5 with a secret of *jnx*. The backbone area must also authenticate LSPs using a simple password of *jnx*.

Backbone authentication is now added and confirmed. The authentication-related additions to a typical backbone router configuration are highlighted next:

```
[edit protocols isis]
lab@r5# show
reference-bandwidth 500m;
level 2 {
    authentication-key "$9$jEkmTOBEhrv"; # SECRET-DATA
    authentication-type simple; # SECRET-DATA
}
interface fe-0/0/0.0 {
    level 2 disable;
```

```
    level 1 {
        hello-authentication-key "$9$H.fz1IcSeW"; # SECRET-DATA
        hello-authentication-type md5; # SECRET-DATA
    }
}
interface fe-0/0/1.0 {
    level 2 disable;
    level 1 {
        hello-authentication-key "$9$EORSlM2gJZjq"; # SECRET-DATA
        hello-authentication-type md5; # SECRET-DATA
    }
}
interface all {
    level 1 disable;
    level 2 {
        hello-authentication-key "$9$5znCyrvMX-"; # SECRET-DATA
        hello-authentication-type md5; # SECRET-DATA
    }
}
```

Backbone authentication is confirmed by verifying the status of adjacencies (hello authentication) and the presence of IS-IS routes (LSP authentication):

```
[edit protocols isis]
lab@r4# run show isis adjacency
Interface            System            L State       Hold (secs) SNPA
as0.0                r5                2 Up               20
fe-0/0/1.0           0100.0000.6002  1 Down              24   0:a0:c9:b2:f8:cb
so-0/1/0.100         r3                2 Up               25


[edit protocols isis]
lab@r4# run show isis route | match /32
10.0.3.3/32       2     55     3 int  so-0/1/0.100 r3
10.0.3.5/32       2     55     1 int  as0.0        r5
```

A working authentication configuration for a typical level 1 router is shown here with authentication-related additions highlighted:

```
[edit protocols isis]
lab@r1# show
reference-bandwidth 500m;
interface all {
```

```
        hello-authentication-key "$9$MexL7Vji.mT3"; # SECRET-DATA
        hello-authentication-type md5; # SECRET-DATA
        level 2 disable;
}
```

Hello authentication in level 1 areas can be confirmed by verifying the correct adjacency status:

```
[edit]
lab@r2# run show isis adjacency
Interface            System       L State       Hold (secs) SNPA
fe-0/0/1.0           r4           1 Up                   25  0:90:69:6b:30:1
fe-0/0/2.0           r3           1 Up                   19  0:90:69:6d:98:1
fe-0/0/3.0           r1           1 Up                   25  0:a0:c9:6f:7b:84
```

Results such as these indicate that hello authentication has been correctly configured in level 1 areas. We next examine a working configuration example for the following case study requirements:

- Backbone area routes must be summarized into area 49.0001.

- The subnet between r3 and T1 must appear in area 49.0003 as an internal route. Ensure that no adjacencies can be established on this subnet.

The summarization and leaking of routes into area 49.0001 requires the use of policy and the definition of an aggregate route, as shown next in the configuration of r5, which highlights the configuration additions needed for this task:

```
[edit]
lab@r5# show routing-options
static {
    route 10.0.200.0/24 next-hop 10.0.1.102;
}
aggregate {
    route 10.0.2.0/23;
}
```

The policy needed to advertise an aggregate route into a level 1 area is shown here:

```
[edit]
lab@r5# show policy-options
policy-statement summ {
    term 1 {
        from {
            protocol aggregate;
            route-filter 10.0.2.0/23 exact;
        }
```

```
        to level 1;
        then accept;
    }
}
```

The export policy must be applied to IS-IS as *export* for it to have any effect:

```
[edit]
lab@r5# show protocols isis export
export summ;
```

The correct operation of route summarization and leaking is easily confirmed on area 49.0001 routers:

```
[edit]
lab@r6# run show route 10.0.2/23

inet.0: 14 destinations, 14 routes (14 active, 0 holddown, 0 hidden)
+ = Active Route, - = Last Active, * = Both

10.0.2.0/23          *[IS-IS/160] 00:02:56, metric 15, tag 1
                      > to 10.0.8.6 via fe-0/1/0.0
```

Setting r3's fe-0/0/2 interface to *passive* ensures the 172.16.0.12/30 prefix is advertised into the backbone area as an internal route while also guarding against IS-IS adjacency formation:

```
[edit protocols isis]
lab@r3# show interface fe-0/0/2
passive;
level 1 disable;
```

It is a good idea to explicitly disable level 1 operation on this interface because its specific mention in the configuration results in its not being affected by the presence of the `interface all level 1 disable` clause. To confirm proper behavior, we verify that the route to 172.16.0.12/30 is present in the backbone as an IS-IS internal level 2 route:

```
[edit]
lab@r5# run show route 172/8

inet.0: 26 destinations, 26 routes (26 active, 0 holddown, 0 hidden)
+ = Active Route, - = Last Active, * = Both

172.16.0.12/30       *[IS-IS/18] 02:10:36, metric 8, tag 2
                      > to 10.0.2.2 via at-0/2/1.35
```

Correct operation can also be verified by examining r3's level 2 LSP:

```
[edit]
lab@r5# run show isis database r3 detail
IS-IS level 1 link-state database:

IS-IS level 2 link-state database:

r3.00-00  Sequence: 0x2b, Checksum: 0x475a, Lifetime: 3551 secs. . .
```

IP prefix:	10.0.2.0/30 Metric:	3 Internal
IP prefix:	172.16.0.12/30 Metric:	5 Internal
IP prefix:	10.0.4.0/30 Metric:	5 Internal
IP prefix:	10.0.4.12/30 Metric:	. . .

These results confirm that backbone routers are correctly seeing the 172.16.0.12/30 prefix as an internal level 2 IS-IS route, in accordance with the case study criteria. The correct LSP's lifetime, currently at 3551 seconds, is also highlighted here. We now address the following criteria:

- Redistribute the 10.0.5/24 route into the backbone while ensuring that area 49.0002–attached routers see a metric of at least 100.

- Except for r5, ensure that no single router or link failure will isolate r1, r2, or the OSPF router.

Achieving these requirements will involve the use of wide metrics for all level 1 area 49.0002 routers (including r3 and r4), and a route redistribution policy on both r1 and r2. Both routers must redistribute the prefix to ensure that a router failure will not sever communications between the OSPF router and the 10.0.5/24 prefix. Keep in mind that while this example is taken from r1, r2 will require similar modifications:

```
[edit]
lab@r1# show protocols isis
export direct;
reference-bandwidth 500m;
lsp-lifetime 3600;
level 1 wide-metrics-only;
interface all {
    hello-authentication-key "$9$MexL7Vji.mT3"; # SECRET-DATA
    hello-authentication-type md5; # SECRET-DATA
    level 2 disable;
}

[edit]
lab@r1# show policy-options
```

```
policy-statement direct {
    term 1 {
        from {
            protocol direct;
            route-filter 10.0.5.0/24 exact;
        }
        then {
            metric 101;
            accept;
        }
    }
}
```

The results are confirmed on r3, where we expect to see both r1 and r2 as viable next hops and a metric greater than *100* for the 10.0.5/24 route:

```
[edit protocols isis]
lab@r3# run show route 10.0.5/24

inet.0: 27 destinations, 27 routes (27 active, 0 holddown, 0 hidden)
+ = Active Route, - = Last Active, * = Both

10.0.5.0/24         *[IS-IS/15] 00:01:34, metric 106, tag 1
                      to 10.0.4.14 via fe-0/0/0.0
                    > to 10.0.4.2 via fe-0/0/1.0
```

The use of wide metrics in area 49.0002 results in the automatic redistribution of the 10.0.5/24 prefix into the backbone area because the route will no longer be seen as an external prefix by the attached routers. Therefore, an IS-IS export policy is not required on r3 and r4 for this particular aspect of the case study. You must take care, however, to ensure that subsequent export policy applications to r3 and r4 correctly take this prefix into account. The following command confirms the route's presence in the backbone:

```
[edit]
lab@r5# run show route 10.0.5/24

inet.0: 37 destinations, 37 routes (37 active, 0 holddown, 0 hidden)
+ = Active Route, - = Last Active, * = Both

10.0.5.0/24         *[IS-IS/18] 00:01:21, metric 64, tag 2
                    > to 10.0.2.10 via as1.0
```

The use of narrow metrics, which support the route type attribute, would have necessitated a route-leaking policy on area 49.0002's attached routers to ensure the route injection into the backbone area. The route's presence in r5, and the correct metric value displayed by area 49.0002 routers, confirms that the requirements for redistributing the 10.0.5/24 route have been met. Next, we will examine the configuration needed to meet the following criteria:

- r5 and r6 must use a level 1 priority of *0*.
- Ensure that r7 never functions as a pseudonode when its adjacencies are up.
- Set the level 1 preference in area 49.0001 to *155*.

With r5 and r6 set to a level 1 priority of *0*, you will need to ensure that r7's priority is also set to *0* and that its MAC addresses are numerically lower than those used by r5 or r6 to prevent it from being elected a DIS. The following configuration prevents r7 from becoming the DIS, and correctly sets the IS-IS level 1 internal route preference in accordance with the case study requirements. The route preference and level 1 priority configuration is also needed on r5 and r6:

```
[edit]
lab@r7# show protocols isis
reference-bandwidth 500m;
lsp-lifetime 3600;
level 1 preference 155;
interface all {
    hello-authentication-key "$9$j5kmTOBEhrv"; # SECRET-DATA
    hello-authentication-type md5; # SECRET-DATA
    level 2 disable;
    level 1 priority 0;
}
```

The following highlights call out r7's new MAC addresses:

```
[edit]
lab@r7# show interfaces fe-0/3/0
mtu 4000;
mac 00.00.00.00.00.11;
unit 0 {
    family inet {
        address 10.0.8.2/30;
    }
    family iso;
}
```

```
[edit]
lab@r7# show interfaces fe-0/3/1
mac 00.00.00.00.00.22;
unit 0 {
```

```
    family inet {
        address 10.0.8.10/30;
    }
    family iso;
}
```

The OSPF–to–IS-IS redistribution tasks must be completed before the level 1 preference modification can be confirmed. Viewing r7's IS-IS adjacencies and interface specifics to confirm the correct priority settings on r5, r6, and r7, and to verify that r7 is not functioning as a DIS, can be performed right away:

```
[edit]
lab@r7# run show isis interface
IS-IS interface database:
Interface        L CirID Level 1 DR   Level 2 DR    L1/L2 Metric
fe-0/3/0.0       1  0x2  r6.03        Disabled      5/5
fe-0/3/1.0       1  0x3  r5.03        Disabled      5/5
lo0.0            0  0x1  Passive      Disabled      0/0
```

These results confirm that r7 is currently not functioning as a DIS on any of its IS-IS interfaces. The following command allows you to confirm the required priority setting on r6 and r5:

```
[edit]
lab@r7# run show isis adjacency detail
r6
  Interface: fe-0/3/0.0, Level: 1, State: Up, Expires in 8 secs
  Priority: 0, Up/Down transitions: 3, Last transition: 00:08:03 ago
  Circuit type: 1, Speaks: IP, IPv6, MAC address: 0:a0:c9:69:c1:e4
  LAN id: r6.03, IP addresses: 10.0.8.1

r5
  Interface: fe-0/3/1.0, Level: 1, State: Up, Expires in 7 secs
  Priority: 0, Up/Down transitions: 5, Last transition: 00:08:04 ago
  Circuit type: 1, Speaks: IP, IPv6, MAC address: 0:90:69:69:70:1
  LAN id: r5.03, IP addresses: 10.0.8.9
```

The confirmation of the correct priority setting on r5 and r6, coupled with the knowledge that r7's level 1 interfaces have also had their MAC addresses manually set, confirms that the requirements for this configuration task have been met.

The following case study criteria will now be addressed:

- You may not modify or view the OSPF router's configuration.
- Configure r6 and r7 to advertise the IS-IS default route to the OSPF router. Ensure that the OSPF router can load balance over the default route.

- Configure r6 and r7 to redistribute OSPF routes learned from the OSPF router into IS-IS.
- Ensure that no single router or link failure will isolate r1, r2, or the OSPF router.
- You must not have suboptimal routing between r6, r7, and the OSPF router.

The OSPF–to–IS-IS redistribution task is made somewhat complex by the fact that you are not able to view or modify the OSPF router's configuration. To complete this task, you will need to perform a fair bit of reverse engineering, or develop some really good psychic skills! The following trace configuration will be used to get the ball rolling on r7, which should tell you something about this author's belief in ESP:

```
[edit]
lab@r7# show protocols ospf
traceoptions {
    file ospf;
    flag hello detail;
    flag error detail;
}
area 0.0.0.0 {
    interface fe-0/3/3.0;
}
```

After committing, monitor the trace file for clues to the OSPF router's configuration, which are highlighted next:

```
lab@r7# run monitor start ospf

[edit]
lab@r7#
*** ospf ***
May 22 23:31:22 OSPF sent Hello 172.16.40.6 -> 224.0.0.5 (fe-0/3/3.0)
May 22 23:31:22   Version 2, length 44, ID 10.0.9.7, area 0.0.0.0
May 22 23:31:22   checksum 0xe81c, authtype 0
May 22 23:31:22   mask 255.255.255.252, hello_ivl 10, opts 0x2, prio 128
May 22 23:31:22   dead_ivl 40, DR 0.0.0.0, BDR 0.0.0.0
May 22 23:31:23 OSPF packet ignored: area mismatch (0.0.0.2) from 172.16.40.5
May 22 23:31:23 OSPF rcvd Hello 172.16.40.5 -> 224.0.0.5 (fe-0/3/3.0)
May 22 23:31:23   Version 2, length 44, ID 192.168.0.1, area 0.0.0.2
May 22 23:31:23   checksum 0x6061, authtype 1  —> simple
May 22 23:31:23   mask 255.255.255.252, hello_ivl 10, opts 0x8, prio 128
May 22 23:31:23   dead_ivl 40, DR 172.16.40.5, BDR 0.0.0.0
```

The highlighted entries reveal that the OSPF router is in area 2, and that it has been configured for simple password-based authentication (type 1). Though not overtly obvious, you can also detect that the OSPF router is coding the options field with 0x08 while r7 is sending a 0x02. Knowing that the options field is used by OSPF to indicate area types and options, and knowing that r6 is set to area 0, which must be a transit area, you can assume that the OSPF router has been set to consider area 2 as some type of non-transit area such as a stub or NSSA. To obtain the correct authentication secret, you must perform traffic monitoring using the detail switch:

```
[edit]
lab@r7# run monitor traffic interface fe-0/3/3 detail
Listening on fe-0/3/3                    Simple key
23:40:57.778943  In 172.16.40.5 > 224.0.0.5:  OSPFv2-hello 44: rtrid 192.168.0.1
area 0.0.0.2 auth "pass^@^@^@^@" mask 255.255.255.252 int 10 pri 128 dead 40 dr
172.16.40.5 nbrs [tos 0xc0]  [ttl 1] (id 12499)
23:40:59.147114 Out 172.16.40.6 > 224.0.0.5:  OSPFv2-hello 44: rtrid 10.0.9.7
backbone E mask 255.255.255.252 int 10 pri 128 dead 40 dr 172.16.40.6 nbrs [tos
0xc0]  [ttl 1] (id 8628)
^C
2 packets received by filter
0 packets dropped by kernel
```

Armed with this information, we reconfigure r7 using the correct area and authentication parameters. In this case, we take a guess and decide to configure the area as a stub, based on the previously noted settings in the OSPF options field:

```
[edit protocols ospf]
lab@r7# delete area 0

[edit protocols ospf]
lab@r7# set area 2 authentication-type simple

[edit protocols ospf]
lab@r7# set area 2 interface fe-0/3/3

[edit protocols ospf]
lab@r7# set area 2 stub

[edit protocols ospf]
lab@r7# set area 2 interface fe-0/3/3 authentication-key pass
```

The modified configuration is displayed:

```
[edit protocols ospf]
lab@r7# show
traceoptions {
    file ospf;
```

```
    flag hello detail;
    flag error detail;
    flag packets detail;
}
area 0.0.0.2 {
    stub;
    authentication-type simple; # SECRET-DATA
    interface fe-0/3/3.0 {
        authentication-key "$9$6vcM/pBIRSeMXhS"; # SECRET-DATA
    }
}
```

After committing, you look for the required OSPF adjacency:

```
[edit protocols ospf]
lab@r7# run show ospf neighbor


[edit protocols ospf]
lab@r7#
```

No joy. OK, so perhaps instead of being a stub area, area 2 is set to operate as a NSSA? It's easy enough to find out by making the following change:

```
[edit protocols ospf]
lab@r7# set area 2 nssa


[edit protocols ospf]
lab@r7# commit
commit complete
```

The OSPF adjacency status is again checked:

```
[edit protocols ospf]
lab@r7# run show ospf neighbor
  Address        Interface        State    ID          Pri  Dead
  172.16.40.5    fe-0/3/3.0       Full     192.168.0.1  128   39
```

Great! The adjacency is up, which means r7 should now be receiving the routes that need to be redistributed into IS-IS. This policy statement matches on the 192.168.*x*/24 routes and advertises them into IS-IS when applied as export to IS-IS:

```
[edit]
lab@r6# show protocols isis export
export ospf-isis;
```

```
[edit]
lab@r6# show policy-options
policy-statement ospf-isis {
    term 1 {
        from {
            route-filter 192.168.0.0/22 longer;
        }
        then accept;
    }
    term 2 {
        from {
            route-filter 0.0.0.0/0 exact;
        }
        then reject;
    }
}
```

Term 2, which rejects the re-advertisement of the default route (in the case that it is coupled through the OSPF router), is not really needed because the default export policy will not redistribute OSPF routes into IS-IS. Still, it never hurts to be extra safe when dealing with route redistribution, so its inclusion is highly recommended. The OSPF export policy needed to redistribute the IS-IS default route to the OSPF router should look something like the following:

```
[edit]
lab@r6# show policy-options policy-statement isis-ospf
term 1 {
    from {
        route-filter 0.0.0.0/0 exact;
    }
    then accept;
}
```

After applying the *ospf-isis* and *isis-ospf* export policies to r6, the reason for requiring the change to the IS-IS level 1 preference in area 49.0001 becomes obvious. Changing the IS-IS level 1 preference as directed will cause r6 or r7 to prefer the default route being re-advertised by the OSPF router, which in turn will result in an extra hop when forwarding packets to the 10.0.5/24 subnet from either r6 or r7. Such a situation is shown next, where we see that r7 has chosen the OSPF default route over the IS-IS default route. At the time of this capture, both r6 and r7 have been configured to redistribute the IS-IS default into OSPF.

In this example, r6 has chosen the IS-IS default as the active route, while r7 has been fooled into accepting the OSPF default that is coupled through the OSPF router due to the level 1 preference modification:

```
[edit]
lab@r6# run show route | match 0.0.0.0/0
0.0.0.0/0              *[IS-IS/155] 01:08:38, metric 5, tag 1

[edit]
lab@r7# run show route | match 0.0.0.0/0

inet.0: 21 destinations, 28 routes (21 active, 0 holddown, 0 hidden)
+ = Active Route, - = Last Active, * = Both

0.0.0.0/0              *[OSPF/150] 00:01:50, metric 5, tag 1
                       > to 172.16.40.5 via fe-0/3/3.0
                       [IS-IS/155] 01:09:32, metric 5, tag 1
                       > to 10.0.8.9 via fe-0/3/1.0
```

Because r7 has chosen the OSPF default, the *isis-ospf* export policy will have no effect because the currently active default route was learned through OSPF and, as such, will not be redistributed back into OSPF. This situation would result in point loss on the JNCIP exam both for having suboptimal routing and for the fact that the OSPF router cannot load balance over the default route because only r6 will be listed as the default route's next hop, as shown next:

```
lab@ospf> show route

inet.0: 20 destinations, 20 routes (20 active, 0 holddown, 0 hidden)
+ = Active Route, - = Last Active, * = Both

0.0.0.0/0              *[OSPF/150] 00:03:19, metric 5, tag 1
                       > to 172.16.40.2 via fe-0/0/0.0
```

Because you cannot apply import policy to block the reception of the default route from the OSPF router, your only real choice here is to adjust the OSPF AS external route preference so that r6 and r7 once again prefer the IS-IS default route, which has a preference of *155* in this example. It is worth noting that the 192.168.*x*/24 routes being redistributed into IS-IS as level 1 externals will not cause problems if the preference associated with OSPF external routes is numerically lower, and therefore more preferred, than the default IS-IS level 1 external preference value of *160*. So the OSPF external preference on r6 and r7 should be set to a value that is higher than *155* but lower than *160*.

Based on the modified IS-IS level 1 preference value, setting the OSPF external preference to *159* on both r6 and r7 allows us to keep the default IS-IS level 1 external preference:

```
[edit]
lab@r6# set protocols ospf external-preference 159
```

After committing the change, r6 and r7 once again prefer the IS-IS default route to the OSPF default route, so both routers correctly export the IS-IS default into OSPF. This produces the required load-balancing behavior at the OSPF router and eliminates the suboptimal routing issue:

```
lab@ospf> show route

inet.0: 20 destinations, 20 routes (20 active, 0 holddown, 0 hidden)
+ = Active Route, - = Last Active, * = Both

0.0.0.0/0          *[OSPF/150] 00:00:43, metric 5, tag 1
                      to 172.16.40.2 via fe-0/0/0.0
                    > to 172.16.40.6 via fe-0/0/1.0
```

The last issue with the OSPF redistribution task is the need to somehow advertise the 172.16.40.0/29 prefixes used by the OSPF domain into area 49.0001. This can be accomplished by running passive IS-IS on these interfaces, or by modifying the IS-IS export policy so that it also redistributes these routes. The latter approach is reflected in this modified IS-IS export policy, which uses the longer match type to catch both of the OSPF subnets in a single route filter term:

```
[edit policy-options policy-statement ospf-isis]
lab@r6# show
term 1 {
    from {
        route-filter 192.168.0.0/22 longer;
        route-filter 172.16.40.0/29 longer;
    }
    then accept;
}
term 2 {
    from {
        route-filter 0.0.0.0/0 exact;
    }
    then reject;
}
```

With the modified IS-IS export policy on both r6 and r7, we expect to see that r5 can load balance to the 192.168.*x*/24 routes, which indicates that both level 1 routers are correctly redistributing the OSPF routes into IS-IS:

```
[edit]
lab@r5# run show route 192.168.0/24

inet.0: 34 destinations, 34 routes (34 active, 0 holddown, 0 hidden)
+ = Active Route, - = Last Active, * = Both

192.168.0.0/24     *[IS-IS/160] 00:00:03, metric 5, tag 1
                    > to 10.0.8.5 via fe-0/0/0.0
                      to 10.0.8.10 via fe-0/0/1.0
192.168.0.1/32     *[IS-IS/160] 00:00:03, metric 6, tag 1
                    > to 10.0.8.5 via fe-0/0/0.0
                      to 10.0.8.10 via fe-0/0/1.0
```

With the mutual route redistribution apparently working, traceroutes are performed to confirm the required OSPF router to 10.0.5/24 subnet reachability:

```
lab@ospf> traceroute 10.0.5.1
traceroute to 10.0.5.1 (10.0.5.1), 30 hops max, 40 byte packets
 1  172.16.40.6 (172.16.40.6)  0.211 ms  0.167 ms  0.113 ms
 2  10.0.8.9 (10.0.8.9)  0.333 ms  0.304 ms  0.279 ms
 3  *^C
```

Well, these results are certainly less than stellar. A quick look at r3 sheds some light on the nature of the problem:

```
lab@r3> show route 192/8

lab@r3>
```

The absence of the redistributed routes in the backbone results from the JUNOS software IS-IS implementation's default policy of not leaking level 1 external prefixes into the level 2 backbone. This is remedied with the highlighted policy modification made to r5's IS-IS export policy:

```
[edit policy-options policy-statement summ]
lab@r5# show
term 1 {
    from {
        protocol aggregate;
        route-filter 10.0.2.0/23 exact;
    }
```

```
        to level 1;
        then accept;
}
term 2 {
    from {
            protocol isis;
            level 1;
            external;
    }
    to level 2;
    then accept;
}
```

After the change is committed, the traceroute is retested:

```
lab@ospf> traceroute 10.0.5.1
traceroute to 10.0.5.1 (10.0.5.1), 30 hops max, 40 byte packets
 1  172.16.40.6 (172.16.40.6)  0.191 ms  0.123 ms  0.095 ms
 2  10.0.8.9 (10.0.8.9)  0.351 ms  0.293 ms  0.277 ms
 3  10.0.2.10 (10.0.2.10)  0.413 ms  0.695 ms  0.381 ms
 4  10.0.4.10 (10.0.4.10)  0.362 ms  0.701 ms  0.383 ms
 5  10.0.5.1 (10.0.5.1)  0.363 ms  0.700 ms  0.379 ms
```

Since the OSPF router is currently forwarding through r7, it is wise to also confirm the forwarding path from r6:

```
[edit]
lab@r6# run traceroute 10.0.5.1
traceroute to 10.0.5.1 (10.0.5.1), 30 hops max, 40 byte packets
 1  10.0.8.6 (10.0.8.6)  0.360 ms  0.297 ms  0.233 ms
 2  10.0.2.10 (10.0.2.10)  0.528 ms  0.495 ms  0.358 ms
 3  10.0.4.10 (10.0.4.10)  0.357 ms  0.647 ms  0.372 ms
 4  10.0.5.1 (10.0.5.1)  0.362 ms  0.683 ms  0.373 ms
```

The results indicate that IS-IS–to–OSPF route redistribution is working in accordance with the specified criteria. Before you consider this task complete, you should verify forwarding paths between r6, r7, and the OSPF router:

```
[edit]
lab@r7# run traceroute 10.0.9.6
traceroute to 10.0.9.6 (10.0.9.6), 30 hops max, 40 byte packets
 1  172.16.40.5 (172.16.40.5)  0.269 ms  0.196 ms  0.112 ms
 2  10.0.9.6 (10.0.9.6)  0.198 ms  0.185 ms  0.157 ms
```

The extra hop through the OSPF router is not good. This situation exists because both r6 and r7 are advertising a stub route to the interface that is sourcing their RID, and this stub route is being coupled through the OSPF router with a better preference than the IS-IS route for the same prefix:

```
[edit]
lab@r7# run show route 10.0.9.6

inet.0: 21 destinations, 24 routes (21 active, 0 holddown, 0 hidden)
+ = Active Route, - = Last Active, * = Both

10.0.9.6/32         *[OSPF/10] 00:08:42, metric 2
                    > to 172.16.40.5 via fe-0/3/3.0
                    [IS-IS/160] 00:36:16, metric 5, tag 1
                    > to 10.0.8.1 via fe-0/3/0.0
```

While this issue could be resolved with preference adjustments, the cleanest fix is to manually configure the RID on both r6 and r7 as shown next:

```
[edit]
lab@r6# set routing-options router-id 10.0.9.6
```

After the change, you confirm that forwarding is now optimal:

```
[edit]
lab@r7# run traceroute 10.0.9.6
traceroute to 10.0.9.6 (10.0.9.6), 30 hops max, 40 byte packets
 1  10.0.9.6 (10.0.9.6)  0.201 ms  0.133 ms  0.100 ms
```

The forwarding problems caused by the automatic route advertisement for the interface used to provide the OSPF router ID could have easily been missed. This example should emphasize the need for JNCIP candidates to constantly check and re-check their work because of the difficulties of actually being able to predict this type of behavior.

To complete this case study, the following task must now be addressed:

- Summarize all routes (internal and external) into the backbone area.

Summarization of level 1 routes will require the local definition of one or more aggregate routes, and a corresponding policy that will block specific prefixes while advertising the aggregates into level 2 only. The following changes to r3 and r4 address the summarization of area 49.0002's routes:

```
[edit]
lab@r3# show routing-options
static {
    route 10.0.200.0/24 next-hop 10.0.1.102;
```

```
}
aggregate {
    route 10.0.4.0/22;
}
[edit]
lab@r3# show policy-options
policy-statement summ {
    term 1 {
        from {
            route-filter 10.0.5.0/24 exact;
        }
        to level 2;
        then accept;
    }
    term 2 {
        from {
            protocol aggregate;
            route-filter 10.0.4.0/22 exact;
        }
        to level 2;
        then accept;
    }
    term 3 {
        from {
            route-filter 10.0.4.0/22 longer;
        }
        to level 2;
        then reject;
    }
}
```

In this policy, `term 3` negates the default IS-IS policy of exporting IS-IS level 1 internals to level 2, which serves to suppress the more specific routes associated with area 49.0002. The second term is carefully written to ensure that the aggregate for area 49.0002 is injected only into the backbone area. The ordering of terms is significant in this policy because `term 3` will match and subsequently reject the 10.0.5/24 route if it is processed before `term 1`. The *summ* policy must be applied to r3 and r4 as an IS-IS export before it will have any effect:

```
[edit]
lab@r3# show protocols isis export
export summ;
```

The results are verified by checking the backbone to confirm the presence of the aggregate and the absence of the more specific contributing routes, except the 10.0.5/24 prefix, which must be leaked into the backbone:

```
[edit]
lab@r5# run show route 10.0.4/22


inet.0: 32 destinations, 32 routes (32 active, 0 holddown, 0 hidden)
+ = Active Route, - = Last Active, * = Both

10.0.4.0/22        *[IS-IS/165] 00:04:29, metric 11, tag 2
                    > to 10.0.2.10 via as1.0
10.0.5.0/24        *[IS-IS/18] 00:04:40, metric 64, tag 2
                    > to 10.0.2.10 via as1.0
```

Load-balancing from r5 to area 49.0002 is not occurring because of the metric differences between r3's at-0/1/0 and r4's as0 interfaces, which are using metrics of *3* and *1*, respectively. Load-balancing could be achieved by adjusting the metrics of these links, but this is not a requirement in this case study.

Summarizing the routes from area 49.0001 requires the same technique, but care must be taken to also include an aggregate for the 192.168.*x*/24 routes originating in the OSPF router because the summarization requirements apply to both internal and external IS-IS routes. The following capture highlights the changes needed on r5 to correctly summarize area 49.0001 routes:

```
lab@r5# show routing-options aggregate
route 10.0.2.0/23;
route 10.0.8.0/21;
route 192.168.0.0/22;


[edit]
lab@r5# show policy-options
policy-statement summ {
    term 1 {
        from {
            protocol aggregate;
            route-filter 10.0.2.0/23 exact;
        }
        to level 1;
        then accept;
    }
    term 2 {
        from {
```

```
            route-filter 10.0.8.0/21 longer;
            route-filter 192.168.0.0/22 longer;
        }
        to level 2;
        then reject;
    }
    term 3 {
        from {
            protocol aggregate;
            route-filter 10.0.8.0/21 exact;
            route-filter 192.168.0.0/22 exact;
        }
        to level 2;
        then accept;
    }
}
```

The results are now confirmed on a backbone router:

```
lab@r3> show route 10.0.8.0

inet.0: 25 destinations, 25 routes (25 active, 0 holddown, 0 hidden)
+ = Active Route, - = Last Active, * = Both

10.0.8.0/21        *[IS-IS/165] 00:02:32, metric 13, tag 2
                    > to 10.0.2.1 via at-0/1/0.35


lab@r3> show route 192/8

inet.0: 25 destinations, 25 routes (25 active, 0 holddown, 0 hidden)
+ = Active Route, - = Last Active, * = Both

192.168.0.0/22     *[IS-IS/165] 00:02:36, metric 13, tag 2
                    > to 10.0.2.1 via at-0/1/0.35
```

These results confirm that summarization into the IS-IS backbone has been correctly configured. Before calling it quits, it is recommended that you once again verify the required connectivity between the 10.0.5/24 subnet and the OSPF router:

```
lab@ospf> traceroute 10.0.5.2
traceroute to 10.0.5.2 (10.0.5.2), 30 hops max, 40 byte packets
 1  172.16.40.6 (172.16.40.6)  0.207 ms  0.121 ms  0.093 ms
```

```
2  10.0.8.9 (10.0.8.9)  0.344 ms   0.290 ms   0.277 ms
3  *^C
```

This is a good example of why assumptions should never be made in the JNCIP lab! Though not necessarily by design, you are likely to find that the layered nature of the configuration tasks can result in the need to modify existing configurations, which in turn can lead to the "breaking" of previously confirmed network functionality. In this case, the modification of r5's policy, which was intended to achieve the case study's summarization requirements, failed to take into account the prefixes associated with the OSPF subnets, thereby making the routes unreachable for backbone routers. The highlighted changes to r5's IS-IS export policy resolves the remaining issue:

```
[edit]
lab@r5# show routing-options aggregate
route 10.0.2.0/23;
route 10.0.8.0/21;
route 192.168.0.0/22;
route 172.16.40.0/29;

[edit]
lab@r5# show policy-options
policy-statement summ {
    term 1 {
        from {
            protocol aggregate;
            route-filter 10.0.2.0/23 exact;
        }
        to level 1;
        then accept;
    }
    term 2 {
        from {
            route-filter 10.0.8.0/21 longer;
        }
        to level 2;
        then reject;
    }
    term 3 {
        from {
            protocol aggregate;
            route-filter 10.0.8.0/21 exact;
            route-filter 192.168.0.0/22 exact;
            route-filter 172.16.40.0/29 exact;
```

```
        }
        to level 2;
        then accept;
    }
}
```

This author has opted to summarize the OSPF subnets because the case study requirements make it clear that both internal and external IS-IS routes are to be summarized, and it is better to be safe than sorry. With the modified policy in place on r5, connectivity to the 10.0.5/24 subnet is restored and the goals of this case study achieved:

```
lab@ospf> traceroute 10.0.5.2
traceroute to 10.0.5.2 (10.0.5.2), 30 hops max, 40 byte packets
 1  172.16.40.6 (172.16.40.6)  0.193 ms  0.122 ms  0.093 ms
 2  10.0.8.9 (10.0.8.9)  0.332 ms  0.291 ms  0.277 ms
 3  10.0.2.10 (10.0.2.10)  0.336 ms  0.308 ms  0.305 ms
 4  10.0.5.2 (10.0.5.2)  0.254 ms  0.232 ms  0.217 ms
```

IS-IS Case Study Configurations

The modified configuration stanzas needed to complete the IS-IS case study are provided in Listings 4.4 through 4.10 for all routers in the test bed, with the IS-IS related changes highlighted.

Listing 4.4: *r1* IS-IS Related Configuration
```
[edit]
lab@r1# show interfaces
fe-0/0/1 {
    vlan-tagging;
    unit 200 {
        vlan-id 200;
        family inet {
            address 10.0.4.14/30;
        }
        family iso;
    }
}
fe-0/0/2 {
    fastether-options {
        source-filtering;
        source-address-filter {
            00:a0:c9:6f:70:0d;
        }
```

```
        }
    unit 0 {
        family inet {
            address 10.0.4.5/30;
        }
        family iso;
    }
}
fxp0 {
    unit 0 {
        family inet {
            address 10.0.1.1/24;
        }
    }
}
lo0 {
    unit 0 {
        family inet {
            address 10.0.6.1/32;
        }
        family iso {
            address 49.0002.0100.0000.6001.00;
        }
    }
}


[edit]
lab@r1# show policy-options
policy-statement direct {
    term 1 {
        from {
            protocol direct;
            route-filter 10.0.5.0/24 exact;
        }
        then {
            metric 101;
            accept;
        }
    }
}
```

```
[edit]
lab@r1# show protocols isis
export direct;
reference-bandwidth 500m;
lsp-lifetime 3600;
level 1 wide-metrics-only;
interface all {
    hello-authentication-key "$9$MexL7Vji.mT3"; # SECRET-DATA
    hello-authentication-type md5; # SECRET-DATA
    level 2 disable;
}
```

Listing 4.5: *r2* IS-IS Related Configuration

```
[edit]
lab@r2# show interfaces
fe-0/0/1 {
    speed 100m;
    link-mode half-duplex;
    fastether-options {
        no-flow-control;
    }
    unit 0 {
        family inet {
            address 10.0.4.10/30;
        }
        family iso;
    }
}
fe-0/0/2 {
    unit 0 {
        family inet {
            address 10.0.4.2/30;
        }
        family iso;
    }
}
fe-0/0/3 {
    fastether-options {
        source-filtering;
        source-address-filter {
            00:a0:c9:6f:7b:84;
```

```
            }
        }
        unit 0 {
            family inet {
                address 10.0.4.6/30;
            }
            family iso;
        }
    }
    fxp0 {
        unit 0 {
            family inet {
                address 10.0.1.2/24;
            }
        }
    }
    lo0 {
        unit 0 {
            family inet {
                address 10.0.6.2/32;
            }
            family iso {
                address 49.0002.0100.0000.6002.00;
            }
        }
    }

[edit]
lab@r2# show policy-options
policy-statement direct {
    term 1 {
        from {
            protocol direct;
            route-filter 10.0.5.0/24 exact;
        }
        then {
            metric 101;
            accept;
        }
    }
}
```

```
[edit]
lab@r2# show protocols isis
export direct;
reference-bandwidth 500m;
lsp-lifetime 3600;
level 1 wide-metrics-only;
interface all {
    hello-authentication-key "$9$TF6ArlMWxd"; # SECRET-DATA
    hello-authentication-type md5; # SECRET-DATA
    level 2 disable;
}
```

Listing 4.6: *r3* **IS-IS Related Configuration**

```
[edit]
lab@r3# show routing-options
static {
    route 10.0.200.0/24 next-hop 10.0.1.102;
}
aggregate {
    route 10.0.4.0/22;
}


[edit]
lab@r3# show interfaces
fe-0/0/0 {
    vlan-tagging;
    unit 0 {
        vlan-id 200;
        family inet {
            mtu 1496;
            address 10.0.4.13/30;
        }
        family iso;
    }
}
fe-0/0/1 {
    unit 0 {
        family inet {
            address 10.0.4.1/30;
        }
        family iso;
```

```
        }
    }
    fe-0/0/2 {
        unit 0 {
            family inet {
                address 172.16.0.13/30;
            }
            family iso;
        }
    }
    at-0/1/0 {
        atm-options {
            vpi 0 maximum-vcs 17;
            vpi 5 maximum-vcs 36;
            ilmi;
        }
        unit 35 {
            vci 5.35;
            shaping {
                cbr 50m;
            }
            oam-period 10;
            oam-liveness {
                up-count 2;
                down-count 2;
            }
            family inet {
                address 10.0.2.2/30;
            }
            family iso;
        }
    }
    so-0/2/0 {
        hold-time up 30 down 30;
        encapsulation frame-relay;
        lmi {
            n392dte 2;
            n393dte 3;
            t391dte 15;
            lmi-type itu;
```

```
    }
    unit 100 {
        dlci 100;
        family inet {
            address 10.0.2.5/30;
        }
        family iso;
    }
}
fxp0 {
    unit 0 {
        family inet {
            address 10.0.1.3/24;
        }
    }
}
lo0 {
    unit 0 {
        family inet {
            address 10.0.3.3/32;
        }
        family iso {
            address 49.0002.0100.0000.3003.00;
        }
    }
}

[edit]
lab@r3# show policy-options
policy-statement summ {
    term 1 {
        from {
            route-filter 10.0.5.0/24 exact;
        }
        to level 2;
        then accept;
    }
    term 2 {
        from {
            protocol aggregate;
```

```
                route-filter 10.0.4.0/22 exact;
        }
            to level 2;
            then accept;
        }
    term 3 {
        from {
                route-filter 10.0.4.0/22 longer;
        }
            to level 2;
            then reject;
        }
}

[edit]
lab@r3# show protocols isis
export summ;
reference-bandwidth 500m;
lsp-lifetime 3600;
level 2 {
    authentication-key "$9$DCH.500REyK"; # SECRET-DATA
    authentication-type simple; # SECRET-DATA
}
level 1 wide-metrics-only;
interface fe-0/0/0.0 {
    level 2 disable;
    level 1 {
        hello-authentication-key "$9$qPT3REyrvL"; # SECRET-DATA
        hello-authentication-type md5; # SECRET-DATA
    }
}
interface fe-0/0/1.0 {
    level 2 disable;
    level 1 {
        hello-authentication-key "$9$FzZb6CuKvLX-w"; # SECRET-DATA
        hello-authentication-type md5; # SECRET-DATA
    }
}
interface fe-0/0/2.0 {
    passive;
```

```
        level 1 disable;
}
interface all {
    level 1 disable;
    level 2 {
        hello-authentication-key "$9$JeUi.AtOBEy"; # SECRET-DATA
        hello-authentication-type md5; # SECRET-DATA
    }
}
```

Listing 4.7: *r4* **IS-IS Related Configuration**

```
[edit]
lab@r4# show routing-options
static {
    route 10.0.200.0/24 next-hop 10.0.1.102;
}
aggregate {
    route 10.0.4.0/22;
}

[edit]
lab@r4# show interfaces
fe-0/0/1 {
    speed 100m;
    link-mode half-duplex;
    fastether-options {
        no-flow-control;
    }
    unit 0 {
        family inet {
            address 10.0.4.9/30;
        }
        family iso;
    }
}
so-0/1/0 {
    dce;
    hold-time up 30 down 30;
    encapsulation frame-relay;
    lmi {
        n392dce 2;
```

```
                n393dce 3;
                t392dce 25;
                lmi-type itu;
            }
        unit 100 {
            dlci 100;
            family inet {
                address 10.0.2.6/30;
            }
            family iso;
        }
    }
so-0/1/1 {
    sonet-options {
        path-trace r4-jnx;
        aggregate as0;
    }
}
so-0/1/2 {
    sonet-options {
        path-trace r4-jnx;
        aggregate as0;
    }
}
as0 {
    aggregated-sonet-options {
        minimum-links 2;
        link-speed oc3;
    }
    unit 0 {
        family inet {
            address 10.0.2.10/30;
        }
        family iso;
    }
}
fxp0 {
    unit 0 {
        family inet {
            address 10.0.1.4/24;
```

```
        }
    }
}
lo0 {
    unit 0 {
        family inet {
            address 10.0.3.4/32;
        }
        family iso {
            address 49.0002.0100.0000.3004.00;
        }
    }
}

[edit]
lab@r4# show policy-options
policy-statement summ {
    term 1 {
        from {
            route-filter 10.0.5.0/24 exact;
        }
        to level 2;
        then accept;
    }
    term 2 {
        from {
            protocol aggregate;
            route-filter 10.0.4.0/22 exact;
        }
        to level 2;
        then accept;
    }
    term 3 {
        from {
            route-filter 10.0.4.0/22 longer;
        }
        to level 2;
        then reject;
    }
}
```

```
[edit]
lab@r4# show protocols isis
export summ;
reference-bandwidth 500m;
lsp-lifetime 3600;
level 2 {
    authentication-key "$9$E7eSlM2gJZjq"; # SECRET-DATA
    authentication-type simple; # SECRET-DATA
}
level 1 wide-metrics-only;
interface fe-0/0/1.0 {
    level 2 disable;
    level 1 {
        hello-authentication-key "$9$jdkmTOBEhrv"; # SECRET-DATA
        hello-authentication-type md5; # SECRET-DATA
    }
}
interface all {
    level 1 disable;
    level 2 {
        hello-authentication-key "$9$vsc8xdDjq.5F"; # SECRET-DATA
        hello-authentication-type md5; # SECRET-DATA
    }
}
```

Listing 4.8: *r5* **IS-IS Related Configuration**

```
[edit]
lab@r5# show routing-options
static {
    route 10.0.200.0/24 next-hop 10.0.1.102;
}
aggregate {
    route 10.0.2.0/23;
    route 10.0.8.0/21;
    route 192.168.0.0/22;
    route 172.16.40.0/29;
}
```

```
[edit]
lab@r5# show interfaces
fe-0/0/0 {
```

```
    unit 0 {
        family inet {
            address 10.0.8.6/30;
        }
        family iso;
    }
}
fe-0/0/1 {
    unit 0 {
        family inet {
            address 10.0.8.9/30;
        }
        family iso;
    }
}
so-0/1/0 {
    sonet-options {
        path-trace r5-jnx;
        aggregate as1;
    }
}
so-0/1/1 {
    sonet-options {
        path-trace r5-jnx;
        aggregate as1;
    }
}
at-0/2/1 {
    atm-options {
        vpi 0 maximum-vcs 17;
        vpi 5 maximum-vcs 36;
        ilmi;
    }
    unit 35 {
        vci 5.35;
        shaping {
            cbr 50m;
        }
        oam-period 10;
        oam-liveness {
```

```
                up-count 2;
                down-count 2;
            }
            family inet {
                address 10.0.2.1/30;
            }
            family iso;
        }
    }
}
as1 {
    aggregated-sonet-options {
        minimum-links 2;
        link-speed oc3;
    }
    unit 0 {
        family inet {
            address 10.0.2.9/30;
        }
        family iso;
    }
}
fxp0 {
    unit 0 {
        family inet {
            address 10.0.1.5/24;
        }
    }
}
lo0 {
    unit 0 {
        family inet {
            address 10.0.3.5/32;
        }
        family iso {
            address 49.0001.0100.0000.3005.00;
        }
    }
}
```

```
[edit]
lab@r5# show policy-options
policy-statement summ {
    term 1 {
        from {
            protocol aggregate;
            route-filter 10.0.2.0/23 exact;
        }
        to level 1;
        then accept;
    }
    term 2 {
        from {
            route-filter 10.0.8.0/21 longer;
        }
        to level 2;
        then reject;
    }
    term 3 {
        from {
            protocol aggregate;
            route-filter 10.0.8.0/21 exact;
            route-filter 192.168.0.0/22 exact;
            route-filter 172.16.40.0/29 exact;
        }
        to level 2;
        then accept;
    }
}

lab@r5# show protocols isis
export summ;
reference-bandwidth 500m;
lsp-lifetime 3600;
level 2 {
    authentication-key "$9$jEkmTOBEhrv"; # SECRET-DATA
    authentication-type simple; # SECRET-DATA
}
level 1 preference 155;
interface fe-0/0/0.0 {
```

```
        level 2 disable;
        level 1 {
            hello-authentication-key "$9$H.fz1IcSeW"; # SECRET-DATA
            hello-authentication-type md5; # SECRET-DATA
            priority 0;
        }
    }
    interface fe-0/0/1.0 {
        level 2 disable;
        level 1 {
            hello-authentication-key "$9$EORS1M2gJZjq"; # SECRET-DATA
            hello-authentication-type md5; # SECRET-DATA
            priority 0;
        }
    }
    interface all {
        level 1 disable;
        level 2 {
            hello-authentication-key "$9$5znCyrvMX-"; # SECRET-DATA
            hello-authentication-type md5; # SECRET-DATA
        }
    }
```

Listing 4.9: *r6* **IS-IS Related Configuration**

```
[edit]
lab@r6# show interfaces
fe-0/1/0 {
    unit 0 {
        family inet {
            address 10.0.8.5/30;
        }
        family iso;
    }
}
fe-0/1/1 {
    mtu 4000;
    unit 0 {
        family inet {
            address 10.0.8.1/30;
        }
        family iso;
```

```
        }
    }
    fe-0/1/3 {
        unit 0 {
            family inet {
                address 172.16.40.2/30;
            }
        }
    }
    fxp0 {
        unit 0 {
            family inet {
                address 10.0.1.6/24;
            }
        }
    }
    lo0 {
        unit 0 {
            family inet {
                address 10.0.9.6/32;
            }
            family iso {
                address 49.0001.0100.0000.9006.00;
            }
        }
    }
}
[edit]
lab@r6# show routing-options
static {
    route 10.0.200.0/24 next-hop 10.0.1.102;
}
router-id 10.0.9.6;

[edit]
lab@r6# show policy-options
policy-statement isis-ospf {
    term 1 {
        from {
            route-filter 0.0.0.0/0 exact;
        }
```

```
            then accept;
        }
}
policy-statement ospf-isis {
    term 1 {
        from {
            route-filter 192.168.0.0/22 longer;
            route-filter 172.16.40.0/29 longer;
        }
        then accept;
    }
    term 2 {
        from {
            route-filter 0.0.0.0/0 exact;
        }
        then reject;
    }
}
[edit]
lab@r6# show protocols
isis {
    export ospf-isis;
    reference-bandwidth 500m;
    lsp-lifetime 3600;
    level 1 preference 155;
    interface all {
        hello-authentication-key "$9$NoVs4PfzF/t"; # SECRET-DATA
        hello-authentication-type md5; # SECRET-DATA
        level 2 disable;
        level 1 priority 0;
    }
}
ospf {
    external-preference 159;
    export isis-ospf;
    area 0.0.0.2 {
        nssa;
        authentication-type simple; # SECRET-DATA
        interface fe-0/1/3.0 {
            authentication-key "$9$Byn1clKvLNVYWL"; # SECRET-DATA
```

```
        }
    }
}
```

Listing 4.10: *r7* IS-IS Related Configuration
```
[edit]
lab@r7# show interfaces
fe-0/3/0 {
    mtu 4000;
    mac 00.00.00.00.00.11;
    unit 0 {
        family inet {
            address 10.0.8.2/30;
        }
        family iso;
    }
}
fe-0/3/1 {
    mac 00.00.00.00.00.22;
    unit 0 {
        family inet {
            address 10.0.8.10/30;
        }
        family iso;
    }
}
fe-0/3/3 {
    unit 0 {
        family inet {
            address 172.16.40.6/30;
        }
    }
}
fxp0 {
    unit 0 {
        family inet {
            address 10.0.1.7/24;
        }
    }
}
lo0 {
```

```
    unit 0 {
        family inet {
            address 10.0.9.7/32;
        }
        family iso {
            address 49.0001.0100.0000.9007.00;
        }
    }
}
[edit]
lab@r7# show routing-options
static {
    route 10.0.200.0/24 next-hop 10.0.1.102;
}
router-id 10.0.9.7;

[edit]
lab@r7# show policy-options
policy-statement isis-ospf {
    term 1 {
        from {
            route-filter 0.0.0.0/0 exact accept;
        }
    }
}
policy-statement ospf-isis {
    term 1 {
        from {
            route-filter 192.168.0.0/22 longer;
            route-filter 172.16.40.0/29 longer;
        }
        then accept;
    }
    term 2 {
        from {
            route-filter 0.0.0.0/0 exact;
        }
        then reject;
    }
}
```

```
[edit]
lab@r7# show protocols
isis {
    export ospf-isis;
    reference-bandwidth 500m;
    lsp-lifetime 3600;
    level 1 preference 155;
    interface all {
        hello-authentication-key "$9$j5kmTOBEhrv"; # SECRET-DATA
        hello-authentication-type md5; # SECRET-DATA
        level 2 disable;
        level 1 priority 0;
    }
}
ospf {
    external-preference 159;
    export isis-ospf;
    area 0.0.0.2 {
        nssa;
        authentication-type simple; # SECRET-DATA
        interface fe-0/3/3.0 {
            authentication-key "$9$6vcM/pBIRSeMXhS"; # SECRET-DATA
        }
    }
}
```

Spot the Issues: Review Questions

The following review questions are based on the topology shown earlier in Figure 4.4.

1. Will the following IS-IS configuration correctly configure interface fe-0/0/0 for IS-IS level 1 operation only?

    ```
    [edit protocols isis]
    lab@r5# show
    interface fe-0/0/0.0 {
        level 1 hello-interval 10;
    }
    interface all {
        level 2 disable;
    }
    ```

2. The following configuration results in an IS-IS adjacency to r3 and r4, but no routes are installed and the LSDB contains no LSP from these routers. What is a likely cause for this symptom?

    ```
    [edit protocols isis]
    lab@r5# show
    export summ;
    reference-bandwidth 500m;
    lsp-lifetime 3600;
    level 2 {
        authentication-key "$9$qP5FREy8X-"; # SECRET-DATA
        authentication-type simple; # SECRET-DATA
    }
    level 1 preference 155;
    interface fe-0/0/0.0 {
        level 2 disable;
        level 1 {
            hello-authentication-key "$9$H.fz1IcSeW"; # SECRET-DATA
            hello-authentication-type md5; # SECRET-DATA
        }
    }
    interface fe-0/0/1.0 {
        level 2 disable;
        level 1 {
            hello-authentication-key "$9$EORS1M2gJZjq"; # SECRET-DATA
            hello-authentication-type md5; # SECRET-DATA
        }
    }
    ```

```
interface all {
    level 1 disable;
    level 2 {
        hello-authentication-key "$9$5znCyrvMX-"; # SECRET-DATA
        hello-authentication-type md5; # SECRET-DATA
    }
}
```

3. You have incorrectly specified the IP address for r5's at-0/12/1.35 interface, as highlighted next. Will an IS-IS adjacency still be possible?

```
[edit interfaces at-0/2/1]
lab@r5# show
atm-options {
    vpi 0 maximum-vcs 17;
    vpi 5 maximum-vcs 36;
    ilmi;
}
unit 35 {
    vci 5.35;
    shaping {
        cbr 50m;
    }
    oam-period 10;
    oam-liveness {
        up-count 2;
        down-count 2;
    }
    family inet {
        address 10.0.20.1/30;
    }
    family iso;
}
```

4. What is missing from the IS-IS configuration shown next?

```
[edit protocols isis]
lab@r5# show
export summ;
reference-bandwidth 500m;
lsp-lifetime 3600;
level 2 {
    authentication-key "$9$jEkmTOBEhrv"; # SECRET-DATA
```

```
        authentication-type simple; # SECRET-DATA
    }
    level 1 preference 155;
    interface fe-0/0/0.0 {
        level 2 disable;
        level 1 {
            hello-authentication-key "$9$H.fz1IcSeW"; # SECRET-DATA
            hello-authentication-type md5; # SECRET-DATA
        }
    }
    interface fe-0/0/1.0 {
        level 2 disable;
        level 1 {
            hello-authentication-key "$9$EORS1M2gJZjq"; # SECRET-DATA
            hello-authentication-type md5; # SECRET-DATA
        }
    }
    interface at-0/2/1.35 {
        level 1 disable;
        level 2 {
            hello-authentication-key "$9$WcqXNbiHmPQn"; # SECRET-DATA
            hello-authentication-type md5; # SECRET-DATA
        }
    }
    interface as1.0 {
        level 2 {
            hello-authentication-key "$9$d7w2a5T3nCu"; # SECRET-DATA
            hello-authentication-type md5; # SECRET-DATA
        }
        level 1 disable;
    }
```

5. Your goal is to advertise a 10.0.4/22 summary to level 2 areas only. Will the following policy achieve this requirement?

```
[edit]
lab@r3# show policy-options
policy-statement summ {
    term 1 {
        from {
            route-filter 10.0.4.0/22 longer;
        }
```

```
        to level 2;
        then reject;
    }
    term 2 {
        from {
            protocol aggregate;
            route-filter 10.0.4.0/22 exact;
        }
        then accept;
    }
}
```

6. You have decided to save some time by using a configuration group intended to configure the iso family on your router's interface with less typing. What could go wrong, based on the following configuration?

```
[edit]
lab@r2# show groups
iso {
    interfaces {
        <*> {
            unit <*> {
                family iso;
            }
        }
    }
}

[edit]
lab@r2# show interfaces apply-groups
apply-groups iso;

[edit]
lab@r2# show protocols isis
export direct;
reference-bandwidth 500m;
lsp-lifetime 3600;
level 1 wide-metrics-only;
interface all {
    hello-authentication-key "$9$TF6ArlMWxd"; # SECRET-DATA
    hello-authentication-type md5; # SECRET-DATA
    level 2 disable;
}
```

Spot the Issues: Answers

1.   No, this configuration will result in level 1 and level 2 operation on the fe-0/0/0 interface. The specific mention of interface fe-0/0/0 exempts it from the `interface all level 2 disable` statement. You will need to specifically disable level 2 operation on this interface.

2.   The most likely cause is mismatched LSP authentication as configured under the level 2 stanza. Hello authentication must be properly configured for the adjacency to form. To test if this is the cause, you could delete backbone area authentication-related entries, perform protocol tracing, or configure the `no-authentication-check` option.

3.   Depending on the JUNOS software version, the answer will be *yes* or *no*. The 5.2.*x* JUNOS software used in this test bed will permit the IS-IS adjacency to form. Unlike OSPF, the IS-IS protocol does not understand IP addressing, and can therefore allow an IS-IS adjacency when IP subnet parameters have been mismatched. This aspect of IS-IS is well worth noting, because troubleshooting issues that relate to simple IP addressing mistakes are made more difficult when the operator believes that the presence of an IS-IS adjacency provides vindication of the interface's IP properties.

4.   The lack of an `interface all` term, and specific mention of the router's lo0 interface, means that the router will have no ISO NET (assuming you have correctly assigned the NET to the router's lo0 interface). The IS-IS protocol will not function without a NET. In this case, protocol tracing will report errors as shown next:

```
May 29 04:42:41 task_receive_packet: task IS-IS I/O from index 5 addr
0.a0.c9.69.c5.27 socket 11 length 62
May 29 04:42:41 ERROR: received IIH but have no local sysid .
```

5.   No. The lack of a `to level` 2 clause in term 2 will result in the summary route being advertised into all IS-IS levels.

6.   Your configuration group's wild-card syntax will match on all router interfaces and logical units, which includes the router's fxp0 interface. The use of `interface all` in the IS-IS stanza will in turn enable IS-IS operation on all such ISO-capable interfaces. This can lead to the formation of IS-IS adjacencies over the OoB network, which has the potential of catastrophic disruption considering the black holes that will occur when a router forwards packets destined for a remote router over an fxp0 adjacency. To alleviate this problem, you could rewrite the wild-card expression to be more selective or you could specifically disable the router's fxp0 interface under the IS-IS stanza. Both approaches are demonstrated next in the context of r2's case study configuration. The first example has the wild-card expression carefully written such that it will match only on the correct router interfaces (fe-0/0/1 through fe-0/0/3):

```
[edit groups iso]
lab@r2# show
iso {
    interfaces {
        "<fe-[1-3]>" {
```

```
            unit <*> {
                family iso;
            }
        }
    }
}
```

The second approach compensates for the use of a sloppy wild-card expression (<*>) by explicitly disabling interfaces that should not run IS-IS:

```
[edit]
lab@r2# show protocols
isis {
    export direct;
    reference-bandwidth 500m;
    lsp-lifetime 3600;
    level 1 wide-metrics-only;
    interface fe-0/0/0.0 {
        disable;
    }
    interface all {
        hello-authentication-key "$9$TF6ArlMWxd"; # SECRET-DATA
        hello-authentication-type md5; # SECRET-DATA
        level 2 disable;
    }
    interface fxp0.0 {
        disable;
    }
}
```

Chapter

5

IBGP Configuration and Testing

JNCIP LAB SKILLS COVERED IN THIS CHAPTER:

- ✓ **IBGP peering**
  - ▪ IBGP policy
- ✓ **IBGP authentication**
- ✓ **Route reflection**
- ✓ **Confederations**
- ✓ **IBGP timers and various other "knobs"**

This chapter provides examples of JNCIP-level Internal Border Gateway Protocol (IBGP) configuration scenarios, as well as examples of the verification methods that can be used to confirm proper IBGP protocol operation. It is assumed that the configurations of the routers in your test bed are currently based on the case study criteria presented at the end of the initial system configuration, interface, and IS-IS chapters, as you will now be adding IBGP to your test bed and a functional Interior Gate Protocol (IGP) is required for proper IBGP operation. If you are unsure of the state of your routers, you should compare your configurations against those provided in the case studies at the end of Chapters 1, 2, and 4. You should also verify that all of your router interfaces and IS-IS IGP are operational before proceeding.

Because IBGP does not really care about the particulars of your IGP, these BGP configuration tasks could easily be applied to a test bed running OSPF. The use of IS-IS is highly recommended, however, as this will simplify the task of following the IS-IS–based examples in this chapter.

The proper operation of IBGP will play a critical role in the overall success of your JNCIP lab exam, as problems with IBGP will impact the operation of subsequent External Border Gateway Protocol (EBGP) and BGP-related policy tasks. A successful JNCIP candidate must possess the practical skills and protocol knowledge necessary to proficiently configure and troubleshoot the IBGP protocol in a variety of network scenarios as demonstrated in this chapter.

This chapter concludes with a case study designed to closely approximate a typical JNCIP IBGP configuration scenario. The results of key operational mode commands are provided in the case study analysis section so that you can also compare the behavior of your network to a known good example. Example router configurations that meet all case study requirements are provided at the end of the case study for comparison with your own configurations.

Initial IBGP Peering

For proper operation, the IBGP protocol requires a full mesh of peering sessions or the use of route reflection and/or confederations. Our first IBGP example will involve a conventional full IBGP mesh, with peering established between router loopback addresses for maximum stability.

You begin your IBGP configuration example with the network topology shown in Figure 5.1, which recounts the multi-level IS-IS configuration left over from Chapter 4, "IS-IS Configuration and Testing." You will use this topology as the starting point for your IBGP configuration tasks.

Referring to Figure 5.1, you can see that each router in the test bed will require six IBGP peering definitions to ensure the requisite full IBGP mesh, and that each router has a single static route that is to be advertised into IBGP to test connectivity and forwarding paths. To complete this configuration example, your IBGP configuration must meet the following criteria:

- Ensure that the loss of any individual interface does not disrupt a router's IBGP sessions.

- All routers must log IBGP session establishment and tear down actions to a file called r*n*-bgp where *n* equals the router number.

- Advertise the 192.168.*x*/24 static routes into IBGP.

- Your network must use optimal forwarding paths.

- Your AS number is 65412.

FIGURE 5.1   IBGP full mesh peering

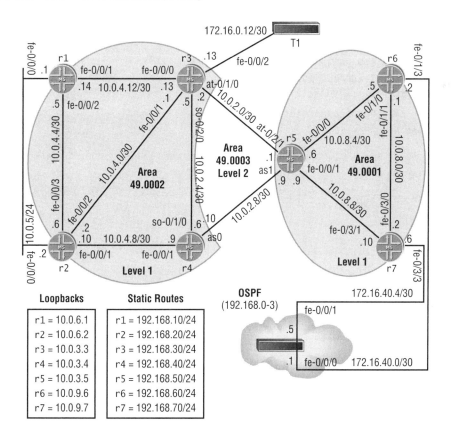

You begin by configuring the IBGP peering sessions on r1. The following commands define the local AS number:

```
[edit routing-options]
lab@r1# set autonomous-system 65412
```

The next set of commands creates a BGP peer group called *internal*, and defines the IBGP peering sessions to the other six routers based on their loopback addresses. Loopback-based peering is required to guarantee that the loss of an individual interface will not disrupt your IBGP sessions:

```
[edit routing-options]
lab@r1# top
```

```
[edit]
lab@r1# edit protocols bgp group internal
```

```
[edit protocols bgp group internal]
lab@r1# set type internal
```

```
[edit protocols bgp group internal]
lab@r1# set local-address 10.0.6.1
```

```
[edit protocols bgp group internal]
lab@r1# set neighbor 10.0.6.2
```

The last command should be repeated using each of the remaining router's lo0 addresses, with the results being the peering configuration shown next:

```
[edit protocols bgp group internal]
lab@r1# show
type internal;
local-address 10.0.6.1;
neighbor 10.0.6.2;
neighbor 10.0.3.3;
neighbor 10.0.3.4;
neighbor 10.0.3.5;
neighbor 10.0.9.6;
neighbor 10.0.9.7;
```

Use of the local-address option is critical here, because failing to include this knob for a given IBGP router pairing will result in the inability to establish the loopback-based peering session. Though such a session can be established when just one of the paired routers makes use of this option, its inclusion on all routers is highly recommended so that either peer can initiate the IBGP session.

The following commands address the session logging aspects of the example by configuring the tracing of BGP connection state transitions to a file called *rn-bgp*. Using the log-updown option under [edit protocols bgp] would result in connection state changes being written to the /var/log/messages file, which would violate the restrictions of this example. It is also suggested that you configure the trace parameters at the group or neighbor level, as a global application could result in the unintentional logging of EBGP connection state changes in a later lab scenario:

```
[edit protocols bgp group internal]
lab@r1# set traceoptions file r1-bgp
```

```
[edit protocols bgp group internal]
lab@r1# set traceoptions flag state detail
```

The completed tracing stanza is now shown:

```
[edit protocols bgp group internal]
lab@r1# show traceoptions
file r1-bgp;
flag state detail;
```

IBGP Policy

The use of policy to effect route redistribution and to manipulate route attributes has been demonstrated in Chapters 3 and 4 for the RIP, OSPF, and IS-IS protocols. The use of policy for BGP is similar to the examples provided for other protocols, but you should consider that with BGP, policies can be applied as both import and export, and can be applied at the global, group, or neighbor levels. Many candidates fail to recognize that JUNOS software executes the *most specific* policy *only*, which means that the presence of a neighbor policy will exempt that neighbor from the actions specified in any group or global policy application.

You should recall that the default policy for BGP is to accept all received routes that pass incoming sanity checks (no AS path loops), and to advertise all active BGP routes to all BGP peers while obeying IBGP rules that prevent a BGP speaker from re-advertising IBGP-learned routes to other IBGP speakers. (The use of route reflection mitigates these restrictions, as discussed in the "IBGP Route Reflection" section later in this chapter.)

 BGP policy mistakes often occur when an exam candidate attempts to link multiple policies together but fails to notice that one or more of these policies make use of an accept action, which when encountered causes all remaining policy processing to terminate. The same thing can happen with multiterm policies, but seeing multiple terminating actions in the same policy statement will often provide a clue as to what is wrong. If you plan on using one policy to, say, set local preference, and another to set the BGP next hop, it is suggested that you avoid the use of the accept action until the last policy, or that you rely on the default BGP policy of accepting all BGP routes so that your policies do not require an explicit accept action. Advertising non-BGP derived routes will require an explicit accept action because the default BGP policy will not accept these routes.

Policy in BGP is used to redistribute routes and to set various BGP and non-BGP attributes such as local preference, Multi-Exit Discriminator (MED), communities, global preference, etc. Various BGP policy applications will be provided throughout this chapter and Chapter 6, "EBGP Configuration and Testing."

The static route definition and policy statement shown next define the 192.168.10/24 static route and the policy needed to selectively match on, and then accept, this prefix for redistribution into another routing protocol. The use of reject as a next hop for the static route is suggested, because this will allow pings and traceroutes to complete with a "destination unreachable" message:

```
[edit]
lab@r1# show routing-options static
route 10.0.200.0/24 next-hop 10.0.1.102;
route 192.168.10.0/24 reject;

[edit]
lab@r1# show policy-options policy-statement ibgp
term 1 {
    from {
        protocol static;
        route-filter 192.168.10.0/24 exact;
    }
    then accept;
}
```

The *ibgp* policy is then applied as export to the *internal* peer group, which puts it into effect for all six of r1's IBGP peers. In this example, you could also have applied the policy globally, or multiple times—once under each peer—if you are so inclined to practice your typing skills:

```
[edit]
lab@r1# set protocols bgp group internal export ibgp
```

The initial BGP configuration for r1 is now displayed:

```
[edit]
lab@r1# show protocols bgp
group internal {
    type internal;
    traceoptions {
        file r1-bgp;
        flag state detail;
    }
    local-address 10.0.6.1;
    export ibgp;
```

```
    neighbor 10.0.6.2;
    neighbor 10.0.3.3;
    neighbor 10.0.3.4;
    neighbor 10.0.3.5;
    neighbor 10.0.9.6;
    neighbor 10.0.9.7;
}
```

You will need to replicate the BGP, static route, Autonomous System (AS) number, and IBGP export policy–related configuration on the remaining routers before proceeding to the next section. The use of `load merge terminal` for the BGP stanza is highly recommended, considering that all routers require the same basic configuration. You will need to edit the local address and neighbor statements to reflect the particulars of each router before performing the merge operation, however. To simplify the edits associated with the cut-and-paste approach, you can include a peering session to the local router so that all seven routers use a common list that includes all routers in the test bed. This will result in an `active` connection on each router because you cannot establish an IBGP session to yourself.

Verify Initial IBGP Peering and Policy

After committing the initial IBGP configuration on all seven routers, you confirm that the BGP sessions have been correctly established:

```
[edit]
lab@r1# run show bgp summary
Groups: 1 Peers: 6 Down peers: 0
Table          Tot Paths  Act Paths Suppressed    History Damp State    Pending
inet.0                6          6          0          0          0          0
Peer             AS      InPkt     OutPkt    OutQ   Flaps Last Up/Dwn
State|#Active/Received/Damped...
10.0.3.3       65412        32         33       0       0   15:08 1/1/0
0/0/0
10.0.3.4       65412        30         30       0       0   13:41 1/1/0
0/0/0
10.0.3.5       65412        28         28       0       0   12:49 1/1/0
0/0/0
10.0.6.2       65412        38         39       0       0   17:44 1/1/0
0/0/0
10.0.9.6       65412        25         25       0       0   11:12 1/1/0
0/0/0
10.0.9.7       65412        23         23       0       0   10:05 1/1/0
0/0/0
```

The presence of six IBGP sessions, all in the established state, along with the peer references to lo0 addresses, indicates that the initial IBGP peering sessions have been correctly established.

You can also see that each session is reporting one received route, which is also active, so indications are also positive with regard to your IBGP export policy and static route definitions. To confirm proper IBGP route advertisement, you examine the BGP routes on r2:

```
[edit]
lab@r2# run show route protocol bgp

inet.0: 22 destinations, 22 routes (22 active, 0 holddown, 0 hidden)
+ = Active Route, - = Last Active, * = Both

192.168.10.0/24    *[BGP/170] 00:21:51, MED 0, localpref 100, from 10.0.6.1
                      AS path: I
                    > to 10.0.4.5 via fe-0/0/3.0
192.168.30.0/24    *[BGP/170] 00:19:02, MED 0, localpref 100, from 10.0.3.3
                      AS path: I
                      to 10.0.4.9 via fe-0/0/1.0
                    > to 10.0.4.1 via fe-0/0/2.0
192.168.40.0/24    *[BGP/170] 00:17:45, MED 0, localpref 100, from 10.0.3.4
                      AS path: I
                    > to 10.0.4.9 via fe-0/0/1.0
                      to 10.0.4.1 via fe-0/0/2.0
192.168.50.0/24    *[BGP/170] 00:16:53, MED 0, localpref 100, from 10.0.3.5
                      AS path: I
                      to 10.0.4.9 via fe-0/0/1.0
                    > to 10.0.4.1 via fe-0/0/2.0
192.168.60.0/24    *[BGP/170] 00:15:15, MED 0, localpref 100, from 10.0.9.6
                      AS path: I
                      to 10.0.4.9 via fe-0/0/1.0
                    > to 10.0.4.1 via fe-0/0/2.0
192.168.70.0/24    *[BGP/170] 00:14:09, MED 0, localpref 100, from 10.0.9.7
                      AS path: I
                    > to 10.0.4.9 via fe-0/0/1.0
                      to 10.0.4.1 via fe-0/0/2.0

iso.0: 1 destinations, 1 routes (1 active, 0 holddown, 0 hidden)
```

The output indicates that r2 has learned the 192.168.*x*/24 routes from the remote routers through IBGP. Because r2 receives two equal-cost next hops for the IS-IS level 1 default, many of the BGP routes show two viable IS-IS forwarding next hops, as expected. Displaying the routes that are being sent or received from various IBGP peers can also test your IBGP export policy:

```
lab@r1> show route receive-protocol bgp 10.0.9.7
```

```
inet.0: 21 destinations, 21 routes (21 active, 0 holddown, 0 hidden)
+ = Active Route, - = Last Active, * = Both

192.168.70.0/24
10.0.9.7                    0         100 I

iso.0: 1 destinations, 1 routes (1 active, 0 holddown, 0 hidden)

lab@r1> show route advertising-protocol bgp 10.0.9.7

inet.0: 21 destinations, 21 routes (21 active, 0 holddown, 0 hidden)
+ = Active Route, - = Last Active, * = Both

192.168.10.0/24
Self                        0         100 I
```

The results confirm the correct IBGP export policy on r1 and r7, because it confirms that both are correctly exporting their respective static routes. The next confirmation step is to conduct a few traceroutes to verify that all is well with the forwarding paths through your AS. The nature of IS-IS routing may cause packets to incur an "extra hop" now and then (due to level 1 routers always choosing the metrically closest attached router and the way summaries are being injected into the backbone), so the presence of a less-than-ideal path does not automatically indicate problems with BGP forwarding paths:

```
[edit]
lab@r7# run traceroute 192.168.10.1
traceroute to 192.168.10.1 (192.168.10.1), 30 hops max, 40 byte packets
 1  10.0.8.9 (10.0.8.9)  0.346 ms  0.259 ms  0.218 ms
 2  10.0.2.10 (10.0.2.10)  0.297 ms  0.252 ms  0.234 ms
 3  10.0.4.10 (10.0.4.10)  0.406 ms  0.676 ms  0.375 ms
 4  10.0.4.5 (10.0.4.5)  0.359 ms  0.684 ms  0.379 ms
 5  10.0.4.5 (10.0.4.5)  0.353 ms !H  0.670 ms !H  0.372 ms !H

[edit]
lab@r7# run traceroute 192.168.20.1
traceroute to 192.168.20.1 (192.168.20.1), 30 hops max, 40 byte packets
 1  10.0.8.9 (10.0.8.9)  0.333 ms  0.250 ms  0.216 ms
 2  10.0.2.10 (10.0.2.10)  0.275 ms  0.250 ms  0.236 ms
 3  10.0.4.10 (10.0.4.10)  0.667 ms  0.679 ms  0.377 ms
 4  10.0.4.10 (10.0.4.10)  0.362 ms !H  0.681 ms !H  0.371 ms !H
```

The forwarding path from r7 to the 192.168.10/24 and 192.168.20/24 prefixes is working as expected. An extra hop is observed when forwarding to 192.168.10/24 due to r5's desire to forward all packets that match the summary route for area 49.0003 to r4, as shown by the presence of the 10.0.2.10 hop in both traceroutes. This behavior is expected due to r4 advertising a lower metric for its as0 interface when compared to r3's metric for its at-0/1/0.35 interface. You will recall that in the IS-IS case study there was no requirement that r5 be able to load balance to the 10.0.4/22 summary route, and even if it could, the hashing function used to select one of the two equal-cost next hops would likely just reverse the situation at best.

Knowing when forwarding inefficiencies are the result of configuration mistakes, rather than normal and expected protocol behavior, is a valuable skill that can prevent you from wasting time trying to resolve "issues" that cannot be fixed. To confirm IBGP connection state logging, you monitor the log file before or after you have cleared your IBGP sessions. You should observe output similar to that shown here:

```
[edit]
lab@r1# run clear bgp neighbor
Cleared 6 connections

[edit]
lab@r1# run monitor start r1-bgp

[edit]
lab@r1# ]
*** r1-bgp ***
Jun 12 16:51:22 bgp_event: peer 10.0.3.3 (Internal AS 65412) old state Active
event ConnectRetry new state Connect
Jun 12 16:51:22 bgp_event: peer 10.0.3.3 (Internal AS 65412) old state Connect
event Open new state OpenSent
Jun 12 16:51:22 bgp_event: peer 10.0.3.3 (Internal AS 65412) old state OpenSent
event RecvOpen new state OpenConfirm
Jun 12 16:51:22 bgp_read_message: 10.0.3.3 (Internal AS 65412): 0 bytes buffered
Jun 12 16:51:22 bgp_event: peer 10.0.3.3 (Internal AS 65412) old state
OpenConfirm event RecvKeepAlive new state Established
Jun 12 16:51:26 bgp_event: peer 10.0.3.4 (Internal AS 65412) old state Active
event ConnectRetry new state Connect
Jun 12 16:51:26 bgp_event: peer 10.0.3.4 (Internal AS 65412) old state Connect
event Open new state OpenSent
Jun 12 16:51:26 bgp_event: peer 10.0.3.4 (Internal AS 65412) old state OpenSent
event RecvOpen new state OpenConfirm
Jun 12 16:51:26 bgp_read_message: 10.0.3.4 (Internal AS 65412): 0 bytes buffered
Jun 12 16:51:26 bgp_event: peer 10.0.3.4 (Internal AS 65412) old state
OpenConfirm event RecvKeepAlive new state Established
```

This output indicates that IBGP connection state tracing has been properly configured. The various confirmation checks performed thus far indicate that you have met all objectives for the IBGP full mesh configuration example.

IBGP Authentication

JUNOS software supports authentication of BGP messages based on either IPSec or an MD5 checksum. IPSec-related configuration is beyond the scope of this book, leaving MD5 as your only option at present. MD5-based authentication can be applied globally, at the group level, or for individual neighbors. To complete this configuration example, you must add IBGP authentication according to the following requirements:

- r2, r3, and r4 authenticate to each other using key *jni*.

- All other routers authenticate using key *jnx*.

Configure Authentication

The following commands correctly configure IBGP authentication on r3. Note that a combination of group and neighbor commands has been used to minimize typing:

```
[edit protocols bgp group internal]
lab@r3# set authentication-key jnx
```

```
[edit protocols bgp group internal]
lab@r3# set neighbor 10.0.3.4 authentication-key jni
```

```
[edit protocols bgp group internal]
lab@r3# set neighbor 10.0.3.5 authentication-key jni
```

The resulting BGP stanza on r3 is shown, and committed:

```
[edit protocols bgp group internal]
lab@r3# show
type internal;
traceoptions {
    file r3-bgp;
    flag state detail;
}
local-address 10.0.3.3;
authentication-key "$9$-zbYof5F39p"; # SECRET-DATA
export ibgp;
neighbor 10.0.6.1;
neighbor 10.0.6.2;
```

```
neighbor 10.0.3.4 {
    authentication-key "$9$-5bYof5Fn/t"; # SECRET-DATA
}
neighbor 10.0.3.5 {
    authentication-key "$9$yLxeMXaJDikP"; # SECRET-DATA
}
neighbor 10.0.9.6;
neighbor 10.0.9.7;

[edit protocols bgp group internal]
lab@r3# commit
commit complete
```

The result of this configuration is that all neighbors lacking an authentication setting will now inherit the group's authentication values such that all routers will use key *jnx* except r3, r4, and r5, which will use key *jni*. Because r3 is the only router currently set to authenticate IBGP messages, we expect to see that it has lost its BGP sessions:

```
[edit protocols bgp group internal]
lab@r3# run show bgp summary
Groups: 1 Peers: 6 Down peers: 6
Table          Tot Paths  Act Paths Suppressed    History Damp State    Pending
inet.0                 0          0          0          0          0          0
Peer             AS      InPkt     OutPkt      OutQ   Flaps Last Up/Dwn
State|#Active/Received/Damped...
10.0.3.4       65412          0          0         0         0      3:08 Connect
10.0.3.5       65412          0          0         0         0      3:08 Connect
10.0.6.1       65412          0          0         0         0      3:08 Connect
10.0.6.2       65412          0          0         0         0      3:08 Connect
10.0.9.6       65412          0          0         0         0      3:08 Connect
10.0.9.7       65412          0          0         0         0      3:08 Connect
```

You must now add compatible authentication values in the remaining routers so that all BGP sessions can once again be established. As a guide, the authentication-related BGP configuration of r1 is shown next:

```
[edit protocols bgp group internal]
lab@r1# set authentication-key jnx
```

The resulting BGP stanza for r1 is displayed:

```
[edit protocols bgp group internal]
lab@r1# show
type internal;
```

```
traceoptions {
    file r1-bgp;
    flag state detail;
}
local-address 10.0.6.1;
authentication-key "$9$oGZDk9CuOIc"; # SECRET-DATA
export ibgp;
neighbor 10.0.6.2;
neighbor 10.0.3.3;
neighbor 10.0.3.4;
neighbor 10.0.3.5;
neighbor 10.0.9.6;
neighbor 10.0.9.7;
```

With r1 set to correctly authenticate, we expect to see it successfully establish an IBGP session to r3:

```
[edit protocols bgp group internal]
lab@r1# run show bgp neighbor 10.0.3.3
Peer: 10.0.3.3+1130   AS 65412 Local: 10.0.6.1+179    AS 65412
  Type: Internal     State: Established    Flags: <>
  Last State: OpenConfirm   Last Event: RecvKeepAlive
  Last Error: None
  Export: [ ibgp ]
  Options: <Preference LocalAddress HoldTime AuthKey LogUpDown Refresh>
  Authentication key is configured
  Local Address: 10.0.6.1 Holdtime: 90 Preference: 170
  Number of flaps: 0
  Peer ID: 10.0.3.3        Local ID: 10.0.6.1        Active Holdtime: 90
  Keepalive Interval: 30
  NLRI advertised by peer: inet-unicast
  NLRI for this session: inet-unicast
  Peer supports Refresh capability (2)
  Table inet.0 Bit: 10000
    Send state: in sync
    Active prefixes: 1
    Received prefixes: 1
    Suppressed due to damping: 0
  Last traffic (seconds): Received 17   Sent 17   Checked 17
  Input messages:  Total 6      Updates 1      Refreshes 0      Octets 176
  Output messages: Total 7      Updates 1      Refreshes 0      Octets 195
  Output Queue[0]: 0
```

This display confirms that the r1-r3 IBGP session has been established and that authentication is in effect, as highlighted in the capture.

Verify IBGP Authentication

To verify that authentication is working, you need only confirm that your sessions are in the established state. Authentication problems manifest themselves as connections stuck in the connect or active states. It is easy to tell when authentication is in use, and you should always try reassigning the MD5 key if you suspect authentication mismatches. Problems often occur when authentication is applied globally, or at the group level, as you may wind up inadvertently configuring authentication for peers that are not using authentication. Displaying the BGP neighbor status, even for sessions that are "broken," will confirm whether or not authentication is configured for that peer, based on whether the keyword Authkey is present in the list of options for that session.

With your IBGP authentication correctly configured on all seven routers, you expect to see that all BGP sessions have once again been correctly established:

```
[edit protocols bgp group internal]
lab@r3# run show bgp summary
Groups: 1 Peers: 6 Down peers: 0
Table          Tot Paths  Act Paths Suppressed    History Damp State    Pending
inet.0              6          6              0          0         0           0
Peer              AS      InPkt     OutPkt     OutQ    Flaps Last Up/Dwn
State|#Active/Received/Damped...
10.0.3.4        65412       5          6         0        0      1:40 1/1/0
0/0/0
10.0.3.5        65412       3          5         0        0      1:20 1/1/0
0/0/0
10.0.6.1        65412       44         46        0        0     21:18 1/1/0
0/0/0
10.0.6.2        65412       7          8         0        0      2:37 1/1/0
0/0/0
10.0.9.6        65412       6          7         0        0      2:19 1/1/0
0/0/0
10.0.9.7        65412       2          3         0        0       23 1/1/0
0/0/0
```

IBGP Route Reflection

Route reflection is used to eliminate the need for a full IBGP mesh by allowing routers with cluster IDs configured in a given peer group to readvertise routes to clients associated with that group. A Juniper Networks route reflector can have multiple cluster IDs configured, and can act as a reflector for one group of clients and as a client for a higher-level route reflector as part of a hierarchical route reflection topology.

Configure Route Reflection

To complete this configuration example, you will need to configure a route reflection topology that complies with the following criteria:

- You must configure at least three clusters and at least two route reflectors.
- You must use physical address peering in at least one of your clusters.
- The failure of any link must not break the route reflection topology.
- The route reflection topology must not impose suboptimal routing or black holes.
- Authentication and logging settings from the previous section must remain in effect.

Before starting your configuration, it is suggested that you first design a route reflection topology that meets all specified criteria. Figure 5.2 provides an example of such a topology.

FIGURE 5.2   Suggested route reflection topology

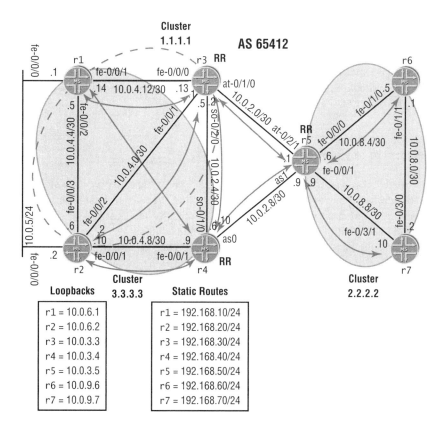

The three cluster IDs shown meet the required number of route reflection clusters, and having r3, r4, and r5 act as route reflectors also complies with the example's design requirements. The tricky aspect to this design is the requirement that you IBGP-peer to physical addresses in one of your clusters, while also ensuring that the failure of a single link will not break the reflection topology. Having r1 and r2 IBGP-peer with both r3 and r4 allows them to maintain one of their IBGP sessions in the event of an interface failure at either r3 or r4. But placing both r3 and r4 in the same cluster would be a mistake in this case, because doing so will cause r3 and r4 to ignore updates that carry their common cluster ID. This will result in missing routes on one of the reflectors should a peering interface fail on one of the two route reflectors that serve clients r1 or r2, which would violate the redundancy aspects of your design requirements.

In addition to the above points, you will need to maintain a full mesh of IBGP sessions between the route reflectors (r3, r4, and r5) while eliminating the unneeded IBGP sessions among route reflector clients. The arrows in Figure 5.2 represent the required IBGP peering relationships for this particular design.

While r5 obviously represents a single point of failure for cluster 2.2.2.2, the requirements state that your network must survive only the failure of individual links. If r4 and r5 are both configured with a cluster ID of 2.2.2.2, the presence of a cluster ID attribute with value 2.2.2.2 in route updates sent from r5 will cause the corresponding route to be ignored by r4, which in turn means that r4 will not be able to reflect these routes into clusters 1.1.1.1 or 3.3.3.3. The "no black holes" aspect of this example would be difficult, if not impossible, to achieve with this particular design, should r4 be configured with a cluster ID of 2.2.2.2 with the IBGP peering sessions shown, because this would result in black holes for the IBGP routes originated by r6 and r7 from the perspective of r4. This problem could be resolved by configuring r6 and r7 to also IBGP-peer with r4, but why bother with additional peering sessions when it is far simpler to just omit the cluster-id statement from r4?

Physical Interface Peering for IBGP?

The requirement that you peer to physical addresses in one of the clusters, while still providing tolerance for interface failures, is a bit unrealistic, in that the current best practice for IBGP designs would recommend that you always use loopback-based peering. This restriction is present so that an evaluation can be made regarding the candidate's understanding of route reflection design, and the different ways that cluster IDs can be assigned to route reflectors that serve a common set of clients. Being able to design a reflection topology that compensates for a less-than-ideal choice of peering interface is a valid skill, and one that all true IBGP "experts" should possess.

The design shown in Figure 5.2 is perhaps the more straightforward solution given these requirements, but other designs are certainly possible. For example, Figure 5.3 provides an alternative, if somewhat more complex, topology that also meets all specified restrictions as part of a hierarchical reflection design.

In the alternative topology, cluster 1.1.1.1 clients r1 and r2 have a single lo0-based peering session to one of the route reflectors that serve cluster 1.1.1.1. While this design does not tolerate a failure of either r3 or r4, it does provide the requisite link failure tolerance due to the use of lo0 peering. r5 provides reflection services for the network's core, which eliminates the need for an IBGP peering session between r3 and r4. You must use lo0-based IBGP peering in cluster 2.2.2.2 to meet the link failure redundancy requirements.

Clusters 3.3.3.3 and 4.4.4.4 are where things get interesting. The need to accommodate interface-based peering in at least one of your clusters forces a somewhat complex design, in which r6 acts as a reflector for client r7 using cluster ID 3.3.3.3 while r7 acts as a reflector for client r6 using cluster ID 4.4.4.4. r5 views both r6 and r7 as non-clients, while r6 and r7 both view r5 as a non-client.

FIGURE 5.3   An alternative route reflection topology

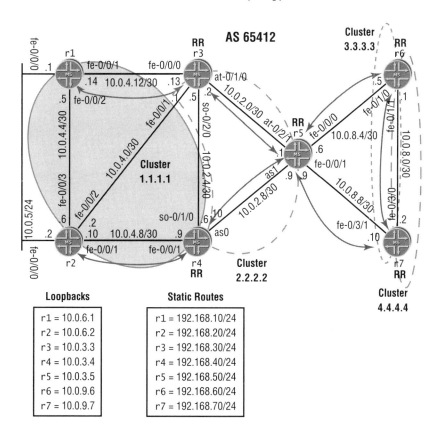

While a design that pairs two route reflectors in such fashion is a bit contrived, it is a viable route reflection topology that meets all provided restrictions. Besides, you have to admit that the operator who is capable of devising such a solution has more than proven their understanding of route reflector operation through a demonstration of their ability to design around aspects of a network that may be beyond their direct control.

Configure Clusters 1.1.1.1 and 3.3.3.3

The following commands correctly configure r4 as a route reflector for cluster ID 3.3.3.3, eliminate the now-unneeded IBGP peering definitions, and reconfigure the remaining neighbor statements to reflect interface-based peering according to the topology shown earlier in Figure 5.2. You begin by renaming the existing peer group to *cluster-3333* to avoid possible confusion down the road:

```
[edit protocols bgp]
lab@r4# rename group internal to group cluster-3333
```

```
[edit protocols bgp]
lab@r4# edit group cluster-3333
```

```
[edit protocols bgp group cluster-3333]
lab@r4# delete neighbor 10.0.3.3
```

```
[edit protocols bgp group cluster-3333]
lab@r4# delete neighbor 10.0.3.5
```

```
[edit protocols bgp group cluster-3333]
lab@r4# delete neighbor 10.0.9.6
```

```
[edit protocols bgp group cluster-3333]
lab@r4# delete neighbor 10.0.9.7
```

After deleting the unneeded neighbor statements, you use the CLI's rename function to configure the interface-based peering definitions for r1 and r2:

```
[edit protocols bgp group cluster-3333]
lab@r4# rename neighbor 10.0.6.1 to neighbor 10.0.4.5
```

[handwritten: → R1 physical add]

```
[edit protocols bgp group cluster-3333]
lab@r4# rename neighbor 10.0.6.2 to neighbor 10.0.4.10
```

[handwritten: → R2 physical add. Typical should use lo add. not physical add.]

And now the cluster ID is assigned:

```
[edit protocols bgp group cluster-3333]
lab@r4# set cluster 3.3.3.3
```

[handwritten: ↓ cluster-id set on RR]

The configuration of r4's cluster 3.3.3.3 peer group is shown. Note that the `local-address` option is no longer required due to the use of interface peering; in fact, leaving the `local-address` set to the r4's lo0 address would now prevent the establishment of IBGP sessions in cluster 3.3.3.3:

```
[edit protocols bgp group cluster-3333]
lab@r4# show
type internal;
traceoptions {
    file r4-bgp;
    flag state detail;
}
authentication-key "$9$G3jkPpu1Icl"; # SECRET-DATA
export ibgp;    ·
cluster 3.3.3.3;
neighbor 10.0.4.5;
neighbor 10.0.4.10;
```

The following stanza correctly configures r3 for operation as a route reflector for cluster 1.1.1.1 and also specifies interface-based peering to r1 and r2:

```
[edit protocols bgp group cluster-1111]
lab@r3# show
type internal;
traceoptions {
    file r3-bgp;
    flag state detail;
}
authentication-key "$9$G3jkPpu1Icl"; # SECRET-DATA
export ibgp;
cluster 1.1.1.1;
neighbor 10.0.4.14;
neighbor 10.0.4.2;
```

The interface peering definitions differ slightly between r3 and r4 due to the desire that each router peer to the "closest" interface possible while avoiding the use of the same physical interface for both peering sessions. To provide the required redundancy for single interface or link failures, r4 is told to peer to r1's fe-0/0/2 address while r3 peers to the address associated with r1's fe-0/0/1.200 address in this example.

With both of the cluster's route reflectors configured, you can now delete the unneeded neighbor statements from cluster 1.1.1.1 and 3.3.3.3 clients. A working configuration for r1 is shown here. Note that the only changes required on the route reflector clients are the deletion of neighbor statements that do not relate to the client's route reflectors, and the need to redefine the remaining peering sessions to evoke the required interface-based peering:

```
[edit]
lab@r1# show protocols bgp
group internal {
    type internal;
    traceoptions {
        file r1-bgp;
        flag state detail;
    }
    authentication-key "$9$oGZDk9CuOIc"; # SECRET-DATA
    export ibgp;
    neighbor 10.0.4.13;
    neighbor 10.0.4.9;
}
```

The configuration of r2 is similar to that of r1, but you will need to configure r2's peering definitions so they are compatible with the interface peering statements in place on r3 and r4.

Configure Cluster 2.2.2.2

The following commands correctly reconfigure r5 as a route reflector for cluster ID 2.2.2.2, and eliminate the now-unneeded IBGP peering definitions. Once again we start by renaming the existing group to *cluster-2222* to avoid confusion down the road:

```
[edit protocols bgp]
lab@r5# rename group internal to group cluster-2222

[edit protocols bgp]
lab@r5# edit group cluster-2222

[edit protocols bgp group cluster-2222]
lab@r5# delete neighbor 10.0.3.3

[edit protocols bgp group cluster-2222]
lab@r5# delete neighbor 10.0.3.4

[edit protocols bgp group cluster-2222]
lab@r5# delete neighbor 10.0.6.1

[edit protocols bgp group cluster-2222]
lab@r5# delete neighbor 10.0.6.2
```

```
[edit protocols bgp group cluster-2222]
lab@r5# set cluster 2.2.2.2
```

The cluster-2222 peer group is now displayed:

```
[edit protocols bgp group cluster-2222]
lab@r5# show
type internal;
traceoptions {
    file r5-bgp;
    flag state detail;
}
local-address 10.0.3.5;
authentication-key "$9$km5FIRSyK8"; # SECRET-DATA
export ibgp;
cluster 2.2.2.2;
neighbor 10.0.9.6;
neighbor 10.0.9.7;
```

The only change needed for clients in cluster 2.2.2.2 is the removal of the now-unnecessary neighbor statements. A working configuration for r6 is shown:

```
[edit protocols bgp group internal]
lab@r6# show
type internal;
traceoptions {
    file r6-bgp;
    flag state detail;
}
local-address 10.0.9.6;
authentication-key "$9$6xvJCpBW87Nb2"; # SECRET-DATA
export ibgp;
neighbor 10.0.3.5;
```

r7 requires a similar configuration before you proceed to the next section.

Configure IBGP in the Core

With all three clusters correctly configured, you now define a new IBGP group for the full mesh of IBGP connections needed in the core. The following commands correctly create and configure the core peer group on r3:

```
[edit protocols bgp]
lab@r3# edit group core
```

```
[edit protocols bgp group core]
lab@r3# set type internal local-address 10.0.3.3
```

 All three RR Peer with each other.

```
[edit protocols bgp group core]
lab@r3# set neighbor 10.0.3.4
```

```
[edit protocols bgp group core]
lab@r3# set neighbor 10.0.3.5
```

```
[edit protocols bgp group core]
lab@r3# set authentication-key jni
```

You will also need to apply the BGP export policy to the *core* peer group, as failing to do so will cause the 192.168.*x*/24 routes owned by the core routers to be omitted in the updates they send to the other core routers:

```
[edit protocols bgp]
lab@r3# set group core export ibgp
```

> **TIP** Do not forget to add the required IBGP state transition tracing to the newly created *core* group, because you must still log all IBGP state changes. Details of this type are easy to overlook while pounding away on the keyboard, so always be on your guard.

The new peer group for IBGP core routers is shown next:

```
[edit protocols bgp]
lab@r3# show group core
type internal;
traceoptions {
    file r3-bgp;
    flag state detail;
}
local-address 10.0.3.3;
authentication-key "$9$tOrrO1h7Nbs2a"; # SECRET-DATA
export ibgp;
neighbor 10.0.3.4;
neighbor 10.0.3.5;
```

Before moving to the following verification section, you should create and commit similar core router IBGP group definitions on r4 and r5.

Verify Route Reflection

The following commands are used to verify your route reflection topology. We start by verifying that all BGP sessions are established:

```
[edit]
lab@r3# run show bgp summary
Groups: 2 Peers: 4 Down peers: 0
```

Table	Tot Paths	Act Paths	Suppressed	History	Damp State	Pending
inet.0	8	6	0	0	0	0

Peer	AS	InPkt	OutPkt	OutQ	Flaps	Last Up/Dwn	State|#Active/Received/Damped...
10.0.3.4	65412	237	236	0	0	1:52:42 1/3/0	0/0/0
10.0.3.5	65412	228	234	0	0	1:52:38 3/3/0	0/0/0
10.0.4.2	65412	116	124	0	0	57:04 1/1/0	0/0/0
10.0.4.14	65412	49	55	0	2	23:08 1/1/0	0/0/0

The output confirms that all of r3's IBGP sessions have been correctly established, which is a good sign to be sure. Though the results are not shown here, you should issue the same command on all of the routers to verify that each shows the expected number of sessions, and that the sessions are in the established state.

You next confirm that no routes have been lost as a result of the reconfiguration and deployment of route reflection, beginning with r1:

```
[edit]
lab@r1# run show route protocol bgp 192/8 | match 192.168 | count
Count: 6 lines
```

The results indicate that r1 has learned six 192.168-related prefixes through the BGP protocol. Considering that there are six other routers in the test bed, and that they should all be sending a single 192.168.*x*/24 static route through IBGP, the output confirms that r1 is not missing routes due to the deployment of route reflection. The same command is now issued on a few other routers. It is recommended that you test all routers before deciding your network is healthy:

```
[edit protocols bgp]
lab@r5# run show route protocol bgp 192/8 | match 192.168 | count
Count: 6 lines
```

r5 also has all the IBGP routes. You now perform a quick check on r6 and r7:

```
[edit protocols bgp group internal]
lab@r6# run show route protocol bgp 192/8 | match 192.168 | count
Count: 6 lines
```

```
[edit protocols bgp group cluster-2222]
lab@r7# run show route protocol bgp 192/8 | match 192.168 | count
Count: 6 lines
```

Great, all routers now display the expected number of BGP routes. You then confirm that the failure of r3's fe-0/0/0 interface will not result in black holes because of your route reflection design. We begin by verifying that r3 is receiving two IBGP advertisements for routes that belong to clusters 1.1.1.1 and 3.3.3.3:

```
[edit]
lab@r3# run show route protocol bgp 192.168.10/24

inet.0: 31 destinations, 33 routes (31 active, 0 holddown, 0 hidden)
+ = Active Route, - = Last Active, * = Both

192.168.10.0/24    *[BGP/170] 00:33:59, MED 0, localpref 100
                      AS path: I
                    > to 10.0.4.14 via fe-0/0/0.0
                     [BGP/170] 00:04:14, MED 0, localpref 100, from 10.0.3.4
                      AS path: I
                    > to 10.0.4.14 via fe-0/0/0.0
```

r3 is receiving advertisements for the 192.168.10/24 prefix from r1 directly, and through the route reflection services of r4. Had you assigned the same cluster ID to both r3 and r4, you would only see the route learned directly from r1.

```
[edit]
lab@r3# run show route protocol bgp 192.168.20/24

inet.0: 31 destinations, 33 routes (31 active, 0 holddown, 0 hidden)
+ = Active Route, - = Last Active, * = Both

192.168.20.0/24    *[BGP/170] 01:07:58, MED 0, localpref 100
                      AS path: I
                    > to 10.0.4.2 via fe-0/0/1.0
                     [BGP/170] 00:04:17, MED 0, localpref 100, from 10.0.3.4
                      AS path: I
                    > to 10.0.4.2 via fe-0/0/1.0
```

The 192.168.20/24 route owned by r2 also correctly shows two viable IBGP advertisements. You next deactivate r3's fe-0/0/0 interface to break the r1–r3 IBGP peering session, with the goal of confirming that r3 will install the 192.168.10/24 route learned from r4 as the active route:

```
[edit]
lab@r3# deactivate interfaces fe-0/0/0


[edit]
lab@r3# commit
commit complete


[edit]
lab@r3# run show route protocol bgp 192.168.10/24 detail

inet.0: 30 destinations, 31 routes (30 active, 0 holddown, 0 hidden)
192.168.10.0/24 (1 entry, 1 announced)
        *BGP    Preference: 170/-101
                Source: 10.0.3.4
                Nexthop: 10.0.4.2 via fe-0/0/1.0, selected
                Protocol Nexthop: 10.0.4.5 Indirect nexthop: 83b9198 28
                State: <Active Int Ext>
                Local AS: 65412 Peer AS: 65412
                Age: 4:32      Metric: 0      Metric2: 10
                Task: BGP_65412.10.0.3.4+1070
                Announcement bits (3): 0-KRT 2-BGP.0.0.0.0+179 3-Resolve inet.0
                AS path: I (Originator)Cluster list:  3.3.3.3
                AS path: Originator ID: 10.0.6.1
                Localpref: 100
                Router ID: 10.0.3.4
```

As planned, r3 still has a route to 192.168.10/24. Because the protocol next hop of 10.0.4.5 is unchanged by the reflection activities of r4, we expect that a traceroute to the 192.168.10/24 route will succeed, albeit with an extra hop through r2:

```
[edit]
lab@r3# run traceroute 192.168.10.1
traceroute to 192.168.10.1 (192.168.10.1), 30 hops max, 40 byte packets
 1  10.0.4.2 (10.0.4.2)  0.646 ms  0.454 ms  0.402 ms
 2  10.0.4.5 (10.0.4.5)  0.493 ms  0.492 ms  0.464 ms
 3  10.0.4.5 (10.0.4.5)  0.485 ms !H  0.495 ms !H  0.470 ms !H
```

Good, the use of two different cluster IDs has resulted in the required network redundancy, despite the use of IBGP interface–based peering, which is normally not recommended due to the very lack of fault tolerance that this design compensates for. You should activate r3's fe-0/0/0 interface before proceeding.

You now verify that both r3 and r4 are reflecting routes from cluster 2.2.2.2 to the clients in clusters 1.1.1.1 and 3.3.3.3. Recall that a decision was made earlier to not associate r4 with cluster 2.2.2.2 to produce this very behavior:

```
[edit]
lab@r2# run show route protocol bgp 192.168.70.1

inet.0: 22 destinations, 29 routes (22 active, 0 holddown, 0 hidden)
+ = Active Route, - = Last Active, * = Both

192.168.70.0/24    *[BGP/170] 03:37:10, MED 0, localpref 100, from 10.0.4.1
                      AS path: I
                    > to 10.0.4.9 via fe-0/0/1.0
                    [BGP/170] 02:33:24, MED 0, localpref 100
                      AS path: I
                    > to 10.0.4.9 via fe-0/0/1.0
```

Excellent! Both r3 and r4 are advertising routes from cluster 2.2.2.2 to the clients in clusters 1.1.1.1 and 3.3.3.3. In this topology, the definition of cluster ID 2.2.2.2 on r4 would have resulted in r2 seeing only one IBGP advertisement for the 192.168.70/24 prefix, which would be coming from r3, and a complete lack of cluster 2.2.2.2 routes on r4. You now deactivate r5's ATM interface to confirm that your route reflection topology does not produce suboptimal routing:

```
[edit]
lab@r5# deactivate interfaces at-0/2/1

[edit]
lab@r5# commit
commit complete
```

Once again, we examine r2's route to 192.168.70/24:

```
[edit]
lab@r2# run show route protocol bgp 192.168.70.1

inet.0: 22 destinations, 29 routes (22 active, 0 holddown, 0 hidden)
+ = Active Route, - = Last Active, * = Both

192.168.70.0/24    *[BGP/170] 03:37:10, MED 0, localpref 100, from 10.0.4.1
                      AS path: I
```

```
> to 10.0.4.9 via fe-0/0/1.0
[BGP/170] 02:33:24, MED 0, localpref 100
  AS path: I
> to 10.0.4.9 via fe-0/0/1.0
```

Hmm. Nothing has changed. With the ATM link down between r3 and r5, and r3's advertisement selected as the active route, you might anticipate that traffic sourced from r2 and destined to 192.168.70/24 destinations will now experience an extra hop through r3.

Does this mean there is a flaw in your reflection topology or is this situation a non-issue? It is not uncommon to see test requirements that may cause a candidate's attention to be focused on what appears to be a problem with the current task, when in reality the issue may relate to a completely different aspect of your configuration, or might even be perfectly normal behavior, and therefore not an issue at all.

This "symptom" appears because both r3 and r4 are generating equal-cost IS-IS default routes (through the attached bit in their LSPs) into area 49.0002. Since backbone routes are not leaked into area 49.0002, the loss of r5's ATM interface goes undetected because r1 and r2 rely on the IS-IS default route to reach all inter-area destinations anyway. With two equal-cost default routes directing all traffic out of area 49.0002, you would expect to find that r2 cannot select the best IBGP path based on IGP metric differences, which causes the tie to be broken by selecting the BGP speaker with the lowest RID as the active route. The fact that r3's RID is lower than r4's explains why r2 (and r1) will always select r3's BGP advertisements over r4's for destinations that lie outside of their IS-IS level 1 area. Displaying detailed information for the 192.168.70/24 route confirms this theory:

```
[edit]
lab@r2# run show route protocol bgp 192.168.70.1 detail

inet.0: 22 destinations, 29 routes (22 active, 0 holddown, 0 hidden)
192.168.70.0/24 (2 entries, 1 announced)
      *BGP    Preference: 170/-101
              Source: 10.0.4.1
              Nexthop: 10.0.4.9 via fe-0/0/1.0, selected
              Protocol Nexthop: 10.0.9.7 Indirect nexthop: 83d83b8 51
              State: <Active Int Ext>
              Local AS: 65412 Peer AS: 65412
              Age: 3:48:08    Metric: 0      Metric2: 5
              Task: BGP_65412.10.0.4.1+179
              Announcement bits (2): 0-KRT 2-Resolve inet.0
              AS path: I (Originator)Cluster list: 1.1.1.1 2.2.2.2
              AS path: Originator ID: 10.0.9.7
              Localpref: 100
              Router ID: 10.0.3.3
```

```
BGP    Preference: 170/-101
       Source: 10.0.4.9
       Nexthop: 10.0.4.9 via fe-0/0/1.0, selected
       Protocol Nexthop: 10.0.9.7 Indirect nexthop: 83d83b8 51
       State: <NotBest Int Ext>
       Inactive reason: Router ID
       Local AS: 65412 Peer AS: 65412
       Age: 2:44:22    Metric: 0        Metric2: 5
       Task: BGP_65412.10.0.4.9+1069
       AS path: I (Originator)Cluster list:  3.3.3.3 2.2.2.2
       AS path: Originator ID: 10.0.9.7
       Localpref: 100
       Router ID: 10.0.3.4
```

The real irony here is that forwarding from r2 to the 192.168.70/24 prefix is unaffected by r2's choice of which BGP update to install as active because both updates indicate the same protocol next hop of 10.0.9.7! This is one reason why extra thought should be given to rewriting the BGP next hop for IBGP routes. Doing so on r3 in this example would have resulted in r2 forwarding packets to r3, and this behavior can result in suboptimal forwarding paths. The results of a traceroute from r2 to 192.168.70/24 confirm that r3 is not actually in the forwarding path, despite its advertisement being selected as the active route. So, like the old saying goes, "if it's not broken, don't fix it!"

```
[edit]
lab@r2# run traceroute 192.168.70.1
traceroute to 192.168.70.1 (192.168.70.1), 30 hops max, 40 byte packets
 1  10.0.4.9 (10.0.4.9)  0.348 ms  0.248 ms  0.219 ms
 2  10.0.2.9 (10.0.2.9)  0.288 ms  0.247 ms  0.235 ms
 3  10.0.8.10 (10.0.8.10)  0.235 ms  0.203 ms  0.191 ms
 4  10.0.8.10 (10.0.8.10)  0.194 ms !H  0.204 ms !H  0.193 ms !H
```

With r5's ATM interface still deactivated, we confirm that all routers still show the required number of BGP routes, and test forwarding with a traceroute or two:

```
[edit protocols bgp group cluster-2222]
lab@r7# run show route protocol bgp 192/8 | match 192.168 | count
Count: 6 lines
```

```
[edit]
lab@r3# run show route protocol bgp 192/8 | match 192.168 | count
Count: 6 lines
```

```
[edit]
```

```
lab@r1# run show route protocol bgp 192/8 | match 192.168 | count
Count: 6 lines
```

The routers still show all the IBGP routes, which is good. You now issue some traceroutes to determine the forwarding paths through your network:

```
[edit]
lab@r7# run traceroute 192.168.10.1
traceroute to 192.168.10.1 (192.168.10.1), 30 hops max, 40 byte packets
 1  10.0.8.9 (10.0.8.9)  0.337 ms  0.250 ms  0.218 ms
 2  10.0.2.10 (10.0.2.10)  0.276 ms  0.246 ms  0.235 ms
 3  10.0.4.10 (10.0.4.10)  0.182 ms  0.168 ms  0.156 ms
 4  10.0.4.5 (10.0.4.5)  0.716 ms  0.686 ms  0.361 ms
 5  10.0.4.5 (10.0.4.5)  0.357 ms !H  0.679 ms !H  0.371 ms !H
[edit]
lab@r7# run traceroute 192.168.20.1
traceroute to 192.168.20.1 (192.168.20.1), 30 hops max, 40 byte packets
 1  10.0.8.9 (10.0.8.9)  0.361 ms  0.248 ms  0.219 ms
 2  10.0.2.10 (10.0.2.10)  0.287 ms  0.251 ms  0.238 ms
 3  10.0.4.10 (10.0.4.10)  0.183 ms  0.169 ms  0.157 ms
 4  10.0.4.10 (10.0.4.10)  0.161 ms !H  0.171 ms !H  0.157 ms !H
```

You are likely to think that the "extra" hop encountered in the traceroute to the 192.168.10/24 prefix is the result of the ATM interface outage on r5, but reactivating the interface will not change the forwarding path to cluster 1.1.1.1 and 3.3.3.3 destinations due to r5 seeing a lower metric for the 10.0.4/22 summary through its aggregated SONET link to r4. You next trace the route to 192.168.30/24, which is owned by r3:

```
[edit]
lab@r7# run traceroute 192.168.30.1
traceroute to 192.168.30.1 (192.168.30.1), 30 hops max, 40 byte packets
 1  10.0.8.9 (10.0.8.9)  0.352 ms  0.247 ms  0.217 ms
 2  10.0.2.10 (10.0.2.10)  0.279 ms  0.249 ms  0.235 ms
 3  10.0.2.5 (10.0.2.5)  0.308 ms  0.266 ms  0.252 ms
 4  10.0.2.5 (10.0.2.5)  0.260 ms !N  0.267 ms !N  0.257 ms !N
```

The extra hop encountered when tracing to the 192.168.30/24 route originated by r3 is attributable to the ATM interface deactivation, however. Results like these indicate that you have met the specified requirements for the route reflection example.

Do not forget to reactivate r5's ATM interface when you are satisfied that your design meets the stated redundancy requirements, because its absence may cause problems in subsequent lab steps. Forgetting to re-enable an interface in the actual lab could lead to massive point loss and a resulting lack of joy at the conclusion of your day. You might try using the confirmed option when you commit these types of changes, as this will cause the router to automatically roll back and commit the rollback 1 file. This technique can be a real lifesaver in the event that you get distracted and forget to issue the rollback yourself.

IBGP Confederations

Confederations are another technique that can be used to eliminate the need for a full mesh of IBGP connections. In operation, you divide your AS into multiple subconfederations. Routers within a subconfederation require either full mesh or route reflection connectivity, while the subconfederations themselves are tied together using a special type of EBGP, called C-BGP. C-BGP operates like EBGP, with the exception that certain IBGP attributes, such as local preference, and the BGP next hop, are conveyed unchanged between the subconfederations.

Each subconfederation requires a unique AS number, called the *confederation member AS*, and will also require a real AS number, referred to as the *confederation AS*, which will be used when interfacing to routers that belong to a nonconfederation member AS. Lastly, each router in a confederation requires a complete list of all the autonomous system's confederation member AS values, so that C-BGP and EBGP updates can be handled appropriately after matching the remote peer's AS value against the complete list of known confederation members.

Configure a Confederation

To complete this configuration example, you need to deploy a confederation topology that meets the following criteria:

- Your confederation AS is 65412.
- Use AS numbers in the range of 65000 to 65003 for confederation member AS values.
- The failure of any link must not cause the loss of BGP routes (black holes) or the disruption of BGP sessions.
- The confederation topology must not impose suboptimal routing.
- You must have at least three subconfederations.
- Support loopback interface–based peering for all IBGP and C-BGP sessions.
- Continue to redistribute the 192.168.*x*/24 static routes through BGP.

Before starting your configuration, it is suggested that you first establish a design for a confederation topology that meets all specified criteria. Figure 5.4 provides an example of such a topology.

FIGURE 5.4   Suggested confederation topology

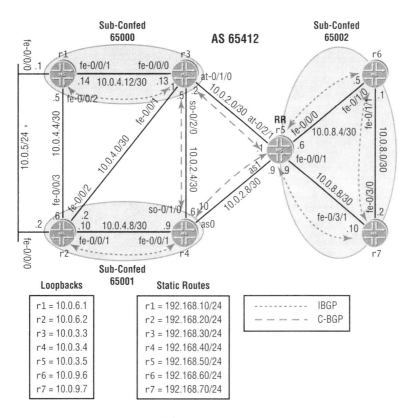

Figure 5.4 provides an example of a confederation topology that meets the requirements of the configuration example in a relatively straightforward way. IBGP sessions within a subconfederation are shown with small dashes while the C-BGP sessions used between subconfederations are shown with large dashes. The IBGP/C-BGP connections shown represent the minimum number of BGP sessions required to meet the failover requirements of the example. The loss of the Fast Ethernet link between r1 and r3, for example, will not prevent the lo0-based peering session from being established over another path that uses a different set of interfaces; this inherent fault tolerance is the principal benefit and motivation to loopback-based peering. Additional C-BGP sessions could be added to your design—for example, between r1 and r2—but the added redundancy will not earn you any extra points in this example.

Once again, r5 represents a single point of failure that would isolate routers in subconfederation 65002; your design must tolerate only individual interface and link failures, however. The example topology will not impose any route inefficiencies that can be blamed on your BGP design, but you should not be surprised to find that some paths incur extra hops due to the nature of IS-IS level 1 routing.

Figure 5.5 provides an alternative topology that also meets the stated design requirements. The use of lo0 peering means that some of the C-BGP connections shown are really not needed to satisfy the link and interface failure requirements of this configuration example, but a little added insurance has never hurt anyone.

FIGURE 5.5   An alternative confederation topology

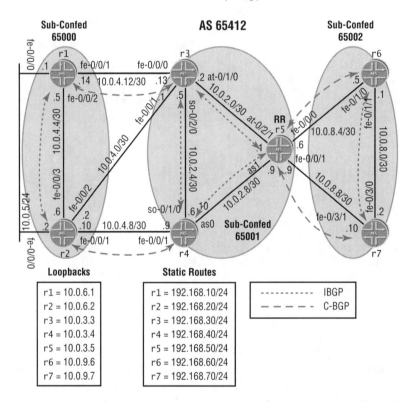

Before starting your configuration, delete your existing BGP stanza to avoid confusion and to better simulate the thrill of embarking on a new lab scenario.

Configure Subconfederation 65000

The following commands correctly configure r1 for the confederation topology shown earlier in Figure 5.4. You begin by deleting the leftover route reflection configuration, because it would otherwise just get in your way:

```
[edit]
lab@r1# delete protocols bgp
```

```
[edit]
lab@r1# edit protocols bgp group 65000

[edit protocols bgp group 65000]
lab@r1# set type internal local-address 10.0.6.1

[edit protocols bgp group 65000]
lab@r1# set neighbor 10.0.3.3
```

The stipulations for this scenario do not require MD5-based authentication or BGP connection state tracing, so neither has been deployed. Also note that the peer group for subconfederation 65000 members is set to run IBGP through the declaration that the group's type is internal. To complete r1's BGP stanza, you must now apply the *ibgp* export policy to effect static route redistribution:

```
[edit protocols bgp group 65000]
lab@r1# set export ibgp
```

The completed BGP stanza for r1 is shown next:

```
[edit protocols bgp group 65000]
lab@r1# show
type internal;
local-address 10.0.6.1;
export ibgp;
neighbor 10.0.3.3;
```

To finish r1's configuration, you now define the confederation AS and confederation member AS numbers as shown in the following:

```
[edit routing-options]
lab@r1# set autonomous-system 65000
```
→ different for each Confederation

```
[edit routing-options]
lab@r1# set confederation 65412
```
→ Same for each Confederation

```
[edit routing-options]
lab@r1# set confederation members 65000

[edit routing-options]
lab@r1# set confederation members 65001

[edit routing-options]
lab@r1# set confederation members 65002
```

You should list all the AS numbers that will be used by AS 65421 confederation members, being sure to include the router's own subconfederation AS number as well. Because r1 uses only IBGP peering in this example, the confederation-related configuration in r1 is not strictly necessary. However, including these statements now causes no harm, and will prove especially useful should r1 later pick up a C-BGP peering session. The completed `routing-options` stanza for r1 is displayed next:

```
[[edit routing-options]
lab@r1# show
static {
    route 10.0.200.0/24 next-hop 10.0.1.102;
    route 192.168.10.0/24 reject;
}
autonomous-system 65000;
confederation 65412 members [ 65000 65001 65002 ];
```

To complete the configuration of subconfederation 65000, the following configuration statements are entered on r3:

```
[edit]
lab@r3# delete protocols bgp

[edit]
lab@r3# edit protocols bgp group 65000

[edit protocols bgp group 65000]
lab@r3# set type internal local-address 10.0.3.3

[edit protocols bgp group 65000]
lab@r3# set neighbor 10.0.6.1

[edit protocols bgp group 65000]
lab@r3# set export ibgp
```

As with r1, you must now reassign r3's AS number and list all the confederation AS members that belong to the confederated AS 65412 using the following configuration statements:

```
[edit routing-options]
lab@r1# set autonomous-system 65000

[edit routing-options]
lab@r3# set confederation 65412
```

```
[edit routing-options]
lab@r3# set confederation members 65000

[edit routing-options]
lab@r3# set confederation members 65001

[edit routing-options]
lab@r3# set confederation members 65002
```

The modified portions of r3's configuration are now displayed with highlights added:

```
[edit]
lab@r3# show routing-options
static {
    route 10.0.200.0/24 next-hop 10.0.1.102;
    route 192.168.30.0/24 reject;
}
aggregate {
    route 10.0.4.0/22;
}
autonomous-system 65000;
confederation 65412 members [ 65000 65001 65002 ];
                    ↙ Global AS
[edit]
lab@r3# show protocols bgp
group 65000 {
    type internal;
    local-address 10.0.3.3;
    export ibgp;
    neighbor 10.0.6.1;
}
```

After committing the changes to r1 and r3, we expect to see that an IBGP session is established, and that each router advertises its 192.168.*x*/24 static route to its peer:

```
[edit]
lab@r3# run show bgp summary
Groups: 1 Peers: 1 Down peers: 0
Table          Tot Paths  Act Paths Suppressed    History Damp State    Pending
inet.0                 1          1          0          0          0          0
Peer             AS      InPkt    OutPkt    OutQ   Flaps Last Up/Dwn
State|#Active/Received/Damped...
10.0.6.1      65000          7         8       0       0     2:11 1/1/0
0/0/0
```

```
[edit]
lab@r3# run show route protocol bgp

inet.0: 27 destinations, 27 routes (27 active, 0 holddown, 0 hidden)
+ = Active Route, - = Last Active, * = Both

192.168.10.0/24    *[BGP/170] 00:02:16, MED 0, localpref 100, from 10.0.6.1
                       AS path: I
                    > to 10.0.4.14 via fe-0/0/0.0

iso.0: 1 destinations, 1 routes (1 active, 0 holddown, 0 hidden)
```

The establishment of the r1–r3 IBGP session and the presence of the IBGP-learned route provides an indication that all is well with subconfederation 65000. We will worry about bringing up the C-BGP links once subconfederations 65001 and 65002 are also operational.

Configure Subconfederations 65001 and 65002

The configuration needed by r2 to function as a member of subconfederation 65001 is shown here with changes highlighted:

```
[edit]
lab@r2# show routing-options
static {
    route 10.0.200.0/24 next-hop 10.0.1.102;
    route 192.168.20.0/24 reject;
}
autonomous-system 65001;
confederation 65412 members [ 65000 65001 65002 ];

[edit]
lab@r2# show protocols bgp
group 65001 {
    type internal;
    local-address 10.0.6.2;
    export ibgp;
    neighbor 10.0.3.4;
}
```

The configuration of r4 is similar to those of r2 and r3. The completed configuration for r4 is shown here with highlights:

```
[edit]
lab@r4# show routing-options
```

```
static {
    route 10.0.200.0/24 next-hop 10.0.1.102;
    route 192.168.40.0/24 reject;
}
aggregate {
    route 10.0.4.0/22;
}
autonomous-system 65001;
confederation 65412 members [ 65000 65001 65002 ];

[edit]
lab@r4# show protocols bgp
group 65001 {
    type internal;
    local-address 10.0.3.4;
    export ibgp;
    neighbor 10.0.6.2;
}
```

As before, you expect to see a single IBGP session established between r2 and r4 when you have committed the changes on both routers:

```
[edit]
lab@r4# run show bgp summary
Groups: 1 Peers: 1 Down peers: 0
Table          Tot Paths  Act Paths Suppressed    History Damp State   Pending
inet.0                 1          1          0          0         0          0
Peer             AS      InPkt     OutPkt     OutQ   Flaps Last Up/Dwn
State|#Active/Received/Damped...
10.0.6.2       65001        13         15        0       0     5:36 1/1/0
0/0/0

[edit]
lab@r4# run show route protocol bgp

inet.0: 28 destinations, 28 routes (28 active, 0 holddown, 0 hidden)
+ = Active Route, - = Last Active, * = Both

192.168.20.0/24    *[BGP/170] 00:05:41, MED 0, localpref 100, from 10.0.6.2
                      AS path: I
                    > to 10.0.4.10 via fe-0/0/1.0

  iso.0: 1 destinations, 1 routes (1 active, 0 holddown, 0 hidden)
```

Results like these indicate that subconfederation 65001 is also working properly. Routers in subconfederation 65002 will require the same type of configuration changes. The highlighted configuration changes shown here are from r5:

```
edit]
lab@r5# show routing-options
static {
    route 10.0.200.0/24 next-hop 10.0.1.102;
    route 192.168.50.0/24 reject;
}
aggregate {
    route 10.0.2.0/23;
    route 10.0.8.0/21;
    route 192.168.0.0/22;
    route 172.16.40.0/29;
}
autonomous-system 65002;
confederation 65412 members [ 65000 65001 65002 ];


[edit]
lab@r5# show protocols bgp
group 65002 {
    type internal;
    local-address 10.0.3.5;
    export ibgp;
    neighbor 10.0.9.6;
    neighbor 10.0.9.7;
}
```

The primary difference between the configuration of r5 compared to that of r3 or r4 is the need for you to define two internal peers in the form of r6 and r7. When similar confederation-related configuration changes have been committed in r6 and r7, we expect to see two IBGP sessions in the established state on each router in subconfederation 65002, as shown next:

```
[edit]
lab@r5# run show bgp summary
Groups: 1 Peers: 2 Down peers: 0
Table          Tot Paths  Act Paths Suppressed    History Damp State    Pending
inet.0                 2          2          0          0         0           0
```

```
Peer              AS     InPkt     OutPkt    OutQ    Flaps Last Up/Dwn
State|#Active/Received/Damped...
10.0.9.6        65002      4        6        0        0     1:18 1/1/0
0/0/0
10.0.9.7        65002      3        4        0        0       35 1/1/0
0/0/0


[edit]
lab@r5# run show route protocol bgp


inet.0: 33 destinations, 33 routes (33 active, 0 holddown, 0 hidden)
+ = Active Route, - = Last Active, * = Both


192.168.60.0/24    *[BGP/170] 00:01:24, MED 0, localpref 100, from 10.0.9.6
                      AS path: I
                    > to 10.0.8.5 via fe-0/0/0.0
192.168.70.0/24    *[BGP/170] 00:00:41, MED 0, localpref 100, from 10.0.9.7
                      AS path: I
                    > to 10.0.8.10 via fe-0/0/1.0
```

Configure C-BGP Links

With each subconfederation operational, it is time to link them together using C-BGP, which, as mentioned previously, is a special type of EBGP. The tricky part here is the need to enable the multihop option on the C-BGP peering sessions to support the loopback-based peering required in this example. The multihop option is needed here because EBGP will only peer over a directly connected interface (by setting the IP packet's TTL to 1) by default.

The next set of commands creates a c-bgp group on r5, and correctly configures this group to peer with r3 and r4:

C-BGP is a special EBGP peering

```
[edit protocols bgp group c-bgp]
lab@r5# set type external local-address 10.0.3.5
```

EBGP TTI is 1 by default.

```
[edit protocols bgp group c-bgp]
lab@r5# set neighbor 10.0.3.3


[edit protocols bgp group c-bgp]
lab@r5# set neighbor 10.0.3.3 peer-as 65000


[edit protocols bgp group c-bgp]
lab@r5# set neighbor 10.0.3.4
```

```
[edit protocols bgp group c-bgp]
lab@r5# set neighbor 10.0.3.4 peer-as 65001
```

```
[edit protocols bgp group c-bgp]
lab@r5# set multihop
```

The *c-bgp* group differs from previous examples in this section in that the group's type needs to be set to `external`. Peers listed in an external peer group require an association with the remote peer's AS number. When the router recognizes that peers in AS 65000 and 65001 are members of its own confederation, it will modify its EBGP behavior so as to adhere to confederation EBGP (C-BGP) protocol behavior.

You now apply the *ibgp* export policy so that r5 will advertise its 192.168.50/24 static route to members of the *c-bgp* group using its C-BGP session:

```
[edit protocols bgp group c-bgp]
lab@r5# set export ibgp
```

The completed C-BGP–related configuration for r5 is shown next:

```
[edit protocols bgp group c-bgp]
lab@r5# show
type external;
multihop;          Need for loopback Peering for EBGP & C-BGP peering.
local-address 10.0.3.5;
export ibgp;
neighbor 10.0.3.3 {
    peer-as 65000;
}
neighbor 10.0.3.4 {
    peer-as 65001;
}
```

Remote peer AS numbers can be specified at the global, group, or neighbor levels as desired. The use of neighbor-level `peer-as` definitions allows you to have a single BGP peer group that supports EBGP peering sessions with remote peers that belong to different ASs. To complete the configuration of the C-BGP links, you need to configure a similar peer group on r3 and r4 using the same commands shown for r5. The *c-bgp* group configuration for r3 is shown here for reference:

```
[edit]
lab@r3# show protocols bgp group c-bgp
type external;
multihop;
local-address 10.0.3.3;
```

```
export ibgp;
neighbor 10.0.3.4 {
    peer-as 65001;
}
neighbor 10.0.3.5 {
    peer-as 65002;
}
```

Verify Confederation Operation

The following commands are used to verify your confederation topology. We start by verifying that all BGP sessions have been correctly established. Based on the topology shown earlier in Figure 5.4, we expect that r3 will have three BGP sessions, one running IBGP and the other two running C-BGP:

```
[edit]
lab@r3# run show bgp summary
Groups: 2 Peers: 3 Down peers: 0
Table          Tot Paths  Act Paths Suppressed     History Damp State    Pending
inet.0               6          6          0           0          0          0
Peer             AS      InPkt    OutPkt    OutQ   Flaps Last Up/Dwn
State|#Active/Received/Damped...
10.0.3.4       65001      111       112      0      0      48:20 2/2/0
0/0/0
10.0.3.5       65002      114       111      0      0      48:16 3/3/0
0/0/0
   10.0.6.1      65000       23        29      0      3      10:15 1/1/0
0/0/0
```

The output confirms that r3 has the expected number of BGP sessions and that they have all been correctly established. Though not shown, you should issue the same command on all routers in the test bed to verify that each shows the expected number of sessions, and that the sessions are all in the established state. You now confirm that no routes have been lost due to the deployment of your confederation, beginning with r1:

```
[edit]
lab@r1# run show route protocol bgp 192/8 | match 192.168 | count
Count: 6 lines
```

The output once again confirms that r1 has learned six 192.168-related prefixes through the BGP protocol. Considering that there are six other routers in the test bed, and that they should all be sending a single 192.168.*x*/24 static route through a combination of IBGP and C-BGP, these results confirm that r1's ability to route to these destinations has not been impacted by the deployment of your confederation. The same command is now issued on a few other routers; it is recommended that you test all routers before deciding your network is healthy:

```
[edit]
lab@r5# run show route protocol bgp 192/8 | match 192.168 | count
Count: 6 lines
```

Good, r5 also displayed the expected number of BGP-learned routes. The same command is now issued on r7:

```
lab@r7# run show route protocol bgp 192/8 | match 192.168 | count
Count: 6 lines
```

Great—all routers are displaying the expected number of BGP routes. You now confirm that forwarding paths are optimal or, at the very least, that your forwarding paths have not been negatively impacted by your confederation design. You start by analyzing r2's view of the routes owned by subconfederation 65002:

```
[edit]
lab@r2# run show route protocol bgp 192.168.60/24

inet.0: 22 destinations, 22 routes (22 active, 0 holddown, 0 hidden)
+ = Active Route, - = Last Active, * = Both

192.168.60.0/24     *[BGP/170] 01:13:58, MED 0, localpref 100, from 10.0.3.4
                       AS path: (65000 65002) I
                       to 10.0.4.9 via fe-0/0/1.0
                     > to 10.0.4.1 via fe-0/0/2.0
```

It would seem that r2 has learned the 192.168.60/24 route from BGP speaker 10.0.3.4 (r3), which provides the C-BGP connectivity for subconfederation 65001. The use of IS-IS level 1 routing results in r2 believing there are two equal-cost paths that can be used to reach r4's loopback address. In reality, the 10.0.4.9 forwarding path is shorter than having r2 forward through r3 via 10.0.4.1. r2's misconception is the result of Multi-Level IS-IS operation, so this output does not indicate a problem with your confederation design.

You may find it odd that the AS path sequence lists the AS numbers associated with subconfederations 65000 and 65002, because this implies that r4 has learned the route through r3 instead of r5, which may seem counterintuitive. This warrants additional investigation, so you move over to r4 and issue the same command:

```
[edit]
lab@r4# run show route 192.168.70/24

inet.0: 29 destinations, 34 routes (29 active, 0 holddown, 0 hidden)
+ = Active Route, - = Last Active, * = Both
```

```
192.168.70.0/24    *[BGP/170] 00:00:27, MED 0, localpref 100, from 10.0.3.3
                      AS path: (65000 65002) I
                   > to 10.0.2.9 via as0.0
                    [BGP/170] 00:00:23, MED 0, localpref 100, from 10.0.3.5
                      AS path: (65002) I
                   > to 10.0.2.9 via as0.0
```

Very interesting: r4 indicates that it has learned the route from both r3 and r5, and has selected the advertisement that was learned from r3 as the active route. Forwarding packets through r3 to reach r5 would be less than ideal with this topology, especially because the IS-IS level 2 backbone is not reliant on a default route. Careful inspection of the display indicates that the forwarding next hop will be 10.0.2.9 via r4's as0 interface, which indicates that regardless of which route was chosen as active, the forwarding path will be from r4 to r5, which is as optimal as you can get. But wait, how can r4 install the route learned from r3 with the intent of forwarding through r5?

The answer lies in understanding BGP's use of the advertising router, protocol next hop, and forwarding next-hop fields. The advertising router is just that—the router ID of the BGP speaker that has advertised the route. The protocol next hop identifies the router to which packets should be forwarded if the route is considered best and becomes active. BGP's support of third-party next hops means that the advertising router and protocol next hops need not be the same. The forwarding next hop is the result of the recursive lookup of the protocol next hop, and therefore indicates the preferred IGP next hop that is used to forward toward the advertised protocol next hop. The various next hops used by BGP are highlighted in this capture:

```
[edit]
lab@r4# run show route 192.168.70/24 detail

inet.0: 29 destinations, 34 routes (29 active, 0 holddown, 0 hidden)
192.168.70.0/24 (2 entries, 1 announced)
        *BGP    Preference: 170/-101
                Source: 10.0.3.3
                Nexthop: 10.0.2.9 via as0.0, selected
                Protocol Nexthop: 10.0.9.7 Indirect nexthop: 83e93b8 57
                State: <Active Int Ext>
                Local AS: 65001 Peer AS: 65000
                Age: 5:02      Metric: 0      Metric2: 11
                Task: BGP_65000.10.0.3.3+179
                Announcement bits (3): 0-KRT 4-BGP.0.0.0.0+179 5-Resolve inet.0
                AS path: (65000 65002) I
                Localpref: 100
                Router ID: 10.0.3.3
         BGP    Preference: 170/-101
                Source: 10.0.3.5
                Nexthop: 10.0.2.9 via as0.0, selected
```

→ ‡Next hop on a
preserved
C-BGP Connection.

```
Protocol Nexthop: 10.0.9.7 Indirect nexthop: 83e93b8 57
State: <NotBest Int Ext>
Inactive reason: Router ID
Local AS: 65001 Peer AS: 65002
Age: 4:58        Metric: 0        Metric2: 11
Task: BGP_65002.10.0.3.5+179
AS path: (65002) I
Localpref: 100
Router ID: 10.0.3.5
```

The use of C-BGP on the EBGP links connecting r3, r4, and r5 results in a modified EBGP behavior that preserves the original protocol next hop in the route updates sent over the C-BGP sessions. Because the protocol next hop is the same (10.0.9.7) in the advertisements generated by both r3 and r4, and because the IGP resolves this route to a forwarding next hop of 10.0.2.9, it makes no difference whether r4 chooses the route advertised by r3 over the route being advertised by r5. The previous capture also indicates why r3's advertisement was selected as the active route. The active route selection process outcome has been decided by choosing the speaker with the lowest RID value because all other aspects of the route's attributes are otherwise equal.

A traceroute issued at both r4 and r3 confirms optimal forwarding over the IS-IS level 2 backbone to destinations in subconfederation 65002:

```
[edit]
lab@r4# run traceroute 192.168.70.1
traceroute to 192.168.70.1 (192.168.70.1), 30 hops max, 40 byte packets
 1  10.0.2.9 (10.0.2.9)  0.761 ms  0.614 ms  0.507 ms
 2  10.0.8.10 (10.0.8.10)  0.447 ms  0.441 ms  0.415 ms
 3  10.0.8.10 (10.0.8.10)  0.426 ms !H  0.436 ms !H  0.419 ms !H
```

r4's path is optimal so you check up on r3's forwarding path:

```
[edit]
lab@r3# run traceroute 192.168.70.1
traceroute to 192.168.70.1 (192.168.70.1), 30 hops max, 40 byte packets
 1  10.0.2.1 (10.0.2.1)  1.082 ms  1.138 ms  0.994 ms
 2  10.0.8.10 (10.0.8.10)  1.004 ms  0.771 ms  1.112 ms
 3  10.0.8.10 (10.0.8.10)  1.041 ms !H  0.963 ms !H  1.096 ms !H
```

These results indicate that forwarding paths have not been impacted by your confederation topology. However, the use of IS-IS level 1 routing can cause routers in area 49.0002 to make a less-than-ideal choice with regard to which attached router they install as the forwarding next hop for their default routes.

Real World Scenario

Nothing Is Perfect...

While developing this section, this author observed that both r4 and r5 were incorrectly computing an IS-IS metric of *10* for their aggregated SONET interfaces after a reboot (recall that the previous IS-IS case study had the metric automatically calculated based on a 500Mbps bandwidth). The higher metric setting was in turn causing r4 to forward packets destined for r5, r6, and r7 through r3, which is a suboptimal path. This condition is shown next, where the route to r7's loopback address is examined on r4:

```
[edit]
lab@r4# run show route 10.0.9.7


inet.0: 29 destinations, 34 routes (29 active, 0 holddown, 0 hidden)
+ = Active Route, - = Last Active, * = Both


10.0.8.0/21        *[IS-IS/165] 01:55:34, metric 16, tag 2
                    > to 10.0.2.5 via so-0/1/0.100
[edit]
lab@r4# run show isis interface
IS-IS interface database:
Interface          L CirID Level 1 DR    Level 2 DR       L1/L2 Metric
as0.0              2   0x1 Disabled      Point to Point        10/10
fe-0/0/1.0         1   0x2 r2.02         Disabled               5/5
lo0.0              0   0x1 Disabled      Passive                0/0
so-0/1/0.100       2   0x1 Disabled      Point to Point         3/3
```

After observing the anomaly, this author tried bouncing the as0 interface by deactivating and reactivating it, but the problem persisted. After confirming that the IS-IS stanza had not changed, and that the interface still displayed a speed of 311,040Kbps (a minimum of two OC-3 interfaces are required in the aggregated bundle), a routing daemon restart was performed and the problem was cleared:

```
[edit]
lab@r4# run restart routing
Routing protocol daemon started, pid 725


[edit]
lab@r4# run show isis interface
IS-IS interface database:
```

Interface	L	CirID	Level 1 DR	Level 2 DR	L1/L2 Metric
as0.0	2	0x1	Disabled	Point to Point	1/1
fe-0/0/1.0	1	0x2	0000.0000.0000.02	Disabled	5/5
lo0.0	0	0x1	Disabled	Passive	0/0
so-0/1/0.100	2	0x1	Disabled	Point to Point	3/3

The moral to this story is that nothing is perfect, and routers, being the complex systems that they are, provide no exception to this rule. A JNCIP exam candidate is expected to know that "stuff happens," and to be able to perform daemon restart and router reboots when operational anomalies are encountered. This particular issue was reproducible, and further investigation confirmed that a Problem Report (PR) had already been filed to correct the problem.

Restart Selectively to Minimize Disruption

Rather than restarting the whole routing daemon, which restarts all routing protocols, you will normally get a faster recovery (and less network disruption) if you can restart just the protocol that is misbehaving. This approach is demonstrated next:

```
[edit]
lab@r4# run show isis interface
IS-IS interface database:
Interface          L CirID Level 1 DR       Level 2 DR      L1/L2 Metric
as0.0              2   0x1 Disabled         Point to Point      10/10
fe-0/0/1.0         1   0x2 r2.02            Disabled             5/5
lo0.0              0   0x1 Disabled         Passive              0/0
so-0/1/0.100       2   0x1 Disabled         Point to Point       3/3


[edit]
lab@r4# deactivate protocols isis


[edit]
lab@r4# commit
commit complete


[edit]
lab@r4# rollback 1
load complete
```

```
[edit]
lab@r4# commit
commit complete


[edit]
lab@r4# run show isis interface
IS-IS interface database:
Interface          L CirID Level 1 DR          Level 2 DR        L1/L2 Metric
as0.0              2   0x1 Disabled            Point to Point       1/1
fe-0/0/1.0         1   0x2 0000.0000.0000.02 Disabled             5/5
lo0.0              0   0x1 Disabled            Passive             0/0
so-0/1/0.100       2   0x1 Disabled            Point to Point       3/3
```

As with the route reflection example, you may want to deactivate a few strategic interfaces to confirm that the network fails over to an optimal path, as determined by the remaining links. In this example, you once again deactivate r3's ATM interface to verify that it correctly begins forwarding through r4 when routing to subconfederation 65002 destinations:

```
[edit]
lab@r3# run traceroute 192.168.70.1
traceroute to 192.168.70.1 (192.168.70.1), 30 hops max, 40 byte packets
 1   10.0.2.6 (10.0.2.6)  0.684 ms  0.542 ms  0.494 ms
 2   10.0.2.9 (10.0.2.9)  0.579 ms  9.033 ms  0.533 ms
 3   10.0.8.10 (10.0.8.10)  0.449 ms  0.449 ms  0.430 ms
 4   10.0.8.10 (10.0.8.10)  0.441 ms !H  0.455 ms !H  0.431 ms !H
```

With the r3–r5 ATM link down, r3 forwards through r4 as expected, so it looks like r3 has chosen the best of the remaining paths, which in the end is all you can really ask of a router's control plane. After activating the ATM interface on r5, you quickly verify forwarding from r6 to subconfederation 65000 destinations:

```
lab@r6> traceroute 192.168.10.1
traceroute to 192.168.10.1 (192.168.10.1), 30 hops max, 40 byte packets
 1   10.0.8.6 (10.0.8.6)  0.345 ms  0.290 ms  0.234 ms
 2   10.0.2.10 (10.0.2.10)  0.286 ms  0.259 ms  0.243 ms
 3   10.0.4.10 (10.0.4.10)  0.175 ms  0.170 ms  0.156 ms
 4   10.0.4.5 (10.0.4.5)  0.552 ms  0.690 ms  0.378 ms
 5   10.0.4.5 (10.0.4.5)  0.361 ms !H  0.685 ms !H  0.375 ms !H
```

All seems perfect until r5 hands the packet to r4 at hop 2, because this decision results in extra router hops for the packet. A look at r5's routing table confirms that it forwards through r4 when attempting to reach all destinations in the level 1 area 49.0002.

```
[edit]
lab@r5# run show route 10.0.4/22

inet.0: 32 destinations, 36 routes (30 active, 0 holddown, 2 hidden)
+ = Active Route, - = Last Active, * = Both

10.0.4.0/22        *[IS-IS/165] 00:16:42, metric 11, tag 2
                    > to 10.0.2.10 via as1.0
10.0.5.0/24        *[IS-IS/18] 00:16:42, metric 64, tag 2
                    > to 10.0.2.10 via as1.0
```

As pointed out in Chapter 4, this condition is the result of a lower interface metric on the r4–r5 aggregated SONET interface, which causes r5 to prefer the summary route advertised by r4 over the same route as advertised by r3. The metric value of *11* would indicate that the summary route is injected into the level 2 backbone with a metric of *10* (which is the default), because the aggregated SONET link is known to have an automatically computed IS-IS metric of *1*. Downing the aggregated link and comparing the new route metric, which should be 10 + 3, or *13*, confirms that it is "normal" IS-IS behavior, and not your confederation design, that is to blame for the extra hops in this example:

```
[edit]
lab@r5# run show route 10.0.4/22

inet.0: 30 destinations, 34 routes (28 active, 0 holddown, 2 hidden)
+ = Active Route, - = Last Active, * = Both

10.0.4.0/22        *[IS-IS/165] 00:00:04, metric 13, tag 2
                    > to 10.0.2.2 via at-0/2/1.35
10.0.5.0/24        *[IS-IS/18] 00:00:04, metric 66, tag 2
                    > to 10.0.2.2 via at-0/2/1.35
```

Your confederation is working perfectly, so after activating r5's as1 aggregated SONET interface, you should congratulate yourself for a job well done!

Save Confederation Configuration

The working confederation configurations on all routers should now be saved for use in Chapter 6, "EBGP Configuration and Testing." The save command demonstrated next should be issued at the [edit] hierarchy on r1 through r7; make sure you take note of the specific filename used for easy restoration in the future:

```
[edit]
lab@r4# save confed-r4
Wrote 267 lines of configuration to 'confed-r4'
```

Miscellaneous IBGP Timers and Knobs

You should be familiar with all IBGP options and available knobs before attempting your lab examination. This section demonstrates how some of the remaining IBGP configuration parameters may be deployed in a lab scenario. Virtual Private Network (VPN) and multicast-related options, both of which relate to the support of non-IPv4 unicast address families, are beyond the scope of this book.

Figure 5.6 documents the topology for this section and shows that the OSPF router has been brought back into the fray.

FIGURE 5.6   Miscellaneous IBGP timers and knobs

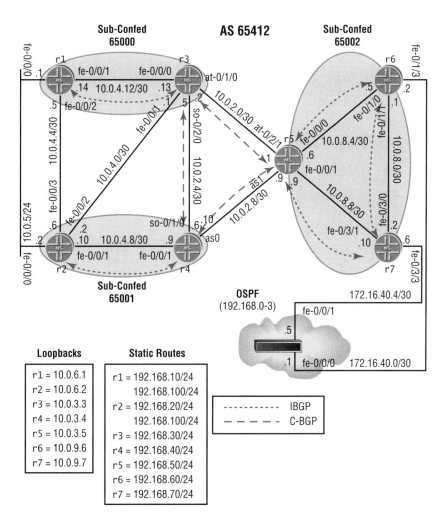

To complete this section, you must configure your network in accordance with the following tasks:

- Redistribute the 192.168.*x*/24 routes from the OSPF router into BGP so that r5 selects the BGP routes as active, and is able to load balance to these routes. You must not modify the existing IS-IS configuration on r5, r6, and r7.

- Configure the IBGP peering session between r3 and r4 so that r3 uses a 60-second keepalive interval.

- Configure r4 to be passive for IBGP and C-BGP connections.

- Configure r1 and r2 to redistribute a 192.168.100/24 static route into IBGP and ensure that all other routers forward through r1 when its IBGP session is up.

- Use a community to ensure that other routers will not forward the 192.168.100/24 route outside your AS.

IBGP Preference and Load Balancing

The first task will require modifications to the *ibgp* export policy on r6 and r7, BGP preference adjustments on r5, and the use of the multipath option for IBGP. The following statements modify the export policy used by IBGP on r6. We begin by displaying the current state of the *ibgp* policy:

```
[edit policy-options policy-statement ibgp]
lab@r6# show
term 1 {
    from {
        protocol static;
        route-filter 192.168.60.0/24 exact;
    }
    then accept;
}
```

You now add a new term to the *ibgp* export policy that will match on, and accept, the 192.168.*x*/24 routes coming from the OSPF router:

```
[edit policy-options policy-statement ibgp]
lab@r6# set term 2 from protocol ospf
```

```
[edit policy-options policy-statement ibgp]
lab@r6# set term 2 from route-filter 192.168.0/21 longer
```

```
[edit policy-options policy-statement ibgp]
lab@r6# set term 2 then accept
```

After committing the changes on r6, you confirm that the OSPF routes are being redistributed into IBGP:

```
[edit policy-options policy-statement ibgp]
lab@r6# run show route advertising-protocol bgp 10.0.3.5

inet.0: 29 destinations, 33 routes (29 active, 0 holddown, 0 hidden)
+ = Active Route, - = Last Active, * = Both

192.168.0.0/24
172.16.40.1             0           100 I
192.168.0.1/32
172.16.40.1             1           100 I
192.168.1.0/24
172.16.40.1             0           100 I
192.168.2.0/24
172.16.40.1             0           100 I
192.168.3.0/24
172.16.40.1             0           100 I
192.168.4.0/24
172.16.40.1             0           100 I
192.168.60.0/24
Self                    0           100 I
```

The display confirms that the OSPF routes are now being sent to r5 through IBGP, so your export policy is working as designed. It is interesting to see that r6 is advertising a third-party next hop of 172.16.40.1. This is normal behavior for BGP running on a broadcast interface, because other BGP speakers might have a direct connection to the OSPF subnet and this would allow IBGP speakers to forward packets directly to the OSPF router, even though the OSPF router does not even speak BGP!

After similar modifications are made to r7, you confirm that r5 is receiving equal-cost BGP routes from both r6 and r7:

```
[edit]
lab@r5# run show route 192.168.1/24

inet.0: 40 destinations, 54 routes (40 active, 0 holddown, 0 hidden)
+ = Active Route, - = Last Active, * = Both

192.168.1.0/24      *[IS-IS/155] 00:22:09, metric 5, tag 1
                       to 10.0.8.5 via fe-0/0/0.0
                     > to 10.0.8.10 via fe-0/0/1.0
```

```
[BGP/170] 00:21:27, MED 0, localpref 100, from 10.0.9.6
  AS path: I
> to 10.0.8.10 via fe-0/0/1.0
[BGP/170] 00:22:24, MED 0, localpref 100, from 10.0.9.7
  AS path: I
> to 10.0.8.5 via fe-0/0/0.0
```

Good, there are two sets of IBGP routes, but IBGP load balancing will be difficult considering that r5 has selected the IS-IS routes as active. To remedy this, you will need to modify the BGP preference on r5 so that BGP routes are preferred to IS-IS level 1 externals, which by default have a global preference of 160. The default IS-IS preference value was changed to 155 as part of the case study in Chapter 5. Adjusting the preference for IS-IS is also feasible, but disallowed by your rules of engagement for this scenario. Given these restrictions, you opt to adjust the BGP preference by the minimum amount required to make the BGP routes preferred over the IS-IS level 1 externals:

```
[edit]
lab@r5# set protocols bgp preference 154
```

After the commit, you once again examine r5's routing table with your attention focused on the routes generated by the OSPF router:

```
[edit]
lab@r5# run show route 192.168.1/24

inet.0: 40 destinations, 54 routes (40 active, 0 holddown, 0 hidden)
+ = Active Route, - = Last Active, * = Both

192.168.1.0/24    *[BGP/154] 00:25:53, MED 0, localpref 100, from 10.0.9.6
                     AS path: I
                   > to 10.0.8.10 via fe-0/0/1.0
                    [BGP/159] 00:26:50, MED 0, localpref 100, from 10.0.9.7
                     AS path: I
                   > to 10.0.8.5 via fe-0/0/0.0
                    [IS-IS/155] 00:01:06, metric 5, tag 1
                   > to 10.0.8.5 via fe-0/0/0.0
                     to 10.0.8.10 via fe-0/0/1.0
```

Great—the IBGP routes are now preferred over the IS-IS alternatives, which is a big step forward in completing this aspect of your configuration. To complete this task, you must now enable IBGP load balancing with the multipath option to allow r5 to load balance to the OSPF prefixes using IBGP routes. Before making the change shown next, note that the currently active IBGP routes for the 192.168.0/22 prefix list a single IGP forwarding next hop. After enabling multipath, you will expect to see multiple IGP next hops listed for the various 192.168.0/22 OSPF prefixes:

```
[edit]
lab@r5# set protocols bgp group 65002 multipath
```

Now to confirm the correct load-balancing behavior, the 192.168.1/24 route is once again displayed on r5:

```
[edit]
lab@r5# run show route 192.168.1/24

inet.0: 40 destinations, 54 routes (40 active, 0 holddown, 0 hidden)
+ = Active Route, - = Last Active, * = Both

192.168.1.0/24      *[BGP/154] 00:28:12, MED 0, localpref 100, from 10.0.9.6
                       AS path: I
                     > to 10.0.8.10 via fe-0/0/1.0
                       to 10.0.8.5 via fe-0/0/0.0
                     [BGP/154] 00:29:09, MED 0, localpref 100, from 10.0.9.7
                       AS path: I
                     > to 10.0.8.5 via fe-0/0/0.0
                     [IS-IS/155] 00:03:25, metric 5, tag 1
                     > to 10.0.8.5 via fe-0/0/0.0
                       to 10.0.8.10 via fe-0/0/1.0
```

Excellent! Even though r6's lower RID value results in its advertisement being chosen as *the* active IBGP route, multipath operation has allowed a recursive lookup on both of the protocol next hops being advertised by r6 and r7, and the result is the desired load-balancing behavior now observed at r5. Detailed output from a show route command is provided here with the various next hops highlighted:

```
[edit]
lab@r5# run show route 192.168.1/24 detail

inet.0: 40 destinations, 54 routes (40 active, 0 holddown, 0 hidden)
192.168.1.0/24 (3 entries, 1 announced)
        *BGP    Preference: 154/-101
                Source: 10.0.9.6
                Nexthop: 10.0.8.10 via fe-0/0/1.0, selected
                Nexthop: 10.0.8.5 via fe-0/0/0.0
```

```
                    Protocol Nexthop: 172.16.40.1 Indirect nexthop: 83e9440 62
                    Protocol Nexthop: 172.16.40.5 Indirect nexthop: 83e9330 60
                    State: <Active Int Ext>
                    Local AS: 65002 Peer AS: 65002
                    Age: 30:21      Metric: 0       Metric2: 7
                    Task: BGP_65002.10.0.9.6+1032
                    Announcement bits (4): 0-KRT 3-Aggregate 4-BGP.0.0.0.0+179 5-
Resolve inet.0
                    AS path: I
                    Localpref: 100
                    Router ID: 10.0.9.6
          BGP       Preference: 154/-101
                    Source: 10.0.9.7
                    Nexthop: 10.0.8.5 via fe-0/0/0.0, selected
                    Protocol Nexthop: 172.16.40.5 Indirect nexthop: 83e9330 60
                    State: <NotBest Int Ext>
                    Inactive reason: Router ID
                    Local AS: 65002 Peer AS: 65002
                    Age: 31:18      Metric: 0       Metric2: 7
                    Task: BGP_65002.10.0.9.7+1036
                    AS path: I
                    Localpref: 100
                    Router ID: 10.0.9.7
```

. . .

Modify IBGP Timers

The second criterion is not as simple as it may at first seem. This is because the BGP keepalive value is configured indirectly in JUNOS software by setting the session hold time, and because the BGP protocol negotiates the session's hold time such that the lower of the two proposed values (within protocol limits) will always be put into effect. The keepalive interval is always set to one-third of the session's negotiated hold time, so a 60-second keepalive is achieved with a session hold time of 180 seconds. There is no way to have r3 and r4 use different hold times, but the wording of the task may lead you to believe that there is! To accomplish this task, you will need to modify the hold time on both r3 and r4, as shown next:

holdtime = 3x keepal.

```
[edit protocols bgp]
lab@r3# set group c-bgp neighbor 10.0.3.4 hold-time 180
```

You must use care to ensure that you do not apply the modified hold time at either the global or group levels because doing so could affect all of r3's IBGP and C-BGP sessions, which is a situation that would be outside of the parameters of this configuration task. After modifying r4's hold time, the results are confirmed:

```
[edit]
lab@r4# run show bgp neighbor 10.0.3.3
Peer: 10.0.3.3+1049    AS 65000 Local: 10.0.3.4+179    AS 65001
  Type: External    State: Established    Flags: <>
  Last State: OpenConfirm    Last Event: RecvKeepAlive
  Last Error: None
  Export: [ ibgp ]
  Options: <Multihop Preference LocalAddress HoldTime PeerAS Refresh Confed>
  Local Address: 10.0.3.4 Holdtime: 180 Preference: 170
  Number of flaps: 1
  Error: 'Cease' Sent: 0 Recv: 1
  Peer ID: 10.0.3.3        Local ID: 10.0.3.4        Active Holdtime: 180
  Keepalive Interval: 60
  NLRI advertised by peer: inet-unicast
  NLRI for this session: inet-unicast
  Peer supports Refresh capability (2)
  Table inet.0 Bit: 10001
    Send state: in sync
    Active prefixes: 5
    Received prefixes: 5
    Suppressed due to damping: 0
  Last traffic (seconds): Received 0    Sent 0    Checked 2
  Input messages:  Total 1776    Updates 1775    Refreshes 0    Octets 122981
  Output messages: Total 1780    Updates 1778    Refreshes 0    Octets 123202
  Output Queue[0]: 0
```

This display confirms the correct setting of the r3–r4 C-BGP session's keepalive time. The display can also be used to ascertain the session's *configured* hold time versus the value that was actually *negotiated*, because the latter is preceded by the `active` keyword.

Configure Passive Mode

The third task requires that r4 be configured to operate in a passive mode for its IBGP and C-BGP connections. This means that it should never initiate a connection to r2, r3, or r5. This behavior is configured with the `passive` keyword, as shown next:

```
[edit]
lab@r4# set protocols bgp group 65001 passive
```

The results can be confirmed by verifying that the `passive` option is in place for r4's IBGP and C-BGP neighbors:

```
[edit]
lab@r4# run show bgp neighbor 10.0.6.2
Peer: 10.0.6.2+179     AS 65001 Local: 10.0.3.4+1029     AS 65001
  Type: Internal     State: Established     Flags: <>
  Last State: OpenConfirm    Last Event: RecvKeepAlive
  Last Error: None
  Export: [ ibgp ]
  Options: <Preference LocalAddress HoldTime Passive Refresh Confed>
  Local Address: 10.0.3.4 Holdtime: 90 Preference: 170
  Number of flaps: 0
  Peer ID: 10.0.6.2        Local ID: 10.0.3.4        Active Holdtime: 90
  Keepalive Interval: 30
  NLRI advertised by peer: inet-unicast
  NLRI for this session: inet-unicast
  Peer supports Refresh capability (2)
  Table inet.0 Bit: 10000
    Send state: in sync
    Active prefixes: 1
    Received prefixes: 1
    Suppressed due to damping: 0
  Last traffic (seconds): Received 3     Sent 3     Checked 3
  Input messages:  Total 380      Updates 1       Refreshes 0     Octets 7256
  Output messages: Total 95837 Updates 95472    Refreshes 0     Octets 6282903
  Output Queue[0]: 0
```

You could also use protocol tracing or traffic monitoring to verify that r4 does not initiate TCP sessions to port 179, if you are so inclined. Showing the system's connections can also be used to verify that r4 is not initiating BGP connections because the "called" end of a TCP connection accepts packets destined to the well-known port while the "calling" end picks a random port above 1023 for its source port. The indication that the local side of a router's TCP connection is using port 179 confirms that that router did not initiate the connection, as shown in this example of a BGP connection between r4 and r2, where r2 has initiated the BGP connection to r4:

```
[edit]
lab@r4# run show system connections
Active Internet connections (including servers)
Proto Recv-Q Send-Q  Local Address      Foreign Address       (state)
tcp4      0      0  10.0.3.4.179         10.0.6.2.1033        ESTABLISHED
. . .
```

The various displays shown in this section serve to confirm that r4 has been correctly configured for passive operation with its peers.

Use Local Preference and Communities

The requirement that other routers in AS 65412 prefer r1 as the source of the 192.168.100/24 prefix is easily accomplished by adjusting the redistribution policies of r1 or r2 so that other routers see r1 advertising a higher, and therefore more preferred, local preference value. Knowing that the default local preference from r2 will be 100 allows you to achieve your goal by simply having r1 set a local preference value of 101 or higher when redistributing the 192.168.100/24 route into IBGP.

This task also requires that you prevent the advertisement of the 192.168.100/24 prefix outside of your AS through the use of communities. While this can be accomplished using various combinations of user-defined communities and BGP policy, the most straightforward way to address this problem is to use the well-known no-export community. The presence of this community will automatically prevent a community-aware BGP speaker from advertising the route outside a confederation boundary, which means the route will never leave AS 65412 in this case. This sounds like just the ticket for getting one step closer to JNCIP nirvana.

The no-export community is coded as 0x FFFF FF01, or decimal 65,535:65,281. This author's advice is that you make use of the JUNOS software support of predefined symbolic naming for well-known communities, because typing **no-export** is pretty easy compared to your remaining syntax alternatives.

You begin with the baseline redistribution policy for r2, starting with the definition of a named community. Oddly enough, you have to assign a user-defined variable name, which might or might not mimic the predefined JUNOS software name for the well-known community, before you can make use the no-export community in a policy:

```
[edit policy-options]
lab@r2# set community no-export members no-export
```
will not advertise outside AS of 65412

In this example, the user-assigned name matches the JUNOS software syntax for the community's well-known name. You now write the policy that will attach this community when advertising the 192.168.100/24 static route to IBGP peers:

```
[edit policy-options]
lab@r2# edit policy-statement static
```

```
[edit policy-options policy-statement static]
lab@r2# set term 1 from route-filter 192.168.100/24 exact
```

```
[edit policy-options policy-statement static]
lab@r2# set term 1 then community add no-export
```

```
[edit policy-options policy-statement static]
lab@r2# set term 1 then accept
```

The completed policy is now shown:

```
[edit policy-options policy-statement static]
lab@r2# show
term 1 {
    from {
        protocol static;
        route-filter 192.168.100/24 exact;
    }
    then {
        metric 101;
        community add no-export;
        accept;
    }
}
```

The *static* policy is applied to r2's *65001* IBGP peer group as export, which causes r2 to evaluate the *ibgp* and *static* policies when advertising BGP routes to its peers:

```
[edit protocols bgp]
lab@r2# set group 65001 export static
```

Next, you define the static route with a reject next hop and commit your changes:

```
[edit]
lab@r2# set routing-options static route 192.168.100/24 reject
```

```
[edit protocols bgp]
lab@r2# commit
commit complete
```

And now to confirm the results of your community tagging and redistribution policy on r2:

```
[edit]
lab@r2# run show route advertising-protocol bgp 10.0.3.4

inet.0: 29 destinations, 30 routes (29 active, 0 holddown, 0 hidden)
+ = Active Route, - = Last Active, * = Both

192.168.20.0/24
Self                            0            100 I
```

```
192.168.100.0/24
Self                         0         100 I
```

Good, both of the static routes associated with r2 are being redistributed into IBGP. To verify the presence of the community, use the detail switch:

```
[edit]
lab@r2# run show route advertising-protocol bgp 10.0.3.4 192.168.100/24 detail

inet.0: 29 destinations, 30 routes (29 active, 0 holddown, 0 hidden)
192.168.100.0/24 (2 entries, 1 announced)
 BGP group 65001 type Internal
     Nexthop: Self
     MED: 0
     Localpref: 100
     AS path: I
     Communities: no-export
```

The route is being advertised by IBGP with the default local preference setting of *100* and the no-export community is correctly attached. After replicating the policy and static route definition on r1, the *static* policy is modified as highlighted:

```
[edit policy-options]
lab@r1# set policy-statement static term 1 then local-preference 101

[edit policy-options]
lab@r1# show
policy-statement static {
    term 1 {
        from {
            protocol static;
            route-filter 192.168.100/24 exact;
        }
        then {
            metric 101;
            local-preference 101;
            community add no-export;
            accept;
        }
    }
}
```

Once applied to r1's *65000* BGP group as export, the results are verified:

```
[edit]
lab@r1# run show route advertising-protocol bgp 10.0.3.3 192.168.100/24 detail

inet.0: 27 destinations, 27 routes (27 active, 0 holddown, 0 hidden)
192.168.100/24 (1 entry, 1 announced)
 BGP group 65000 type Internal
     Nexthop: Self
     MED: 101
     Localpref: 101
     AS path: I
     Communities: no-export
```

The routing tables of other routers are now analyzed to verify that the local preference causes them to prefer r1 as the source of the 192.168.100/24 route as required:

```
lab@r6> show route 192.168.100/24 detail

inet.0: 30 destinations, 38 routes (30 active, 0 holddown, 0 hidden)
192.168.100.0/24 (1 entry, 1 announced)
        *BGP    Preference: 170/-102
                Source: 10.0.3.5
                Nexthop: 10.0.8.6 via fe-0/1/0.0, selected
                Protocol Nexthop: 10.0.6.1 Indirect nexthop: 8460110 43
                State: <Active Int Ext>
                Local AS: 65002 Peer AS: 65002
                Age: 28:19     Metric: 0      Metric2: 5
                Task: BGP_65002.10.0.3.5+179
                Announcement bits (2): 0-KRT 6-Resolve inet.0
                AS path: (65000) I
                Communities: no-export
                Localpref: 101
                Router ID: 10.0.3.5
```

Well, it does seem that r6 has installed r1's route as active, but what about the fact that r2's advertisement is not even shown? Is this a symptom of a malfunction in r2's export policy? The answer to these questions can be gleaned from the understanding that BGP speakers advertise only active routes to other speakers, and that the lack of a full IBGP mesh between the routers that compose the test bed means that some routers are now reliant on the coupling of IBGP routes through other BGP speakers.

In this case, r1's higher local preference setting is causing r4 to install r1's 192.168.100/24 route as active (which it learns about through the C-BGP peering session to r3), and this in turn causes both r3 and r4 to suppress the advertisement of r2's 192.168.100/24 BGP route in the updates they generate to r5. The route's absence on r5 prevents r6 and r7 from learning r2's advertisement in a similar fashion. Checking r2's routing table confirms that it too prefers r1's BGP route, although the local static route definition on r2 prevents r1's BGP route from becoming active:

```
[edit]
lab@r2# run show route 192.168.100/24 detail


inet.0: 29 destinations, 30 routes (29 active, 0 holddown, 0 hidden)
192.168.100.0/24 (2 entries, 1 announced)
        *Static Preference: 5
                Next hop type: Reject
                State: <Active Int Ext>
                Age: 45:09      Metric: 0
                Task: RT
                Announcement bits (3): 0-KRT 3-BGP.0.0.0.0+179 4-Resolve inet.0
                AS path: I
        BGP    Preference: 170/-102
                Source: 10.0.3.4
                Nexthop: 10.0.4.5 via fe-0/0/3.0, selected
                Protocol Nexthop: 10.0.6.1 Indirect nexthop: 84293b8 57
                State: <Int Ext>
                Inactive reason: Route Preference
                Local AS: 65001 Peer AS: 65001
                Age: 39:17      Metric: 0       Metric2: 5
                Task: BGP_65001.10.0.3.4+179
                AS path: (65000) I
                Communities: no-export
                Localpref: 101
                Router ID: 10.0.3.4
```

By temporarily removing the *static* policy on r1, you can easily confirm that other routers will install r2's advertisement as the active route:

```
[edit]
lab@r1# delete protocols bgp group 65000 export static


[edit]
lab@r1# commit
commit complete
```

With only r2 advertising the 192.168.100/24 prefix, you confirm that other routers have installed r2's route as active:

```
lab@r6> show route 192.168.100/24 detail

inet.0: 30 destinations, 38 routes (30 active, 0 holddown, 0 hidden)
192.168.100.0/24 (1 entry, 1 announced)
        *BGP    Preference: 170/-101
                Source: 10.0.3.5
                Nexthop: 10.0.8.6 via fe-0/1/0.0, selected
                Protocol Nexthop: 10.0.6.2 Indirect nexthop: 8460220 47
                State: <Active Int Ext>
                Local AS: 65002 Peer AS: 65002
                Age: 49:27     Metric: 0      Metric2: 5
                Task: BGP_65002.10.0.3.5+179
                Announcement bits (2): 0-KRT 6-Resolve inet.0
                AS path: (65000 65001) I
                Communities: no-export
                Localpref: 100
                Router ID: 10.0.3.5
```

As expected, r2 has been chosen as the preferred source of the 192.168.100/24 route. r5 is now receiving more or less identical updates from both r3 and r4, but has chosen r3's route as active because of its preferred RID value. As before, both routes carry the same protocol next hop of 10.0.6.2, so forwarding is not impacted by r5 choosing r3 as the preferred source of the route:

```
lab@r5> show route 192.168.100/24 detail

inet.0: 41 destinations, 56 routes (41 active, 0 holddown, 0 hidden)
192.168.100.0/24 (2 entries, 1 announced)
        *BGP    Preference: 154/-101
                Source: 10.0.3.3
                Nexthop: 10.0.2.10 via as1.0, selected
                Protocol Nexthop: 10.0.6.2 Indirect nexthop: 83e92a8 60
                State: <Active Int Ext>
                Local AS: 65002 Peer AS: 65000
                Age: 51:18     Metric: 0      Metric2: 11
                Task: BGP_65000.10.0.3.3+179
                Announcement bits (3): 0-KRT 4-BGP.0.0.0.0+179 5-Resolve inet.0
                AS path: (65000 65001) I
                Communities: no-export
                Localpref: 100
                Router ID: 10.0.3.3
```

```
BGP    Preference: 154/-101
       Source: 10.0.3.4
       Nexthop: 10.0.2.10 via as1.0, selected
       Protocol Nexthop: 10.0.6.2 Indirect nexthop: 83e92a8 60
       State: <NotBest Int Ext>
       Inactive reason: Router ID
       Local AS: 65002 Peer AS: 65001
       Age: 5:25       Metric: 0       Metric2: 11
       Task: BGP_65001.10.0.3.4+179
       AS path: (65001) I
       Communities: no-export
       Localpref: 100
       Router ID: 10.0.3.4
```

With the correct redistribution, community, and local preference settings confirmed, you restore r1's *static* export policy before moving on:

```
[edit]
lab@r1# rollback 1
load complete


[edit]
lab@r1# commit
commit complete
```

Troubleshoot an IBGP Problem

Your test bed is configured according to Figure 5.6, shown earlier, when you notice that r4 and r5 are missing the 192.168.10/24 route from r1:

```
[edit]
lab@r4# run traceroute 192.168.10.1
traceroute to 192.168.10.1 (192.168.10.1), 30 hops max, 40 byte packets
traceroute: sendto: No route to host
 1 traceroute: wrote 192.168.10.1 40 chars, ret=-1
^C
```

You verify that r3 has the 192.168.10/24 route, which indicates the IBGP session to r1 is operational, but you notice that its C-BGP sessions to r4 and r5 are both active:

```
lab@r3> show route protocol bgp 192.168.10/24
```

```
inet.0: 29 destinations, 29 routes (29 active, 0 holddown, 0 hidden)
+ = Active Route, - = Last Active, * = Both


192.168.10.0/24     *[BGP/170] 00:09:46, MED 0, localpref 100, from 10.0.6.1
                      AS path: I
                    > to 10.0.4.14 via fe-0/0/0.0


iso.0: 1 destinations, 1 routes (1 active, 0 holddown, 0 hidden)

lab@r3> show bgp summary
Groups: 2 Peers: 3 Down peers: 2
Table           Tot Paths  Act Paths Suppressed    History Damp State   Pending
inet.0                 2          2          0          0          0          0
Peer            AS       InPkt    OutPkt    OutQ    Flaps Last Up/Dwn
State|#Active/Received/Damped...
10.0.3.4        65001        2         6       0       17        14 Active
10.0.3.5        65002        2         6       0       20        27 Active
10.0.6.1        65000       24        25       0        0    10:39 2/2/0
0/0/0
```

This state of affairs explains the missing route on r4. You decide to trace BGP open messages on r3, and capture the following output:

```
Jun  7 13:15:49 trace_on: Tracing to "/var/log/hrr" started
Jun  7 13:16:03 bgp_send: sending 45 bytes to 10.0.3.4 (External AS 65001)
Jun  7 13:16:03
Jun  7 13:16:03 BGP SEND 10.0.3.3+179 -> 10.0.3.4+1103
Jun  7 13:16:03 BGP SEND message type 1 (Open) length 45
Jun  7 13:16:03 BGP SEND version 4 as 65000 holdtime 180 id 10.0.3.3 parmlen 16
Jun  7 13:16:03 MP capability AFI=1, SAFI=1
Jun  7 13:16:03 Refresh capability, code=128
Jun  7 13:16:03 Refresh capability, code=2
Jun  7 13:16:03 bgp_send: sending 45 bytes to 10.0.3.4 (External AS 65001)
Jun  7 13:16:03
Jun  7 13:16:03 BGP SEND 10.0.3.3+179 -> 10.0.3.4+1103
Jun  7 13:16:03 BGP SEND message type 2 (Update) length 45
Jun  7 13:16:03 BGP SEND flags 0x40 code Origin(1): IGP
Jun  7 13:16:03 BGP SEND flags 0x40 code ASPath(2): 65000
Jun  7 13:16:03 BGP SEND flags 0x40 code NextHop(3): 10.0.3.3
Jun  7 13:16:03 BGP SEND          192.168.10.0/24
```

```
Jun  7 13:16:03 bgp_send: sending 52 bytes to 10.0.3.4 (External AS 65001)
Jun  7 13:16:03
Jun  7 13:16:03 BGP SEND 10.0.3.3+179 -> 10.0.3.4+1103
Jun  7 13:16:03 BGP SEND message type 2 (Update) length 52
Jun  7 13:16:03 BGP SEND flags 0x40 code Origin(1): IGP
Jun  7 13:16:03 BGP SEND flags 0x40 code ASPath(2): 65000
Jun  7 13:16:03 BGP SEND flags 0x40 code NextHop(3): 10.0.3.3
Jun  7 13:16:03 BGP SEND flags 0x80 code MultiExitDisc(4): 0
Jun  7 13:16:03 BGP SEND        192.168.30.0/24
Jun  7 13:16:03 bgp_read_v4_update: receiving packet(s) from 10.0.3.4 (External AS
65001)
Jun  7 13:16:03
Jun  7 13:16:03 BGP RECV 10.0.3.4+1103 -> 10.0.3.3+179
Jun  7 13:16:03 BGP RECV message type 2 (Update) length 59
Jun  7 13:16:03 BGP RECV flags 0x40 code Origin(1): IGP
Jun  7 13:16:03 BGP RECV flags 0x40 code ASPath(2): (65001)
Jun  7 13:16:03 BGP RECV flags 0x40 code NextHop(3): 10.0.3.4
Jun  7 13:16:03 BGP RECV flags 0x80 code MultiExitDisc(4): 0
Jun  7 13:16:03 BGP RECV flags 0x40 code LocalPref(5): 100
Jun  7 13:16:03 BGP RECV        192.168.40.0/24
Jun  7 13:16:03 bgp_path_attr_error: NOTIFICATION sent to 10.0.3.4 (External AS
65001): code 3 (Update Message Error) subcode 11 (AS path attribute problem)
Jun  7 13:16:03 bgp_send: sending 21 bytes to 10.0.3.4 (External AS 65001)
Jun  7 13:16:03
Jun  7 13:16:03 BGP SEND 10.0.3.3+179 -> 10.0.3.4+1103
Jun  7 13:16:03 BGP SEND message type 3 (Notification) length 21
Jun  7 13:16:03 BGP SEND Notification code 3 (Update Message Error) subcode 11 (AS
path attribute problem)
```

You decide to focus on r3's BGP-related configuration because r4 and r5 seem to be working fine. Can you spot the issue in the r3's configuration?

```
[edit]
lab@r3# show protocols bgp
group 65000 {
    type internal;
    local-address 10.0.3.3;
    hold-time 180;
    export ibgp;
    neighbor 10.0.6.1;
```

```
    }
group c-bgp {
    type external;
    traceoptions {
        file hrr;
        flag open detail;
        flag update detail;
    }
    multihop;
    local-address 10.0.3.3;
    export ibgp;
    neighbor 10.0.3.4 {
        hold-time 180;
        peer-as 65001;
    }
    neighbor 10.0.3.5 {
        peer-as 65002;
    }
}
[edit]
lab@r3# show routing-options
static {
    route 10.0.200.0/24 next-hop 10.0.1.102;
    route 192.168.30.0/24 reject;
}
aggregate {
    route 10.0.4.0/22;
}
autonomous-system 65000;
confederation 65412 members [ 6500 6501 6502 ];


[edit]
lab@r3# show policy-options policy-statement ibgp
term 1 {
    from {
        protocol static;
        route-filter 192.168.30.0/24 exact;
    }
```

```
        then accept;
}
```

If you spotted the "fat-finger" typing errors in r3's confederation settings, then you have a good eye for details! The (AS path attribute problem) messages in the trace output also help to diagnose the problem, as the error report clearly indicates that r3 is having a problem with what appears to be a malformed AS path attribute in the update messages sent by r4 (and r5). This is caused by r3 treating r4 and r5 as conventional EBGP peers (because their AS numbers are not configured in the confederation list) while r4 and r5 treat r3 as a C-BGP peer. Different codes are used to identify a conventional AS path segment and a confederation AS path segment—which, in the case of an AS sequence segment type, is coded as 2 and 4, respectively. The differences in AS path segment coding cause the notification messages shown in the trace output and a subsequent teardown of the BGP session.

Summary

This chapter detailed several IBGP-related configuration tasks that represent JNCIP-level lab assignments. You should now be comfortable with the configuration and verification of full mesh, route reflection, and confederation applications of the BGP protocol, and you should be able to use routing policy to effect route redistribution and to adjust IBGP attributes such as local preference and community strings. Because IBGP peering is almost always implemented between router loopback addresses, you must be able to effectively use the *local-address* option, and make use of the *multihop* keyword as needed on C-BGP links to support lo0-based peering. This chapter also provided an IBGP load-balancing example that made use of the *multipath* option to permit the installation of multiple IGP forwarding next hops when presented with otherwise equal IBGP updates for the same prefix from two or more IBGP speakers.

A successful JNCIP exam candidate must be proficient with all things IBGP, because the operation of EBGP, and the overall effectiveness of your BGP-related policy, will depend in large part on the successful deployment of a functional IBGP infrastructure.

Case Study: IGBP

The IBGP case study is designed to emulate a typical JNCIP-level IBGP configuration scenario. In the interest of "mixing things up," you will be adding the IBGP-related case study configuration to the interface and OSPF-related case study configurations produced at the end of Chapters 2 and 3, respectively. The multi-area OSPF topology is shown in Figure 5.7 so you can reacquaint yourself with it.

FIGURE 5.7 OSPF case study topology

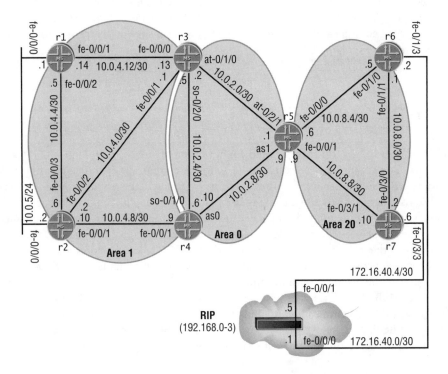

Because you will now be using OSPF as your IGP, you should load and commit your saved OSPF case study configurations from Chapter 3 to ensure that your routers will look and behave like the examples shown here. Before starting the IBGP case study, you should verify the correct operation of all routers, interfaces, OSPF, and the RIP router, using the confirmation steps outlined in the case study at the end of Chapter 3. You may also want to review the OSPF case study requirements to refresh your memory as to the specifics of the IGP that will now support your IBGP configurations.

You will need to refer to the criteria listing and the information contained in Figure 5.8, the case study topology, for the information you will need to complete this case study. It is expected that a JNCIP exam candidate will be able to complete this case study in approximately one hour, with the result being an IBGP design and configuration that exhibits no serious operational problems. Sample configurations from all seven routers are provided at the end of the case study for comparison with your own configurations. Because multiple solutions are usually possible, differences between the provided examples and your own configurations do not always indicate that mistakes have been made. Because you are graded on the overall functionality of your network and its conformity to the specified configuration criteria, various operational mode commands are included so that you may compare the behavior of your network to a known good example.

FIGURE 5.8   IBGP case study topology

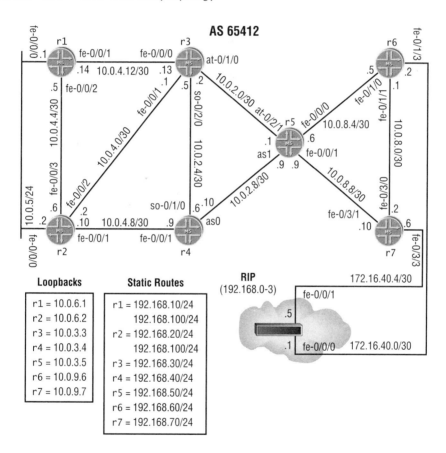

To complete this case study, your IBGP configuration must meet the following criteria:

- Your IBGP design must be added to the OSPF case study configuration from Chapter 3.
- Deploy two confederations using AS 65000 and 65001.
- Use route reflection in each confederation. Your design must use exactly two unique cluster IDs and no more than three route reflectors.
- Suppress reflection in one of the clusters.

- Ensure that your design will tolerate the failure of any single link/interface, and the failure of either r3 or r4.

- You must use loopback-based IBGP peering within each cluster, and interface peering for C-BGP links.

- Authenticate all IBGP sessions in one of the clusters with key *jnx*.

- Redistribute the static routes shown earlier in Figure 5.7 into IBGP, and using communities, ensure that all routers prefer r2's 192.168.100/24 IBGP route. You must not alter the default local preference of this route.

- Your IBGP design cannot result in any black holes or suboptimal routing.

- Redistribute a summary of the RIP routes into IBGP from both r6 and r7.

- r5 must IBGP load-balance to the summary route representing the RIP prefixes.

- Make sure that r1 and r2 receive the RIP route summary from r3 and r4 through IBGP. You cannot change any protocol preference values on r3 or r4, and the BGP protocol next hop as seen by r1 and r2 must be the same as that seen by r5.

- Configure r7 to be passive, and ensure that its IBGP sessions operate with a 45-second keepalive interval. No other session keepalive intervals should be modified.

In this case study, the RIP router is preconfigured to advertise the 192.168.0-3/24 routes to both r6 and r7. Please refer back to Chapter 3 for the details of its configuration, if you are curious.

IBGP Case Study Analysis

Each configuration requirement for the case study will now be matched to one or more valid router configurations and commands that can be used to confirm whether your network is operating within the specified case study guidelines. We begin with these criteria because they serve to establish a baseline for your BGP connectivity:

- Deploy two confederations using AS 65000 and 65001.

- Use route reflection in each confederation. Your design must use exactly two unique cluster IDs and no more than three route reflectors.

- Suppress reflection in one of the clusters.

- Ensure that your design will tolerate the failure of any single link/interface, and the failure of either r3 or r5.

- You must use loopback-based IBGP peering within each cluster, and interface peering for C-BGP links.

Before you start pounding away on your routers, it is suggested that you take a few moments to think through your various design alternatives, and that you document your design on paper so that confusion and mistakes are less likely once you begin the act of configuring the network. Figure 5.9 illustrates a workable design that meets all requirements posed for this case study.

FIGURE 5.9   Suggested IBGP design

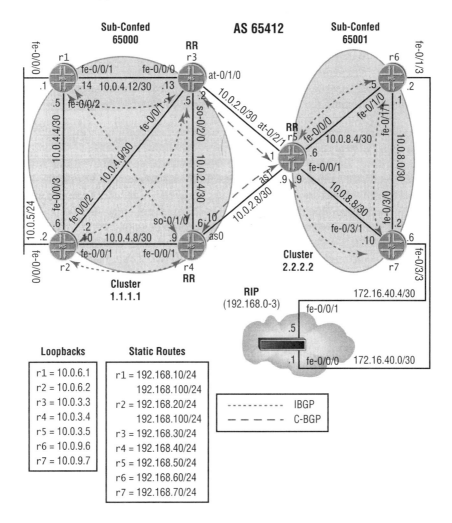

Figure 5.9 shows that r1, r2, r3, and r4 will belong to confederation 65000, and that both r3 and r4 will act as route reflectors for this cluster. r5, r6, and r7 will be in confederation 65001 with r5 acting as the cluster's route reflector. The extra IBGP peering session shown between r6 and r7 will accommodate the lack of reflection in this cluster. Lastly, the C-BGP sessions between r3, r4, and r5 will connect the two subconfederations with the required level of redundancy, despite the fact that your C-BGP connections must use interface peering.

The two C-BGP connections in the core provide the required redundancy due to the way a route reflector handles the reflection of routes from non-clients. Because a route reflector only adds its cluster ID when it is reflecting routes received from one of its clients, r4 will not add its cluster ID when it reflects the routes received from r5 into cluster 1.1.1.1. This means that r3 will not lose any BGP routes if the r3–r5 C-BGP session should fail because it will receive the same routes through the reflection services of r4, and the lack of cluster ID 1.1.1.1 in these routes allows them to be accepted by r3. Routes received from cluster 1.1.1.1 clients will have cluster ID 1.1.1.1 attached when reflected between r3 and r4, but this is not an issue because each of the cluster's route reflectors will also receive these routes directly over its IBGP peering sessions to the cluster's clients.

Although other logical BGP topologies that meet these requirements almost certainly exist, the solution shown in Figure 5.9 is one of the most straightforward designs.

C-BGP Peering to Physical Interfaces?

While there is nothing "illegal" about configuring C-BGP sessions to peer with physical addresses, this is normally not done due to the added redundancy benefits one gains from loopback peering. A previous configuration example in this chapter demonstrated lo0-based C-BGP peering, so in the interest of full coverage and in keeping you on your toes, this case study requires that you use interface-based C-BGP peering. Requirements such as these are designed to force a candidate into deviating from "run-of-the-mill" network designs, which in turn provides a mechanism that allows proctors to objectively gauge the candidate's depth of understanding with regard to a given protocol's operation and network design alternatives.

We begin our analysis with the basic IBGP configuration for r1:

```
[edit]
lab@r1# show routing-options
static {
    route 10.0.200.0/24 {
        next-hop 10.0.1.102;
        no-readvertise;
    }
}
autonomous-system 65000;
confederation 65412 members [ 65000 65001 ];

[edit]
lab@r1# show protocols bgp
group 65000 {
    type internal;
    local-address 10.0.6.1;
    neighbor 10.0.3.3;
    neighbor 10.0.3.4;
}
```

There is nothing real surprising here. r1 must IBGP-peer with both r3 and r4 using lo0 peering, and r1 has been correctly configured to peer between loopback addresses with the correct local-address and neighbor definitions. r1 belongs to AS 65000, which has been properly configured as a subconfederation of AS 65412. The configuration of r2 is virtually identical and is therefore not shown here. We next look at the basic IBGP and C-BGP configuration for r4:

```
[edit]
lab@r4# show routing-options
static {
    route 10.0.200.0/24 {
        next-hop 10.0.1.102;
        no-readvertise;
    }
}
autonomous-system 65000;
confederation 65412 members [ 65000 65001 ];

[edit]
lab@r4# show protocols bgp
group 65000 {
    type internal;
    local-address 10.0.3.4;
    cluster 1.1.1.1;
    neighbor 10.0.3.3;
    neighbor 10.0.6.1;
    neighbor 10.0.6.2;
}
group c-bgp {
    type external;
    neighbor 10.0.2.9 {
        peer-as 65001;
    }
}
```

The configuration of r4 shows that it has an internal IBGP group called *65000*, and that it will function as a route reflector for this group using cluster ID 1.1.1.1. You can also see that r4 will have three IBGP peering sessions, one each to r1, r2, and r3. The *c-bgp* group has been correctly set as an external peer group, and the neighbor definitions accommodate the interface peering required in this case study. The use of interface-based peering for C-BGP means that the local-address and multihop options are not needed. In fact, configuring a local address that differs from the default behavior of using the egress interface's IP address will prevent the C-BGP sessions from being established! The correct AS number has also been configured for peer 10.0.3.5 in this example. Because the configuration of r3 is virtually identical, it is not shown here.

r5's basic IBGP and C-BGP configuration is examined next:

```
[edit]
lab@r5# show routing-options
static {
    route 10.0.200.0/24 {
        next-hop 10.0.1.102;
        no-readvertise;
    }
}
autonomous-system 65001;
confederation 65412 members [ 65000 65001 ];


[edit]
lab@r5# show protocols bgp
group 65001 {
    type internal;
    local-address 10.0.3.5;
    cluster 2.2.2.2;
    no-client-reflect;
    neighbor 10.0.9.6;
    neighbor 10.0.9.7;
}
group c-bgp {
    type external;
    neighbor 10.0.2.2 {
        peer-as 65000;
    }
    neighbor 10.0.2.10 {
        peer-as 65000;
    }
}
```

The confederation-related configuration of r5 is similar to those of r3 and r4. The primary difference is the use of *65001* as r5's autonomous system number. Note that all routers in the test bed have been configured with a common list of AS 65412 confederation members. The 65001 internal peer group has been assigned cluster ID 2.2.2.2, making r5 a route reflector. The no-client-reflect option has been enabled to prevent r5 from reflecting routes to the clients in this group. The *c-bgp* group lists the interface addresses of both r3 and r4, which provides the necessary redundancy should a failure of r3, r4, or one of the peering interfaces occur.

Finally, we look at the basic IBGP configuration for r6. The configuration of r7 will be nearly identical.

```
[edit]
lab@r6# show routing-options
static {
    route 10.0.200.0/24 {
        next-hop 10.0.1.102;
        no-readvertise;
    }
}
aggregate {
    route 192.168.0.0/22;
}
autonomous-system 65001;
confederation 65412 members [ 65000 65001 ];


[edit]
lab@r6# show protocols bgp
group 65001 {
    type internal;
    local-address 10.0.9.6;
    neighbor 10.0.3.5;
    neighbor 10.0.9.7;
}
```

Because cluster 2.2.2.2's route reflector has been configured to not reflect routes, you must include an IBGP peering session between r6 and r7, as highlighted, or you could have black holes. Before proceeding, you should confirm that all IBGP and C-BGP peering sessions have been correctly established. This capture, taken from r3, shows the expected number of IBGP and C-BGP sessions and confirms that they are in the established state. The lack of BGP export policy results in a lack of route advertisements over the BGP peering sessions at this time, however.

```
[edit]
lab@r3# run show bgp summary
Groups: 2 Peers: 4 Down peers: 0
Table          Tot Paths  Act Paths Suppressed    History Damp State    Pending
inet.0                22          9          0          0          0          0
Peer              AS       InPkt     OutPkt    OutQ   Flaps Last Up/Dwn
State|#Active/Received/Damped...
10.0.2.1       65001         13         14       0       2       9 1/4/0
0/0/0
```

10.0.3.4	65000	5493	5501	0	0	53:12 3/5/0
0/0/0						
10.0.6.1	65000	108	3389	0	0	53:04 1/2/0
0/0/0						
10.0.6.2	65000	112	3384	0	0	53:00 4/11/0
0/0/0						

You will now add authentication to your network in accordance with the following requirement:

- Authenticate all IBGP sessions in one of the clusters with key *jnx*.

In this case, this author has opted to add authentication to cluster 2.2.2.2, simply because it will involve less typing overall. The following capture highlights the authentication information that has been added to *r5*'s *65001* IBGP group; similar statements will be needed on *r6* and *r7*. You must use caution to ensure that you do not inadvertently add authentication to the *c-bgp* group, such as would occur if you carelessly apply the authentication-key statement at the global level.

```
[edit protocols bgp]
lab@r5# show
group 65001 {
    type internal;
    local-address 10.0.3.5;
    authentication-key "$9$GsjkPpu1Icl"; # SECRET-DATA
    cluster 2.2.2.2;
    no-client-reflect;
    neighbor 10.0.9.6;
    neighbor 10.0.9.7;
}
group c-bgp {
    type external;
    neighbor 10.0.2.2 {
        peer-as 65000;
    }
    neighbor 10.0.2.10 {
        peer-as 65000;
    }
}
```

You can determine that authentication is working properly when you see that the IBGP sessions have been correctly reestablished in subconfederation 65001. You will now address the following case study requirement:

- Redistribute the static routes shown earlier in Figure 5.9 into IBGP, and using communities, ensure that all routers prefer *r2*'s 192.168.100/24 IBGP route. You may not alter the default local preference of this route.

You begin this task by defining each router's static route(s), and by defining a basic BGP export policy such as the example shown here:

```
[edit policy-options]
lab@r1# show policy-statement ibgp
term 1 {
    from {
        protocol static;
        route-filter 192.168.0.0/16 longer;
    }
    then accept;
}
```

After defining all static routes and applying your BGP export policy on all routers, verifying the presence of the 192.168.*x*/24 and 192.168.100/24 routes quickly assesses the general health of your network. In this case study, this author has opted to apply the export policy once, at the global level, which causes static route redistribution for all IBGP and C-BGP peers:

```
[edit]
lab@r4# run show route protocol bgp | match 192.168 | count
Count: 7 lines
```

The indication that there are seven 192.168/16 BGP routes confirms your static route definitions and the proper operation of your basic IBGP export policy. To quickly validate r3's redistribution of its static route, and to verify the particulars of what routes are being advertised, the `terse` switch is used on r5 as shown next:

```
[edit]
lab@r5# run show route protocol bgp terse

inet.0: 34 destinations, 41 routes (34 active, 0 holddown, 0 hidden)
+ = Active Route, - = Last Active, * = Both
```

A Destination	P Prf	Metric 1	Metric 2	Next hop	AS path
* 192.168.10.0/24	B 170	100	0	>as1.0 at-0/2/1.35	(65000) I
	B 170	100	0	>as1.0 at-0/2/1.35	(65000) I
* 192.168.20.0/24	B 170	100	0	as1.0 >at-0/2/1.35	(65000) I
	B 170	100	0	as1.0 >at-0/2/1.35	(65000) I

```
* 192.168.30.0/24    B 170      100         0 >10.0.2.2      (65000) I
                     B 170      100         0 >at-0/2/1.35   (65000) I
* 192.168.40.0/24    B 170      100         0 >10.0.2.10     (65000) I
                     B 170      100         0 >as1.0         (65000) I
* 192.168.60.0/24    B 170      100         0 >10.0.8.5              I
* 192.168.70.0/24    B 170      100         0 >10.0.8.10             I
* 192.168.100.0/24   B 170      100         0 >as1.0         (65000) I
                                              at-0/2/1.35
                     B 170      100         0 >as1.0         (65000) I
                                              at-0/2/1.35
```

With basic redistribution working, you now tackle the "routers must prefer r2's advertisement using communities" issue, without modifying the route's local preference. This is accomplished by defining a unique community tag at r2 according to the algorithm <as-number:router-number>, and by instructing r2 to attach this community only to the 192.168.100.0/24 route through the *ibgp* export modifications shown with highlights. Other routers will match on this community tag to set the route's preference to a value lower (and therefore more preferred) than the default BGP preference setting of 170, as described later in this section.

```
[edit]
lab@r2# show policy-options policy-statement ibgp
term 1 {
    from {
        protocol static;
        route-filter 192.168.0.0/16 longer;
        route-filter 192.168.100.0/24 exact next term;
    }
    then accept;
}
term 2 {
    from {
        route-filter 192.168.100.0/24 exact;
    }
    then {
        community add r2;
        accept;
    }
}
```

```
[edit]
lab@r2# show policy-options community r2
members 65412:2;
```

Next, you define the *r2* community on r3 and r4, and you write a BGP import policy that will match on this community with the intent of setting a preference setting less than 170 in these routers. Because r1 and r2 will use their local static route in lieu of any learned BGP routes, there is no need to address their configurations further. Similarly, r6 and r7 will fall into "line" with whatever route is chosen as active by r5, and because r5 will receive updates only for the active routes as selected by r3 and r4, you will not need the community definition or *prefer-2* import policy on r5, r6, or r7. Defining the *r2* community and *prefer-2* import policy on all routers should not cause any operation impact, however. The modifications to r3's configuration are shown next. Similar changes are needed for r4.

```
[edit]
lab@r3# show policy-options policy-statement prefer-2
term 1 {
    from community r2;
    then {
        preference 20;
    }
}
```

```
[edit]
lab@r3# show policy-options community r2
members 65412:2;
```

```
[edit]
lab@r3# show protocols bgp import
import prefer-2;
```

In this example, the *prefer-2* policy has been applied globally, even though it is needed only on the peering session to r2. This global application should cause no harm, because only r2 is attaching this community. To confirm the correct behavior, we display r3's route table entry for the 192.168.100/24 route:

```
[edit]
lab@r3# run show route 192.168.100/24

inet.0: 38 destinations, 50 routes (37 active, 0 holddown, 2 hidden)
+ = Active Route, - = Last Active, * = Both
```

```
192.168.100.0/24    *[BGP/20] 00:44:33, MED 0, localpref 100, from 10.0.6.2
                        AS path: I
                      > to 10.0.4.2 via fe-0/0/1.0
                       [BGP/170] 00:45:51, MED 0, localpref 100, from 10.0.6.1
                        AS path: I
                      > to 10.0.4.14 via fe-0/0/0.0
```

These results confirm that r2's route is preferred, despite r1 having the lower, and therefore more preferred, RID assignment. Also note that both routes correctly display the default local preference setting, as required by your case study restrictions. The results from r5 confirm that both r3 and r4 have selected r2's route, which means r5 will automatically fall into line, which is good because it really has little other choice in the matter:

```
[edit]
lab@r5# run show route 192.168.100/24

inet.0: 34 destinations, 41 routes (34 active, 0 holddown, 0 hidden)
+ = Active Route, - = Last Active, * = Both

192.168.100.0/24    *[BGP/170] 00:09:27, MED 0, localpref 100, from 10.0.2.2
                        AS path: (65000) I
                      > via as1.0
                        via at-0/2/1.35
                       [BGP/170] 00:09:23, MED 0, localpref 100, from 10.0.2.10
                        AS path: (65000) I
                      > via as1.0
                        via at-0/2/1.35
```

Though not shown in this display, the protocol next hop for both routes is 10.0.6.2, which proves that r2's advertisement has beaten out r1's. The correct protocol next hop is confirmed on r7 with use of the `detail` switch:

```
[edit]
lab@r7# run show route 192.168.100/24 detail

inet.0: 37 destinations, 38 routes (37 active, 0 holddown, 0 hidden)
192.168.100.0/24 (1 entry, 1 announced)
        *BGP    Preference: 170/-101
                Source: 10.0.3.5
                Nexthop: 10.0.8.9 via fe-0/3/1.0, selected
                Protocol Nexthop: 10.0.6.2 Indirect nexthop: 846e198 51
                State: <Active Int Ext>
                Local AS: 65001 Peer AS: 65001
```

```
Age: 10:37      Metric: 0       Metric2: 46
Task: BGP_65001.10.0.3.5+1055
Announcement bits (2): 0-KRT 6-Resolve inet.0
AS path: (65000) I
Communities: 65412:2
Localpref: 100
Router ID: 10.0.3.5
```

Before considering this task complete, you should temporarily remove r2's 192.168.100/24 static route to confirm that packets start going to r1:

```
[edit]
lab@r2# delete routing-options static route 192.168.100.0/24

[edit]
lab@r2# commit confirmed 5
commit complete
```

With r2 no longer advertising the 192.168.100/24 route (at least for the next five minutes or so), you reissue the show route command on r7:

```
[edit]
lab@r7# run show route 192.168.100/24 detail

inet.0: 37 destinations, 38 routes (37 active, 0 holddown, 0 hidden)
192.168.100.0/24 (1 entry, 1 announced)
        *BGP    Preference: 170/-101
                Source: 10.0.3.5
                Nexthop: 10.0.8.9 via fe-0/3/1.0, selected
                Protocol Nexthop: 10.0.6.1 Indirect nexthop: 846e110 50
                State: <Active Int Ext>
                Local AS: 65001 Peer AS: 65001
                Age: 12:11      Metric: 0       Metric2: 46
                Task: BGP_65001.10.0.3.5+1055
                Announcement bits (2): 0-KRT 6-Resolve inet.0
                AS path: (65000) I
                Localpref: 100
                Router ID: 10.0.3.5
```

The output confirms that failures of r2 will cause the route advertised by r1 to become active. You may notice some extra hops if you trace the route from r6 or r7 to the 192.168.100/24 prefix, as shown here:

```
[edit]
lab@r7# run traceroute 192.168.100.1
traceroute to 192.168.100.1 (192.168.100.1), 30 hops max, 40 byte packets
 1   10.0.8.9 (10.0.8.9)  0.339 ms  0.247 ms  0.216 ms
 2   10.0.2.10 (10.0.2.10)  0.286 ms  0.245 ms  0.231 ms
 3   10.0.4.10 (10.0.4.10)  0.173 ms  0.166 ms  0.169 ms
 4   10.0.4.5 (10.0.4.5)  0.483 ms  0.700 ms  0.379 ms
 5   10.0.4.5 (10.0.4.5)  0.363 ms !H  0.700 ms !H  0.372 ms !H
```

This behavior can be attributed to r5's OSPF load-balancing behavior to the 10.0.4/22 summary, which in this case has resulted in the use of r4 and the aggregated SONET interface when forwarding to the protocol next hop 10.0.6.1, as shown next:

```
[edit]
lab@r5# run show route 192.168.100/24

inet.0: 35 destinations, 44 routes (35 active, 0 holddown, 0 hidden)
+ = Active Route, - = Last Active, * = Both

192.168.100.0/24   *[BGP/170] 00:28:54, MED 0, localpref 100, from 10.0.3.3
                      AS path: (65000) I
                    > via as1.0
                      via at-0/2/1.35
                    [BGP/170] 00:11:19, MED 0, localpref 100, from 10.0.3.4
                      AS path: (65000) I
                    > via as1.0
                      via at-0/2/1.35
```

These results confirm that the extra hops in the traceroute are not the result of your IBGP design or its implementation. The next criterion to be addressed in the case study is:

- Redistribute a summary of the RIP routes into IBGP from both r6 and r7.

This requirement is easily accomplished with the highlighted modifications to the *ibgp* export policy on r6 and r7. Note that a 192.168.0/22 aggregate was already defined as part of the OSPF case study for redistribution into OSPF:

```
[edit policy-options policy-statement ibgp]
lab@r6# show
term 1 {
    from {
```

```
        protocol static;
        route-filter 192.168.0.0/16 longer;
    }
    then accept;
}
term 2 {
    from {
        protocol aggregate;
        route-filter 192.168.0.0/22 exact;
    }
    then accept;
}
```

We confirm the results at r5, where we expect to see BGP advertisements from both r6 and r7 reporting the summary route for the RIP prefixes:

```
[edit]
lab@r5# run show route 192.168.0/22

inet.0: 34 destinations, 44 routes (34 active, 0 holddown, 0 hidden)
+ = Active Route, - = Last Active, * = Both

192.168.0.0/22     *[OSPF/150] 00:00:06, metric 0, tag 0
                    > to 10.0.8.5 via fe-0/0/0.0
                      to 10.0.8.10 via fe-0/0/1.0
                    [BGP/170] 00:03:34, localpref 100, from 10.0.9.6
                      AS path: I
                    > to 10.0.8.5 via fe-0/0/0.0
                    [BGP/170] 00:03:30, localpref 100, from 10.0.9.7
                      AS path: I
                    > to 10.0.8.10 via fe-0/0/1.0
```

With r6 and r7 correctly sending the RIP summary to r5 through IBGP, the next requirement in the case study is the load-balancing behavior at r5 in accordance with this requirement:

- r5 must IBGP load-balance to the summary route representing the RIP prefixes.

With equal-cost IGP paths already in place between r5 and the source of the RIP routes, you will need to enable multipath in the 65000 peer group to facilitate the desired load balancing for IBGP. You will also need to adjust protocol preferences so that r5 prefers the BGP routing source to OSPF externals because the default preference assignments result in r5 choosing the OSPF routing source. The necessary changes to r5's configuration are highlighted here:

```
[edit]
lab@r5# show protocols bgp group 65001
```

```
type internal;
local-address 10.0.3.5;
authentication-key "$9$GsjkPpu1Icl"; # SECRET-DATA
cluster 2.2.2.2;
no-client-reflect;
multipath;
neighbor 10.0.9.6;
neighbor 10.0.9.7;
```

```
[edit]
lab@r5# show protocols ospf external-preference
external-preference 171;
```

Note that you could have achieved identical results by adjusting the BGP preference lower instead of making the OSPF protocol's higher. Proper operation is confirmed by verifying that the BGP route is now active, and that it has installed both of the IGP next hops that result from the recursive lookup of the protocol next hops 10.0.9.6 and 10.0.9.7 as advertised by r6 and r7, respectively:

```
[edit]
lab@r5# run show route 192.168.0/22
```

```
inet.0: 34 destinations, 43 routes (34 active, 0 holddown, 0 hidden)
+ = Active Route, - = Last Active, * = Both
```

```
192.168.0.0/22     *[BGP/170] 00:06:31, localpref 100, from 10.0.9.6
                      AS path: I
                    > to 10.0.8.5 via fe-0/0/0.0
                      to 10.0.8.10 via fe-0/0/1.0
                     [BGP/170] 00:06:03, localpref 100, from 10.0.9.7
                      AS path: I
                    > to 10.0.8.10 via fe-0/0/1.0
                     [OSPF/171] 00:06:15, metric 0, tag 0
                    > to 10.0.8.5 via fe-0/0/0.0
                      to 10.0.8.10 via fe-0/0/1.0
```

Compared to the previous display, the additional IGP next hops used to support IBGP load balancing are clearly evident. Your next challenge is to accommodate this stipulation:

- Make sure that r1 and r2 receive the RIP route summary from r3 and r4 through IBGP. You cannot change any protocol preference values on r3 or r4, and the BGP protocol next hop as seen by r1 and r2 must be the same as that seen by r5.

Because you cannot alter the global preference of BGP or OSPF on r3 and r4, you will have a problem getting the 192.168.0/22 BGP route received from r5 to be considered active. Simply redistributing the route from OSPF would result in r3 and r4 listing their own RIDs in the protocol next-hop field, thereby causing the protocol next hop at r1 and r2 to differ from the true protocol next hop as advertised by r6 and r7.

The best way out of this dilemma is to deploy the `advertise-inactive` knob to goad r3 and r4 into advertising a BGP route that is not active due to route preference. Policy will not be needed here, because the default IBGP export policy on the route reflectors causes BGP routes received from non-clients to be advertised to their clients, as listed in the BGP groups that are enabled for route reflection via the `cluster-id` keyword. The default BGP export behavior will therefore get the route to r1 and r2 as required. Besides, no amount of policy can ever be used to force the advertisement of a non-active route anyway.

The highlighted change to r3's configuration should also be added to r4's configuration:

```
[edit]
lab@r3# show protocols bgp group 65000
type internal;
local-address 10.0.3.3;
advertise-inactive;
cluster 1.1.1.1;
neighbor 10.0.6.1;
neighbor 10.0.6.2;
neighbor 10.0.3.4;
```

Confirmation of this task is quite easy. It is suggested that you first verify that r3 and r4 still prefer the OSPF route, which confirms that global preference values have not been altered (or at least that such alterations have had no net effect on your network), and then confirm that the routes are being advertised to r1 and r2 with the protocol next hop unchanged:

```
[edit]
lab@r3# run show route 192.168.0/22 detail

inet.0: 37 destinations, 43 routes (37 active, 0 holddown, 0 hidden)
192.168.0.0/22 (2 entries, 1 announced)
        *OSPF   Preference: 150
                Nexthop: via at-0/1/0.35, selected
                State: <Active Int Ext>
                Local AS: 65000
                Age: 3:38      Metric: 0       Tag: 0
                Task: OSPF
                Announcement bits (3): 0-KRT 3-BGP.0.0.0.0+179 4-Resolve inet.0
                AS path: I
```

```
        BGP     Preference: 170/-101
                Source: 10.0.2.1
                Nexthop: via at-0/1/0.35, selected
                Protocol Nexthop: 10.0.9.6 Indirect nexthop: 842b220 59
                State: <Int Ext>
                Inactive reason: Route Preference
                Local AS: 65000 Peer AS: 65001
                Age: 10:45      Metric2: 26
                Task: BGP_65001.10.0.2.1+179
                AS path: (65001) IAggregator: 65001 10.0.9.6
                Localpref: 100
                Router ID: 10.0.3.5
```

You can see that the BGP route is inactive in deference to the lower preference value associated with OSPF, and that the protocol next hop identifies r6 as the originator of the route. You now confirm that the 192.168.0/22 summary route is present in r1 as a BGP route with the protocol next hop as originally advertised by r6:

```
lab@r1> show route 192.168.0/22 detail

inet.0: 26 destinations, 36 routes (26 active, 0 holddown, 0 hidden)
192.168.0.0/22 (2 entries, 1 announced)
        *BGP    Preference: 170/-101
                Source: 10.0.3.3
                Nexthop: 10.0.4.13 via fe-0/0/1.200, selected
                Protocol Nexthop: 10.0.9.6 Indirect nexthop: 83e1198 44
                State: <Active Int Ext>
                Local AS: 65000 Peer AS: 65000
                Age: 13:32      Metric2: 11
                Task: BGP_65000.10.0.3.3+179
                Announcement bits (2): 0-KRT 2-Resolve inet.0
                AS path: (65001) IAggregator: 65001 10.0.9.6
                Localpref: 100
                Router ID: 10.0.3.3
        BGP     Preference: 170/-101
                Source: 10.0.3.4
                Nexthop: 10.0.4.13 via fe-0/0/1.200, selected
                Protocol Nexthop: 10.0.9.6 Indirect nexthop: 83e1198 44
                State: <NotBest Int Ext>
                Inactive reason: Cluster list length
                Local AS: 65000 Peer AS: 65000
                Age: 3:54       Metric2: 11
```

```
                    Task: BGP_65000.10.0.3.4+179
                    AS path: (65001) I (Originator)Aggregator: 65001 10.0.9.6
                    AS path: Cluster list:  1.1.1.1
                    AS path: Originator ID: 10.0.3.3
                    Localpref: 100
                    Router ID: 10.0.3.4
```

Good going—both r3 and r4 are advertising the route to client r1 in accordance with the specified restrictions. To complete the case study, you must now address the last requirement:

- Configure r7 to be passive, and ensure that its IBGP sessions operate with a 45-second keepalive interval. No other session keepalive intervals should be modified.

The changes needed on r5, r6, and r7 are highlighted next. You will need to adjust the BGP hold-time for all routers that IBGP-peer with r7, being careful to not modify the hold-time at either the group or global levels on r5 and r6, because you are not supposed to modify the hold-time parameters for sessions that do not involve r7. You need to modify the hold parameters on both sides of the peering session because BGP will choose the lesser of the hold times proposed during session negotiations with other routers:

```
[edit]
lab@r7# show protocols bgp
export ibgp;
group 65001 {
    type internal;
    local-address 10.0.9.7;
    hold-time 135;
    passive;
    authentication-key "$9$.fQnEhr1MX"; # SECRET-DATA
    neighbor 10.0.3.5;
    neighbor 10.0.9.6;
}
```

The required change to r6's configuration is highlighted next:

```
[edit protocols bgp]
lab@r6# show
export ibgp;
group 65001 {
    type internal;
    local-address 10.0.9.6;
    authentication-key "$9$TF6Ar1MWxd"; # SECRET-DATA
    neighbor 10.0.3.5;
    neighbor 10.0.9.7 {
```

```
    hold-time 135;
  }
}
```

The correct session hold time is easy enough to verify:

```
[edit protocols bgp]
lab@r7# run show bgp neighbor | match hold
  Options: <Preference LocalAddress HoldTime AuthKey Refresh Confed>
  Local Address: 10.0.9.7 Holdtime: 135 Preference: 170
  Peer ID: 10.0.3.5        Local ID: 10.0.9.7       Active Holdtime: 135
  Options: <Preference LocalAddress HoldTime AuthKey Refresh Confed>
  Local Address: 10.0.9.7 Holdtime: 135 Preference: 170
  Peer ID: 10.0.9.6        Local ID: 10.0.9.7       Active Holdtime: 135
```

You should compare these results to those displayed for sessions that do not involve r7 to make sure you have not mistakenly altered the hold-time of other sessions. The hold-time for all other BGP sessions should remain at the 30-second default.

IBGP Case Study Configurations

The modified configuration stanzas needed to complete the IBGP case study are in Listings 5.1 through 5.7, for all routers in the test bed, with changes highlighted.

Listing 5.1: *r1* IBGP-Related Configuration
```
[edit]
lab@r1# show protocols bgp
export ibgp;
group 65000 {
    type internal;
    local-address 10.0.6.1;
    neighbor 10.0.3.3;
    neighbor 10.0.3.4;
}
[edit]
lab@r1# show routing-options
static {
    route 10.0.200.0/24 {
        next-hop 10.0.1.102;
        no-readvertise;
    }
    route 192.168.10.0/24 reject;
    route 192.168.100.0/24 reject;
```

```
}
autonomous-system 65000;
confederation 65412 members [ 65000 65001 ];

[edit]
lab@r1# show policy-options
policy-statement external {
    term 1 {
        from {
            route-filter 10.0.5.0/24 exact;
        }
        then {
            metric 10;
            tag 420;
            external {
                type 1;
            }
            accept;
        }
    }
    term 2 {
        then reject;
    }
}
policy-statement ibgp {
    term 1 {
        from {
            protocol static;
            route-filter 192.168.0.0/16 longer;
        }
        then accept;
    }
}
```

Listing 5.2: *r2* **IBGP-Related Configuration**
```
[edit]
lab@r2# show protocols bgp
export ibgp;
group 65000 {
    type internal;
    local-address 10.0.6.2;
```

```
    neighbor 10.0.3.3;
    neighbor 10.0.3.4;
}

[edit]
lab@r2# show routing-options
static {
    route 10.0.200.0/24 {
        next-hop 10.0.1.102;
        no-readvertise;
    }
    route 192.168.20.0/24 reject;
    route 192.168.100.0/24 reject;
}
autonomous-system 65000;
confederation 65412 members [ 65000 65001 ];

[edit]
lab@r2# show policy-options
policy-statement external {
    term 1 {
        from {
            route-filter 10.0.5.0/24 exact;
        }
        then {
            metric 10;
            tag 420;
            external {
                type 1;
            }
            accept;
        }
    }
    term 2 {
        then reject;
    }
}
policy-statement ibgp {
    term 1 {
        from {
```

```
                protocol static;
                route-filter 192.168.0.0/16 longer;
                route-filter 192.168.100.0/24 exact next term;
            }
        then accept;
    }
    term 2 {
        from {
            route-filter 192.168.100.0/24 exact;
        }
        then {
            community add r2;
            accept;
        }
    }
}
community r2 members 65412:2;
```

Listing 5.3: *r3* IBGP-Related Configuration
```
[edit]
lab@r3# show protocols bgp
import prefer-2;
export ibgp;
group 65000 {
    type internal;
    local-address 10.0.3.3;
    advertise-inactive;
    cluster 1.1.1.1;
    neighbor 10.0.6.1;
    neighbor 10.0.6.2;
    neighbor 10.0.3.4;
}
group c-bgp {
    type external;
    multihop;
    neighbor 10.0.2.1 {
        peer-as 65001;
    }
}
```

```
[edit]
lab@r3# show routing-options
static {
    route 10.0.200.0/24 {
        next-hop 10.0.1.102;
        no-readvertise;
    }
    route 192.168.30.0/24 reject;
}
autonomous-system 65000;
confederation 65412 members [ 65000 65001 ];

[edit]
lab@r3# show policy-options
policy-statement ibgp {
    term 1 {
        from {
            protocol static;
            route-filter 192.168.0.0/16 longer;
        }
        then accept;
    }
}
policy-statement prefer-2 {
    term 1 {
        from community r2;
        then {
            preference 20;
        }
    }
}
community r2 members 65412:2;
```

Listing 5.4: *r4* **IBGP-Related Configuration**

```
[edit]
lab@r4# show protocols bgp
import prefer-2;
export ibgp;
group 65000 {
    type internal;
    local-address 10.0.3.4;
```

```
    advertise-inactive;
    cluster 1.1.1.1;
    neighbor 10.0.3.3;
    neighbor 10.0.6.1;
    neighbor 10.0.6.2;
}
group c-bgp {
    type external;
    neighbor 10.0.2.9 {
        peer-as 65001;
    }
}

[edit]
lab@r4# show routing-options
static {
    route 10.0.200.0/24 {
        next-hop 10.0.1.102;
        no-readvertise;
    }
    route 192.168.40.0/24 reject;
}
autonomous-system 65000;
confederation 65412 members [ 65000 65001 ];

[edit]
lab@r4# show policy-options
policy-statement ibgp {
    term 1 {
        from {
            protocol static;
            route-filter 192.168.0.0/16 longer;
        }
        then accept;
    }
}
policy-statement prefer-2 {
    term 1 {
        from community r2;
        then {
```

```
            preference 20;
        }
    }
}
community r2 members 65412:2;
```

Listing 5.5: *r5* **IBGP-Related Configuration**

```
[edit]
lab@r5# show protocols
bgp {
    export ibgp;
    group 65001 {
        type internal;
        local-address 10.0.3.5;
        authentication-key "$9$GsjkPpu1Icl"; # SECRET-DATA
        cluster 2.2.2.2;
        no-client-reflect;
        multipath;
        neighbor 10.0.9.6;
        neighbor 10.0.9.7;
    }
    group c-bgp {
        type external;
        neighbor 10.0.2.2 {
            peer-as 65000;
        }
        neighbor 10.0.2.10 {
            peer-as 65000;
        }
    }
}
ospf {
    external-preference 171;
    reference-bandwidth 1g;
    area 0.0.0.0 {
        authentication-type md5; # SECRET-DATA
        interface lo0.0;
        interface at-0/2/1.35 {
            authentication-key "$9$LaA7dskqf5F/" key-id 1; # SECRET-DATA
        }
        interface as1.0 {
```

```
                metric 6;
                authentication-key "$9$LBa7dskqf5F/" key-id 1; # SECRET-DATA
            }
        }
    area 0.0.0.20 {
        area-range 172.16.40.0/28;
        area-range 10.0.8.0/21;
        interface fe-0/0/0.0;
        interface fe-0/0/1.0;
    }
}

[edit]
lab@r5# show routing-options
static {
    route 10.0.200.0/24 {
        next-hop 10.0.1.102;
        no-readvertise;
    }
    route 192.168.50.0/24 reject;
}
autonomous-system 65001;
confederation 65412 members [ 65000 65001 ];

[edit]
lab@r5# show policy-options
policy-statement ibgp {
    term 1 {
        from {
            protocol static;
            route-filter 192.168.0.0/16 longer;
        }
        then accept;
    }
}
```

Listing 5.6: *r6* IBGP-Related Configuration

```
[edit]
lab@r6# show protocols bgp
export ibgp;
group 65001 {
```

```
    type internal;
    local-address 10.0.9.6;
    authentication-key "$9$TF6ArlMWxd"; # SECRET-DATA
    neighbor 10.0.3.5;
    neighbor 10.0.9.7 {
        hold-time 135;
    }
}

[edit]
lab@r6# show routing-options
static {
    route 10.0.200.0/24 {
        next-hop 10.0.1.102;
        no-readvertise;
    }
    route 192.168.60.0/24 reject;
}
aggregate {
    route 192.168.0.0/22;
}
autonomous-system 65001;
confederation 65412 members [ 65000 65001 ];

[edit]
lab@r6# show policy-options
policy-statement rip-in {
    term 1 {
        from {
            protocol rip;
            route-filter 192.168.0.0/22 orlonger;
        }
        then accept;
    }
    term 2 {
        then reject;
    }
}
policy-statement ospf-out {
    term 1 {
```

```
        from {
            protocol aggregate;
            route-filter 192.168.0.0/22 exact;
        }
        then accept;
    }
    term 2 {
        then reject;
    }
}
policy-statement rip-out {
    term 1 {
        from {
            protocol ospf;
            route-filter 10.0.5.0/24 exact;
        }
        then accept;
    }
    term 2 {
        then reject;
    }
}
policy-statement ibgp {
    term 1 {
        from {
            protocol static;
            route-filter 192.168.0.0/16 longer;
        }
        then accept;
    }
    term 2 {
        from {
            protocol aggregate;
            route-filter 192.168.0.0/22 exact;
        }
        then accept;
    }
}
```

Listing 5.7: *r7* **IBGP-Related Configuration**
[edit]

```
lab@r7# show protocols bgp
export ibgp;
group 65001 {
    type internal;
    local-address 10.0.9.7;
    hold-time 135;
    authentication-key "$9$.fQnEhrlMX"; # SECRET-DATA
    neighbor 10.0.3.5;
    neighbor 10.0.9.6;
}

[edit]
lab@r7# show routing-options
static {
    route 10.0.200.0/24 {
        next-hop 10.0.1.102;
        no-readvertise;
    }
    route 192.168.70.0/24 reject;
}
aggregate {
    route 192.168.0.0/22;
}
autonomous-system 65001;
confederation 65412 members [ 65000 65001 ];

[edit]
lab@r7# show policy-options
policy-statement rip-in {
    term 1 {
        from {
            protocol rip;
            route-filter 192.168.0.0/22 orlonger;
        }
        then accept;
    }
    term 2 {
        then reject;
    }
}
```

```
policy-statement ospf-out {
    term 1 {
        from {
            protocol aggregate;
            route-filter 192.168.0.0/22 exact;
        }
        then accept;
    }
    term 2 {
        then reject;
    }
}
policy-statement rip-out {
    term 1 {
        from {
            protocol ospf;
            route-filter 10.0.5.0/24 exact;
        }
        then accept;
    }
    term 2 {
        then reject;
    }
}
policy-statement ibgp {
    term 1 {
        from {
            protocol static;
            route-filter 192.168.0.0/16 longer;
        }
        then accept;
    }
    term 2 {
        from {
            protocol aggregate;
            route-filter 192.168.0.0/22 exact;
        }
        then accept;
    }
}
```

Spot the Issues: Review Questions

1. You are having problems establishing IBGP sessions between r3, r1, and r2 in the topology shown earlier in Figure 5.2. Can you spot the problem in r3's configuration?

```
[edit]
lab@r3# show protocols bgp
local-address 10.0.3.3;
group core {
    type internal;
    traceoptions {
        file r3-bgp;
        flag state detail;
    }
    authentication-key "$9$tOrr01h7Nbs2a"; # SECRET-DATA
    export ibgp;
    neighbor 10.0.3.4;
    neighbor 10.0.3.5;
}
group cluster-1111 {
    type internal;
    traceoptions {
        file r3-bgp;
        flag state detail;
    }
    authentication-key "$9$G3jkPpu1Icl"; # SECRET-DATA
    export ibgp;
    cluster 1.1.1.1;
    neighbor 10.0.4.14;
    neighbor 10.0.4.2;
}
```

2. Your goal is to advertise the 192.168.20/24 and 192.168.100/24 static routes into IBGP while attaching the *r2* community only to 192.168.100/24, as per this chapter's case study. Will the following policy work without any snags?

```
[edit]
lab@r2# show policy-options policy-statement ibgp
term 1 {
    from {
        protocol static;
```

```
            route-filter 192.168.0.0/16 longer;
            route-filter 192.168.100.0/24 exact next term;
        }
        then accept;
    }
    term 2 {
        then {
            community add r2;
            accept;
        }
    }
}
```

3. You are having problems getting BGP sessions established on r5 using the topology shown earlier in Figure 5.4. Any ideas?

```
[edit]
lab@r5# show routing-options
static {
    route 10.0.200.0/24 next-hop 10.0.1.102;
    route 192.168.50.0/24 reject;
}
aggregate {
    route 10.0.2.0/23;
    route 10.0.8.0/21;
    route 192.168.0.0/22;
    route 172.16.40.0/29;
}
autonomous-system 65412;
confederation 65412 members [ 65000 65001 65002 ];

[edit]
lab@r5# show protocols bgp
group 65002 {
    type internal;
    local-address 10.0.3.5;
    export ibgp;
    neighbor 10.0.9.6;
    neighbor 10.0.9.7;
}
group c-bgp {
    type external;
```

```
        multihop;
        local-address 10.0.3.5;
        export ibgp;
        neighbor 10.0.3.3 {
            peer-as 65000;
        }
        neighbor 10.0.3.4 {
            peer-as 65001;
        }
    }
```

4. A route exists in both OSPF and IBGP. You need to advertise it to a BGP peer without altering the protocol next hop. How can you accomplish this?

5. Will the following configuration support C-BGP peering between loopback addresses?

```
[edit]
lab@r5# show protocols bgp
group 65002 {
    type internal;
    local-address 10.0.3.5;
    export ibgp;
    neighbor 10.0.9.6;
    neighbor 10.0.9.7;
}
group c-bgp {
    type external;
    local-address 10.0.3.5;
    export ibgp;
    neighbor 10.0.3.3 {
        peer-as 65000;
    }
    neighbor 10.0.3.4 {
        peer-as 65001;
    }
}

[edit]
lab@r5# show routing-options
```

```
static {
    route 10.0.200.0/24 next-hop 10.0.1.102;
    route 192.168.50.0/24 reject;
}
aggregate {
    route 10.0.2.0/23;
    route 10.0.8.0/21;
    route 192.168.0.0/22;
    route 172.16.40.0/29;
}
autonomous-system 65002;
confederation 65412 members [ 65000 65001 65002 ];
```

6. Why will the following policy not advertise the 192.168.100/24 static route with a modified local preference?

```
[edit policy-options policy-statement static]
lab@r2# show
term 1 {
    from {
        protocol static;
        route-filter 192.168.20.0/24 exact;
    }
    then accept;
}
term 2 {
    from {
        protocol static;
        route-filter 192.168.100.0/24 orlonger;
    }
    then {
        local-preference 120;
    }
}
```

Spot the Issues: Answers

1. The global application of the local-address statement in r3's configuration is affecting the behavior of both the *core* and *cluster-1111* peer groups. With this configuration, r3 sources packets from its lo0 address when attempting to connect with r1 and r2, and this conflicts with their interface peering definitions, causing them to declare that r3's packets belong to an undefined peer. You can resolve this by removing the global application of local-address and reapplying it under the *core* group, or by applying the local-address statement at the neighbor level in the cluster-1111 group, being careful to specify the correct interface addresses, as shown next:

```
[edit protocols bgp group cluster-1111]
lab@r3# show
type internal;
traceoptions {
    file r3-bgp;
    flag state detail;
}
authentication-key "$9$G3jkPpu1Icl"; # SECRET-DATA
export ibgp;
cluster 1.1.1.1;
neighbor 10.0.4.14 {
    local-address 10.0.4.13;
}
neighbor 10.0.4.2 {
    local-address 10.0.4.1;
}
```

2. Well, not quite. It is true that the 192.168.20/24 route will be advertised without the *r2* community, and that the 192.168.100/24 route will be advertised with the *r2* community, but unfortunately, the *match all* nature of term 2 will result in r2's advertisement of *every* other active route in its routing table with the *r2* community attached. While some might argue that the policy meets the stated objectives, blatantly advertising OSPF and direct routes when a lab scenario does not call for such redistribution can result in point loss for not adhering to the specified goals. You can also encounter operational problems when routes are leaked with no reason. For example, think about what might happen in a complex internetworking topology should r2 suddenly start announcing a default route with a "prefer me" community attached to all its IBGP peers?

3. The problem here lies in r5's confederation and autonomous system–related configuration. The operator has incorrectly specified its autonomous system number as 65412 when it should have been 65002. This is causing the open messages it sends to its IBGP and C-BGP peers to indicate that it belongs to AS number 65412, which the peers see as an unauthorized connection attempt. The confederation AS number should only be seen by EBGP peers, but this configuration exposes all peers to the network's real AS number.

4. You could change protocol preferences to cause the BGP route to become active so that it is eligible for export. If preference adjustment is not possible, you will need to use the `advertise-inactive` option to instruct BGP to send the "best" BGP routes, even though some may currently be inactive because of the presence of a route with equal specificity having been learned through a protocol with a lower global preference.

5. No. The default behavior of EBGP will only support peering over a directly connected subnet. C-BGP peering between lo0 addresses requires the use of the `multihop` option in addition to the correct use of the `local-address` statement.

6. The issue with this policy lies in the absence of an `accept` action in term 2. You do not need to include an accept action for routes that are learned through BGP, because the default export policy for BGP is to advertise all BGP routes. You must include an explicit `accept` action to cause the redistribution of routes from all other protocol sources into BGP, however. As written, the 192.168.100/24 has a local preference attribute of 120 associated with it, but upon encountering the default BGP export policy the route meets up with a `reject` action and is therefore never exported.

Chapter 6

EBGP Configuration and Testing

JNCIP LAB SKILLS COVERED IN THIS CHAPTER:

- ✓ **EBGP peering**
  - Multihop and multipath
  - EBGP authentication
- ✓ **Routing policy**
  - Route damping
  - Martian filters
  - Local preference, MED, next hop self, etc.
- ✓ **Miscellaneous EBGP knobs**

This chapter details JNCIP-level EBGP and service provider (SP) routing policy configuration scenarios, and provides examples of the verification methods that can be used to confirm proper EBGP and policy operation. It is assumed that the configurations of the routers in your test bed currently reflect the case study criteria presented at the end of Chapter 5, "IBGP Configuration and Testing," which was built on top of the router configurations created during the OSPF case study in Chapter 3, "OSPF Configuration and Testing." You will now be adding EBGP functionality to your test bed, and a functional IGP and IBGP configuration is required for proper EBGP and routing policy operation. If you are unsure as to the state of your routers, you should compare your configurations against those provided in the case studies at the end of Chapters 1, 2, 3, and 5. Verify that all of your router interfaces, your OSPF IGP, and your IBGP case study configuration are operational before proceeding.

EBGP may need the services of your IGP to resolve next hops, but like IBGP, it does not really care about the particulars of your IGP so the EBGP configuration tasks presented in this chapter could easily be applied to a test bed running IS-IS, or even RIP! Using the OSPF case study configuration is highly recommended, however, because this will simplify the task of following the OSPF-based examples presented in this chapter.

Proper EBGP operation is a significant factor in the overall success of your network. Making serious mistakes with EBGP will impact your ability to demonstrate proper routing policy, and may even cause your network to operate erratically due to the large number of routes present in a complete BGP routing table. The reader should bear in mind that it can be difficult to fully separate the operation of IBGP and EBGP. Due to their interdependence, the configuration specifics of one may cause problems in the other. A good example would be the typical need for a next hop self policy on IBGP peering sessions to prevent unusable next hops from producing hidden BGP routes. A JNCIP exam candidate must be proficient in the configuration, testing, and troubleshooting of all things BGP if the candidate's resulting SP policy is to have any chance of working correctly.

Although the application of routing policy has been demonstrated throughout this book, most of your policy-related activities in the JNCIP examination are likely to be associated with the need to handle and process EBGP routes in typical SP fashion. In the end, you will likely agree that this chapter involves more routing policy–related activities than actual EBGP configuration, despite the chapter's "EBGP" title.

This chapter concludes with a case study designed to closely approximate a typical JNCIP routing policy and EBGP configuration scenario. The results of key operational mode commands are provided in the case study analysis section so that you can also compare the behavior of your network to a known good example. Sample router configurations that meet all case study requirements are provided at the end of the case study for comparison with your own configurations.

Initial EBGP Peering

The overall operation of your network at the end of this chapter will depend on the complex interplay of your IGP, IBGP, EBGP, and routing policy configurations. Their interdependency creates a sequencing problem because an EBGP peering session may be useless until you apply the appropriate EBGP policy and IBGP policy modifications to your network. Dealing with your EBGP peering definitions, your EBGP policy statements, and any required IBGP policy modifications all at once is a reasonable thing to do, but there is also merit in addressing these tasks sequentially. In the sequential approach, you first concentrate on getting your EBGP peering sessions up, then worry about your EBGP policy, and then deal with any IBGP modifications necessitated by the relative success of the first two tasks. This chapter is organized according to the latter philosophy, in part because the author feels it is a sound approach, but also because it simplifies the chapter's organization.

You will therefore begin with the configuration and verification of all the EBGP peering sessions in your network. After the EBGP peering sessions are operational, you will add a variety of EBGP import and export policy statements. Based on the overall operation of your EBGP policy, you will next decide what, if any, IBGP policy modifications are needed to achieve the synergistic operation that is required in an SP network. We start by reviewing the state of your network at the conclusion of the IBGP chapter's case study, which is shown in Figure 6.1. You will use this topology as the starting point for your EBGP configuration tasks.

You may want to review the case study configuration requirements from Chapter 5 to reacquaint yourself with the network that will now serve as the basis of your EBGP configuration activities. Figure 6.2 provides the information you will need to establish your EBGP peering sessions. The loopback addresses of all EBGP peers can be pinged (when routing policy is working), using a target address that is based on the prefix range owned by the remote AS in the form of $x.x.0.1$, such that C1's lo0 address will be 200.200.0.1, for example. In the actual JNCIP examination, the EBGP peer routers are not accessible by the candidate. To closely approximate the actual examination environment, this chapter does not detail the specifics of the EBGP peer router configurations. In general, each EBGP peer has the necessary EBGP peering configuration and one or more static routes that are advertised once the EBGP session is established. Some of these routes may consist of Martians or other prefixes that should be filtered at the edge of your autonomous system as specified by the details of your test scenario.

You will be able to follow the details of this chapter without the benefit of the extra routers that make up the various EBGP peers that are shown in Figure 6.1, but for maximum benefit at least some of the peers should be present in your test bed. This author was able to reduce the number of stand-alone EBGP routers needed by using multiple BGP routing instances.

As shown in Figure 6.2, your AS will now form EBGP sessions to various Customer, Transit, and Peer routers identified respectively on the figure as C, T, and P routers. To complete this section, you must configure your network to meet the following EBGP peering criteria:

- Establish all EBGP peering sessions shown with the following criteria:
  - You must be able to load balance over the two links connecting r4 to C1.
  - You must be able to load balance from r3 to T1 and T2.

- The P1 router is configured with a single neighbor statement. You must configure r1 and r2 to peer with P1 while ensuring that the failure of either r1 or r2 does not result in chronic loss of the routes advertised by P1.

- The T2 router uses authentication with secret *ebgp*.

- You must not view or modify the configurations of your EBGP peers.

- Static routes are permitted to accommodate EBGP load balancing only. These routes cannot be redistributed into your network.

FIGURE 6.1 IBGP case study topology

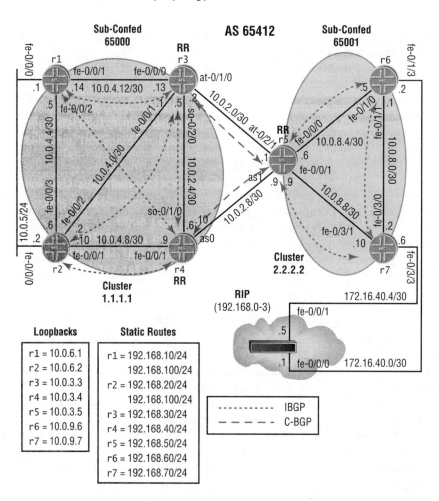

FIGURE 6.2   EBGP topology

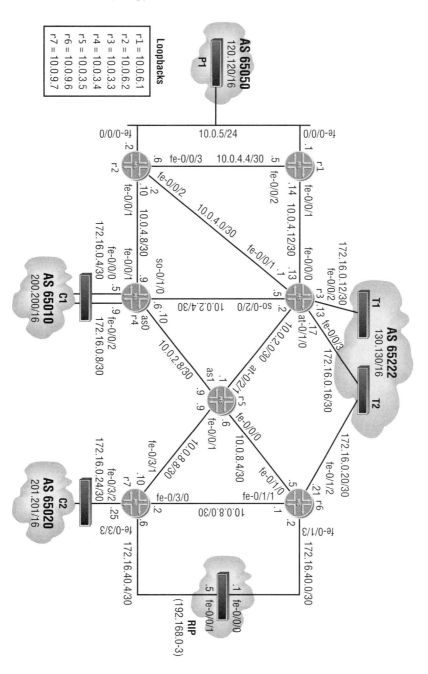

C2 EBGP Peering

You begin by configuring the EBGP peering session to C2, because this session represents the most straightforward of the EBGP peering tasks. The following commands create a new peer group called *c2* and correctly configure the group to peer with router C2:

```
[edit]
lab@r7# edit protocols bgp group c2

[edit protocols bgp group c2]
lab@r7# set type external neighbor 172.16.0.26

[edit protocols bgp group c2]
lab@r7# set peer-as 65020
```

The new peer group is displayed:

```
[edit protocols bgp group c2]
lab@r7# show
type external;
peer-as 65020;
neighbor 172.16.0.26;
```

To save time, you can omit the type statement in an EBGP peer group because the presence of the peer-as statement implies an external peer type.

After committing, the EBGP session status is analyzed:

```
[edit]
lab@r7# run show bgp summary
Groups: 2 Peers: 3 Down peers: 1
Table          Tot Paths  Act Paths Suppressed    History Damp State    Pending
inet.0                 8          7          0          0          0          0
Peer              AS      InPkt     OutPkt     OutQ    Flaps Last Up/Dwn
State|#Active/Received/Damped...
172.16.0.26    65020          0          0        0        0        5 Idle
10.0.3.5       65001        184        184        0        0  2:14:17 6/6/0
0/0/0
10.0.9.6       65001      25754        189        0        0  2:17:08 1/2/0
0/0/0
```

The session's `idle` status normally indicates that the router has no idea how to go about establishing the BGP session. This is a condition that typically results from not being able to route a connection request packet to the peer. This is confirmed with a quick ping test:

```
[edit]
lab@r7# run ping 172.16.0.26
PING 172.16.0.26 (172.16.0.26): 56 data bytes
ping: sendto: No route to host
ping: sendto: No route to host
^C
--- 172.16.0.26 ping statistics ---
2 packets transmitted, 0 packets received, 100% packet loss
```

The results confirm the routing problem. Because the EBGP peering address should be associated with a directly connected interface route, the status of r7's fe-0/3/2 interface is checked:

```
[edit]
lab@r7# run show interfaces fe-0/3/2 terse
Interface       Admin Link Proto Local              Remote
fe-0/3/2        up    up
```

The output confirms that the problem is caused by the lack of IP address configuration on r7's fe-0/3/2 interface. The correct address is now assigned and the change is committed:

```
[edit interfaces fe-0/3/2]
lab@r7# set unit 0 family inet address 172.16.0.25/30
```

```
[edit]
lab@r7# commit
commit complete
```

After waiting for a little while (30 seconds or so), the EBGP session status is again displayed:

```
[edit]
lab@r7# run show bgp summary
Groups: 2 Peers: 3 Down peers: 0
Table          Tot Paths  Act Paths Suppressed    History Damp State    Pending
inet.0               18        17          0          0         0           0
Peer             AS    InPkt    OutPkt    OutQ   Flaps Last Up/Dwn
State|#Active/Received/Damped...
172.16.0.26   65020       6        13      0       0      0 10/10/0
0/0/0
10.0.3.5      65001     194       195      0       0   2:21:51 6/6/0
0/0/0
```

```
10.0.9.6       65001    25764       200     0    0    2:24:42 1/2/0
0/0/0
```

The r7-to-C2 EBGP session has been established, and the display indicates the reception of 10 routes from C2 and that all of them have been installed as active. You just have to dig that! It is not a bad idea to also display the routes being received for each EBGP peering session because your future policy configuration will be impacted by what is, or is not, being advertised by your external peers:

```
[edit]
lab@r7# run show route receive-protocol bgp 172.16.0.26

inet.0: 48 destinations, 50 routes (48 active, 0 holddown, 0 hidden)
+ = Active Route, - = Last Active, * = Both

0.0.0.0/0
172.16.0.26             0               65020 62 39 I
64.0.0.0/7
172.16.0.26             0               65020 I
201.201.0.64/26
172.16.0.26             0               65020 I
201.201.1.0/24
172.16.0.26             0               65020 I
201.201.2.0/24
172.16.0.26             0               65020 I
201.201.3.0/24
172.16.0.26             0               65020 I
201.201.4.0/24
172.16.0.26             0               65020 I
201.201.5.0/24
172.16.0.26             0               65020 I
201.201.6.0/24
172.16.0.26             0               65020 I
201.201.7.0/24
172.16.0.26             0               65020 I
```

An interesting, if somewhat motley, collection of routes is being advertised by C2. The listing includes several 201.201/16–related prefixes, a default route, and a few other "nasties" that might necessitate future policy action to be sure.

C1 EBGP Peering

You now configure the r4-to-C1 peering session. In order to load balance over the two physical links, you will need to define a loopback-based peering session and the static routing needed to resolve the lo0 peering address to the appropriate physical next hops. This peer group also requires the `multihop` option to support the indirect lo0-based peering. The following commands create and configure the `c1` peer group on r4:

```
[edit protocols bgp group c1]
lab@r4# set type external neighbor 200.200.0.1
```

```
[edit protocols bgp group c1]
lab@r4# set peer-as 65010
```

```
[edit protocols bgp group c1]
lab@r4# set multihop
```
— *Since Peering is external and to loopback address*

The `c1` group is displayed:

```
[edit protocols bgp group c1]
lab@r4# show
type external;
multihop;
peer-as 65010;
neighbor 200.200.0.1;
```

You next configure and display the static routing needed to resolve C1's loopback address. The use of brackets allows you to specify the multiple next hops that are associated with the static route's destination on a single command line, if so desired:

```
[edit routing-options static]
lab@r4# set route 200.200.0.1 next-hop [172.16.0.6 172.16.0.10]
```

```
[edit routing-options static]
lab@r4# show
route 10.0.200.0/24 {
    next-hop 10.0.1.102;
    no-readvertise;
}
route 192.168.40.0/24 reject;
route 200.200.0.1/32 next-hop [ 172.16.0.6 172.16.0.10 ];
```

To complete the configuration of r4, you must assign the correct addresses to its fe-0/0/0 and fe-0/0/2 interfaces:

```
[edit interfaces]
lab@r4# set fe-0/0/0 unit 0 family inet address 172.16.0.5/30
```

```
[edit interfaces]
lab@r4# set fe-0/0/2 unit 0 family inet address 172.16.0.9/30
```

The status of the new peering session is displayed after the changes have been committed on r4:

```
[edit]
lab@r4# run show bgp summary
Groups: 3 Peers: 5 Down peers: 1
Table          Tot Paths  Act Paths Suppressed    History Damp State    Pending
inet.0              10        7          0            0         0           0
Peer            AS      InPkt     OutPkt    OutQ   Flaps Last Up/Dwn
State|#Active/Received/Damped...
200.200.0.1    65010        0          8       0       0       3:03 Active
10.0.2.9       65001      353      25780      0       0   2:51:20 3/4/0
0/0/0
10.0.3.3       65000    25872       5203      0       0   2:49:16 1/2/0
0/0/0
10.0.6.1       65000      339      25779      0       0   2:49:20 1/2/0
0/0/0
10.0.6.2       65000      343      25780      0       0   2:50:31 2/2/0
0/0/0
```

Due to the use of a fixed 30-second retry timer, BGP sessions can take what may seem an inordinate amount of time to become established. After making changes to a BGP peering configuration, you should make it a point to wait a minute or two before deciding whether the problem has been fixed. Some candidates are so "hyped-up" that they may alter a newly modified (and perhaps working) configuration, and in so doing break it again, because their instant gratification timer expires before the BGP retry time-out. This condition is especially true if the changes affect your IGP, as is the case when restarting rpd or clearing adjacencies, because BGP will now have to wait for the IGP to converge before it can even get started.

Troubleshoot EBGP Peering

The active indication in the previous screen capture indicates that r4 is actively trying to establish the EBGP session to C1, but considering that the condition has persisted for over a minute in this author's test bed, the prognosis for this connection suddenly entering the established state is starting to look mighty grim. Ping testing is used to determine if the problem relates to the physical layer, interface addressing, or static route definitions:

```
[edit]
lab@r4# run ping 172.16.0.6 count 1
PING 172.16.0.6 (172.16.0.6): 56 data bytes
64 bytes from 172.16.0.6: icmp_seq=0 ttl=255 time=0.596 ms

--- 172.16.0.6 ping statistics ---
1 packets transmitted, 1 packets received, 0% packet loss
round-trip min/avg/max/stddev = 0.596/0.596/0.596/0.000 ms

[edit]
lab@r4# run ping 172.16.0.10 count 1
PING 172.16.0.10 (172.16.0.10): 56 data bytes
64 bytes from 172.16.0.10: icmp_seq=0 ttl=255 time=0.599 ms

--- 172.16.0.10 ping statistics ---
1 packets transmitted, 1 packets received, 0% packet loss
round-trip min/avg/max/stddev = 0.599/0.599/0.599/0.000 ms
```

The 172.16.0.4/30 and 172.16.0.8/30 subnets appear to be functional, which vindicates your interface configuration and their physical and link-level operation. You now test reachability to C1's loopback address:

```
[edit]
lab@r4# run ping 200.200.0.1 count 1
PING 200.200.0.1 (200.200.0.1): 56 data bytes
64 bytes from 200.200.0.1: icmp_seq=0 ttl=255 time=0.605 ms

--- 200.200.0.1 ping statistics ---
1 packets transmitted, 1 packets received, 0% packet loss
round-trip min/avg/max/stddev = 0.605/0.605/0.605/0.000 ms
```

Because the r4-to-C1 peering session must be established between loopback addresses, it is a good idea to evoke the local switch in order to source the ping from r4's loopback address.

This confirms that C1 also has the static routing needed to support the lo0-based peering session in place:

```
[edit]
lab@r4# run ping 200.200.0.1 local 10.0.3.4 count 1
PING 200.200.0.1 (200.200.0.1): 56 data bytes
64 bytes from 200.200.0.1: icmp_seq=0 ttl=255 time=0.612 ms

--- 200.200.0.1 ping statistics ---
1 packets transmitted, 1 packets received, 0% packet loss
round-trip min/avg/max/stddev = 0.612/0.612/0.612/0.000 ms
```

All four of the ping tests succeed, which provides a strong indication that the problem relates to the EBGP peering definition for C1 on r4. Although the astute reader will likely already know what is wrong with r4's configuration, an example of EBGP tracing is provided to demonstrate its utility in times like these. The following highlighted capture shows the tracing configuration that has been added to r4; note that the tracing is applied only to the c1 peer group to minimize trace output clutter and the router's processing burden:

```
[edit protocols bgp group c1]
lab@r4# show
type external;
traceoptions {
    file c1;
    flag open detail;
}
multihop;
peer-as 65010;
neighbor 200.200.0.1;
```

Key portions of the trace output are shown next. Can you spot the problem?

```
[edit]
lab@r4#
*** c1 ***
Jun 18 12:36:54 bgp_send: sending 45 bytes to 200.200.0.1 (External AS 65010)
Jun 18 12:36:54
Jun 18 12:36:54 BGP SEND 172.16.0.5+1074 -> 200.200.0.1+179
Jun 18 12:36:54 BGP SEND message type 1 (Open) length 45
Jun 18 12:36:54 BGP SEND version 4 as 65412 holdtime 90 id 10.0.3.4 parmlen 16
Jun 18 12:36:54 MP capability AFI=1, SAFI=1
Jun 18 12:36:54 Refresh capability, code=128
```

```
Jun 18 12:36:54 Refresh capability, code=2
Jun 18 12:36:54
Jun 18 12:36:54 BGP RECV 200.200.0.1+179 -> 172.16.0.5+1074
Jun 18 12:36:54 BGP RECV message type 1 (Open) length 29
Jun 18 12:36:54 BGP RECV version 4 as 65010 holdtime 90 id 200.200.0.1 parmlen 0
Jun 18 12:36:54
Jun 18 12:36:54 BGP RECV 200.200.0.1+179 -> 172.16.0.5+1074
Jun 18 12:36:54 BGP RECV message type 3 (Notification) length 21
Jun 18 12:36:54 BGP RECV Notification code 2 (Open Message Error) subcode 5
(authentication failure)

*** monitor and syslog output disabled, press ESC-Q to enable ***
```

If you noted the fact that r4 is incorrectly sourcing its TCP connection from its physical inter-face address, as opposed to its loopback address, then you are spot on. The last few lines of trace output indicate that C1 is rejecting r4's open message because it is presenting itself as *172.16.0.5*, which is an undefined peer. Because BGP was originally intended to operate between autonomous networks, the protocol is designed to require explicit declaration of peers as a means for enhanc-ing security, in that the lack of a corresponding peer statement will prevent the establishment of unauthorized BGP sessions. This aspect of EBGP accounts for the authentication-related error message generated when an unknown peer attempts to establish a BGP session.

JUNOS software supports BGP peer declarations that are based on address blocks, instead of host addresses using the allow keyword. For example, specifying allow 10/8 would permit BGP sessions from any BGP speaker with a 10.*x.x.x* address while "promiscuous" operation can be achieved by specifying an address of 0.0.0.0. Normally the passive keyword is used in conjunction with the allow keyword because the lack of explicit peer definitions prevents the local router from being able to successfully initiate BGP connections.

Because the local-address statement has "conveniently" been omitted from C1's configura-tion, you must include this statement on r4 or the session will never be established. The following configuration adds the required local-address statement, and deletes the trace configuration because its purpose has been served:

```
[edit protocols bgp group c1]
lab@r4# delete traceoptions

[edit protocols bgp group c1]
lab@r4# set local-address 10.0.3.4
```

The modified stanza is displayed next with the change highlighted:

```
[edit protocols bgp group c1]
lab@r4# show
type external;
```

```
multihop;
local-address 10.0.3.4;
peer-as 65010;
neighbor 200.200.0.1;
```

The status of the C1 EBGP session is again displayed a minute or so after you have committed the changes on r4:

```
[edit protocols bgp group c1]
lab@r4# run show bgp summary
Groups: 3 Peers: 5 Down peers: 0
Table          Tot Paths  Act Paths Suppressed   History Damp State   Pending
inet.0              22        19          0          0          0          0
Peer             AS    InPkt    OutPkt   OutQ   Flaps Last Up/Dwn
State|#Active/Received/Damped...
200.200.0.1   65010     5         9       0       0       15 12/12/0
0/0/0
10.0.2.9      65001    518      25947     0       0    4:13:45 3/4/0
0/0/0
10.0.3.3      65000    26037     5370     0       0    4:11:41 1/2/0
0/0/0
10.0.6.1      65000    504      25946     0       0    4:11:45 1/2/0
0/0/0
10.0.6.2      65000    508      25947     0       0    4:12:56 2/2/0
0/0/0
```

Good, the r4–C1 EBGP session has been established. You decide to display the routes being received from C1 to confirm what you are dealing with and whether the correct load-balancing behavior has been achieved:

```
[edit protocols bgp group c1]
lab@r4# run show route receive-protocol bgp 200.200.0.1

inet.0: 48 destinations, 52 routes (48 active, 0 holddown, 0 hidden)
+ = Active Route, - = Last Active, * = Both


32.0.0.0/16
200.200.0.1              0              65010 420 I
200.200.0.0/24
200.200.0.1              0              65010 I
200.200.0.0/28
200.200.0.1              0              65010 I
200.200.1.0/24
200.200.0.1              0              65010 I
```

```
200.200.2.0/24
200.200.0.1                   0                   65010 I
200.200.3.0/24
200.200.0.1                   0                   65010 I
200.200.4.0/24
200.200.0.1                   0                   65010 I
200.200.5.0/24
200.200.0.1                   0                   65010 I
200.200.5.128/25
200.200.0.1                   0                   65010 I
200.200.6.0/24
200.200.0.1                   0                   65010 I
200.200.7.0/24
200.200.0.1                   0                   65010 I
```

As with C2, there appears to be an interesting assortment of routes being advertised by C1—you will revisit the specifics of these routes later when creating and applying your EBGP policy. To confirm load balancing, verify that both r4's fe-0/0/0 and fe-0/0/2 interfaces are listed as the forwarding next hops for the routes that are learned from C1:

```
[edit protocols bgp group c1]
lab@r4# run show route protocol bgp 200.200.0.0/24

inet.0: 48 destinations, 52 routes (48 active, 0 holddown, 0 hidden)
+ = Active Route, - = Last Active, * = Both

200.200.0.0/24      *[BGP/170] 00:08:08, MED 0, localpref 100, from 200.200.0.1
                       AS path: 65010 I
                     > to 172.16.0.6 via fe-0/0/0.0
                       to 172.16.0.10 via fe-0/0/2.0
200.200.0.0/28      *[BGP/170] 00:08:08, MED 0, localpref 100, from 200.200.0.1
                       AS path: 65010 I
                     > to 172.16.0.6 via fe-0/0/0.0
                       to 172.16.0.10 via fe-0/0/2.0
```

Both forwarding next hops are correctly displayed, indicating that the r4–C1 EBGP session is now operating correctly.

P1 EBGP Peering

This section deals with the configuration of the EBGP session between r1, r2, and the P1 router. This task is made complex by the indication that P1 is configured with a *single* EBGP peering definition and the requirement that the failure of either r1 or r2 should not result in a long-term loss of P1's routes within your network. Because BGP does not support point-to-multipoint modes of operation, peering two routers to a machine configured with a single neighbor statement may seem to verge on the impossible.

To get the ball rolling, the following configuration is committed on r1 to reverse engineer P1's address assignment and BGP neighbor definition. The neighbor address has been chosen at random from the 10.0.5/24 subnet to allow the trace-related configuration to commit.

```
[edit protocols bgp group p1]
lab@r1# show
type external;
traceoptions {
    file p1;
    flag open detail;
}
peer-as 65050;
neighbor 10.0.5.10;
```

Unfortunately, the trace output affords you little help in this case:

```
Jun 18 21:58:35 bgp_connect_complete: error connecting to 10.0.5.10 (External AS
65050): Socket is not connected
```

Looks like it may be time to throw r1's fe-0/0/0 interface into promiscuous mode to see if anything of interest is hitting the wire:

```
[edit]
lab@r1# run monitor traffic interface fe-0/0/0
Listening on fe-0/0/0
22:09:50.950616 Out VID [7: 150] 10.0.5.1 > 224.0.0.18:  ip-proto-112 20
. . .
22:09:58.020679 Out VID [7: 150] 10.0.5.1 > 224.0.0.18:  ip-proto-112 20
22:09:58.351962  In VID [0: 150] 10.0.5.254.1045 > 10.0.5.200.bgp: S
3318404620:3318404620(0) win 16384 <mss 1456,nop,wscale 0,nop,nop,timestamp
1984619 0> [tos 0xc0]
22:09:59.030732 Out VID [7: 150] 10.0.5.1 > 224.0.0.18:  ip-proto-112 20
. . .
```

The highlighted entry provides the information being sought. The output confirms that P1's address is 10.0.5.254, and that it has been configured to peer with 10.0.5.200, which is the VRRP virtual IP (VIP) address shared by r1 and r2. The requirement that both r1 and r2 should peer to a router with a single neighbor statement, and that the failure of either r1 or r2 should not disrupt this peering session, suddenly becomes feasible when illuminated by this newfound information.

To test the hypothesis that P1 is supposed to (or even can) peer with the VIP address shared by r1 and r2, you make the highlighted changes to r1's configuration:

```
[edit protocols bgp group p1]
lab@r1# show
type external;
traceoptions {
    file p1;
    flag open detail;
}
local-address 10.0.5.200;
peer-as 65050;
neighbor 10.0.5.254;
```

A few minutes after the changes are committed, the session is still down so something else must be amiss. Analyzing the **p1** trace file uncovers another clue:

```
Jun 18 22:28:54 task_addr_local: task BGP_65050.10.0.5.254 address 10.0.5.200:
Can't assign requested address
Jun 18 22:28:54 bgp_select_myaddr: peer 10.0.5.254 (External AS 65050) local
address 10.0.5.200 unavailable, connection failed
```

Seems like r1 is having trouble sourcing packets from its VIP address. Displaying the VRRP status confirms that it is the current master, however:

```
[edit protocols bgp group p1]
lab@r1# run show vrrp summary
Interface   Unit   Group   Type   Address        Int state   VR state
fe-0/0/0    0      1       lcl    10.0.5.1       up          master
                           vip    10.0.5.200
```

Any ideas? Another invaluable clue is obtained by r2's indication that pings to the VIP address fail:

```
[edit]
lab@r2# run ping 10.0.5.200 count 1
PING 10.0.5.200 (10.0.5.200): 56 data bytes
^C
--- 10.0.5.200 ping statistics ---
1 packets transmitted, 0 packets received, 100% packet loss
```

Examining r2's ARP cache confirms that r1 has responded to ARP request for the VIP address:

```
[edit]
lab@r2# run show arp | match 10.0.5.200
00:00:5e:00:01:01 10.0.5.200      10.0.5.200              fe-0/0/0.0
```

At this point, you should recall that, according to the VRRP standard, with the exception of ARP replies, a router can respond to traffic addressed to the VIP only when it is the VRRP group's master and when the VIP is actually assigned to one of its interfaces. You should also recall that JUNOS software provides a knob that allows a router to respond to traffic sent to the VIP address, even though this address is not assigned to any of its interfaces. This sounds like an option worth exploring, so the following change is committed:

```
[edit interfaces fe-0/0/0 unit 0 family inet address 10.0.5.1/24]
lab@r1# set vrrp-group 1 accept-data
```

A minute or so later, the BGP session status on r1 is again displayed:

```
[edit]
lab@r1# run show bgp summary
Groups: 2 Peers: 3 Down peers: 0
Table          Tot Paths  Act Paths Suppressed    History Damp State    Pending
inet.0             38         26         0            0         0          0
Peer             AS      InPkt     OutPkt    OutQ   Flaps Last Up/Dwn
State|#Active/Received/Damped...
10.0.3.3       65000      46        40        0      2    17:12 3/8/0
0/0/0
10.0.3.4       65000      48        39        0      2    17:12 13/20/0
0/0/0
10.0.5.254     65050      19        26        0      0    6:03 10/10/0
0/0/0
```

Excellent! The change to the VRRP configuration has done the trick. You will need to define a similar p1 peering group on r2, being sure to also add the `accept-data` option to r2's VRRP configuration. You should also remove the BGP tracing configuration from r1 before proceeding. After committing the changes on r2, deactivate r1's fe-0/0/0 interface to confirm that the VRRP mastership changes and that the EBGP session follows the VIP over to r2. Before deactivating r1's interface, the VRRP status and P1 peering session are displayed on r2:

```
lab@r2# run show vrrp summary
Interface   Unit  Group  Type  Address        Int state   VR state
Fe-0/0/0     0     1     lcl   10.0.5.2        up          backup
                          vip   10.0.5.200
[edit protocols bgp]
lab@r2# run show bgp summary | match 10.0.1.254
10.0.1.254     65050      0         0         0      0             22 Active
```

After r1's fe-0/0/0 interface is deactivated, the change in r2's VRRP status is confirmed:

```
[edit protocols bgp]
lab@r2# run show vrrp summary
Interface   Unit  Group  Type  Address         Int state   VR state
fe-0/0/0    0     1      lcl   10.0.5.2        up          master
                         vip   10.0.5.200
```

The VIP is now owned by r2, so in a few minutes we expect to see the P1 EBGP session roll over to r2. The EBGP session must be torn down and reestablished as a result of the VRRP mastership change, so it may take a minute or two before r2 begins displaying routes from the P1 router. During the transition and reestablishment of the EBGP session, the routes learned from the P1 router will be withdrawn from your network. As long as the EBGP session successfully rolls over to r2, the loss of P1's EBGP routes will be short-term, which is in accordance with the configuration criteria presented in this section:

```
[edit protocols bgp group p1]
lab@r2# run show bgp summary | match 10.0.5.254
10.0.5.254   65050        9        16      0      0         18 10/10/0       0/0/0
```

The output confirms that the EBGP session has followed the VIP as planned. After restoring r1's fe-0/0/0 interface, confirm that the BGP session successfully rolls back to r1 and display the routes being advertised by P1 using the **source-gateway** switch:

```
[edit]
lab@r1# run show route protocol bgp source-gateway 10.0.5.254

inet.0: 46 destinations, 56 routes (43 active, 0 holddown, 3 hidden)
+ = Active Route, - = Last Active, * = Both

120.120.0.0/24    *[BGP/170] 00:00:33, MED 0, localpref 100
                     AS path: 65050 I
                  > to 10.0.5.254 via fe-0/0/0.0
120.120.1.0/24    *[BGP/170] 00:00:33, MED 0, localpref 100
                     AS path: 65050 I
                  > to 10.0.5.254 via fe-0/0/0.0
120.120.2.0/24    *[BGP/170] 00:00:33, MED 0, localpref 100
                     AS path: 65050 I
                  > to 10.0.5.254 via fe-0/0/0.0
120.120.3.0/24    *[BGP/170] 00:00:33, MED 0, localpref 100
                     AS path: 65050 I
                  > to 10.0.5.254 via fe-0/0/0.0
```

```
120.120.4.0/24     *[BGP/170] 00:00:33, MED 0, localpref 100
                      AS path: 65050 I
                    > to 10.0.5.254 via fe-0/0/0.0
120.120.5.0/24     *[BGP/170] 00:00:33, MED 0, localpref 100
                      AS path: 65050 I
                    > to 10.0.5.254 via fe-0/0/0.0
120.120.6.0/24     *[BGP/170] 00:00:33, MED 0, localpref 100
                      AS path: 65050 I
                    > to 10.0.5.254 via fe-0/0/0.0
120.120.7.0/24     *[BGP/170] 00:00:33, MED 0, localpref 100
                      AS path: 65050 I
                    > to 10.0.5.254 via fe-0/0/0.0
120.120.69.128/25  *[BGP/170] 00:00:33, MED 0, localpref 100
                      AS path: 65050 I
                    > to 10.0.5.254 via fe-0/0/0.0
```

The establishment of an EBGP session that successfully tracks the VIP address associated with r1 and r2 confirms that you have successfully configured r1 and r2 to peer with the P1 router.

T2 EBGP Peering

This section details the configuration of the EBGP session between r6 and transit provider T2. There is nothing particularly fancy about this task because EBGP authentication is configured in the same manner as that demonstrated for IBGP in Chapter 5. The following commands are entered on r6 to configure the t2 peer group:

```
[edit protocols bgp group t2]
lab@r6# set type external neighbor 172.16.0.22
```

```
[edit protocols bgp group t2]
lab@r6# set peer-as 65222 authentication-key ebgp
```

The completed t2 peer group configuration is displayed:

```
lab@r6# show
type external;
authentication-key "$9$vxvWLNVb2UDkwY"; # SECRET-DATA
peer-as 65222;
neighbor 172.16.0.22;
```

You now assign the correct IP address to r6's fe-0/1/2 interface:

```
[edit interfaces fe-0/1/2]
lab@r6# set unit 0 family inet address 172.16.0.21/30
```

The BGP session status is displayed a few minutes after committing the changes on r6:

```
[edit]
lab@r6# run show bgp summary
Groups: 2 Peers: 3 Down peers: 0
Table          Tot Paths  Act Paths Suppressed    History Damp State    Pending
inet.0            111230     111218          0          0        0           0
Peer              AS     InPkt     OutPkt    OutQ    Flaps Last Up/Dwn
State|#Active/Received/Damped...
172.16.0.22     65222     26760      26970       0        0       13:00 111235/
111235/0        0/0/0
10.0.3.5        65001       858      49247       0        0     7:02:43 16/16/0
0/0/0
10.0.9.7        65001       572      52301       0        0     7:05:31 1/13/0
0/0/0
```

The EBGP session to T2 has been established, which indicates that compatible authentication settings are in effect. And no, that is not a typo in the screen capture; r6 really is receiving 111,235 routes from T2!

As with the actual JNCIP examination, this author's test bed has been outfitted with a live BGP feed that carries a full Internet routing table. From here on out, the stakes have been significantly raised, because what might otherwise be classified as an innocuous mistake can now prove disastrous with this many routes floating around in your AS.

Having a full Internet routing table adds realism, complexity, and danger to the JNCIP examination. The realism and complexity aspects are the natural side effects of having so many darned routes to filter and parse through when looking for a particular route or community value. From now on, you should plan on filtering the output of show route commands so that the JUNOS software CLI does as much of the work for you as possible. The "danger" aspect relates to the fact that making a mistake, such as redistributing over 100,000 BGP routes into RIP, can lead to unexpected behavior and the possible meltdown of your network!

The well-written and modular nature of JUNOS software coupled with the ASIC-based design of the M-series and T-series routers creates a synergistic combination proven to carry more routes, converge faster, and be more stable than any other vendor's equipment produced to date. Even so, the complex nature of a routing system coupled with the myriad ways in which various features can be configured and combined results in every network being a little distinct, to say the least. Although this author has intentionally redistributed a full Internet routing table into OSPF successfully several times during classroom demonstrations, the key words in that statement are "classroom" and "intentional." Generally speaking, the time-constrained JNCIP lab environment is not the best place to conduct stress testing of a Juniper Networks router!

By way of example, instances have been observed in which setting next hop self in an EBGP *import* policy can result in an rpd core dump, while the same policy applied to a router with a paltry 18 routes results in nothing worse than having 18 routes that are hidden due to unusable next hops. The attentive reader should have noticed that the instructions provided in this chapter have guided the reader in the careful application of BGP tracing (for example, tracing just the problematic neighbor or group instead of applying the trace configuration at the global level), and have repeatedly advised you to remove tracing configurations after they have served their purpose.

To be clear, there is nothing wrong with leaving a tracing configuration in place that is selective and applied at a neighbor level, but applying a `flag all detail` tracing configuration globally, with this many routes being bandied about, can significantly delay network convergence and result in a slew of other problems ranging from scheduler slips to mysterious operation that cannot be reproduced. To put this into perspective, most experienced operators would consider typing the Cisco IOS command `debug all` to be the work of a fool, even on a router with only a few dozen routes, while in contrast it is more realistic to routinely trace BGP operation on Juniper Networks routers with full Internet routing feeds. The point is to use common sense when tracing by trying to be as selective as you can, both in the definition of what is being flagged for tracing, as well as where the tracing stanza is configured (i.e., at the global, group, or neighbor hierarchical levels).

Also, you should consider deactivating or deleting the tracing stanza if you sense that the router begins acting "funny" after the trace configuration is committed. This author once saw a candidate who was tracing all BGP packets at the global level and who repeatedly restarted routing and rebooted the routers that were thought to be misbehaving. These actions served only to exacerbate the problems, however, because the constant teardown and reestablishment of the BGP sessions resulted in an ongoing tsunami of BGP packets to be traced.

T1 EBGP Peering

This section describes the configuration of the EBGP session between r3 and the T1 and T2 routers. The need for load balancing to the routes advertised by the T1 and T2 routers necessitates the use of the `multipath` option. The following commands are entered on r3 to configure the t1–t2 peer group:

```
[edit protocols bgp group t1-t2]
lab@r3# set type external peer-as 65222
```

```
[edit protocols bgp group t1-t2]
lab@r3# set neighbor 172.16.0.14
```

```
[edit protocols bgp group t1-t2]
lab@r3# set neighbor 172.16.0.18
```

```
[edit protocols bgp group t1-t2]
lab@r3# set multipath
```

The resulting t1–t2 peer group is displayed:

```
[edit protocols bgp group t1-t2]
lab@r3# show
```

```
type external;
peer-as 65222;
multipath;
neighbor 172.16.0.14;
neighbor 172.16.0.18;
```

The interface addressing needed for r3 to peer with T1 and T2 is now configured:

```
[edit interfaces]
lab@r3# set fe-0/0/2 unit 0 family inet address 172.16.0.13/30
```

```
[edit interfaces]
lab@r3# set fe-0/0/3 unit 0 family inet address 172.16.0.17/30
```

After committing, you confirm that the EBGP sessions to T1 and T2 have been correctly established:

```
[edit protocols bgp]
lab@r3# run show bgp summary
Groups: 3 Peers: 6 Down peers: 0
Table          Tot Paths  Act Paths Suppressed    History Damp State    Pending
inet.0            222495     222484          0          0         0           0
Peer             AS     InPkt     OutPkt     OutQ   Flaps Last Up/Dwn
State|#Active/Received/Damped...
172.16.0.14     65222     21036      21150        0       0      4:23 111229/
111230/0        0/0/0
172.16.0.18     65222     19635      19857        0       0      4:14 111230/
111230/0        0/0/0
10.0.2.1        65001      1887      68370     0     0   8:01:33 1/4/0
0/0/0
10.0.3.4        65000      7028      71753     0     0   9:35:31 12/17/0
0/0/0
10.0.6.1        65000       515      46115     0     2   3:50:32 10/12/0
0/0/0
10.0.6.2        65000      1155      72274     0     0   9:35:28 2/2/0
0/0/0
```

The output confirms the established state of both EBGP sessions and that each of the peering sessions has contributed almost the exact same number of active routes to the tune of some 111,229 prefixes. The fact that both sessions display this level of concordance between the number of received and active routes provides a good indication that multipath load balancing is working, but a careful operator will analyze at least one of the routes to verify that the protocol and forwarding next hops associated with T1 and T2 are actually listed:

```
[edit protocols bgp group t1-t2]
lab@r3# run show route 3/8 detail
```

```
inet.0: 111284 destinations, 222518 routes (111282 active, 0 holddown, 3 hidden)
3.0.0.0/8 (2 entries, 1 announced)
        *BGP    Preference: 170/-101
                Source: 172.16.0.14
                Nexthop: 172.16.0.14 via fe-0/0/2.0, selected
                Nexthop: 172.16.0.18 via fe-0/0/3.0
                Protocol Nexthop: 172.16.0.14 Indirect nexthop: c4f3440 73
                Protocol Nexthop: 172.16.0.18 Indirect nexthop: c4f3550 75
                State: <Active Ext>
                Local AS: 65000 Peer AS: 65222
                Age: 6:16        Metric2: 0
                Task: BGP_65222.172.16.0.14+179
                Announcement bits (3): 0-KRT 3-BGP.0.0.0.0+179 4-Resolve inet.0
                AS path: 65222 10458 14203 3967 7018 80 I
                Localpref: 100
                Router ID: 130.130.0.1
         BGP    Preference: 170/-101
                Source: 172.16.0.18
                Nexthop: 172.16.0.18 via fe-0/0/3.0, selected
                Protocol Nexthop: 172.16.0.18 Indirect nexthop: c4f3550 75
                State: <NotBest Ext>
                Inactive reason: Router ID
                Local AS: 65000 Peer AS: 65222
                Age: 3:57        Metric2: 0
                Task: BGP_65222.172.16.0.18+1317
                AS path: 65222 10458 14203 3967 7018 80 I
                Localpref: 100
                Router ID: 130.130.0.2
```

The highlighted portions of the capture confirm that while T1's advertisement has been selected as the active route because of its lower router ID, both of the protocol and forwarding next hops associated with the routes received from the T1 and T2 routers are listed under the active route. This output confirms that the load-balancing requirements for the multiple EBGP peering sessions supported by r3 have been met. By way of comparison, the same route is now displayed after the multipath option has been removed from r3:

```
[edit protocols bgp group t1-t2]
lab@r3# run show route 3/8 detail
```

```
inet.0: 111285 destinations, 222522 routes (111283 active, 9218 holddown, 3 hidden)
3.0.0.0/8 (2 entries, 2 announced)
        *BGP    Preference: 170/-101
```

```
                    Source: 172.16.0.18
                    Nexthop: 172.16.0.18 via fe-0/0/3.0, selected
                    Protocol Nexthop: 172.16.0.18 Indirect nexthop: c4f3550 75
                    State: <Active Ext>
                    Local AS: 65000 Peer AS: 65222
                    Age: 11:04     Metric2: 0
                    Task: BGP_65222.172.16.0.18
                    Announcement bits (3): 0-KRT 3-BGP.0.0.0.0+179 4-Resolve inet.0
                    AS path: 65222 10458 14203 3967 7018 80 I
                    Localpref: 100
                    Router ID: 130.130.0.2
          BGP       Preference: 170/-101
                    Source: 172.16.0.14
                    Protocol Nexthop: 172.16.0.14 Indirect nexthop: c4f3440 73
                    Protocol Nexthop: 172.16.0.18 Indirect nexthop: c4f3550 75
                    State: <Delete Ext>
                    Inactive reason: Unusable path
                    Local AS: 65000 Peer AS: 65222
                    Age: 2  Metric2: 0
                    Task: BGP_65222.172.16.0.14
                    Announcement bits (1): 3-BGP.0.0.0.0+179
                    AS path: 65222 10458 14203 3967 7018 80 I
                    Localpref: 100
                    Router ID: 130.130.0.1
```

By contrasting this capture with the previous example, you can easily spot the additional next hops that result when multipath is correctly configured. The BGP summary output also clearly shows that r3 has installed only routes from router T1 when multipath has been omitted from the t1–t2 stanza:

```
[edit protocols bgp]
lab@r3# run show bgp summary
Groups: 3 Peers: 6 Down peers: 0
Table          Tot Paths  Act Paths Suppressed    History Damp State    Pending
inet.0            222499     111250          0          0         0        4263
Peer             AS     InPkt     OutPkt     OutQ   Flaps Last Up/Dwn
State|#Active/Received/Damped...
172.16.0.14    65222    20210       3806    13766      0          47 111231/
111232/0       0/0/0
172.16.0.18    65222    19576       4053    13272      0          43 3/
111232/0         0/0/0
10.0.2.1    65001   1898    68464   33343      0    8:07:03 1/4/0
0/0/0
```

10.0.3.4	65000	7039	71847	33343	0	9:41:01 3/17/0
0/0/0						
10.0.6.1	65000	526	46209	33343	2	3:56:02 10/12/0
0/0/0						
10.0.6.2	65000	1166	72368	33343	0	9:40:58 2/2/0
0/0/0						

Make sure that you restore the multipath option to r3's configuration before proceeding to the next section.

EBGP and Policy

Various policy applications have been demonstrated throughout this book. Chapter 5 provided an overview of the default BGP policy and the rules of applying policies at the global, group, and neighbor levels of the BGP configuration hierarchy. You should recall that the default policy for BGP is to accept all received BGP routes that pass incoming sanity checks (no AS path loops), and to advertise all active BGP routes to all BGP peers while obeying IBGP rules that prevent a BGP speaker from readvertising IBGP-learned routes to other IBGP speakers except where exempted by the use of route reflection.

This chapter will focus on the use of routing policy for common EBGP-related issues such as route damping, setting next hop self, and the filtering and tagging of routes that are learned from other ASs.

Note that all of your routers currently have, at a minimum, a simple static route redistribution policy that should be applied only to your IBGP and C-BGP connections. If you have applied your IBGP policy globally, then you will need to apply your EBGP policy at the EBGP group or neighbor levels to ensure that EBGP peers are not subjected to your IBGP policy. In this section, you will create policies for use with your EBGP peers and modify your existing IBGP policy as needed. Bear in mind that policy cannot activate a route that is hidden, nor will it allow you to advertise a hidden route. Also, a given route can be accepted or rejected only once in its policy processing—a fact that can make the ordering of your policies (or policy terms) extremely important because once a route is rejected (or accepted), it is not possible to subject that route to additional policy evaluation unless you are using Boolean policy groupings. The use of Boolean policy groupings is a technique rarely used in production networks and is therefore considered outside the scope of this book.

EBGP Import Policy

This section outlines various requirements that can be achieved with one or more policies that are applied as input to the EBGP peering sessions in your AS. In some cases, a given policy can be applied as import, export, or as both import and export for a particular peering session. Although some of the policies outlined in this section could be applied to EBGP as an export policy, this chapter breaks down the policy assignments into import and export sections to improve the chapter's structure and organization.

Route Damping

Route damping is used to suppress the advertisement of a prefix that has been advertised and withdrawn, or has had its attributes changed, too often in a given period of time. Route damping can be applied only to EBGP due to the need for consistent routing within a given AS. Route damping requires the use of policy when the default damping parameters need to be modified or when you wish to damp only certain routes. To complete this configuration example, you must add EBGP damping according to the following requirements.

- Damp routes received from T1 and T2 according to these criteria:

  - Damp all prefixes with a mask length equal to or greater than 17 more aggressively than routes with a mask length between 9 and 16, inclusive.

  - Damp routes with a mask length between 0 and 8, inclusive, less than routes with a mask length greater than 8.

  - Do not damp the 17.128.0.0/9 prefix at all.

It would be wise to begin this task with knowledge of the default damping parameters in JUNOS software because the default damping class can be used to save yourself some work. As of JUNOS software release 5.2, the default damping parameters are:

- Decay half-life (when reachable) = 15 minutes
- Maximum hold-down time = 60 minutes
- Reuse threshold = 750
- Cut-off (suppress) threshold = 3000

By creating three custom damping profiles, one that is more aggressive, one that is less aggressive, and another that disables damping altogether, you can use these default parameters to achieve the four damping classes required in this task. The following commands create the `aggressive` damping profile:

```
[edit policy-options]
lab@r3# set damping aggressive half-life 30
```

```
[edit policy-options]
lab@r3# set damping aggressive suppress 2500
```

In this example, increasing the `half-life` parameter or decreasing the `suppress` parameter, relative to those in the default damping class, is sufficient to achieve your aggressive damping goal. Doing both simply creates a profile that is all the more aggressive. Rather than a lower `suppress` setting, you could also opt to configure a `reuse` threshold that is lower (and therefore harder to reach) than the default. The next command creates the `timid` damping profile that will cause associated routes to have their figure of merit decreased by half every five minutes, which allows their figure of merit to decay below the profile's default `reuse` setting of 750 significantly faster than routes subjected to the default or `aggressive` damping classes:

```
[edit policy-options]
lab@r3# set damping timid half-life 5
```

This next statement creates a damping profile called `dry` with damping disabled. This is important because all EBGP routes are subject to damping once it is enabled with the `damping` keyword, thus making a disabled damping profile the only way to exempt certain EBGP routes from the wrath of the damping daemon (which is technically part of rpd):

```
[edit policy-options]
lab@r3# set damping dry disable
```

The three custom damping profiles are now displayed:

```
[edit policy-options]
lab@r3# show | find damp
damping aggressive {
    half-life 30;
    suppress 2500;
}
damping timid {
    half-life 5;
}
damping dry {
    disable;
}
```

You now write a policy called `damp` that employs route filters to match prefix lengths to one of the custom damping classes. Remember that a prefix can only be subjected to one set of damping parameters; therefore the ordering of your terms can be the difference between success and failure:

```
[edit policy-options policy-statement damp term 1]
lab@r3# set from route-filter 17.128.0.0/9 exact damping dry
[edit policy-options policy-statement damp term 1]
lab@r3# set from route-filter 0/0 prefix-length-range /0-/8 damping timid

[edit policy-options policy-statement damp term 1]
lab@r3# set from route-filter 0/0 prefix-length-range /17-/32 damping aggressive
```

The `damp` policy is now displayed:

```
[edit policy-options policy-statement damp term 1]
lab@r3# show
from {
    route-filter 17.128.0.0/9 exact damping dry;
```

```
    route-filter 0.0.0.0/0 prefix-length-range /0-/8 damping timid;
    route-filter 0.0.0.0/0 prefix-length-range /17-/32 damping aggressive;
}
```

Note that routes with a prefix length in the range between /9 and /16 will not match any of the route filter statements, causing them to be subjected to the default damping profile. This configuration provides the required low, medium, and high damping behavior relative to a route's prefix length while also providing the necessary exemption for the 17.128/9 prefix. You must now enable EBGP damping, and apply the damp policy as import to all routers that have EBGP peering sessions to routers T1 and T2:

```
[edit protocols bgp]
lab@r3# set damping
```

```
[edit protocols bgp]
lab@r3# set group t1-t2 import damp
```

The modified configuration for r3 is shown next with the changes highlighted:

```
[edit protocols bgp]
lab@r3# show
damping;
import prefer-2;
export ibgp;
group 65000 {
    type internal;
    local-address 10.0.3.3;
    advertise-inactive;
    cluster 1.1.1.1;
    neighbor 10.0.6.1;
    neighbor 10.0.6.2;
    neighbor 10.0.3.4;
}
group c-bgp {
    type external;
    neighbor 10.0.2.1 {
        peer-as 65001;
    }
}
group t1-t2 {
    type external;
```

```
    import damp;
    peer-as 65222;
    multipath;
    neighbor 172.16.0.14;
    neighbor 172.16.0.18;
}
```

You will need to define the same damping profiles and damping-related policy on r6 before proceeding. Do not forget to enable damping and apply the policy as shown for r3!

 It is worth noting that the damp policy does not make use of an accept terminating action so that the routes are still candidates for further policy manipulation after being subjected to one of the damping profiles. It is suggested that you avoid the use of accept when writing a BGP policy intended to process BGP routes because all such routes that are not explicitly rejected will be accepted by the default policy after all user policies have been processed. Including an accept action in the damp policy would cause all of the routes to be accepted, thereby making them immune to any additional policies that you later apply as part of a policy chain. If you are predisposed to not relying on default actions, you can always add an explicit "accept all BGP routes" policy at the end of your policy chains with similar effects.

Verify Damping

The verification of damping is easy when you have control over the remote system that is advertising the routes. In this case, you can modify the advertising router's policy to effect the advertisement and withdrawal of a given prefix while monitoring its figure of merit and damping status. Having a live Internet feed almost guarantees that a certain degree of route flap will always be present, and the following command verifies that routes are being hidden due to damping:

```
[edit]
lab@r3# run show route damping suppressed

inet.0: 111327 destinations, 222600 routes (111198 active, 0 holddown, 256 hidden)
+ = Active Route, - = Last Active, * = Both

62.109.0.0/19        [BGP ] 01:59:22, localpref 100
                        AS path: 65222 10458 14203 701 6453 8470 15487 I
                     > to 172.16.0.14 via fe-0/0/2.0
                        [BGP ] 01:59:08, localpref 100
. . .
```

The predicted collapse of the Internet due to routing instability must surely be imminent because over 250 routes have been hidden due to damping! Displaying the details of damped routes provides useful information:

```
[edit]
lab@r3# run show route damping suppressed 62.109.0.0/19 detail

inet.0: 111328 destinations, 222602 routes (111150 active, 0 holddown, 354 hidden)
62.109.0.0/19 (2 entries, 0 announced)
        BGP                 /-101
                Source: 172.16.0.14
                Nexthop: 172.16.0.14 via fe-0/0/2.0, selected
                Protocol Nexthop: 172.16.0.14 Indirect nexthop: c4f3440 76
                State: <Hidden Ext>
                Local AS: 65000 Peer AS: 65222
                Age: 2:02:24    Metric2: 0
                Task: BGP_65222.172.16.0.14+179
                AS path: 65222 10458 14203 701 6453 8470 15487 I
                Localpref: 100
                Router ID: 130.130.0.1
                Merit (last update/now): 2976/1873
                damping-parameters: aggressive
                Last update:        00:20:09 First update:        00:45:22
                Flaps: 6
                Suppressed. Reusable in:        00:39:40
```

The highlights in this capture indicate that the displayed route has a mask length that is equal to or greater than a /17, and confirms that it has been correctly mapped to the aggressive damping profile. You can also see the route's current (and last) figure of merit value, and when the route is expected to become active if it remains stable. Locating a damped route with a /16 mask confirms that the default parameters are in effect:

```
[edit]
lab@r3# run show route damping suppressed detail | match 0/16
138.184.0.0/16 (2 entries, 0 announced)
139.179.0.0/16 (2 entries, 0 announced)
146.249.0.0/16 (2 entries, 0 announced)
147.248.0.0/16 (2 entries, 0 announced)
150.184.0.0/16 (2 entries, 0 announced)
```

```
[edit]
lab@r3# run show route damping suppressed 139.179.0.0/16 detail
inet.0: 111329 destinations, 222604 routes (111029 active, 0 holddown, 598 hidden)
139.179.0.0/16 (2 entries, 0 announced)
        BGP                     /-101
                Source: 172.16.0.18
                Nexthop: 172.16.0.18 via fe-0/0/3.0, selected
                Protocol Nexthop: 172.16.0.18 Indirect nexthop: c4f34c8 77
                State: <Hidden Ext>
                Local AS: 65000 Peer AS: 65222
                Age: 2:06:34    Metric2: 0
                Task: BGP_65222.172.16.0.18+179
                AS path: 65222 10458 14203 3967 3561 701 11331 13263 8466 I
                Localpref: 100
                Router ID: 130.130.0.2
                Merit (last update/now): 5199/3761
                Default damping parameters used
                Last update:        00:07:05 First update:        00:50:11
                Flaps: 11
                Suppressed. Reusable in:        00:35:00
                Preference will be: 170
                History entry.  Expires in:        01:00:20
```

You might also try some fancy logical OR groupings or cascaded piping to simplify the determination of what damping profile is being used for routes with a given mask length:

```
lab@r3> show route damping suppressed detail | match "0 announced|damp"
62.176.64.0/22 (2 entries, 0 announced)
                damping-parameters: aggressive
                damping-parameters: aggressive
62.176.96.0/21 (2 entries, 0 announced)
                damping-parameters: aggressive
                damping-parameters: aggressive
62.181.64.0/18 (2 entries, 0 announced)
                damping-parameters: aggressive
                damping-parameters: aggressive
63.233.200.0/24 (2 entries, 0 announced)
                damping-parameters: aggressive
                damping-parameters: aggressive
```

```
64.94.183.0/24 (2 entries, 0 announced)
              damping-parameters: aggressive
              damping-parameters: aggressive
. . .
```

In a pinch, you can clear your EBGP neighbors a few times to simulate flaps, and watch the damped route count shoot skyward. This capture was taken after clearing r3's BGP neighbors four times:

```
lab@r3> show bgp summary
Groups: 3 Peers: 6 Down peers: 0
Table          Tot Paths  Act Paths Suppressed   History Damp State   Pending
inet.0            222585        29     222188       544    222548           0
Peer              AS     InPkt    OutPkt    OutQ   Flaps Last Up/Dwn
State|#Active/Received/Damped...
172.16.0.14    65222    21493        22       0       4      49 6/
111275/111092        0/0/0
172.16.0.18    65222    19588        22       0       4      49 6/
111275/111092        0/0/0
10.0.2.1       65001       13    22      0       4      49 0/4/4
0/0/0
10.0.3.4       65000       15    20      0       4      49 4/17/0
0/0/0
10.0.6.1       65000        5    23      0       6      49 11/12/0
0/0/0
10.0.6.2       65000        4    23      0       4      49 2/2/0
0/0/0
```

This display would indicate that you have managed to damp virtually every route in the global Internet. When satisfied that your EBGP routes are correctly associated with a damping profile, you can issue the `clear bgp damping` operational mode command to restore an active status to your damped routes, which will return your customer's Internet connectivity to a semblance of normal operation.

Martian Filtering

The next configuration task involves the application of route filters and AS path regx matching to control the routes to be accepted from your EBGP peers. A JNCIP exam candidate is expected to know that RFC 1918 defines a set of well-known, local use–only addresses, and that ISPs filter such routes upon ingress to avoid wasting resources processing routes that no one on the public Internet can ever hope to reach. Further, routes that identify the network with all 0's or 1's, such as 128.0/16 and 128.255/16, are reserved by the IANA and are sometimes called "guard nets" because they are the first and last network numbers within a particular classfull addressing space. These routes are often referred to as *Martians* because they are considered un-routable and do not belong in a well-designed network, so their presence indicates some type of alien invasion from the perspective of a service provider!

Some ISPs define a superset of routes they consider *bogus,* with the individual members of this group termed *bogons,* which is interpreted as "the elementary particles of bogosity," as defined by http://info.astrian.net/jargon/terms/b/bogon.html. The group of bogons will normally include things like RFC 1918 routes, prefixes with masks longer than a /24, prefixes from the 0–127 (class "A") space with masks less than a /8, default routes, and so on.

Juniper Networks routers come from the factory with a Martian table containing well-known bogons such as the all 1's and all 0's guard nets. While the default entries cannot be removed, the operator can override them by adding specific entries associated with an allowed action. The show route table martians command can be used to view the list of predefined Martian routes.

To complete this section, you must address the following filtering requirements.

- Filter routes from EBGP peers according to these criteria:

  - No default route or any 0.*x* prefix with a mask length up to /7

  - No RFC 1918 routes

  - No prefixes longer than /24 from peer and transit sites; customer sites may send prefixes up to /28

  - No customer routes that do not originate in that customer's AS

  - No 0–127 routes with prefix lengths less than /8

The following policy will do the job for non-customer-attached routers such as r1 and r3:

```
[edit]
lab@r1# show policy-options policy-statement bogons
term 1 {
    from {
        route-filter 0.0.0.0/0 through 0.0.0.0/7 reject;
        route-filter 0.0.0.0/1 prefix-length-range /1-/7 reject;
    }
}
term 2 {
    from {
        route-filter 0.0.0.0/0 prefix-length-range /25-/32 reject;
        route-filter 172.16.0.0/12 orlonger reject;
        route-filter 192.168.0.0/16 orlonger reject;
        route-filter 10.0.0.0/8 orlonger reject;
    }
}
```

The first term eliminates the default route and any prefix with all 0's in the first 7 bits of the high-order byte with the classic use, and pretty much *only* recommended use, of the through match type. Term 2 starts by rejecting any routes with mask lengths longer than /25 and also eliminates RFC 1918 routes. The bogons policy must be applied to r1's EBGP peer as an import policy before it can take effect:

```
[edit]
lab@r1# show protocols bgp group p1
type external;
local-address 10.0.5.200;
import bogons;
peer-as 65050;
neighbor 10.0.5.254;
```

A similar policy should be applied to the EBGP peers on r2, r3, and r6 before moving on. The following policy addresses the needs of customer-attached routers like r7. The highlights call out the modifications made to support a customer-attached router:

```
[edit policy-options policy-statement bogons]
lab@r7# show
term 1 {
    from {
        route-filter 0.0.0.0/0 through 0.0.0.0/7 reject;
        route-filter 0.0.0.0/1 prefix-length-range /1-/7 reject;
    }
}
term 2 {
    from {
        route-filter 0.0.0.0/0 prefix-length-range /29-/32 reject;
        route-filter 172.16.0.0/12 orlonger reject;
        route-filter 192.168.0.0/16 orlonger reject;
        route-filter 10.0.0.0/8 orlonger reject;
    }
}
term 3 {
    from as-path c2;
    then next policy;
}
term 4 {
    then reject;
}

[edit policy-options]
lab@r7# show as-path c2
".* 65020";
```

The modifications to the **bogons** filter permits prefixes up to 28 bits in length, and defines an AS regular expression that matches any routes with AS 65020 as the first entry in the AS path attribute, because the originating AS is always listed first in a route's AS path. The regular expression begins with a "match all" wildcard sequence to ensure that AS path prepending at C2 will not result in the rejection of C2's routes. Term 4 rejects all routes not matching term 3. The route-filtering policy is applied as import to r7's EBGP peering session:

```
[edit protocols bgp]
lab@r7# set group c2 import bogons

[edit protocols bgp]
lab@r7# show group c2
type external;
import bogons;
peer-as 65020;
neighbor 172.16.0.26;
```

The highlighted changes shown here are needed for the application of the **bogons** policy to r4:

```
policy-statement bogons {
    term 1 {
        from {
            route-filter 0.0.0.0/0 through 0.0.0.0/7 reject;
            route-filter 0.0.0.0/1 prefix-length-range /1-/7 reject;
        }
    }
    term 2 {
        from {
            route-filter 0.0.0.0/0 prefix-length-range /29-/32 reject;
            route-filter 172.16.0.0/12 orlonger reject;
            route-filter 192.168.0.0/16 orlonger reject;
            route-filter 10.0.0.0/8 orlonger reject;
        }
    }
    term 3 {
        from as-path c1;
        then next policy;
    }
    term 4 {
        then reject;
    }
```

```
}
as-path c1 ".* 65010";
```

Do not forget to apply the bogons policy as import to r4's EBGP peering session before moving on to the verification section.

Verify Martian Filters

The operation of your Martian filters can be verified by displaying the routes received from your EBGP peers, both with and without the hidden switch. Routes that are rejected by your import policy will be hidden and listed among any other routes that may be hidden for different reasons. To demonstrate, consider the case of the EBGP peering session to the P1 router, where you start by displaying the received routes that are not hidden:

```
[edit]
lab@r1# run show route source-gateway 10.0.5.254

inet.0: 110887 destinations, 110908 routes (110880 active, 0 holddown, 8 hidden)
+ = Active Route, - = Last Active, * = Both

3.4.0.0/20       *[BGP/170] 04:19:30, MED 0, localpref 100
                    AS path: 65050 I
                  > to 10.0.5.254 via fe-0/0/0.0
120.120.0.0/24   *[BGP/170] 04:19:30, MED 0, localpref 100
                    AS path: 65050 I
                  > to 10.0.5.254 via fe-0/0/0.0
120.120.1.0/24   *[BGP/170] 04:19:30, MED 0, localpref 100
                    AS path: 65050 I
                  > to 10.0.5.254 via fe-0/0/0.0
120.120.2.0/24   *[BGP/170] 04:19:30, MED 0, localpref 100
                    AS path: 65050 I
                  > to 10.0.5.254 via fe-0/0/0.0
120.120.3.0/24   *[BGP/170] 04:19:30, MED 0, localpref 100
                    AS path: 65050 I
                  > to 10.0.5.254 via fe-0/0/0.0
120.120.4.0/24   *[BGP/170] 04:19:30, MED 0, localpref 100
                    AS path: 65050 I
                  > to 10.0.5.254 via fe-0/0/0.0
120.120.5.0/24   *[BGP/170] 04:19:30, MED 0, localpref 100
                    AS path: 65050 I
                  > to 10.0.5.254 via fe-0/0/0.0
```

```
120.120.6.0/24      *[BGP/170] 04:19:30, MED 0, localpref 100
                       AS path: 65050 I
                     > to 10.0.5.254 via fe-0/0/0.0
120.120.7.0/24      *[BGP/170] 04:19:30, MED 0, localpref 100
                       AS path: 65050 I
                     > to 10.0.5.254 via fe-0/0/0.0
```

The prefixes listed do not match any of the entries on your AS's bogon list, which indicates a good start. Now display the hidden routes that are received over the P1 EBGP peering session:

```
[edit]
lab@r1# run show route source-gateway 10.0.5.254 hidden

inet.0: 110860 destinations, 110881 routes (110853 active, 0 holddown, 8 hidden)
+ = Active Route, - = Last Active, * = Both

0.0.0.0/0           [BGP ] 04:21:10, MED 0, localpref 100
                       AS path: 65050 I
                     > to 10.0.5.254 via fe-0/0/0.0
0.0.0.0/4           [BGP ] 04:21:10, MED 0, localpref 100
                       AS path: 65050 I
                     > to 10.0.5.254 via fe-0/0/0.0
6.0.0.0/7           [BGP ] 04:21:10, MED 0, localpref 100
                       AS path: 65050 I
                     > to 10.0.5.254 via fe-0/0/0.0
120.120.69.128/25   [BGP ] 04:21:10, MED 0, localpref 100
                       AS path: 65050 I
                     > to 10.0.5.254 via fe-0/0/0.0
172.17.0.0/24       [BGP ] 04:21:10, MED 0, localpref 100
                       AS path: 65050 I
                     > to 10.0.5.254 via fe-0/0/0.0
192.168.4.0/24      [BGP ] 04:21:10, MED 0, localpref 100
                       AS path: 65050 I
                     > to 10.0.5.254 via fe-0/0/0.0
```

The routes that are hidden include a default route, a 0/4 prefix, some RFC 1918 prefixes, and a 120.120.69.128/25 prefix that exceeds the specified 24-bit mask length. This output confirms the correct operation of the bogons policy at r1.

The same commands should be used to verify the customer-attached router bogons policy at r4 and r7. This output shows the hidden routes on r7. Use of the source-gateway switch ensures that the output will be limited to the routes being advertised by the C2 router:

```
[edit protocols bgp]
lab@r7# run show route source-gateway 172.16.0.26 hidden
```

```
inet.0: 110882 destinations, 110885 routes (53 active, 0 holddown, 110830 hidden)
+ = Active Route, - = Last Active, * = Both

0.0.0.0/0           [BGP ] 01:41:44, MED 0, localpref 100
                      AS path: 65020 65020 62 39 I
                    > to 172.16.0.26 via fe-0/3/2.0
64.0.0.0/7          [BGP ] 01:41:45, MED 0, localpref 100
                      AS path: 65020 65020 I
                    > to 172.16.0.26 via fe-0/3/2.0
201.201.0.7/32      [BGP ] 01:34:09, MED 0, localpref 100
                      AS path: 65020 65020 I
                    > to 172.16.0.26 via fe-0/3/2.0
210.210.16.128/26   [BGP ] 01:32:34, MED 0, localpref 100
                      AS path: 65020 65020 65010 I
                    > to 172.16.0.26 via fe-0/3/2.0
```

All of the hidden routes match the defined bogon criteria; the 210.210.16.128/26 route has been filtered because of the indication that it originated in AS 65010.

Community Tagging

Your next configuration task requires that you add community strings to the routes learned over your EBGP peering sessions based on the site's designation as transit, peer, or customer. To complete this section, you must configure your routers in accordance with the following requirement:

- Tag all EBGP routes based on the peer type that advertises them

To minimize the potential for mistakes and confusion down the road, you should, before starting your configuration, establish a plan detailing all the community values you will use. Table 6.1 lists the community values chosen for this example.

TABLE 6.1   Community Value Assignments

Peer Designation	Community Value
Transit	65412:100
Peer	65412:200
Customer	65412:300

With the community plan firmly established, start by defining all three communities on each router. Do this up front, because only defined communities can be referenced in a policy statement and you will likely need to use policy-based community matches on one or more of the community strings at some future point. The following commands define all three communities on r6:

```
[edit policy-options]
lab@r6# set community transit members 65412:100

[edit policy-options]
lab@r6# set community peers members 65412:200

[edit policy-options]
lab@r6# set community customers members 65412:300
```

The community definitions are shown next:

```
[edit policy-options]
lab@r6# show | find comm
community customers members 65412:300;
community peers members 65412:200;
community r2 members 65412:2;
community transit members 65412:100;
. . .
```

These community definitions should be replicated on all remaining EBGP-peering routers before proceeding. The next step is to write an import policy that adds the appropriate community tag based on the EBGP peer's designation. The following policy accommodates routers that connect to customer sites:

```
[edit policy-options policy-statement community]
lab@r7# show
term 1 {
    from protocol bgp;
    then {
        community add customers;
    }
}
```

The community policy is applied to r7's EBGP peering session, creating a chain of import policies. Ordering of the individual policies is not significant in this case due to the lack of accept actions in the policies created thus far:

```
[edit]
lab@r7# show protocols bgp group c2
type external;
import [ bogons community ];
```

```
peer-as 65020;
neighbor 172.16.0.26;
```

Verify Community Tagging

The verification of community tagging policies is a simple process. The only complicating factor is the fact that you should now have numerous hidden routes on many of your routers, which means that you may have trouble finding all community tags on all routers, at least with the current state of your network. You can check the local routing table of each EBGP peering router to confirm that the routes were correctly tagged upon ingress. It is safe to assume that the community string will be still present when they are exported to your IBGP peers, unless, of course, you decide to explicitly strip the communities using an IBGP export policy. The following command verifies correct route tagging at routers peering with peer site P1:

```
[edit]
lab@r3# run show route source-gateway 172.16.0.14 detail

inet.0: 111798 destinations, 223542 routes (110827 active, 0 holddown, 1937 hidden)
3.0.0.0/8 (2 entries, 1 announced)
        *BGP    Preference: 170/-101
                Source: 172.16.0.14
                Nexthop: 172.16.0.14 via fe-0/0/2.0, selected
                Nexthop: 172.16.0.18 via fe-0/0/3.0
                Protocol Nexthop: 172.16.0.14 Indirect nexthop: 849d000 53
                Protocol Nexthop: 172.16.0.18 Indirect nexthop: 849d110 56
                State: <Active Ext>
                Local AS: 65000 Peer AS: 65222
                Age: 6:18:44    Metric2: 0
                Task: BGP_65222.172.16.0.14+1230
                Announcement bits (3): 0-KRT 3-BGP.0.0.0.0+179 4-Resolve inet.0
                AS path: 65222 10458 14203 701 1239 80 I
                Communities: 65412:100
                Localpref: 100
                Router ID: 130.130.0.1
```

You can also use the CLI match function to display community tags and route prefixes as shown next:

```
[edit]
lab@r3# run show route source-gateway 172.16.0.14 detail | match
"announced|comm"
3.0.0.0/8 (2 entries, 1 announced)
                Communities: 65412:100
```

```
4.0.0.0/8 (2 entries, 1 announced)
            Communities: 65412:100
6.0.0.0/20 (2 entries, 1 announced)
            Communities: 65412:100
6.3.0.0/18 (2 entries, 1 announced)
            Communities: 65412:100
. . .
```

To confirm that your IBGP export policies are not altering the community tags, you can display the routes being advertised or received over IBGP sessions, or simply display the IGP peer's routing table. In this example, the `hidden` switch is needed on r5 because the routes it has received from r7 are hidden due to next hop problems:

```
[edit]
lab@r5# run show route 201.201/16 hidden detail | match com
            Communities: 65412:300
            Communities: 65412:300
            Communities: 65412:300
            Communities: 65412:300
            Communities: 65412:300
            Communities: 65412:300
            Communities: 65412:300
```

These results confirm that the community tagging at r3 and r7 are working as per your instructions. You should test the remaining routers before moving to the next section.

EBGP (and IBGP) Export Policy

The majority of this section outlines configuration requirements that can be achieved with one or more policies that are applied as export to the various EBGP peering sessions in your AS. Once you have successfully advertised an aggregate for your AS's address space to your EBGP peers, you should be able to conduct ping testing to verify the forwarding paths through your network.

You begin this section by adjusting your IBGP export policy to eliminate the numerous hidden routes present on most routers.

Repair Hidden Routes

To complete this task, you must configure IBGP export policies that meet the following requirements:

- You can have no black holes.
- All routers must be able to route to all EBGP destinations.
- You cannot have suboptimal routing.
- The 172.16.*x.x* prefixes must not appear in your IGP.

You start by confirming that you currently have a hidden route issue by displaying r5's route table:

```
lab@r5# run show route

inet.0: 112321 destinations, 224602 routes (43 active, 0 holddown, 224542 hidden)
+ = Active Route, - = Last Active, * = Both

3.4.0.0/20          *[BGP/170] 00:27:01, MED 0, localpref 100, from 10.0.2.2
                       AS path: (65000) 65050 I
                     > via as1.0
                     [BGP/170] 00:27:53, MED 0, localpref 100, from 10.0.2.10
                       AS path: (65000) 65050 I
                     > via as1.0
. . .
```

Yes, with 224,542 hidden routes on r5 it would seem that your network does indeed have some. Currently, the majority of these routes are hidden due to lack of reachability within your AS for the 172.16.*x.x* prefixes used to support your EBGP peering sessions. This theory is confirmed with the following command:

```
[edit]
lab@r5# run show route resolution unresolved detail
Table inet.0
144.160.0.0/24
        Protocol Nexthop: 172.16.0.14
        Indirect nexthop: 0 -
. . .
```

The first entry shows a protocol next hop of 172.16.0.14, which identifies T1 as the source of this particular route. The issue here is that your IGP cannot resolve this prefix, so the route is unusable:

```
[edit]
lab@r5# run show route 172.16.0.14

[edit]
lab@r5#
```

These routes are not hidden on r3 or r6 because they are directly connected to the EBGP peering links and so can resolve the associated EBGP next hop without the need for a recursive IGP lookup. While you can resolve this problem by running a passive IGP on your EBGP interface, or by redistributing the direct EBGP interface routes into your IGP, both approaches would cause 172.16.*x.x* routes in your IGP and this is not permitted in this example. Static routes could also fix the problem but, being bad form, they too are not allowed in this case. This leaves only one choice, and that is to adjust your IBGP export policy to set next hop self on the routes learned from external peers.

The incorrect use of a next hop self policy can result in suboptimal routing, or hidden routes when incorrectly applied as an import policy, so you should put some thought into your next hop self plan before boldly embarking on this task. For example, consider Figure 6.3, which shows a simplified route reflection topology and a sample policy for setting next hop self.

FIGURE 6.3 Incorrect use of a next hop self policy

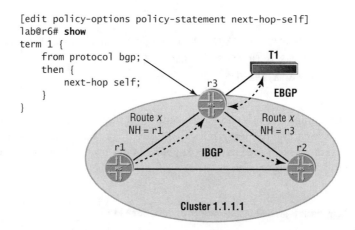

In Figure 6.3, a simple next hop self policy has been applied as export to the IBGP group containing r1 and r2. In this example, r3 is a route reflector serving r1 and r2 as clients. The problem with this particular policy is the lack of distinction between BGP routes learned internally vs. those learned externally, with the result being that r3 is now overwriting the BGP next hop in the routes it reflects between clients r1 and r2. This results in the clients having to forward through the route reflector, which is suboptimal routing in the face of the direct link that exists between r1 and r2.

The highlighted changes in the ibgp policy circumvent this problem by including the neighbor keyword as part of the match criteria for term 3 in the ibgp policy. Another workable alternative for this example would be to use community-based match criteria to determine when the BGP next hop should be overwritten. The policy shown next is designed for use by r3:

```
[edit policy-options policy-statement ibgp]
lab@r3# show
term 1 {
    from {
        protocol static;
        route-filter 192.168.0.0/16 longer;
    }
```

```
        then accept;
}
term 2 {
    from {
        protocol aggregate;
        route-filter 10.0.0.0/8 exact;
    }
    then accept;
}
term 3 {
    from {
        protocol bgp;
        neighbor [ 172.16.0.14 172.16.0.18 ];
    }
    then {
        next-hop self;
    }
}
```

You should create similar policies on all EBGP-peering routers before proceeding. This example has you modify the existing ibgp policy so there is no need to apply another policy to your IBGP peer groups. Also, because the 10.0.5/24 network used to support the EBGP peering to P1 is being redistributed into your IGP, next hop self policies are not required on r1 and r2. Applying a next hop self policy to r1 and r2 will not impair the operation of your network, however. Make sure that you specify a neighbor value of 200.200.0.1 in r4's next hop self policy to accommodate r4's loopback-based peering session to C1.

Verify Next Hop Self

After committing the new policy on r3, you again examine the number of hidden routes on r5:

```
[edit]
lab@r5# run show route

inet.0: 112138 destinations, 336318 routes (112129 active, 0 holddown, 112085 hidden)
+ = Active Route, - = Last Active, * = Both

3.0.0.0/8           *[BGP/170] 02:36:12, localpref 100
                      AS path: (65000) 65222 10458 3944 2914 7018 80 I
                    > to 10.0.2.2 via at-0/2/1.35
                     [BGP/170] 00:02:13, localpref 100, from 10.0.2.10
```

```
                    AS path: (65000) 65222 10458 3944 2914 7018 80 I
                  > via at-0/2/1.35
```

Good, the current count of 112,085 hidden routes is a far sight better than the previous 224,542! Looking at one of the route's details confirms that r3 is advertising its IBGP peering address as the protocol next hop for the routes it is learning from T1 and T2:

```
[edit]
lab@r5# run show route 3/8 detail

inet.0: 112138 destinations, 336320 routes (112129 active, 0 holddown, 112087 hidden)
3.0.0.0/8 (3 entries, 1 announced)
        *BGP    Preference: 170/-101
                Source: 10.0.2.2
                Nexthop: 10.0.2.2 via at-0/2/1.35, selected
                Protocol Nexthop: 10.0.2.2 Indirect nexthop: 8466330 55
                State: <Active Int Ext>
                Local AS: 65001 Peer AS: 65000
                Age: 2:38:18    Metric2: 0
                Task: BGP_65000.10.0.2.2+179
                Announcement bits (3): 0-KRT 3-BGP.0.0.0.0+179 4-Resolve inet.0
                AS path: (65000) 65222 10458 3944 2914 7018 80 I
                Communities: 2914:420 3944:380 65412:100
                Localpref: 100
                Router ID: 10.0.3.3
. . .
```

After committing the IBGP next hop self policy changes on all routers with EBGP peers, you again look at the number of hidden routes on r5:

```
[edit]
lab@r5# run show route

inet.0: 112155 destinations, 336373 routes (112155 active, 0 holddown, 0 hidden)
+ = Active Route, - = Last Active, * = Both

3.0.0.0/8         *[BGP/170] 02:44:03, localpref 100
                    AS path: (65000) 65222 10458 3944 2914 7018 80 I
                  > to 10.0.2.2 via at-0/2/1.35
                   [BGP/170] 00:10:04, localpref 100, from 10.0.2.10
                    AS path: (65000) 65222 10458 3944 2914 7018 80 I
                  > via at-0/2/1.35
```

```
[BGP/170] 02:44:01, localpref 100, from 10.0.9.6
  AS path: 65222 10458 3944 2914 7018 80 I
> to 10.0.8.5 via fe-0/0/0.0
```
. . .

r5 is now free of hidden routes, which is a very good sign. You should inspect all routers for hidden routes before moving on to be sure that all of your policy modifications are working as expected. To complete this section, we verify that route reflectors are not overwriting IBGP next hops by examining the 192.168.10/24 route's next hop after it has been reflected through r3:

```
[edit]
lab@r2# run show route 192.168.10/24 detail

inet.0: 112162 destinations, 224307 routes (112161 active, 0 holddown, 2 hidden)
192.168.10.0/24 (2 entries, 1 announced)
      *BGP    Preference: 170/-101
              Source: 10.0.3.3
              Nexthop: 10.0.4.5 via fe-0/0/3.0, selected
              Protocol Nexthop: 10.0.6.1 Indirect nexthop: 8466198 56
              State: <Active Int Ext>
              Local AS: 65000 Peer AS: 65000
              Age: 2:47:20    Metric: 0       Metric2: 10
              Task: BGP_65000.10.0.3.3+1035
              Announcement bits (2): 0-KRT 4-Resolve inet.0
              AS path: I (Originator)Cluster list:  1.1.1.1
              AS path: Originator ID: 10.0.6.1
              Localpref: 100
              Router ID: 10.0.3.3
```
. . .

The output confirms that the selective nature of your next hop policies will not result in sub-optimal routing through your AS.

Route Filtering

To complete this task, you must configure policies that meet the following requirements:
- Advertise an aggregate route for the 10/8 space to all peers
- Advertise customer routes to all EBGP peers
- Advertise transit and peer routes to all customers
- Advertise peer routes to transit providers
- Filter all other routes to EBGP peers

Customer Site Export Policy

To get the ball rolling, you start with the export policy needed by your customer-attached routers, r4 and r7. This policy addresses the route advertisement requirements for routers attached to customer sites:

```
[edit policy-options policy-statement cust-export]
lab@r7# show
term 1 {
    from {
        protocol aggregate;
        route-filter 10.0.0.0/8 exact;
    }
    then accept;
}
term 2 {
    from community [ customers transit peers ];
    then next policy;
}
```

The cust-export policy example uses term 1 to match on and explicitly accept a local aggregate route definition. The accept action is needed for this route because the default BGP policy will not accept non-BGP routes. Term 2 leverages your community tagging efforts to simplify the act of ensuring that customer sites will get the routes learned from transit, peer, and customer EBGP peering sessions. Route filters could have also been used, but this approach involves more work and is somewhat prone to error when compared to the community-based matching example shown here.

Note that because you need to advertise all BGP routes to your customers, you really needed only term 1 in this policy. The routes learned from other customer, transit, and peer locations would be advertised to C2 by default.

The cust-export policy is now applied as export to r7's c2 peer group:

```
[edit]
lab@r7# set protocols bgp group c2 export cust-export
```

Before committing the changes, you also define the 10/8 aggregate:

```
[edit]
lab@r7# set routing-options aggregate route 10/8
```

The cust-export policy can be applied to r4 with no modifications. You may want to use the load merge terminal option to reduce typing requirements. Do not forget to define the aggregate and apply the policy as export on r4 before proceeding.

Verify Customer Site Export Policy

To verify your policy, you display the routes advertised to a customer router. Keep in mind that hidden routes cannot be advertised, so you should make sure that any hidden route problems have been resolved before verifying your EBGP export policies. Start by determining whether the aggregate for your AS is being correctly advertised:

```
[edit]
lab@r7# run show route advertising-protocol bgp 172.16.0.26 10/8

inet.0: 110886 destinations, 110889 routes (54 active, 0 holddown, 110833 hidden)
+ = Active Route, - = Last Active, * = Both

10.0.0.0/8
Self                                    I
```

The aggregate is present, so the presence of peer routes is now verified:

```
[edit]
lab@r7# run show route advertising-protocol bgp 172.16.0.26 120.120/16

inet.0: 110889 destinations, 110892 routes (54 active, 0 holddown, 110836 hidden)
+ = Active Route, - = Last Active, * = Both

120.120.0.0/24
Self                            (65000) 65050 I
120.120.1.0/24
Self                            (65000) 65050 I
120.120.2.0/24
Self                            (65000) 65050 I
. . .
```

Peer routes are going out as required. You now verify that C1's routes are also being sent to C2:

```
[edit]
lab@r7# run show route advertising-protocol bgp 172.16.0.26 200.200/16

inet.0: 112183 destinations, 224301 routes (112179 active, 0 holddown, 4 hidden)
+ = Active Route, - = Last Active, * = Both

200.200.0.0/16
Self                            65222 10458 14203 701 4230 I
200.200.0.0/24
Self                            (65000) 65010 I
```

```
200.200.0.0/28
Self                                    (65000) 65010 I
200.200.1.0/24
Self                                    (65000) 65010 I
. . .
```

C1's routes are being sent to C2 as required. You now verify that transit provider routes are also being advertised:

```
[edit]
lab@r7# run show route advertising-protocol bgp 172.16.0.26 130.130/16


inet.0: 112184 destinations, 224303 routes (112180 active, 0 holddown, 4 hidden)
+ = Active Route, - = Last Active, * = Both


130.130.0.0/16
Self                            65222 I
```

With the advertisement of all EBGP routes and your network's aggregate confirmed, the last check is to make sure that you are not advertising any 192.168/16 prefixes:

```
[edit]
lab@r7# run show route advertising-protocol bgp 172.16.0.26 192.168/16


inet.0: 110843 destinations, 110845 routes (44 active, 0 holddown, 110799 hidden)
+ = Active Route, - = Last Active, * = Both


192.168.20.0/24
Self                                    (65000) I
192.168.30.0/24
Self                                    (65000) I
192.168.40.0/24
Self                                    (65000) I
. . .
```

Whoa! The 192.168/16 routes are not supposed to be going out to customers! Catching "simple" mistakes like this before grading commences can make a fair bit of difference in your final score. r7 is advertising the 192.168/16 routes it has learned through its IBGP sessions, because your customer export policy never explicitly rejected them, which results in their acceptance by BGP's default policy. Adding a term quickly rectifies this situation:

```
[edit policy-options policy-statement cust-export]
lab@r7# set term 3 from route-filter 192.168/16 orlonger reject
```

```
[edit policy-options policy-statement cust-export]
lab@r7# commit
commit complete
```

Wise operators always take a moment to verify their fixes:

```
[edit]
lab@r7# run show route advertising-protocol bgp 172.16.0.26 192.168/16

[edit]
lab@r7#
```

Ah, perfect. Don't forget to make this change on r4's cust-export policy also!

Peer Site Export Policy

Based on the relative success of your customer export policy, you decide to use the same approach for routers that peer with P1. The following policy looks like it will meet the export requirements for the EBGP peering session to peer router P1:

```
[edit policy-options policy-statement peer-export]
lab@r1# show
term 1 {
    from {
        protocol aggregate;
        route-filter 10.0.0.0/8 exact;
    }
    then accept;
}
term 2 {
    from community transit;
    then reject;
}
term 3 {
    from {
        route-filter 192.168.0.0/16 orlonger reject;
    }
}
```

In this example, term 1 serves to advertise a local aggregate while term 2 explicitly rejects any routes with the transit community string. Term 3, on the other hand, reflects your ability to learn from the mistakes that were made on r7's customer export policy by explicitly filtering the 192.168/16 routes. Routes from customer and other peer locations (if there were additional peers in the test bed) will not match either of the peer-export policy terms, and will therefore filter through to the default BGP policy, where they will be advertised to P1. You now apply the peer-export policy to r1's EBGP peer group as export:

```
[edit protocols]
lab@r1# set bgp group p1 export peer-export
```

To complete this task, you define the 10/8 aggregate as was done for r7:

```
[edit]
lab@r1# set routing-options aggregate route 10/8
```

You commit your changes and decide to test the policy before you configure r2 with the same policy solution, which turns out to be a smart move on your part.

Verify Peer Site Export Policy

You display the routes being sent to the P1 router to verify that the peer-export policy meets all specified restrictions. Once again, hidden routes will not be advertised so their presence can impact the results of your verification tests. You start by verifying the aggregate for your AS is being advertised:

```
[edit]
lab@r1# run show route advertising-protocol bgp 10.0.5.254 10/8

inet.0: 110845 destinations, 110866 routes (110838 active, 0 holddown, 8 hidden)
+ = Active Route, - = Last Active, * = Both

10.0.0.0/8
Self                                    I
```

Good, the aggregate is going out as required. You next verify that you are not sending any 192.168/16 routes to the P1 router:

```
[edit]
lab@r1# run show route advertising-protocol bgp 10.0.5.254 192.168/16

[edit]
lab@r1#
```

Good, no 192.168/16 prefixes are being sent, which is in accordance with the specified restrictions. Next, display active BGP routes on r1 to get an idea of what other prefixes can be used to test your peer export policy:

```
[edit]
lab@r1# run show route protocol bgp
```

```
inet.0: 33 destinations, 35 routes (28 active, 0 holddown, 6 hidden)
+ = Active Route, - = Last Active, * = Both

3.4.0.0/20          *[BGP/170] 06:50:12, MED 0, localpref 100
                       AS path: 65050 I
                     > to 10.0.5.254 via fe-0/0/0.0
120.120.0.0/24      *[BGP/170] 06:50:12, MED 0, localpref 100
                       AS path: 65050 I
                     > to 10.0.5.254 via fe-0/0/0.0
. . .
120.120.7.0/24      *[BGP/170] 06:50:12, MED 0, localpref 100
                       AS path: 65050 I
```

This output seems a bit odd, because r1 claims to have only 35 routes, of which only 6 are hidden. Further, the only BGP routes returned are those that are learned from P1. What has happened to all your IBGP routes? Deciding to investigate this a bit further, you display BGP summary information and find yourself wishing you had worn some protective undergarments into the lab:

```
[edit]
lab@r1# run show bgp summary
Groups: 2 Peers: 3 Down peers: 2
Table           Tot Paths  Act Paths Suppressed    History Damp State    Pending
inet.0                 15          9          0          0         0          0
Peer              AS    InPkt    OutPkt    OutQ   Flaps Last Up/Dwn
State|#Active/Received/Damped...
10.0.3.3       65000    48738       653       0       4       24:20 Active
10.0.3.4       65000      670       653       0       4       24:21 Active
10.0.5.254     65050    47387     47313       0       2    6:54:15 9/15/0
0/0/0
```

It would seem that, somehow, your recent actions have disrupted your IBGP sessions, or that you have experienced a hardware failure. Ping tests to the lo0-based IBGP peering addresses of r3 and r4 fail, but pings to the addresses within the OSPF area succeed:

```
[edit]
lab@r1# run ping 10.0.3.3
PING 10.0.3.3 (10.0.3.3): 56 data bytes
ping: sendto: No route to host
^C
--- 10.0.3.3 ping statistics ---
1 packets transmitted, 0 packets received, 100% packet loss
```

```
[edit]
lab@r1# run ping 10.0.4.1 count 1
PING 10.0.4.1 (10.0.4.1): 56 data bytes
64 bytes from 10.0.4.1: icmp_seq=0 ttl=254 time=0.615 ms

--- 10.0.4.1 ping statistics ---
1 packets transmitted, 1 packets received, 0% packet loss
round-trip min/avg/max/stddev = 0.615/0.615/0.615/0.000 ms
```

Displaying the route to the unreachable loopback addresses illuminates the nature of your dilemma:

```
[edit]
lab@r1# run show route 10.0.3.3

inet.0: 33 destinations, 35 routes (28 active, 0 holddown, 6 hidden)
+ = Active Route, - = Last Active, * = Both

10.0.0.0/8         *[Aggregate/130] 00:29:22
                      Reject
```

It would seem that the local aggregate definition, which worked so well for r4 and r7, has resulted in a serious problem when applied to routers in OSPF area 1. This is because area 1 is functioning as an NSSA with summaries filtered at the ABRs, which in turn has caused the local aggregate to come back as the longest, and therefore the best, match for all destinations outside of area 1. Because an aggregate route can point to only discard or reject next hops, you have managed to black-hole your connectivity to destinations in other OSPF areas. Looks like you will need to find another way to get the 10/8 summary route into r1 and r2.

The first reaction of many candidates is to try adjusting global protocol preferences, but this approach is futile at best, because routers always use the longest match when forwarding packets, regardless of the route's preference. After wasting time with preference adjustments, many candidates will decide to define the aggregate on an ABR, because these routers carry full OSPF routing information, which results in the aggregate route not being used in deference to the more specific routes they carry. To get things moving, you delete the 10/8 aggregate route definition from r1:

```
[edit]
lab@r1# delete routing-options aggregate route 10.0.0.0/8
```

You next define the same aggregate route on r3 and adjust r3's IBGP export policy to advertise the aggregate, as shown next with highlights:

```
[edit routing-options]
lab@r3# set aggregate route 10/8
```

```
[edit policy-options policy-statement ibgp]
lab@r3# show
term 1 {
    from {
        protocol static;
        route-filter 192.168.0.0/16 longer;
    }
    then accept;
}
term 2 {
    from {
        protocol aggregate;
        route-filter 10.0.0.0/8 exact;
    }
    then accept;
}
```

After waiting for the reestablishment of the r1–r3 IBGP session, you confirm the summary route's presence on r1 as a BGP route:

```
[edit]
lab@r1# run show route 10/8 | match 10.0.0.0/8

[edit]
```

The aggregate route is not returned. You might want to use the hidden switch to see if it is actually being sent to r1:

```
[edit]
lab@r1# run show route 10.0.0.0 hidden detail

inet.0: 110836 destinations, 110858 routes (110828 active, 0 holddown, 10 hidden)
10.0.0.0/8 (2 entries, 0 announced)
        BGP    Preference: 170/-101
               Next hop type: Unusable
               State: <Hidden Int Ext>
               Local AS: 65000 Peer AS: 65000
               Age: 7:36
               Task: BGP_65000.10.0.3.4+1070
               AS path: I (Originator)Aggregator: 65000 10.0.3.3
               AS path: Cluster list:  1.1.1.1
```

```
                    AS path: Originator ID: 10.0.3.3
                    Localpref: 100
                    Router ID: 10.0.3.4
          BGP       Preference: 170/-101
                    Next hop type: Unusable
                    State: <Hidden Int Ext>
                    Local AS: 65000 Peer AS: 65000
                    Age: 7:36
                    Task: BGP_65000.10.0.3.3+1069
                    AS path: IAggregator: 65000 10.0.3.3
                    Localpref: 100
                    Router ID: 10.0.3.3
```

The 10/8 summary route has been sent to r1, but unfortunately it has been hidden due to next hop resolution problems. Newer versions of JUNOS software will not allow a more specific route to recurse through a less specific route, because this behavior could lead to recursion loops. If the aggregate route were to be installed as active on r1, the following conditions would exist:

- 10/8 is reachable through 10.0.3.3.

- 10.0.3.3 is reachable through 10/8.

This situation would be unproductive at best, so the router chooses to hide the 10/8 prefix to prevent the formation of a recursion loop.

Your best bet at extricating yourself from this quagmire is to define a generated route on r1 (and ultimately r2) that, unlike an aggregate route, can forward over the next hop associated with the primary contributing route, thus preventing the formation of a black hole. The generated route is defined on r1:

```
[edit]
lab@r1# set routing-options generate route 10/8
```

After the commit, you confirm that area 0 loopback addresses are no longer being black-holed, and that you have an active 10/8 summary available for export to P1:

```
[edit]
lab@r1# run show route protocol aggregate

inet.0: 110848 destinations, 110871 routes (110840 active, 1 holddown, 10 hidden)
+ = Active Route, - = Last Active, * = Both

10.0.0.0/8          *[Aggregate/130] 00:00:04
                     > to 10.0.4.6 via fe-0/0/2.0
```

```
[edit]
lab@r1# run show route 10.0.3.3

inet.0: 110847 destinations, 110870 routes (110840 active, 0 holddown, 10 hidden)
+ = Active Route, - = Last Active, * = Both

10.0.0.0/8          *[Aggregate/130] 00:00:12
                    > to 10.0.4.6 via fe-0/0/2.0
```

The results indicate that you have definitely taken a step in the right direction. The only issue now is the fact that the generated route's primary contributing route (10.0.4.0/30) causes traffic to be forwarded from r1 to r3 by way of r2:

```
[edit]
lab@r1# run show route protocol aggregate detail

inet.0: 110856 destinations, 110879 routes (110849 active, 0 holddown, 10 hidden)
10.0.0.0/8 (3 entries, 1 announced)
        *Aggregate Preference: 130
                Nexthop: 10.0.4.6 via fe-0/0/2.0, selected
                State: <Active Int Ext>
                Age: 4:03
                Task: Aggregate
                Announcement bits (3): 0-KRT 3-BGP.0.0.0.0+179 4-Resolve inet.0
                AS path: I
                            Flags: Generate Depth: 0        Active
                Contributing Routes (3):
                        10.0.4.0/30          proto OSPF
                        10.0.4.8/30          proto OSPF
                        10.0.6.2/32          proto OSPF
```

```
[edit]
lab@r1# run traceroute 10.0.3.3
traceroute to 10.0.3.3 (10.0.3.3), 30 hops max, 40 byte packets
 1  10.0.4.6 (10.0.4.6)  0.222 ms  0.186 ms  0.114 ms
 2  10.0.3.3 (10.0.3.3)  0.479 ms  0.432 ms  0.409 ms
```

This is a real dilemma, because a route can only contribute to a generated route when it is associated with a forwarding next hop, which means that r1's directly connected broadcast interfaces are not allowed to contribute, as indicated by their absence in the output of the show route protocol aggregate detail command. Because the numerically lowest route with a valid next hop is chosen as the generated route's primary contributor, r1 forwards packets that match the generated route as if it were forwarding to the 10.0.4.0/30 primary contributor's subnet.

The preferred way to resolve the suboptimal routing problem would be to define a static route to the 10.0.4.0/30 subnet that points to r3 as a next hop, because forcing 10.0.4.0/30 traffic from r1 through r3 is really no worse than having the same traffic transit r2. Before applying any static route, you should first verify whether static routes are permitted in your lab scenario because the capricious use of static routing may result in point loss. In this example, a single static route on r1 and r2 to circumvent this problem is permitted, so the route is defined:

```
[edit routing-options]
lab@r1# set static route 10.0.4.0/30 next-hop 10.0.4.13

[edit]
lab@r1# commit
commit complete
```

And now to confirm the results:

```
[edit]
lab@r1# run show route protocol aggregate detail

inet.0: 110855 destinations, 110879 routes (110848 active, 0 holddown, 10 hidden)
10.0.0.0/8 (3 entries, 1 announced)
        *Aggregate Preference: 130
                Nexthop: 10.0.4.13 via fe-0/0/1.200, selected
                State: <Active Int Ext>
                Age: 18:53
                Task: Aggregate
                Announcement bits (3): 0-KRT 3-BGP.0.0.0.0+179 4-Resolve inet.0
                AS path: I
                                Flags: Generate Depth: 0        Active
                Contributing Routes (3):
                        10.0.4.0/30             proto Static
                        10.0.4.8/30             proto OSPF
                        10.0.6.2/32             proto OSPF
```

In an effort to savor the sweet smell of your hard-fought success, you again test if you are correctly advertising the 10/8 summary to P1:

```
[edit]
lab@r1# run show route advertising-protocol bgp 10.0.5.254 10.0.0.0

inet.0: 110861 destinations, 110885 routes (110854 active, 0 holddown, 10 hidden)
+ = Active Route, - = Last Active, * = Both
```

10.0.0.0/8
Self   I

 Real World Scenario

Another Solution to the "Aggregate Route Problem"

Another solution to the hidden aggregate route problem described in this section, without using generated or static routes, is to use policy to alter the BGP next hop associated with the aggregate route so that the associated BGP next hop is no longer resolved through the summary route. The following policy statement, applied to r3, will cause the BGP next hop for the 10/8 aggregate route to be 10.0.4.13. Because this address is present in the IS-IS level 1 area (and in an OSPF totally stubby area), the advertised BGP next hop will no longer need to recurse through the 10/8 aggregate, allowing it to become active. The following policy term, when applied as part of an IBGP export policy, will achieve this goal:

```
[edit policy-options policy-statement ibgp-export term agg-route]
lab@r3# show
from {
    route-filter 10.0.0.0/8 exact;
}
then {
    next-hop 10.0.4.13;
```

Because of the next hop self policy deployed at the beginning of this section, you can test the remainder of your `peer-export` policies because there should be no hidden routes on r1. You start by confirming that no transit provider routes are being advertised:

```
[edit]
lab@r1# run show route advertising-protocol bgp 10.0.5.254 130.130/16
```

```
[edit]
```

The 130.130/16 route advertised by your transit provider is active on r1 and is correctly omitted from r1's EBGP advertisements to P1. You now verify that customer routes are being correctly advertised:

```
[edit]
lab@r1# run show route advertising-protocol bgp 10.0.5.254 200.200/16
```

```
inet.0: 112180 destinations, 224336 routes (112175 active, 0 holddown, 8 hidden)
+ = Active Route, - = Last Active, * = Both

200.200.0.0/24
Self                                         65010 I
200.200.0.0/28
Self                                         65010 I
. . .


[edit]
lab@r1# run show route advertising-protocol bgp 10.0.5.254 201.201/16

inet.0: 112184 destinations, 224344 routes (112179 active, 0 holddown, 8 hidden)
+ = Active Route, - = Last Active, * = Both

201.201.1.0/24
Self                                (65001) 65020 65020 I
201.201.2.0/24
Self                                (65001) 65020 65020 I
. . .
```

The output confirms that C1 and C2 routes are being sent to P1 in accordance with the example criteria.

Transit Provider Export Policy

To complete this task, you need to define and apply your transit provider EBGP export policy at r3 and r6. A working policy for r3's T1 and T2 peering sessions is shown next:

```
[edit policy-options]
lab@r3# show policy-statement transit-export
term 1 {
    from {
        protocol aggregate;
        route-filter 10.0.0.0/8 exact;
    }
    then accept;
}
term 2 {
    from community [ peers transit ];
    then reject;
}
term 3 {
```

```
    from {
        route-filter 192.168.0.0/16 orlonger reject;
    }
}
```

Rather than accepting customer-tagged routes and explicitly rejecting all other BGP routes, this policy matches on, and rejects, BGP routes with the transit and peers communities, which is why the 192.168/16 route filter in term 3 is needed to suppress advertisement of the 192.168.*x*/24 routes r3 has learned from its IBGP peers. Inclusion of the transit community in term 2 prevents the default JUNOS software behavior of advertising routes back to the EBGP peer from which they were received, and ensures that transit routes that might be coupled between r3 and r6 (using IBGP) are not inadvertently re-advertised to your transit providers.

The highlights show the changes needed in r3's configuration to apply the transit-export policy and define the local aggregate:

```
[edit]
lab@r3# show protocols bgp group t1-t2
type external;
import [ damp bogons community ];
export transit-export;
peer-as 65222;
multipath;
neighbor 172.16.0.14;
neighbor 172.16.0.18;

[edit]
lab@r3# show routing-options
static {
    route 10.0.200.0/24 {
        next-hop 10.0.1.102;
        no-readvertise;
    }
    route 192.168.30.0/24 reject;
}
aggregate {
    route 10.0.0.0/8;
}
autonomous-system 65000;
confederation 65412 members [ 65000 65001 ];
```

You should adapt these policy changes and the related configuration changes for use in r6 before proceeding.

Verify Transit Provider Export Policy

You can verify the transit provider export policy in the same manner as demonstrated for peer and customer sites. The policy should result in the advertisement of a 10/8 and the 200.200/16 and 201.201/16 routes from customer sites, as shown next in this edited capture:

```
[edit]
lab@r6# run show route advertising-protocol bgp 172.16.0.22

inet.0: 117782 destinations, 229860 routes (112139 active, 2 holddown, 5645 hidden)
+ = Active Route, - = Last Active, * = Both

10.0.0.0/8
Self                               I
200.200.0.0/24
Self                               (65000) 65010 I
. . .
201.201.4.0/24
Self                               65020 65020 I
201.201.5.0/24
Self                               65020 65020 I
. . .
```

As required, only the 10/8 aggregate and the routes learned from the C1 and C2 peering sessions are being sent to T1.

Confirm Forwarding Paths

Before calling your EBGP policy efforts a success, you should take a few moments to trace the routes from various points in your AS to the destinations advertised by your EBGP peers. Most exam candidates opt to trace the route to each EBGP peer's loopback address, because the other routes coming from your EBGP peers may point to discard next hops that will prevent the trace from completing. The aggregate for your AS must be correctly advertised before traceroute and ping testing can succeed. Also, your test bed will lack actual Internet connectivity, so despite the full Internet routing table you will not be able to reach Internet destinations. When tracing the routes, attention should be placed on the forwarding paths taken through your network because problems with next hop self policies or active BGP sessions can be discovered when the traces either fail or are observed to take convoluted paths. The following captures are taken from r5 and show successful traceroutes to various EBGP peer loopback addresses.

```
[edit]
lab@r5# run traceroute 120.120.0.1
traceroute to 120.120.0.1 (120.120.0.1), 30 hops max, 40 byte packets
 1  10.0.2.10 (10.0.2.10)  0.661 ms  0.543 ms  0.507 ms
```

```
 2  10.0.4.10 (10.0.4.10)  0.444 ms  0.446 ms  0.428 ms
 3  120.120.0.1 (120.120.0.1)  0.613 ms  0.590 ms  0.569 ms

[edit]
lab@r5# run traceroute 130.130.0.1
traceroute to 130.130.0.1 (130.130.0.1), 30 hops max, 40 byte packets
 1  10.0.2.2 (10.0.2.2)  1.165 ms  1.115 ms  1.081 ms
 2  130.130.0.1 (130.130.0.1)  0.989 ms  1.503 ms  1.074 ms

[edit]
lab@r5# run traceroute 130.130.0.2
traceroute to 130.130.0.2 (130.130.0.2), 30 hops max, 40 byte packets
 1  10.0.2.2 (10.0.2.2)  1.296 ms  1.129 ms  1.086 ms
 2  172.16.0.14 (172.16.0.14)  0.991 ms  0.976 ms  1.097 ms
 3  130.130.0.2 (130.130.0.2)  0.819 ms  0.965 ms  1.083 ms

[edit]
lab@r5# run traceroute 201.201.0.1
traceroute to 201.201.0.1 (201.201.0.1), 30 hops max, 40 byte packets
 1  10.0.8.5 (10.0.8.5)  0.624 ms  0.443 ms  0.405 ms
 2  10.0.8.2 (10.0.8.2)  0.498 ms  0.490 ms  0.474 ms
 3  201.201.0.1 (201.201.0.1)  0.587 ms  0.568 ms  0.549 ms
```

Miscellaneous EBGP Timers and Knobs

The EBGP protocol supports many of the same timers and miscellaneous options that were discussed in the previous IBGP chapter. This section will focus on options that are unique to EBGP. The use of local-as and remove-private are not demonstrated here because they are required in the chapter's case study and so will be illustrated in that section.

To complete this section, you must configure your network in accordance with the following tasks:

- Peer P1 has incorrectly prepended your AS number to one of its routes. You must configure your network to accept this route.

- Use policy so that packets forwarded by T2 will tend to use the 172.16.0.20/30 link to r6 without prepending AS numbers.

- Without using policy, make sure that all routers in your AS use r3 when forwarding to transit destinations.

AS Loops

Your routers will discard any route that contains the local AS number in the AS path list by default. Such routes are not stored in the Routing Information Base (RIB), so they will not be displayed, even with the `hidden` switch. Setting `keep all` will cause them to be retained, but the AS loop condition will prevent the route from becoming active. To complete this objective, you must tell r1 and r2 that they should accept routes that contain the local AS number in the path:

```
[edit routing-options]
lab@r1# set autonomous-system loops 2
```

```
[edit routing-options]
lab@r1# commit
commit complete
```

Note that you will need to set the `loops` parameter to at least 2, because the default setting of 1 means that a route can cross a given AS only once, and for this route to be accepted, you must indicate that it can cross the local AS twice. After committing, you attempt to verify the route is now present and active:

```
[edit routing-options]
lab@r1# run show route 120.120/16 | match 65412
```

```
[edit routing-options]
lab@r1#
```

It would seem that *attempt* was the right word, because the output from the command indicates that no routes received from P1 contain the local AS number. Before chasing the proverbial wild goose, you should clear the BGP session to force P1 to re-advertise its routes. This action is needed because a BGP speaker will advertise a given route only once due to BGP's reliance on the error correction and acknowledged delivery services of its TCP-based transport. Therefore, if the receiving peer chooses not to install a prefix in its incoming RIB, due to a failed sanity check involving AS loops, for example, then you will need to have the remote peer re-advertise its routes to get things working. JUNOS software support for BGP refresh allows the soft clearing of a BGP neighbor whereby r1 will request that P1 resend all of its advertised routes without having to tear down the established connection:

```
[edit routing-options]
lab@r1# run clear bgp neighbor 10.0.5.254 soft-inbound
```

```
[edit routing-options]
lab@r1# run show route 120.120/16 | match 65412
                    AS path: 65050 65412
```

I

After the soft clearing, a route with the local AS number is now present and active in r1. Before proceeding, you must remember to adjust r2's configuration also, else the failure of r1 will result in the loss of this route.

Influence Incoming Traffic Flow

With AS path prepending not permitted, the second criterion requires that you set the MED attribute in the routes advertised to your transit providers in such a way that T2 will choose the routes advertised by r6 over the same routes as sent from r3. The tricky part of this task relates to the fact that lower MED values are preferred (unlike local preference), and that the absence of the MED attribute is interpreted by JUNOS software as a MED value of 0, which is the lowest MED value possible. Operators lacking experience with the MED attribute will often define a policy on r6 that sets the MED to some value and call it a day. Having only r6 send a MED will automatically result in T2 using the routes advertised by r3, due to the absence of the MED attribute being interpreted as a value of 0. Such a condition results in a behavior that is the exact opposite of what you are trying to achieve.

While you could write policies that instruct both r3 and r6 to attach the MED attribute, being careful to make sure that r3's MED value is higher than r6's, the simplest solution is to have only r3 attach the MED attribute. This will leverage the fact that r6's routes, which will lack the MED attribute, will be interpreted as having a lower MED value. Based on the requirements of this task, it is recommended that you apply your MED policy on r3 in such a way that it will affect only the routes sent to T2. You must also be careful to make sure that all advertised routes have the MED correctly attached. The policy example shown here will attach the MED only to customer routes, due to the local 10/8 aggregate being accepted in term 1 *before* the MED action in term 4 is ever analyzed:

```
[edit policy-options policy-statement transit-export]
lab@r3# show
term 1 {
    from {
        protocol aggregate;
        route-filter 10.0.0.0/8 exact;
    }
    then accept;
}
term 2 {
    from community [ peers transit ];
    then reject;
}
term 3 {
    from {
        route-filter 192.168.0.0/16 orlonger reject;
    }
}
```

```
}
term 4 {
    then {
        metric 100;
    }
}
```

You could choose to modify the existing `transit-export` policy to include the MED action, but you should first copy it (with a new name) so that you can later apply the modified MED-related export policy to the r3–T2 peering session only. Another alternative is to create a new policy for MED-related activities, which is the approach taken here. The new `med` policy is displayed next:

```
[edit]
lab@r3# show policy-options policy-statement med
term 1 {
    then {
        metric 100;
    }
}
```

The `med` policy is not protocol source–specific, because listing `from protocol bgp` in term 1, for example, would prevent the 10/8 aggregate from having the correct MED attached. Putting an `accept` action in a `match all` policy such as this one would result in every active route being exported to T2, which proves that attention to detail is what JUNOS software routing policy is all about. You now apply the `med` policy to r3 so that it will only affect the T2 peering session, as shown next:

```
[edit protocols bgp]
lab@r3# show group t1-t2
type external;
import [ damp bogons community ];
export transit-export;
peer-as 65222;
multipath;
neighbor 172.16.0.14;
neighbor 172.16.0.18 {
    export med;
}
```

The problem now is that you have exempted T2 from the `t1-t2` group's `transit-export` policy because of the neighbor-level application of the `med` policy. The absence of a neighbor-level import policy means that all neighbors listed in the `t1-t2` group will still process the `damp`, bogons, and community policies, however. To correct this situation, you add the transit-export policy at the 172.16.0.18 neighbor level, as shown next:

```
[edit protocols bgp]
lab@r3# show group t1-t2
type external;
import [ damp bogons community ];
export transit-export;
peer-as 65222;
multipath;
neighbor 172.16.0.14;
neighbor 172.16.0.18 {
    export [ med transit-export ];
}
```

One last point that bears mentioning is that the nature of the transit-export policy requires that the new med policy be evaluated first. If the med policy is processed after the transit-export policy, the 10/8 aggregate will not have the MED attribute attached because of its acceptance by the transit-export policy's first term. You can rearrange the order of chained policies by using the CLI's insert feature when needed.

This capture shows the state of T2's path selection before you commit the med policy changes:

```
[edit]
lab@T2# run show route 10/8

inet.0: 117445 destinations, 117483 routes (117445 active, 0 holddown, 0 hidden)
+ = Active Route, - = Last Active, * = Both

10.0.0.0/8          *[BGP/170] 00:18:05, localpref 100
                      AS path: 65412 I
                    > to 172.16.0.17 via fe-0/0/2.0
                     [BGP/170] 02:22:03, localpref 100
                      AS path: 65412 I
                    > to 172.16.0.21 via fe-0/0/1.0
                     [BGP/170] 07:47:04, localpref 100
                      AS path: 65412 I
                    > to 10.0.1.65 via fe-0/0/0.0
```

T2 currently prefers the 10/8 advertisement from r3 because of its lower router ID. After committing your changes on r3, you can easily confirm the correct setting of the MED attribute in r3's advertisements to T2:

```
[edit]
```

```
lab@r3# run show route advertising-protocol bgp 172.16.0.18 detail | match MED
    MED: 100
    MED: 100

    . . .

    MED: 100
```

The same approach is used to confirm that the MED attribute is not attached to the routes being advertised to T1:

```
[edit]
lab@r3# run show route advertising-protocol bgp 172.16.0.14 detail | match MED

[edit]
lab@r3#
```

The output confirms that your MED-related policy modifications are spot on. Though you may not have access to external routers during the actual examination, in this test bed you do, so why not take some time to verify that T2's forwarding behavior has been modified by your med policy on r3?

```
[edit]
lab@T2# run show route 10/8

inet.0: 117454 destinations, 117492 routes (117454 active, 0 holddown, 0 hidden)
+ = Active Route, - = Last Active, * = Both

10.0.0.0/8          *[BGP/170] 02:26:48, localpref 100
                       AS path: 65412 I
                    > to 172.16.0.21 via fe-0/0/1.0
                     [BGP/170] 07:51:49, localpref 100
                       AS path: 65412 I
                    > to 10.0.1.65 via fe-0/0/0.0
                     [BGP/170] 00:00:02, MED 100, localpref 100
                       AS path: 65412 I
                    > to 172.16.0.17 via fe-0/0/2.0
```

T2 now forwards traffic through r6 instead of r3, indicating that your med policy application to r3 has correctly altered the results of the active route selection process on T2. This results in the redirection of traffic from T2 onto the T2–r6 peering link instead of the RID-based decision that had resulted in the use of the T2–r3 link.

This particular MED application could have been performed without using policy by specifying the metric-out keyword in r3's BGP configuration stanza at the T2 neighbor level. Policy is normally the preferred way to set MED because it provides greater granularity and increased flexibility with MED settings. MED values set through policy override the MED values configured under the BGP stanza. One alternative r3 configuration that meets the requirements of this task would be as follows. Note the lack of a med policy, and the fact that both of r3's sessions to transit providers now execute the same export policy defined at the group level:

```
[edit protocols bgp group t1-t2]
lab@r3# show
type external;
import [ damp bogons community ];
export transit-export;
peer-as 65222;
multipath;
neighbor 172.16.0.14;
neighbor 172.16.0.18 {
    metric-out 100;
}
```

(handwritten annotations: MeD Value in BGP-stanza overrides BGP stanza. → MeD Policy)

Set Local Preference Directly

The last requirement can be achieved by setting the local preference of r3's c-bgp peer group directly so that routing policy is not involved. You can also set local preference in the 65000 peer group, but this is not needed, as r3's lower RID already causes r1 and r2 to select r3's routes as active. The suggested change will also affect the local preference setting of the 192.168.x/24 routes that originate in subconfederation 65000, but this does not alter packet forwarding due to r3 having a preferred RID when compared to r4. The prefer-2 import policy on r3 and r4 continues to ensure that packets addressed to the 192.168.100/24 prefix, as advertised by both r1 and r2, are still forwarded to r2.

Before adjusting r3's local preference, confirm that r7 forwards through the metrically closer r6 for transit destinations:

```
[edit]
lab@r7# run show route 4/8

inet.0: 112338 destinations, 114557 routes (112334 active, 0 holddown, 4 hidden)
+ = Active Route, - = Last Active, * = Both

4.0.0.0/8          *[BGP/170] 00:00:29, localpref 100, from 10.0.9.6
                      AS path: 65222 10458 3944 2914 1 I
                    > to 10.0.8.1 via fe-0/3/0.0
                    [BGP/170] 01:32:09, localpref 100, from 10.0.3.5
                      AS path: (65000) 65222 10458 3944 2914 1 I
                    > to 10.0.8.9 via fe-0/3/1.0
```

The highlighted change is now committed on r3:

```
[edit]
lab@r3# show protocols bgp group c-bgp
type external;
local-preference 200;
neighbor 10.0.2.1 {
    peer-as 65001;
}
```

You confirm the effects of the change at r7:

```
[edit]
lab@r7# run show route 4/8

inet.0: 112339 destinations, 198459 routes (112332 active, 60391 holddown, 4 hidden)
+ = Active Route, - = Last Active, * = Both

4.0.0.0/8            *[BGP/170] 01:34:19, localpref 200, from 10.0.3.5
                      AS path: (65000) 65222 10458 3944 2914 1 I
                      > to 10.0.8.9 via fe-0/3/1.0
```

The output confirms that the route's local preference has been altered, and that the modified local preference value has resulted in the desired forwarding behavior at r7. Traceroute testing shows that even r6 has installed r3's routes, despite it having a direct EBGP peering session with T2!

```
[edit]
lab@r6# run traceroute 130.130.0.1
traceroute to 130.130.0.1 (130.130.0.1), 30 hops max, 40 byte packets
 1  10.0.8.6 (10.0.8.6)  0.417 ms  0.330 ms  0.251 ms
 2  10.0.2.2 (10.0.2.2)  1.230 ms  1.016 ms  0.887 ms
 3  130.130.0.1 (130.130.0.1)  0.379 ms  0.677 ms  0.397 ms
```

The various screen outputs confirm that you have met the requirements of the "Miscellaneous EBGP Timers and Knobs" section.

Summary

This chapter detailed EBGP and ISP policy–related configuration tasks that are similar to typical JNCIP-level lab assignments. You should be comfortable with the configuration and verification of interface and loopback-based EBGP peering configurations as well as with the configuration of EBGP load balancing and multipath applications. A JNCIP exam candidate must be proficient with the use of routing policy to control route advertisements to EBGP peers, to filter routes received from EBGP peers, and to perform various tasks such as community tagging, setting MED, supporting AS loops, and the general manipulation of BGP route attributes.

This chapter demonstrated how the act of advertising an aggregate route for your AS, which at first glance seems to be a trivial task, can in fact be very difficult when the interplay between IBGP, EBGP, and OSPF stub area routing are brought together in such a way that their interactions can be difficult to predict. The moral to this story is to never assume anything and constantly re-check your work. Sometimes a small configuration change, like defining a local aggregate on routers in a stub area, can have a disastrous impact on your network's overall operation. A prepared exam candidate will periodically perform quick status checks on previously confirmed aspects of the network's operation to better their chances of finding these types of problems before the test proctor encounters them while grading the exam.

Case Study: EBGP

The EBGP case study is designed to emulate a typical JNCIP-level EBGP and ISP policy configuration scenario. In the interest of "mixing things up," you will configure the EBGP case study using the IBGP confederation topology demonstrated in Chapter 5. The Multi-Level IS-IS topology that will support your IBGP and EBGP sessions stems from the Chapter 4 case study and is shown in Figure 6.4 so you that may reacquaint yourself with it.

FIGURE 6.4   Multi-Level IS-IS topology from Chapter 4 case study

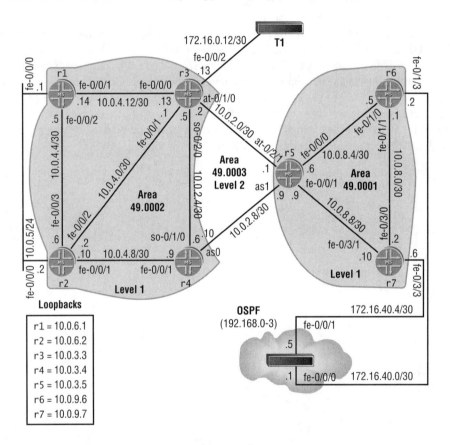

You should load and commit the saved IBGP confederation configurations produced in the "IBGP Confederations" section of Chapter 5 to ensure that your routers will look and behave like the examples shown here. Before starting the EBGP case study, you should verify the correct operation of all routers, interfaces, IS-IS, and the OSPF router using the confirmation steps outlined in the case study at the end of Chapter 4. You may want to review the IS-IS case study requirements to refresh your memory as to the specifics of the IGP that now supports your EBGP case study configuration.

Figure 6.5 shows the IBGP confederation topology from Chapter 5 that serves as your EBGP case study starting point. Before starting this case study, confirm proper IBGP operation using the confirmation steps provided in the "IBGP Confederation" section of Chapter 5.

FIGURE 6.5   IBGP confederation topology from Chapter 5

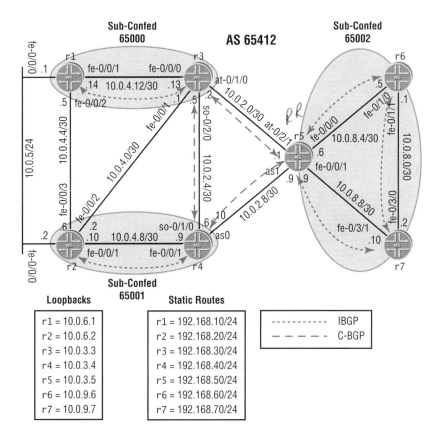

You will want to refer to the criteria listing and the information shown in Figure 6.6, the EBGP case study topology, for the information you will need to complete this case study. It is expected that a JNCIP exam candidate will be able to complete this case study in approximately two hours, with the completed EBGP and ISP policy configuration resulting in a network with no serious connectivity or operational problems. Sample configurations from all seven routers are provided at the end of the case study for comparison with your own configurations. Because multiple solutions are usually possible, differences between the provided examples and your own configurations do not always indicate that mistakes have been made. Because you are graded on the overall functionality of your network and its conformity to the specified configuration criteria, various operational mode commands are included so that you can compare the behavior of your network to a known good example.

FIGURE 6.6 EBGP case study topology

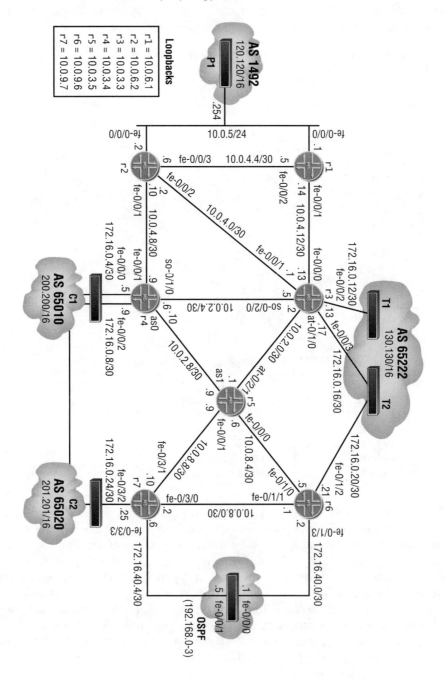

To complete this case study, your EBGP configuration must meet the following criteria.

- Your EBGP and policy configuration must be added to the IBGP confederation example from Chapter 5.

- Establish EBGP peering sessions according to the following criteria:

  - EBGP load balance over the two links connecting r4 to C1.
  - EBGP load balance from r3 to T1 and T2.
  - The P1 router must peer to both r1 and r2 using interface addresses.
  - The C1 router uses authentication with secret *jnx*.
  - The C2 router has been incorrectly set to peer with AS 65413. You must bring up the EBGP session without modifying the C2 router's configuration.
  - r4 must write to the syslog when C1 advertises more than 10 IPv4 unicast routes.

- Policy requirements

  - Originate three advertisements to EBGP peers reflecting your 10/8 space, the OSPF router's routes, and the OSPF subnets.
  - You cannot use generated routes, but a single static route is permitted on both r1 and r2. Interface or link failures cannot disrupt P1's connectivity.
  - Prepend *64512 64512* to all routes received from P1. Ensure that transit providers do not receive these AS numbers.
  - Use communities to tag routes based on the EBGP peering point where they are learned. Ensure that routes learned from each peering point can be uniquely identified.
  - Remove all communities received from the P1 router.
  - Without using policy, make sure you do not install any 192.0.2/24 test-net prefixes from EBGP peers as active routes.
  - Accept all customer routes that have originated in customer sites to accommodate the C1–C2 EBGP peering shown in Figure 6.6.
  - Accept no routes with prefixes longer than a /26.
  - Use local preference so that customer routes are preferred over transit routes.
  - Do not accept any default routes or RFC 1918 routes from EBGP peers.
  - Send peer EBGP routes to all sites. Do not send transit provider routes to peers.
  - Customers receive all EBGP routes, and all sites receive customer EBGP routes.
  - r6 must advertise a MED to T2 based on its IGP metrics.
  - Damp transit provider routes based on prefix length according to these criteria:
    - Prefix lengths 0–8 = No damping
    - Prefix lengths 9–16 = 20-minute half-life and reuse of 1000
    - Prefix lengths 17–32 = 25-minute half-life and reuse of 1500
    - 210.0/16 or longer = No damping

- All routers in your AS should forward through r2 to reach peer prefixes when r2 is operational.

- Ensure that transit providers use the r6 peering link when forwarding traffic to customer destinations without setting MED on r3.

- You cannot have any black holes or suboptimal routing.

EBGP Case Study Analysis

Each configuration requirement for the case study will now be matched to one or more valid router configurations and commands that can be used to confirm whether your network is operating within the specified case study guidelines. We begin with these criteria, as they serve to establish baseline for your BGP connectivity:

- Establish EBGP peering sessions according to the following requirements:

  - EBGP load balance over the two links connecting r4 to C1.

  - EBGP load balance from r3 to T1 and T2.

  - The P1 router must peer to both r1 and r2 using interface addresses.

  - The C1 router uses authentication with secret *jnx*.

  - The C2 router has been incorrectly set to peer with AS 65413. You must bring up the EBGP session without modifying the C2 router's configuration.

  - r4 must write to the syslog when C1 advertises more than 10 IPv4 unicast routes.

r1 and *r2* EBGP Peering

We begin our analysis with the EBGP peering configuration for r1. r2's P1 peering configuration is identical and is not shown here.

```
[edit]
lab@r1# show protocols bgp group p1
type external;
neighbor 10.0.5.254 {
    peer-as 1492;
}
```

The P1 peering session is then confirmed to be operational:

```
[edit]
lab@r1# run show bgp summary
Groups: 2 Peers: 2 Down peers: 1
Table          Tot Paths  Act Paths Suppressed    History Damp State    Pending
inet.0                15         14          0          0         0           0
```

```
Peer              AS      InPkt    OutPkt    OutQ   Flaps Last Up/Dwn
State|#Active/Received/Damped...
10.0.3.3        65000    39001        91       0      1      10:17 Active
10.0.5.254       1492       31       36       0      0   11:48 14/15/0
0/0/0
```

The P1 peering session is established, but the establishment of the EBGP session to P1 has caused the loss of the IBGP session to r3. Further analysis confirms this is due to the presence of a Martian route being received from P1:

```
[edit]
lab@r1# run show route 10.0.3.3

inet.0: 29 destinations, 30 routes (29 active, 0 holddown, 0 hidden)
+ = Active Route, - = Last Active, * = Both

0.0.0.0/4          *[BGP/170] 00:11:50, MED 0, localpref 100
                      AS path: 1492 I
                    > to 10.0.5.254 via fe-0/0/0.0
```

Your subsequent Martian filtering activities at r1 and r2 will resolve this problem.

r4 EBGP Peering

A working EBGP peering stanza for r4 is shown next. Note the presence of the multihop and local-address statements needed to support the loopback-based EBGP peering session to C1:

```
[edit]
lab@r4# show protocols bgp group c1
type external;
multihop;
local-address 10.0.3.4;
family inet {
    unicast {
        prefix-limit {
            maximum 10;
        }
    }
}
peer-as 65010;
neighbor 200.200.0.1 {
    authentication-key "$9$n2/i9tOMWx7VY"; # SECRET-DATA
}
```

The `prefix-limit` related configuration will result in syslog entries when more than 10 unicast IPv4 routes are advertised by C1. Adding the `teardown` option would cause r4 to clear the connection when the prefix limit is exceeded, which is a behavior that is outside the requirements of this study. The static routing needed to back up the loopback peering is shown next, as are the correct interface address assignments for r4's EBGP peering to C1:

```
[edit]
lab@r4# show routing-options static
route 10.0.200.0/24 next-hop 10.0.1.102;
route 192.168.40.0/24 reject;
route 200.200.0.1/32 next-hop [ 172.16.0.6 172.16.0.10 ];


[edit]
lab@r4# show interfaces fe-0/0/0
unit 0 {
    family inet {
        address 172.16.0.5/30;
    }
}


[edit]
lab@r4# show interfaces fe-0/0/2
unit 0 {
    family inet {
        address 172.16.0.9/30;
    }
}
```

Proper EBGP session establishment to C1 is confirmed:

```
lab@r4# run show bgp summary
Groups: 3 Peers: 4 Down peers: 1
Table          Tot Paths  Act Paths Suppressed    History Damp State    Pending
inet.0               19         15          0          0          0          0
Peer              AS      InPkt     OutPkt    OutQ   Flaps Last Up/Dwn
State|#Active/Received/Damped...
200.200.0.1    65010        113        115       0       0    54:04 12/12/0
0/0/0
10.0.3.3       65000      39102      39110       0       0  1:36:14 4/4/0
0/0/0
10.0.3.5       65002        180        183       0       1  1:23:19 0/4/0
0/0/0
10.0.6.2       65001         38      38950       0       1  1:16:48 Active
```

Considering that 12 prefixes have been advertised by C1, you can confirm the prefix-limit configuration by examining the messages file:

```
[edit]
lab@r4# run show log messages | match prefix
Jun 25 11:22:54 r4 rpd[580]: 200.200.0.1 (External AS 65010): Configured maximum
prefix-limit(10) exceeded for inet-unicast nlri: 12
```

r7 EBGP Peering

The fact that C2 has been misconfigured with regard to r7's AS number, coupled with your inability to modify C2's configuration, means that you will need to use the local-as option to allow r7 to "appear" as if it belongs to a different AS. A working c2 stanza for r7 is shown next along with the required interface configuration:

```
[edit protocols bgp]
lab@r7# show group c2
type external;
local-as 65413;
neighbor 172.16.0.26 {
    peer-as 65020;
}
```

```
[edit]
lab@r7# show interfaces fe-0/3/2
unit 0 {
    family inet {
        address 172.16.0.25/30;
    }
}
```

The EBGP peering session to C2 is confirmed to be operational:

```
[edit]
lab@r7# run show bgp summary
Groups: 2 Peers: 3 Down peers: 0
Table          Tot Paths  Act Paths Suppressed    History Damp State   Pending
inet.0               17        16          0           0        0           0
Peer             AS      InPkt    OutPkt    OutQ   Flaps Last Up/Dwn
State|#Active/Received/Damped...
172.16.0.26    65020      61        65        0       0     27:57 12/13/0
0/0/0
10.0.3.5       65002     276       269        0       1    2:12:29 3/3/0
0/0/0
```

```
10.0.9.6        65002       290      295      0      0    2:24:52 1/1/0
0/0/0
```

r6 EBGP Peering

r6's EBGP peering is relatively straightforward. A working t2 stanza along with the necessary interface configuration is shown next:

```
lab@r6# show group t2
type external;
neighbor 172.16.0.22 {
    peer-as 65222;
}


[edit]
lab@r6# show interfaces fe-0/1/2
unit 0 {
    family inet {
        address 172.16.0.21/30;
    }
}
```

After the commit EBGP session establishment to T2 is confirmed:

```
[edit protocols bgp]
lab@r6# run show bgp summary
Groups: 2 Peers: 3 Down peers: 0
```

Table	Tot Paths	Act Paths	Suppressed	History	Damp State	Pending
inet.0	117565	117564	0	0	0	0

Peer	AS	InPkt	OutPkt	OutQ	Flaps	Last Up/Dwn	State|#Active/Received/Damped...
172.16.0.22	65222	30723	30800	0	0	19	117548/117549/0
							0/0/0
10.0.3.5	65002	289	30999	0	1	2:18:19	3/3/0 0/0/0
10.0.9.7	65002	306	22767	27816	1	2:30:38	13/13/0 0/0/0

r3 EBGP Peering

r3's EBGP peering stanza requires use of the multipath option to accommodate load balancing. A working t1–t2 stanza and the necessary interface configuration statements are shown next:

```
[edit protocols bgp group t1-t2]
lab@r3# show
```

```
type external;
peer-as 65222;
multipath;
neighbor 172.16.0.14;
neighbor 172.16.0.18;

[edit]
lab@r3# show interfaces fe-0/0/2
unit 0 {
    family inet {
        address 172.16.0.13/30;
    }
    family iso;
}

[edit]
lab@r3# show interfaces fe-0/0/3
unit 0 {
    family inet {
        address 172.16.0.17/30;
    }
}
```

The family iso setting on r3's fe-0/0/2 interface was called for in Chapter 5 to allow the advertisement of the 172.16.0.12/30 prefix as an IS-IS level 2 internal prefix. The presence of this route within your network does not preclude the use of a next hop self policy on r3 during subsequent policy-related configuration, but it does mean that r3 only really needs next hop self configuration for the peering session to T2.

r3's EBGP sessions to T1 and T2 are now confirmed:

```
[edit]
lab@r3# run show bgp summary
Groups: 3 Peers: 5 Down peers: 1
Table          Tot Paths  Act Paths Suppressed    History Damp State    Pending
inet.0           235105     235103          0          0         0            0
Peer               AS      InPkt     OutPkt    OutQ   Flaps Last Up/Dwn
State|#Active/Received/Damped...
172.16.0.14      65222      22123      24654       0       0     6:52 117544/
117544/0         0/0/0
172.16.0.18      65222      21138      23863       0       0     6:48 117545/
117545/0         0/0/0
10.0.3.4         65001      64029      63704       0       1  2:55:14 11/13/0
0/0/0
```

```
10.0.3.5       65002     23228     24350    0     1     2:42:24 3/3/0
0/0/0
10.0.6.1       65000        85     39002    0     1     2:35:48 Active
```

Proper multipath operation is confirmed by seeing the same number of active routes attributed to both of the T1 and T2 peering sessions.

EBGP Import Policy and Martian Filtering

This section highlights the EBGP import policy and Martian filtering configurations for all routers in the test bed. We begin with the following case study requirement:

- Without using policy, ensure that you do not install any 192.0.2/24 test-net prefixes from EBGP peers as active routes.

The inability to use routing policy and route filters means that you will have to configure the Martian table of each router in order to deny 192.168.0.2/24 routes as shown next:

```
[edit]
lab@r6# set routing-options martians 192.0.2/24 orlonger
```

After the commit, the Martian table for inet.0 is shown, and a 192.0.2/24 route received from T2 is confirmed as hidden. The use of orlonger for the match type is recommended to ensure that no test-net prefixes will be accepted:

```
[edit]
lab@r6# run show route martians table inet.0

inet.0:
            0.0.0.0/0 exact -- allowed
            0.0.0.0/8 orlonger -- disallowed
            127.0.0.0/8 orlonger -- disallowed
            128.0.0.0/16 orlonger -- disallowed
            191.255.0.0/16 orlonger -- disallowed
            192.0.0.0/24 orlonger -- disallowed
            223.255.255.0/24 orlonger -- disallowed
            240.0.0.0/4 orlonger -- disallowed
            192.0.2.0/24 orlonger -- disallowed
```

```
[edit]
lab@r6# run show route 192.0.2/24 hidden

inet.0: 117589 destinations, 235127 routes (117588 active, 0 holddown, 1 hidden)
+ = Active Route, - = Last Active, * = Both
```

```
192.0.2.0/24        [BGP ] 00:04:01, MED 0, localpref 100
                       AS path: 65222 I
                    > to 172.16.0.22 via fe-0/1/2.0
```

The next EBGP import policy task relates to route damping in accordance with the following requirements.

- Damp transit provider routes based on prefix length according to these criteria:
  - Prefix lengths 0–8 = No damping
  - Prefix lengths 9–16 = 20-minute half-life and reuse of 1000
  - Prefix lengths 17–32 = 25-minute half-life and reuse of 1500
  - 210.0/16 or longer = No damping

The policy and damping profile definitions shown for r6 correctly configure the router for the specified damping requirements:

```
[edit]
lab@r6# show policy-options | find damp
policy-statement damp {
    term 1 {
        from {
            route-filter 200.0.0.0/16 orlonger damping none;
            route-filter 0.0.0.0/0 prefix-length-range /0-/8 damping none;
            route-filter 0.0.0.0/0 prefix-length-range /9-/16 damping low;
            route-filter 0.0.0.0/0 prefix-length-range /17-/32 damping high;
        }
    }
}
damping none {
    disable;
}
damping high {
    half-life 25;
    reuse 1500;
}
damping low {
    half-life 20;
    reuse 1000;
}
```

To put damping into effect, the highlighted changes are needed in r6's BGP stanza. The `damping` keyword could have been applied globally if desired because it will affect only EBGP peering sessions:

```
[edit]
lab@r6# show protocols bgp
group 65002 {
    type internal;
    local-address 10.0.9.6;
    export ibgp;
    neighbor 10.0.9.7;
    neighbor 10.0.3.5;
}
group t2 {
    type external;
    damping;
    import damp;
    neighbor 172.16.0.22 {
        peer-as 65222;
    }
}
```

Before proceeding, be sure to replicate the damping-related changes shown for r6 on r3. To verify damping, you can clear your EBGP neighbor sessions several times and then display hidden routes, or use the `show route damping suppressed` command. Displaying hidden routes with the `detail` switch will allow you to see what damping parameters a given prefix is being subjected to, which allows you to confirm the proper prefix to damping profile mappings.

We now examine the case study's criteria for route filtering and tagging, beginning with the context of a customer-attached router:

- Use communities to tag routes based on the EBGP peering point where they are learned. Ensure that routes learned from each peering point can be uniquely identified.
- Accept all customer routes that have originated in customer sites to accommodate the C1–C2 EBGP peering shown earlier in Figure 6.6.
- Accept no routes with prefixes longer than a /26.
- Use local preference so that customer routes are preferred over transit routers.
- Do not accept any default routes or RFC 1918 routes from EBGP peers.
- Remove all communities received from the P1 router.

Table 6.2 contains this author's choice of a unique community-tagging scheme that meets the case study's requirements.

TABLE 6.2 Community Value Assignments

Peer Designation	Community Base
Transit	65412:10*x*
Peer	65412:20*x*
Customer	65412:30*x*

The plan here is to code the last digit of the community value with the number associated with each peer such that P1 will be identified by the community value of 65412:201, for example.

Customer-Attached Routers *r4* and *r7*

The policy, community, and AS path definitions shown next will accommodate the import policy needs of r4 and r7. Note that the local preference setting required to ensure that customer routes will be preferred over transit providers, which will use the default value of 100, has been incorporated into the cust-filter-in policy:

```
[edit policy-options policy-statement cust-filter-in]
lab@r4# show
term rfc1918 {
    from {
        route-filter 10.0.0.0/8 orlonger reject;
        route-filter 192.168.0.0/16 orlonger reject;
        route-filter 172.16.0.0/12 orlonger reject;
        route-filter 0.0.0.0/0 through 0.0.0.0/32 reject;
    }
}
term kill-27-or-longer {
    from {
        route-filter 0.0.0.0/0 prefix-length-range /27-/32 reject;
    }
}
term tag-c1 {
    from as-path cust-1;
```

```
    then {
        community add cust-1;
    }
}
term tag-c2 {
    from as-path cust-2;
    then {
        community add cust-2;
    }
}
term prefer-cust {
    from as-path [ cust-1 cust-2 ];
    then {
        local-preference 101;
        next policy;
    }
}
term kill-rest {
    then reject;
}

[edit policy-options]
lab@r4# show | match 65412
community cust-1 members 65412:301;
community cust-2 members 65412:302;
community peer-1 members 65412:201;
community trans-1 members 65412:101;
community trans-2 members 65412:102;

[edit policy-options]
lab@r4# show | match 650
as-path cust-1 ".* 65010";
as-path cust-2 ".* 65020";
```

The AS path regx definitions and the specifics for their use in the cust-filter-in policy provide the required local preference modification action for customer routes that may be re-advertised by customer sites after being coupled through the C1–C2 EBGP connection shown earlier in Figure 6.6. The kill-rest term rejects routes that have not matched the prefer-cust term, thereby eliminating any routes that did not originate in a customer network.

The policy-related changes made on r4 need to be copied over to r7 before proceeding to the next set of criteria.

Peer-Attached Routers *r1* and *r2*

Routers that peer with P1 have a similar need for community definitions and Martian filtering, but also have the following unique requirements:

- Prepend *64512 64512* to all routes received from P1. Ensure that transit providers do not receive these AS numbers.

- Ensure that all routers in your AS forward through r2 to reach peer prefixes when r2 is operational.

- Remove all communities received from the P1 router.

The peer-filter-in policy statement shown next will accommodate the import route filtering, community stripping, and AS path prepending needs of r1. The term ordering is important because placing the no-comms term after the tag-p1 term will result in the removal of your community tags as well as those that may have been present in the routes received from P1:

```
[edit]
lab@r1# show policy-options policy-statement peer-filter-in
term rfc1918 {
    from {
        route-filter 10.0.0.0/8 orlonger reject;
        route-filter 192.168.0.0/16 orlonger reject;
        route-filter 172.16.0.0/12 orlonger reject;
        route-filter 0.0.0.0/0 through 0.0.0.0/32 reject;
    }
}
term kill-27-or-longer {
    from {
        route-filter 0.0.0.0/0 prefix-length-range /27-/32 reject;
    }
}
term no-comms {
    then {
        community delete all-comms;
    }
}
term tag-p1 {
    from as-path peer-1;
    then {
        community add peer-1;
        as-path-prepend "64512 64512";
    }
}
```

You must define your named communities and AS paths in order to commit the peer-filter-in policy:

```
[edit]
lab@r1# show policy-options community all-comms
members *:*;

[edit]
lab@r1# show policy-options | match 65412
community cust-1 members 65412:301;
community cust-2 members 65412:302;
community peer-1 members 65412:201;
community trans-1 members 65412:101;
community trans-2 members 65412:102;

[edit]
lab@r1# show policy-options | match 1492
as-path peer-1 ".* 1492";
```

The peer-filter-in policy must be applied as import to the P1 EBGP peer group before proceeding. The highlighted addition of the prefer-2 term adapts r1's import policy for use at r2. The new term ensures that all routers in your network will prefer r2 to r1 when forwarding to provider prefixes. r1's community and AS path definitions will need to be carried over to r2 as well:

```
[edit]
lab@r1# show policy-options policy-statement peer-filter-in
term rfc1918 {
    from {
        route-filter 10.0.0.0/8 orlonger reject;
        route-filter 192.168.0.0/16 orlonger reject;
        route-filter 172.16.0.0/12 orlonger reject;
        route-filter 0.0.0.0/0 through 0.0.0.0/32 reject;
    }
}
term kill-27-or-longer {
    from {
        route-filter 0.0.0.0/0 prefix-length-range /27-/32 reject;
    }
}
term no-comms {
    then {
```

```
            community delete all-comms;
        }
    }
    term tag-p1 {
        from as-path peer-1;
        then {
            community add peer-1;
            as-path-prepend "64512 64512";
        }
    }
    term prefer-2 {
        from community peer-1;
        then {
            local-preference 101;
        }
    }
}
```

The peer-filter-in policy's successful filtering of the default routes advertised by P1 allows r1 and r2 to reestablish their IBGP session to the level 1 area's attached routers r3 and r4, respectively. The correct AS path prepending behavior and, in the case of r2, the modified local preference values, are easy to verify:

```
[edit]
lab@r2# run show route advertising-protocol bgp 10.0.3.4

inet.0: 117260 destinations, 117261 routes (117256 active, 0 holddown, 5 hidden)
+ = Active Route, - = Last Active, * = Both

3.4.0.0/20
10.0.5.254              0        101 64512 64512 1492 I
6.0.0.0/7
10.0.5.254              0        101 64512 64512 1492 I
120.120.0.0/24
10.0.5.254              0        101 64512 64512 1492 I
120.120.1.0/24
10.0.5.254              0        101 64512 64512 1492 I
. . .
192.168.20.0/24
Self                    0        100 I
```

The output confirms that r2 is correctly adjusting local preference and performing its AS path prepending operations on the routes learned from the P1 peering session only. Successful community removal and the addition of locally-defined communities can be verified as shown next:

```
[edit]
lab@r2# run show route advertising-protocol bgp 10.0.3.4 detail | match comm
        Communities: 65412:201
        Communities: 65412:201
        Communities: 65412:201
        Communities: 65412:201
        Communities: 65412:201
        Communities: 65412:201
        Communities: 65412:201
        Communities: 65412:201
        Communities: 65412:201
        Communities: 65412:201
        Communities: 65412:201
        Communities:
```

The output confirms that only the locally added communities are now attached to the routes. If P1 had added any communities, they are gone now! To complete the configuration of these import policy tasks, you must enable the remove-private option on r3 and r6 so that transit providers do not receive the private AS numbers added by r1 and r2. Be careful to apply remove-private only to the peer group containing the router's EBGP peers, because removing the private AS numbers associated with your subconfederation can break things in a really bad way:

```
[edit protocols bgp]
lab@r3# show
group 65000 {
    type internal;
    local-address 10.0.3.3;
    hold-time 180;
    export ibgp;
    neighbor 10.0.6.1;
}
group c-bgp {
    type external;
    multihop;
    local-address 10.0.3.3;
    export ibgp;
    neighbor 10.0.3.4 {
        peer-as 65001;
```

```
    }
    neighbor 10.0.3.5 {
        peer-as 65002;
    }
}
group t1-t2 {
    type external;
    damping;
    import damp;
    remove-private;
    peer-as 65222;
    multipath;
    neighbor 172.16.0.14;
    neighbor 172.16.0.18;
}
```

Because the removal of locally added private AS numbers and the addition of the confederation AS number occurs *after* the processing of the show route advertising protocol bgp <neighbor> command, you might opt to rely on faith when attempting to confirm that you have successfully removed the private AS numbers in the EBGP advertisements being sent to transit providers. In fact, the command output shown next could easily lead a candidate into believing that remove-private does not work, or worse, it might lead them down the path of unnecessary reconfigurations when there are better things for the exam candidate to be spending time on:

```
[edit protocols bgp]
lab@r3# run show route advertising-protocol bgp 172.16.0.14 120.120.2/24

inet.0: 117696 destinations, 235334 routes (117650 active, 0 holddown, 95 hidden)
+ = Active Route, - = Last Active, * = Both

120.120.2.0/24
Self                                 (65001) 64512 64512 1492 I
```

As an alternative to the "just have faith" approach, you can monitor BGP advertisements in the reverse (receive) direction, after enabling keep all on r3 or r6 to leverage the JUNOS software behavior of advertising EBGP routes back to their source.

After enabling keep all at the global level of r3's BGP stanza, we verify that peer router P1's routes, as echoed by T1 back to r3, have the expected AS path. You may need to soft-clear the EBGP sessions to the transit providers so they will re-advertise routes that previously failed incoming sanity checks:

```
[edit protocols bgp]
lab@r3# run show route receive-protocol bgp 172.16.0.14 120.120.2/24 hidden
```

```
inet.0: 117687 destinations, 470620 routes (117673 active, 0 holddown, 235331 hidden)
+ = Active Route, - = Last Active, * = Both


120.120.2.0/24
172.16.0.13                              65222 65412 1492 I
```

Be sure to remove the keep all setting when you are satisfied that all is working as required, and do not forget to add remove-private to the EBGP peer group containing T2 on r6.

Transit-Attached Routers *r3* and *r6*

To complete this task, you need to apply a Martian filtering and community tagging policy to r3 and r6. Because r3 is dual-homed with EBGP peers in the same remote AS, you will have trouble adding the required peer-based community tags using AS path regx matching due to the transit routes having the same AS path. A sample policy for r3 is shown next with highlights calling out its use of neighbor-based matching for its community tagging operations:

```
[edit policy-options]
lab@r3# show policy-statement transit-filter-in
term rfc1918 {
    from {
        route-filter 10.0.0.0/8 orlonger reject;
        route-filter 192.168.0.0/16 orlonger reject;
        route-filter 172.16.0.0/12 orlonger reject;
    }
}
term kill-27-or-longer {
    from {
        route-filter 0.0.0.0/0 prefix-length-range /27-/32 reject;
    }
}
term tag-t1 {
    from neighbor 172.16.0.14;
    then {
        community add trans-1;
    }
}
term tag-t2 {
    from neighbor 172.16.0.18;
    then {
        community add trans-2;
    }
}
```

A similar policy should be added to r6, although r6 can make use of AS path regx if you desire. The same set of community definitions shown for the other routers should also be added to r3 and r6 before proceeding to the next section. Once again, do not forget to apply your `transit-filter-in` policy as import to the EBGP peer group on both r3 and r6.

CONFIRM IMPORT POLICY

You should display the active and hidden routes being received from each EBGP peer to confirm the effects of your Martian filters, community tagging, community removal, and local preference settings before proceeding to the next section.

EBGP Export Policy and Hidden Route Repair

This section addresses your remaining EBGP and IBGP export policy–related tasks. You begin with the following criterion, which is somewhat all-encompassing:

- You cannot have any black holes or suboptimal routing.

The lack of next hop self policies, coupled with the restrictions that surround your ability to advertise the majority of the 172.16/12 networks used to support your EBGP peerings, has resulted in a number of hidden routes and the corresponding potential for inefficient routing. Recall that the specifics of your setup currently have r3 running a passive IS-IS instance on the fe-0/0/2 interface, which allows next-hop resolution for transit routes within your AS. The suboptimal routing situation can be observed on r7, which has only installed transit routes learned from the r3–T1 peering due to its inability to resolve the BGP next hop associated with the advertisements coming from r6:

```
[edit]
lab@r7# run show route 130.130/16 hidden detail


inet.0: 117617 destinations, 235039 routes (117567 active, 98 holddown, 65789 hidden)
130.130.0.0/16 (1 entry, 0 announced)
          BGP     Preference: 170/-101
                  Next hop type: Unusable
                  State: <Hidden Int Ext>
                  Local AS: 65002 Peer AS: 65002
                  Age: 1:37:14    Metric: 0
                  Task: BGP_65002.10.0.9.6+179
                  AS path: 65222 I
                  Localpref: 100
                  Router ID: 10.0.9.6
```

Having r7 forward all transit traffic through r5 and r3, when it could have taken a single hop through r6, is not optimal:

```
[edit]
lab@r7# run traceroute 130.130.0.1
```

```
traceroute to 130.130.0.1 (130.130.0.1), 30 hops max, 40 byte packets
 1  10.0.8.9 (10.0.8.9)  0.400 ms  0.329 ms  0.254 ms
 2  10.0.2.2 (10.0.2.2)  0.791 ms  0.592 ms  0.918 ms
 3  * * *
^C
```

In this case, the traceroute fails because the 10/8 aggregate for your AS has not yet been exported to EBGP peers. To fix these hidden routes, you must either adjust your existing IBGP export policy or write a new one that will selectively overwrite the BGP next hop on routes learned from EBGP peers. As mentioned in the chapter body, care should be taken to ensure you do not alter the next hop on routes learned from IBGP because this behavior could lead to suboptimal routing for internal destinations. The highlighted policy changes in r3's existing `ibgp` policy leverage your community tags to provide the desired EBGP next-hop rewrite behavior:

```
[edit policy-options policy-statement ibgp]
lab@r3# show
term 1 {
    from {
        protocol static;
        route-filter 192.168.30.0/24 exact;
    }
    then accept;
}
term 2 {
    from community [ trans-1 trans-2 ];
    then {
        next-hop self;
    }
}
```

The logical OR function of term 2's community-matching criteria will result in r3 setting itself as the next hop for routes tagged with either the 65412:101 or 65412:102 communities. An alternative approach would be to define a new, regx-based, community that matches on the occurrence of either transit provider community tag, which allows you to list a single named community in your policy, as shown next:

```
community trans-1-2-a members 65412:10.;
community trans-1-2-b members 65421:101-2;


...
term 2 {
    from community trans-1-2-a;
    then {
```

```
        next-hop self;
    }
}
```

You should define similar next hop self–related IBGP export policies for all routers with EBGP peers, with the exception of r1 and r2 because their EBGP peering subnet is already being redistributed, into IS-IS before you proceed to the next section. Be sure to match on both customer site communities at r4 and r7 to accommodate routes coupled through the C1–C2 EBGP peering session. After committing changes on all affected routers, you retest the path from r7 to the 130.130.0.1 prefix to confirm that it can now forward optimally through r6:

```
[edit]
lab@r7# run traceroute 130.130.0.1
traceroute to 130.130.0.1 (130.130.0.1), 30 hops max, 40 byte packets
 1  10.0.8.1 (10.0.8.1)  0.300 ms  0.209 ms  0.123 ms
 2  *^C
```

After you have successfully exported your 10/8 aggregate, the traceroute should complete normally. You should verify that no routers have hidden routes caused by unreachable next hops before proceeding. Looking at the state of a router like r5 provides a quick indication of the overall success of your hidden route repair efforts:

```
[edit]
lab@r5# run show route

inet.0: 112736 destinations, 337716 routes (112736 active, 0 holddown, 0 hidden)
+ = Active Route, - = Last Active, * = Both

3.0.0.0/8          *[BGP/170] 02:06:16, localpref 100, from 10.0.3.3
                      AS path: (65000) 65222 10458 3944 2914 7018 80 I
                    > to 10.0.2.2 via at-0/2/1.35
. . .
```

We now examine solutions for the following EBGP export policy requirements:

- Originate three NLRI advertisements to EBGP peers reflecting your 10/8 space, the OSPF router's routes, and the OSPF subnets, without altering the `routing-options` stanza on r3, r4, r6, and r7.

- You must not use generated routes, but a single static route is permitted on both r1 and r2. Individual interface or link failures cannot disrupt the connectivity to P1.

r3, r4, r6, and r7

The requirement that you advertise aggregate routes, without modifying the `routing-options` stanza on r3, r4, r6, and r7, means that you will have to define a 10/8 aggregate on r5, and then adjust its IBGP export policy to advertise the new 10/8 aggregate along with its existing

192.168.0/22 and 172.16.40/29 aggregates to all other routers through IBGP. The default EBGP export policy will function to have all three aggregates re-advertised to transit and customer sites, assuming that the IBGP advertisements are active and that you have not negated the default EBGP policy, as per the examples provided in this chapter. The following ibgp policy change and aggregate route definition on r5 creates the necessary aggregate route advertisement behavior:

```
[edit]
lab@r5# show policy-options policy-statement ibgp
term 1 {
    from {
        protocol static;
        route-filter 192.168.50.0/24 exact;
    }
    then accept;
}
term 2 {
    from {
        protocol aggregate;
        route-filter 10.0.0.0/8 exact;
        route-filter 192.168.0.0/22 exact;
        route-filter 172.16.40.0/29 exact;
    }
    then accept;
}
```

```
[edit]
lab@r5# show routing-options aggregate
route 10.0.2.0/23;
route 10.0.8.0/21;
route 192.168.0.0/22;
route 172.16.40.0/29;
route 10.0.0.0/8;
```

The results should be confirmed for all transit and customer peering points before you move on to dealing with r1 and r2. The following output confirms that r4 is not advertising the 192.168.0/22 and 172.16.40/29 routes because of a protocol preference problem caused by r5's redistribution of the same routes into the level 2 IS-IS backbone:

```
[edit]
lab@r4# run show route advertising-protocol bgp 200.200.0.1 192.168.0/22
```

```
[edit]
lab@r4# run show route advertising-protocol bgp 200.200.0.1 172.16.40/29
```

```
[edit]
lab@r4# run show route 192.168.0/22

inet.0: 112467 destinations, 224853 routes (112465 active, 0 holddown, 2 hidden)
+ = Active Route, - = Last Active, * = Both

192.168.0.0/22     *[IS-IS/165] 03:25:27, metric 11, tag 2
                    > to 10.0.2.9 via as0.0
                    [BGP/170] 01:02:11, localpref 100, from 10.0.3.5
                      AS path: (65002) I
                    > to 10.0.2.9 via as0.0
```

The addition of advertise-inactive to r4's BGP stanza allows the router to advertise the best BGP routes that are inactive due to protocol preference, which resolves this problem nicely. Applying the option at the EBGP peer group level will prevent the advertisement of the inactive summary routes to r2, so be sure to apply the advertise-inactive option at the global level (or multiple times within each peer group):

```
[edit]
lab@r4# set protocols bgp advertise-inactive

[edit]
lab@r4# commit
commit complete

[edit]
lab@r4# run show route advertising-protocol bgp 200.200.0.1 172.16.40/29

inet.0: 112491 destinations, 224898 routes (112486 active, 3 holddown, 2 hidden)
+ = Active Route, - = Last Active, * = Both

172.16.40.0/29
Self                                    (65002) I
```

Based on these results, you should make a point of adding the advertise-inactive option to r3 also. This option is not needed on r6 and r7 because the 192.168.0/22 and 172.16.40/29 aggregate routes are not leaked into their level 1 IS-IS area by r5, which causes r5's IBGP advertisement of the 192.168.0/22 and 172.16.40/29 route to be active. The correct behavior for summary route advertisements to EBGP peers is observed at r6:

```
[edit]
lab@r6# run show route advertising-protocol bgp 172.16.0.22 10/8
```

```
inet.0: 117883 destinations, 228894 routes (113047 active, 0 holddown, 4843 hidden)
+ = Active Route, - = Last Active, * = Both


10.0.0.0/8
Self                                    I


[edit]
```
lab@r6# **run show route advertising-protocol bgp 172.16.0.22 172.16.40/29**

```
inet.0: 117883 destinations, 228895 routes (113045 active, 0 holddown, 4846 hidden)
+ = Active Route, - = Last Active, * = Both


172.16.40.0/29
Self                                    I


[edit]
```
lab@r6# **run show route advertising-protocol bgp 172.16.0.22 192.168.0/22**

```
inet.0: 117883 destinations, 228895 routes (113045 active, 0 holddown, 4846 hidden)
+ = Active Route, - = Last Active, * = Both


192.168.0.0/22
Self                                    I
```

r1 and r2

Both r1 and r2 should have active 192.168.0/22 and 172.16.40/29 BGP routes, so the default
policy should already result in their advertisements to the P1 router:

```
[edit]
```
lab@r2# **run show route advertising-protocol bgp 10.0.5.254 192.168.0/22**

```
inet.0: 110768 destinations, 110769 routes (110764 active, 0 holddown, 5 hidden)
+ = Active Route, - = Last Active, * = Both


192.168.0.0/22
Self                               (65000 65002) I


[edit]
```
lab@r2# **run show route advertising-protocol bgp 10.0.5.254 172.16.40/29**

```
inet.0: 110768 destinations, 110769 routes (110764 active, 0 holddown, 5 hidden)
+ = Active Route, - = Last Active, * = Both
```

```
172.16.40.0/29
Self                                        (65000 65002) I
```

The problem with these routers involves getting the 10/8 aggregate sent. Both routers have hidden this route to prevent recursion loops, as discussed in the "Verify Peer Site Export Policy" section earlier in this chapter. The case study's criteria indicate that you cannot use generated routes, which was the approach chosen in the "Verify Peer Site Export Policy" section, but do permit a single static route on each of these routers as long as the failure of a single interface or link does not isolate the P1 router. Defining a 10/8 static route that points to discard or reject would be no better than an aggregate route, in that the presence of such a route would black-hole destinations outside of the level 1 IS-IS area.

Based on the requirements, it would seem that your best bet will be to define a static route that makes use of qualified next hops so that the failure of the primary forwarding path will cause traffic to follow one or more qualified next hops that are attached to the static route. The commands needed to define the static route with a qualified next hop on r1 are shown next:

```
[edit routing-options static]
lab@r1# set route 10/8 next-hop 10.0.4.13
```

```
[edit routing-options static]
lab@r1# set route 10/8 qualified-next-hop 10.0.4.6 preference 10
```

The results from a similar configuration on r2 are displayed:

```
[edit routing-options static]
lab@r2# run show route 10/8
```

```
inet.0: 110644 destinations, 110647 routes (110641 active, 0 holddown, 5 hidden)
+ = Active Route, - = Last Active, * = Both
```

```
10.0.0.0/8          *[Static/5] 00:00:04
                     > to 10.0.4.9 via fe-0/0/1.0
                     [Static/10] 00:00:04
                     > to 10.0.4.1 via fe-0/0/2.0
```

With an active 10/8 prefix that provides the required redundancy, all that is required to finish this section is the creation (and application) of a simple static route redistribution policy on r1 and r2. The policy example, and its application as *export* shown here, do the job:

```
[edit]
lab@r1# show policy-options policy-statement p1-export
```

```
term 1 {
    from {
        protocol static;
        route-filter 10.0.0.0/8 exact;
    }
    then accept;
}
```

```
[edit]
lab@r1# show protocols bgp group p1
type external;
import peer-filter-in;
export p1-export;
neighbor 10.0.5.254 {
    peer-as 1492;
}
```

After committing the policy definition and application as *export* to the p1 peer group, the 10/8 advertisement is confirmed:

```
[edit]
lab@r1# run show route advertising-protocol bgp 10.0.5.254 10/8

inet.0: 110627 destinations, 110641 routes (110624 active, 0 holddown, 5 hidden)
+ = Active Route, - = Last Active, * = Both

10.0.0.0/8
Self                                    I
```

With all routers adverting the three summaries for the prefixes in your AS, you should be able to conduct traceroute and ping testing to the loopback addresses of all external peers. A few examples of proper forwarding behavior as taken from r5 are shown next. This router is chosen because of its lack of EBGP peering sessions.

```
lab@r5> traceroute 120.120.0.1
traceroute to 120.120.0.1 (120.120.0.1), 30 hops max, 40 byte packets
 1  10.0.2.10 (10.0.2.10)  0.734 ms  0.557 ms  0.502 ms
 2  10.0.4.10 (10.0.4.10)  0.436 ms  0.432 ms  0.415 ms
 3  120.120.0.1 (120.120.0.1)  0.613 ms  0.927 ms  0.612 ms

lab@r5> traceroute 130.130.0.1
traceroute to 130.130.0.1 (130.130.0.1), 30 hops max, 40 byte packets
```

```
1   10.0.2.2 (10.0.2.2)  1.194 ms  0.843 ms  1.047 ms
2   130.130.0.1 (130.130.0.1)  0.994 ms  1.021 ms  1.077 ms

lab@r5> traceroute 200.200.0.1
traceroute to 200.200.0.1 (200.200.0.1), 30 hops max, 40 byte packets
1   10.0.2.10 (10.0.2.10)  0.597 ms  0.552 ms  0.513 ms
2   200.200.0.1 (200.200.0.1)  0.567 ms  0.471 ms  0.459 ms

lab@r5> traceroute 201.201.0.1
traceroute to 201.201.0.1 (201.201.0.1), 30 hops max, 40 byte packets
1   10.0.8.10 (10.0.8.10)  0.534 ms  0.438 ms  0.400 ms
2   201.201.0.1 (201.201.0.1)  0.507 ms  0.487 ms  0.482 ms
```

More Than One Way to Skin a Cat

The "aggregate route in a stub/level 1 area" problem was solved twice in this chapter: once with a generated route, and again in this section with a qualified next hop static route. Other creative solutions to this problem include the following:

- Although definitely unorthodox, establishing multi-hop EBGP sessions from r3 and r4 to the P1 router will allow you to advertise the necessary summary routes. Whether this will work depends on the P1 router being preconfigured with the statements needed to permit these peerings, however.

- Converting a totally stubby area into a stub area by removing the no-summaries option, or in the case of IS-IS level 1 areas, applying an appropriate L2–L1 route leaking policy, both result in the presence of more-specific routes that will prevent a local aggregate from creating a black hole.

- Yet another solution involves the application of an IBGP export policy on backbone area routers to effect the redistribution of backbone area IGP routes to the routers in your IS-IS level 1 or OSPF totally stubby area.

- As mentioned previously in this chapter, you could also adjust the IBGP export policy on the stub area's ABRs so that the BGP next hop associated with the aggregate route is set to a prefix that is internal to the stub area instead of the default loopback interface–based router ID.

You will need to read the specified criteria carefully to determine which, if any, of the options demonstrated in this chapter are permitted during a given JNCIP lab exercise. Always ask the proctor for clarification when there is any doubt as to the restrictions imposed on a given lab scenario.

With the corrected aggregate route advertisement behavior confirmed, the following case study criteria will be analyzed.

▪   Send peer EBGP routes to all sites. Do not send transit provider EBGP routes to peer P1.

▪   Customers receive all EBGP routes, and all sites receive customer EBGP routes.

Because the default BGP policy already advertises all active BGP routes, most routers only require an EBGP export policy that will block the 192.168.*x*.0/24 routes (being redistributed from static into IBGP from each router) to satisfy their route filtering requirements. This policy will work for customer and transit provider attached routers:

```
[edit]
lab@r4# show policy-options policy-statement no-192-24s
term 1 {
    from {
        route-filter 192.168.0.0/16 prefix-length-range /24-/32 reject;
    }
}
```

```
[edit]
lab@r4# show protocols bgp group c1
type external;
multihop;
local-address 10.0.3.4;
import cust-filter-in;
family inet {
    unicast {
        prefix-limit {
            maximum 10;
        }
    }
}
export no-192-24s;
peer-as 65010;
neighbor 200.200.0.1 {
    authentication-key "$9$n2/i9tOMWx7VY"; # SECRET-DATA
}
```

When applied to EBGP peers as shown, proper operation is confirmed:

```
[edit]
lab@r4# run show route advertising-protocol bgp 200.200.0.1 192.168.70/24
```

```
[edit]
lab@r4# run show route advertising-protocol bgp 200.200.0.1 192.168.0/22

inet.0: 112821 destinations, 225592 routes (112819 active, 0 holddown, 2 hidden)
+ = Active Route, - = Last Active, * = Both

192.168.0.0/22
Self                                    (65000 65002) I
```

For r1 and r2, you now adjust the existing **p1-export** policy so that it blocks the routes learned from your transit providers as well as the 192.168.*x*/24 prefixes. To filter the transit routes, you could write the policy to match on the unique communities assigned to each transit provider, or you could opt for an AS path regx to leverage the fact that all transit routes have the transit network's AS in common.

The AS path regx approach is demonstrated here because community-based route filtering was shown in the body of this chapter. The highlighted changes to the **p1-export** policy combined with the correct AS path regx will correctly filter the transit and 192.168.*x*/24 routes from the EBGP advertisements sent to P1:

```
[edit policy-options policy-statement p1-export]
lab@r1# show
term 1 {
    from {
        protocol static;
        route-filter 10.0.0.0/8 exact;
    }
    then accept;
}
term 2 {
    from as-path trans;
    then reject;
}
term 3 {
    from {
        route-filter 192.168.0.0/16 prefix-length-range /24-/32;
    }
    then reject;
}

[edit policy-options]
lab@r1# show as-path trans
".* 65222 .*";
```

Many exam candidates would think that all routes coming from transit providers should begin with *65222* and that an AS path regx like *65222 .** would therefore work to filter these routes. While this might be true for a full mesh or pure route reflection topology, the use of a confederation means these routes may very well contain your network's subconfederation AS numbers when received by r1 and r2 as shown here:

```
[edit]
lab@r2# run show route aspath-regex ".* 65222 .*"

inet.0: 112978 destinations, 112981 routes (112975 active, 0 holddown, 5 hidden)
+ = Active Route, - = Last Active, * = Both

3.0.0.0/8          *[BGP/170] 08:33:08, localpref 100, from 10.0.3.4
                      AS path: (65000) 65222 10458 3944 2914 7018 80 I
                    > to 10.0.4.9 via fe-0/0/1.0
4.0.0.0/8          *[BGP/170] 08:33:08, localpref 100, from 10.0.3.4
                      AS path: (65000) 65222 10458 3944 2914 1 I
                    > to 10.0.4.9 via fe-0/0/1.0
```

Making assumptions can lead to the commission of "simple" mistakes when in the JNCIP lab. Most successful JNCIP exam candidates have developed work habits that result in their always taking the time to verify the effects of their configurations and policies, because after all, everybody who has ever made an assumption has been proven wrong at some point! The following commands are used to confirm proper P1 export policy operation:

```
[edit]
lab@r1# run show route advertising-protocol bgp 10.0.5.254 | match 65222

[edit]
lab@r1# run show route advertising-protocol bgp 10.0.5.254 192.168.60/24

[edit]
lab@r1#
```

Good, no transit or 192.168.60/24 routes are present. Now to verify the advertisement of the customer routes:

```
[edit]
lab@r1# run show route advertising-protocol bgp 10.0.5.254 200.200.2/24

inet.0: 112960 destinations, 112963 routes (112957 active, 0 holddown, 5 hidden)
+ = Active Route, - = Last Active, * = Both
```

```
200.200.2.0/24
Self                                    (65001) 65010 I
```

```
[edit]
lab@r1# run show route advertising-protocol bgp 10.0.5.254 201.201.0/24
```

```
inet.0: 112960 destinations, 112963 routes (112957 active, 0 holddown, 5 hidden)
+ = Active Route, - = Last Active, * = Both
```

```
201.201.0.0/24
Self                                    (65001 65002 65413) 65020 I
```

Routes from both customer sites are being sent. Combined with previous confirmation of the required summary route advertisements, this behavior indicates that you have accomplished the goals of this section. To finish this case study, you have the following requirements to deal with:

- r6 must advertise a MED to T2 based on its IGP metrics.
- Ensure that transit providers use the r6 peering link when forwarding traffic to customer destinations without setting MED on r3.

The first item requires the configuration of a direct MED setting on r3 that will track the IGP cost for each prefix advertised. The highlighted change instructs r6 to set the MED to equal its current IGP cost to each destination:

```
[edit protocols bgp group t2]
lab@r6# show
type external;
metric-out igp;
damping;
import [ damp transit-filter-in ];
export no-192-24s;
remove-private;
neighbor 172.16.0.22 {
    peer-as 65222;
}
```

Displaying the MED setting in the routes advertised from r6 to T2 and comparing the value to the IGP metric for a given route confirms that this requirement has been met:

```
[edit]
lab@r6# run show route advertising-protocol bgp 172.16.0.22 10/8 detail
```

```
inet.0: 117914 destinations, 230419 routes (112632 active, 0 holddown, 5291 hidden)
10.0.0.0/8 (1 entry, 1 announced)
```

```
BGP group t2 type External
    Nexthop: Self
    MED: 15
    AS path: I
    Aggregator: 65002 10.0.3.5
    Communities:

[edit]
lab@r6# run show route resolution 10/8
Table inet.3 Nodes 0
10.0.0.0/8 Originating RIB: inet.0
  Metric: 15  Node path count: 1
  Indirect nexthops: 1
        Protocol Nexthop: 10.0.3.5 Metric: 15
        Indirect nexthop: 84ed110 122
        Indirect path forwarding nexthops: 1
            Nexthop: 10.0.8.6 via fe-0/1/0.0
```

The last requirement is to make transit providers T1 and T2 prefer the T2–r6 peering point when forwarding to customer prefixes, without setting MED on r3. T2 currently prefers the r3 peering point due to its preferred MED setting. Recall that no MED equals 0, so having r6 advertise any non-zero MED makes it less attractive to T2. Even without MED, r3's lower RID would still cause it to be the active source of your customer's routes. The current customer prefix forwarding behavior at T2 is shown here:

```
lab@T2> show route 200.200.1/24 detail

inet.0: 117819 destinations, 342989 routes (117819 active, 0 holddown, 112543 hidden)
200.200.1.0/24 (3 entries, 1 announced)
        *BGP    Preference: 170/-101
                Source: 172.16.0.17
                Nexthop: 172.16.0.17 via fe-0/0/2.0, selected
                State: <Active Ext>
                Local AS: 65222 Peer AS: 65412
                Age: 8:04:18
                Task: BGP_65412.172.16.0.17+1026
                Announcement bits (3): 0-KRT 3-BGP.0.0.0.0+179 4-Resolve inet.0
                AS path: 65412 I
                Communities: 65412:301
                Localpref: 100
                Router ID: 10.0.3.3
```

```
BGP    Preference: 170/-101
       Source: 10.0.1.65
       Nexthop: 10.0.1.65 via fe-0/0/0.0, selected
       Protocol Nexthop: 10.0.1.65 Indirect nexthop: 8426000 46
       State: <NotBest Int Ext>
       Inactive reason: Interior > Exterior > Exterior via Interior
       Local AS: 65222 Peer AS: 65222
       Age: 8:04:18    Metric2: 0
       Task: BGP_65222.10.0.1.65+179
       AS path: 65412 I
       Communities: 65412:301
       Localpref: 100
       Router ID: 130.130.0.1
BGP    Preference: 170/-101
       Source: 172.16.0.21
       Nexthop: 172.16.0.21 via fe-0/0/1.0, selected
       State: <NotBest Ext>
       Inactive reason: Not Best in its group
       Local AS: 65222 Peer AS: 65412
       Age: 11:36      Metric: 15
       Task: BGP_65412.172.16.0.21+179
       AS path: 65412 I
       Communities: 65412:301
       Localpref: 100
       Router ID: 10.0.9.6
```

Because you cannot configure r3 to send a less attractive MED to T2, you need to find a tie-breaking condition that is evaluated before MED in the active route selection process that you can control from r3. If you are thinking "AS path prepending," then this author thinks you are thinking right!

The new prepend policy statement is designed to have r3 add two extra copies of your network's AS number to any customer routes it sends to T1 or T2.

```
[edit]
lab@r3# show policy-options policy-statement prepend
term 1 {
    from community [ cust-1 cust-2 ];
    then as-path-prepend "65412 65412";
}
```

Note that having r3 prepend the routes it sends to T2, but not to T1, will result in T2 choosing to forward through T1, which in turn will forward through r3 to reach customer prefixes due to the higher MED settings T2 sees in the routes coming from r6. A correct application of the prepend policy is shown next:

```
[edit]
lab@r3# show protocols bgp group t1-t2
type external;
damping;
import [ damp transit-filter-in ];
export [ no-192-24s prepend ];
remove-private;
peer-as 65222;
multipath;
neighbor 172.16.0.14;
neighbor 172.16.0.18;
```

The desired forwarding behavior is now observed on T2:

```
lab@T2> show route 200.200.1/24 detail

inet.0: 117738 destinations, 343163 routes (117738 active, 0 holddown, 112633 hidden)
200.200.1.0/24 (2 entries, 1 announced)
        *BGP    Preference: 170/-101
                Source: 172.16.0.21
                Nexthop: 172.16.0.21 via fe-0/0/1.0, selected
                State: <Active Ext>
                Local AS: 65222 Peer AS: 65412
                Age: 59:16       Metric: 15
                Task: BGP_65412.172.16.0.21+179
                Announcement bits (3): 0-KRT 3-BGP.0.0.0.0+179 4-Resolve inet.0
                AS path: 65412 I
                Communities: 65412:301
                Localpref: 100
                Router ID: 10.0.9.6
         BGP    Preference: 170/-101
                Source: 172.16.0.17
                Nexthop: 172.16.0.17 via fe-0/0/2.0, selected
                State: <Ext>
                Inactive reason: AS path
                Local AS: 65222 Peer AS: 65412
                Age: 12:05
                Task: BGP_65412.172.16.0.17+1035
```

```
                    AS path: 65412 65412 65412 I
                    Communities: 65412:301
                    Localpref: 100
                    Router ID: 10.0.3.3
```

Verifying that you have met the customer traffic weighting requirements is more difficult if you do not have access to the transit routers. You can easily observe the presence of prepended AS numbers in your advertisements to transit providers, but knowing how the remote routers react to them is another story.

```
[edit]
lab@r3# run show route advertising-protocol bgp 172.16.0.18 200.200.1/24

inet.0: 117757 destinations, 242451 routes (112934 active, 0 holddown, 15949 hidden)
+ = Active Route, - = Last Active, * = Both

200.200.1.0/24
Self                              65412 65412 [65000] (65001) 65010 I
```

By enabling keep all on r3 (and performing a soft clearing of its EBGP peers), you can display the routes that T1 is advertising to r3, and from this information reverse engineer that it has not chosen the route with prepended AS numbers. The keep all option is needed to allow the storage of routes with AS path loops in the router's RIB-in, as you expect to see T1 re-advertising the 200.200.1/24 route back to r3, and whether it was learned from r3 or r6, the local AS number will be present:

```
[edit]
lab@r3# run show route receive-protocol bgp 172.16.0.14 200.200.1/24 hidden

inet.0: 117762 destinations, 461223 routes (112905 active, 1 holddown, 235466 hidden)
+ = Active Route, - = Last Active, * = Both

200.200.1.0/24
172.16.0.14                       65222 65412 I
```

The presence of the transit provider's AS number and the single occurrence of the local AS number indicate that T1 has installed the customer routes it receives from T2—otherwise you would see r3's routes echoed back. Knowing that r3 is prepending AS numbers in the routes it sends to both of its transit providers, coupled with the knowledge that the routes they re-advertise do not contain any prepended AS numbers, provide compelling proof that they both have decided to install the route learned from r6 as the active route. The deactivation of r6's EBGP peering session provides definitive proof, because soon after you will begin to observe that both T1 and T2 begin re-advertising routes with the prepended AS numbers:

```
[edit]
lab@r6# deactivate protocols bgp group t2

[edit]
lab@r6# commit
commit complete

[edit]
lab@r3# run show route receive-protocol bgp 172.16.0.14 200.200.1/24 hidden
detail

inet.0: 117898 destinations, 460474 routes (112395 active, 0 holddown, 235788 hidden)
200.200.1.0/24 (3 entries, 1 announced)
     Nexthop: 172.16.0.13
     AS path: 65222 65412 65412 65412 I (Looped: 65000)
     Communities: 65412:301
```

Final Confirmation

The complexity of this case study would make the printing of all required verification steps and the corresponding operational mode output cumbersome for the reader and expensive for the forest that would have to be sacrificed to print the extra pages. This section provided key examples of how you can monitor the operation of your BGP configuration and related policies. Before considering a case study of this magnitude complete, validate your work by asking yourself the following questions:

- Are all your IBGP and EBGP sessions still established?
- Are there any hidden routes due to unreachable next hops?
- Are you exporting the correct routes to all peers?
- Have you filtered routes from each peer according to the defined list of Martians?
- Are the required MED, local preference, prepended AS numbers, and community tags present?
- Do you still have full reachability to internal destinations over optimal paths?
- Can all your routers trace the route to each EBGP peer's loopback address using optimal paths? Did you remember to verify connectivity from the OSPF router to your EBGP peers?
- Is damping working?
- Are IBGP and EBGP load balancing working?

EBGP Case Study Configurations

The modified configuration stanzas needed to complete the EBGP case study as built on top of the chapter confederation topology are shown in Listings 6.1 through 6.7 for all routers in the test bed, with changes highlighted.

Listing 6.1: *r1* **EBGP-Related Configuration**

```
[edit]
lab@r1# show protocols bgp
group 65000 {
    type internal;
    local-address 10.0.6.1;
    export ibgp;
    neighbor 10.0.3.3;
}
group p1 {
    type external;
    import peer-filter-in;
    export p1-export;
    neighbor 10.0.5.254 {
        peer-as 1492;
    }
}

[edit]
lab@r1# show routing-options
static {
    route 10.0.200.0/24 next-hop 10.0.1.102;
    route 192.168.10.0/24 reject;
    route 10.0.0.0/8 {
        next-hop 10.0.4.13;
        qualified-next-hop 10.0.4.6 {
            preference 10;
        }
    }
}
martians {
    192.0.2.0/24 orlonger;
}
autonomous-system 65000;
confederation 65412 members [ 65000 65001 65002 ];
```

```
[edit]
lab@r1# show policy-options
policy-statement direct {
    term 1 {
        from {
            protocol direct;
            route-filter 10.0.5.0/24 exact;
        }
        then {
            metric 101;
            accept;
        }
    }
}
policy-statement ibgp {
    term 1 {
        from {
            protocol static;
            route-filter 192.168.10.0/24 exact;
        }
        then accept;
    }
}
policy-statement peer-filter-in {
    term rfc1918 {
        from {
            route-filter 10.0.0.0/8 orlonger reject;
            route-filter 192.168.0.0/16 orlonger reject;
            route-filter 172.16.0.0/12 orlonger reject;
            route-filter 0.0.0.0/0 through 0.0.0.0/32 reject;
        }
    }
    term kill-27-or-longer {
        from {
            route-filter 0.0.0.0/0 prefix-length-range /27-/32 reject;
        }
    }
    term no-comms {
        then {
            community delete all-comms;
```

```
                }
          }
     term tag-p1 {
          from as-path peer-1;
          then {
                community add peer-1;
                as-path-prepend "64512 64512";
          }
     }
}
policy-statement p1-export {
     term 1 {
          from {
                protocol static;
                route-filter 10.0.0.0/8 exact;
          }
          then accept;
     }
     term 2 {
          from as-path trans;
          then reject;
     }
     term 3 {
          from {
                route-filter 192.168.0.0/16 prefix-length-range /24-/32;
          }
          then reject;
     }
}
community all-comms members *:*;
community cust-1 members 65412:301;
community cust-2 members 65412:302;
community peer-1 members 65412:201;
community trans-1 members 65412:101;
community trans-2 members 65412:102;
as-path peer-1 ".* 1492";
as-path trans ".* 65222 .*";
```

Listing 6.2: *r2* **EBGP-Related Configuration**
```
lab@r2# show protocols bgp
group 65001 {
```

```
    type internal;
    local-address 10.0.6.2;
    export ibgp;
    neighbor 10.0.3.4;
}
group p1 {
    type external;
    import peer-filter-in;
    export p1-export;
    neighbor 10.0.5.254 {
        peer-as 1492;
    }
}

[edit]
lab@r2# show routing-options
static {
    route 10.0.200.0/24 next-hop 10.0.1.102;
    route 192.168.20.0/24 reject;
    route 10.0.0.0/8 {
        next-hop 10.0.4.9;
        qualified-next-hop 10.0.4.1 {
            preference 10;
        }
    }
}
martians {
    192.0.2.0/24 orlonger;
}
autonomous-system 65001;
confederation 65412 members [ 65000 65001 65002 ];

[edit]
lab@r2# show policy-options
policy-statement direct {
    term 1 {
        from {
            protocol direct;
            route-filter 10.0.5.0/24 exact;
        }
        then {
```

```
                metric 101;
                accept;
            }
        }
    }
policy-statement ibgp {
    term 1 {
        from {
            protocol static;
            route-filter 192.168.20.0/24 exact;
        }
        then accept;
    }
}
policy-statement peer-filter-in {
    term rfc1918 {
        from {
            route-filter 10.0.0.0/8 orlonger reject;
            route-filter 192.168.0.0/16 orlonger reject;
            route-filter 172.16.0.0/12 orlonger reject;
            route-filter 0.0.0.0/0 through 0.0.0.0/32 reject;
        }
    }
    term kill-27-or-longer {
        from {
            route-filter 0.0.0.0/0 prefix-length-range /27-/32 reject;
        }
    }
    term no-comms {
        then {
            community delete all-comms;
        }
    }
    term tag-p1 {
        from as-path peer-1;
        then {
            community add peer-1;
            as-path-prepend "64512 64512";
        }
    }
```

```
    term prefer-2 {
        from community peer-1;
        then {
            local-preference 101;
        }
    }
}
policy-statement p1-export {
    term 1 {
        from {
            protocol static;
            route-filter 10.0.0.0/8 exact;
        }
        then accept;
    }
    term 2 {
        from as-path trans;
        then reject;
    }
    term 3 {
        from {
            route-filter 192.168.0.0/16 prefix-length-range /24-/32;
        }
        then reject;
    }
}
community all-comms members *:*;
community cust-1 members 65412:301;
community cust-2 members 65412:302;
community peer-1 members 65412:201;
community trans-1 members 65412:101;
community trans-2 members 65412:102;
as-path peer-1 ".* 1492";
as-path trans ".* 65222 .*";
```

Listing 6.3: *r3* **EBGP-Related Configuration**

```
[edit]
lab@r3# show protocols bgp
advertise-inactive;
group 65000 {
    type internal;
```

```
        local-address 10.0.3.3;
        hold-time 180;
        export ibgp;
        neighbor 10.0.6.1;
    }
    group c-bgp {
        type external;
        multihop;
        local-address 10.0.3.3;
        export ibgp;
        neighbor 10.0.3.4 {
            peer-as 65001;
        }
        neighbor 10.0.3.5 {
            peer-as 65002;
        }
    }
    group t1-t2 {
        type external;
        damping;
        import [ damp transit-filter-in ];
        export [ no-192-24s prepend ];
        remove-private;
        peer-as 65222;
        multipath;
        neighbor 172.16.0.14;
        neighbor 172.16.0.18;
    }

[edit]
lab@r3# show interfaces fe-0/0/3
unit 0 {
    family inet {
        address 172.16.0.17/30;
    }
}

[edit]
lab@r3# show routing-options
static {
```

```
    route 10.0.200.0/24 next-hop 10.0.1.102;
    route 192.168.30.0/24 reject;
}
martians {
    192.0.2.0/24 orlonger;
}
aggregate {
    route 10.0.4.0/22;
}
autonomous-system 65000;
confederation 65412 members [ 65000 65001 65002 ];

[edit]
lab@r3# show policy-options
policy-statement summ {
    term 1 {
        from {
            route-filter 10.0.5.0/24 exact;
        }
        to level 2;
        then accept;
    }
    term 2 {
        from {
            protocol aggregate;
            route-filter 10.0.4.0/22 exact;
        }
        to level 2;
        then accept;
    }
    term 3 {
        from {
            route-filter 10.0.4.0/22 longer;
        }
        to level 2;
        then reject;
    }
}
policy-statement ibgp {
    term 1 {
```

```
        from {
            protocol static;
            route-filter 192.168.30.0/24 exact;
        }
        then accept;
    }
    term 2 {
        from community [ trans-1 trans-2 ];
        then {
            next-hop self;
        }
    }
}
policy-statement damp {
    term 1 {
        from {
            route-filter 200.0.0.0/16 orlonger damping none;
            route-filter 0.0.0.0/0 prefix-length-range /0-/8 damping none;
            route-filter 0.0.0.0/0 prefix-length-range /9-/16 damping low;
            route-filter 0.0.0.0/0 prefix-length-range /17-/32 damping high;
        }
    }
}
policy-statement transit-filter-in {
    term rfc1918 {
        from {
            route-filter 10.0.0.0/8 orlonger reject;
            route-filter 192.168.0.0/16 orlonger reject;
            route-filter 172.16.0.0/12 orlonger reject;
        }
    }
    term kill-27-or-longer {
        from {
            route-filter 0.0.0.0/0 prefix-length-range /27-/32 reject;
        }
    }
    term tag-t1 {
        from neighbor 172.16.0.14;
        then {
            community add trans-1;
```

```
                }
          }
      term tag-t2 {
            from neighbor 172.16.0.18;
            then {
                  community add trans-2;
            }
        }
    }
policy-statement no-192-24s {
    term 1 {
          from {
              route-filter 192.168.0.0/16 prefix-length-range /24-/32 reject;
          }
      }
    }
policy-statement prepend {
    term 1 {
          from community [ cust-1 cust-2 ];
          then as-path-prepend "65412 65412";
      }
    }
community cust-1 members 65412:301;
community cust-2 members 65412:302;
community peer-1 members 65412:201;
community trans-1 members 65412:101;
community trans-2 members 65412:102;
damping none {
    disable;
}
damping high {
    half-life 25;
    reuse 1500;
}
damping low {
    half-life 20;
    reuse 1000;
}
```

Listing 6.4: *r4* **EBGP-Related Configuration**
```
[edit]
lab@r4# show protocols bgp
advertise-inactive;
group 65001 {
    type internal;
    local-address 10.0.3.4;
    export ibgp;
    neighbor 10.0.6.2;
}
group c-bgp {
    type external;
    multihop;
    local-address 10.0.3.4;
    export ibgp;
    neighbor 10.0.3.3 {
        peer-as 65000;
    }
    neighbor 10.0.3.5 {
        peer-as 65002;
    }
}
group c1 {
    type external;
    multihop;
    local-address 10.0.3.4;
    import cust-filter-in;
    family inet {
        unicast {
            prefix-limit {
                maximum 10;
            }
        }
    }
    export no-192-24s;
    peer-as 65010;
    neighbor 200.200.0.1 {
        authentication-key "$9$n2/i9tOMWx7VY"; # SECRET-DATA
    }
}
```

```
[edit]
lab@r4# show interfaces fe-0/0/0
unit 0 {
    family inet {
        address 172.16.0.5/30;
    }
}

[edit]
lab@r4# show interfaces fe-0/0/2
unit 0 {
    family inet {
        address 172.16.0.9/30;
    }
}

[edit]
lab@r4# show routing-options
static {
    route 10.0.200.0/24 next-hop 10.0.1.102;
    route 192.168.40.0/24 reject;
    route 200.200.0.1/32 next-hop [ 172.16.0.6 172.16.0.10 ];
}
martians {
    192.0.2.0/24 orlonger;
}
aggregate {
    route 10.0.4.0/22;
}
autonomous-system 65001;
confederation 65412 members [ 65000 65001 65002 ];

[edit]
lab@r4# show policy-options
policy-statement summ {
    term 1 {
        from {
            route-filter 10.0.5.0/24 exact;
        }
        to level 2;
```

```
            then accept;
        }
        term 2 {
            from {
                protocol aggregate;
                route-filter 10.0.4.0/22 exact;
            }
            to level 2;
            then accept;
        }
        term 3 {
            from {
                route-filter 10.0.4.0/22 longer;
            }
            to level 2;
            then reject;
        }
    }
}
policy-statement ibgp {
    term 1 {
        from {
            protocol static;
            route-filter 192.168.40.0/24 exact;
        }
        then accept;
    }
    term 2 {
        from community [ cust-1 cust-2 ];
        then {
            next-hop self;
        }
    }
}
policy-statement cust-filter-in {
    term rfc1918 {
        from {
            route-filter 10.0.0.0/8 orlonger reject;
            route-filter 192.168.0.0/16 orlonger reject;
            route-filter 172.16.0.0/12 orlonger reject;
            route-filter 0.0.0.0/0 through 0.0.0.0/32 reject;
        }
```

```
        }
    term kill-27-or-longer {
        from {
            route-filter 0.0.0.0/0 prefix-length-range /27-/32 reject;
        }
    }
    term tag-c1 {
        from as-path cust-1;
        then {
            community add cust-1;
        }
    }
    term tag-c2 {
        from as-path cust-2;
        then {
            community add cust-2;
        }
    }
    term prefer-cust {
        from as-path [ cust-1 cust-2 ];
        then {
            local-preference 101;
            next policy;
        }
    }
    term kill-rest {
        then reject;
    }
}
policy-statement no-192-24s {
    term 1 {
        from {
            route-filter 192.168.0.0/16 prefix-length-range /24-/32 reject;
        }
    }
}
community cust-1 members 65412:301;
community cust-2 members 65412:302;
community peer-1 members 65412:201;
community trans-1 members 65412:101;
```

```
community trans-2 members 65412:102;
as-path cust-1 ".* 65010";
as-path cust-2 ".* 65020";
```

Listing 6.5: *r5* **EBGP-Related Configuration**
```
[edit]
lab@r5# show routing-options
static {
    route 10.0.200.0/24 next-hop 10.0.1.102;
    route 192.168.50.0/24 reject;
}
martians {
    192.0.2.0/24 orlonger;
}
aggregate {
    route 10.0.2.0/23;
    route 10.0.8.0/21;
    route 192.168.0.0/22;
    route 172.16.40.0/29;
    route 10.0.0.0/8;
}
autonomous-system 65002;
confederation 65412 members [ 65000 65001 65002 ];

[edit]
lab@r5# show policy-options
policy-statement summ {
    term 1 {
        from {
            protocol aggregate;
            route-filter 10.0.2.0/23 exact;
        }
        to level 1;
        then accept;
    }
    term 2 {
        from {
            route-filter 10.0.8.0/21 longer;
        }
        to level 2;
```

```
            then reject;
        }
        term 3 {
            from {
                protocol aggregate;
                route-filter 10.0.8.0/21 exact;
                route-filter 192.168.0.0/22 exact;
                route-filter 172.16.40.0/29 exact;
            }
            to level 2;
            then accept;
        }
    }
    policy-statement ibgp {
        term 1 {
            from {
                protocol static;
                route-filter 192.168.50.0/24 exact;
            }
            then accept;
        }
        term 2 {
            from {
                protocol aggregate;
                route-filter 10.0.0.0/8 exact;
                route-filter 192.168.0.0/22 exact;
                route-filter 172.16.40.0/29 exact;
            }
            then accept;
        }
    }
    community cust-1 members 65412:301;
    community cust-2 members 65412:302;
    community peer-1 members 65412:201;
    community trans-1 members 65412:101;
    community trans-2 members 65412:102;
```

Listing 6.6: *r6* **EBGP-Related Configuration**
```
[edit]
lab@r6# show protocols bgp
group 65002 {
```

```
    type internal;
    local-address 10.0.9.6;
    export ibgp;
    neighbor 10.0.9.7;
    neighbor 10.0.3.5;
}
group t2 {
    type external;
    metric-out igp;
    damping;
    import [ damp transit-filter-in ];
    export no-192-24s;
    remove-private;
    neighbor 172.16.0.22 {
        peer-as 65222;
    }
}

[edit]
lab@r6# show interfaces fe-0/1/2
unit 0 {
    family inet {
        address 172.16.0.21/20;
    }
}

[edit]
lab@r6# show routing-options
static {
    route 10.0.200.0/24 next-hop 10.0.1.102;
    route 192.168.60.0/24 reject;
}
martians {
    192.0.2.0/24 orlonger;
}
router-id 10.0.9.6;
autonomous-system 65002;
confederation 65412 members [ 65000 65001 65002 ];
```

```
[edit]
lab@r6# show policy-options
policy-statement isis-ospf {
    term 1 {
        from {
            route-filter 0.0.0.0/0 exact;
        }
        then accept;
    }
}
policy-statement ospf-isis {
    term 1 {
        from {
            route-filter 192.168.0.0/22 longer;
            route-filter 172.16.40.0/29 longer;
        }
        then accept;
    }
    term 2 {
        from {
            route-filter 0.0.0.0/0 exact;
        }
        then reject;
    }
}
policy-statement ibgp {
    term 1 {
        from {
            protocol static;
            route-filter 192.168.60.0/24 exact;
        }
        then accept;
    }
    term 2 {
        from community trans-2;
        then {
            next-hop self;
        }
    }
}
```

```
policy-statement damp {
    term 1 {
        from {
            route-filter 200.0.0.0/16 orlonger damping none;
            route-filter 0.0.0.0/0 prefix-length-range /0-/8 damping none;
            route-filter 0.0.0.0/0 prefix-length-range /9-/16 damping low;
            route-filter 0.0.0.0/0 prefix-length-range /17-/32 damping high;
        }
    }
}
policy-statement transit-filter-in {
    term rfc1918 {
        from {
            route-filter 10.0.0.0/8 orlonger reject;
            route-filter 192.168.0.0/16 orlonger reject;
            route-filter 172.16.0.0/12 orlonger reject;
        }
    }
    term kill-27-or-longer {
        from {
            route-filter 0.0.0.0/0 prefix-length-range /27-/32 reject;
        }
    }
    term tag-t2 {
        from neighbor 172.16.0.22;
        then {
            community add trans-2;
        }
    }
}
policy-statement no-192-24s {
    term 1 {
        from {
            route-filter 192.168.0.0/16 prefix-length-range /24-/32 reject;
        }
    }
}
community cust-1 members 65412:301;
community cust-2 members 65412:302;
community peer-1 members 65412:201;
```

```
community trans-1 members 65412:101;
community trans-2 members 65412:102;
damping none {
    disable;
}
damping high {
    half-life 25;
    reuse 1500;
}
damping low {
    half-life 20;
    reuse 1000;
}
```

Listing 6.7: *r7* **EBGP-Related Configuration**

```
[edit]
lab@r7# show protocols bgp
group 65002 {
    type internal;
    local-address 10.0.9.7;
    export ibgp;
    neighbor 10.0.9.6;
    neighbor 10.0.3.5;
}
group c2 {
    type external;
    import cust-filter-in;
    export no-192-24s;
    local-as 65413;
    neighbor 172.16.0.26 {
        peer-as 65020;
    }
}

[edit]
lab@r7# show interfaces fe-0/3/2
unit 0 {
    family inet {
        address 172.16.0.25/30;
    }
}
```

```
[edit]
lab@r7# show routing-options
static {
    route 10.0.200.0/24 next-hop 10.0.1.102;
    route 192.168.70.0/24 reject;
}
martians {
    192.0.2.0/24 orlonger;
}
router-id 10.0.9.7;
autonomous-system 65002;
confederation 65412 members [ 65000 65001 65002 ];

[edit]
lab@r7# show policy-options
policy-statement isis-ospf {
    term 1 {
        from {
            route-filter 0.0.0.0/0 exact accept;
        }
    }
}
policy-statement ospf-isis {
    term 1 {
        from {
            route-filter 192.168.0.0/22 longer;
            route-filter 172.16.40.0/29 longer;
        }
        then accept;
    }
    term 2 {
        from {
            route-filter 0.0.0.0/0 exact;
        }
        then reject;
    }
}
policy-statement ibgp {
    term 1 {
        from {
```

```
            protocol static;
            route-filter 192.168.70.0/24 exact;
        }
        then accept;
    }
    term 2 {
        from community [ cust-1 cust-2 ];
        then {
            next-hop self;
        }
    }
}
policy-statement cust-filter-in {
    term rfc1918 {
        from {
            route-filter 10.0.0.0/8 orlonger reject;
            route-filter 192.168.0.0/16 orlonger reject;
            route-filter 172.16.0.0/12 orlonger reject;
            route-filter 0.0.0.0/0 through 0.0.0.0/32 reject;
        }
    }
    term kill-27-or-longer {
        from {
            route-filter 0.0.0.0/0 prefix-length-range /27-/32 reject;
        }
    }
    term tag-c1 {
        from as-path cust-1;
        then {
            community add cust-1;
        }
    }
    term tag-c2 {
        from as-path cust-2;
        then {
            community add cust-2;
        }
    }
    term prefer-cust {
        from as-path [ cust-1 cust-2 ];
```

```
        then {
            local-preference 101;
            next policy;
        }
    }
    term kill-rest {
        then reject;
    }
}
policy-statement no-192-24s {
    term 1 {
        from {
            route-filter 192.168.0.0/16 prefix-length-range /24-/32 reject;
        }
    }
}
community cust-1 members 65412:301;
community cust-2 members 65412:302;
community peer-1 members 65412:201;
community trans-1 members 65412:101;
community trans-2 members 65412:102;
as-path cust-1 ".* 65010";
as-path cust-2 ".* 65020";
```

Spot the Issues: Review Questions

1. Why is the policy producing hidden routes when applied as an input policy for an EBGP peer?

   ```
   [edit policy-options]
   lab@r6# show policy-statement transit-filter-in
   term rfc1918 {
       from {
           route-filter 10.0.0.0/8 orlonger reject;
           route-filter 192.168.0.0/16 orlonger reject;
           route-filter 172.16.0.0/12 orlonger reject;
       }
   }
   term kill-27-or-longer {
       from {
           route-filter 0.0.0.0/0 prefix-length-range /27-/32 reject;
       }
   }
   term tag-t2 {
       from neighbor 172.16.0.22;
       then {
           community add trans-2;
       }
   }
   term nhs {
       then {
           next-hop self;
       }
   }
   ```

2. Your goal is to prepend your AS number to the routes that r3 is sending to T2 only. Will the following EBGP export policy achieve this goal?

   ```
   [edit policy-options policy-statement prepend-T2]
   lab@r3# show
   term 1 {
       from protocol bgp;
   ```

```
        to neighbor 172.16.0.18;
        then as-path-prepend "65412 65412";
    }
```

3. Why is this configuration not damping any routes?

```
[edit]
lab@r6# show protocols bgp
group 65002 {
    type internal;
    local-address 10.0.9.6;
    export ibgp;
    neighbor 10.0.9.7;
    neighbor 10.0.3.5;
}
group t2 {
    type external;
    metric-out igp;
    import [ damp transit-filter-in ];
    export no-192-24s;
    remove-private;
    neighbor 172.16.0.22 {
        peer-as 65222;
    }
}

[edit]
lab@r6# show policy-options | find damp
policy-statement damp {
    term 1 {
        from {
            route-filter 200.0.0.0/16 orlonger damping none;
            route-filter 0.0.0.0/0 prefix-length-range /0-/8 damping none;
            route-filter 0.0.0.0/0 prefix-length-range /9-/16 damping low;
            route-filter 0.0.0.0/0 prefix-length-range /17-/32 damping high;
        }
    }
}
. . .
```

```
damping none {
    disable;
}
damping high {
    half-life 25;
    reuse 1500;
}
damping low {
    half-life 20;
    reuse 1000;
}
```

4. Why is this policy not setting the local preference value in customer routes to 101?

```
[edit policy-options]
lab@r4# show policy-statement cust-filter-in
term rfc1918 {
    from {
        route-filter 10.0.0.0/8 orlonger reject;
        route-filter 192.168.0.0/16 orlonger reject;
        route-filter 172.16.0.0/12 orlonger reject;
        route-filter 0.0.0.0/0 through 0.0.0.0/32 reject;
    }
}
term kill-27-or-longer {
    from {
        route-filter 0.0.0.0/0 prefix-length-range /27-/32 reject;
    }
}
term tag-c1 {
    from as-path cust-1;
    then {
        community add cust-1;
        accept;
    }
}
term tag-c2 {
    from as-path cust-2;
    then {
        community add cust-2;
```

```
        accept;
    }
}
term prefer-cust {
    from as-path [ cust-1 cust-2 ];
    then {
        local-preference 101;
        next policy;
    }
}
term kill-rest {
    then reject;
}
```

5. What is wrong with this EBGP case study configuration for r3?

```
[edit protocols bgp]
lab@r3# show
advertise-inactive;
remove-private;
group 65000 {
    type internal;
    local-address 10.0.3.3;
    hold-time 180;
    export ibgp;
    neighbor 10.0.6.1;
}
group c-bgp {
    type external;
    multihop;
    local-address 10.0.3.3;
    export ibgp;
    neighbor 10.0.3.4 {
        peer-as 65001;
    }
    neighbor 10.0.3.5 {
        peer-as 65002;
    }
}
```

```
group t1-t2 {
    type external;
    damping;
    import [ damp transit-filter-in ];
    export [ no-192-24s prepend ];
    peer-as 65222;
    multipath;
    neighbor 172.16.0.14;
    neighbor 172.16.0.18;
}
```

6. You are testing forwarding paths at the end of this chapter's case study. Do the extra hops in the traceroute indicate some type of BGP problem?

```
[edit]
lab@r2# run traceroute 130.130.0.1
traceroute to 130.130.0.1 (130.130.0.1), 30 hops max, 40 byte packets
 1  10.0.4.9 (10.0.4.9)  0.354 ms  0.259 ms  0.222 ms
 2  10.0.2.5 (10.0.2.5)  0.281 ms  0.243 ms  0.229 ms
 3  130.130.0.1 (130.130.0.1)  0.189 ms  0.172 ms  0.160 ms
```

Spot the Issues: Answers

1. The use of next hop self on an input policy would create a routing loop so such routes will be hidden. You should only attempt to overwrite the BGP next hop as part of an IBGP export policy.

2. No. The `to neighbor` match condition is a synonym for `from neighbor` when used in an import policy and is ignored when used in an export policy. The 5.2 code release used in this test bed resulted in no routes being prepended when policies like this were used. You would need to eliminate the `to` condition and apply the resulting policy as a T2 neighbor-level export to achieve the goal of prepending the routes sent to T2 but not T1.

3. The operator has neglected to enable damping with the `damping` keyword in the BGP stanza. The `damping` option should be applied either globally or at the `t2` peer group level.

4. The `accept` actions in the `tag-c1` and `tag-c2` terms are causing matching routes to break out of further policy processing so that they do not encounter the `prefer-cust` term.

5. The application of `remove-private` will break your IBGP confederation by removing the private AS numbers used by the member ASs. Care should be taken to apply this option only to EBGP peers when used in a confederation environment.

6. It is hard to say for sure, but in this case the extra hop is caused by the 10/8 static route that points to `r4` as the primary next hop. Similar forwarding inefficiencies will result when routers in a stub or level 1 area decide to install one default route from one ABR/attached router rather than another. Knowing when extra hops indicate a problem and when they are simply the "nature of the beast" is an invaluable skill. These captures prove that BGP is not to blame for the suboptimal routing:

```
[edit]
lab@r2# run show route 130.130.0.1 detail

inet.0: 111625 destinations, 111628 routes (111622 active, 0 holddown, 5
hidden)
130.130.0.0/16 (1 entry, 1 announced)
        *BGP    Preference: 170/-101
                Source: 10.0.3.4
                Nexthop: 10.0.4.9 via fe-0/0/1.0, selected
                Protocol Nexthop: 10.0.3.3 Indirect nexthop: 8429198 56
                State: <Active Int Ext>
                Local AS: 65001 Peer AS: 65001
                Age: 1:56:27    Metric: 0       Metric2: 0
                Task: BGP_65001.10.0.3.4+1035
                Announcement bits (2): 0-KRT 4-Resolve inet.0
```

```
                    AS path: (65000) 65222 I
                    Communities: 65412:101
                    Localpref: 100
                    Router ID: 10.0.3.4

[edit]
lab@r2# run show route 10.0.3.3

inet.0: 111606 destinations, 111609 routes (111603 active, 0 holddown, 5
hidden)
+ = Active Route, - = Last Active, * = Both

10.0.0.0/8         *[Static/5] 02:13:08
                    > to 10.0.4.9 via fe-0/0/1.0
                    [Static/10] 02:13:59
                    > to 10.0.4.1 via fe-0/0/2.0
```

Glossary

1X   First phase of third-generation (3G) mobile wireless technology for CDMA2000 networks.

1XEV   Evolutionary phase for 3G for CDMA2000 networks, divided into two phases: 1XEV-DO (data only) and 1XEV-DV (data and voice).

2-Way   Adjacency state for OSPF that shows bidirectional communication between two neighbors has been established.

3GPP   Third-generation Partnership Project. Created to expedite the development of open, globally accepted technical specifications for the Universal Mobile Telecommunications System (UMTS).

A

accept   JUNOS software syntax command used in a routing policy or a firewall filter. It halts the logical processing of the policy or filter when a set of match conditions is met. The specific route is placed into the routing table or announced to a neighbor. An IP packet is forwarded to the next hop along the network path.

action   Within a routing policy or firewall filter, an action denotes a specific function to perform on a route or IP packet.

active route   Route chosen by a router from all routes in the routing table to reach a specific destination. Active routes are installed into the forwarding table.

add/drop multiplexer (ADM)   SONET functionality that allows lower-level signals to be dropped from a high-speed optical connection.

address match conditions   The use of an IP address as a match criterion in a routing policy or a firewall filter.

Address Resolution Protocol (ARP)   Protocol for mapping IP addresses to MAC addresses.

adjacency   Link-state network neighbor status that represents two neighbors who have exchanged their link-state database information with each other.

Adjacency-RIB-In   Logical software table that contains BGP routes received from a specific neighbor.

Adjacency-RIB-Out   Logical software table that contains BGP routes to be sent to a specific neighbor.

aggregation   Combination of groups of routes that share the same most significant bits into a single entry in the routing table.

Alternate Priority Queuing (APQ)   Dequeuing method that has a special queue, similar to SPQ, which is visited each time the scheduler moves from one low priority queue to another low priority queue. The packets in the special queue still have a predictable latency, although the upper limit of the delay is higher than that with SPQ. Since the other configured queues share the remaining service time, queue starvation is usually avoided. See also *Strict Priority Queuing (SPQ)*.

American National Standards Institute (ANSI)   The United States' representative to the ISO. See also *International Organization for Standardization (ISO)*.

application-specific integrated circuit (ASIC)   Specialized processors that perform specific functions on the router.

area   Routing subdomain that maintains detailed routing information about its own internal composition and that maintains routing information that allows it to reach other routing sub-domains. In IS-IS, an area corresponds to a Level 1 subdomain. In IS-IS and OSPF, an area is a set of contiguous networks and hosts within an Autonomous System that have been administratively grouped together.

area border router   Router that belongs to more than one area. Used in OSPF. See also *Open Shortest Path First (OSPF)*.

ASBR Summary LSA   OSPF link-state advertisement sent by an ABR to advertise the router ID of an ASBR across an area boundary. See also *Autonomous System boundary router*.

AS external-link advertisements   OSPF link-state advertisement sent by AS boundary routers to describe external routes that they know. These link-state advertisements are flooded throughout the AS (except for stub areas).

AS path   In BGP, the path to a destination. The path consists of the AS numbers of all domains a packet must go through to reach a destination.

Asynchronous Transfer Mode (ATM)   A high-speed multiplexing and switching method utilizing fixed-length cells of 53 octets to support multiple types of traffic.

ATM adaptation layer (AAL)   A series of protocols enabling various types of traffic, including voice, data, image, and video, to run over an ATM network.

ATM Line Interface (ALI)   Interface between ATM and 3G systems. See also *Asynchronous Transfer Mode (ATM)*.

atomic   Smallest possible operation. An atomic operation is performed either entirely or not at all. For example, if machine failure prevents a transaction from completing, the system is rolled back to the start of the transaction, with no changes taking place.

attempt   OSPF adjacency state seen in a Non-Broadcast Multi-Access (NBMA) network that means the local router is to send a unicast hello packet to a neighbor for which it has not yet received any protocol packets.

authentication center (AUC)   Part of the Home Location Register (HLR) in 3G systems, the AUC performs computations to verify and authenticate the user of mobile phones.

Authentication Header (AH)   A component of the IPSec protocol used to verify that the contents of a packet have not been changed, and to validate the identity of the sender. The actual packet data is not protected. See also *encapsulating security payload (ESP)*.

Automatic Protection Switching (APS)   Technology used by SONET ADMs to protect against circuit faults between the ADM and a router and to protect against failing routers. See also *add/drop multiplexer (ADM)*.

Autonomous System (AS)   A set of routers under a single technical administration. Each AS normally uses a single Interior Gateway Protocol (IGP) and metrics to propagate routing information within the set of routers. Also called *routing domain*.

Autonomous System boundary router   In OSPF, routers that import routing information external to the protocol into the link-state database.

Autonomous System external-link advertisements   OSPF link-state advertisement sent by Autonomous System boundary routers to describe external routes that they know. These link-state advertisements are flooded throughout the Autonomous System (except for stub areas).

Autonomous System path   In BGP, the path to a destination. The path consists of the Autonomous System numbers of all the domains a packet must pass through to reach a destination.

auto-RP   One of three methods of electing and announcing the rendezvous point to group address mapping in a multicast network. A vendor-proprietary specification supported by the JUNOS software.

B

backbone area   In OSPF, an area that consists of all networks in area ID 0.0.0.0, their attached routers, and all area border routers.

backbone router   An OSPF router with all operational interfaces within area 0.0.0.0.

backplane   On an M40 router, component of the Packet Forwarding Engine that distributes power, provides signal connectivity, manages shared memory on FPCs, and passes outgoing data cells to FPCs. See also *flexible PIC concentrator (FPC)*.

backup   Denotes a Routing Engine in a dual Routing Engine chassis that is not currently controlling the router's operations.

backup designated router   An OSPF router on a broadcast segment that monitors the operation of the designated router and takes over its functions in the event of a failure.

bandwidth   The range of transmission frequencies a network can use, expressed as the difference between the highest and lowest frequencies of a transmission channel. In computer networks, greater bandwidth indicates faster data-transfer rate capacity.

base station controller (BSC)   Key network node in 3G systems that supervises the functioning and control of multiple base transceiver stations.

base station subsystem (BSS)   Composed of the base transceiver station (BTS) and base station controller (BSC).

Base Station System GPRS Protocol (BSSGP)   Processes routing and quality-of-service (QoS) information for the BSS.

base transceiver station (BTS)   Mobile telephony equipment housed in cabinets and co-located with antennas. Also known as a *radio base station*.

Bellcore   Bell Communications Research. Research and development organization created after the divestiture of the Bell System. It is supported by the regional Bell holding companies (RBHCs), which own the regional Bell operating companies (RBOCs).

Bellman-Ford algorithm   Algorithm used in distance-vector routing protocols to determine the best path to all routes in the network.

bit error rate test (BERT)   A test that can be run on an electrical point-to-point interface (T1, E1, T3, E3, etc.) to determine whether it is operating properly.

bit field match conditions   The use of fields in the header of an IP packet as match criteria in a firewall filter.

bootstrap router   The single router in a multicast network responsible for distributing candidate rendezvous point information to all PIM-enabled routers.

Border Gateway Protocol (BGP)   Exterior Gateway Protocol used to exchange routing information among routers in different Autonomous Systems.

broadcast   Operation of sending network traffic from one network node to all other network nodes.

Building Integrated Timing Source (BITS)   Dedicated timing source that synchronizes all equipment in a particular building.

bundle   Collection of software that makes up a JUNOS software release.

C

call detail record (CDR)   A record containing data (such as origination, termination, length, and time of day) unique to a specific call.

candidate configuration   A file maintained by the JUNOS software containing all changes to the router's active configuration. It becomes the active configuration when a user issues the `commit` command.

candidate-RP-advertisements   Information sent by routers in a multicast network when they are configured as a local rendezvous point. This information is unicast to the BSR for the multicast domain.

CDMA2000   Radio transmission and backbone technology for the evolution to third-generation (3G) mobile networks.

cell tax   Describes the physical transmission capacity used by header information when sending data packets in an ATM network. Each ATM cell uses a 5-byte header.

CFM   Cubic feet per minute. Measure of air flow in volume per minute.

Challenge Handshake Authentication Protocol (CHAP)   A protocol that authenticates remote users. CHAP is a server-driven, three-step authentication mechanism that depends on a shared secret password that resides on both the server and the client.

channel service unit/data service unit (CSU/DSU)   The channel service unit connects a digital phone line to a multiplexer or other digital signal device. The data service unit connects a DTE to a digital phone line.

chassis daemon (chassisd)   JUNOS software process responsible for managing the interaction of the router's physical components.

circuit cross-connect (CCC)   A JUNOS software feature that allows you to configure transparent connections between two circuits.

Cisco-RP-Announce   Message advertised into a multicast network by any router configured as a local rendezvous point in an auto-RP network. It is advertised in a dense-mode fashion to the 224.0.1.39 multicast group address.

Cisco-RP-Discovery   Message advertised by the mapping agent in an auto-RP network. It contains the rendezvous point to multicast group address assignments for the domain. It is advertised in a dense-mode fashion to the 224.0.1.40 multicast group address.

class of service (CoS)   The method of classifying traffic on a packet-by-packet basis to provide different service levels to different traffic. See also *type of service (ToS)*.

classless interdomain routing (CIDR)   A method of specifying Internet addresses in which you explicitly specify the bits of the address to represent the network address instead of determining this information from the first octet of the address.

client peer   In a BGP route reflection network, a member of a cluster that is not the route reflector. See also *nonclient peer*.

cluster   In BGP, a set of routers that have been grouped together. A cluster consists of at least one system that acts as a route reflector, along with any number of client peers. The client peers mainly receive their route information from the route reflector system. Routers in a cluster do not need to be fully meshed.

Code Division Multiple Access (CDMA)   Technology for digital transmission of radio signals between, for example, a mobile telephone and a base transceiver station (BTS).

command completion   Function of the router's command-line interface that allows a user to enter only the most significant characters in any command. Users access this function through the spacebar or Tab key.

command-line interface (CLI)   The user's interface to the JUNOS software through a console, Telnet, or SSH session.

common language equipment identifier (CLEI)   Inventory code used to identify and track telecommunications equipment.

community   In BGP, a group of destinations that share a common property. Community information can be included as one of the path attributes in BGP update messages.

Competitive Local Exchange Carrier (CLEC)   (Pronounced "see-lek") Company that competes with the already established local telecommunications business by providing its own network and switching.

complete sequence number PDU (CSNP)   Packet that contains a complete list of all the LSP headers in the IS-IS database.

confederation   In BGP, a group of small Autonomous Systems that appears to external Autonomous Systems to be a single Autonomous System.

configuration mode   JUNOS software mode allowing a user to alter the router's current configuration.

Connect   BGP neighbor state where the local router has initiated the TCP session and is waiting for the remote peer to complete the TCP connection.

Connectionless Network Protocol (CLNP)   ISO-developed protocol for OSI connectionless network service. CLNP is the OSI equivalent of IP.

Connector Interface Panel (CIP)   On an M40e or M160 router as well as on a T320 or T640 routing node the panel that contains connectors for the Routing Engines, BITS interfaces, and alarm relay contacts.

constrained path   In traffic engineering, a path determined using the CSPF algorithm. The ERO carried in the RSVP packets contains the constrained path information.

Constrained Shortest Path First (CSPF)   An MPLS algorithm that has been modified to take into account specific restrictions when calculating the shortest path across the network.

context-sensitive help   Function of the router's command-line interface that allows a user to request information on the JUNOS software command hierarchy. It is accessed in both operational as well as configuration modes.

contributing routes   Active IP routes in the routing table that share the same most significant bits and are more specific than an aggregate or generate route.

Control Board (CB)   On a T640 routing node, part of the host subsystem that provides control and monitoring functions for router components.

core   The central backbone of the network.

craft interface   Mechanisms used by a Communication Workers of America craftsperson to operate, administer, and maintain equipment or provision data communications. On a Juniper Networks router, the craft interface allows you to view status and troubleshooting information and perform system control functions.

customer edge device (CE device)   Router or switch in the customer's network that is connected to a service provider's provider edge (PE) router and participates in a Layer 3 or Layer 2 VPN.

customer premises equipment (CPE)   Telephone or other service provider equipment located at a customer site.

Customized Application of Mobile Enhance Logic (CAMEL)   ETSI standard for GSM networks that enhances the provision of Intelligent Network services.

D

daemon   Background process that performs operations on behalf of the system software and hardware. Daemons normally start when the system software is booted, and they run as long as the software is running. In the JUNOS software, daemons are also referred to as processes.

damping   Method of reducing the number of update messages sent between BGP peers, thereby reducing the load on these peers without adversely affecting the route convergence time for stable routes. The protocol accomplishes this by not advertising unstable routes.

data circuit-terminating equipment (DCE)   An RS-232-C device, typically used for a modem or printer, or a network access and packet switching node.

data-link connection identifier (DLCI)   Identifier for a Frame Relay virtual connection (also called a logical interface).

data service unit (DSU)   A device used to connect a DTE to a digital phone line. Converts digital data from a router to voltages and encoding required by the phone line. See also *channel service unit/data service unit (CSU/DSU)*.

Data Terminal Equipment (DTE)   The RS-232-C interface that a computer uses to exchange information with a serial device.

Database Description packet   OSPF packet type used in the formation of an adjacency. It sends summary information about the local router's database to the neighboring router.

dcd   The JUNOS software interface process, called the Device Control Daemon.

deactivate   A method of modifying the router's active configuration. Portions of the hierarchy marked as inactive using this command are ignored during the router's commit process as if they were not configured at all.

dead interval   The amount of time an OSPF router maintains a neighbor relationship before declaring that neighbor as no longer operational. The JUNOS software uses a default value of 40 seconds for this timer.

default address   Router address that is used as the source address on unnumbered interfaces.

default route   Route used to forward IP packets when a more specific route is not present in the routing table. Often represented as 0.0.0.0 /0, the default route is sometimes referred to as the route of last resort.

denial of service (DoS)   System security breach in which network services become unavailable to users.

dense mode   A method of forwarding multicast traffic to interested listeners. Dense mode forwarding assumes that the majority of hosts on the network wish to receive the multicast data. Routers flood packets and prune back unwanted traffic every 3 minutes.

dense wavelength-division multiplexing (DWDM)   Technology that enables data from different sources to be carried together on an optical fiber, with each signal carried on its own separate wavelength.

designated router   In OSPF, a router selected by other routers that is responsible for representing the local segment to the remainder of the network, which reduces the amount of network traffic and the size of the routers' topological databases.

destination prefix length   The number of bits used for the network portion of a CIDR IP address.

Differentiated Services Codepoint (DSCP)   The use of the first 6 bits of the IPv4 Type of Service byte. The use of the DSCP for classifying traffic allows an administrator to have 64 unique service levels in the network.

Diffie-Hellman   A public key scheme, invented by Whitfield Diffie and Martin Hellman, used for sharing a secret key without communicating secret information, thus precluding the need for a secure channel. Once correspondents have computed the secret shared key, they can use it to encrypt communications.

Diffserv   Differentiated Service (based on RFC 2474). Diffserv uses the ToS byte to identify different packet flows on a packet-by-packet basis. Diffserv adds a Class Selector Codepoint (CSCP) and a Differentiated Services Codepoint (DSCP).

Dijkstra algorithm   See *shortest path first (SPF)*.

direct routes   See *interface routes*.

disable   A method of modifying the router's active configuration. Portions of the hierarchy marked as disabled (mainly router interfaces) cause the router to use the configuration but stop the pertinent operation of the configuration.

discard   JUNOS software syntax command used in a routing policy or a firewall filter. It halts the logical processing of the policy or filter when a set of match conditions is met. The specific route or IP packet is dropped from the network silently. It may also be a next-hop attribute assigned to a route in the routing table.

distance-vector   Method used in Bellman-Ford routing protocols to determine the best path to all routes in the network. Each router determines the distance (metric) to the destination as well as the vector (next hop) to follow.

Distance Vector Multicast Routing Protocol (DVMRP)   Distributed multicast routing protocol that dynamically generates IP multicast delivery trees using a technique called reverse path multicasting (RPM) to forward multicast traffic to downstream interfaces.

Distributed Buffer Manager ASICs   Juniper Networks ASIC responsible for managing the router's packet storage memory.

Down   OSPF adjacency state that is the starting state for the protocol.

drop profile   Drop probabilities for different levels of buffer fullness that are used by RED to determine if a packet is dropped from a queue or transmitted out an interface.

dual inline memory module (DIMM)   A 168-pin memory module that supports 64-bit data transfer.

Dynamic Host Configuration Protocol (DHCP)   Allocates IP addresses dynamically so that they can be reused when they are no longer needed.

dynamic label-switched path   An MPLS network path established by signaling protocols such as RSVP or LDP.

dynamic random access memory (DRAM)   Storage source on the router that can be accessed quickly by a process.

E

edge router   In MPLS, a router located at the beginning or end of a label-switching tunnel. When at the beginning of a tunnel, an edge router applies labels to new packets entering the tunnel. When at the end of a tunnel, the edge router returns to forwarding the packets using the destination IP address. See also *Multiprotocol Label Switching (MPLS)*.

editor macros (Emacs)   Shortcut keystrokes used within the router's command-line interface. These macros move the cursor and delete characters based on the specific sequence specified.

egress router   In MPLS, the last router in a label-switched path (LSP). See also *ingress router*.

electromagnetic interference (EMI)   Any electromagnetic disturbance that interrupts, obstructs, or otherwise degrades or limits the effective performance of electronics or electrical equipment.

Electronic Industries Association (EIA)   A United States trade group that represents manufacturers of electronics devices and sets standards and specifications.

embedded OS software   Software used by a Juniper Networks router to operate the physical router components.

encapsulating security payload (ESP)   A fundamental component of IPSec-compliant VPNs, ESP specifies an IP packet's encryption, data integrity checks, and sender authentication, which are added as a header to the IP packet. See also *Authentication Header (AH)*.

end system   In IS-IS, the network entity that sends and receives packets.

Equipment Identity Register (EIR)   Mobile network database that contains information about devices using the network.

Established   BGP neighbor state that represents a fully functional BGP peering session.

exact   JUNOS software routing policy match type that represents only the route specified in a route filter.

exception packet   An IP packet not processed by the normal packet flow through the Packet Forwarding Engine. Exception packets include local delivery information, expired TTL packets, or packets with an IP option specified.

Exchange   OSPF adjacency state that means the two neighboring routers are actively sending Database Description packets to each other to exchange their database contents.

Exchange Carriers Standards Association (ECSA)   A standards organization created after the divestiture of the Bell System to represent the interests of interexchange carriers.

explicit path   See *signaled path*.

Explicit Route Object (ERO)   Extension to RSVP that allows an RSVP Path message to traverse an explicit sequence of routers that is independent of conventional shortest-path IP routing.

export   To place routes from the routing table into a routing protocol.

ExStart   OSPF adjacency state where the neighboring routers negotiate who is in charge of the synchronization process.

Exterior Gateway Protocol (EGP)   The original exterior gateway protocol used to exchange routing information among routers in different Autonomous Systems. EGP was replaced by BGP as the size and complexity of the Internet grew.

External BGP (EBGP)   BGP configuration in which sessions are established between routers in different ASs.

external metric   A cost included in a route when OSPF exports route information from external Autonomous Systems. There are two types of external metrics: Type 1 and Type 2.

F

far-end alarm and control (FEAC)   Signal used to send alarm or status information from the far-end terminal back to the near-end terminal and to initiate loopbacks at the far-end terminal from the near-end terminal.

fast reroute   Mechanism for automatically rerouting traffic on an LSP if a node or link in an LSP fails, thus reducing the loss of packets traveling over the LSP.

field-replaceable unit (FRU)   Router component that customers can replace onsite.

firewall   A security gateway positioned between two different networks, usually between a trusted network and the Internet. A firewall ensures that all traffic that crosses it conforms to the organization's security policy. Firewalls track and control communications, deciding whether to pass, reject, discard, encrypt, or log them. Firewalls also can be used to secure sensitive portions of a local network.

first in, first out (FIFO)   Queuing and buffering method where the first data packet stored in the queue is the first data packet removed from the queue. All JUNOS software interface queues operate in this mode by default.

flap damping   See *damping*.

flapping   See *route flapping*.

flexible PIC concentrator (FPC)   An interface concentrator on which PICs are mounted. An FPC inserts into a slot in a Juniper Networks router. See also *physical interface card (PIC)*.

floating static route   A route that should be used only when all dynamically learned versions of that same route are no longer in the routing table.

flood and prune   Method of forwarding multicast data packets in a dense-mode network. This process repeats itself every 3 minutes.

flow control action   JUNOS software syntax used in a routing policy or a firewall filter. It alters the default logical processing of the policy or filter when a set of match conditions is met.

forwarding class   Internal router designation that represents the queuing service offered to IP packets matching some set of criteria. The forwarding class is assigned to a packet when it enters the router and can be modified by a routing policy or a firewall filter.

Forwarding Engine Board (FEB) In M5 and M10 routers, provides route lookup, filtering, and switching to the destination port.

forwarding information base See *forwarding table*.

forwarding table JUNOS software forwarding information base (FIB). The JUNOS routing protocol process installs active routes from its routing tables into the Routing Engine forwarding table. The kernel copies this forwarding table into the Packet Forwarding Engine, which is responsible for determining which interface transmits the packets.

Frame Relay Layer 2 encoding and addressing mechanism that uses a DLCI to segment logical circuits on a physical transmission media.

from JUNOS software command syntax that contains match criteria in a routing policy or a firewall filter.

Full OSPF adjacency state that represents a fully functional neighbor relationship.

fxp0 JUNOS software permanent interface used for out-of-band network access to the router.

fxp1 JUNOS software permanent interface used for communications between the Routing Engine and the Packet Forwarding Engine.

fxp2 JUNOS software permanent interface used for communications between the Routing Engine and the Packet Forwarding Engine. This interface is not present on all routers.

G

Garbage Collection timer Timer used in a distance-vector network that represents the time remaining before a route is removed from the routing table.

Gateway GPRS Support Node (GGSN) Router that serves as a gateway between mobile networks and packet data networks.

G-CDR GGSN call detail record. Collection of charges in ASN.1 format that is eventually billed to a mobile station user.

General Packet Radio Service (GPRS) Packet-switched service that allows full mobility and wide area coverage as information is sent and received across a mobile network.

generated route A summary route that uses an IP address next hop to forward packets in an IP network. A generated route is functionally similar to an aggregated route.

Global System for Mobile Communications (GSM) A standard for mobile communications networks that delivers high quality and secure mobile voice and data services with full roaming capabilities across the world.

GPRS Tunneling Protocol (GTP) Protocol that transports IP packets between an SGSN and a GGSN.

GPRS Tunneling Protocol Control (GTP-C) Protocol that allows an SGSN to establish packet data network access for a mobile station.

GPRS Tunneling Protocol User (GTP-U) Protocol that carries mobile station user data packets.

group A collection of related BGP peers.

group address The IP address used as the destination address in a multicast IP packet. It functionally represents the senders and interested receivers for a particular multicast data stream.

H

hash A one-way function that takes a message of any length and produces a fixed-length digest. In security, a message digest is used to validate that the contents of a message have not been altered in transit. The Secure Hash Algorithm (SHA-1) and Message Digest 5 (MD5) are commonly used hashes.

Hashed Message Authentication Code (HMAC) A mechanism for message authentication that uses cryptographic hash functions. HMAC can be used with any iterative cryptographic hash function—for example, MD5 or SHA-1—in combination with a secret shared key. The cryptographic strength of HMAC depends on the properties of the underlying hash function.

hello interval The amount of time an OSPF router sends a hello packet to each adjacent neighbor. The JUNOS software uses a default value of 10 seconds for this timer.

hello mechanism Process used by an RSVP router to enhance the detection of network outages in an MPLS network.

High-Level Data Link Control (HDLC) An International Telecommunication Union (ITU) standard for a bit-oriented data link layer protocol on which most other bit-oriented protocols are based.

High-Speed Circuit-Switched Data (HSCSC) Circuit-switched wireless data transmission for mobile users, at data rates up to 38.4Kbps.

hold down A timer used by distance-vector protocols to prevent the propagation of incorrect routing knowledge to other routers in the network.

hold time Maximum number of seconds allowed to elapse between the time a BGP system receives successive keepalive or update messages from a peer.

Home Location Register (HLR) Database containing information about a subscriber and the current location of a subscriber's mobile station.

Host Membership Query   IGMP packet sent by a router to determine whether interested receivers exist on a broadcast network for multicast traffic.

Host Membership Report   IGMP packet sent by an interested receiver for a particular multicast group address. Hosts send Report messages when they first join a group or in response to a Query packet from the local router.

host module   On an M160 router, provides routing and system management functions of the router. Consists of the Routing Engine and Miscellaneous Control Subsystem (MCS).

host subsystem   On a T640 routing node, provides routing and system-management functions of the router. Consists of a Routing Engine and an adjacent Control Board (CB).

I

Idle   The initial BGP neighbor state where the local router is refusing all incoming session requests.

import   To install routes from the routing protocols into a routing table.

inet.0   Default JUNOS software routing table for IPv4 unicast routes.

inet.1   Default JUNOS software routing table for storing the multicast cache for active data streams in the network.

inet.2   Default JUNOS software routing table for storing unicast IPv4 routes specifically used to prevent forwarding loops in a multicast network.

inet.3   Default JUNOS software routing table for storing the egress IP address of an MPLS label-switched path.

inet.4   Default JUNOS software routing table for storing information generated by the Multicast Source Discovery Protocol (MSDP).

inet6.0   Default JUNOS software routing table for storing unicast IPv6 routes.

infinity metric   A metric value used in distance-vector protocols to represent an unusable route. For RIP, the infinity metric is 16.

ingress router   In MPLS, the first router in a label-switched path (LSP). See also *egress router*.

init   OSPF adjacency state where the local router has received a hello packet but bidirectional communication is not yet established.

insert   JUNOS software command that allows a user to reorder terms in a routing policy or a firewall filter. It may also be used to change the order of a policy chain.

Institute of Electronic and Electrical Engineers (IEEE)   The international professional society for electrical engineers that sets standards for networking technologies.

Integrated Drive Electronics (IDE)   Type of hard disk on the Routing Engine.

inter-AS routing   Routing of packets among different ASs. See also *External BGP (EBGP)*.

intercluster reflection   In a BGP route reflection network, the redistribution of routing information by a route reflector system to all nonclient peers (BGP peers not in the cluster). See also *route reflection*.

interface cost   Value added to all received routes in a distance-vector network before placing them into the routing table. The JUNOS software uses a cost of 1 for this value.

interface routes   Routes that are in the routing table because an interface has been configured with an IP address. Also called *direct and local routes*.

Interior Gateway Protocol (IGP)   A routing protocol designed to operate within the confines of an administrative domain. Examples include the Routing Information Protocol (RIP), Open Shortest Path First (OSPF), and Intermediate System to Intermediate System (IS-IS).

intermediate system   In IS-IS, the network entity that sends and receives packets and that can also route packets.

Intermediate System-to-Intermediate System (IS-IS)   Link-state, interior gateway routing protocol for IP networks that also uses the shortest path first (SPF) algorithm to determine routes.

Internal BGP (IBGP)   BGP configuration in which sessions are established between routers in the same AS.

Internal Ethernet   Another name for the `fxp1` and `fxp2` interfaces that provide communications between the Routing Engine and the Packet Forwarding Engine.

International Electrotechnical Commission (IEC)   See *International Organization for Standardization (ISO)*.

International Mobile Station Equipment Identity (IMEI)   A unique code used to identify an individual mobile station to a GSM network.

International Mobile Subscriber Identity (IMSI)   Information that identifies a particular subscriber to a GSM network.

International Organization for Standardization (ISO)   Worldwide federation of standards bodies that promotes international standardization and publishes international agreements as International Standards.

International Telecommunications Union (ITU)   Formerly known as the CCITT, group supported by the United Nations that makes recommendations and coordinates the development of telecommunications standards for the entire world.

Internet Assigned Numbers Authority (IANA)   Regulatory group that maintains all assigned and registered Internet numbers, such as IP and multicast addresses.

Internet Control Message Protocol (ICMP)   Used in router discovery, ICMP allows router advertisements that enable a host to discover addresses of operating routers on the subnet.

Internet Engineering Task Force (IETF)   International community of network designers, operators, vendors, and researchers concerned with the evolution of the Internet architecture and the smooth operation of the Internet.

Internet Group Management Protocol (IGMP)   Multicast protocol used for router-to-host communications. Hosts use IGMP to request multicast data streams from the network. Routers use IGMP to determine whether group members are still present on the local segment.

Internet Key Exchange (IKE)   The key management protocol used in IPSec, IKE combines the ISAKMP and Oakley protocols to create encryption keys and security associations.

Internet Processor ASIC   Juniper Networks ASIC responsible for using the forwarding table to make routing decisions within the Packet Forwarding Engine. The Internet Processor ASIC also implements firewall filters.

Internet Protocol (IP)   The protocol used for sending data from one point to another on the Internet.

Internet Protocol Security (IPSec)   The industry standard for establishing VPNs, IPSec comprises a group of protocols and algorithms that provide authentication and encryption of data across IP-based networks.

Internet Security Association and Key Management Protocol (ISAKMP)   A protocol that allows the receiver of a message to obtain a public key and use digital certificates to authenticate the sender's identity. ISAKMP is designed to be key exchange independent; that is, it supports many different key exchanges. See also *Internet Key Exchange (IKE)* and *Oakley*.

Internet service provider (ISP)   Company that provides access to the Internet and related services.

intra-AS routing   The routing of packets within a single AS. See also *Internal BGP (IBGP)*.

I/O Manager ASIC   Juniper Networks ASIC responsible for segmenting data packets into 64-byte J-cells and for queuing result cells prior to transmission.

J

jbase   JUNOS software package containing updates to the kernel.

jbundle   JUNOS software package containing all possible software package files.

J-cell   A 64-byte data unit used within the Packet Forwarding Engine. All IP packets processed by a Juniper Networks router are segmented into J-cells.

jdocs   JUNOS software package containing the documentation set.

jitter   Small random variation introduced into the value of a timer to prevent multiple timer expirations from becoming synchronized.

jkernel   JUNOS software package containing the basic components of the software.

Join message   PIM message sent hop-by-hop upstream towards a multicast source or the RP of the domain. It requests that multicast traffic be sent downstream to the router originating the message.

jpfe   JUNOS software package containing the Embedded OS software for operating the Packet Forwarding Engine.

jroute   JUNOS software package containing the software used by the Routing Engine.

K

keepalive   BGP packet used to maintain a peering session with a neighbor.

kernel   The basic software component of the JUNOS software. It operates the various daemons used to control the router's operations.

kernel forwarding table   See *forwarding table*.

L

label   In MPLS, a 20-bit unsigned integer in the range 0 through 1048575, used to identify a packet traveling along an LSP.

Label Distribution Protocol (LDP)   A signaling protocol used to establish an MPLS label-switched path. LDP uses the IGP shortest-path cost to each egress router in the network and is not capable of utilizing traffic-engineering concepts.

label object   An RSVP message object that contains the label value allocated by the next downstream router.

label pop operation   Function performed by an MPLS router in which the top label in a label stack is removed from the data packet.

label push operation   Function performed by an MPLS router in which a new label is added to the top of the data packet.

label request object   An RSVP message object that requests each router along the path of an LSP to allocate a label for forwarding purposes.

label swap operation   Function performed by an MPLS router in which the top label in a label stack is replaced with a new label before forwarding the data packet to the next-hop router.

label-switched path (LSP)   Sequence of routers that cooperatively perform MPLS operations for a packet stream. The first router in an LSP is called the ingress router, and the last router in the path is called the egress router. An LSP is a point-to-point, simplex connection from the ingress router to the egress router. (The ingress and egress routers cannot be the same router.)

label switching   See *Multiprotocol Label Switching (MPLS)*.

label-switching router (LSR)   A router on which MPLS is enabled and is thus capable of processing label-switched packets.

label values   A 20-bit field in an MPLS header used by routers to forward data traffic along an MPLS label-switched path.

Lightweight Directory Access Protocol (LDAP)   Software protocol used for locating resources on a public or private network.

line loopback   A method used to troubleshoot a problem with a physical transmission media. A transmission device in the network sends the data signal back to the originating router.

link   Communication path between two neighbors. A link is up when communication is possible between the two end points.

link-state acknowledgment   OSPF data packet used to inform a neighbor that a link-state update packet has been successfully received.

link-state advertisement (LSA)   OSPF data structure that is advertised in a link-state update packet. Each LSA uniquely describes a portion of the OSPF network.

link-state database   All routing knowledge in a link-state network is contained in this database. Each router runs the SPF algorithm against this database to locate the best network path to each destination in the network.

link-state PDU (LSP)   Packets that contain information about the state of adjacencies to neighboring systems in an IS-IS network.

link-state request list   A list generated by an OSPF router during the exchange of database information while forming an adjacency. Advertised information by a neighbor that the local router doesn't contain is placed onto this list.

link-state request packet   OSPF data packet that a router uses to request database information from a neighboring router.

link-state update   OSPF data packet that contains one or multiple LSAs. It is used to advertise routing knowledge into the network.

loading   OSPF adjacency state where the local router is sending link-state request packets to its neighbor and is awaiting the appropriate link-state updates from that neighbor.

local preference   Optional BGP path attribute carried in internal BGP update packets that indicates the degree of preference for an external route.

local significance   Concept used in an MPLS network where the label values are unique only between two neighbor routers.

Local-RIB   Logical software table that contains BGP routes used by the local router to forward data packets.

logical operator   Characters used in a firewall filter to represent a Boolean AND or OR operation.

longer   JUNOS software routing policy match type that represents all routes more specific than the given subnet, but not the given subnet itself. It is similar to a mathematical greater-than operation.

loose   In the context of traffic engineering, a path that can use any route or any number of other intermediate (transit) points to reach the next address in the path. (Definition from RFC 791, modified to fit LSPs.)

loose hop   Router in an MPLS named-path that is not required to be directly connected to the local router.

M

management daemon (mgd)   JUNOS software process responsible for managing all user access to the router.

Management Ethernet   Another name for the fxp0 interface that provides out-of-band access to the router.

Management Information Base (MIB)   Definition of an object that can be managed by SNMP.

mapping agent   A router used in an auto-RP multicast network to select the rendezvous point for all multicast group addresses. This information is then advertised to all other routers in the domain.

Martian address   Network address about which all information is ignored.

Martian routes   Network routes about which information is ignored. The JUNOS software doesn't allow Martian routes to reside in the inet.0 routing table.

mask   See *subnet mask*.

master   The router in control of the OSPF database exchange during an adjacency formation.

match   A logical concept used in a routing policy or a firewall filter. It denotes the criteria used to find a route or IP packet before performing some action.

match type   JUNOS software syntax used in a route filter to better describe the routes that should match the policy term.

maximum transmission unit (MTU)   Limit on segment size for a network.

MBone   Internet multicast backbone. An interconnected set of subnetworks and routers that support the delivery of IP multicast traffic. The MBone is a virtual network that is layered on top of sections of the physical Internet.

mean time between failure (MTBF)   Measure of hardware component reliability.

mesh   Network topology in which devices are organized in a manageable, segmented manner with many, often redundant, interconnections between network nodes.

message aggregation   An extension to the RSVP specification that allows neighboring routers to bundle up to 30 RSVP messages into a single protocol packet.

Message Digest 5 (MD5)   A one-way hashing algorithm that produces a 128-bit hash. See also *Secure Hash Algorithm (SHA-1)*.

midplane   Forms the rear of the PIC cage on M5 and M10 routers and the FPC card cage on M20, M40e, M160, and T640 platforms. Provides data transfer, power distribution, and signal connectivity.

Miscellaneous Control Subsystem (MCS)   On the M40e and M160 routers, provides control and monitoring functions for router components and SONET clocking for the router.

mobile network access subsystem (MAS)   GSN application subsystem that contains the access server.

mobile point-to-point control subsystem (MPS)   GSN application subsystem that controls all functionality associated with a particular connection.

mobile station   A mobile device, such as a cellular phone or a mobile personal digital assistant (PDA).

Mobile Station Integrated Services Digital Network Number (MSISDN)   Number that callers use to reach a mobile services subscriber.

Mobile Switching Center (MSC)   Provides origination and termination functions to calls from a mobile station user.

mobile transport subsystem (MTS)   GSN application subsystem that implements all the protocols used by the GSN.

multicast   Operation of sending network traffic from one network node to multiple network nodes.

multicast distribution tree   The data path between the sender (host) and the multicast group members (receiver or listener).

Multiple Exit Discriminator (MED)   Optional BGP path attribute consisting of a metric value that is used to determine the exit point to a destination when all other factors in determining the exit point are equal.

Multiprotocol BGP (MBGP)   An extension to BGP that allows you to exchange routing knowledge from multiple NLRI within and between BGP ASs.

Multiprotocol Label Switching (MPLS)   Mechanism for engineering network traffic patterns that functions by assigning to network packets short labels that describe how to forward them through the network. Also called *label switching*. See also *traffic engineering*.

N

named-path   JUNOS software syntax that specifies a portion or the entire network path that should be used as a constraint in signaling an MPLS label-switched path.

neighbor   Adjacent system reachable by traversing a single subnetwork. An immediately adjacent router. A system to which a BGP session is established. Also called a *peer*.

network entity title (NET)   Network address defined by the ISO network architecture and used in CLNS-based networks.

network layer reachability information (NLRI)   Information that is carried in BGP packets and is used by MBGP.

network-link advertisement   An OSPF link-state advertisement flooded throughout a single area by designated routers to describe all routers attached to the DR's local segment.

network LSA   OSPF link-state advertisement sent by the DR on a broadcast or NBMA segment. It advertises the subnet associated with the DR's segment.

network service access point (NSAP)   Connection to a network that is identified by a network address.

Network Summary LSA   OSPF link-state advertisement sent by an ABR to advertise internal OSPF routing knowledge across an area boundary.

Network Time Protocol (NTP)   Protocol used to synchronize computer clock times on a network.

Next Hop   BGP attribute that specifies the router to send packets to for a particular set of routes.

nonclient peer   In a BGP route reflection network, a BGP peer that is not a member of a cluster. See also *client peer*.

notification cell   JUNOS software data structure generated by the Distributed Buffer Manager ASIC that represents the header contents of an IP packet. The Internet Processor ASIC uses the notification cell to perform a forwarding table lookup.

Notification message   BGP message that informs a neighbor about an error condition and then possibly terminates the BGP peering session.

not-so-stubby area (NSSA)   In OSPF, a type of stub area in which external routes can be flooded.

n-selector   Last byte of an ISO Network Entity Title (NET) address.

Null Register message   A PIM message sent by the first hop router to the RP. It informs the RP that the local source is still actively sending multicast packets into the network should future interested listeners send a Join message to the RP.

numeric range match conditions   The use of numeric values (protocol and port numbers) in the header of an IP packet as match criteria in a firewall filter.

O

Oakley   A key determination protocol based on the Diffie-Hellman algorithm that provides added security, including authentication. Oakley was the key-exchange algorithm mandated for use with the initial version of ISAKMP, although various algorithms can be used. Oakley describes a series of key exchanges called "modes" and details the services provided by each; for example, Perfect Forward Secrecy for keys, identity protection, and authentication. See also *Internet Security Association and Key Management Protocol (ISAKMP)*.

Open message   BGP message that allows two neighbors to negotiate the parameters of the peering session.

OpenConfirm   BGP neighbor state that shows a valid Open message was received from the remote peer.

OpenSent   BGP neighbor state that shows an Open message was sent to the remote peer and the local router is waiting for an Open message to be returned.

Open Shortest Path First (OSPF)   A link-state IGP that makes routing decisions based on the shortest path first (SPF) algorithm (also referred to as the Dijkstra algorithm).

Open System Interconnection (OSI)   Standard reference model for how messages are transmitted between two points on a network.

operational mode   JUNOS software mode allowing a user to view statistics and information concerning the router's current operating status.

Optical Carrier (OC)   In SONET, Optical Carrier levels indicate the transmission rate of digital signals on optical fiber.

Origin   BGP attribute that describes the believability of a particular route. The router that first places the route into BGP should attempt to accurately describe the source of the route.

orlonger   JUNOS software routing policy match type that represents all routes more specific than the given subnet, including the given subnet itself. It is similar to a mathematical greater-than-or-equals-to operation.

OSPF Hello packet Message sent by each OSPF router to each adjacent neighbor. It is used to establish and maintain the router's neighbor relationships.

overlay network Network design seen where a logical Layer 3 topology (IP subnets) is operating over a logical Layer 2 topology (ATM PVCs). Layers in the network do not have knowledge of each other, and each requires separate management and operation.

P

package A collection of files that make up a JUNOS software component.

packet data protocol (PDP) Network protocol, such as IP, used by packet data networks connected to a GPRS network.

Packet Forwarding Engine The architectural portion of the router that processes packets by forwarding them between input and output interfaces.

Packet Loss Priority (PLP) Internal router designation that represents a greater probability of dropping a particular IP packet based on configured class of service settings. The priority is assigned to a packet when it enters the router and can be modified by a firewall filter.

partial sequence number PDU (PSNP) Packet that contains only a partial list of the LSP headers in the IS-IS link-state database.

path attribute Information about a BGP route, such as the route origin, AS path, and next-hop router.

PathErr RSVP message that indicates an error has occurred along an established LSP. The message is advertised upstream toward the ingress router and it doesn't remove any RSVP soft state from the network.

PathTear Message RSVP message that indicates the established LSP and its associated soft state should be removed by the network. The message is advertised downstream hop-by-hop toward the egress router.

path-vector protocol A routing protocol definition that describes the direction to the destination and the network path used to reach the destination. This often describes the functionality of BGP.

peer An immediately adjacent router with which a protocol relationship has been established. Also called a *neighbor*.

penultimate hop popping (PHP) A mechanism used in an MPLS network that allows the transit router prior to the egress to perform a label pop operation and forward the remaining data (often a native IPv4 packet) to the egress router.

penultimate router The last transit router prior to the egress router in an MPLS label-switched path.

Perfect Forward Secrecy (PFS)   A condition derived from an encryption system that changes encryption keys often and ensures that no two sets of keys have any relation to each other. The advantage of PFS is that if one set of keys is compromised, only communications using those keys are at risk. An example of a system that uses PFS is *Diffie-Hellman*.

Peripheral Component Interconnect (PCI)   Standard, high-speed bus for connecting computer peripherals. Used on the Routing Engine.

permanent virtual circuit (PVC)   A logical Layer 2 connection between two network devices. The network path is preengineered and configured on each device in the network supporting the PVC.

Personal Computer Memory Card International Association (PCMCIA)   Industry group that promotes standards for credit card–size memory or I/O devices.

Physical Interface Card (PIC)   A network interface–specific card that can be installed on a FPC in the router.

PIC I/O Manager ASIC   Juniper Networks ASIC responsible for receiving and transmitting information on the physical media. It performs media-specific tasks within the Packet Forwarding Engine.

PLP bit   Packet Loss Priority bit. Used to identify packets that have experienced congestion or are from a transmission that exceeded a service provider's customer service license agreement. This bit can be used as part of a router's congestion control mechanism and can be set by the interface or by a filter.

policing   Applying rate limits on bandwidth and burst size for traffic on a particular interface or IPv4 prefix.

Policing Equivalence Classes (PEC)   In traffic policing, a set of packets that is treated the same by the packet classifier.

pop   Removal of the last label, by a router, from a packet as it exits an MPLS domain.

Point-to-Point Protocol (PPP)   Link-layer protocol that provides multiprotocol encapsulation. It is used for link-layer and network-layer configuration.

poison reverse   Method used in distance-vector networks to avoid routing loops. Each router advertises routes back to the neighbor it received them from with an infinity metric assigned.

policy chain   The application of multiple routing policies in a single location. The policies are evaluated in a predefined manner and are always followed by the default policy for the specific application location.

precedence bits   The first three bits in the ToS byte. On a Juniper Networks router, these bits are used to sort or classify individual packets as they arrive at an interface. The classification determines the forwarding class to which the packet is directed upon transmission.

preference   Desirability of a route to become the active route. A route with a lower preference value is more likely to become the active route. The preference is an arbitrary value in the range 0 through 4,294,967,295 that the routing protocol process uses to rank routes received from different protocols, interfaces, or remote systems.

preferred address   On an interface, the default local address used for packets sourced by the local router to destinations on the subnet.

prefix-length-range   JUNOS software routing policy match type representing all routes that share the same most significant bits. The prefix length of the route must also lie between the two supplied lengths in the route filter.

primary address   On an interface, the address used by default as the local address for broadcast and multicast packets sourced locally and sent out the interface.

primary contributing route   The contributing route with the numerically smallest prefix and smallest JUNOS software preference value. This route is the default next hop used for a generated route.

primary interface   Router interface that packets go out when no interface name is specified and when the destination address does not imply a particular outgoing interface.

protocol address   The logical Layer 3 address assigned to an interface within the JUNOS software.

protocol data unit (PDU)   The basic data structure used by the IS-IS routing protocol to form adjacencies and exchange routing information.

protocol families   The grouping of logical properties within an interface configuration. The JUNOS software supports the `inet`, `iso`, `mpls`, and `inet6` families.

Protocol Independent Multicast (PIM)   A protocol-independent multicast routing protocol. PIM sparse mode routes to multicast groups that might span wide-area and interdomain internets. PIM dense mode is a flood-and-prune protocol.

protocol preference   A 32-bit value assigned to all routes placed into the routing table. It is used as a tiebreaker when multiple exact routes are placed into the table by different protocols.

provider edge (PE) router   A router in the service provider's network that can have customer edge (CE) devices connected and that participates in a virtual private network (VPN).

provider router   Router in the service provider's network that does not attach to a customer edge (CE) device.

Prune message   PIM message sent upstream to a multicast source or the RP of the domain. It requests that multicast traffic stop being transmitted to the router originating the message.

public land mobile network (PLMN)   A telecommunications network for mobile stations.

push   Addition of a label or stack of labels, by a router, to a packet as it enters an MPLS domain.

Q

quad-wide   A type of PIC that combines the PIC and the FPC within a single FPC slot.

qualified next hop   A next hop for a static route that allows a second next hop for the same static route to have different metric and preference properties than the original.

quality of service (QoS)   Performance, such as transmission rates and error rates, of a communications channel or system.

querier router   PIM router on a broadcast subnet responsible for generating IGMP Query messages for the segment.

R

radio frequency interference (RFI)   Interference from high-frequency electromagnetic waves emanating from electronic devices.

radio network controller (RNC)   Manages the radio part of the network in UMTS.

Random Early Detection (RED)   Gradual drop profile for a given class that is used for congestion avoidance. RED tries to anticipate incipient congestion and reacts by dropping a small percentage of packets from the head of the queue to ensure that a queue never becomes full.

rate limiting   See *policing*.

rate policing   See *policing*.

receive   A next hop for a static route that allows all matching packets to be sent to the Routing Engine for processing.

record route object (RRO)   An RSVP message object that notes the IP address of each router along the path of an LSP.

recursive lookup   A method of consulting the routing table to locate the actual physical next hop for a route when the supplied next hop is not directly connected.

regional Bell operating company (RBOC)   (Pronounced "are-bock") Regional telephone companies formed as a result of the divestiture of the Bell System.

Register message   PIM message unicast by the first hop router to the RP that contains the multicast packets from the source encapsulated within its data field.

Register Stop message   PIM message sent by the RP to the first hop router to halt the sending of encapsulated multicast packets.

reject   A next hop for a configured route that drops all matching packets from the network and returns an ICMP message to the source IP address. Also used as an action in a routing policy or a firewall filter.

Remote Authentication Dial-In User Service (RADIUS)   Authentication method for validating users who attempt to access the router using Telnet.

rename   JUNOS software command that allows a user to change the name of a routing policy, a firewall filter, or any other variable character string defined in the router's configuration.

Request for Comments (RFC)   Internet standard specifications published by the Internet Engineering Task Force.

Rendezvous Point (RP)   For PIM-SM, a router acting as the root of the shared distribution tree.

Request message   RIP message used by a router to ask for all or part of the routing table from a neighbor.

resolve   A next hop for a static route that allows the router to perform a recursive lookup to locate the physical next hop for the route.

Resource Reservation Protocol (RSVP)   Resource reservation setup protocol designed to interact with integrated services on the Internet.

Response message   RIP message used to advertise routing information into a network.

result cell   JUNOS software data structure generated by the Internet Processor ASIC after performing a forwarding table lookup.

ResvConf message   RSVP message that allows the egress router to receive an explicit confirmation message from a neighbor that its Resv message was received.

ResvErr message   RSVP message that indicates an error has occurred along an established LSP. The message is advertised downstream toward the egress router and it doesn't remove any RSVP soft state from the network.

ResvTear message   RSVP message that indicates the established LSP and its associated soft state should be removed by the network. The message is advertised upstream toward the ingress router.

reverse path forwarding   Method used in a multicast routing domain to prevent forwarding loops.

reverse path multicasting (RPM)   Routing algorithm used by DVMRP to forward multicast traffic.

route filter   JUNOS software syntax used in a routing policy to match an individual route or a group of routes.

route flapping   Situation in which BGP systems send an excessive number of update messages to advertise and withdraw reachability of the same NLRI.

route identifier   IP address of the router from which a BGP, IGP, or OSPF packet originated.

route redistribution   A method of placing learned routes from one protocol into another protocol operating on the same router. The JUNOS software accomplishes this with a routing policy.

route reflection   In BGP, configuring a group of routers into a cluster and having one system act as a route reflector, redistributing routes from outside the cluster to all routers in the cluster. Routers in a cluster do not need to be fully meshed.

Router ID   An IP address used by a router to uniquely identify itself to a routing protocol. This address may or may not be equal to a configured interface address.

router-link advertisement   OSPF link-state advertisement flooded throughout a single area by all routers to describe the state and cost of the router's links to the area.

router LSA   OSPF link-state advertisement sent by each router in the network. It describes the local router's connected subnets as well as their metric values.

Router Priority   A numerical value assigned to an OSPF or an IS-IS interface that is used as the first criterion in electing the designated router or designated intermediate system, respectively.

routing domain   See *Autonomous System (AS)*.

Routing Engine   Architectural portion of the router that handles all routing protocol processes, as well as other software processes that control the router's interfaces, some of the chassis components, system management, and user access to the router.

Routing Information Base (RIB)   A logical data structure used by BGP to store routing information.

Routing Information Protocol (RIP)   Distance-vector Interior Gateway Protocol that makes routing decisions based on hop count.

routing instance   A collection of routing tables, interfaces, and routing protocol parameters. The set of interfaces belongs to the routing tables and the routing protocol parameters control the information in the routing tables.

routing protocol daemon (rpd)   JUNOS software routing protocol process (daemon). User-level background process responsible for starting, managing, and stopping the routing protocols on a Juniper Networks router.

routing table   Common database of routes learned from one or more routing protocols. All routes are maintained by the JUNOS routing protocol process.

RSVP Path message   RSVP message sent by the ingress router downstream toward the egress router. It begins the establishment of a soft state database for a particular label-switched path.

RSVP Resv message   RSVP message sent by the egress router upstream toward the ingress router. It completes the establishment of the soft state database for a particular label-switched path.

RSVP signaled LSP   A label-switched path that is dynamically established using RSVP Path and Resv messages.

S

Secure Hash Algorithm (SHA-1)   A widely used hash function for use with Digital Signal Standard (DSS). SHA-1 is more secure than MD5.

secure shell (SSH)   A protocol that provides a secured method of logging in to a remote network system.

security association (SA)   An IPSec term that describes an agreement between two parties about what rules to use for authentication and encryption algorithms, key exchange mechanisms, and secure communications.

Security Parameter Index (SPI)   A portion of the IPSec Authentication Header that communicates which security protocols, such as authentication and encryption, are used for each packet in a VPN connection.

segmentation and reassembly (SAR)   Method used in ATM to transform IP packets into ATM cells and cells into IP packets.

Serving GPRS Support Node (SGSN)   Device in the mobile network that requests PDP contexts with a GGSN.

Session Announcement Protocol (SAP)   Used with multicast protocols to handle session conference announcements.

session attribute object   RSVP message object that is used to control the priority, preemption, affinity class, and local rerouting of the LSP.

Session Description Protocol (SDP)   Used with multicast protocols to handle session conference announcements.

shared tree   The multicast forwarding tree established from the RP to the last hop router for a particular group address.

shim header   The name used to describe the location of the MPLS header in a data packet. The JUNOS software always places (shims) the header between the existing Layers 2 and 3 headers.

Short Message Service (SMS)   GSM service that enables short text messages to be sent to and from mobile telephones.

shortest path first (SPF)   An algorithm used by IS-IS and OSPF to make routing decisions based on the state of network links. Also called the *Dijkstra algorithm*.

shortest-path tree   The multicast forwarding tree established from the first hop router to the last hop router for a particular group address.

show route advertising-protocol   JUNOS software command that displays the routes sent to a neighbor for a particular protocol.

show route receive-protocol   JUNOS software command that displays the routes received from a neighbor for a particular protocol.

signaled path   In traffic engineering, an explicit path; that is, a path determined using RSVP signaling. The ERO carried in the packets contains the explicit path information.

Signaling System 7 (SS7)   Protocol used in telecommunications for delivering calls and services.

Simple Network Management Protocol (SNMP)   Protocol governing network management and the monitoring of network devices and their functions.

simplex interface   An interface that assumes that packets it receives from itself are the result of a software loopback process. The interface does not consider these packets when determining whether the interface is functional.

soft state   A database structure maintained by an RSVP router to store information about a particular label-switched path.

SONET Clock Generator (SCG)   On a M40e or M160 router as well as on a T320 or T640 routing node, the SCG provides Stratum 3 clock signal for the SONET/SDH interfaces. It also provides external clock inputs.

source-based tree   The multicast forwarding tree established from the source of traffic to all interested receivers for a particular group address. It is often seen in a dense-mode forwarding environment.

source-specific multicasting   As part of the IGMPv3 specification, it allows an end host to request multicast traffic for a group address from a specific source of traffic.

sparse mode   A method of operating a multicast domain where sources of traffic and interested receivers meet at a central rendezvous point. A sparse-mode network assumes that there are very few receivers for each group address.

Split Horizon   Method used in distance-vector networks to avoid routing loops. Each router does not advertise routes back to the neighbor it received them from.

static label-switched path (static LSP)   See *static path*.

static path   In the context of traffic engineering, a static route that requires hop-by-hop manual configuration. No signaling is used to create or maintain the path. Also called a *static LSP*.

static route   A configured route that includes a route and a next hop. It is always present in the routing table and doesn't react to topology changes in the network.

static RP   One of three methods of learning the rendezvous point to group address mapping in a multicast network. Each router in the domain must be configured with the required RP information.

strict   In the context of traffic engineering, a route that must go directly to the next address in the path. (Definition from RFC 791, modified to fit LSPs.)

strict hop   Routers in an MPLS named path that are required to be directly connected to the previous router in the configured path.

Strict Priority Queuing (SPQ) Dequeuing method that provides a special queue that is serviced until it is empty. The traffic sent to this queue tends to maintain a lower latency and more consistent latency numbers than traffic sent to other queues. See also *Alternate Priority Queuing (APQ)*.

stub area In OSPF, an area through which, or into which, AS external advertisements are not flooded.

subnet mask The number of bits of the network address used for the network portion of a Class A, Class B, or Class C IP address.

summary-link advertisement OSPF link-statement advertisement flooded throughout the advertisement's associated areas by area border routers to describe the routes that they know about in other areas.

Switch Interface Board (SIB) On a T320 or T640 routing node, provides the switching function to the destination Packet Forwarding Engine.

Switching and Forwarding Module (SFM) On an M40e or M160 router, a component of the Packet Forwarding Engine that provides route lookup, filtering, and switching to FPCs.

Synchronous Digital Hierarchy (SDH) CCITT variation of SONET standard.

Synchronous Optical Network (SONET) High-speed synchronous network specification developed by Bellcore and designed to run on optical fiber. STS-1 is the basic building block of SONET. Approved as an international standard in 1988. See also *Synchronous Digital Hierarchy (SDH)*.

Synchronous Transport Module (STM) CCITT specification for SONET at 155.52Mbps.

Synchronous Transport Signal (STS) Level 1 Basic building block signal of SONET, operating at 51.84Mbps. Faster SONET rates are defined as STS-*n*, where *n* is a multiple of 51.84Mbps. See also *Synchronous Optical Network (SONET)*.

sysid System identifier. A portion of the ISO Network Entity Title (NET) address. The sysid can be any 6 bytes that are unique throughout a domain.

syslog A method for storing messages to a file for troubleshooting or record-keeping purposes. It can also be used as an action within a firewall filter to store information to the `messages` file.

System Control Board (SCB) On an M40 router, the part of the Packet Forwarding Engine that performs route lookups, monitors system components, and controls FPC resets.

System Switching Board (SSB) On an M20 router, Packet Forwarding Engine component that performs route lookups and component monitoring and monitors FPC operation.

T

TCP port 179   The well-known port number used by BGP to establish a peering session with a neighbor.

tcpdump   A Unix packet monitoring utility used by the JUNOS software to view information about packets sent or received by the Routing Engine.

Terminal Access Controller Access Control System Plus (TACACS+)   Authentication method for validating users who attempt to access the router.

terminating action   An action in a routing policy or firewall filter that halts the logical software processing of the policy or filter.

terms   Used in a routing policy or firewall filter to segment the policy or filter into smaller match and action pairs.

through   JUNOS software routing policy match type representing all routes that fall between the two supplied prefixes in the route filter.

Timeout timer   Used in a distance-vector protocol to ensure the current route is still usable for forwarding traffic. The JUNOS software uses a default value of 120 seconds.

token-bucket algorithm   Used in a rate-policing application to enforce an average bandwidth while allowing bursts of traffic up to a configured maximum value.

totally stubby area   An OSPF area type that prevents Type 3, 4, and 5 LSAs from entering the non-backbone area.

traffic engineering   Process of selecting the paths chosen by data traffic in order to balance the traffic load on the various links, routers, and switches in the network. (Definition from `http://www.ietf.org/internet-drafts/draft-ietf-mpls-framework-04.txt`.) See also *Multiprotocol Label Switching (MPLS)*.

transient interfaces   Interfaces that can be moved from one location in the router to another. All customer-facing interfaces are considered transient in nature.

transit area   In OSPF, an area used to pass traffic from one adjacent area to the backbone or to another area if the backbone is more than two hops away from an area.

transit router   In MPLS, any intermediate router in the LSP between the ingress router and the egress router.

Transmission Control Protocol (TCP)   Works in conjunction with Internet Protocol (IP) to send data over the Internet. Divides a message into packets and tracks the packets from the point of origin.

transport mode   An IPSec mode of operation in which the data payload is encrypted but the original IP header is left untouched. The IP addresses of the source or destination can be modified if the packet is intercepted. Because of its construction, transport mode can be used only when the communication endpoint and cryptographic endpoint are the same. VPN gateways that provide encryption and decryption services for protected hosts cannot use transport mode for protected VPN communications. See also *tunnel mode*.

triggered updates   Used in a distance-vector protocol to reduce the time for the network to converge. When a router has a topology change, it immediately sends the information to its neighbors instead of waiting for a timer to expire.

Triple-DES   A 168-bit encryption algorithm that encrypts data blocks with three different keys in succession, thus achieving a higher level of encryption. Triple-DES is one of the strongest encryption algorithms available for use in VPNs.

Tspec Object   RSVP message object that contains information such as the bandwidth request of the LSP as well as the minimum and maximum packets supported.

tunnel   Private, secure path through an otherwise public network.

tunnel mode   An IPSec mode of operation in which the entire IP packet, including the header, is encrypted and authenticated and a new VPN header is added, protecting the entire original packet. This mode can be used by both VPN clients and VPN gateways, and protects communications that come from or go to non-IPSec systems. See also *transport mode*.

Tunnel PIC   A physical interface card that allows the router to perform the encapsulation and decapsulation of IP datagrams. The Tunnel PIC supports IP-IP, GRE, and PIM register encapsulation and decapsulation. When the Tunnel PIC is installed, the router can be a PIM rendezvous point (RP) or a PIM first-hop router for a source that is directly connected to the router.

type of service (ToS)   The method of handling traffic using information extracted from the fields in the ToS byte to differentiate packet flows.

U

UMTS Terrestrial Radio Access Network (UTRAN)   The WCDMA radio network in UMTS.

unicast   Operation of sending network traffic from one network node to another individual network node.

uninterruptible power supply (UPS)   Device that sits between a power supply and a router (or other piece of equipment) that prevents undesired power-source events, such as outages and surges, from affecting or damaging the device.

unit   JUNOS software syntax that represents the logical properties of an interface.

Universal Mobile Telecommunications System (UMTS)   Third-generation (3G), packet-based transmission of text, digitized voice, video, and multimedia, at data rates up to 2Mbps.

Update message   BGP message that advertises path attributes and routing knowledge to an established neighbor.

Update timer   Used in a distance-vector protocol to advertise routes to a neighbor on a regular basis. The JUNOS software uses a default value of 30 seconds.

upto   JUNOS software routing policy match type representing all routes that share the same most significant bits and whose prefix length is smaller than the supplied subnet in the route filter.

User Datagram Protocol (UDP)   Layer 4 protocol that provides an unreliable, connectionless service between two end IP hosts.

V

vapor corrosion inhibitor (VCI)   Small cylinder packed with the router that prevents corrosion of the chassis and components during shipment.

virtual circuit   Represents a logical connection between two Layer 2 devices in a network.

virtual circuit identifier (VCI)   A 16-bit field in the header of an ATM cell that indicates the particular virtual circuit the cell takes through a virtual path. Also called a *logical interface*.

virtual link   In OSPF, a link created between two routers that are part of the backbone but are not physically contiguous.

virtual local area network (VLAN)   A grouping of end hosts within a single IP subnet. These hosts usually reside on multiple physical segments and are connected through a Layer 2 Ethernet switched network.

virtual path   A combination of multiple virtual circuits between two devices in an ATM network.

virtual path identifier (VPI)   The 8-bit field in the header of an ATM cell that indicates the virtual path the cell takes. See also *virtual circuit identifier (VCI)*.

virtual private network (VPN)   A private data network that makes use of a public TCP/IP network, typically the Internet, while maintaining privacy with a tunneling protocol, encryption, and security procedures.

Virtual Router Redundancy Protocol (VRRP)   On Fast Ethernet and Gigabit Ethernet interfaces, allows you to configure virtual default routers.

W

wavelength-division multiplexing (WDM)   Technique for transmitting a mix of voice, data, and video over various wavelengths (colors) of light.

Wideband Code Division Multiple Access (WCDMA)   Radio interface technology used in most third-generation systems.

weighted round-robin (WRR)   Scheme used to decide the queue from which the next packet should be transmitted.

Index

Note to the Reader: Throughout this index **boldfaced** page numbers indicate primary discussions of a topic. *Italicized* page numbers indicate illustrations.

Numbers

1X phase, 620
1XEV phase, 620
2-Way adjacency state, 620
3GPP (Third-Generation Partnership Project), 620
802.3ad link aggregation, 101

A

AAL (ATM Adaptation Layer), 89, 621
ABRs (Area Border Routers) in OSPF
    address summarization, 194–195
    defined, 621
    multi-area configuration, 154, 157
    NSSAs, 193
    stub areas, 179
    TSAs, 187
accept actions
    defined, 620
    in EBGP, 508, 526
    in IBGP, 377
    in IS-IS, 302
accept-data option
    in EBGP, 496
    in VLAN and VRRP configuration, 103
access reject messages, 17
actions, 620
active connections in IBGP, 379
active keyword, 427
active routes, 620
active state
    in EBGP peering, 489
    in IBGP authentication, 386
add/drop multiplexer (ADM), 620
Address Resolution Protocol (ARP)
    caches
        in EBGP peering, 496
        in MAC address filtering, 112

defined, 620
    for Ethernet interfaces, 102
address summarization, **194–197**
addresses
    in EBGP peering, 491
    IP. *See* IP addresses
    MAC
        in Ethernet interfaces, 101, **111–113**
        in IS-IS, 278, 314–315
    match conditions, 620
    in POS interfaces, 68
    in unnumbered interfaces, 124–125
adjacencies
    defined, 620
    in IS-IS, **272–274, 276**, 323
    in OSPF, 156, 160, **164–166, 225–227**
Adjacency-RIB-In table, 620
Adjacency-RIB-Out table, 620
ADM (add/drop multiplexer), 620
Advanced SSH Options dialog box, 13
advertise-inactive option
    in EBGP, 575
    in IBGP, 457
advertisements
    in EBGP
        import policy, 505
        route filtering, 526
    in IBGP, 380–382, 415–416
    link-state. *See* LSAs (link-state advertisements) in OSPF
AFIs (Authority and Format Identifiers), 258
aggregate routes
    defined, 620
    in EBGP
        case study, 573–574, 577, 579–580
        filtering, 532, 534–537
aggregated interfaces
    Ethernet, **114–117**, *114*
    SONET, **117–119**
aggressive damping, 505
AHs (Authentication Headers), 622
alarm configuration, **33–34**

ALI (ATM Line Interface), 621
all keyword in IS-IS, 265
allow-commands option, 18
allow keyword
    in EBGP peering, 491
    in user accounts, 10
Alternate Priority Queuing (APQ), 621
Amnesiac prompt, 5
ANSI (American National Standards
    Institute), 621
application-specific integrated circuits
    (ASICs), 621
APQ (Alternate Priority Queuing), 621
APS (Automatic Protection Switching), 622
area 1 configuration, **161**
area 49.0001, *257, 257*
area 49.0002, *257, 257*
    authenticating, **282–283, 286**
    configuring, **270**
    verifying, **271**
area 49.0003
    configuring, **287–290**, *287*
    verifying, **290**
Area Border Routers (ABRs) in OSPF
    address summarization, 194–195
    defined, 621
    multi-area configuration, 154, 157
    NSSAs, 193
    stub areas, 179
    TSAs, 187
area-range option, 194–196
area routing subdomains, 621
ARP (Address Resolution Protocol)
    caches
        in EBGP peering, 496
        in MAC address filtering, 112
    defined, 620
    for Ethernet interfaces, 102
asbrsummary option, 182
ASICs (application-specific integrated
    circuits), 621
ASs (Autonomous Systems)
    AS numbers
        in EBGP, 587–588
        in IBGP, 375–377, 379, 402, 405–406,
            412, 414

ASBR-summary LSAs
    defined, 621
    in stub areas, 179, 182
boundary routers, 201
    address summarization, 196
    defined, 622
    NSSAs, 188
    with RIP, 219
defined, 622
in EBGP, **542–543**
external-link advertisements, 621
IGP routing in, 154
paths, 581–582, 621–622
asterisks (*) for NTP servers, 26–27
ATM (Asynchronous Transfer Mode), **89**, *90*
    defined, 621
    ILMI operation with, **95–97**
    with IS-IS, 277
    logical properties for, **91–93**
    multipoint connections for, **97–98**, *97*
    physical properties for, **90–91**
    summary, **100**
    traffic shaping for, **98–100**
    verifying, **93–97**
ATM Adaptation Layer (AAL), 89, 621
ATM Line Interface (ALI), 621
atomic operations, 621
attached bit, 314
attempt adjacency state, 621
AUC (authentication center), 622
auth file, 21
authentication
    in IBGP
        case study, 448
        configuring, **383–386**
        verifying, **386**
    in IS-IS, **278**
        area 49.0002, **282–283, 286**
        case study, **324–326**
        r3 and r4, **280–282**
        r5, **278–280**
        troubleshooting, **283–286**
    in OSPF, **173–175**
        protocol tracing, **177–178**
        verifying, **176–177**
    in RADIUS, 11, 15–16, 47
    for root account, **11–12**

for users, 47
in VRRP, **107–111**
authentication center (AUC), 622
Authentication Headers (AHs), 622
authentication-key option, 174
authentication-order list, 15–16
authentication-type option, 174
Authkey keyword, 386
Authority and Format Identifiers (AFIs), 258
authorization messages, 20
auto-RP method, 622
Automatic Protection Switching (APS), 622
Autonomous Systems (ASs). *See* ASs
(Autonomous Systems)

B

-b flag in ssh-keygen, 13
backbone areas, 622
backbone authentication, **324–326**
backbone routers, 622
backplanes, 622
backup designated routers, 622
backups, 622
bandwidth, 623
base station controllers (BSCs), 623
base station subsystems (BSSs), 623
Base Station System GPRS Protocol
(BSSGP), 623
base transceiver stations (BTSs), 623
BCD (Binary Coded Decimal) format, 258
Bellcore organization, 623
Bellman-Ford algorithm, 623
BERTs (bit error rate tests)
in ATM, 90
defined, 623
BGP (Border Gateway Protocol), 623
bidirectional keepalives, 72
bidirectional redistribution, 310
Binary Coded Decimal (BCD) format, 258
bit error rate tests (BERTs)
in ATM, 90
defined, 623
bit field match conditions, 623
BITS (Building Integrated Timing Source), 623
bogons group and policy, **512–516**

bogus routes, 512
book, this. *See JNCIP Study Guide*
boot-server option, 25–27
bootstrap routers, 623
Border Gateway Protocol (BGP), 623
broadcasts, 623
BSCs (base station controllers), 623
BSSGP (Base Station System GPRS
Protocol), 623
BSSs (base station subsystems), 623
BTSs (base transceiver stations), 623
Buchsteiner, Josef, xxix
Building Integrated Timing Source (BITS), 623
bundles, 623
burst threshold in leaky bucket rate
limiting, 120
bypass-routing option, 126

C

C-BGP
for confederations, 402–404, *403–404*
configuring, **411–413**
with physical interfaces, 444
C-bit parity, 90
C1 peering, **487–488, 555–557**
C2 peering, **484–486**
call detail records (CDRs), 623
CAMEL (Customized Application of Mobile
Enhance Logic), 626
candidate configurations, 624
candidate-RP-advertisements, 624
categories hierarchy in SNMP, 23
CB (Control Board), 626
CBR (Constant Bit Rate) parameter, 98–99
CCCs (circuit cross-connects), 624
CDMA (Code Division Multiple Access), 625
CDMA2000 transmission and backbone
technology, 624
CDRs (call detail records), 623
CE (customer edge) devices, 626
cell encapsulation mode, 90
cell tax, 624
CFM (cubic feet per minute), 624
channel service unit/data service unit
(CSU/DSU), 624

CHAP (Challenge Handshake Authentication
    Protocol)
  defined, 624
  for PPP, 85–88
chassis alarm configuration, 33–34
chassis daemon (chassisd), 624
checksums in ATM, 90
CIDR (classless interdomain routing), 624
CIP (Connector Interface Panel), 625
circuit cross-connects (CCCs), 624
cisco-hdlc keepalives, 69, 71
Cisco-RP-Announce messages, 624
Cisco-RP-Discovery messages, 624
class of service (CoS), 624
classless interdomain routing (CIDR), 624
clear bgp damping command, 511
clear bgp neighbor command, 382, 542
clear interfaces statistics command, 121, 124
clear isis database command, 316
clear line command, 7
clear ospf neighbor command, 164
clearing terminal server sessions, 6–8
CLECs (Competitive Local Exchange
    Carriers), 625
CLEIs (common language equipment
    identifiers), 625
CLI (command-line interface), 625
client peers, 624
clients keyword, 23
CLNP (Connectionless Network Protocol), 625
clock selection and synchronization in NTP
  configuring, 24–25, 50–51
  defined, 640
  verifying, 25–28
clocking with POS interfaces, 65
cluster-id keyword, 457
clusters in IBGP
  1.1.1.1 and 3.3.3.3, 390–392
  2.2.2.2, 392–393
  cluster IDs, 386–388
  defined, 625
Code Division Multiple Access (CDMA), 625
command completion, 625
command-line interface (CLI), 625
command prompts, hostnames for, 9
commit and-quit command, 9, 16
common language equipment identifiers
    (CLEIs), 625

communities
  defined, 625
  in EBGP, 517–520
  in IBGP, 429–435
community strings, 23
Competitive Local Exchange Carriers
    (CLECs), 625
complete sequence number PDU (CSNP), 625
confederation AS, 402
confederation member AS, 402
confederations in IBGP, 402
  configuring, 402–404, 403–404
    C-BGP links, 411–413
    subconfederation 65000, 404–408
    subconfederations 65001 and 65002,
      408–411
  defined, 625
  saving, 420
  verifying, 413–420
configuration groups, 48–49
configuration mode, 625
configured hold times, 427
confirmed option, 402
connect state
  defined, 625
  in IBGP authentication, 386
Connectionless Network Protocol (CLNP), 625
Connector Interface Panel (CIP), 625
console connections for terminal servers, 3–5, 4
Constant Bit Rate (CBR) parameter, 98–99
constrained paths, 625
Constrained Shortest Path First (CSPF)
    algorithm, 625
context-sensitive help, 626
contributing routes, 626
Control Board (CB), 626
core
  defined, 626
  in IBGP route reflection, 393–394
CoS (class of service), 624
count function, 162
CPE (customer premises equipment), 626
craft interface mechanisms, 626
CRC with POS interfaces, 65
Create Identity File option, 13
CSNP (complete sequence number PDU), 625
CSPF (Constrained Shortest Path First)
    algorithm, 625

CSU compatibility mode, 90
CSU/DSU (channel service unit/data service unit), 624
cubic feet per minute (CFM), 624
customer edge (CE) devices, 626
customer premises equipment (CPE), 626
customer sites
    in community tagging, 517–518
    in route filtering, **526–529**
Customized Application of Mobile Enhance Logic (CAMEL), 626
cut and paste in system configuration, **37–41**
cut-off threshold in route damping, 505

D

daemon processes, 626
damping
    defined, 626
    in EBGP, **505–511**, 561–562
data circuit-terminating equipment (DCE), 626
data communications equipment (DCE), 71–72, 75, 78
data-link connection identifiers (DLCIs)
    defined, 626
    for Frame Relay, 71–73, 76
data service units (DSUs), 626
data terminal equipment (DTE)
    defined, 626
    for Frame Relay, 71–72, 75, 78
database description packets
    defined, 627
    for OSPF, 165
date command, 26
dcd (Device Control Daemon) interface process, 627
DCE (data circuit-terminating equipment), 626
DCE (data communications equipment), 71–72, 75, 78
deactivate interfaces command, 397–398
deactivate method, 627
deactivate protocols isis command, 418
deactivate unit command, 100
dead intervals, 627
debug all option, 500
decay half-life in damping, 505
default addresses, 627

default-lsa option, 190
default-metric option, 180, 191
default routes, 627
delays for NTP synchronization, 26–27
delete address command, 274
delete file messages authorization command, 20
delete keepalives command, 72
delete neighbor command, 390, 392
delete no-authentication-check command, 286
delete protocols bgp command, 404, 406
delete protocols bgp group command, 433
delete routing-options command, 39
delete routing-options aggregate command, 532
delete traceoptions command, 491
Denial of service (DoS) attacks
    defined, 627
    IS-IS settings for, 314
dense mode, 627
dense wavelength-division multiplexing (DWDM), 627
deny command, 10
deny-commands option, 18
Designated Intermediate System (DIS), 261–262, **278**
Designated Routers (DRs)
    defined, 627
    for IS-IS, 278
    for NBMA, 170–171
    for OSPF, 166
destination keyword
    for POS, 69
    for PPP, 83
destination prefix length, 627
detail option
    for communities, 431
    for IS-IS, 262
Device Control Daemon (dcd) interface process, 627
DHCP (Dynamic Host Configuration Protocol), 628
Differentiated Services Codepoint (DSCP), 627
Diffie-Hellman public key scheme, 627
Diffserv Differentiated Service, 627
DIMMs (dual inline memory modules), 628
DIS (Designated Intermediate System), 261–262, **278**
disable method, 628
disabled option, 506

discard command
  defined, 628
  in leaky bucket rate limiting, 120
discontiguous subnets, 194
distance vector-based routing
  defined, 628
  in OSPF configuration, 154
Distance Vector Multicast Routing Protocol
    (DVMRP), 628
Distributed Buffer Manager ASICs, 628
DLCIs (data-link connection identifiers)
  defined, 626
  for Frame Relay, 71–73, 76
DoS (Denial of service) attacks
  defined, 627
  IS-IS settings for, 314
Down adjacency state, 628
DRAM (dynamic random access memory), 628
drop profiles, 628
DRs (Designated Routers)
  defined, 627
  for IS-IS, 278
  for NBMA, 170–171
  for OSPF, 166
DSCP (Differentiated Services Codepoint), 627
DSUs (data service units), 626
DTE (data terminal equipment)
  defined, 626
  for Frame Relay, 71–72, 75, 78
dual inline memory modules (DIMMs), 628
duplicate RIDs, 64
DVMRP (Distance Vector Multicast Routing
    Protocol), 628
DWDM (dense wavelength-division multi-
    plexing), 627
Dynamic Host Configuration Protocol
    (DHCP), 628
dynamic label-switched paths, 628
dynamic random access memory (DRAM), 628

E

EBGP (External BGP), **480**
  case study, **550–554**, *551–552*
    confirmation, **588**
    hidden route repair, **571–588**
    Martian filtering, **560–571**
  peering, **554–560**
    r1, **589–591**
    r2, **591–594**
    r3, **594–598**
    r4, **599–603**
    r5, **603–604**
    r6, **604–608**
    r7, **608–611**
  defined, 630
  peering in, **481–482**, *482–483*
    C1, **487–488**
    C2, **484–486**
    P1, **493–498**
    T1, **500–504**
    T2, **498–500**
    troubleshooting, **489–493**
  policy in, **504**
    export. *See* export policies
    forwarding path confirmation, **540–541**
    import. *See* import policies
  summary, **549**
  timers and knobs in, **541**
    AS loops, **542–543**
    incoming traffic flow, **543–547**
    local preferences, **547–548**
ECSA (Exchange Carriers Standards
    Association), 629
edge routers, 628
edit group command, 390, 392–393
edit interfaces command, 92
edit policy-options command, 181
edit policy-options policy-statement command
  in IS-IS, 306
  in OSPF, 189
edit policy-statement command, 429
edit protocols bgp group command
  in EBGP, 484
  in IBGP, 405–406
edit protocols bgp group interval
    command, 376
edit unit command, 104
editor macros (Emacs), 629
EGP (Exterior Gateway Protocol), 629
egress routers, 629
EIA (Electronic Industries Association), 629
802.3ad link aggregation, 101
EIR (Equipment Identity Register), 629
electromagnetic interference (EMI), 629

Electronic Industries Association (EIA), 629
eligible keyword, 169–170
Emacs (editor macros), 629
embedded OS software, 629
emergency-level messages, 20
EMI (electromagnetic interference), 629
encapsulating security payload (ESP), 629
encapsulation
    in ATM, 93
    in Ethernet interfaces, 101
    in Frame Relay
        configuring, **71–79**
        point-to-multipoint connections,
            80–82, *81*
        verifying, **79–80**
    in leaky bucket rate limiting, 119
    with POS interfaces, 65–66
    PPP, **82–88**, *83*
encryption in ATM, 90
end system entities, 629
end-to-end ATM switches, *95*
Equipment Identity Register (EIR), 629
EROs (Explicit Route Objects), 629
escape sequence for IOS prompt, 6
ESP (encapsulating security payload), 629
Established neighbor state
    defined, 629
    in EBGP peering, 489
Ethernet interfaces, **101**
    aggregated, **114–117**, *114*
    logical properties for, **102–103**
    MAC address filtering in, **111–113**
    physical properties for, **101**, *102*
    summary, **114**
    VLAN and VRRP configuration for
        r1, **103–105**
        r2, **105–107**
    VRRP authentication and tracking in,
        107–111
exact match type, 629
exception packets, 629
Exchange adjacency state, 629
Exchange Carriers Standards Association
    (ECSA), 629
EXEC mode passwords, 3
exit command, 15
Explicit Route Objects (EROs), 629

export policies
    EBGP, **520**
        hidden route repair, **520–525**, *522*,
            571–588
        route filtering, **525–540**
    IBGP
        confederations, 412
        r5, 423–424
        r6, 422–423
    OSPF, **218–221**, 231–235
ExStart adjacency state, 629
extensive option
    for leaky bucket rate limiting, 121
    for POS interfaces, 67
Exterior Gateway Protocol (EGP), 629
External BGP. *See* EBGP (External BGP)
external LSA generation, **181–182**
external metrics, 630
external option for confederations, 412

F

far-end alarm and control (FEAC) signal, 630
Fast Ethernet PICs, 101
fast reroute mechanism, 630
fastether-options option, 101
faulty hardware, 2
FEAC (far-end alarm and control) signal, 630
FEB (Forwarding Engine Board), 631
field-replaceable units (FRUs), 630
FIFO (first in, first out) queuing and buffering
    method, 630
filtering
    in EBGP, **525**
        customer site, **526–529**
        Martian, **511–517**, 560–571
        peer site, **529–538**
        transit provider, **538–540**
    in Ethernet, 101, **111–113**
firewalls, 630
first in, first out (FIFO) queuing and buffering
    method, 630
flag all detail option, 500
flexible PIC concentrators (FPCs), 630
floating static routes, 630
flood and prune method, 630

flood ping testing
  for ATM traffic shaping, 99
  for leaky bucket rate limiting, 122–123
  for POS interfaces, 70–71
flow control
  defined, 630
  for Ethernet interfaces, 101
flushing IS-IS LSBDs, 316
forwarding class designation, 630
Forwarding Engine Board (FEB), 631
forwarding next-hop field, 415
forwarding path confirmation, **540–541**
forwarding tables, 631
FPCs (flexible PIC concentrators), 630
frame checksums, 90
Frame Relay
  defined, 631
  for POS
    configuring, **71–79**
    point-to-multipoint connections,
      80–82, *81*
    verifying, **79–80**
frame-relay encapsulation type, 71
framing with POS interfaces, 65–66
from command, 631
from next-hop option, 216
FRUs (field-replaceable units), 630
FTP servers, 30–32
Full adjacency state, 164, 631
fxp0 interface, 260, 631
fxp1 interface, 631
fxp2 interface, 631

G

G-CDRs (GGSN call detail records), 631
Garbage Collection timer, 631
General Packet Radio Service (GPRS), 631
generated routes, 631
GGSN (Gateway GPRS Support Node), 631
GGSN call detail records (G-CDRs), 631
Gigabit Ethernet PICs, 101
gigether-options option, 101
global preferences for OSPF, **218–221**
Global System for Mobile Communications
  (GSM), 631
GPRS (General Packet Radio Service), 631

GPRS Tunneling Protocol (GTP), 632
GPRS Tunneling Protocol Control
  (GTP-C), 632
GPRS Tunneling Protocol User (GTP-U), 632
group addresses, 632
groups, 632
GSM (Global System for Mobile
  Communications), 631
GTP (GPRS Tunneling Protocol), 632
GTP-C (GPRS Tunneling Protocol
  Control), 632
GTP-U (GPRS Tunneling Protocol User), 632
guard nets, 511

H

half/full duplex mode, 101
half-life in route damping, 505
Hashed Message Authentication Code
  (HMAC), 632
hashes, 632
HDLC (High-Level Data Link Control)
  defined, 632
  with POS interfaces, 65–66
hello intervals, 632
hello mechanism
  defined, 632
  in IS-IS, 262, **324–326**
  in OSPF, 156
hello timers, 262
hidden route repair, **520–525**, *522*, **571–588**
hidden switch, 515
High-Level Data Link Control (HDLC)
  defined, 632
  with POS interfaces, 65–66
High-Speed Circuit-Switched Data
  (HSCSC), 632
HLR (Home Location Register), 632
HMAC (Hashed Message Authentication
  Code), 632
HMAC-MD5-based authentication, 278
hold down timers, 632
hold times
  defined, 632
  in IBGP, 426–427
  in IS-IS, 262
  in POS interfaces, 65–66, 68

Home Location Register (HLR), 632
host addresses for POS interfaces, 69
host keys, accepting, 14, *14*
host mappings, **4–5**
Host Membership Query packets, 633
Host Membership Report packets, 633
host modules, 633
host subsystems, 633
hostnames
    for command prompts, 9
    for OoB management network
        configuration, 8
    for routers, 44
HSCSC (High-Speed Circuit-Switched
    Data), 632
HSRP (Hot Standby Router Protocol), 101

I

I/O Manager ASIC, 635
IANA (Internet Assigned Numbers
    Authority), 634
IBGP (Internal Border Gateway Protocol), **374**
    authentication
        configuring, 383–386
        verifying, **386**
    case study, 440–441, *440–441*
        authentication, **448**
        design alternatives, **442–444**, *443*
        load-balancing, **455–456**
        passive mode, **459–460**
        r1, 444–445, 460–461
        r2, 461–463
        r3, 463–464
        r4, 445–446, 464–466
        r5, 446, 466–467
        r6, 447–448, 467–469
        r7, 469–471
        route redistribution, 448–455
        route summaries, 456–459
    confederations, **402**
        configuring, **402–413**, *403–404*
        saving, **420**
        verifying, 413–420
    defined, 634
    export policy
        confederations, 412

r5, 423–424
r6, 422–423
IGP operation for, 154
peering
    initial setup, **374–377**, *375*
    policies, **377–383**
redistribution policy, **429–432**
route reflection, **386–387**
    configuring, **387–394**, *387*, *389*
    verifying, 395–402
summary, **439**
timers and knobs, **421–422**, *421*
    load balancing, **422–426**
    local preferences and communities in,
        429–435
    passive mode configuration, **427–429**
    timer modifications, **426–427**
troubleshooting, **435–439**
ibgp export policy, 412
ICMP (Internet Control Message Protocol), 635
IDE (Integrated Drive Electronics), 634
idle neighbor state
    defined, 633
    in EBGP, 485
IEEE (Institute of Electronic and Electrical
    Engineers), 633
IETF (Internet Engineering Task Force), 635
IGMP (Internet Group Management
    Protocol), 635
ignore-attached-bit option, 314
IGP (Interior Gateway Protocol), 154, 374, 634
IKE (Internet Key Exchange) protocol, 635
ILMI (Integrated Local Management Interface),
    89–90, **95–97**
IMEI (International Mobile Station Equipment
    Identity), 634
import policies
    in EBGP, **504**
        community tagging, **517–520**
        Martian filtering, **511–517**, **560–571**
        route damping, **505–511**
    in RIP, **216–218**
importing routes, 633
IMSI (International Mobile Subscriber Identity)
    information, 634
IN-ARP (Inverse ARP)
    in ATM, 98
    in Frame Relay, 80, 82

incoming traffic flow in EBGP, **543–547**

inet.0 routing table, 633

inet.1 routing table, 633

inet.2 routing table, 633

inet.3 routing table, 633

inet.4 routing table, 633

inet protocol for unnumbered interfaces, 125

inet6.0 routing table, 633

infinity metric, 633

ingress routers, 633

init adjacency state, 633

insert command, 633

Institute of Electronic and Electrical Engineers (IEEE), 633

Integrated Drive Electronics (IDE), 634

Integrated Local Management Interface (ILMI), 89–90, **95–97**

inter-AS routing, 634

intercluster reflection, 634

interdependency in EBGP peering, 481

interface all keyword, 265

interface configurations

    aggregated interfaces

        Ethernet, **114–117**, *114*

        SONET, **117–119**

    ATM. *See* ATM (Asynchronous Transfer Mode)

    case study, **129–131**, *129*

        r1, **131–133**

        r2, **133–136**

        r3, **136–139**

        r4, **139–141**

        r5, **142–145**

        r6, **146–147**

        r7, **148**

    Ethernet. *See* Ethernet interfaces

    leaky bucket rate limiting

        configuring, **119–121**

        verifying, **121–124**, *122–123*

    lo0 interface

        configuring, **60–61**

        verifying, **61–64**

    POS. *See* POS (Packet Over SONET) interfaces

    summary, **128**

    unnumbered interfaces, **124–125**, *125*

        configuring, **125–126**

        verifying, **126**

interface costs, 634

interface keyword, 23

interface routes, 634

interface-to-level mappings, 322–323

Interior Gateway Protocol (IGP), 154, 374, 634

Intermediate System-to-Intermediate System. *See* IS-IS (Intermediate System-to-Intermediate System)

Intermediate Systems (ISs), 634

Internal Border Gateway Protocol. *See* IBGP (Internal Border Gateway Protocol)

Internal Ethernet, 634

internal timing with POS interfaces, 65

International Mobile Station Equipment Identity (IMEI), 634

International Mobile Subscriber Identity (IMSI) information, 634

International Organization for Standardization (ISO), 634

International Telecommunications Union (ITU), 634

Internet Assigned Numbers Authority (IANA), 634

Internet Control Message Protocol (ICMP), 635

Internet Engineering Task Force (IETF), 635

Internet Group Management Protocol (IGMP), 635

Internet Key Exchange (IKE) protocol, 635

Internet Processor ASIC, 635

Internet Protocol (IP), 635

Internet Protocol Security (IPSec)

    defined, 635

    in IBGP, 383

Internet routing tables with EBGP, 499

Internet Security Association and Key Management Protocol (ISAKMP), 635

Internet service providers (ISPs), 635

intra-AS routing, 635

Inverse ARP (IN-ARP)

    in ATM, 98

    in Frame Relay, 80, 82

inverse-arp keyword, 98

IOS prompt, escape sequence for, 6

IP (Internet Protocol), 635

IP addresses

    and adjacency, **276**

    in ATM, 89

    for Ethernet interfaces, 102

for loopback interfaces, 60, 62–63
for OoB management network
    configuration, 8
rename feature for, **127–128**
for VRRP, 106
IPCP (IPv4 Control Protocol), 84
IPSec (Internet Protocol Security)
defined, 635
in IBGP, 383
IPv4 Control Protocol (IPCP), 84
IS-IS (Intermediate System-to-Intermediate
    System), **256**
    authentication, 278
      area 49.0002, **282–283**, 286
      r3 and r4, **280–282**
      r5, **278–280**
      troubleshooting, **283–286**
    case study, 319–324, *320*
      authentication, **324–326**
      OSPF routers, **331–340**
      priority in, **330–331**
      r1, **345–347**
      r2, **347–349**
      r3, **349–353**
      r4, **353–356**
      r5, **356–360**
      r6, **360–363**
      r7, **363–365**
      route redistribution, **328–330**
      route summarization, **326–328**, **340–345**
    defined, 634
    knobs in, **313–316**
    multi-level. *See* multi-level IS-IS
      configuration
    network types, **277–278**
    routing policies
      area 49.0003 configuration,
        287–290, *287*
      route leaking, **286–293**
      route redistribution. *See* route
        redistribution
      summarization, **286–290**, **293–297**
    summary, **318**
ISAKMP (Internet Security Association and Key
    Management Protocol), 635
ISO (International Organization for
    Standardization), 634
iso protocol family, 258

ISPs (Internet service providers), 635
ISs (Intermediate Systems), 634
ITU (International Telecommunications
    Union), 634

J

J-cell data unit, 635
jbase package, 635
jbundle package, 30, 635
jdocs package, 635
jinstall package, 30–32
jitter, 636
jkernel package, 636
JNCIP Study Guide (this book)
    author/technical editors, xxix
    CD contents, xxviii–xxix
    how to use, xxviii
    overview of, xxv
    scope of, xxvi
    what it covers, xxvi–xxvii
    what to know before starting, xxv–xxvi
JNTCP (Juniper Networks Technical
    Certification Program)
    defined, **xv**
    ERX Edge Routers track, xv
    exam-taking tips, xxiii–xxv
    M-series Routers & T-series Routing
      Platforms track
      Certified Internet Associate, xv, xvi–xvii
      Certified Internet Expert, xvi, xix
      Certified Internet Professional, xv,
        xviii–xix
      Certified Internet Specialist, xv, xvii–xviii
      overview of, xv-xvi, *xvi*
    nondisclosure agreement, xxi
    recertification requirements, xx–xxi
    registering for exams, xix–xx
    resources
      CertManager website, xxii
      Groupstudy mailing list/website, xxiii
      JNTCP website, xxi–xxii
      overview of, xxi
      Techcenter website, xxiii
      technical documentation, xxii
      training courses, xxii
Join messages, 636

jpfe package, 636
jroute package, 30, 636
jumbo frames, 101
Juniper Networks Technical Certification
        Program. *See* JNTCP

K

keep all option, 542, 587
keepalives
    for ATM, 89
    defined, 636
    for Frame Relay, 71–72
    for IBGP, 426
    for PPP, 85
kernel component, 636
kill-rest option, 564
knobs
    in EBGP, **541**
        AS loops, **542–543**
        incoming traffic flow, **543–547**
        local preferences, **547–548**
    in IBGP, **421–422**, *421*
        load balancing, **422–426**
        local preferences and communities in,
            429–435
        passive mode configuration, **427–429**
        timer modifications, **426–427**
    in IS-IS, **313–316**
    in OSPF, **222–225**, *225*

L

-l flag in ssh-keygen, 13
lab accounts
    configuring, **14–15**
    parameters for, 11
    verifying, **15–17**
Label Distribution Protocol (LDP), 636
label objects, 636
label pop operations, 636
label push operations, 636
label request objects, 636
label swap operations, 636
label-switched paths (LSPs), 637

label-switching routers (LSRs), 637
label values, 637
labels, 636
LCP (Link Control Protocol), 83–88
LDAP (Lightweight Directory Access
        Protocol), 637
LDP (Label Distribution Protocol), 636
leaky bucket rate limiting
    configuring, **119–121**
    verifying, **121–124**, *122–123*
leaky routes in IS-IS, **286–290**
    case study, **326–328**
    configuring, **290–292**
    verifying, **292–293**
Lightweight Directory Access Protocol
        (LDAP), 637
line build testing, 90
line loopback method, 637
Link Control Protocol (LCP), 83–88
link keyword, 23
link-level encapsulation, 65
link-state acknowledgments, 637
link-state advertisements. *See* LSAs (link-state
        advertisements) in OSPF
link-state databases. *See* LSDBs (link-state
        databases)
Link State Protocol Data Units (LSPs)
    defined, 637
    in IS-IS, 256, 297, 316
link-state request lists, 637
link-state request packets, 637
link-state updates, 637
links
    defined, 637
    virtual, **198–201**, *198*
LMI (Local Management Interface), 71, 74–75
lo0 interface
    configuring, **60–61**
    verifying, **61–64**
load balancing
    in EBGP, 501–502
    in IBGP, **422–426**, 455–456
    in OSPF, 223, 241–242
load merge terminal command, 39–40
    in EBGP, 526
    in IBGP, 379
    in RIP, 212
load override terminal command, 38

loading adjacency state, 637
local-address option
    in EBGP, 491
    in IBGP, 376, 391
local AS number, 375–377
local-as option, 557
Local Management Interface (LMI), 71, 74–75
local passwords
    for lab account, 16–17
    for users, 47
local preferences
    in BGP, 637
    in EBGP, **547–548**
    in IBGP, **429–435**
Local-RIB table, 638
local significance concept, 638
local time zone setting, **27–28**
log-updown option, 376
logging in as root, 5, 47
logical operators, 638
logical properties
    for ATM interfaces, **91–93**
    for Ethernet interfaces, **102–103**
    for POS interfaces, **68–69**
logical units
    for ATM, 91, 96–97
    for IS-IS, 321–322
    loopback interfaces for, 60
    for POS interfaces, 68
longer match type, 638
loopback-based peering, 376
loopback interfaces, **60–64**
loopbacks and loopback addresses
    in ATM, 90
    in EBGP, 482, *482–483*
    in Ethernet interfaces, 101
    in IBGP, 376
        confederations, 403–404, *403–404*
        route reflection, 387, *387*, 389, *389*
    in IS-IS, 324
    in OSPF, 155, 230
    in stub areas, 181
    in TSAs, 186
loops
    in EBGP, **542–543**
    in RIP, 219
loops parameter, 542
loose hops, 638

loose paths, 638
LSAs (link-state advertisements) in OSPF,
    154–155, 179, 201
    in address summarization, 196
    defined, 637
    in LSDB, 182, 185
    in NSSAs, 188, 193
    in stub areas, 179, **181–182**
    in TSAs, 187
    in virtual links, 199
LSDBs (link-state databases)
    defined, 637
    in IS-IS, 263, 316
    in OSPF, 154, 179
        LSAs in, 182, 185
        in NSSAs, 193
LSPs (label-switched paths), 637
LSPs (Link State Protocol Data Units)
    defined, 637
    in IS-IS, 256, 297, 316
LSRs (label-switching routers), 637

M

MAC addresses
    in Ethernet interfaces, 101, **111–113**
    in IS-IS, 278, 314–315
maintenance, **28–30**
management daemon (mgd), 638
Management Ethernet, 638
Management Information Bases (MIBs), 638
mapping agents, 638
mappings
    for IS-IS, 322–323
    symbolic name, **4–5**
Martian routes and addresses
    defined, 638
    in EBGP, **511–517, 560–571**
    table for, 126
    for unnumbered interfaces, 124–125
MAS (mobile network access subsystem), 639
master routers, 638
match function
    for community tagging, 519
    defined, 638
    for OSPF database routers, 162
match types, 638

maximum burst, 98
maximum hold-down time, 505
maximum queue depth, 98
maximum transmission units (MTUs)
    defined, 639
    in Ethernet interfaces, 101
    in POS interfaces, 65, 68
maximum-vci option, 92
maximum-vcs option, 91
MBGP (Multiprotocol BGP), 640
MBone backbone, 639
MCS (Miscellaneous Control Subsystem), 639
MD5 (Message Digest 5) authentication
    defined, 639
    for IBGP, 383
    for IS-IS, 285
    for OSPF, 173–174
    for VRRP, 107–109
mean time between failure (MTBF), 639
MED (Multiple Exit Discriminator)
    defined, 639
    in EBGP
        case study, 583–586
        traffic flow, 543–546
meshes
    defined, 639
    in IBGP, 374, 375
message aggregation, 639
Message Digest 5. See MD5 (Message Digest 5)
    authentication
messages file, 20–21
metric-out keyword, 546
metrics
    in IS-IS, 302–304
    in OSPF, 222–225, 225
mgd (management daemon), 638
mget FTP transfer option, 31–32
MIBs (Management Information Bases), 638
midplanes, 639
Miscellaneous Control Subsystem (MCS), 639
mobile network access subsystem (MAS), 639
mobile point-to-point control subsystem
    (MPS), 639
Mobile Station Integrated Services Digital
    Network Number (MSISDN), 639
mobile stations, 639
Mobile Switching Centers (MSCs), 639
mobile transport subsystem (MTS), 639

monitor interface command, 123
monitor start command, 382
monitor start isis command, 273, 285
monitor start ospf command, 172–173, 177
monitor start vrrp command, 111
monitor traffic command
    for Frame Relay, 74–75, 79–80
    for NTP server synchronization, 26
monitor traffic interface command
    for EBGP, 494
    for Frame Relay, 74–76
    for IS-IS, 283–284
    for OSPF, 176
    for PPP, 84–85, 87
    for SNMP, 24
Moyer, Peter, xxix
MPLS (Multiprotocol Label Switching)
    mechanism, 640
MPS (mobile point-to-point control
    subsystem), 639
MSCs (Mobile Switching Centers), 639
MSISDN (Mobile Station Integrated Services
    Digital Network Number), 639
MTBF (mean time between failure), 639
MTS (mobile transport subsystem), 639
MTUs (maximum transmission units)
    defined, 639
    in Ethernet interfaces, 101
    in POS interfaces, 65, 68
multi-area OSPF configuration, 154–155, 155
    adjacency problems in, 164–166
    area 1, 161
    r3, 159–160
    r4, 155–157
    r5, 157–159
    verifying, 161–164
multi-level IS-IS configuration, 256–257, 257
    adjacency in, 272–274, 276
    area 49.0002, 270–271
    IP addressing in, 276
    PDU support in, 258–260
    r3, 267–270
    r5, 264–267
    routing instances in, 260–261
    timers in, 262
    verifying, 261–263, 272, 274–275
multicast distribution trees, 639
multicast-dlci option, 277

multicast operations
    defined, 639
    Frame Relay, 277
multihop option, 411
multipath option
    in EBGP, 500–503
    in IBGP load balancing, 424–425
Multiple Exit Discriminator (MED)
    defined, 639
    in EBGP
        case study, 583–586
        traffic flow, 543–546
multipoint keyword
    for ATM, **97–98**, *97*
    for Frame Relay, 81–82
    for IS-IS, 277
    for OSPF, 166–167
multipoint-destination keyword, 98
multipoint network types, **166–168**, *167*
Multiprotocol BGP (MBGP), 640
Multiprotocol Label Switching (MPLS) mech-
    anism, 640
multiterm policies in IBGP, 377
mutual route redistribution, 297

N

n-selectors, 641
named-path software syntax, 640
narrow metrics, 302, 304
NBMA network types
    OSPF, **168–172**, *168*
    troubleshooting, **172–173**, *172*
negotiated hold times, 427
neighbors, 640
netmasks for loopback interfaces, 60
NETs (network entity titles)
    defined, 640
    in IS-IS, 258
network interface registration, 89
network layer reachability information
    (NLRI), 640
network-link advertisements, 640
network LSAs, 640
network management
    configuring, **22–23**
    verifying, **23–24**

network service access points (NSAPs), 640
Network Summary LSAs, 640
Network Time Protocol (NTP)
    configuring, **24–25**, 50–51
    defined, 640
    verifying, **25–28**
network-to-network interface (NNI), 72
network types
    IS-IS, **277–278**
    OSPF, **168–173**, *168*, *172*
Next Hop attribute, 640
next-hop option, 487
next hops
    for confederations, 415–416
    for OoB management network configu-
        ration, 10
    self policy, **522–525**
NLPID encapsulation, 93
NLRI (network layer reachability
    information), 640
NMBA (non-broadcast multi-access)
    topology, 80
NNI (network-to-network interface), 72
no-authentication-check option, 278, 283, 286
no-export community, 429, 431
no-keepalives option, 85
no-readvertise tags, 10
no-summaries option in OSPF
    NSSAs, 190–191
    TSAs, 187
non-broadcast multi-access (NMBA)
    topology, 80
non-Martian addresses for unnumbered
    interfaces, 124
nonclient peers, 640
notification cells, 640
Notification messages, 640
NSAPs (network service access points), 640
NSSAs (not-so-stubby areas), **188**
    configuring, **188–191**
    defined, 641
    verifying, **191–194**
NTP (Network Time Protocol)
    configuring, **24–25**, 50–51
    defined, 640
    verifying, **25–28**
ntpdate command, 25

Null Register messages, 641
numeric range match conditions, 641

O

Oakley protocol, 641
OAM (Operations, Administration, and
     Management)
  keepalives, 89
  loopback cells, 95
OC (Optical Carrier), 641
offsets for NTP server synchronization, 26
1X phase, 620
1XEV phase, 620
OoB (Out of Band) management
  configuring, 44–45
  network configuration, 8–10
  for terminal servers, 3, *4*
Open messages, 641
Open Shortest Path First (OSPF). *See* OSPF
     (Open Shortest Path First) protocol
Open System Interconnection (OSI)
     standard, 641
OpenConfirm neighbor state, 641
OpenSent neighbor state, 641
operational modes, 641
Operations, Administration, and
     Management (OAM)
  keepalives, 89
  loopback cells, 95
ops account
  configuring, **17–18**
  parameters for, 11
  verifying, **19**
Optical Carrier (OC), 641
Origin attribute, 641
orlonger match type
  defined, 641
  in EBGP, 560
OSI (Open System Interconnection)
     standard, 641
OSPF (Open Shortest Path First) protocol,
     154, 440
  address summarization in, **194–197**
  adjacency in, **225–227**

authentication, 173–175
  protocol tracing, 177–178
  verifying, 176–177
case study, 228–231, *228*
  export policies, 231–235
  r1, 243–244
  r2, 244–245
  r3, 245–246
  r4, 246
  r5, 246–247
  r6, 247–248
  r7, 249–250
  RIP, 237–243
  summarization, 235–237
defined, 641
in IS-IS route redistribution, 299–300
  case study, 331–340
  r6, 305–310
  r7, 310–311
  verifying, 311–313
load balancing in, 223, 241–242
loopback addresses in, 230
metrics and knobs for, **222–225**, *225*
multi-area configuration, 154–155, *155*
  adjacency problems in, 156, 160,
       164–166
  area 1, **161**
  r3, 159–160
  r4, 155–157
  r5, 157–159
  verifying, 161–164
network types, **166**
  multipoint, **166–168**, *167*
  NBMA, **168–172**, *168*
  troubleshooting, 172–173
not-so-stubby areas in, **188**
  configuring, **188–191**
  defined, 641
  verifying, **191–194**
RIDs in, 230
routing policies for, **201–202**, *202*
  redistribution, **204–212**
  verifying, **213–221**, *214–215*
stub areas in, **179**
  configuring, **182–184**
  defined, 650
  deployment of, **180–181**, *180*

external LSA generation for, **181–182**
totally stubby, **179–180, 186–188**
summary, **227**
virtual links in, **198–201**, *198*
OSPF Hello packets, 642
Out of Band (OoB) management
configuring, 44–45
network configuration, **8–10**
for terminal servers, 3, *4*
out testing in ATM, 90
overlay networks, 642
overload option, 223–224

P

P1 peering, **493–498, 554–555**
packages, 30, 642
packet data protocol (PDP), 642
packet flood ping testing
for ATM traffic shaping, 99
for leaky bucket rate limiting, 122–123
for POS interfaces, 70–71
Packet Forwarding Engine, 642
packet loops in RIP, 213
Packet Loss Priority (PLP), 642
Packet Loss Priority (PLP bit), 643
Packet Over SONET. *See* POS (Packet Over SONET) interfaces
PAP (Password Authentication Protocol), 85
parity in ATM, 90
partial sequence number PDU (PSNP), 642
passive mode
in EBGP, 491
in IBGP, **427–429**, 459–460
in OSPF, 160
Password Authentication Protocol (PAP), 85
password keyword, 16
passwords
EXEC mode, 3, 6
in IS-IS, 279
for lab accounts, 16–17
for users, 47
path attribute, 642
path-vector protocols, 642
PathErr messages, 642
PathTear Messages, 642

payload scrambling
in ATM, 90
in POS interfaces, 65
PCI (Peripheral Component Interconnect) standard, 643
PCMCIA (Personal Computer Memory Card International Association), 643
PDP (packet data protocol), 642
PDUs (protocol data units)
defined, 644
in IS-IS, **258–260**
PE (provider edge) routers, 644
peak bit rate, 98
PECs (Policing Equivalence Classes), 643
peer-as option, 412
peer-export option, 530
peer sites
in community tagging, 517–518
in route filtering, **529–538**
peering
defined, 642
in EBGP, **481–482**, *482–483*
C1, **487–488**
C2, **484–486**
case study, **554–560**
P1, **493–498**
T1, **500–504**
T2, **498–500**
troubleshooting, **489–493**
in IBGP
initial setup, **374–377**, *375*
policies, **377–383**
penultimate hop popping (PHP) mechanism, 642
penultimate routers, 642
Perfect Forward Secrecy (PFS), 643
performance of OSPF, 179
Peripheral Component Interconnect (PCI) standard, 643
permanent virtual circuits (PVCs)
in ATM, 89
defined, 643
for Frame Relay, 71
Personal Computer Memory Card International Association (PCMCIA), 463
PFS (Perfect Forward Secrecy), 643
PHP (penultimate hop popping) mechanism, 642

Physical Interface Cards (PICs), 643
physical interface peering
  with C-BGP, 444
  in IBGP, 388
Physical Layer Convergence Protocol
  (PLCP), 90
physical properties
  for ATM interfaces, **90–91**
  for Ethernet interfaces, **101**, *102*
  for POS interfaces, **65–68**
PIC I/O Manager ASIC, 643
PICs (Physical Interface Cards), 643
PIM (Protocol Independent Multicast)
  protocol, 644
ping size command, 99–100
ping testing
  for ATM
    traffic shaping, 99–100
    virtual circuits, 94–95
  for EBGP
    peering, 489–490, 495
    route filtering, 531–532
  for IS-IS, 272
  for leaky bucket rate limiting, 122–123
  for loopback interfaces, 61
  for MAC address filtering, 113
  for OoB management network
    configuration, 10
  for ops account, 19
  for POS interfaces, 70–71
  for unnumbered interfaces, 126
PLCP (Physical Layer Convergence
  Protocol), 90
PLMNs (public land mobile networks), 644
PLP (Packet Loss Priority), 642
PLP bit (Packet Loss Priority) bit, 643
point-to-multipoint connections, 80–82, *81*
Point-to-Point Protocol (PPP)
  defined, 643
  for POS interfaces
    CHAP authentication for, 85–88
    configuring, **82–83**, *83*
    verifying, **83–85**
poison reverse method, 643
policies
  EBGP, **504**
    export. *See* export policies
    import. *See* import policies

IBGP, 377–383
OSPF routing, **201–202**, *202*
  redistribution, **204–212**
  verifying, **213–221**, *214–215*
policing, 643
Policing Equivalence Classes (PECs), 643
policy chains, 643
poll expectation timers, 78
poll-interval parameter, 169
polls for Frame Relay, 77–78
popping, 643
POS (Packet Over SONET) interfaces, **64**, *65*
  encapsulation options for
    Frame Relay, **71–82**, *81*
    PPP, **82–88**, *83*
  logical properties of, **68–69**
  physical properties of, **65–68**
  summary, **89**
  verifying, **69–71**
PPP (Point-to-Point Protocol)
  defined, 643
  for POS interfaces
    CHAP authentication for, **85–88**
    configuring, **82–83**, *83*
    verifying, **83–85**
ppp-options option, 86
precedence bits, 643
preferences
  defined, 644
  in EBGP, **547–548**
  in IBGP, **422–426**, **429–435**
preferred addresses
  defined, 644
  with loopback interfaces, 62
prefix advertising, 505
prefix-length-range match type, 644
prefix-limit option, 556–557
prepend policy option, *585–586*
primary addresses
  defined, 644
  with loopback interfaces, 62–63
primary contributing routes, 644
primary interfaces, 644
primary option, 63
priorities
  for DR, 171
  in IS-IS, **330–331**
  in VRRP, 104, 108, 110–111

privileged EXEC mode passwords, 3, 6
protocol addresses, 644
protocol data units (PDUs)
    defined, 644
    in IS-IS, **258–260**
protocol families, 644
Protocol Independent Multicast (PIM)
    protocol, 644
protocol next hops for confederations, 415
protocol preference value, 644
protocol tracing
    in IS-IS authentication, **285**
    in OSPF authentication, **177–178**
    in SNMP, 24
provider edge (PE) routers, 644
provider routers, 644
Prune messages, 644
PSNP (partial sequence number PDU), 642
.pub extension, 13
public keys, 11, 13
public land mobile networks (PLMNs), 644
PVCs (permanent virtual circuits)
    in ATM, 89
    defined, 643
    for Frame Relay, 71

Q

QoS (quality of service), 645
quad-wide PICs, 645
qualified next hops, 645
querier routers, 645

R

r1 router
    in ATM, 98
    in EBGP
        case study, **554–555, 576–591**
        Martian filtering, **512–513**
        P1 peering, **493–498**
    in Ethernet interfaces
        physical configuration, 101, *102*
        VLAN and VRRP configuration,
        103–105

in Frame Relay, **80–82,** *81*
in IBGP, **375–377**
    authentication, **384–385**
    case study, **444–445, 460–461**
    redistribution policy, **431–432**
    route reflection, **391–392**
    subconfederations, **404–406**
in interface configuration case study, 130,
    132–133
in IS-IS
    case study, **345–347**
    route redistribution, **300–305**
in OSPF
    case study, **243–244**
    NSSAs, **188–190**
    redistribution policies, **204–205**
    stub areas, 184
r2 router
    in ATM, 98
    in EBGP
        case study, **554–555, 565–570, 576–588,**
        591–594
        P1 peering, **493–498**
    in Ethernet interfaces
        physical configuration, 101, *102*
        VLAN and VRRP configuration,
        105–107
    in Frame Relay, **80–82,** *81*
    in IBGP
        case study, **461–463**
        redistribution policy, **429–431**
        route reflection, **392**
        subconfederations, **408**
    in interface configuration case study, 130,
        133–136
    in IS-IS
        case study, **347–349**
        route redistribution, **300–305**
    in OSPF
        case study, **244–245**
        redistribution policies, **204–205**
        stub areas, 184
r3 router
    in ATM
        logical properties, **91–95**
        multipoint connections, 98
        traffic shaping, **98–100**
    CHAP for, **85–88**

in EBGP
  case study, 558–560, 570–571, 573–576,
    594–598
  damping, 505–511
  hidden route repair, 522–523
  local preferences, 547–548
  Martian filtering, 512–513
  route filtering, 538–539
  T1 peering, 500–504
  traffic flow, 543–547
in Ethernet interfaces
  aggregated, 115–116
  MAC address filtering, 112–113
in Frame Relay
  configuration for, 72–78
  point-to-multipoint connections,
    80–82, 81
in IBGP
  authentication, 383–384
  case study, 463–464
  hold time, 426–427
  route reflection, 391, 393–394
  subconfederations, 406–408
ILMI changes for, 95–97
in interface configuration case study,
  130, 136–139
in IS-IS, 267–268
  authentication, 280–282
  case study, 349–353
  verifying, 268–270
leaky bucket rate limiting for, 119–124,
  122–123
loopback interfaces for, 61–64
in OSPF
  address summarization, 195–196
  case study, 245–246
  configuring, 159–161
  NBMA, 169–170
  stub areas, 183
  verifying, 160–161
in POS, for, 66–71
in PPP, 83–85, 83
in SONET interface, 117–119
r4 router, 98
  in ATM, 93–95
  CHAP for, 85–88
  in EBGP
    C1 peering, 487–488

case study, 555–557, 563–570, 573–576,
  599–603
in Frame Relay, 75–78
in IBGP, 445–446
  case study, 464–466
  hold time, 427
  passive mode, 427–429
  route reflection, 391
  subconfederations, 408–409
in interface configuration case study,
  130–131, 139–141
in IS-IS
  authentication, 280–282
  case study, 353–356
  PDUs, 258–260
  routing instances, 260–261
  verifying, 261–263
loopback interfaces for, 61
in OSPF
  case study, 246
  configuring, 155–156
  NBMA, 169–170
  stub areas, 183
  verifying, 157
in PPP, 83–85, 83
r5 router
  in EBGP
    case study, 603–604
    hidden route repair, 521–525
  in IBGP, 446
    case study, 466–467
    export policy, 423–424
    route reflection, 392–393
    subconfederations, 410–412
  in interface configuration case study, 131,
    142–145
  in IS-IS, 264–265
    authentication, 278–280
    case study, 356–360
    multi-level, 257, 257
    verifying, 265–267
  in OSPF
    address summarization, 195, 197
    authentication, 175–177
    case study, 246–247
    configuring, 157–158
    NBMA, 169–170
    protocol tracing, 177–178

verifying, **158–159**
virtual links, 198–201
r6 router
  in EBGP
    case study, **558, 573–576, 604–608**
    route filtering, 539–540
    T2 peering, **498–500**
  in IBGP, 447–448
    case study, **467–469**
    export policy, 422–423
  in interface configuration case study, 131,
    146–147
  in IS-IS
    area 49.0002, 270–271
    case study, **360–363**
    multi-level, 257, *257*
    route redistribution, 305–310
  in OSPF configuration
    case study, **247–248**
    redistribution policies and RIP, 205–210
r7 router
  in EBGP
    C2 peering, **484–486**
    case study, **557–558, 563–564, 573–576,**
    608–611
    community tagging, 518–519
    Martian filtering, 513–515
    route filtering, 526–527
  in IBGP, **469–471**
  in interface configuration case study,
    131, **148**
  in IS-IS
    area 49.0002, 270–271
    authentication, 282
    case study, **363–365**
    multi-level, 257, *257*
    route redistribution, **310–311**
  in OSPF
    case study, **249–250**
    redistribution policies and RIP, **210–215**
    static routes, **181–182**
radio frequency interference (RFI), 645
radio network controllers (RNCs), 645
RADIUS (Remote Authentication Dial-In User
    Service) authentication, 47
  defined, 646
  for lab account, **14–17**

for root account, 11
simulating failures in, 15–16
Random Early Detection (RED) profile, 645
rapid ping tests
  for ATM traffic shaping, 99
  for leaky bucket rate limiting, 122–123
  for POS interfaces, 70–71
RBOCs (regional Bell operating
    companies), 645
RE (Routing Engine)
  defined, 647
  for flood pings, 122
  redundancy support in, 33
read-write keyword, 23
receive hops, 645
record route objects (RROs), 645
recursive lookups, 645
RED (Random Early Detection) profile, 645
redistribution. *See* route redistribution
redundancy configuration, **33–34**
regional Bell operating companies
    (RBOCs), 645
Register messages, 645
Register Stop messages, 645
reject hops, 645
reject option, 378, 430
Remote Authentication Dial-In User Service
    (RADIUS) authentication, 47
  defined, 646
  for lab account, **14–17**
  for root account, 11
  simulating failures in, 15–16
remove-private option, 568
rename command
  for addresses, 64
  defined, 646
  for mistake correction, **127–128**
rename group internal command, 390, 392
rename neighbor command, 390
rename unit command, 64
Rendezvous Points (RPs), 646
Request for Comments (RFC), 646
Request messages, 646
request system snapshot command, 33–34
resolve hops, 646
Resource Reservation Protocol (RSVP), 646
Response messages, 646
restart routing command, 417

restarts, selective, **418–419**
restrict keyword, 188
result cells, 646
ResvConf messages, 646
ResvErr messages, 646
ResvTear messages, 646
retry parameter for RADIUS, 14
retry timers in EBGP, 488
reuse threshold in route damping, 505
reverse engineering, 317
reverse path forwarding method, 646
reverse path multicasting (RPM), 646
reverse telnet sessions, switching among, **6**
Reynolds, Harry, xxix
RFC (Request for Comments), 646
RFI (radio frequency interference), 645
RIBs (Routing Information Bases), 647
RIDs (Router IDs)
    defined, 647
    in IS-IS, 309
    loopback interfaces for, 60, 64
    in OSPF, 155–157, 230
    for unnumbered interfaces, 124
RIP (Routing Information Protocol)
    defined, 647
    import policies for, **216–218**
    in OSPF, 237–243
RIP router configuration for OSPF, 202–204
    r6, **205–210**
    r7, **210–212**
RNCs (radio network controllers), 645
Rogan, Jason, xxix
rollback command, 418, 435
root accounts
    configuring, **11–12**, *14*
    verifying, **12–14**, *12*
root user
    logins with, 5, 47
    parameters for, 11
route advertisements
    in EBGP, 526
    in IBGP, 380–382
route damping, **505–511**
route filtering
    defined, 646
    in EBGP, **525**
        customer site, **526–529**

peer site, **529–538**
    transit provider, **538–540**
route flapping, 646
route identifiers, 646
route leaking in IS-IS, **286–290**
    case study, **326–328**
    configuring, **290–292**
    verifying, **292–293**
route redistribution
    defined, 647
    in IBGP, **429–432**, **448–455**
    in IS-IS, **297–298**, *298*
        case study, **328–330**
        OSPF router configuration, **299–300**
        r1 and r2, **300–305**
        r6, **305–310**
        r7, **310–311**
        troubleshooting, **301–305**
        verifying, **311–313**
    in OSPF, 201
        r1 and r2, **204–205**
        r6, **205–210**
        r7, **210–212**
        verifying, **213–221**, *214–215*
route reflection in IBGP, 386–387
    configuring, **387–390**, *387*, *389*
        clusters 1.1.1.1 and 3.3.3.3, **390–392**
        clusters 2.2.2.2, **392–393**
        in core, **393–394**
    defined, 647
    verifying, **395–402**
route repair, hidden, **520–525**, *522*, **571–588**
route summarization. *See* summarization
route tagging, 201
Router IDs (RIDs)
    defined, 647
    in IS-IS, 309
    loopback interfaces for, 60, 64
    in OSPF, 155–157, 230
    for unnumbered interfaces, 124
router-link advertisements, 647
router LSAs, 647
Router Priority, 647
routers
    as broadcast NTP clients, 50
    hostnames for, 44
    problems with, **417–418**

routing daemon restart command, 417
Routing Engine (RE)
    defined, 647
    for flood pings, 122
    redundancy support in, 33
Routing Information Bases (RIBs), 647
Routing Information Protocol (RIP), 647
routing instances
    defined, 647
    in IS-IS, 260–261
routing-options option
    for confederations, 406
    for OSPF configuration, 156
    for RIP, 203
routing-options stanza, 39
routing-options static option
routing policies
    in IS-IS
        route leaking, **286–293**
        route redistribution. *See* route
            redistribution
        summarization, **286–290, 293–297**
    in OSPF, **201–202**, *202*
        redistribution, **204–212**
        RIP router configuration, 202–204
        verifying, **213–221**, *214–215*
routing tables, 647
rpd (routing protocol daemon), 647
RPM (reverse path multicasting), 646
RPs (Rendezvous Points), 646
RROs (record route objects), 645
RSA public keys, 11
RSVP (Resource Reservation Protocol), 646
RSVP Path messages, 647
RSVP Resv messages, 647
RSVP signaled LSPs, 647

S

SAP (Session Announcement Protocol), 648
SAR (segmentation and reassembly) method
    in ATM, 89, 91
    defined, 648
SAs (security associations), 648
save command, 420
saving confederations, **420**

scalability
    in IS-IS, 256
    in OSPF, 154, 179
SCB (System Control Board), 650
SCG (SONET Clock Generator), 649
SDH (Synchronous Digital Hierarchy) standard
    defined, 650
    with POS interfaces, 65–66
SDP (Session Description Protocol), 648
secret keys, 13
Secure Hash Algorithm (SHA-1), 648
secure shell (SSH) protocol
    defined, 648
    password authentication, **11–12**, *12*
    session settings, 12
    SSH key pairs, **12–14**, *14*
SecureCRT application, 13
SecureCRT Key Generation Wizard, 13
security associations (SAs), 648
Security Parameter Index (SPI), 648
segment switches in ATM, 95
segmentation and reassembly (SAR) method
    in ATM, 89, 91
    defined, 648
selective restarts, **418–419**
Serving GPRS Support Node (SGSN)
    devices, 648
Session Announcement Protocol (SAP), 648
session attribute objects, 648
Session Description Protocol (SDP), 648
session hold time, 426
set address command
    in IS-IS, 258, 274
    in POS, 69
set aggregate route command, 532
set aggregated-devices command, 115
set aggregated-ether-options command, 115
set area 0 authentication-type md5
    command, 174
set area 0 interface command, 155, 157–159
set area 1 interface command, 158, 161
set area 10 stub command, 183–184
set area-range command, 195–196
set as0 command, 258
set atm-options ilmi command, 95
set atm-options vpi command, 90, 95
set authentication-key command, 25

set authentication-key jni command, 394
set authentication-key jnx command, 383–384
set authentication-order command, 15
set authentication-type simple command, 174
set autonomous-system command
    in EBGP, 542
    in IBGP, 375, 405–406
set bgp group command, 530
set chassis fpc command, 66
set chassis redundancy command, 33
set class ops command, 17
set cluster command, 390, 393
set community customers members
        command, 518
set community no-export command, 429
set community peers members command, 518
set community test authorization command, 23
set community transit members command, 518
set confederation command, 405–406
set confederation members command, 405, 407
set damping command, 507
set damping aggressive half-life command, 505
set damping aggressive suppress command, 505
set damping dry disable command, 506
set damping timid half-life command, 505
set date command, 26
set dce command, 75
set encapsulation command
    for ATM, 92
    for Frame Relay, 81
    for POS, 66
set encapsulation frame-relay command, 72
set export ibgp command, 405–406, 412
set family command, 92
set file auth archive files command, 20
set file auth authorization info command, 20
set from route-filter command, 506
set group command
    in EBGP, 507
    in IBGP, 430
set group c2 import command, 514
set group core command, 394
set group rip neighbor command, 205, 217
set group rip preference command, 218
set hold-time command, 66
set interface all command, 270, 282
set interface as1 command, 264
set interface as1.0 command, 278–279

set interface at-0/2/1.35 command, 279
set interface fe-0/0/0 command, 279
set interface lo0 command, 264, 274
set interfaces command, 8, 85–86
set isis interface command, 316
set keepalives command, 66
set level 2 command, 270, 278
set lmi lmi-type itu command, 72, 75
set lmi t391dte command, 77
set lmi t392dce command, 78
set lo0 unit command, 61
set local-address command
    in EBGP, 491
    in IBGP, 376
set login user lab command, 14
set mac command, 113, 315
set mtu command, 69
set multihop command
    in EBGP, 487
    in IBGP, 412
set multipoint-destination command, 81–82
set multpath command, 500
set neighbor command
    in EBGP, 500
    in IBGP
        authentication, 383
        confederations, 405–406, 411–412
        core, 394
        peering, 376
set no-authentication-check command, 278
set nssa command, 190
set ops command, 17
set ospf area command, 306
set peer-as command, 484, 487, 498
set policy-statement static command, 431
set protocols bgp group interval command, 378
set protocols bgp group multipath
        command, 425
set protocols bgp group passive command, 427
set protocols bgp preference command, 424
set protocols isis ignore-attached-bit
        command, 314
set protocols isis interface command, 315
set protocols isis level 1 command, 263
set protocols ospf export command, 181,
        189, 207
set protocols ospf overload command, 224
set protocols rip group command, 208

set radius-server command, 14
set root-authentication command, 11
set route command, 487
set routing-options aggregate route
    command, 526
set routing-options generate route
    command, 534
set routing-options router-id command, 309
set routing-options static route command, 430
set server command, 25
set shaping command, 99
set sonet-options command, 66, 120
set source-address-filter command, 112
set source-filtering command, 112
set ssh-rsa command, 11
set static route command
    in EBGP, 536
    in OSPF, 181
set stub no-summaries command, 187
set system authentication-order password
    command, 16
set system host-name command, 8
set system processes command, 33
set system services ssh command, 11
set system services telnet command, 8
set system time-zone command, 28
set term command
    for NSSAs, 189
    for static routes, 181
set term 1 command, 429–430
set term 2 command, 422
set traceoptions file command, 377
set traceoptions flag command, 377
set track interface command, 108
set transit-delay command, 225
set transmit-bucket command, 120
set trusted-key command, 25
set type external local-address command, 411
set type external neighbor command, 484,
    487–498
set type external peer-as command, 500
set type internal command, 376
set type internal local-address, 394, 405–406
set unit command
    for EBGP, 485, 498
    for Frame Relay, 72, 81–82
    for loopback interfaces, 62–63

for PPP, 83
for VRRP, 103–106
set user ops command, 17
set vci command, 92
set virtual-link command, 199–200
set vlan-tagging command, 101, 114
set vrrp-group command, 103–104, 106,
    108, 496
SFM (Switching and Forwarding Module), 650
SGSN (Serving GPRS Support Node)
    devices, 648
SHA-1 (Secure Hash Algorithm), 648
shared trees, 648
shim headers, 648
Short Message Service (SMS), 648
shortest path first (SPF) algorithm, 648
shortest-path trees, 648
show access command, 86
show arp command, 496
show authentication-order command, 15
show bgp neighbor command
    for authentication, 385
    for passive mode, 428
    for timers, 427
show bgp summary command
    in EBGP
        C1 peering, 488, 492
        C2 peering, 484–486
        damping, 511
        P1 peering, 496–497
        route filtering, 531
        T1 peering, 501, 503–504
        T2 peering, 499
    in IBGP
        authentication, 384, 386
        confederations, 407, 409–411, 413
        peering, 279
        route reflection, 395
show chassis aggregated-devices command
    for Ethernet, 116
    for SONET, 117
show chassis alarm command, 34
show chassis alarms command, 28
show chassis environment command, 28–29
show chassis fpc command, 66
show chassis hardware command, 29
show chassis redundancy command, 34
show class ops command, 18

show group c2 command, 514
show group core command, 394
show group t1-t2 command, 544–545
show ilmi command, 97
show interfaces command, 9
  in ATM, 91
  in EBGP, 485
  in Ethernet, 116
  in Frame Relay, 73–74, 79–80
  in ILMI, 96–97
  in leaky bucket rate limiting, 120, 124
  in loopback interfaces, 61
  in ops account, 18
  in OSPF, **166–167**, 299–300
  in POS interfaces, 65–67
  in PPP, 84, 86–87
  in SONET, 117–119
  in VRRP, 106–109
show interfaces as0 command, 259–260
show interfaces fxp0 command, 260
show interfaces lo0 command, 62–63, 259–260,
  288–290
show interfaces terse command, 268
show isis adjacency command, 274
  area 49.0002, 271, 282–283
  r3, 269
  r4, 261
show isis adjacency detail command, 266
show isis database command
  area 49.0002, 271
  r3, 269
  r4, 263
  redistribution, 303
  summarization, 295–296
show isis database detail command, 266
show isis hostname command, 275, 290
show isis interface command, 272–273, 315,
  418–419
  r3, 268–269
  r4, 261
  r5, 265
show isis interface detail command, 262–263
show lo0 command, 61
show log auth command, 21
show login user command, 15
show ntp associations command, 25, 27
show ospf database asbrsummary
  command, 182

show ospf database detail command, 157
show ospf database extern command, 182,
  185, 217
show ospf database netsummary command,
  186–187, 191
show ospf database netsummary area
  command, 159, 222–223
show ospf database netsummary extensive
  command, 199
show ospf database nssa detail command,
  191–192
show ospf database router command, 178
show ospf database router advertising-router
  command, 160–161
show ospf database router area 0
  command, 162
show ospf database router detail command,
  224–225
show ospf interface command, 173
  r3, 160
  r4, 157
  r5, 158, 175, 177–178
show ospf interface detail command, 157, 167
show ospf interface extensive command,
  170–171
show ospf neighbor command
  r3, 160, 163, 168, 173
  r5, 159, 163, 178
  r6, 161
  r7, 163, 166
show ospf neighbor detail command, 171–172
show policy-options command, 189, 203, 211
show policy-options policy-statement command
  in IBGP, 378
  in IS-IS, 294
  in OSPF, 299
  in RIP, 216
show policy-options policy-statement bogons
  command, 512
show policy-options policy-statement med
  command, 544
show policy-statement command, 216,
  218–219
show policy-statement transit-export
  command, 538
show protocols bgp command, 378
  for confederations, 408–410
  for route reflection, 392

show protocols bgp group command, 413

show protocols bgp group c-bgp command, 412, 548

show protocols bgp group c2 command, 518–519

show protocols bgp group export command, 378

show protocols bgp group p1 command, 513

show protocols bgp group t1-t2 command, 539

show protocols isis command, 288–290

show protocols isis export command, 292, 295

show protocols ospf command, 169

show protocols ospf area command, 198

show protocols ospf detail command, 167

show protocols ospf traceoptions command, 164

show protocols rip command, 202, 217

show radius-server command, 15

show root-authentication command, 12

show route command
  in EBGP, 501–503
    AS loops, 542
    community tags, 520
    hidden route repair, 521, 523–525
    local preferences, 547–548
    route filtering, 533–534
    traffic flow, 545–546
  in IBGP
    confederations, 414–415, 420
    load balancing, 423–425
    local preferences, 432–434

show route advertising-protocol command, 648

show route advertising-protocol bgp command
  in EBGP
    incoming traffic flow, 546
    route filtering, 536–538
    site export policy, 527–530, 538
    transport provider export policy, 540
  in IBGP
    peering 381
    preferences, 423, 430–432

show route damping command, 508–511

show route protocol aggregate command, 534–535

show route protocol aggregate detail command, 535–536

show route protocol bgp command
  in EBGP
    peer site export policy, 530–531
    peering, 493
  in IBGP, 380
    for confederations, 408–409, 413–414
    for route reflection, 395–401

show route protocol bgp source-gateway command, 497–498

show route protocol isis command, 269–270, 272, 274–275, 290–292

show route protocol ospf command, 162–163, 185–187, 195

show route protocol rip command, 206

show route receive-protocol command, 648

show route receive-protocol bgp command
  in EBGP, 486, 492–493
  in IBGP, 380–381

show route resolution command, 521

show route source-gateway command, 515–516, 519–520

show route table martians command, 512

show routing-options command, 39–40
  in EBGP, 539
  in IBGP, 378, 407–408, 410
  in OSPF, 299
  in RIP, 203

show routing-options aggregate command, 295

show system command, 9

show system authentication-order command, 16

show system connections command, 23–24, 428–429

show system processes command, 34

show system services command, 12

show system syslog command, 20

show system uptime command, 27–28

show traceoptions command
  in IBGP, 377
  in IS-IS, 273, 285

show user ops command, 18

show version command, 29–30, 32

show vrrp summary command, 105, 107, 110, 495–497

show vrrp track command, 110

SIB (Switch Interface Board), 650

SIDs (System IDs)
  defined, *650*
  in IS-IS, 257–258
signaled paths, 649
Signaling System 7 (SS7) protocol, 649
simplex interface, 649
SMS (Short Message Service), 648
SNMP (Simple Network Management
  Protocol)
  configuring, **22–23**, 49
  defined, 649
  verifying, **23–24**
SNPA (Subnetwork Point of Attachment), 278
soft state structure, 649
software upgrades, **30–32**
software versions, 29–30
SONET (Synchronous Optical Network)
  specification
  aggregated, **117–119**
  defined, *650*
SONET Clock Generator (SCG), 649
source address filtering, 101
source-based trees, 649
source-filtering option, 111
source-gateway option, 515–516
source-specific multicasting, 649
source switch, 309
sparse mode, 649
SPF (shortest path first) algorithm, 648
SPI (Security Parameter Index), 648
Split Horizon method
  defined, 649
  with RIP, 219
SPQ (Strict Priority Queuing), 650
SS7 (Signaling System 7) protocol, 649
SSB (System Switching Board), 650
SSH (secure shell) protocol
  defined, 648
  password authentication, **11–12**, *12*
  session settings, 12
  SSH key pairs, **12–14**, *14*
ssh-keygen command, 13
SSH Quick Connect dialog box, 12–13, *12*
stanzas, cutting and pasting, **39–41**
star topology, 166
static ARP entries, 102
static paths, 649

static routes
  defined, 649
  in EBGP, 482, *482*
    case study, *577*
    route filtering, *536*
  in IBGP, 378–379
    confederations, 403–404, *403–404*
    route reflection, 387, *387*, 389, *389*
  in lab exams, **222**
  for OoB management network
    configuration, 10
  in OSPF
    NSSAs, 188
    RIP, 209
    stub areas, 181–182
    TSAs, 186
static RP method, 649
STMs (Synchronous Transport Modules), 650
strict hop routers, 649
Strict Priority Queuing (SPQ), 650
strict routes, 649
STS (Synchronous Transport Signal)
  Level 1, 650
stub areas in OSPF, **179**
  configuring, **182–184**
  defined, *650*
  deploying, **180–181**, *180*
  external LSA generation for, **181–182**
  totally stubby, **179–180**, **186–188**
subconfederation 65000, **404–408**
subconfederations 65001 and 65002, **408–411**
subnets and subnet masks
  defined, *650*
  in OSPF, 194
  for POS interfaces, 69
  for static routes, 210
Subnetwork Point of Attachment (SNPA), 278
summarization
  in IBGP, 456–459
  in IS-IS, 286–290
    case study, **326–328**, **340–345**
    configuring, **293–295**
    verifying, **295–297**
  in OSPF
    case study, 235–237
    configuring, **194–197**
summary-link advertisements, 650
summary LSAs, 179

supernetting, 194
superuser login class, 14
suppress threshold in route damping, 505
sustained bit rate, 98
Switch Interface Board (SIB), 650
switching among reverse telnet sessions, **6**
Switching and Forwarding Module (SFM), 650
symbolic name mappings, **4–5**
synchronization in NTP
    configuring, **24–25**, 50–51
    defined, 640
    verifying, **25–28**
Synchronous Digital Hierarchy (SDH) standard
    defined, 650
    with POS interfaces, 65–66
Synchronous Optical Network (SONET)
    specification
    aggregated, **117–119**
    defined, 650
Synchronous Transport Modules (STMs), 650
Synchronous Transport Signal (STS)
    Level 1, 650
sysids (system identifiers)
    defined, 650
    in IS-IS, 257–258
syslog method, 650
syslog parameters
    configuring, **20–21**, 45
    verifying, **21–22**
system clocks for NTP server
    synchronization, 26
system configuration
    case study, **42**
        completed configuration, **51–54**
        examples, **43–51**
        requirements, **42–43**
    cut and paste for, **37–41**
    initial, **34–37**
    summary, **41**
System Control Board (SCB), 650
System IDs (SIDs)
    defined, 650
    in IS-IS, 257–258
system snapshots, 33–34
System Switching Board (SSB), 650

T

-t flag in ssh-keygen, 13
T1 peering, **500–504**
T2 peering, **498–500**
T3 C-bit parity, 90
T391 poll timer, 78
T392 poll expectation timer, 78, 141
TACACS+ (Terminal Access Controller Access
    Control System Plus) authentication, 651
tagging
    community, **517–520**
    VLAN, 101, 103–105
TCP (Transmission Control Protocol), 651
TCP port 179, 651
tcpdump utility
    defined, 651
    for Frame Relay, 74
teardown option, 556
telnet service and terminal servers, **2–3**
    clearing, **6–8**
    console connections for, **3–5**, *4*
    for OoB management network
        configuration, 8
    for router access, 3, 5
    switching among, **6**
Terminal Access Controller Access Control
    System Plus (TACACS+)
    authentication, 651
terminating actions, 651
terms, 651
text editors, 37
3GPP (Third-Generation Partnership
    Project), 620
through match type, 512, 651
time synchronization in NTP
    configuring, **24–25**, 50–51
    defined, 640
    verifying, **25–28**
time zone settings, 27–28
timeout parameter, 14
Timeout timers, 651
timers and knobs
    in EBGP, **541**
        AS loops, **542–543**
        incoming traffic flow, **543–547**
        local preferences, **547–548**

in IBGP, 421–422, *421*
   load balancing, **422–426**
   local preferences and communities,
      429–435
   passive mode configuration, **427–429**
   timer modifications, **426–427**
  in IS-IS, **262**
timid damping, 505
TLVs (Type Length Values), 276
TNSSAs (Totally Not-So-Stubby Areas), 188
token-bucket algorithm, 651
ToS (type of service) method, 652
Totally Stubby Areas (TSAs)
  defined, 651
  in OSPF, **179–180**, **186–188**
traceroute command
  in EBGP
   forwarding path confirmation, 540–541
   local preferences, 548
   route filtering, 535
  in IBGP
   confederations, 416, 419
   peering, 381–382
   route reflection, 397, 400–401
  in IS-IS
   configuration, 275
   route redistribution, 304–305, 309–310,
     312–313
  in OSPF
   NSSAs, 194
   RIP, 208–209, 213, 220–221
   TSAs, 187–188
  for unnumbered interfaces, 126
  for virtual links, 201
tracing
  IS-IS authentication, **285**
  in OSPF
   adjacency problems, 164–165
   authentication, **177–178**
tracking in VRRP, **107–111**
traffic engineering, 651
traffic shaping, 89, **98–100**
transient interfaces, 651
transit areas, 651
transit-delay setting, 225
transit routers, 651

transit sites
  in community tagging, 517–518
  in route filtering, 538–540
Transmission Control Protocol (TCP), 651
transport mode, 652
trap group operation, 24
triggered updates, 652
Triple-DES encryption algorithm, 652
troubleshooting
  EBGP peering, **489–493**
  IBGP, **435–439**
  IS-IS
   authentication, **283–286**
   route redistribution, **301–305**
  OSPF network types, **172-173**
TSAs (Totally Stubby Areas), **179–180,**
  186–188
Tspec Object, 652
tunnel mode, 652
Tunnel PICs, 652
tunnels, 652
2-Way adjacency state, 620
Type Length Values (TLVs), 276
type of service (ToS) method, 652

U

UBR (Unspecified Bit Rate), 91, 98
UDP (User Datagram Protocol), 653
UMTS (Universal Mobile Telecommunications
  System), 653
UMTS Terrestrial Radio Access Network
  (UTRAN), 652
UNI (User-to-Network Interface) DCE, 89
uninterruptible power supplies (UPSs), 652
unit numbers for Frame Relay, 73
units, 652
Universal Mobile Telecommunications System
  (UMTS), 653
unnumbered interfaces, 124–125, *125*
  configuring, **125–126**
  verifying, **126**
Unspecified Bit Rate (UBR), 91, 98
Update messages, 653
Update timers, 653
upgrades, software, **30–32**

UPSs (uninterruptible power supplies), 652
upto match type, 653
user accounts, **10–14**, *12*, *14*, **45–48**
User Datagram Protocol (UDP), 653
User-to-Network Interface (UNI) DCE, 89
UTC time zone, 27
UTRAN (UMTS Terrestrial Radio Access
    Network), 652

V

vapor corrosion inhibitors (VCIs), 653
VBR (Variable Bit Rate) parameter, 98
VC (virtual-circuit)-based multiplexing, 89
VCI-to-IP address mapping, 98
VCIs (vapor corrosion inhibitors), 653
VCIs (virtual circuit identifiers)
    in ATM, 90–91, 93
    defined, 653
VCs
    for ATM, 90
    defined, 653
verifying
    ATM interfaces, **93–97**
    in EBGP
        community tagging, **519–520**
        customer site export policy, **527–529**
        damping, **508–511**
        Martian filtering, **515–517**
        next hop self, **523–525**
        peer site export policy, **530–538**
        transit provider export policy, **540**
    Frame Relay, **79–80**
    in IBGP
        authentication, **386**
        confederations, **413–420**
        peering and policies, **379–383**
        route reflection, **395–402**
    in IS-IS
        area 49.0002, **271**
        area 49.0003, **290**
        multi-level, **261–263**
        overall, **272**, **274–275**
        r3, **268–270**
        r5, **265–267**
        route leaking, **292–293**

    route redistribution, **311–313**
    summarization, **295–297**
lab accounts, **15–17**
leaky bucket rate limiting, **121–124**,
    122–123
lo0 interface, **61–64**
MAC address filtering, **113**
NTP, **25–28**
ops account, **19**
in OSPF
    authentication, **176–177**
    external LSA generation, **182**
    NSSAs, **191–194**
    overall, **161–164**
    r3, **160–161**
    r4, **157**
    r5, **158–159**
    routing policies, **213–221**, *214–215*
    stub areas, **184–186**
    totally stubby areas, **187–188**
POS interfaces, **69–71**
PPP, **83–85**
root accounts, **12–14**, *12*, *14*
SNMP, **23–24**
syslog parameters, **21–22**
unnumbered interfaces, **126**
VRRP
    configuration, **107**
    interface tracking, **109–111**
versions, software, 29–30
VIP (Virtual IP) addresses
    in EBGP peering, 496
    in Ethernet interfaces, 102
    for VRRP, 106
virtual-circuit (VC)-based multiplexing, 89
virtual circuit identifiers (VCIs)
    in ATM, 90–91, 93
    defined, 653
virtual circuits (VCs)
    for ATM, 90
    defined, 653
Virtual IP (VIP) addresses
    in EBGP peering, 496
    in Ethernet interfaces, 102
    for VRRP, 106
virtual links
    defined, 653
    in OSPF, **198–201**, *198*

virtual local area networks (VLANs)
   defined, 653
   for Ethernet interfaces
      r1, **103–105**
      r2, **105–107**
virtual path identifiers (VPIs)
   in ATM, 93
   defined, 653
virtual paths (VPs)
   in ATM, 90–91
   defined, 653
virtual private networks (VPNs), 653
Virtual Router Redundancy Protocol (VRRP)
   defined, 653
   in EBGP peering, 495–497
   for Ethernet, 101
      authentication and tracking, **107–111**
      r1, **103–105**
      r2, **105–107**
VLAN IDs for Ethernet interfaces, 102–103
VLAN tagging
   for Ethernet interfaces, 101
   for VLAN and VRRP configuration,
      103–105
VLANs (virtual local area networks)
   defined, 653
   for Ethernet interfaces
      r1, **103–105**
      r2, **105–107**

voice/data integration, 89
VPIs (virtual path identifiers)
   in ATM, 93
   defined, 653
VPNs (virtual private networks), 653
VPs (virtual paths)
   in ATM, 90–91
   defined, 653
VRRP (Virtual Router Redundancy Protocol)
   defined, 653
   for Ethernet interfaces, 101
      authentication and tracking, **107–111**
      r1, **103–105**
      r2, **105–107**

W

WCDMA (Wideband Code Division Multiple
   Access), 654
WDM (wavelength-division multiplexing), 654
weighted round-robin (WRR) scheme, 654
wide metrics, 302–303
wide-metrics-only option, 303–304
Wideband Code Division Multiple Access
   (WCDMA), 654
WRR (weighted round-robin) scheme, 654

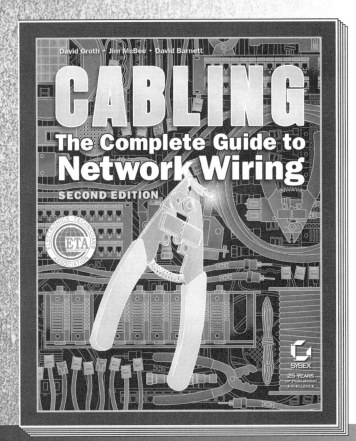

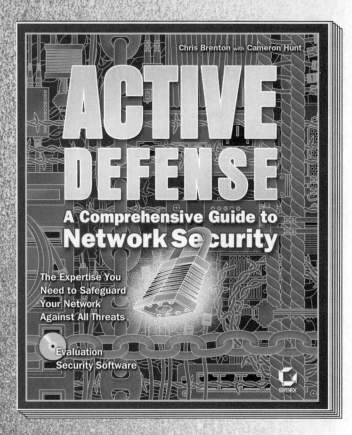

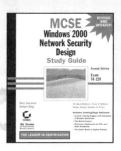 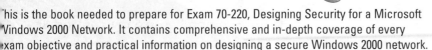

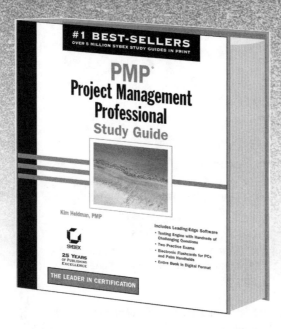

TELL US WHAT YOU THINK!

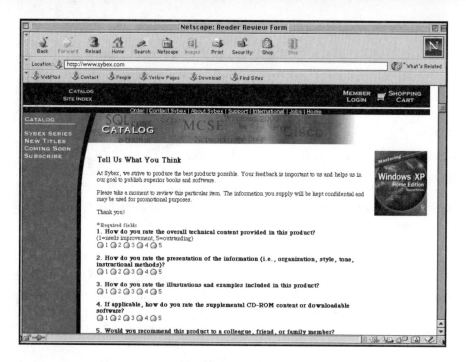

Your feedback is critical to our efforts to provide you with the best books and software on the market. Tell us what you think about the products you've purchased. It's simple:

1. Go to the Sybex website.
2. Find your book by typing the ISBN or title into the Search field.
3. Click on the book title when it appears.
4. Click **Submit a Review.**
5. Fill out the questionnaire and comments.
6. Click **Submit.**

With your feedback, we can continue to publish the highest quality computer books and software products that today's busy IT professionals deserve.

www.sybex.com

SYBEX Inc. • 1151 Marina Village Parkway, Alameda, CA 94501 • 510-523-8233